THE MAKING OF SOUTH AFRICAN LEGAL CULTURE 1902–1936

Fear, Favour and Prejudice

The development of the South African legal system in the early twentieth century was crucial to the establishment and maintenance of the systems that underpinned the racist state, including control of the population, the running of the economy, and the legitimisation of the regime. Martin Chanock's highly illuminating and definitive perspective on that development examines all areas of the law including criminal law and criminology; the Roman-Dutch law; the state's African law; land, labour and 'rule of law' questions. His revisionist analysis of the construction of South African legal culture illustrates the larger processes of legal colonisation, while the consideration of the interaction between imported doctrine and legislative models with local contexts and approaches also provides a basis for understanding the re-fashioning of law under circumstances of post-colonialism and globalisation.

MARTIN CHANOCK is Professor of Law and Legal Studies at La Trobe University, Melbourne, Australia. His publications include *Law, Custom and Social Order. The Colonial Experience in Malawi and Zambia* (1985), and *Unconsummated Union. Britain, Rhodesia and South Africa 1900–1945* (1977).

THE MAKING OF SOUTH AFRICAN LEGAL CULTURE 1902–1936 FEAR, FAVOUR AND PREJUDICE

MARTIN CHANOCK

La Trobe University, Australia

CAMBRIDGE
UNIVERSITY PRESS

PUBLISHED BY THE PRESS SYNDICATE OF THE UNIVERSITY OF CAMBRIDGE
The Pitt Building, Trumpington Street, Cambridge, United Kingdom

CAMBRIDGE UNIVERSITY PRESS
The Edinburgh Building, Cambridge, CB2 2RU, UK   www.cup.cam.ac.uk
40 West 20th Street, New York, NY 10011–4211, USA   www.cup.org
10 Stamford Road, Oakleigh, Melbourne 3166, Australia
Ruiz de Alarcón 13, 28014 Madrid, Spain

First published 2001

Printed in the United Kingdom at the University Press, Cambridge

Typeface 10.5pt/14pt Minion.   System 3b2   [CE]

A catalogue record for this book is available from the British Library

Library of Congress Cataloguing in Publication data
Chanock, Martin.
The making of South African legal culture, 1902–1936: fear, favour, and
prejudice / Martin Chanock.
p.   cm.
ISBN 0 521 79156 1 (hb)
1. Law – South Africa – History.   I. Title.
KTL120.C48   2000
349.68–dc21   00–037893

ISBN 0 521 79156 1 hardback

For Jennifer, Abigail, Alice and Rebecca
And to the memory of Edward Roux

CONTENTS

PREFACE

When I first thought of writing this book towards the end of the 1980s the apartheid regime in South Africa was in a state of violent disintegration. The state itself had become increasingly 'lawless' and the courts had become arenas for political theatre. In the face of state lawlessness there was much anxiety among lawyers who looked both forward towards an ideal future for law and justice in a democratic state and backwards towards an idealised version of what South Africa's law had been like before its corruption by the apartheid and the security state. It seemed to me, though, that there was little on which to base an understanding of South Africa's legal past that could consider the law on anything but its own terms as a body of authoritative doctrine, a story which usually concentrated heavily on the history of the unique development of the white private law. Indeed texts and courses that treated legal history placed South Africa's legal past in Rome and Renaissance Europe rather than in European law's encounter with Africa and with the context of the rule of white over African which was the overriding factor in the development of the legal system. My first aim, therefore, was to try to situate an account of South Africa's legal history firmly within this local context, and to try to provide the beginnings of a re-mapping and the indication of a new archive for the interpretation of South African law.

Soon after I began, the dramatic process of the collapse of apartheid and the unanticipated negotiated transition towards democracy began. As the present changed, so did the past. The issues that now presented themselves were seen through a lens not of violent disintegration, but of the hopeful, and painful, processes of reconstructing the state. These processes re-shaped my project, which became increasingly concerned with the analysis of law in the process of state construction, for it was this that seemed to be of most interest for the present and future in which, to confess to a heresy for a historian, I was most interested. It became clear that it was most important to illustrate first how law, however much its imagery works through long pasts, continuities, inheritances and authoritative doctrines, is, like any complex cultural activity, always in the process of making, of contemporary creation. Secondly I have tried to show that in this making there was no authoritative rule-producing voice but a multiplicity of voices and dialogues both within and outside the state. For it is through these concepts – of making and multiplicity – that the processes of the legal past become a part of the legal future. Finally, while I had begun with the intention of emphasising the localness of South Africa's legal history, it became plain, again through the lens of contemporary developments, that I was writing also about a larger process of legal colonisation – a transfer of ideas, images, doctrine, institutions and legislative models – which was taking place globally during the period I cover. These themes became an essential part of the framing of a narrative that would have meaning in the current period of globalisation, renewed legal imperialism, and the re-formation of states.

While I have opened the book with a series of narratives which exemplify the essential themes in the legal culture, I have discussed the methodological questions in a more systematic way in the second chapter. I have taken my period of state construction to be the years between the end of the South African War and the achievement of consensus among the white ruling elites on the basis of 'segregation'. The substantive parts of the book attempt a comprehensive picture of the law. It starts with colonial policing and 'law and order' rather than with Roman law; it illustrates the simultaneity and connectedness of the making of Roman-Dutch and African customary law; and underlines the importance of the state's project of segregation in all of the law. The final chapter leaps over the intervening years to take up these questions in their current context.

ACKNOWLEDGEMENTS

In the course of the long preparation of this book I was fortunate to have
the academic hospitality of a number of institutions which it is my
pleasure to acknowledge here. I began this work in the Centre for African
Studies in Cambridge, and my thanks go to the then Director, John
Spender. In the other Cambridge I was a Visitor in the Department of
History at Harvard, under the auspices of the late Leroy Vail. While on
leave from La Trobe University on a subsequent occasion I had a home in
the Department of Sociology and Anthropology at Wellesley College, and
much conversation to think about with Sally Merry and Susan Silbey.
Subsequently Julius Nyang'oro made me welcome in the Centre for
African Studies at the University of North Carolina in Chapel Hill, while
Cynthia and Alan Dessen gave me their house to work in. In South Africa
I began many years ago using the resources of the Centre for African
Studies, and the Faculty of Law at the University of the Witwatersrand,
and I am grateful to the then Dean of Law, Carol Lewis, for assistance, to
Charles van Onselen for generous access to materials, to the late Etienne
Mureinik for stimulating and thoughtful insights into what I should have
been doing, and to Adam Gordon for assistance with research. In the early
stages of the project Hugh Corder was of substantial assistance, both
intellectually and practically, and he was so again when I concluded the
research during a period as a visiting scholar at the University of Cape
Town's Faculty of Law. Danie Visser as Dean arranged my visit to Cape
Town, and added to his role as an exemplar for the writing of legal
history. Much of academic work is in conversation, and while it is
invidious to pick some out there are conscious traces in this work of
conversations with Rick Abel, Penny Andrews, John Brigham, Sandra
Burman, Dennis Davis, Stephen Ellman, Christine Harrington, Shula
Marks, Thandabantu Nhlapo and Howard Venable. In the course of an

exchange before the project began Arthur Chaskalson, with an expression of great alarm, told me that if that was what I thought, I ought to write a book about it. Tony Blackshield advised me as I hesitated between different histories that I should write about South Africa rather than Australia. Finally one comes closer to home. Finola O'Sullivan at the Press has been very helpful, and I am most grateful to my copy-editor, Mary Starkey. I have learned much from listening to colleagues in La Trobe's School of Law and Legal Studies which is the home of a formidable group of interdisciplinary legal scholars. The Australia Research Council has provided financial support, and La Trobe University the indispensable periods of research leave. Kate Chanock's editorial skills and intellectual insights have palpably shaped the manuscript. Finally there is the question of a dedication. Those South African lawyers who worked with such commitment and talent for justice during the apartheid years, and since in the processes of re-making law, deserve to be honoured. However, fearing that I might not get around to writing another book I offer this to my children, and ask them to share the customary familial dedication with someone whose writing introduced me to counter-narrative in South African history and who was for me in many respects when I was young, an exemplary South African.

ABBREVIATIONS

AC   Appeal Court (UK)
AD   Appellate Division
CPD   Cape Provincial Division
EDC   Eastern Districts Courts
EDL   Eastern Districts Local Division
GWLD   Griqualand West Local Division
ICU   Industrial and Commercial Workers' Union
NAC   Native Appeal Court
NHC   Natal Native High Court
NPD   Natal Provincial Division
OPD   Orange Free State Provincial Division
SALJ   South African Law Journal
SALT   South African Law Times
SC   Select Committee
TPD   Transvaal Provincial Division
TS   Transvaal Supreme Court
UG   Union Government

PART I

Puzzles, paradigms and problems

1

Four stories

The Union of South Africa, created in 1910, was an unstable state. It was the political outcome of the South African War between the Afrikaner Republics and the British empire. Though the war had ended in 1902, the issues over which it was fought were not laid to rest, and continued to call into question the legitimacy of the new state for decades. In addition to Afrikaner republicanism the state had to face a powerful new challenge from the largely British South African white labour movement, and the elemental task of maintaining white rule over the black majority. In the period after 1902 the country faced several major political revolts. In Natal a Zulu rebellion was defeated in 1906. In the Transvaal strikes by white workers led to violence which necessitated repression by military action in 1905–07, 1913–1914 and 1918, and which culminated in an attempt at revolution in 1922. In 1915 an Afrikaner republican revolt in the armed forces brought civil war to areas of the country. It is in this period of state making in a fiercely contested polity that South African legal culture and the legal system were developed.

This book locates the history of the formation of South African law in late nineteenth and early twentieth-century South Africa rather than, as other studies have done,[1] in Rome or Renaissance Europe. It places the

[1] E.g. Hahlo and Kahn 1968; Hosten 1983. Where the 'law' is situated in time and place is fundamental. The latter text, for example, begins with theories of law in Graeco-Roman times and then moves through medieval canon law; natural law; the Renaissance and English legal positivism; the European historical school and American realism. History begins with Roman law; then the twelfth-century Roman law revival; Germanic customary law and the reception of Roman law in the feudal Netherlands and the Dutch Republic. Only on p. 186 is South Africa reached, while the twentieth century is discussed on pp. 204–10. South African legal historiography is still largely trapped as a sub-category of white colonial and national narrative, from which the rest of South African historical writing has freed itself over the past three decades. But this latter historiography has not focused on the state (among exceptions are Posel 1991, Evans 1997 and Duncan 1995). Social and economic history and national and

3

development of this law within the context of the making of the South African state with a constitutional and statutory framework derived from the British imperial and colonial repertoire. And it shows how, by this state, two interdependent systems of private law were developed – Roman-Dutch law and African customary law. It tells not of the mono-logue of a developing legal 'system', but emphasises the multi-vocality and dissonance of a legal culture within a state based on racial dominance. The book is an account not simply of South Africa, but of the expansion of European law in the colonial period, a significant time of legal globalisa-tion. This account was written after another period of intense conflict, and the subsequent creation of another new South African state, and it tries to provide a frame within which to understand the connections between state making and legal culture, now proceeding in a post-colonial context as a part of a new globalising law. To illustrate the themes of the book I begin with four stories, chosen from a vast range of possibilities, in order to underline that legal history is a myriad of narratives, each set in its own context. A conventional methodological introduction follows in chapter 2.

A trial

In November 1921 Enoch Mgijima and 140 others, some on crutches and with limbs missing, all with numbered cardboard tickets dangling from their necks, were tried for sedition and public violence in Queenstown.[2] Nearly two hundred people had been killed: the survivors were on trial. Unable to afford a barrister, they were, with special leave of the court for the first time in over fifty years, defended by a local solicitor. There was rather more specialised expertise on the Crown's side. The prosecutor (who had 'a vast amount of experience of large native trials') had conducted the Crown case in the trial of the Zulu King, Dinizulu, and prosecuted in other major cases following the Natal rebellion, and had prosecuted the Indians charged after the Natal strike of 1913.

I present here only the story as seen through the prism of the legal

---

class struggle have been the major concerns, rather than the complexity of the state and its bureaucratic enterprises. This focus may change as the new state, no longer a hostile force, embarks on its project of reconstruction.

[2] My account is based on the reports in *The Star* for December 1921, in particular Judge Graham's summing up reported on 6 December.

proceedings, with their power to mould and to mock, and to shape not only a narrative but a frame of meaning. Exhibited in court were swords, scabbards made of paraffin tins, assegais and knobkerries, as well as Enoch Mgijima's robes of office, seized from his home. 'One of the robes was a resplendent affair of cerise silk, edged with gold lace. There were three caps. One roughly in the shape of a cardinal's cap, was made of blue plush, with a crown of scarlet. It was encircled with four thin strips of gold lace, and at intervals were four large stars.' Also on exhibit were Enoch's dreams. Prominent in evidence of seditious dreaming was his vision of two white goats fighting, and a baboon which had seized them both and crushed them. The court accepted the evidence that to Mgijima 'the white goats were the Europeans, and . . . the other animal was the natives, and that it meant that the white people should be crushed by the natives' (Graham JP's summing up).

The actual point of conflict between the so-called Israelites and the state was occasioned by the illegal occupation by sect members of a part of the commonage of the densely populated location at Bulhoek. In essence Mgijima and his followers defied an ejection order. There was intense pressure on the limited land available for African occupation around Queenstown (see chapter 15). Title holders in the location had small areas for cultivation, and made use of a common for pasture. Pressure on such grazing land was intense in the Eastern Cape where the population had outstripped the land available under the 'Glen Grey system' of title, and illegal occupation and cultivation were far from uncommon. The occupation had first been reported to the Department of Native Affairs in 1914, the year after the passing of the Land Act and the time of maximum hysteria among both white and black over the rights of Africans to land. When the head of the Native Affairs Department, Edward Barrett, visited the area in 1920 he found a situation in which control over the occupation of land in the location had virtually broken down. Several hundred people were squatting on the common. But, while he admitted that he had been 'amazed' at the extent of the settlement that had taken place due to 'imperfect' administration of the land laws, he had seen 'similar troubles' in other locations. Pragmatically the officials tried to register the occupants, rather than moving to eject them by force. Barrett even engaged in ideological debate with Enoch Mgijima. He admitted Mgijima's claim that the ground was 'God's ground' and that the Bible said that 'the earth was the Lord's and the fullness thereof'. On his part he wielded the alternative text of Romans chapter 13 ('Let every soul be subject unto the higher powers . . . the powers that be are ordained of God. Whosoever therefore resisteth the power, resisteth the ordinance of God'). However for Barrett the real text to be deployed was the Locations Ordinance, while for the Israelites it was increasingly in the world of religious injunction that the issue of the search for land on which to live, and the battle against the white state's prohibitions, were to be situated. Enoch preached, according to the evidence of followers, that after the conflict they would go to Jerusalem on a wagon that 'travelled in the air . . . those who were freed would go . . . Those who escaped when the whole earth was set on fire would get onto that wagon and be borne away.' 'What were you to be freed from?' asked Graham aggressively. 'Why were you anxious to go to Jerusalem?' 'I wanted to go there to rest,' said the witness, evoking the longing to escape the harshness of South African life rather than the will to rebel. 'The time has come,' said another. 'We have seen by the Watchman that Jehovah is coming down with his armies.'

The moment of the killings was confusing. Confronted by the police, and in a hail of fire, the Israelites ran forward. In the recollection of one witness 'there was all dust and confusion and we didn't know what we were doing'. But another strand of the evidence also told of a narrative more purposeful than confusion and the promise of Jerusalem. According to an African police witness one of the accused had spoken to him about the contemporary disturbances in Johannesburg and Port Elizabeth and asked, 'Does it not stir your hearts to see the blood of your brothers being spilt?' Another had attended a meeting at which one of the accused had preached against further tax paying and proclaimed that 'we have grown tired of being under the rule of the white man'. Other evidence concerned the colonial staples – driving the British into the sea and bullets turning to water. Enoch Mgijima, according to Graham, had 'preached that the hour of the black man was coming'. Graham mocked the defendants in his summing up. They had been attracted to the sect, he thought, by 'the indiscriminate kissing that went on between men and women' (the 'holy kiss' had been made much of by the press) and 'the entire absence of any work must have been a great attraction'. But they had more than the usually attributed characteristics of promiscuity and laziness; they were also revolutionaries. What bound these people together, said Graham, was not religion, which was a 'cloak' but 'the real bond . . . was the crazy notion that the day was coming when the black man was to have his freedom'. Like the Israelites the court magnified the local moment. Each instant of confusion and defiance was never far, in the minds of the rulers, from a wholesale black rebellion. This is why the ultimate cause of the disaster, in Graham's view, was the weakness showed by those in authority. Allowing the initial occupation to continue had been a 'sign of weakness', showing that local officials had 'no authority' over those under their charge. A 'vacillation, a shirking of responsibility' had characterised the dealings of the higher officials who had come into contact with the Israelites. Dr Livingstone was quoted as authority for the proposition that black men should not be threatened with firearms unless there was intention to use them. The initial show of force by the police, which had failed, was condemned. The effect had been 'deplorable'. There was no other instance, said Graham, 'in the long record of native disturbances' where nearly a hundred 'armed and disciplined men were compelled to retreat before a body of natives armed with swords, assegais and knobkerries'. The attempts of the then political authorities to negotiate a way out of the impasse were considerable. The Secretary for Native Affairs had come; so had the members of the Native Affairs Commission; and they had brought a delegation of prominent Africans, including Tengo Jabavu and Pellem, and there had been a serious prospect of a meeting with the Prime Minister. In the end the judge, while finding no fault with the police on the day of the massacre, condemned the processes of negotiation: 'All seemed to have forgotten that in dealing with the natives a legacy of sorrow and blood invariably follows in the wake of misplaced clemency.' Even Sir James Innes, who has the reputation of having been the most 'liberal' of South Africa's senior judges during this period, could only record in his memoirs that Bulhoek was an instance 'of the impressionability of the Bantu race, and of its recklessness when aroused, which lawyers and administrators would do well to bear in mind' (Rose-Innes 1949: 283). The government learned from Judge Graham's views about strength and weakness. Barrett, despised as weak, lost his job as Secretary for Native Affairs. Colonel Truter, who had commanded the slaughter, became the national commander of the police.

An execution

In November 1922 Samuel (Taffy) Long was sentenced to death by a special criminal court. Long had lived in his moments of violence inside another millennial dream and mounted the gallows singing 'The Red Flag'. While in this case the victorious were not to be carried away from a burning earth in a flying wagon, but would inherit a classless and exploitation-free world (and, in the local formulation of the ideal, a white South Africa), there were vital parallels in both the local impulse to erase the existing injustices and the link with a larger external doctrinal canon of total redemption. The murder of which he had been convicted arose out of the events of the attempted revolution, inspired and led by white labour, on the Rand. In the course of the revolt nearly two hundred and fifty people were killed. Special courts, created so that offences arising out of the rebellion would not come before juries, later convicted eighteen men of murder, and sixty-seven of treason and sedition (Simons and Simons 1969: 296). Of the four men who were hanged, it was Long's case that created the most controversy. Long was tried twice. The killing had not taken place in the heat of the moment, but had been the result of a 'trial' of a local grocer as a suspected spy after which Long had carried out the death sentence. At his first trial the court comprising Dove-Wilson, de Waal and Stratford failed to reach a verdict. The government ordered a second trial, which was presided over by judges Mason, de Villiers and Curlewis. This court found Long guilty and sentenced him to death.

While the court made no public recommendation for mercy it addressed a confidential recommendation to the Governor-General, Prince Arthur of Connaught, with whom lay the royal prerogative of mercy. The judges unanimously recommended commutation of the sentence 'having regard to the circumstances of the time . . . and to the fact that the accused purported to carry out what was apparently the sentence of a Court Martial' (SA Archives GG S1/6525).[3] The Governor-General consulted his ministers. Cabinet discussed the case and advised unanimously that the sentence be carried out. Jan Smuts, the Prime Minister, rejected the judges' argument that Long had had no personal animosity against the accused, observing that 'neither had Stassen [who had already been executed in relation to strike related killings] against the Natives whose lives he took', and, with an aim at imperial sensitivities, 'neither, if an analogy be drawn, have the Irish rebels against the people they do to death'.

---

[3] This account is based on the dispatch sent by the Governor-General to the Secretary of State on 15 November 1922 (SA Archives GG: S1/6525).

Constitutionally the prerogative of mercy was the Governor-General's alone 'according to his own deliberate judgement, whether the members of the Executive concur therein or otherwise' (Royal Instructions: Article IX). 'There were', he wrote, 'only two courses open to me. I had to decide between the judges who are regarded as impartial and experienced administrators and the politicians who are believed to be biassed by party policy and party prejudice.' Initially it appeared as if he would accept the judges' recommendations. Three judges had failed to agree as to Long's guilt, and three had recommended mercy. But the Prime Minister threatened that if this was done he would resign. He gave

> a very interesting and convincing exposition of the problem . . . the general theme of his argument being *salus populi suprema lex*. Had this been an isolated murder, he said, he would not have disputed the opinion of the judges. But he contended that the crimes committed during the rebellion were of an extraordinary nature involving something more than the purely legal view. High policy was affected. For years past the progress of South Africa had been arrested by frequent outbursts of lawlessness and revolution . . . the country had reached a world position that demanded some evidence of permanent stability . . . [and needed to] demonstrate clearly that any attempt to overthrow constituted authority would be severely dealt with . . .
> Speaking of the judges he confessed he was unable to understand what considerations had induced them to recommend mercy. He could only attribute their action to nervous strain brought about by continuous work on these capital cases.

The exercise of the prerogative in Southern Africa had been politically charged before. Lord Gladstone had been publicly vilified for his intervention in what was known in South Africa as a 'black peril' case, i.e. a rape of a white woman by a black man. More to the point, Smuts reminded the Governor-General that the Governor of Natal had wished to go against the Natal government over sentences after the Zulu rebellion of 1906, but had been humiliated into backing down by that government's threat of retaliation.

In the face of this Connaught abandoned his inclination towards the judges. But he persuaded Smuts to allow the Judge-President of the Court, Sir Arthur Mason, to explain the judges' reasons to the Executive Council. When the council met, Connaught opened the proceedings by announcing that he supported the ministers. Mason then spoke. In the words of Connaught's account:

> In the first place he contended that the Government could not absolve itself from a measure of blame inasmuch as he believed the policy adopted in this and previous disturbances was to some extent responsible for the strikers having recourse to armed resistance. With regard to Long he claimed that five out of six of the judges who sat on the case were in favour of commutation of the sentence for the following reasons. Fordsburg was being held by the strikers against the Government forces with little prospect of ultimate success. 'Spy mania' was rife and the Court was convinced that Long and his associates honestly believed that Marais was guilty of spying and had attempted to indicate their positions to the police.

Long, he continued, was an instrument in the hands of a court martial composed of 'strike ringleaders' and subject to 'the excitement prevailing at the time'. The ministers were unmoved and the sentence of death was confirmed. In his final remarks Connaught denied that he had surrendered his prerogative to ministerial threat, claiming that there had really been no difference of opinion. He concluded with observations on the constitution. Whereas, he wrote, 'in the United States, Canada and Australia the Constitution is supreme, the Act of Union, in letter and spirit, endeavours to subordinate the Constitution to Parliament'. The government, in other words, had to prevail.

These stories contain many strands which we shall follow in this book. The second illustrates above all the primacy of reasons of state, of the early invocation by the Prime Minister of the maxim that the safety of the state was the supreme law. It displays too the ambivalent position of the judges: accorded some respect, yet without final power. We can see too that judiciary and executive did not necessarily have predetermined structural stances. In the Bulhoek trial it was the executive that had leaned towards leniency and the Judge-President who had bayed for punishment, while in Long's case the positions were reversed. And it shows the combination of the respect for legal niceties, and formalism, with the willingness to discard them. Long's trial was one of a number of political trials during the period covered by this book in which issues of the legitimacy and the basis of existence of the state were concentrated in a single trial. The trial of Dinizulu, the Zulu monarch, for treason in 1906, was one; that of Jopie Fourie, the Defence Force officer executed for treason in 1915, was another; the trial of the survivors of Bulhoek a third. The fragility of the state, and the relationship between force and law, in these and hundreds of other 'political cases' were the background against which legal doctrine was developed (see part II). The role of judicial institutions, and legal doctrine, in the face of political unrest and revolution remained a feature of South African legal history throughout the history of the white-ruled state. And we can see also hints of other contemporary themes. The view that the constitutional design of the Union entailed the supremacy of the government over the constitution was to be affirmed in the struggle between the Appeal Court and the government in the 1950s. And, of perennial relevance, the expressed need of the state to demonstrate internationally that it could maintain law and order continued to be an ingredient of South African legalism.

The structure of oppression, and of struggle, gave a form to both stories. In both the localness of the struggle, in Fordsburg and in Bulhoek, was linked by all the participants to a larger cosmology of struggle, victory and defeat. The local event was transformed into a larger one by linking the limited actions to a vast pattern beyond: of the redemption of the world, of proletarian revolution, a final setting to right and crushing of wrong, which gave meaning to the local events. The state's response was in a similar manner made up of the mundane and the apocalyptic: the application of the criminal law, and the defence of the white race and its civilisation. In these acts of rebellion it is not surprising that the conflict should quickly become dramatised and enlarged. But, given the overall framework of oppression, this possibility was immanent in a very wide range of legal encounters. Two dreams of redemption, the brotherhood of man, and the coming of Christ, and two languages, the words of 'The Red Flag' sung on the gallows, and the sermons on flying to Jerusalem, embodying the visions, white and black, of a life beyond the oppressions of South Africa, both ended in courts to be evaluated by the language of the laws of sedition, treason and crime. In this confrontation, where the overwhelming anxiety of those who controlled the legal institutions was to protect authority, there were no echoes in the law of the visions of justice presented to it, no traces of a common link or language between rule and justice. It is here that we might begin our understanding of the meaning, in South Africa, of government under law.

A case at common law

In the first two stories we saw how legal actors and institutions confronted alternative dreams of justice. In both cases the core issue was the authority of the state. In one the audience was internal and African. In another it was white, and both internal and international. In both cases a message – the implacable will of the state to rule – can be distilled. My third story is of a different kind, far divorced from the high stakes and dramatic circumstances of rebellion, death and state power. It also raises questions about the audience for legal discourse and decisions in a different way, one which must lead towards the posing of questions about the 'rationality' of law, even within a quintessentially 'legal–rational' system. It concerns a simple dispute over a rural commercial transaction, which raised problems in the law of contract which found their way to the Appellate Division. The law of contract does, of course, embody a millennial dream of a kind, of the voluntary reaching of agreement, without oppression, between freely contracting parties, but it also embodies an ideology of compulsion which as I shall show in this book was to be of great significance as a legal weapon in the South African social order, as much a part of domination as the power to execute and imprison. But in all three of the stories what I want to draw attention to is the extreme disjunctures that exist between the world of the law and those of its subjects, gaps which require more from our understanding of law than a simple faith that they can be explained either in terms of legal doctrine or setting the law in its social context. In *Long*'s the circumstances concerned the conduct of a trial claimed to be valid in a revolutionary context. The state said he had committed murder and hanged him. But mutual comprehension was complete, though the worlds of justification were vastly different. In the case of the Israelites there was little mutual comprehension and no way of bridging the gap between the fiery chariot rising to heaven and the court which could have resort only to oppressive ridicule. In the third of the stories the gap is of a different kind. It is simply that the parties could not have begun to imagine the nature of the legal reasoning that would be applied to their dispute.

As this book will show, while South African judges developed the Roman-Dutch law as the common law of the country, the state made considerable efforts to keep Africans confined within a customary law of their own believed to be more suited to their stage of evolution. However, within a setting of economic integration between black and white this created all sorts of difficulties. What was clear, however, was that the whites' Roman-Dutch law always applied to transactions between African and white. Such disputes did not often reach the appellate courts, and I have chosen one of the rare ones that did in order to raise questions about the relationship (if any) between formal legal discourses and 'society'.

In 1916 an African farmer named Mapenduka in the Eastern Cape bought 152 bags of maize from a white trader called Ashington for £109. Peasant farmers were no longer self-sufficient in food. Selling part of their crop after harvest to meet their tax burden, as well as to buy newly available goods, they frequently found themselves re-purchasing maize at higher prices later in the year. As they more often than not had little money income and no assets other than stock, Africans who sold and bought grains in this disadvantageous exchange typically found themselves deeply in debt. Sometimes traders would treat the debt as an advance against labour services, and a sort of peonage developed. In other cases traders acted as labour agents who recruited their debtors as mine labourers. In others it was common to pledge stock against future payment. In this case Mapenduka pledged six oxen, a cow, a calf and a horse. He was not able to meet his debt when it fell due. Ashington believed that the property in the pledged stock passed to him. However, some time later Mapenduka was in a position to meet his debt, tendered £109, and claimed return of the stock. But only one ox remained in Ashington's possession. Mapenduka sued him for the difference between the amount of the debt and what he claimed was the value of the stock, a sum of £51.

He lost. Hutton J accepted Ashington's version of the history of the transaction and the evidence of a local auctioneer that Mapenduka's valuation was 'absurd for native oxen', and that they were worth no more than the debt owing *(Mapenduka v Ashington 1918 EDL 299* at 307). But the judge had also to deal with the claim that a contract by which the creditor took possession of pledged property on default of payment was oppressive and therefore void. Both parties, it appeared from the evidence, had believed that ownership of the goods would pass if the debt was not paid. In giving judgment he added to the usual citations from Voet and van der Linden a mixture of civil and common law authorities – Donat's *Civil Law,* and Storey on *Bailments* and *Equity Jurisprudence* (308). He was reluctant to find the contract void and also quoted approvingly the dictum of Sir George Jessel:

> You are not to extend arbitrarily those rules which say that a given contract is void as being against public policy because if there is one thing more than another public policy requires, it is that men of full age and competent understanding shall have the utmost liberty of contracting, and that their contracts, when entered into freely and voluntarily, shall be held sacred and shall be enforced by courts of justice. (309)

Denied political equality and deemed to be racially inferior and culturally backward, Mapenduka and other Africans were nonetheless of 'full age and competent understanding' in relation to their contracts.

Mapenduka appealed (*Mapenduka v Ashington 1919 AD 343*). In the Appellate Division Judge Hutton's English texts were trumped. The litigants were met with the determination of the judges to develop and display the fully flowering jurisprudence of the Roman-Dutch law. All was not so simple and it took close to twenty pages to show it. De Villiers AJA opened his account with laws going back to the emperor Constantine, as well as quoting Voet, to the effect that pacts which treated the pledged goods as belonging to the creditor were oppressive. On p. 352 he referred to 'a rescript of the Emperors Severus and Antonius probably altered by Tribonian' and four lines in Latin were quoted. De Villiers observed: 'It will be noticed that there is an important difference between the rescripts and the language of Voet.' He pursued the issue of limitation of freedom of contract when the contract was oppressive into the works of Pothier and van Leeuwen (352–3). Maasdorp JA was not to be outdone. He began with Justinian's Code and moved on to the jurists of Germany and France, invoking Carpzovius' 'Law of Saxony' as well as van Gluck and Pothier (357–8). The point as to whether there had to be a price fixed by agreement for the pledge, or a 'just price' was further followed in German jurists Thoasius and Huber (356–9).

It was all a most impressive display of scholarship and typical of the style of judgment of the court in this period. Actually they need not have gone through all of this at all. While the law may have been in some senses on his side, in that the authorities regarded as oppressive a contract in which property in the pledge passed regardless of value, Mapenduka received nothing as the judges accepted the evidence that there was no difference between the value of the pledged stock and the maize. But what is clear is that the judgment could not only have meant nothing to the parties but would also have been unintelligible to most South African legal practitioners. The judges could perhaps be seen to be using the case to develop an area of the law. The rationality and liberality of the Roman-Dutch law was proven, upholding Mapenduka's counsel's legal point, even though it was irrelevant to the result. But, in this most banal and secular of cases what they were also doing was stamping not only their ownership but also their mystical authority as expounders of a theology not approachable by any but a handful of adepts. It was not simply a case of the law being complex – which is normal – but one in which its derivation and language were entirely external to the society it ruled. The very complexity so lovingly displayed set it apart from what was often reiterated about African law in relation to contract, that it was simple, if it existed at all. Standing at the very boundaries of civilisation between those who had law and the lawless, the judges unsheathed their most important weapon, the golden thread of continuity which made them a part of the jurisprudential learning and traditions of Europe.[4]

There are a number of ways in which this judgment can be read. As an exercise in scholarship it can be read with pleasure. But it should also be read with incredulity if one asks why Carpzovius' 'Law of Saxony' or the rescripts of the emperor Severus could have been applied to Mapenduka's oxen. Neither Hutton nor the appellate judges had any thought for the concepts of right and law which might have been in the minds of the litigants. Mapenduka would have been familiar with the local African law relating to loans and pledge of cattle which was applied to disputes between Africans. Probably Ashington would have had a greater familiarity with the local customary law than with the law applied. The narrative here is one of 'whose law', and the court was making very clear that it was not Africa's. And then there is the question of the relationship of law and judges to power. In Long's case the implacable power of the political state overrode the judges. In the second story, the court itself abusively associated itself with the police killings. In Mapenduka's case the court apparently abased itself before the authorities which it called on to exercise

---

[4] This imaginative choice of where to situate the law can be illustrated in another way. In *Lennon Ltd* v *British South African Company 1914 AD 1* the court had to decide whether the doctrine of contributory negligence was a part of South African law. Solomon J said simply it had been 'frequently recognised by our Courts that on this subject there is no essential difference between our law and that of England'. This was not enough for the Chief Justice who wanted to derive the principle from another place: 'In the Digest Ulpian is quoted (7, 2, 9 Sec 4) . . . as laying down that if a slave was killed by persons throwing javelins for amusement Aquilian law was applicable, but not if the slave was passing at an unreasonable time over a field devoted to such exercise.' Can we wonder why it seemed quite natural to him to find the law among careless slaves spoiling their masters' pastime?

its right of final decision. The self-image in the application of the Roman-Dutch law was one in which the judges were subjects of the authority, yet there was no greater exercise of power than the application of these 'authorities' to the transaction between Mapenduka and Ashington.

Rosen has written of Moroccan court settings that speech in them is continuous with that of the rest of society and provides a 'frame for cultural understandings' (see Mertz 1992: 426). Yet in South Africa there was an absolute discontinuity between language in legal settings such as these and language in the rest of the public domain. Such discontinuities between formalist and popular language are present in many legal systems. English judges have had resort to Latin, legal French and Middle English. But here they were a part of the exercise of power by one race over another. This use of language needs to be highlighted at the outset and is underscored by the fact that when state officials other than judges talked about law arcane language was not used at all.

Resistance: an uncommon lawyer

The first of these stories concerns the relationship between courts and people, whose voice is absolutely subordinated; in the second the thematic issues are illustrated in a relationship between state and judges and in it the determinant and dominant voice is that of the state; in the third the judges construe the 'authorities' which appear to dominate both them and the litigants. In the fourth story I look for a different voice, developed in the struggle of subordinated people against law. But I have chosen a lawyer's voice, that of the most significant figure to have practised law in South Africa in this period, because it is crucial to be aware that within the law (though at its very fringes) genuinely alternative voices were formulated and heard. Over the objections of the Natal Law Society M. K. Gandhi was admitted to practice in Natal in 1893. (In the Transvaal, after the war, the Law Society did not oppose his admission.) The story of his assumption of the leadership of the Indian struggle in the Transvaal and Natal has been often told (Gandhi 1928; Swan 1985; Huttenback 1971). The events into which he was drawn were but one facet of the discreditable aspects of the imperial government's restructuring of the Transvaal after the war. It was a feature of that regime that, building on the principle of legal continuity with the former republic, its programme of reform was essentially one of enforcing, with greater efficiency, the discriminatory legal regime about which its propaganda had been so critical before 1899. Gandhi acutely summed up the difference between the administration of the anti-Indian laws in the Boer republic and the Transvaal. The British 'rule of law' meant not greater liberty, but stricter enforcement of rules. In the republic the 'drastic' laws had not been strictly enforced. However, he wrote, 'under the British Constitution . . . if the policy of the Government is liberal, the subjects receive the utmost advantage of its liberality. On the other hand if their policy is oppressive . . . the subjects feel the maximum weight of their heavy hand' (Gandhi 1928: 79–80). The anti-Indian policies of the Republic were stiffened. In its attempt to prevent Indian immigration to the Transvaal Milner's government introduced what came to be known to the Indian community as the Black Act which required registration and fingerprinting of all Asian residents. After the first phase of Indian resistance the law was disallowed by the Colonial Secretary Lord Elgin, but immediately reintroduced and passed in March 1907 when Responsible Government was bestowed upon the Transvaal.

There followed a prolonged campaign of defiance against the law. Among 150 Satyagrahi prisoners in the first batch, Gandhi was sentenced to two months in prison in January 1908. He recorded: 'I was standing as an accused in the very Court where I had often appeared as counsel. But I well remember that I considered the former role as far more honourable than the latter' (137–8). He was summoned from prison after three weeks for the first of many meetings with Smuts, who opened with the curious appeal 'You know I too am a barrister', underlining the English legal education that they had in common (144). He offered, in Gandhi's account, a repeal of the Black Act in return for voluntary registration. The prisoners were released. Amid scenes of violence in which Gandhi was severely assaulted by Indian dissidents, he led the acceptance of registration. But the Act was not repealed. The two men disagreed, not for the last time, over what undertakings had been given. After an impassioned campaign over broken pledges a public burning of the registration certificates took place at a large meeting in August 1908. Gandhi witnessed: 'The Negroes of South Africa take their meals in iron cauldrons resting on four legs. One such cauldron of the largest size available had been . . . set up on a platform . . . in order to burn the certificates.' Over two thousand certificates 'saturated with paraffin' burned (185–7).

The struggle continued. Violence, imprisonment, deportations, marches and hunger strikes swelled the ranks of the Satyagrahis. They grew to include Indian strikers on the Natal coalfields and then the cane estates, whose actions were attacked and suppressed by police and military force. Eventually women were drawn into the realm of public violence. The Indian struggle draws our attention to curious aspects of South African patriarchy. The South African state hesitated over extending the pass laws to African women. The overall willingness to leave and preserve the control of African men over women in the customary law were features of a nervousness about the extent to which state power could be extended in this sphere, and a state willing to allow that subordinate populations were ready and competent to be trusted to exert control, not over themselves, but over 'their' women. The original provisions of the Transvaal 'Black Act', which would have required the fingerprinting of Indian women, were greeted with 'shock' and 'a fit of passion' (94). Faced with the ferocity of the Indian determination to 'protect' their women, the single important concession freely made by the Transvaal government to the Indian resistance was to withdraw its insistence on compulsory fingerprinting of women. Gandhi also relates the eagerness of many women to take part in the Satyagrahi struggle. He was unwilling to send them 'into the firing line', and, he wrote, 'another argument was that it would be derogatory to our manhood if we sacrificed our women in resisting a law which was directed only against men' (251). Only when the struggle against the non-recognition of Indian marriages directly affected women were they permitted to join.

There are other important themes raised by these events. I have noted above the importance in South African legal culture of the processes by which the identities of self and other were established. Gandhi perceived that this was central to the fiercely anti-Indian laws of the Transvaal. He observed that 'a bare-faced selfish or mercantile argument would not satisfy . . . The human intellect delights in inventing specious arguments in order to support injustice.' The argument put forward by whites in South Africa was that 'South Africa is a representative of Western Civilisation, while India is the centre of Oriental culture. Thinkers of the present generation hold that these two civilisations cannot go together.' Thus the Indian question was presented, Gandhi wrote, not simply as trade jealousy or race hatred, but as what he called a 'pseudo-philosophical' and 'hypocritical' opposing of cultures (83–4). Another theme concerns the remnants of British authority in South Africa. A misplaced faith in 'English' justice and the power of the Crown to protect the oppressed in

South Africa was manipulated by the constitution. The myth did serve to mislead African opposition movements until well after the First World War. However, the fact that it was possible in the context and structure of imperial politics to influence South Africa's laws was evident by the interventions of the Indian government in the period after 1910. A third theme to which much attention will be paid in what is to follow concerns the position of Asians in South African law. Because Asians could not, like Africans, be relegated to a different legal regime, but had to be discriminated against within and by the ordinary law, they posed many of the most difficult problems to South Africa's lawyers.

The experience of the campaign, in particular the final phases where the government forced strikers in Natal back to work by police and military action, led Gandhi to reflect further on the nature of South African legality. 'Authority takes the place of law in the last resort,' he wrote. Yet he conceded that it was 'not always objectionable . . . to lay the ordinary law on the shelf'. An authority 'charged with and pledged to the public good' was entitled, when threatened with destruction, to disregard legal restraints. 'But occasions of such a nature must always be rare.' Furthermore, 'the authority in South Africa was not pledged to the public good but existed for the exclusive benefit of Europeans only . . . And therefore the breach of all restraints on the part of such a partisan authority could never be proper or excusable' (288–9).

What was the overall effect of the Satyagraha campaign on the legal culture within which it was waged? It did pose a pointed challenge to the colonial state and its command system of law. As Gandhi said in 1928, 'Whether there is or there is not any law in force, the Government cannot exercise control over us without our co-operation . . . But a Satyagrahi differs . . . if he submits to a restriction he submits voluntarily . . . We are fearless and free' (147). Such an attitude produced in response a greater emphasis on force and punishment. It contributed to the sense of righteous implacability that was the primary spirit of law making and enforcement. The movement truly tested the limits of the law-making and law-enforcing power. As Gandhi wrote in his concluding remarks on his South African experience, capturing the essence of the legal culture: 'A thing acquired by violence can be retained by violence alone' (306).

2

Legal culture, state making and colonialism

Method

One of the problems of enduring interest raised by the unhappy history of the South African state in the twentieth century has been the existence of a legal system clearly based on the liberal forms of law at the heart of a racist and oppressive state. An attempt to understand this immediately raises the question of how to approach relationships between law and other processes of the state.[1] I have tried to write a general history of a period in South African law, rather than about parts of it, and this venture has raised many problems. The first concern with any communication must be audience. Legal history can be written for a predominantly legal audience, as an internal history of the development of doctrine. It can be written for a more general audience in order to explain the arcane world of the 'legal' in accessible ways. It can also be written as a broader contextualised history, both to make the broader audience aware that the law is not arcane and specialised but a part of the polity and culture which must be understood, and also to reinterpret law to the legal audience. But contextualising the study of law assumes in its simplest form a separability between law and politics, economy, society and culture, and this is too simple a model with which to work. Contextualising also raises purely practical problems, those of the feasibility and length of such a venture. A

---

[1] A prerequisite is acknowledgement of my predecessors: those most responsible for initially pointing the way, and from whom, as will become clear, I have derived most inspiration are Simons (1968); Sachs (1973); Dugard (1978); Corder (1984 and 1988); and Visser (1989). Any consideration of South Africa's legal history must begin with these works. The understanding of the development of South African law has been greatly enriched recently by Bennett (1991 and 1995) and Zimmerman and Visser (1996). Prior to this the major compilation was Hahlo and Kahn (1960). For a fuller assessment of the sources for writing South African legal history and a historiographical survey, see Chanock (1989).

project which was to write a general history of 'law' alone would be long enough, the example of Holdsworth's seventeen volumes on the history of English law providing a warning (Holdsworth 1932–66).[2] If context, a conceptually endless account of the entire society, were to be added, the result would be unmanageable, and, more importantly, lose coherence. Clearly some other choices about method and content would have to be made.

Any general legal history comes with the assumption that there is a 'legal system', that is that the different parts are interlinked, and have something important in common. Maitland was convinced that there was a commonality. He wrote:

> Do not get into the way of thinking of law as consisting of a number of independent compartments . . . so that you learn the contents of one compartment and know nothing as to what is in the others. No, law is a body, a living body, every member of which is connected with . . . every other member. (1908: 538–9; quoted in Sugarman and Rubin 1983: 51)

However, as soon as the process of contextualising begins, the more each part of the 'system' is set within the deeper narratives of its own context, the less they appear to have in common. The inherent connections between the stories of the development of such areas as the criminality; family; the growth of corporations; African land; and labour disputes are by no means obvious. To preserve the important sense of connectedness another form of contextualisation is necessary.

Locating the law

It may be that this problem can be approached by focusing on trying to work out how to find the law. There is an easy answer to this: that it is in the statutes, regulations and decisions of the courts, and these are the sources to which lawyers go. But if this is so, even a contextualising study can do no more than explain how various bits of law so defined came to

---

[2] As is evident this is a long book. The prescriptive wisdom of my editor prevented it from being far longer. Some substantive subjects have been sacrificed. One is an account of taxation, a crucial part of state construction. Others were a fuller description of the policing of political opposition; an account of the politics of the construction of the judiciary; and an assessment of Sir James Rose-Innes as a prism through which to consider the dilemmas of the 'liberal' judge in the racist state. The original manuscript contained fuller assessments of the development of doctrine in contract and delict, which have been rendered unnecessary by the publication of Zimmerman and Visser (1996).

be in the law books. Clearly this is one of the things that a legal history must do, but it would reduce a general study to a compendium, and would add little to our understanding of the place of law in any state or social formation. The primary way of dealing with the 'place' of law in this broader sense has been the study of how law 'really works', of 'law in action' as opposed to 'law in the books'. It is evident that no set of rules is self-enforcing, and that huge 'gaps' exist between idealised statements of rules and principles, the practices of the institutions that administer them and actual patterns of public behaviour. Legal language and ideology have not tended to justify law by saying that it is an efficient way of getting things done. Far from using the language of pragmatism (or power) jurists have described law in a language of equity, liberty, justice and rights, clothing the 'drab cruelties' (Arnold 1935: 34) of the everyday exercise of power in an immaculate garment of justice. Thus analysis of how law works has consistently been accompanied by a sense that it has betrayed its promises. The discovery of the 'gap' between the ideal and the real has tended to lead towards theoretical and analytical conclusions that the law is in some senses a facade, masking and legitimising economic and social realities and the abuse of power with a language of rules and justice. My research project began by looking at 'law in action', and at the 'gap', and the ideological uses of law. Any study of South African legal history must immediately be confronted by questions about the coexistence of professed legalism with its accompanying rhetoric of justice, and the racist abuse of power by the state. I tried to approach these questions not with accusations about law as a form of deceptive 'ideology', but by thinking again about the notion that legalism was about the limitation of power, which has been so ingrained in assumptions about law. It became clear that, in the processes of building a new colonial state, law could best be understood as a way of creating powers, of endowing officials with regulated ways of acting, a weapon in the hands of the state rather than a defence against it. Investigating the mechanics of law, rather than its legitimising role, seemed to be more fruitful (particularly as the law was never legitimate in the eyes of most of the population).

Thinking about law in terms of the endowment of powers obliges one to look beyond the sources which lawyers usually use to find out where law really 'is', and it also requires another look at 'law in action', with its focus on what law does. Law is used to justify acts of violence, to allocate resources. But how? Legal forms, style and language need to be contextualised as much as legal acts. How and where in a society is law spoken about? As soon as one asks this question it is obvious that the lawyers 'speaking' about law is only a small part of the discursive universe of law. Not only judges and legislatures speak about law, but so do people at large; religious organisations; the press; special interests such as trade unions and mining and industry; and, most significantly for the purposes of my study, which is an account of state making, so do bureaucrats. I turned, therefore, towards an attempt to generate a concept of a legal culture. A legal culture consists of a set of assumptions, a way of doing things, a repertoire of language, of legal forms and institutional practices. As with all aspects of a culture, it changes in response to new situations, but it also reproduces itself; its new responses fit into its existing forms. This sort of continuity is important to all aspects of culture, but perhaps especially to lawyers who depend on the 'authority' of old texts, precedents and established meanings and constitutional forms. A legal culture, like other aspects of culture, embodies a narrative, encompassing both past and future, which gives meaning to thought and actions. Such an approach to understanding a legal system will focus on process and style, as much as on rules (the lawyers' paradigm), and on discourses within and about law, as much as on outcomes (the 'law in action/realist' paradigm). What I am here calling a legal culture is made up of an interrelated set of discourses about law: some professional, some administrative, some political, some popular. Each understands and represents law in different ways, and each therefore acts differently on it. While the discourses differ, they do not exist in isolation from each other, and they draw upon each other, sometimes critically, sometimes affirmatively. And they are all set within the broader political and social discourses of the state and society.[3] This approach diverts my analysis from a number of paths. It attempts no sort of overall explanation of the interrelationships

[3] Studies of legal culture have, on the whole, tended to emphasise popular legal consciousness, rather than bureaucracy. These issues may be pursued in Merry (1990); *Yale Law Journal* 98 1989; Horwitz (1992: chapter 8). For an exemplary historical study of an aspect of legal culture see Wiener (1990). In drawing attention to the breadth and variety of discourses that constitute a legal culture it is not my intention to indicate that the professional, 'internal' legal discourses are less 'real' than, or should be subordinated to, a more popular consciousness of law. My argument is rather that this formalism must be clearly acknowledged to be a part of a wider spectrum, and not mistaken for all of 'law'. I am also not writing about the falsity of a distinction between 'law' and 'politics', nor suggesting that a 'pretence' that law is apolitical be overcome. The suggestion here is that even when broadly constituted, legal discourses are distinguishable (if not distinct) from political ones.

between law, society and economy, nor of the 'role' of law in politics and society. It also does not proceed from the assumption that legal discourses are a facade to be thrust aside in order to reveal the real world of actions and effects.

In approaching law as a set of interrelated and overlapping discourses care must be taken to convey the distinctness of each. Legal formalism, with its internal logic of rule derivation and the making of decisions by the application of rules to facts, not by considering substantive outcomes, need not be unmasked as anything other than what it is. What needs to be done is to show it as only one part of a working legal culture. The questions then are framed around what the role of formalism was in the making of the new state, in relation to other ways of talking about and doing law. What different ways of talking about law achieve what kinds of ends? In what areas of life do particular ways of doing law dominate? This is not an analysis of legal pluralism of the kind that considers the different legal and normative sub-systems and which usually relates them in some form of hierarchy, but is concerned with the complex relationships between different ways of saying things about law.

Looking for law 'inside the state' in search of an answer to both the 'where' and the 'how' of law yields important insights. From this viewpoint judges and courts, far from being at the centre of legal processes, were peripheral, and occasionally an irritant. The senior officials were the ultimate legal realists: to them law was policy driven and about achieving ends, not about adjudication. This was also, of course, true of the approach of politicians. The tensions and accommodations between the bureaucratic, political and judicial perspectives are keys to understanding South Africa's legal history in this period. The period is one of state making: of putting together a union after a destructive war, and of attempting to endow it with the institutions of an early twentieth-century state. It is very common to deal with the difference in approach between the 'political' and the 'legal' and to consider how to distinguish between the two realms, but less attention has been given to the relationship between the bureaucratic and judicial versions of law. This relationship is a focus of my book, and it is one that makes the judiciary far less prominent in the story. (One should remember also that the judicial function was exercised over most of the population by executive officials.)

The shift to a broader world of legal discourses tends to make understandings more varied and complex. Much of contextualised legal study has been based on a combination of legal realism and versions of functional, structural and materialist social science and has been focused around exploring the ways in which 'society' and 'economy' underlie and explain the content of legal doctrines, and on describing how law 'really works' in practice. (This would not have been so much of a problem if positivist jurisprudence had not so forcefully isolated law. The curious South African combination of this kind of positivism with a historical jurisprudence which placed the history of South African law in Europe and quite out of the local social context dissociated law even further.) But recent currents in social science which have emphasised the power of discursive formations have opened up ways of going beyond this broadly 'realist' project, and yield further ways of approaching the questions of the connections between doctrinal formalism and social order which have been the foundation of so much contextual study of law. My account does not wholly forgo the realist project of illustrating law in practice. But it contextualises the internal discourse of law within a set of related discourses which include 'external' discourses about law, as well as those on economy, politics, evolution, race, history and justice. The discursive construction of lawyers' law is placed within an opened and broadened realm of discourses. It is these multiple discursive sites, along with the institutional practices so constructed, that make up what I have called legal culture.

Legal scholars have generally been at ease with the turn in the social sciences towards the analysis of discourse and texts, because they are accustomed to this kind of process. There are risks of losing touch with a world of events and acts. However, the importance of this approach, it seems to me, is that it displays, in so many ways, that 'law' is never a determined 'given', but that a range of questions and possibilities and choices are always present. It is vital to understand the multi-vocality of something that so often claims to have only one authoritative voice. A. M. Honore once characterised the Roman contribution to law as being that of creating a separate sphere of discourse – of 'conventions restricting the scope of permissible arguments' – which he contrasted with the 'garrulous and undisciplined Greeks' who were 'incapable' of devising such an instrument of control and cohesion (Honore 1974). Clearly the roles of legal formalism and of the Roman-Dutch law were to police the boundaries of acceptable argument in a plural society in the making. This repression can only be transcended if analyses turn towards the garrulity and lack of discipline ascribed to the Greeks. I try to show that the legal culture in the period I am describing was multi-vocal, and that it contained many voices other than those heard and possible choices other than those made. There were also limits to multi-vocality. It is significant that there were no women's voices in any of the sites in which law was talked about: no women lawyers, no women politicians, no women 'experts'. An alliance of patriarchies relegated African women to the bottom of the social structure, and simultaneously elevated and demeaned white women. They became not invisible, but inaudible, to state, polity and law.

Sources

An emphasis on legal culture and on language as much as on actions has implications for sources. While I have said that this approach took me 'inside the state', and that I locate 'law' as much in the discourses of bureaucrats as in those of courts, I have only rarely gone beyond what is on the public record, because a legal culture is within the public realm. Only occasionally do I use archives or private papers to cast light upon an issue. If one goes in search of law beyond the statutes and the law reports, and if one's methodological premise is that all societal discourses on law are sources, then one is faced with a virtually endless range of possibilities, which I have somewhat arbitrarily reduced. I have concentrated upon the published sites in which there was most communication and dialogue between official actors – the politicians, the senior policy makers and officials, 'expert' members of the public and the lawyers – and these are found in the reports of and evidence to parliamentary select committees and commissions of enquiry. I only rarely canvassed how these issues were discussed in the press at large, in the specialised press or periodicals (for example of industry, agriculture or labour), though these would give a better impression of the wider legal culture. In using the conventional legal sources, the law reports, I have dealt with the problem of control of length by focusing largely on those of the Transvaal, and this diminishes any sense of regional variation, as does my exclusion of the work of the provincial councils or municipalities. (Nor, though this is also a slightly different methodological question, have I written about the many disciplinary sub-systems that existed in a range of sites from churches to labour compounds, all of which invoked rules and sanctions, and all of which are a part of the 'legal culture'.)

In this study the words are the events. As I have indicated, the 'discovery' of the 'gap' between legal words and legal acts which was the basis of the realist paradigm led to a view that the focus should be on acts rather than on words. But my approach to the 'gap' has been rather to acknowledge and to employ it to cast a focus back on what the words might mean. If legal words do not describe or determine acts, what kinds of understandings do they encompass? There are also problems about how to read. This used to be a simple matter, in that historians let the text speak for itself, as a simple reflection of the conscious meaning of the author. But ever since, in the post-modern turn, readers became authors, meaning has become more complex, and we have been accustomed to reading what was not in the text, what it had suppressed, and its choices of representation: a way of reading of particular interest in interpreting colonial texts. On the whole I have tried to avoid ambushing my subjects by perverse interpretation, but one point that should be made is that legal texts need to be read simultaneously as if one is both an insider and an outsider. The reader must appreciate their legal reasoning and rationale, but must also ask 'what on earth is going on here?', both engaging and suspending belief.

When I began the project I initially envisaged a study which would deal with three periods: the making of the state, which I conceived of as ending roughly in 1929, the end of the first terms of the National Party–Labour government; the re-making of the state between 1948 and 1961 when apartheid was put in place; and the unravelling of the state in the late 1980s (Chanock 1989). That this was unachievable was soon apparent. The earlier period, however, seems to me to be crucial in that it was the time when all of the institutions, patterns and habits of South Africa's law became established. The creation of separate regimes of law for whites and non-whites, both in common law and by racially discriminatory statutes, were products of this period, as were the styles and forms of law that survived into the 1980s. The first decades of the state became my focus for other reasons. The study was begun when the apartheid state was still in place, and its dramatic collapse not yet envisaged. Even those who thought its end was near did not predict the nature of the transition, and the rapid negotiation of a new legal and constitutional order. In returning to complete the study after a long break, I found that the present had changed the past. As the present changes, so do the historical narratives that lead to and beyond it. And different questions require answers.

Specifically the period which is now the subject of this book has immediate relevance as that in which the South African state was first made. It has an immediacy of connection with a time in which that state is being radically reconstructed.

Content

Two areas of South African legal history have been much written about – constitutional law and the history of private law – and I have not tried to retell the story of these areas. But I have tried to cast them in a new light. The story of the private law, of the common law, has been told as the story of the triumphant creation of an original and indigenous Roman-Dutch law, based on the pre-codified civil law of Europe. The relationship of this law to English common law – both antagonistic and complementary – has been a major theme of these histories (see Zimmerman and Visser 1996). What has always been missing from this history of private law is African law. Where African law has been dealt with at all it has been separated from the history of mainstream law, as if South African common law developed in Europe, or at least in isolation from African law. I have tried to tell this story in a different way. My premise is that in the last part of the nineteenth and the early twentieth centuries two systems of common law were developed in South Africa, and that these must be understood in relation to each other, if either system, and the legal culture as a whole, are to be understood. Thus I have tried to bring the story of the development of African law into the centre of the account of private law, given that it and Roman-Dutch law were, in many important ways, both products of the same time and society, and were discursively closely related in a continuing process of contrasting and differentiating which affected the mutual construction of both systems.

In considering public law I have tried to concentrate on those areas of law that affected most people and which also seemed to be most in need of a general narrative treatment. Quite apart from this they are also essential to trying to illustrate the nature of a 'legal culture' and in coming to terms with Maitland's idea that all of the parts of law are interrelated. The first of these areas is the criminal justice system. Maintaining 'law and order' was an overriding preoccupation. This involves more than giving an account of the criminal law, for its provisions and principles are only a small part of the world that includes policing, prisons and the necessarily related discourses of penology and criminology. These apparatuses of coercion were closely linked to other attempts at control from which most criminal convictions arose – the attempt to impose prohibition of alcohol, and the pass laws which controlled labour contracts, movement and access to urban areas. The latter were really a part of the differentiated regime of labour law, and I have given an extended treatment to labour law as it affected both white and black and related it closely to political conflict and economic analyses of the time. The story of land law has been often (and well) told but it is a part of my account because it is crucial to illustrating the legal culture, and I tell it with a focus on differential regimes of tenure. South African law in the period about which I write was the law of a capitalist society and had a conceptual framework which prioritised concepts of 'market' and 'contract'. Yet (aside from 'law and order') most state activity was about intervention in the market and controlling contract. In the core areas of land and labour it was clear that leaving these areas to market and contract would insufficiently protect white economic interests, and I have tried to illustrate the tensions in the relationship between state, market and law.

In addition to crime, labour, and land, I have also attempted to tell the story of what may be called in shorthand 'administrative law'. In common with other states in the early twentieth century the production of wide-ranging statutes giving discretionary powers to ministers and officials; powers to pass delegated legislation; and excluding the jurisdiction of courts were major features of the law in this period. South African judges coped with what Lord Hewart in England was to call 'the New Despotism' (1929) in a distinctive context in which most of the major state legislative initiatives involved racial considerations. The courts' accommodation to the growth of executive powers and the deployment of conventional legal tools, for example of statutory interpretation, are shown as developing in a particular context. These stories are essential to an understanding of what the 'rule of law' might have meant, and therefore are central to the concept of and analysis of 'legal culture'. But there are other good reasons for this focus. 'Rule of law' issues have long been central to South African law. For decades accusations were made that the formal legalism adhered to by the state (a rule by law) was in fact a betrayal of some other higher concept (Cowan 1961; Mathews 1972; Dugard 1978). Then, in the period in which I began to write this book, when the apartheid state was disintegrating, fear was expressed about 'law' losing its grip altogether

(Davis 1987). The construction of a new basis for a 'rule of law' was essential to the new constitution. Some of the problematic assumptions in all of these debates may be illustrated by looking at the earlier part of the twentieth century.

Colonialism and legal culture

I have also consciously situated this history as an episode in the expansion of European law and the making of a colonial legal culture both before and after nominal independence in 1910.[4] In writing the history of any aspect of a colonised society one has to deal simultaneously with external and internal considerations and the many ways in which they interact. The development of the South African state and its law is not comprehensible outside this colonial context. There is much current interest in the phenomenon of the globalisation of law, and we now have a heightened awareness of the ways in which legal forms and ideas migrate across the globe. The spread of constitutionalism, bills of rights, and rule of law; and of other, market-related law – contract, corporations, intellectual property – are a much commented-upon feature of the current post-cold-war world. If we go back a century we find a similar interest and process. It took place within a different context, one of unabashed and of conscious empire building and lawgiving, but it was a period in which huge transfers of legal institutions and ways of thinking took place. But such transfers, even where there were significant differences in institutional experience and intellectual resources between the imperial centre and the colonies, were not the same as transplants. Each colony in the British empire used, adapted and developed the British endowment in different ways, because they had different populations, different political conflicts and different economies. Yet the successor states developed not only in a continuing conscious relation with Britain, but (during this period) with a high degree of awareness of each other. While the dominant fashion in the writing of the history of the successor

---

[4] In an earlier attempt to understand the processes of legal colonisation (Chanock 1985) I dealt with simpler colonial states and a simpler discursive field – between white administrators and African elders – which constituted the law. In South Africa the colonial state was more complex and the discursive field within which law was constituted was more varied: a white polity divided by class and nationality; a large bureaucracy with diverse and sometimes conflicting interests; a self-conscious legal profession; and a politically weaker African voice than in the rest of colonial Africa.

states of empire has been to emphasise independent and differing trajectories, the era of globalisation and the transcending of the nation-state
gives us an opportunity to de-emphasise self-centred histories, and to
write, not in terms of transplant versus independence, but with a greater
awareness of the relationship between external and indigenous factors in
the making of the new states.

Another initial point may be made about setting an account of South
Africa's legal history within a global context. This book is about law in a
racist state. In this South Africa was not unique. As a part of the British
empire it was a part of a world-wide system of racial and racist rule, in
which both Britain and the other white Dominions endorsed racist law.
Contemporaneously with the South African story told here, a far more
explicitly racist law developed and flourished in the United States. In
addition to the racial bars on immigration, explicitly racist laws banning
racial intermarriage were enacted across the southern states several
decades before such legislation was passed in South Africa. In endorsing
segregation through the 'separate but equal' doctrine the South African
Appellate Division in *Minister of Posts and Telegraphs v Rassool* 1934 AD
167 was nearly four decades behind the United States Supreme Court in
Plessey v Ferguson (163 US 537 1896). Empire, segregation and, at the
close of this period, Nazism, were fundamental parts of the world within
which South Africa's race-based law developed. It was its normality,
rather than its aberrations, that are cause for the deepest concern. Yet
while much of this book is about racism, it is, like law, difficult to pin
down just what and where this is, and how it works. I do not offer any
overall analysis of the place of race in South African society, but I will
venture to state how I have come to approach this part of the story. It is
the state that was the most active proponent in making the racially
divided society. The drive to segregate appears to have been driven by the
white elites and constantly imposed on those elements of white society
that appeared not to value racial identity sufficiently. Much of law was
concerned with forcing the races apart, rather than the legal system
'reflecting' an amorphously and 'naturally' racist society.

In dealing with any aspect of a colonial culture one has to consider the
complex issues of the fusion of the local and the metropolitan. South
African art and literature, for example, and its racist thought, and its law,
not only owe their primary conceptualisations to external discourses, but
developed along with and in relation to them. A notion of South African

legal culture must involve an evaluation of the changing relationship between the external and the local elements of legal developments. In the period of state formation with which I have begun, the influence of English legal practices was enormous, not simply in terms of doctrine and precedent, but in relation to more basic forms. The organisation of the courts and their procedures, the self-conception of the judiciary and the profession, the language and linguistic forms of statute and judgment, all mimicked those of England and other parts of the empire. After nearly a century in which there have been important efforts to diminish this endowment, this remains the case. Of course this is not peculiar to South Africa. Large parts of the world have acquired, and persisted with, the forms of British legalism, while undergoing substantial political changes. In Britain itself the elaborate facade of formalism had been to a degree tempered by juries and a large lay magistracy. But in its colonial version in Africa and Asia where it has usually persisted beyond the end of empire, the formalist facade has tended to operate in isolation from other social forces. Typically it has produced in Africa and in Asia, either acknowledged or unacknowledged, binary systems which relegate the greater part of the population to subordinate systems that have provided little guarantee of legal rights. This dualism, extreme formalism in some areas, almost none in others, has been an important feature of South Africa's law.

I have stressed above that in the study of a colonial society the local must be placed in its wider dimension. But this book is based on another, and, I think, not contradictory, premise, which is that the story of the development of South African law must be told in its specific time and place. In this it distinguishes itself sharply from the tradition of South African legal history which begins its story in Rome and then moves to Renaissance Europe. While texts, and consequently images (and imaginings), of these places are deployed in South Africa, it is the place and the circumstances in which they are re-read that must be the focus of study. The South African Roman-Dutch law was a common law created on an initially flimsy textual base in a politically fraught colonial time and place, and this is where its history must necessarily be located. This is not as simple as it may seem. In South Africa at this time all white knowledges – of theology, economics, anthropology, criminology, and history, and all of the ingredients of law – were derived from outside. (African ideas and law were deemed to be either non-existent or uncivilised.) This is not intended to imply that colonial intellectuals were simpletons. It is the reverse that made the strength of outside influences so strong. Many of the leading judges and lawyers, and senior civil servants, had been (and continued to be) educated in Britain and Europe, and were people of considerable sophistication who kept well abreast of the intellectual developments of their times. Political struggles, and the construction of law, as my opening stories all show, took place in a conscious context of, and in relation to, global ideas and struggles. The South African world had to be described and fashioned with external concepts, derived from and for different places, societies and times. Thus in analysing the relationship between ideas, language and law and any colonial social and economic formation within which they operate, we have an unusually complex task as both external and derived indigenous intellectual formations operate within the local social place. The South African intelligentsia was small and thus it took time for it to construct its own intellectual arena. That the jurists were the first to do so was a considerable achievement. And their tone has ever been self-congratulatory: the Roman-Dutch law, to quote one such exemplar, was 'one of South Africa's most valuable and distinctive assets' (Cowan 1959).

It was also an achievement which involved a complete colonisation of African time and place. South African society had no common law in the historical sense. In the making of a colonial law traditions are neither habitual nor locally presenced: the narratives of habit must be newly created by deploying imported discourses against indigenous practices. The process of creating the new common law depended on a focused scholarly enterprise of retrieval and translation of Roman and Renaissance legal texts. Fidelity to these texts, as embodying the inherent rationality of law, situated this rationality physically, historically and imaginatively in Europe and, specifically, not in Africa. The arcaneness of the texts limited access and comprehension. Few white lawyers had access to them, or could have understood them, in these years. A source of mystery to the white population, they were nonetheless emblematic, an assurance that the white law contained the core of historical rationality, not simply the commands of the advantaged. This law was what Bakhtin has called an authoritative discourse:

> The authoritative word is located in a distanced zone, organically con-
> nected with a past that is felt to be hierarchically higher. It is, so to speak,
> the world of the fathers. Its authority is already *acknowledged* in the past. It

is a prior discourse. It is therefore not a question of choosing it from among other possible discourses that are its equal. (Quoted in Goodrich 1990: 173)

Dialogue and dispute between Europe and Africa was excluded. Africans could not invade the seventeenth century. Nor could they create the future. As Clifford has said: 'These suddenly "backward" people no longer invent local futures . . . [they are] tied to their traditional pasts, inherited structures that either resist or yield to the new but cannot produce it' (1988: 5).

While Europe's past became the future, Africa's present was frozen in an imagined past. The creation of the Roman-Dutch law was mirrored by the simultaneous creation of a customary law with even more limited ownership. Appropriated from Africans, who ceased to be either its authoritative source or transmitters, the state's 'customary law' was impenetrable to nearly all white lawyers and judges as well. The dual cryptic codes were mutually reinforcing creations, foundations of a racist law. The legal rules and concepts which came to be enforced in South Africa's courts under the name of customary law were also essentially the product of this period. Different sets of rules were seen as appropriate for the bearers of a 2,000-year-old legal tradition, and for barbarians who were still infants in evolutionary development. Increasingly these latter rules began to lose their applicability to the real life of Africans as they had access to land drastically reduced, were driven into the cash economy as labourers, and were caught up in the process of urbanisation. One South African tradition had assumed that this would ultimately lead to legal integration. But, just as these economic and social developments intensified, the white state underlined the importance it placed on legal differentiation by passing the 1927 Native Administration Act, which institutionalised, nation wide, separate courts applying separate law. Migrant labour and the gender imbalances in urbanisation, pressure on land and the political and cultural defence of traditionalism gave to many Africans an interest in the symbolism, if not always the substance, of this customary law. But African input into the development and exposition of the customary law administered by the state's courts remained small. Segregated from the 'real' law reports and from the syllabuses of professional legal studies in the universities, a mystical 'expert' field to most lawyers and judges, it was embellished in the cheaply produced and rarely consulted reports of the Native Appeal Courts, and in handbooks of rules for administrators. Yet, if we are to generate an idea of South African legal culture it is important to grasp that it was not just a matter of there being two systems of common law, but that they were interrelated, and that they are not historically comprehensible without each other. The Roman-Dutch law grew in an intimate relationship with English common law, and also in another with customary law. Conversely customary law cannot be understood without its white 'other'. And furthermore neither of these created bodies of common law had much purchase in either of the populations to which they respectively applied. Few identified them, even rhetorically, as the source of their inherent rights. The ideological posture of the English common law, that it was the source of the rights of 'free-born Englishmen', was absent in South Africa where the racialised state was the identifiable source of rights or oppression.

In the period about which I have written the colonial state was being made. When I began this book it was in the process of disintegration, and the questions with which I began were related to trying to understand the pretensions and contradictions in the foundations of its legal order. But now, when that state's fundamental institutions and legacies are being dismantled, a different perspective presents itself. The beginning of the century and its end are both periods of state making, and approaching legality in the light of the challenges of such an enterprise seems apposite. The themes of the tensions between instrumentalism and formalism, and of the re-making of authoritative foundations, appear closely contemporaneous. And there are also unfinished dialogues with the past which are of relevance to the present, and which can now be taken up. We may think of the current processes of land law reform, for example, in terms of Krikler's remark that 'the vanished generation which we thought we had left in the obscurity of the past is . . . before us now, speaking to us as if from the future, demanding resolution of the questions it raised' (1993: 235).

In answering the 'vanished generation', and in retrieving and constructing new narratives, manifold choices will be made, and this brings me back to the notion of legal culture. One should not be trapped with a notion of 'culture' which is too closely linked to social structure or to economy. Cultures are not simply reflections of practices, but are made up of acts of imagination. In representing and re-imagining social narratives the banal world of practice is extended, fantasised and changed. While legal history is conventionally tied to what William Wordsworth called 'the meagre, stale, unprofitable world of custom, law and statute', the concept of legal culture allows us to recognise the place of fantasy and imagination and to appreciate in fresh ways just how strange, indeed extraordinary, many of the things said and done really were. The colonial imagination is necessarily complex because no colonial society is cognitively autonomous or discrete. People must habitually think beyond their immediate locality and local narratives, and link them to other places, times and cultures. Representation and self-representation of the local requires not only reflection or description but, because there are no other resources in the mind of the coloniser with which to confront the local, in a creative interaction with externals. In the creation of colonial narratives, as in the telling of any story, the element of fantasy is necessarily present. By this I mean not fabrication, but myth and illusion about self and others. Legal scholars are familiar with one major fantasy, the world of rights and justice, though it is never thought of in this way because to call something a fantasy is generally taken to reduce its seriousness, rather than being a step towards achieving some form of realisation. South Africa's lawyers usually fantasised in less attractive ways. Judges imagined their roles in terms of the English judiciary, and were thereby enabled to act like them, even though this was an illusion. Imaginative representations of savagery and civilisation were, as we shall see, at the core of much of South Africa's legal culture. The elements of imagination and fantasy are very powerful in the ways in which societies construct their basic narratives, their images of self, and make plausible their most banal and everyday activities. Without an awareness of this, much that is astonishing in this historical account of a legal culture cannot be understood. And without it we cannot creatively imagine a future.

The constitutional frame

I shall not deal at length with the story of constitutional law as the story of the formation of the Union, and subsequent issues, such as the franchise, have been well told (Thompson 1960; Kennedy and Schlosberg 1935; Walker 1962; Tatz 1962). But there is a need for a general outline of some themes.[5] The place to begin this brief account is with the attempt by J. G.

---

[5] We should note that even in embedding racism in its constitution the Union was not perceived to be unique in this period. As Lord Crewe said when defending this aspect of the Act of Union in the parliamentary debate at Westminster: 'In the Australian Commonwealth a similar provision exists' (Kennedy and Schlosberg 1935: 64).

Kotze, who, when he was Chief Justice of the South African Republic and acting under the influence of American constitutional law, tried to hold the state to its constitution by claiming the right in 1895 to declare laws passed by defective procedures to be invalid. He was dismissed by President Kruger, who associated the testing right with the Devil's contest with divine authority (see Corder 1984 and the sources quoted therein). All I shall do is make some points about the aftermath of these events. Kotze received little support among the judiciary of the other colonies (apart from those in the Orange Free State). The main importance of the confrontation was the indirect effect it had on the subsequent constitution. In the formation of the Union both judges and politicians wanted to avoid creating a structure that would invite such struggles. The judges did not yearn when the Union was made for the pivotal position of power which a federal constitution and a consequent 'testing power' would have given to them. It was not simply a matter of judicial timidity. Among the reasons for the eschewing of any testing role was the conceived need for authority to speak in one voice to the subject African population. In the deliberations of the constitutional convention the possibility of creating a federation was extensively discussed, and rejected for, among other reasons, the fear of creating a court with a 'testing right'. F. S. Malan records how he and Smuts were against giving 'semi-legislative' powers to the judiciary, as this could lead to deadlocks between parliament and the court if legislation was declared to be *ultra vires*. What is significant is the example that he gave, a 'great delay which may seriously jeopardise public safety and think what an effect such a state of affairs may have on the Native mind should such a law concern them. To whom will they look as the final Authority, to the Government or to the Supreme Court?' (1951: 35). Innes and Solomon also anticipated that a new supreme court in a federation would mean that 'inter-racial and quasi-political cases . . . were likely to become more frequent if anything like a federal constitution were adopted' (Walker 1925: 454). Smuts characterised giving a federal supreme court the power to 'override an Act of Parliament' as leaving 'the supreme power of government in the hands of an unrepresentative body such as a court of justice'. This, he said, was what was happening in Australia, and would lead to the politicisation of the courts (Cowan 1961: 139, 141). This was closely associated with the view that Africans only understood the implacable authority of chiefs, and that more democratic forms of government were inappropriate, a political view which was given concrete legal form. It was important to close down the discursive sites within which dissent about law could take place, because this was inherently linked to dissent about the legitimacy of authority.[6]

We might consider the importance placed on the appearance of the authority of the law, and its unity with the highest levels of government in the eyes of Africans, in another way, which also illustrates the significance of the attachment to the empire in South African constitutional history. The importance placed on the retention of appeals to the judicial committee of the Privy Council (of which he was a member) by Lord de Villiers, then Chief Justice of the Cape, was illustrated by a letter he wrote to Innes in May 1901. 'I fear', he wrote, 'that there may be an attempt on the part of the Australians to practically abolish appeals from the Australian Court of Appeal and, if this is done, a precedent will be established which it would be difficult to avoid in regard to other Colonies.' He wanted an 'Imperial Court of Appeal' which would be 'a firm link in the chain which binds the Colonies to the Mother Country' (Innes Papers, de Villiers–Innes 21/5/01). De Villiers had, in fact, misjudged the Australian intentions. Far from wishing to break free, they wanted to create a stronger appellate link through the creation of a new court of appeal for the empire as a whole. This proposal was discussed in June 1901 by a conference at the Colonial Office, attended by the British law officers, the Secretary of State for the Colonies and representatives of colonial governments, including Innes, then Cape Attorney-General. He strongly opposed the proposed change. His views are significant in that they show at the highest level a theme which is frequently to be found in judgments concerning Africans, and in political rhetoric, namely the manipulation of the aura of the authority of the monarch in securing African acceptance of white power. 'The great point in South Africa is this', said Innes:

> We do not want the right every subject has to appeal to the Sovereign interfered with in any way. We want a direct appeal to the Crown's person,

---

[6] The belief in speaking with one voice and the anxiety about what subjects might make of public judicial dissent can also be found on the imperial level. In 1901 there were discussions as to whether the practice of not allowing dissenting judgments on the Privy Council should be altered. The Lord Chancellor, Lord Selborne, feared that dissents might tend to create 'great discontents in India and the Colonies'. He was 'activated by the difficulty of satisfying public opinion in India rather than in this country . . . the dissentient judge's opinion might be made the subject of great discussion in India'. This might be permissible in England, but not among 'comparatively half-educated Hindoo lawyers' (see Stephen 1979: 74 note 214 and 75 note 222).

because we think that the prerogative of the Crown, the influence of the Crown, the prestige of the Crown, is a very important factor in binding the Empire together . . . And in regard to local matters at the Cape especially, I think it is valuable that the appeal should be to the Sovereign. There are many important questions involving land, areas of land, native reserves, the rights to those which come before the Supreme Court. We think it very important that we should sometimes be able to tell a native Chief, that in addition to his appealing to three impartial Judges at Cape Town, he can go to the great Chief over the sea and be protected. (Colonial Office, Confidential Prints Miscellaneous 138: 9–10)

William Morcom, on behalf of Natal, added that they too regarded 'the appeal to the Sovereign direct, advised as he has to be by a Judicial Committee on all questions, as appealing strongly to the natives' (14).

South African constitutional law and practice were an integral part of those of the British empire. It became the first of many states in Africa to be endowed with a Westminster-style constitution. This constitution was an Act of the British parliament, which, until the Statute of Westminster in 1931 and the Status of the Union Act in 1934, was a superior legislative body to the parliament it had created in Cape Town.[7] The National Party after its formation in 1914 made much of the fact that the country was not fully independent. While the Westminster parliament did not in this period legislate for South Africa, and Acts passed in Cape Town were not disallowed, as they could have been, and while appeals to the Privy Council were limited and politically unspectacular, in practice the political subordination of the new Union did make a difference (see Chanock 1977). And it was integration within this system that made it highly implausible that a public law and practice governing the relationship of courts to parliament and to the executive different from that of Britain's would develop. The overall Diceyan framework of parliamentary supremacy: the separation of powers and a 'rule of law' in which rights were only located in the common law dominated South African public law (Dicey 1902). There was little doubt that the Governor-General had been

---

[7] Not only was Union legislation theoretically subject to the Colonial Laws Validity Act, and appeal to the Privy Council preserved, but the Act of Union made provision for both compulsory and discretionary reservation of Acts by the Governor-General for the consent of the imperial government. While attention has commonly been paid to Acts that might diminish non-white political rights, the United Kingdom government had ranked other interests as more important. Compulsory reservation was for laws that might impinge upon the Colonial Courts of Admiralty Act and the Merchant Shipping Act.

correct in his analysis of the spirit of the constitution which he gave in *Long's* case (see above). Lord de Villiers had warned the constitutional convention of the dangers of creating a constitution which would 'usurp the functions' of the legislature which it created (Kennedy and Schlosberg 1935: 64). His advice had been taken: the new parliament was sovereign on the model of the parliament at Westminster. This is clear if we consider the analyses that followed the passing of the Statute of Westminster in 1931 which removed the white Dominions from the fetters of the Colonial Laws Validity Act. Canada, Australia and New Zealand, however, did not agree to the repeal of the Colonial Laws Validity Act insofar as their constitutions were concerned, but South Africa had so agreed. As a result, wrote Kennedy and Schlosberg in 1935, 'the constitution of the Union appears to have been made as flexible, as uncontrolled, as easy to amend in every detail as the constitution of the United Kingdom' (1935: 101).[8]

The re-conceiving of this book between 1987 and 1997 led me to look at the overall issue of South African public law in a different way. In 1987, before the breach of the Berlin Wall and the fall of both communism and apartheid, the constitutional questions were already being posed in South Africa in terms of the failure of the British system of absolute parliamentary sovereignty combined with a 'rule of law', and how this might be remedied by the development of a constitutionally entrenched bill of rights. Intellectually the South African debates were then swept up in the huge international project of constructing a constitutional order in post-communist Europe, and post-cold-war Latin America and Africa. The rule of law versus bill of rights issue was partly subsumed (and renamed) within a larger debate about the construction of 'constitutionalism'. The concept of 'constitutionalism', because it involves questions of constitutional law, and the safeguards that limit power and protect rights, as well as the political processes and political culture which make these workable, provides us with a lens through which to view the early decades of the

---

[8] Accordingly, in their view, the Union's parliament could henceforth amend the entrenched clauses of the Act of Union, which had required a two-thirds majority (and which had, *inter alia*, protected the African and Coloured franchises at the Cape) by a simple majority. They noted, however, that 'the rudiment of what may become a new kind of constitutional convention' might develop as a result of declarations by the government and speaker in 1934 that the original procedures would be followed (102). Their view that the entrenched clauses were no longer legally entrenched was supported by other constitutional scholars of the time. It was the unexpected rejection of this interpretation by the Appellate Division in the 1950s that led to its constitutional confrontation with the government (see below and Forsyth 1985).

South African state. So do recent analyses of the nature of that state by Ashforth (1990) and Mamdani (1996). These works emphasise, as does this one, the bifurcated nature of the South African state, and that it essentially began with and continued to refine two constitutional orders – one democratic and one authoritarian – not one. Africans were 'in a sense citizens but not altogether citizens' (Cecil Rhodes (1894), quoted by Ashforth 1990: 45). A question that then emerges is not 'how and why did the system of public law as a whole fail to protect rights?', but a question not about failure but success. For, even given the extremely high level of intra-white political violence – of strikes, civil war, treason and rebellion – a culture of 'constitutionalism' was successfully maintained among and for whites. Limited sanctions in terms of sentences; generous amnesties for political offenders; the maintenance of a very broad arena for freedom of speech and political activity; and the strict patrolling of the limits of the application of statutes which limited freedoms are all features of the polity of the white part of the state. Power was limited to protect white democracy, but not limited where Africans (and Asians) were concerned. Thus I have approached these questions by analysing the realm of administrative law, not by searching only for broad principles, but by focusing on each circumstance with which courts had to deal. It was not inherent faults in the constitutional order such as the absence of a bill of rights, or that the courts debased themselves before parliament, that led the courts to 'fail' to protect constitutional freedoms. Rather it is because they made choices as to which part of the bifurcated state each case belonged to. That state has been best described by Kennedy and Schlosberg, who wrote that 'we have in South Africa, as far as the natives are concerned, an undefined "colony" within a dominion, a "colony" undefined in area, bounded only by the limits of the state itself, where a system of "Crown Colony Government" is in existence within the framework of an entirely independent and advanced state'. An 'executive despotism' was exercised over Africans 'side by side' with the 'trappings' of parliamentary government (1935: 459–60). The really fundamental issue was the franchise. For the enfranchised there was, there had to be, constitutionalism: for those without the vote there did not. In the democratic part of the state, law 'succeeded'. For those for whom it failed, the failure was one of democracy, not of 'law'.

It is with this division of the state in mind that we can conclude this introduction with the different perceptions of the rule of and role of law in the South African state. The notion that law constrained power in the interests of the liberty of the subject was contained in Chief Justice de Villiers' celebrated protest that the 'first and sacred duty' of the courts was 'to administer justice to those who would seek it . . . to administer the laws of the country without fear, favour or prejudice independently of the consequences which ensue' (*In re Kok 1879 Buch 45* at 66). Legal scholars are, along with judges, fond of rhetorical flourishes and South Africa's legal culture is rich with passages of this kind. There were contrasting perceptions that show that the law could be perceived in quite a different way. D. D. T. Jabavu wrote in 1934 that 'South Africa, so far as we aboriginals are concerned, is a country perpetually in the throes of martial law, from which there is no escape' (quoted in Schapera, 1934: 290). For those trapped in this mesh of restrictions the central metaphor of law as a defence against the power of the state was least apposite. Law was rather unchecked authoritative power. Kas Maine expressed it this way: 'Look the Law, if that is the law you follow the law. Don't stand and argue . . . [it is] just like a river in full flood . . . you've got nothing in your hand with which to stem them' (quoted in Bradford 1987: 431).

PART II

Law and order

Police and policing

The police

In popular parlance the police are often referred to as 'the Law', an indication of their prominence in the characterisation of a legal system as far as the public are concerned. This is not only because this is the force on the frontier between coercive law and the people, but because policing involves wide discretions in the exercise of which the criminal law and other controlling laws become a real part of state practice. A study of legality and legal culture must therefore attempt to come to grips with the nature of its police. In a coercive society like South Africa in this period it is an appropriate place to start. Policing South Africa has long been an overtly politicised part of government. The prime characteristic was the combination of policing and defence functions. We may start with the War Office's advice to Lord Kitchener, who commanded the British troops in South Africa during the South African War, that the role of the police was 'continuous and effective occupation', which can serve as the keynote to this chapter (Grundlingh 1991: 169).

During this period the defence function dominated. Once British control had been established in the Transvaal, it was policed by the newly created South African Constabulary under the command of Colonel Baden-Powell. Its methods and organisation were evolved after study of those of the Royal Irish Constabulary, the French Gendarmes and the North West Mounted Police. The entire area of the newly conquered colony was to be regularly patrolled. The special law and order needs of the Transvaal as perceived by Milner were described well by Worsfold. There was first the 'permanent and outstanding menace' of the 'dense masses of semi-civilised Bantu'. Secondly there were two particular possibilities in relation to white criminality: crime and renewed resistance to

British rule. In the rural areas there were 'elements out of which there might easily have arisen in the fastnesses of the Drakensburg a class of outlaws analogous to the Bushrangers which enlivened the criminal annals of Australia' (Worsfold 1913, vol. II: 157, 59, 60). In addition there were the criminal gangs operating in Johannesburg. Thirdly there was the realistic prospect of a Boer rebellion if occupation was not effective. Among the Boer population, Milner wrote in 1904, there were

> numbers of men ruined by the War, disappointed, defeated and even desperate . . . In the absence of a force something far beyond the ordinary civil police force . . . we might have a state of things . . . that would not only terrorise the inhabitants but would give a great shock to the credit of this country throughout the world. (Worsfold 1913, vol II: 166)

The connection between the ability to maintain law and order and the anxiety about the international creditworthiness of the new colony is worthy of note.

The fears of both black and white revolt originally dominated South African policing and dictated the organisation of its police. Militarised constabulary guarded against both black and Afrikaner rebellion, and other forms of civil auxiliaries were brought into being to assist policing during major strikes. And, as the menace of Afrikaner and black 'tribal' rebellions receded, and the military aspect of police organisation was de-emphasised, the political policing of left-wing political organisations was developed. And policing was increasingly concerned not with common-law crime, but statutory crimes peculiar to South African modes of control, in particular the liquor, pass, and masters and servants laws, and the control of trade in gold and diamonds. R. H. Brand, the Secretary of the Inter-colonial Council, commented in 1906 of Transvaal police operations: 'Every farm is visited by a patrol once a month . . . and manifold services are rendered to the farmer in this way . . . a large amount of their time is taken up assisting at the collection of native taxes and checking native passes' (Worsfold 1913, vol. II: 173).

Parallel to this was the development of ordinary civil policing. In 1902 Milner brought Edward Henry, the Commissioner of Indian Police (the originator of the method of classifying fingerprinting) to the Transvaal to organise the new police force, and it was his systems that provided the basis of the working methods for the South African Police when it was established after Union. To deal with international gang crime in Johannesburg Milner imported Major Mavrogodato from Egypt to be the head of the Transvaal CID (Trew 1938: 167; 192–3). In the Cape the forces were divided between local rural police forces and town police; the Cape Mounted Riflemen, who policed the largely black areas in the east; and the Cape Mounted Police, which patrolled outlying rural areas (UG 62 1912: 82). The division between a militarised force whose mission was the preservation of the state and public order and who had no skills in the detection and prevention of crime, and local police who were concerned, among other things, with 'ordinary' crime, was one full of problems for the future. In addition few of the military or the civil police had the necessary linguistic capabilities for any form of detective work.

It was not always easy to separate the aspects of ordinary and political policing in South Africa. The activities of the police were conducted against a backdrop of white racial panics, which sometimes became acute. In the early years there was a series of these concerning Chinese in the Transvaal, Zulus and Indians in Natal, and black rapists, all of which created hysteria about law enforcement. Fear of powerful gangs (with no 'sentimental ideas' about the value of life) among the faceless Chinese labourers in the Transvaal was behind the 'fierce wave of indignation' that swept the Transvaal following murders by Chinese workers who escaped from their compounds. A 'Special Burger Police', the forerunner of many, was created on this occasion (Trew 1938: 109–10). The Zulu Rebellion in Natal created fears in other colonies. In 1913 the Union government faced major strike action by white workers in the Transvaal, and a strike by Indian workers in Natal. On both these occasions, Colonel Trew, then a major in the South African Police, wrote, 'large armed forces had to be employed by the Government to maintain order'. But it was the Indians, whose aims were limited, not the white strikers who were directly confronting the state, who provoked a particular anxiety for the police. There was fear about what would happen if 'thousands of coolies . . . got out of control'. Police fired on strikers. Trew described their 'fanatical rush . . . filled . . . with *bhang*' (marijuana) (1938: 255, 257).

During the general strike in Johannesburg in 1914 a special reserve force was sworn in. Martial law had been proclaimed, and a force of 2,563 reserves sworn in (Trew 1938: 126). The atmosphere in which they operated, and the mission they accomplished, can be gauged from the report of the responsible officer. 'Owing . . . to the presence of thousands of native servants as well as hordes of natives in locations' the work of patrolling was extensive. The reserves 'proved themselves fit guardians of the town . . . This was amply proved by the crowds of natives and others they arrested . . . Absolute safety and security was felt by the suburban inhabitants, particularly by the women' (UG 28 1915: 127). In a general atmosphere of unrest, the task of policing was perceived to be the protection of the white suburbs from the threat, real or imagined, from the black locations. And in doing this, even in a moment of acute class conflict among whites, the white male population could be called upon as a whole. 'I feel it is incumbent on me specially to mention', the report continues, '. . . the cheerful and willing work rendered by the rank and file of the Special Constables. They came forward from every class. The "Magnate" was found side by side with the "Worker" ' (ibid.). During the Afrikaner rebellion in October of 1914 a reserve force of 4,116 was sworn in. The report noted that 'this was the third occasion within a period of 16 months in which the citizens of Johannesburg voluntarily undertook this important duty to meet emergencies of a very serious nature' (129). In the early years of the new state it was not only not easy to separate the political and criminal aspects of policing, or the policing role from the defence role, but there was also no clear line drawn between policing by the professional forces, and by members of the white public.

The Police Act, passed by the Union parliament in 1912, was to a large extent based on the Transvaal Police Act of 1908. Prior to its passage the Chief Commissioner toured rural areas and came back convinced of 'the absolute necessity for the control and direction of police work from some central office' (UG 62 1912: 2). His report gives a picture of the routine activities of policing in the country. In 1911 there were 1,118 rural police in the Cape, 163 of whom were black; and 334 were in the mounted police. The character of the work of the rural police was pithily summed up in his report. The 'most attention . . . outside ordinary cases of drunkenness, petty assaults and the like, is paid to stock thefts and illicit liquor traffic' (4). For the urban police drunkenness was overwhelmingly the major offence charged (6, 7). The main duty of the mounted police was identified as patrolling the country 'to restrict the facilities for stock stealing and to pay proper attention to complaints of losses of stock' (8). Natal policing concentrated heavily on the hut- and poll-tax collection, drunkenness, and breach of the peace, and on labour-related offences arising out of the Indian Immigration Act and the Masters and Servants Law (17).

But it was not these routine policing activities that were uppermost in the minds of the politicians. After Union the police were reorganised and tied closely into the new Defence Force. The government rejected the compelling advice given to it by the Police Commissioner that there should be a single civilian police force. Smuts and Hertzog agreed on the co-ordination of the Police and Defence Bills, and on the creation of the South African Mounted Rifles, 'a military force which incidentally would do police work in the frontier districts in time of peace' (UG 46 1919: 133–7). Five regiments of the SAMR were created with responsibility for policing the Transkei and border areas; southern Natal and the Basutoland border; northern Natal and Zululand; the northern Transvaal; and the north-west Cape. Smuts explained to parliament in 1912 during the debate on the Defence Bill that South Africa required 'a small permanent striking force to deal with emergencies which arise suddenly and which you may nip in the bud' (ibid.: 11). This 'striking force' created, which was attached to the Ministry of Defence and which had responsibility for policing one quarter of the Union, outnumbered the South African Police proper by 4,432 to 4,370 (12). The two forces were tied together by the Police and Defence Acts. Section 8 of the Police Act made provision for the Governor-General '. . . in case of war or other emergency, [to] employ the Force or any part thereof, to assist in the defence of the Union within or outside the same, but in South Africa'. When so deployed the police could come under military command and discipline. Section 11 of the Defence Act defined the permanent force as including 'Persons charged in time of peace with the maintenance of order within the Union', i.e. the police. Section 12 of the Defence Act made the SAMR liable to perform police duties.

Introducing the Police Bill to parliament in 1912 the Minister of Justice, N. J. de Wet, explained that it 'went hand in hand with the Defence Bill. A portion of the police would be constituted a section of the military defence force, but yet the police would form a complete whole' (Hansard 8/5/12). The Police Act created a single national force which was to be the uncomfortable heir to both traditions of South African policing, absorbing the local crime-oriented police forces into a national force with a military character. J. X. Merriman characterised it a 'highly centralised little army' (Hansard 20/5/12). The force was, as E. H. Louw said succinctly in parliament, 'our first line of defence, as is shown during disturbances and riots' (Hansard 20/8/24). These views of policing became entrenched. The Department of Justice, as the then minister, Tielman Roos, was to tell parliament in 1927, had always set itself against the 'village policeman' concept, with the same man being continually stationed at the same place. 'Our position is entirely different from other countries' (Hansard 5/5/27). Policing absorbed 11 per cent of revenue and defence 4.1 per cent. Nonetheless there were calls for a transfer of resources from Defence to Police. The Defence Force, it was pointed out, 'is only based on the assumption of internal disorder'. 'Much of the money which is spent on the [defence] General Staff could be more usefully employed in increasing the police' (Hansard 13/4/27; 6/5/27).

If the police force was not to be primarily either a civilian or a helping service, this was so for whites as well as blacks. One insight into the role envisaged for the police can be gained from the responsible minister's reaction in parliament to the suggestion that women be enrolled in the police force. Women, it was put to him, often did not complain to male police officers, and women police would also be useful in coping with controlling the morals of girls. They were needed, urged Patrick Duncan, to enter 'certain places' to rescue young girls and to help them 'in times of danger and temptation'. The minister, de Wet, however, flatly rejected this. That there were four women police officers in Cape Town was 'an admission of weakness'. What class of women, he asked rhetorically, would undertake police work? The suggestion embodied 'a complete misconception of the duties of the police force' which were to maintain public order and protect lives and property, not to be 'saddled with the duty of the moral reclamation of the people'. This militarisation continued to be attacked in parliament by the Labour member Walter Madeley. Police members, he said, 'objected very strongly to the importation of . . . semi-military tendencies' (Hansard 3/7/20). The following year he was able to return to the attack on this point, with the example of the militarised suppression of the Israelites at Bulhoek where machine guns, field guns, and rifles with fixed bayonets had been used. The Labour concern was that a militarised force would also be available for use in industrial disputes (Hansard 4/6/21).

There were clear tensions also between the needs of an increasingly bureaucratised administration of justice and a militarised police force. The Harrismith magistrate in 1912 recorded that he

> hoped that those imbued with the martial spirit would be removed to the Defence Force. One of the greatest drawbacks of the police force had been

too much aping of the military and too little knowledge of police work. A small knowledge of the laws which applied to minor offences was necessary to make a policeman useful in whatever community he was stationed. (UG 44 1913: 221)

The magistrates also found the police inadequate in other ways. A general impression which can be gained from the magistrates' reports in the early years of Union is the lightness of policing in the rural districts. The commissioner's report for 1911 records: 'At Union and during 1910 the cry for more police was reiterated from every quarter' (UG 62 1912: 82). But while the magistracy was increasingly concerned with efficiency, the political representatives of the white population continued to treasure a different style of policing. As the force became more centralised and bureaucratised, new formal and standardised routines spread from town to country. Yet this drew some complaints. 'The police are concentrated in the towns,' a rural Member of Parliament complained, 'when they get into the country they are so loaded with official documents and unnecessary formalities that they cannot give their attention properly to local conditions' (Hansard 20/8/24).

The magistrate for Barkly West reported in 1915 that 'in regard to policing by the SAMR . . . with them military training came first and police work was quite a secondary consideration and that as the men became imbued with this idea the interests of justice suffered' (UG 28 1915: 79). In 1916 one Natal magistrate confirmed of the SAMR in his district that 'the policemen are soldiers whose knowledge of police duty and elementary law is nil' (UG 36 1918: 89). Another added that they were 'unable to make out an intelligent report in any language' (89/90). Many were illiterate. The Chief Magistrate wrote: 'To fill the ranks from the more uneducated white class may be a way of relief to that class but it is not fair to either the European or the coloured community' (89). The Transvaal reports for the same year take up the same themes energetically. Inefficiency, poor education, deterioration of quality and absence of legal instruction of the new recruits were all referred to as the background for poor policing (113). Elevated notions of public service were not necessarily part and parcel of local culture. A recurring complaint from magistrates concerned police who served in their home districts and who might show partiality to friends and relatives. Another common complaint related to the incapacity of police in conducting prosecutions. 'Few Magistrates presiding over Courts in which police officers are promiscuously deputed to prosecute', wrote the Outdshoorn magistrate in 1915, 'cannot relate cases of gross miscarriage of justice in consequence of the hopeless incompetency of the prosecutor' (UG 39 1918: 65). The police themselves objected to having to carry out the 'onerous' and 'arduous' functions of public prosecution. In 1919 the Public Service Commission agreed with the commissioner that there should be a 'buffer' between police and courts, and that the 'reputation for fairness and impartiality' of the force was being 'compromised' (96). Another frequent remark was that young Afrikaners from rural areas were at sea as police in large urban areas (UG 36 1918: 61).

My purpose in relating these criticisms is to allow a pause to reflect on the different levels of competence and effectiveness of the new state, and the gap between legislative and administrative ambitions and agenda and the actual levels of working of the state machine. Neither the resources nor the capacity of the new state matched the sophistication of the legal and administrative structure which it had borrowed from the imperial power over the years. One of the values of looking at policing, and at the administration of laws, is that it can show how the state was incomplete. The remarks of three Natal magistrates (UG 35 1920: 86), who charac- terised the system as a 'farce', captures some of the sense of the magis- trates' reports on law enforcement in the years after Union. This was a weak state which failed not only in routine administration of law and order, but failed also in those areas to which it devoted the maximum effort – the control of alcohol, and of African migration to urban areas. It is in this gap between ambition and failure that the mechanisms of legality were located.

The employment of black police was always regarded as problematic, not only because of the defence function of the police, but because of the limited range of functions black police could perform. The basic limita- tion perceived was that they could not be used to police or arrest whites, and many felt that they should not be used to patrol any areas but those that were exclusively black. Many rural magistrates urged the greater use of blacks, because of their linguistic knowledge, and their greater capacity to perform detective work among the black population. In the Transvaal black police were used to enforce the pass and tax laws, and in the rural areas to patrol villages and report stock movements. They were also 'frequently employed in the carrying out, under the supervision of white policemen, of raids in locations, compounds, etc.' (UG 62 1912: 43). But there were other issues canvassed, especially in the urban areas. One was that one of the most important functions of urban police was the examination of passes, and it was felt that a largely illiterate black force was unable to do this effectively. Better educated blacks, it was noted in 1913, had been tried in Natal, 'but in almost every case they were found to be untrustworthy'. Nonetheless the extreme difficulties of policing Johannesburg made the use of literate black police seem a desirable option. Another sensitive problem was the tribal make-up of the black force. Colonel Truter, then commanding the Transvaal police, reported in 1912 that Zulus were used for urban policing because they were 'undoubtedly the best material' (ibid.). The Assaults Commission, however, warned that the police 'Zulus do not treat other natives with reasonable sympathy' (UG 39 1913: 29). In 1911 nearly one-third of the Transvaal force of over 3,000 were black police (UG 62 1912: 33).

Recruitment of white police was both a managerial and a political problem. In the Transvaal before Union the make-up of the force was a matter for acute political controversy. After the introduction of Responsible Government a two-year residence qualification was introduced to limit recruitment from England. After Union tensions between English and Afrikaner recruits to the force were rife. The senior ranks of the force were manned either by English speakers or those perceived as supporters of the South African Party. Afrikaners recruited into the lower ranks were not only politically distanced but were alienated by low pay and military-style discipline. Truter explained that great difficulty had been experienced in 'obtaining the right class' of recruit. The majority were 'of Dutch extraction . . . whose educational qualifications left much to be desired', and who required classes in 'reading and writing'. Basically the police were recruiting from the bottom of the white labour market because of competition from the gold-mining industry and other areas offering higher rates of pay to the literate and educated (UG 62 1912: 37). Similar problems with obtaining white recruits with 'any education' were reported from the Free State (73). Reflecting a major grievance in the existing police force about recruitment from outside South Africa, the Transvaal's two-year period of residence became a national requirement. This did not stop disputes about who ought to be in the force. Discussions of how to provide work for the growing poor white population canvassed the desirability of their recruitment into the police, especially when they had been weakened by the outbreak of war, but as a modernised force developed, this was not simple. On the one hand there was constant criticism, often from the magistrates, of the low quality of police recruits and policing. This prompted the raising of the minimum educational standard from Standard 4 to Standard 6. But it also produced a fierce reaction. It was, said a National Party member representing a country district, 'nothing but a concession to the jingoes' (Hansard 3/7/20). Nonetheless the low status of prestige of police work can be gauged from the report of the Bethulie magistrate for 1916 in which he remarked that poor whites would not enlist in the service as it was 'not dignified enough for them' (UG 36 1918: 32). Growing tensions were evident also in the introduction of a colour bar and the demotion of those classified as coloured (Hansard 3/4/18).

A group of senior officers advised the commissioner that this was 'a positive danger to the safety of the State'. The South African force was, they claimed, the lowest paid of the large forces in the empire. They warned of the 'disintegrating influences now being brought to bear upon the Police Force by trade unionism and other disturbing agencies' and of their 'conviction' that should the police of any one division refuse duty, all would follow nationwide (National Archives Jus. 46/605/10. 1923). In November 1918 it was reported that informal mass meetings of police had been held and that new Dutch constables and overseas men with long service were for the first time united (*Rand Daily Mail*, 25/11/18 in ibid.). The crisis in the police force was brought to a head by the strike in the Cape force. While the strike was brought on by the acute economic pressure faced by members of the force as a result of rising inflation and static salaries, it also illustrated the basic divide between uneducated Afrikaner lower ranks, and their English-speaking officers (SC 5 1918: 50). The commissioner, Truter, who threatened the strikers with the 'utmost rigour of the law' and sentences of six months hard labour, affirmed that all the strikers but one were 'Dutchmen' (47–8; 65). He noted the press agitation in Johannesburg against police malpractices and admitted that police 'are inclined to go into debt. Sometimes they arrest natives and take money from them. That is generally the uninitiated young man and is usually the outcome of his upbringing. Of course they are mostly Dutch' (77).

As a culmination of the problems of the police force, and in the context of the general review, the Public Service Commission of Enquiry reported on the police in 1919 (UG 46 1919). They noted that while police everywhere were not representatives of an arbitrary power, but protectors of the rights of all, in South Africa they were 'liable to be called upon at any time to suppress or control civil disturbances' and therefore needed 'certain military training'. 'Both forces may be mobilised for active service in the field and be required to perform military duties' (4). The evidence given to the 1919 commission by senior police officers reflects the same concern as that of the magistrates with the quality of the recruits to the force. It is worth considering at length because of the apprehension of weakness about the forces that defended the white state, and the picture of the whites who were the first line of defence that is conveyed. The Deputy Commissioner in Johannesburg told the commission that 'the force is simply going to the dogs at present . . . We are steering straight on the rocks.' It was pointed out that the age and standard of education (eighteen years and Standard 4) at which recruits were accepted were 'considerably below' those that prevailed in Britain, the Dominions, or Europe, and that their three- to five-month training ('Swedish drill, including locks and holds. Musketry. Foot and Mounted drill. Law. Preliminary lessons in First Aid') was insufficient. The moral strains put upon recruits were too great. The commission concluded:

> It seems beyond doubt that the real reason why recruits of this low standard of age and education are accepted is the fact that it was desired, with the best intentions, to afford a useful and honourable career to Europeans who belong to the 'poor white' and 'bijwoner' classes. *This policy has broken down.* (14)

The commission recommended a minimum educational qualification of Standard 6, and an entry age of at least twenty (15) and the amalgamation of the SAMR with the police in a single force under the control of the Ministry of Justice (19). The unity of defence and policing was breaking: after 1922 it was no longer possible for the Governor-General to assign defence units to policing duties. However the idea that the function of the police was really a defence function remained on the agenda. South Africa's defence problem was internal, wrote R. F. Currey in 1930, and he pleaded for a return to a police force 'trained on military principles' for the 'soldier-policing' of 'native districts' (1930: 370–2). An army was not needed, he argued, as external defence rested on the Royal Navy.

Policing

The frontiers of the state's struggle to establish its version of law and order were the zones of interracial activity. There were two main areas of interracial criminal co-operation which concerned the police. One involved the control of alcohol and the enforcement of the prohibition laws.[1] Another involved the policing of the South African economic crimes of trading in illicit gold and diamonds. The Transvaal law on illicit gold buying was based on the Cape diamond law of 1882 which aimed primarily at the receiver and made possession a felony, placing the onus of proving lawful possession on the accused, and giving wide powers of search and seizure to the police. Policing the liquor, gold and diamond laws was not easy. In all three cases the *modus operandi* depended on a process of trapping, which, Blackburn and Caddell write, 'never had public sympathy or acquiescence' (1911: 132). Police agents, as sellers, would entice offenders, usually poor whites, into the transaction (observed, as the courts insisted on corroboration of what was strictly speaking accomplice evidence, by another policeman). In the case of the liquor transaction, as the essence of the criminal nature of the act was that it needed a white to supply a black, conviction depended on the use of black evidence against white, against which there was strong white public and judicial feeling (see e.g. Blackburn and Caddell 1911: 38).

The Report of the Transvaal Police Commissioner, Truter, for 1911, gives an indication of police problems, and indicates the difficulties the legal definitions imposed on the police. Illicit gold buyers, he wrote, managed to get alloy into the gold purchased. They would have their furnace ready in anticipation of customers. No purchase price would be paid until a silver or copper coin had been added to the gold and melted. As soon as this was done, 'the detectives are powerless', as the excuse was put forward that the metal was melted-down ornaments, and that the gold was in a manufactured state. The Reef was, he said, 'absolutely overstocked' with jewellers and pawnbrokers, many of whom had previous gold law convictions (UG 62 1912: 47–8). Much of the problem with the gold law was put down to foreigners. Foreign devils were consistently on the minds of the police, and the problem of crime was closely connected

---

[1] For a lively early description of the liquor trade and the problems of policing it in the Transvaal see Blackburn and Caddell (1911: chapter 3).

in their minds with the immigration of groups alien to the South African social order. The Transvaal police operated a foreign criminal staff,

> which was principally engaged with matters concerning the foreign element in the Country. There are large numbers of undesirable aliens, including Russian Jews, Syrians, Greeks, Italians, Portuguese and others, who keep restaurants, kaffir eating houses, illicit liquor dens, gambling saloons and opium dens, which are frequented by criminal classes belonging to the white and black races. These places require constant supervision in order to prevent organised crime, illicit liquor and gold dealing and other offences. (50)

He noted that 'local criminals . . . will . . . in time . . . develop into dangerous men of the oversea type that infested the country after the War' (69).

After the outbreak of war in 1914 and the enlistment of many in the police and the withdrawal of the South African Mounted Rifles from policing, many of the rural areas became, to a considerable degree, self-policing, as farmers became honorary police and dealt with stock and black labour and trespass cases (UG 28 1915: 79–80). Nonetheless the Cape magistrates reported wide areas going virtually unpoliced (ibid.). The sense of the inadequacy magistrates and police felt about their capacity to police the large black population comes through regularly in the reports. While there was little sense that matters internal to these communities needed policing, it was around the fringes where violence threatened others, and where theft, particularly of stock, took place, that more police were wanted. Dogs were considered, though the Johannes-burg magistrate wondered about their ability to 'pick one particular native . . . from a group' (UG 36 1918: 62).

It is noteworthy that the main problem seized on as a result of the withdrawal of rural mounted police once war began was not an outbreak of criminal violence, but problems with the enforcement of labour discipline, and this underlines the crucial part that rural policing played in this. The magistrate in Prieska, a centre of General Maritz's rebellion, where the civil government was directly challenged, reported that with the dislocation of policing there were 'complaints by farmers that native servants had deserted in some cases and were difficult to manage in others' (UG 28 1915: 81). In Volksrust 'farmers complained loudly of the disobedience of their servants and the losses of stock, which resulted from the removal of the police' (119). In Natal the major problem raised was that of the failure of tax collection from the black population, which was a policing function.

Alongside the weakness of the state's police, both the state and the large employers of labour developed their own systems of private policing of compounds and plantations. These continued to develop in spite of the scandal about the abuse of whipping of labourers in the mine workers' compounds in the Transvaal under Milner. In Lord Selborne's words, in cases of 'breaches of discipline and trivial offences for which it was not considered necessary to prosecute' compound managers were authorised to inflict 'slight corporal punishment of such a nature as is permitted in schools in England' (Worsfold 1913, vol. II: 361). While the infliction of punishment without formal legal processes was purportedly abandoned, private policing remained. There were numerous references to the problems of policing the mining compounds which were perceived as hotbeds of criminal activity and violence beyond police control. The obsession with the liquor traffic dominated here too. Large amounts of liquor were supplied to, and consumed in, compounds. The Police Commissioner's report for 1912 records: 'The Native Compound Police are utterly unreliable in as far as the suppression of the illicit liquor traffic is concerned . . . they are almost always in the pay of the illicit dealer' (UG 62 1912: 80). On the Natal sugar estates 'there existed a system of privately paid police . . . [for] the large barracks full of frequently quarrelsome and thieving Asiatics. These men were uniformed' (UG 28 1915: 158). In addition much local rural policing depended on the village headmen. In the words of the Cape report for 1916, 'order is principally maintained by the native headmen, who, the Magistrate fears, have not always the respect which they should have for statutory prohibitions' (UG 36 1918: 70).

Surveillance of political subversion was also the duty of the police. What is of note here is the proactive role the police leadership took in proposing new laws for the control of political activity, especially as communists became more active. In April 1921 the Police Commissioner concluded his report on Bolshevism in the Union of South Africa by writing:

> As mentioned in previous reports there is an urgent need for suitable legislation to strengthen the hands of the Executive Government and the Police in dealing with the revolutionary agencies at work . . . The Communists are a very determined party and realise to the full the value of winning our coloured population over . . . To this end the preaching or promulga-

tion of doctrines calculated to cause serious discontent among them, or to inflame or engender in them resentment against the Government should be prohibited under severe penalty.

He distinguished between white and black in relation to the severity of the measures required: 'To the activities carried out among the European community, more latitude can be allowed.' After the political violence of 1922 he reported that the lessons of the Rand rebellion were that 'no efforts should be spared to introduce legislation and administrative machinery to deal with this evil before it again assumes such proportions'. Noting the links which Ivon Jones had with the Communist International, Truter concluded that 'it is highly probable that the Communists in the Union are guided by instructions issued from Russian Headquarters'. They were 'astute enough' to know that the Dominions, especially India and South Africa, were 'particularly vulnerable'. The blacks, wrote Truter, were being told that whites were 'out to make this a white man's country regardless of the interests of the Native races', and that the Cape franchise would be abolished (Truter–Smuts, 8/7/22; 11/8/22).[2]

In his report, after surveying the work of white communists, the activities of the Universal Negro Improvement Association, the Industrial and Commercial Workers' Union (ICU) and the Transvaal Native Congress, the Commissioner wrote: 'The discontent, unrest and lack of employment existing in the country afford ideal scope and opportunity to the Revolutionary agitator . . . We have in our midst agitators whose ability is unquestionable and whose faith in the doctrines of Bolshevism cannot be shaken.' He urged that communist gatherings be suppressed and that 'Bolshevik disciples' born outside the Union be deported. There was continuing concern about the control of immigration of communists. Truter noted in his report of March 1925 (CP/SJ 3/3/25) that there was a danger of an increased influx of 'low class persons' from Russia and the pre-war Russian empire and that 'this is the class of person which is most likely to assist in the fostering of Communist doctrines in our midst'. The immigration authorities ought, therefore, to enquire into the 'attitude towards Bolshevism' of all intended immigrants.

Police also reported on the growth of republican sentiment; political agitation related to publications about the 1915 rebellion; political attacks

---

[2] The following paragraphs are based on correspondence from the Union Archives collected on microfilm by CAMP – the Comparative Africana Microfilm Project.

on participation in the war and the nature of the peace imposed on Germany; as well as on Irish nationalist sympathisers. All these were regarded as sensitive topics. The rationale for monitoring inter-white conflicts was related to white prestige. On the 'inflammatory publications' of the Sinn Fein movement, such as 'English Atrocities in Ireland', the commissioner wrote that the time was coming when it would be necessary to suppress pamphlets of this kind 'as apart from the question of an infringement of the law, they fall into the hands of coloured persons who can read and tend to undermine the prestige of the European race' (PC/SJ 21/2/21).

The Police Commissioner also reported regularly to the Minister of Justice and through him to the Prime Minister on the activities of the African National Congress and other political groups and Zionist churches. But the reports lack the urgency and intensity of the concerns with communism, and, ironically, provided one of the rare ways in which an African political voice could be heard in government. While there were frequent proposals at congresses of the ANC, and meetings of the ICU, and of the Communist Party, that there should be mass actions in defiance of the pass laws, and that the gaols should be filled, the Police Commissioner's reports at no time give any indication that there was concern about campaigns of defiance. However, when it was suspected that there was a connection between the Communist Party and other movements concern intensified. Secret police reports noted the movement towards closer co-operation between the ICU and leading communists. In June 1926 Truter took up the question specifically (CP/SJ 18/6/26). While there was, he said, 'little public indication of an extension of the Communist movement, it is clear that a determined effort . . . is being made to disaffect the native races, and is bearing fruit in the unveiled advocacy by officials of the ICU of the Communist Party's principles'. The followers of the ICU, he wrote, were still primitive, and their opinions were easily moulded by extremists. Serious and far-reaching trouble would come about if this was not checked. 'Legislation to curb freedom of action and speech which is so much abused today, may be unpopular, but the need of it has beyond all doubt been established'.

4

Criminology

As I suggested in chapter 2, comprehension of a legal culture, and the role of legal formalism within it, depends on relating the various discourses about law to each other. To understand the criminal law one must encompass the thinking about crime, criminals and criminality, and penology. Contextualisation means more than setting law or criminology within a background of 'society'. Culler reminds us that contextualisation 'seems to presume that the context is given, and determines the meaning of the act' (1988: ix). But, as he says, 'context is not given but produced'. He suggests instead the notion of 'framing' which 'reminds us that framing is something that we do'. The outcome of framing criminology and criminal law is an illustration of the ways in which apparently scientific and practical areas of knowledge and activities depend on a structured imagination of selves and others. This is of particular interest in the search for an understanding of legalism in a colonial society in which racial differences are central to criminal justice.

At first sight legal preoccupations and discourses, legal methods and techniques, appear to have been strikingly separated from and different from those of criminology and penology. The imperatives of both the situation of white rule in South Africa and of the criminological and penological agenda were urgent, wide and sweeping. Yet the mechanisms of the law could at times be restricting and limiting in relation to the exercise of power. Despite this ostensible difference between purposes and tools, I shall, by showing their complementarity, try to illuminate the nature of legality in the new state. South African discourses on crime were not focused on the immediate political and economic problems of a new, and insecure, independence in a country in which a white minority ruled a black majority. The period in South Africa about which I am writing saw the accelerating motion of an engine of oppression. In the early years of the state there was a huge leap in the numbers sentenced and imprisoned. Very nearly all were black men, prosecuted under the taxation, pass, and masters and servants laws. In these years the process was centred on the Transvaal.[1] The labour of a dispossessed peasantry was being mobilised by mining, industry and an increasingly capitalist agriculture; many were being proletarianised and urbanised under the harshest conditions. The criminalisation of huge numbers in these processes of labour coercion and control of movement and residence was not, however, the primary matter seen and debated when the problems of crime and its control were discussed. These processes were explicitly observed and discussed in the political debates about labour and land. But, while both ideology and institutions were developed within the context of the struggle by the new white state to control blacks in the process of urbanisation, the specific debates about crime drew upon other and quite distinctive discourses. Read now, many of the thoughts discussed here appear both extreme and bizarre. But they were not then an isolated corner of racist thought at odds with liberal and egalitarian principles immanent in Western thought but were expressed from within the common sense of the Western scientific and legal worlds.

In analysing the South African criminology of this period a number of basic features become plain. As in all colonial situations, the parameters of science were imported from Britain, Europe and North America, and discussions of local society remained dependent upon formulations from elsewhere. The external discourses are, however, used to describe particular local situations, which leads to choices, emphases and adaptations. This process of observation and description of the local through external discourses contributes to the air of unreality, to an apparent inability to perceive. Finally, the external discourses were used to describe and to construct difference between criminal and righteous, black and white. When we look at the criminal law we can see the same features. These parallels enable a new approach to be taken to the analysis of the working of criminal law in this period. The framework, concepts and procedures of law (both English and Roman-Dutch) were imported. Different emphases

[1] For an analysis of the figures see Sachs (1973: 162–70). See too van Onselen (1985: 68) for his discussion of the 'dramatic tightening of the bands of a labour repressive system' and the consequent 'explosive increase in the size of the Transvaal prison population'. Between 1912 and 1932 the number of persons of all races prosecuted increased from 46 per thousand to 72.3. The numbers convicted rose from 37.8 per thousand to 63.1 (Simons 1936: 29). Far more acts were criminalised and policing was intensified.

developed and they were given, in the local situation, some new statutory content. The briefest acquaintance with judicial discourse shows its remove from reality; its distance from description; its perception and presentation of the world through singular lenses. And, as in the case of criminology, the interplay between the imported discourses, the local needs and the consequent perceptual distortions produced a criminal law which served to describe and to constitute otherness of a subject population. International discourses float above societies like clouds over a continent. Depending on the local features sometimes they linger and block out the sun; sometimes they just disperse; sometimes there is rain. In the first instance they may prevent the locals from fashioning an understanding of local circumstances; in the third they will raise up a local understanding which has grown up as a result of their influence, but it will be one that will continue to be dependent on external words and concepts.

The international criminological agenda

Thought and writing concerning crime in any society can usefully be considered as a form of ethnography. It is by now a common observation that ethnographical thought is about others and otherness. Ethnographical writing describes, or better, constructs, this otherness, and simultaneously, in opposition, outlines the lineaments of the position of the observer (Boon 1982; Clifford and Marcus 1986). The nature of criminological thought as a form of ethnography becomes very much clearer in colonial and imperial situations. Where the state is white and most of the ruled and most of the criminals are black, the description and construction of criminal otherness is subsumed within a larger discourse about the otherness of the subjects. Thus the received criminological theories were not simply applied but adapted to the South African situations which were perceived and discussed in their terms.[2] Turn-of-the-century criminology in the metropole now reads clearly as one of the scripts of the intensified class warfare there. It had to be adapted for use in colonial

---

[2] Cf. the remarks of van Zyl Smit (1989: 227): criminological ideas 'are incorporated into national criminologies and applied in specific penal practices'. The ideas, he goes on, are 'transformed' in the process of incorporation into these discourses. But the national discourses, particularly in colonial countries, are constantly transformed, in that they are restructured by the ideas prevailing outside.

situations on the periphery. The institutions of the new South African state were made at a time of a revolution in Europe and America in thinking about crime and state responses, and they reflect this thought in an adapted form. I draw attention here first to the adaptations of 'scientific' criminology in South Africa and also to its connections with the anthropological thought of the period. Criminology in South Africa adapted developing themes not so much in order to 'understand' the black criminal but to construct a composite picture of the black/criminal. Western criminology, itself deeply concerned with the construction of otherness, was in South Africa (and also in the USA) easily turned to the construction of racial separateness.

If, as I suggest we should, we think about criminological writing in Europe and North America as a form of ruling-class ethnographic writing about elements of the subject population within, it is not surprising that at the turn of the century it had many close affinities with the developing science of anthropology, which dealt with the subjects without. Both came to be concerned not with common features of humanity but with funda-mental differences which were found in physical and in mental character-istics. In North America there were fixations on the crimogenic nature both of blacks and of the Southern and Eastern European immigrants in the cities, while in Britain preoccupations were with degeneracy and feeble-mindedness among the working-class home population of the empire. These obsessions become particularly important in the South African context. Three other features were vital. Criminology claimed to offer a scientific understanding of crime. In the South African situation it offered, therefore, a justification of a form of oppression without the necessity to resort overtly to the politics of race. The second was the concern with 'physicalism': the search for the roots of crime in 'an aberration or abnormality of the individual's constitution'. The third was the close concern with the nature of the brain. Garland (1985: 111–12, 114) notes that the categories of moral imbecile, moral insanity, degen-eracy and feeble-mindedness were taken over from the new psychiatry and became a basic part of criminological thought. These categories of course converged with and overlapped those in the forefront of anthropological thinking about the different mentality of inferior races. It became hard to separate inherent criminality from the fundamental physical, mental and cultural characteristics of savagery and blackness. Indeed, there was a tendency to collapse the two. As Havelock Ellis wrote in his widely read

The Criminal (first published in 1890), criminals were in a state of 'atavism' and 'constantly reproduced the features of savage character – want of forethought, inaptitude for sustained labour, love of orgy etc.' (quoted in Wiener 1990: 209). The criminal, Ellis elaborated, acted like a savage in a foreign environment: 'a simple and incomplete creature must inevitably tend to adopt those simple and incomplete modes of life which are natural to the savage' (255). This kind of thinking was not confined to theorists. The chairman of the English Prison Commission described habitual criminals in 1875 as having characteristics 'entirely those of the inferior races of mankind – wandering habits, utter laziness, want of moral sense, cunning' (301). If criminals were like savages, then all savages were potentially criminals. Much criminological writing found it hard to deal with black criminals as individual moral actors responding to situations. The situations became less relevant to the explanation of black actions than the inherent nature of blacks. This posed problems for a criminal law organised around the notion of guilty intention in relation to specific acts. As Garland points out, the new penology 'was caught in a contradictory position, *being both for and against determinism*' (1985: 185). If determinism was taken too far, there could be no grounds for punishing a liable offender. South African thinking about crime, I will suggest, had a way of avoiding this problem. It tended towards determinism in relation to black offenders, but to the possibility of amelioration of offending whites. As we shall see this had effects on the policies thought appropriate to deal with whites and with blacks, as well as on the interpretation of criminal intention in the courts, and in the first quarter of the century there was an accelerating movement away from a unitary approach.[3]

While a belief in the innate disposition to violence among primitives was an organising node of explaining black actions, the approach to white crime was different. White criminals were weak or defective individuals. But they could be rescued, particularly if they could be separated from contact with blacks. Contact itself was infectious: criminality spread like a disease from lower races to higher. Garland notes similar concerns in late nineteenth-century England with the 'containment and quarantine' of the 'dangerous classes', and the images of 'danger, demoralisation and con-

---

[3] Van Zyl Smit writes of Afrikaner criminology of the 1940s that while it employed a social emphasis on issues like poverty to explain white crime, it abandoned this focus when it turned to black crime, concentrating there on 'organic differences'. This had long been a feature of South African criminology (1989: 227).

tamination'(1985: 38–41). We might find thinking about the nature of control of disease more useful in understanding attitudes to crime in this context than the more conventional focus on 'social control'. Legislation for the control of infectious diseases was passed during this period and was based on sweeping contaminated blacks out of contact with whites. There were similarities in the responses to the 'crisis' of the rising crime rate in the new cities, where the increasing numbers of black urban residents lived in some places alongside poor whites. These were presented as remedies to infectious pollution as much as defences against the challenges to social order.[4]

Some saw a reverse infection: a spreading of crime from those degraded whites in contact with blacks. This was based upon another stereotype: that of the easily corruptible, mystified and gullible tribal innocent. In this view the ingenuous tribesmen who came to the cities were infected and corrupted by more sophisticated but debased poor whites.[5] It was, said the important 1905 Native Affairs Commission, 'an axiom' that contact with Western civilisation was 'demoralising' for 'primitive races' and introduced 'new forms of sexual immorality, intemperance and dishonesty' (quoted in Simons, 1936: 2). Poor whites were letting the side down in the worst sense. But these whites could be saved because their very debasement was seen as deriving directly from their close contact with blacks. Separation was the cure both for the poor white disease and the infecting of blacks.[6]

---

[4] Compare the frequent demands from magistrates for control of syphilis. The compulsory medical examination of all blacks living in urban areas was suggested (UG 39 1918: 78). In 1913 one Cape magistrate reported having convicted a man who had had syphilis for not submitting to the prescribed treatment. Printed with the heading 'Danger in the household', the report recounts how the accused had engaged himself as a kitchen boy, 'there being no outward sign of the disease' (UG 44 1913: 100). There were many other accounts of infected servants. The Public Health Act passed in 1919 provided, among other matters, for the prevention and suppression of venereal diseases. The onus was placed on those who suffered from them to place themselves under medical treatment. It also provided for compulsory detention and treatment of the infected (see also Swanson 1977).

[5] See Bain (1938: 37–8). Even Simons, the writer in this field most sympathetic to Africans, employed a primal innocence/urban corruption opposition. Men and women, he wrote, 'who themselves, or whose recent ancestors, had been orderly and law abiding in the tribe became hooligans, criminals and prostitutes in the centres of white civilisation' (1936: 1). However, in this formulation the seeds of criminality lay not in the primitive savagery, but in the new oppressions: unemployment and the extremes of poverty and wealth. This was not a common South African analysis.

[6] Cf. again van Zyl Smit on the 1940s: crime-control policies 'based on the science of criminology' demanded the 'strict separation of the races' (1989: 240).

Labour

Debates within the country drew upon the most recent and reformatory of international fashions of thought, and statutes faithfully constructed local versions of laws that had been enacted elsewhere, with a strong preference for British precedents. The construction of the black/criminal was inherent not only in racial rule but also for the control of labour. The development of the systems of control of labour and the quest for a disciplined labour force had long tended to blur the boundary line between not working and criminality (though the blurring of this boundary was, as we shall see below, not a peculiarly South African habit). The vagrancy laws, the pass laws and the confinement of mine workers to compounds, which controlled the movement of labour, and the masters and servants laws, which criminalised the breach of a labour contract, developed into an essential part of this apparatus. The elaborate framework which had been constructed during the latter part of the nineteenth century for controlling the black/criminal/worker made even more pointed the contrast with the uncontrolled zone of freedom along the unsegregated racial frontier in the rapidly growing cities, which came to be regarded as the most dangerous area for the production of crime in South African society.

It is significant that, at first, in the period of reconstruction after the South African War, the transposition of the international agenda led to a blurring of the line between not working and criminality in the case of white workers as well. The Transvaal Indigency Commission, which was composed of imperial ideologues and bureaucrats associated with Lord Milner's post-war regime, had to consider the new problem of the 'poor whites'. How were landless and unskilled whites to fit into the new urban and industrial society? It was accepted as obvious that they could not compete with blacks in the unskilled labour market. The relationship between white poverty and crime was analysed in a chapter of its report entitled 'The Lazy and the Vicious' (TG 11 1908: chapter 3). Johannesburg was presented as an urban running sore, the stage for the corruption of displaced rural whites who there were tempted by the illicit gold and alcohol trades. If a white was convicted, the commission said, the normal prison sentence was too short, because white prisoners should be taught a trade to lift them beyond black competition. In this respect it was noted that 'in other countries indeterminate sentences were coming into vogue'.

But what of those who were simply 'vagrants and loafers'? The 'only way' to deal with this class was 'to make any form of culpable idleness an offence punishable with hard labour'. To do this they urged the use of an old English tool, and recommended the adoption of an English style vagrancy law to apply to whites in the Transvaal (139–40). But they also drew on the more 'progressive' discussions of the problem. The English Departmental Committee on Vagrancy (Cd 2852 1906) was quoted as authority for the view that a vagrant was not a criminal in the ordinary sense but someone requiring detention 'on account of his mode of life'. The Transvaal Commissioners noted that 'the treatment that they need is to be forced to work', that criminal sanctions were insufficient, and that the 'only alternative' was 'a long period of hard labour in a labour colony'. And they invoked not only an English model. The report contains an extended, detailed and approving discussion of labour colonies in Germany, Switzerland and Belgium, which provided for long periods of detention for vagrants and which not only stopped the 'idle and vicious from contaminating each other' but prevented them from 'propagating their kind to prey upon the next generation' (TG 11: 140, 143). It is significant that while the imperial bureaucracy did not distinguish between the criminal propensities of workless whites and blacks, local politicians had to. While white political power prevented the application of these ideas to whites once the country became independent in 1910, there were few obstacles in the way of their enlistment in relation to blacks.

Urbanisation and segregation

The appeal of the new criminological thinking in the South African context is clear when we consider the force of Garland's remark that 'The advantages of criminology lay in its rejection of . . . formal liberal egalitarianism . . . It insisted upon a qualitative differentiation which would trace out the dangerous classes and the real contours of criminality.' Furthermore, as he writes, 'the existence of a class which was constantly criminalised . . . could now be explained by reference to the natural, constitutional propensities of these individuals, thereby excluding all reference to the character of the law, of politics or of social relations' (1985: 130). The analysis of crime was also set in a complex of fears about black urbanisation which included anxiety about black proletarianisation, potential political agitation and competition for jobs. To the rulers of South Africa those most criminally dangerous were quite clearly visible. They were not an undifferentiated mass of blacks but specifically the inhabitants of the racial interface in the urban slums. The targets of South African criminological thinking and policy were not simply the drunks, feeble-minded, vagrants and habitual criminals that inhabited the overseas discipline's world, but those with a specific location in social geography. They were the newly urbanised blacks, the poor whites who mixed with them, and the urban 'coloureds' who were seen to inhabit this dangerous societal habitat. The ecology of this world was seen by police, policy makers and the public to revolve around interracial sex, the provision of alcohol by whites to blacks, and the reverse flow of *dagga* (marijuana). It was a nightmare construction representing the reversal of the South African moral ideal. One of the fundamental aims of the new criminology was anticipation and pre-emption: 'the discovery of the infected members of society *before* their disease has become an actual offence' (H. M. Boies; quoted at ibid.: 132). In South Africa that discovery was easy. The treatment was clear: the destruction of the habitat and the separation of urban blacks and poor whites.

There was a further ingredient to analysis and that was the constant preoccupation of the enforcers of law with the state of mind of the populations in relation to authority, and in the potential for their acceptance of state authority to break down. This was hardly surprising in view of the frequency of rebellions among both white and black. Law enforcement in general was coloured by the possibility of revolt. An important part of this was the fear that the appearance of weakness in white authority, as well as the existence of hostility and division among whites, could have an effect on the 'native mind' and excite disaffection. Rumours of unrest, war, strikes and rebellion were all believed to have extremely dangerous destabilising effects on the 'native mind' even though Africans were not a party to the political struggles involved. This form of anxiety linked with alarmist analysis of crime. In their report for the year 1911 the Transvaal CID observed that:

> The outstanding features in connection with criminal statistics is the steady increase in the number of native criminals; this can only be attributed to the environment of the natives working in the Witwatersrand area. Raw natives from all parts of South Africa are being debauched by all classes of criminals and illicit traders on the Reef, and *the result in the course of time*

is too terrible to contemplate with equanimity. The only solution of this
question is the close compounding of all natives who work on the mining
areas. (UG 62 1912: 45; my emphasis)

The language, as usual, was apocalytpic, the solutions proposed extreme.
Thus it is not so much the figures related to criminal convictions that
seem important as the meaning attached to them, in particular in relation
to the state of the social formation as a whole. It is notable that in relation
to serious crimes most were committed within racial groups, with very
few crimes of violence that crossed the colour line reaching the courts.
Yet, the report continued later, 'The native criminals continue to call for
special attention, and the condition of the country is becoming less safe
every year on their account . . . The necessity for banishing native
criminals from industrial centres . . . is becoming more pressing every
year' (70). The recommendation was the establishing of distant penal
arcadias in 'remote portions of the Union' where offending Africans
'could live in freedom and cultivate the land' instead of being released
back into the urban community. The official, and the public, mind lived
on the edge of an apocalypse in relation to these matters. This atmosphere
was a part of the workings of the criminal justice system.

The criminalised state of urbanised blacks was often contrasted with an
image of a crime-free tribal state. Africans in their natural tribal habitat
were restrained; in towns, where the restraints were not operative, their
natural primitive passions were released. In the tribal world people were
seen as being dominated by taboos, fear of witchcraft and the authority of
the chiefs. As the report of the Commission into Assaults on Women put
it, the black standard of morality 'bears no comparison' with that of
Europeans. Blacks were just emerging from 'barbarism': 'Yet in their
barbarism they have always had a social system and institutions which,
with all their defects, have also had a side which exercises considerable
influence for good. Loyalty to the Chief and to the Tribe has always been
the mainspring of their morality' (UG 39 1913: 13).

The lasting nature of this theme is evident as it is taken up two decades
later by the words of the Native Economic Commission: 'Under their
tribal system discipline was well maintained and the habits so instilled in
them persist today in the majority of natives' (UG 22 1932: para. 776).
Rules of conduct were 'bolstered by fear of the supernatural'. The image of
tribal absolutism, particularly Zulu absolutism, was pervasive and impor-

tant in many discursive contexts in South Africa. The Native Economic Commission took as its touchstone Bryant's *Olden Times in Zululand and Natal* which it quoted at length:

> The one great law that governed there was the law of complete submission to parental authority; and that authority was drastically enforced. Unquestioning, unanswering obedience to the supreme power was demanded without distinction of all alike, of mothers, of sons (some of them already middle aged men with families of their own), of every child . . . And what each inmate of the kraal saw practised by the father, he in turn practised of his own regard, demanding of all his juniors the same measure of obedience as was demanded of him by those above. (Bryant 1929; quoted in Id para. 39)

This image was both generalised and extended: as the commissioners remarked, what Bryant said of the Zulu home obtained generally in black society, and this was being, to the great distress of parents everywhere, undermined by urbanisation and the escape of children into a life of immorality.

The construction of this world was conspicuously resistant to the developments within academic anthropology. It remained the touchstone of popular and official ethnographic descriptions, and permeated into official thinking, policy making and legal institutions. 'The Native's moral and social conduct', Bain wrote, 'is largely controlled by his belief in the power of the spirit world – that all his actions are constantly being watched and judged.' Fear of ancestors, group solidarity and a 'sense of loyalty and submission to authority' ensured proper behaviour (Bain 1938: 43, 50). It was also to be found in psychological writing which contributed to the science of the black mind. As B. J. F. Laubscher, senior psychiatrist in the Union government mental services, wrote: 'The native is a slave to the infantile status of his cultural development.' His fundamental security needs and tribal traditions were 'forces of rectitude' which could not be replaced by European culture. The transition from one culture to another 'requires a number of props and substitutes not at present available'. Emotional situations 'will stimulate the infantile and narcissistic components of the mind' (Laubscher 1937: 59). The infantile state of black culture also meant a deficit in civic responsibility. 'The native has his collective responsibility,' Laubscher wrote, 'but this collective responsibility is limited to his primitive social organisation and does not extend to the conception of a social responsibility embracing the

white man's conception of law' (316). Analyses of this lack of individual
responsibility were common. Simons quotes the Afrikaner criminologist
Willemse, who averred that African criminals existed because the African
was an 'undifferentiated person, a child, a natural man who feels and acts
more than he feels and thinks' (Simons 1936: 50).

In towns with 'controls and restraints lost and no substitute to put in
their place' a precocious individualism took over, constrained neither by
tribal group nor the moral individual conscience that whites had. With
regard to the latter there was 'abundant evidence' that, while Africans had
quickly absorbed white materialism, their 'assimilation of European
spiritual culture has been less rapid' (Bain 1938: 51–2). The theme of a
conscienceless individualism replacing the control of group and chief was
one of the most prominent in discussions of change in relation to the
African population (Chanock 1994). All the commentators, hostile or
sympathetic to the plight of Africans, employed a basic binary imagery
revolving around categories such as innocence/corruption; savage/civi-
lised; authority/lawlessness; purity/impurity. The effect was to render
perceptions of processes more extreme and apocalyptic. This appears
again in another conspicuous and closely related line of analysis, alongside
criminological discourse and often penetrating it, concerning the disintegration of the black family in towns. Individualism was perceived to be
leading to the collapse of the control of the patriarch in African families.
In contrast to the familial peace and observed obligations of tribal life,
urban families were menaced by 'an increasing revolt against parental
control and against the old tribal restrictions concerning sex relations'
(Bain 1938: 52; see further Chanock 1994). The collapse of authority over
women and over the young had important implications for criminology.
For it was seen to be at the root of the growth of two groups of the
inherently deviant: urban black youth and urban black women. While the
first group was troublesome in relation to fairly conventional gang crimes,
the second was of more basic importance. African chiefs and white
officials agreed in sensing that urban black women were the keys to new
dangers (La Hausse 1990: 85, 92). Their independence, combined with
that of the young male workers, seemed to present a fundamental
challenge to the patriarchal family system, though as La Hausse notes
erosion of male control was 'at best temporary' (110). Uncontrolled (and
uncontrollable) black women were also perceived to be at the centre of a
complex of what were considered to be real dangers to whites, the trades

in illicit sex and illicit alcohol. Illicit alcohol sales threatened the fabric of order because of the link with violent crime and also because of the polluting effects of the multi-racial *demi-monde* in which the alcohol trade was situated. Transracial sex imperilled the social and political order itself.

One of the most illuminating documents of the period is the report of the Commission Appointed to Enquire into Assaults on Women (UG 39 1913). While its appointment arose nominally out of a country-wide panic among whites, assiduously inflamed by press and politicians, concerning the perceived rise in the number of assaults by black men on white women, it was a response to a number of coalescing fears about the ability to maintain white security as the pace of black urbanisation quickened. The commission approached the problem in terms of a wide-ranging diagnosis of the spreading disease of interracial contact in the social order as a whole.[7] White women, they noted, were entirely safe in rural areas, where blacks were living in their 'natural environment' under 'tribal control'. We should note again the uncanny stability and continuity of representations of the problems by comparing the later diagnosis of the Native Economic Commission. The problem with urban relationships, in that commission's view, was that they were not wholly structured and, therefore, were full of potential violence. In rural areas, the commissioners wrote, blacks had 'determined' relationships with officials, missionaries, farmers and traders. But in the towns blacks met whites of all classes 'with a large number of whom definite standards of conduct are not a reciprocal rule' and 'explosive passion' was more easily stirred (UG 22 1932: para. 507).

What blacks did to each other was not the focus of criminological discussion. The answer to the violence of black urban crime was not primarily seen to be the policing of black communities, or the basic improvement in living standards, but to lie in the segregation of crimogenic blacks from whites. We can turn again to the Assaults Commission and note its total response to its specific task of investigation. At its core is described an entry into the nightmare of ruling-class white imagination,

---

[7] One should also note the prior report of the Transvaal Indigency Commission of 1908 (TG 11 1908), a source of the view that urban race mixing was itself crimogenic, and which drew particular attention to race mixing among youth and its supposed connection with youth crime.

the urban hell in which all the values of white South Africa were simply
reversed:

> Members of the Commission had an opportunity, under police protection
> and guidance, of visiting some of the slums of Johannesburg . . . and in
> these dwell whites, Chinese, Indians, Natives and others, on terms of
> equality . . . It is not necessary here to dwell on the evils of overcrowding
> as being subversive of decency and morality, or upon the positive vice
> which is being engendered through the poverty stricken condition of these
> people; the lowering of the white race and the loss of respect by the native
> for white people, by this close association of black and white, are the points
> upon which the Commission wishes to lay stress. (23)

Again there was a continuity in the analysis: these views were repeated two
decades later by the Native Economic Commission: 'Natives generally
respect Europeans as a race, but such respect cannot be maintained where
Natives and Europeans live side by side in the appalling slum conditions
existing in most of our large towns' (UG 22 1932: para. 687). Crime was
produced by the existence of this interracial frontier. The answer was to
prise the races apart. Whites could be dragged up: blacks pushed aside or
out. There was an 'imperative and urgent necessity of steps being taken to
uplift the fallen classes of the white races' (23). For blacks the 'evidence
was overwhelmingly in favour of a closed compound system' (i.e. a sort of
imprisonment at the workplace) for mine workers (30) and other
methods of local urban segregation. For blacks convicted of crimes
ordinary sentences were not enough. The Assaults Commission supported
proposals by the police and the Chamber of Mines for detention in
settlements for blacks convicted of serious crimes 'even in circumstances
in which the record of their convictions individually is not such as to
warrant an indeterminate sentence'. And it advocated the 'complete
removal' by deportation of 2,000 suspected dangerous blacks on the
Witwatersrand (33). As we shall see there were definite limitations in the
controlling capacities of the ordinary criminal law. And even where that
law was supported by a huge range of discriminatory statutes it was not an
ideal instrument for the control of crimogenic blacks. Methods by which
they could be dealt with after (and even before) sentence were creatively
developed from the criminological literature in the early years of the state.

But even though a moral order of sorts was granted to the tribal state,
there remained qualifications regarding sexual morality. The Assaults
Commission observed that Africans in the tribal state were 'brought up in

an atmosphere of immorality and lust' (UG 39 1913: 13). In the towns, deprived of the tribal constraints, this was let loose. The Director of Native Labour noted with regard to urbanisation 'the *contaminating* [my emphasis] influences to which they are there subjected (in which dissolute native women play a prominent part) are productive of a large number of natives of the idle, dissolute and criminal classes' (UG 22 1932: para. 779). This analysis could be taken further. Even apart from the presence of blacks, there was, as we have seen, a foreign element of whites considered to be responsible for the corruption of local whites, because, among other things, foreigners were unreliable in relation to racial separation.[8] The immorality squad wrote of its successful 'crusade against foreign pimps'. This had left prostitution on the Reef to be located among 'women who have chosen the life through their own inclinations . . . and the most deplorable surroundings connected therewith are to be found among low class whites, mostly criminals and illicit liquor dealers, who cohabit with native prostitutes' (UG 62 1912: 59, 64). There was a tendency in the analysis of crime to concentrate and telescope immorality in society as all taking place among particular groups who were responsible for all the evils together, not just one. This kind of analysis had two partly contra-dictory effects. As all evils were interconnected, everything had to be eliminated at once in order to eliminate one of them. And, as they all took place among the same target groups, all of the people in these had to be got rid of, so that all evils could be tackled at one swoop. There was a huge difference between the tenor of the reports about crime from urban and those from rural areas: while the former were full of accounts of horror and foreboding of things to come, the rural reports were by and large self-congratulatory on the state of law and order, apart from masters and servants offences, stock theft and alcohol. To both groups of officials urbanisation was clearly the pathological factor. The Port Elizabeth magistrate observed of the process in 1913 that while many Africans led

> sober, industrious and respectable lives . . . I very much fear that each generation will show a falling off as compared with its predecessor. The influences among which young Natives grow up are often unspeakably vile. Mixed up with the Natives are numbers of degraded coloured people of

---

[8] Concentration on the immigrant alien as a pollutant criminalising source was one of the major preoccupations of American criminology of this period. See e.g. Hoag and Williams (1923: 206) where crime is connected to the immigration of racial inferiors, and control of immigration is seen as a vital crime-control measure.

nondescript breed . . . Their influence on the usually healthier minded and bodied Native is deplorable. (UG 44 1913: 302)

Race and mentality

South African criminological thinking took note of the full range of problems discussed overseas, and some writers were attracted to the debates about the physical elements involved in criminality and to the extremities of counter-measures. In an article published in 1909 the 'latest' theories of penology from England were taken up with some gusto. The latest school said that crime had to be grappled with at the expense of the criminal: 'The logical end of their creed is elimination, the natural evolutionary process by which those unfitted or incapable of adapting themselves to their environment must drop out.' While the Italian attempt to identify criminality from physical type had failed, nonetheless there was 'mentally a true criminal type' (C.J.I. 1909: 46 ff.).[9]

Arguments based upon a genetic mental degeneracy linked to crime, while they flourished in a fertile South African soil, did not originate there. What can be called, broadly, the eugenics movement, eugenic discourse, and the role of eugenic measures in controlling crime, were another ideological import. Degeneracy of the race occupied the minds of many social reformers in Britain where racial decline was linked to apocalyptically phrased fears about Empire and its ruling race. Garland notes the 'overlapping target population' of eugenic and criminological programmes: 'the habitual criminal, the inebriate, the feeble minded and the defective' (1985: 148). In South Africa this target population was to be found on the racial frontier, among poor whites, coloureds, and onward into the African population beyond. First those whites who 'overlapped' with blacks were at risk in terms of both the eugenic and criminological programmes. Beyond loomed blackness, delinquent both morally and mentally. Once criminology emphasised the mentality of offenders it was inevitable that discussions in South Africa would construct racial mental-ities differently, and that these constructions would become an inherent part of the courts' understandings of mental intentions and character of accused persons. Nonetheless the main product of eugenic thinking in the

---

[9] Noting this article, entitled 'The Cry of the Abolitionist', is a point at which to observe the silence on the subject of the death penalty which prevailed across the whole range of legal discourse during this period.

criminological field that was popularly touted at the time outside South Africa, compulsory sterilisation for offenders, either sexual offenders, or all offenders, depending on the degree of commitment to the eugenic idea, did not really catch on in South Africa. The contrast with many of the American states is marked in this regard and needs some explanation. In 1910 the *South African Law Journal* noted that the new Californian legislation had given to medical superintendents and prison boards the power to 'asexualise' certain moral offenders by an operation (No author 1910: 508–9). The Assaults Commission, which was specifically asked to look at the question, noted that emasculation of offenders existed in the United States. There, they observed, it was not a means of punishment for a particular offence such as rape, but existed for use on the 'feeble-minded, epileptic, criminal and other defective inmates' (UG 39 1913: 32). Citing the New York law on 'Operations for the Prevention of Procreation' the commission concluded that it was 'not prepared to recommend such operations as mere means of punishment. It would be quite another matter if by legislation the principle embodied in the American Statute above referred to were introduced generally.' The situation might have seemed ripe for the development of a legislative repertoire along these lines, but it was not done. This was because British legislative models dominated in the new state.

Eugenics did, however, have support. One discussion concluded that it should be 'criminal for persons who fall below a certain eugenic standard . . . to give birth to offspring under any circumstances' (De van Hart 1915: 235). Another maintained that 'heredity and atavism between them have produced the criminal recidivist, the throwback in the evolution of mankind'. Statistics showed that 25 per cent of criminals 'have received the criminal taint in their blood'. The new school demanded the 'elimination and isolation of the criminal from society . . . Its action is thorough . . . It clears out the criminal growth root and branch. No seed from it can afterwards be propagated' (C.J.I. 1909: 61–3). We should note again the appeal of the total solution, the rooting out, the easy transition from (a form of) rationality to hysteria. This tendency to slide easily towards extremism was an integral part both of the 'science' of criminology in South Africa and of the official discussion of practical reforms.

In 1911 G. T. Morice, a member of the Bar who had been a judge in the South African Republic and who was later to serve as an acting judge of the Supreme Court in the Transvaal, published an extended discussion of

H. Munsterberg's recent book, *Psychology and Crime*. Morice found it 'satisfactory' that modern German and American experimental psychology rejected Lombrosian ideas that there were physically abnormal people who were 'born to crime'. But while Munsterberg rejected the notion of a born criminal he supplied in its place another explanation which was to have considerable purchase in South Africa. Criminals were, by habit and environment, 'deficient in self control'. As Wiener has described (1990: chapter 3) the contrast between self-mastery and impulse was central to the late Victorian view of criminality. He outlines the concern about moral fitness for the franchise, contrasting Gladstone's listing of the virtues – 'self-command, self-control, respect for order, patience under suffering, confidence in the law, regard for superiors' – with the concern that the working-class character was full of 'unbridled sensuality and riotous animalism'. Self-mastery was linked to physical evolution and heredity. Charles Darwin thought it 'possible . . . even probable, that the habit of self command may . . . be inherited'. The jurist Leslie Stephen thought personal self-command an 'evolutionarily valuable trait' (quoted in ibid.: 144, 161).

This was perfectly adaptable as an explanatory tool to describe the causes of criminality among inferior and childlike races whose lack of self-control was almost axiomatic. There was also, Morice thought, 'a general physical and mental inferiority' which was 'characteristic of criminals compared with those who are higher on the scale of humanity' (Morice 1911: 25–7). This link between criminality and mental backwardness took hold in South African discussions. The Inspector of Prisons wrote, in relation to white offenders, of the 'vast problem' of the 'feeble-minded' which could only be dealt with by 'drastic legislation'. It was not punishment that was required but treatment, and treatment meant a segregation that must necessarily deprive the person of the means of perpetuating his race with those equally if not more unfit. 'South Africa will be wise if she tackles this question early in her life as a nation . . . It is quite as important to preserve the quality of our race in South Africa as the colour or quantity' (Mardall 1913: 428–9).

We have observed the shadowing of 'science' by immanent hysteria, the ways in which rational enquiry could be trapped within extreme paradigms, and the magnetised need to propose total solutions to all problems, which are found both in academic and official discourse. These are all illustrated in an article originally published in the *South African Journal of*

Science by G. T. Morice (1920: 321–2). He considered the chief characteristics of the feeble-minded to be want of intelligence and 'weakness of will' (cf. Munsterburg). The latter led to 'the male drifting into a life of crime . . . and to the female becoming a victim of seduction, the latter a lapse most calamitous for society, as feeblemindedness is hereditary'. Studies by Dr J. Marius Moll, wrote Morice, showed that while only 1 per cent of white children were feeble-minded, 20 per cent of white convicted prisoners were. The Johannesburg probationary officer had found high proportions of feeble-minded among young offenders, and figures of over 20 per cent were given for long-term prisoners in Pretoria, Cape Town and in Sing Sing. As if this was not bad enough, matters escalated. 'In homes for fallen women and among arrested prostitutes the proportion of feeble minded is enormous . . . 90% at the home at Irene, near Pretoria, and figures from other parts of the world make this proportion quite credible.' The problem was yet more extensive: 21 per cent of those relieved by the Unemployment and Relief Board were also 'feebleminded'. The Director of Prisons, Morice noted with approval, was arranging for all European inmates of reformatories and European habitual criminals to be examined by psychiatrists.

But there was an even more serious problem beyond the 90 per cent of feeble-minded fallen women. The form of many of these discussions leads up to the question of how much greater and more serious the problem is when one considers blacks, and how desperate are the measures needed. 'The fact of the great majority of convicts being natives', Morice wrote,

> greatly increases the difficulty of the problem of feeblemindedness in this country. There can be no doubt that feeblemindedness is to be found among native and coloured convicts. *But how is it to be detected?* The tests applied in the case of Europeans are unsuitable. Here is a subject that calls loudly for research. Possibly some of our missionaries will render assistance in the matter. (133; my emphasis)

As feeble-mindedness was hereditary, it was of 'the utmost importance' that the feeble-minded should be sterilised. Morice did not himself draw the conclusion which followed, that given that they made up the overwhelming preponderance of prisoners, there would have to be a large-scale sterilisation of black convicts. But it was there to be drawn.[10] These

---

[10] We might note a closely related concern with a huge and undetected mass of disturbed and potentially criminal Africans expressed by Laubscher. Usually, he wrote, 'psychotic and defective' Africans were only detected when they committed crimes and became 'a nuisance'

ideas were not confined to intellectual journals, but were a part of policy discussions. The 1918 Annual report of the Department of Prisons noted that 'The latest American development in penology is the establishment of psychiatric clinics in connection with the big prisons and with children's courts to determine in how far the criminal or anti-social act of the individual who comes before the criminal courts and ultimately into prison, was really wilful and malicious, or was due to mental defect.' The crucial questions were how many such persons were there in South African prisons and reformatories; and how could the punishment be made to fit the crime? 'Such cases will have to be separated and subjected to special treatment.' One American study found that 28 per cent of prisoners were 'morons'. In Johannesburg a study of 101 young offenders by Dr J. M. Moll found that 11 per cent were mental defectives, which was to be regarded as a minimum. This figure compared with other quoted British and American investigations. Dr Moll's work had by 1918 begun to influence the work of the probation officer in Johannesburg, who had enlisted his testing expertise and had various youths classified as 'morons' and one as a 'moral imbecile' (UG 36 1918: 92–3, 123). By 1932 it had all become commonplace. The Commissioner for Mental Hygiene reported that there was a large amount of insanity and 'mental weakness', which was 'in most cases hereditary' and caused crime among African and mixed-race prisoners (UG 38 1918: 1932; quoted in Simons 1936: 53). C. T. Loram, a prominent spokesman for African interests, also drew on 'science'. His metaphor was military: 'Just as the War needed the chemist, the physicist and the engineer, so the native question needs the human nature scientist.' He concluded, after considering the 'best substantial opinion', that Africans found 'sublimation of original nature' more difficult than Europeans, that for Africans 'the emotions meant more than the intellect' and that therefore 'justice must be simpler, punishment more suitable, rewards more immediate' (Loram 1921–2: 100, 106).

   It is important to be aware that there was a different kind of analysis of black crime available, but the developing scientific understandings did not draw upon it. The report of the Commissioner for Police for 1924/5

to white society. But it was easy for them to live in black rural areas and 'we are forced to the conclusion that the numbers of those mentally disordered living in the kraals must be large . . . Such a state of affairs has far reaching influences, especially in reference to crimes' (1937: 226). In this context see also Gilman (1985: 137 ff.) for discussions in the USA in the 1840s in the context of abolition of slavery which included 'scientific' projections of a huge amount of black insanity and feeble-mindedness. These concerns persisted into the 1880s and 1890s.

observed in a matter-of-fact manner that black criminals were the product of a 'bad environment', 'deplorable living conditions' and 'economic pressure'. The Secretary for Native Affairs, in 1925, considered it 'incontestable' that the 'herding' of Africans into slums was the main reason for the high crime rates (quoted in Simons 1936: 48–9). But these were not the views that dominated scientific or public debate in which it was the essential nature of blacks, whether cultural or psychological, rather than sociological or economic considerations, that explained their criminal acts. White crime, however, was more likely to be given a sociological explanation, usually the presence of blacks. Parliamentary discussions of crime showed the same tendency to slide easily and swiftly from figures to apocalypticism, from law breaking to the whole urgent and all-consuming question of the 'future of the race'. Their tenor is worth brief separate consideration as they illustrate the interpenetration between the discourses of criminologists, bureaucrats and politicians. They inhabited the same conceptual world, though they manipulated the pieces differently. Some of the hostility, especially on the English-speaking side of politics, was directed against the weak link in the white race, the largely Afrikaner poor whites, and the focus was on the growing cities, Johannesburg in particular. As T. W. Smartt told the House of Assembly in May 1912, the spread of crime 'was to a large extent due to the lowest description of the white population who were gathered together in some of the large industrial centres'. He advocated deportation from South Africa wherever possible. Especially of concern were 'the lower class of white women', and their activities made it all the more necessary to separate blacks from white criminal influences. The Rand, he said, was a 'veritable hell on earth' (Hansard 9/5/1912). John X. Merriman built on his analysis of the 'hideous mass of crime' in that 'criminal university' for blacks, Johannesburg, to raise the question of the dangers posed to whites by the emergence of a black criminal class. The Minister of Justice's description of Johannesburg life, with its 'hordes of these criminal, drunken natives about the streets', was accompanied by the wishful suggestion that the remedy was the closed compound for all black workers.

In addition to identifying the urban nightmare, Members of Parliament also picked up the theme of inherent criminality. The member for Three Rivers told the House of Assembly in 1925 that there was a connection between criminality, mental deficiency and heredity. In this case the problem was the 'inherent criminality' of the 'Cape coloured' population.

Combined with this there was also concern about the 'want of discipline', not only among the 'coloureds', but also among whites. But as Afrikaner Nationalist ideology developed, with its imperative of incorporating poor whites into the ruling group, it became clear that in its view poor-white crime was the fault of the blacks. During the period of the first National Party–Labour government between 1924 and 1929, the Minister of Justice, Tielman Roos, was frequently attacked by the parliamentary opposition and the English-language press for his leniency towards white offenders. Yet, as he explained on one occasion, whites drifted into crime in the cities because of unemployment and the 'easier way' of a life of liquor selling. The white lack of discipline and lack of industry which arose were really 'occasioned by the presence of a large native population' (Hansard 6/6/1925).

Perception of others and the creation of self

Having begun with the voices of the controllers of crime, we may now look very briefly at some voices of the controlled. This may help us to think less about the mechanics and institutions of law and more about the ways in which it is a construct and constructor of perceptions of the social order. There were many outraged complaints made over the years by black political organisations about the administration of justice: anger at the unfairness of jury trials with all-white juries; at disproportionate sentencing of whites and blacks; at the aggressive brutality of the police; and at the substance of pass, and of master and servant laws was almost routine.[11] They made no impact on official discourses, policies or practices. But there were other perceptions, judged insane at the time, which seem now to be the truer counterpoint to the hysterical world of the controllers and separators. The 'native insane', wrote Dr Sachs, '*come to the asylum through the gates of the gaol* more often than do the white insane' (my emphasis). They showed 'the syndromes of introversion, *turning away from reality* and inertia. Practically all withdrew from external reality' (my emphasis). Black schizophrenics were 'silent, dull and indifferent' and also displayed delusions of grandeur (Sachs 1933: 707–10).

---

[11] These are copiously reported in the contemporary press. For an account of a part of the world of black crime from its own perspective see van Onselen (1982 and 1985).

Yet we must seriously ask whether they were further turned away from reality in their perceptions than the scientists, criminologists or lawyers. Indeed, they seem now to have spoken with a frightening clarity. One forty-year-old man had seen Satan, and his mother had told him that he was living in 'a dead place'. Dr Sachs wrote: 'The influence of the sense of guilt, of self punishment, in the mechanism of this delusion was obvious. Everybody wanted to kill him (phantastic craving for punishment); he was in a dead place (this punishment already carried out).' A twenty-five-year-old Swazi 'boy' 'said that he was told by Jesus to come here and discharge all the boys. He was sent by Jesus to alter the law which allowed the white people to take the land from the natives . . . Jesus told him to destroy all the white people in this country.' 'A good illustration', the doctor commented, 'of the wish fulfilment element which is equally present in a dream, in a neurotic symptom or in a psychotic delusion.' One fifteen-year-old 'was very much worried by God and Judges who were wandering about in the sky'. Another elderly man also had 'a remarkable delusion of persecution. People wanted to take his land from him' (710–12).

Sometimes ideas of persecution were associated with 'megalomaniac ideals':

> The delusions of grandeur are of the typical father complex desire to be a king. Most of the natives imagined themselves King George or his son. Others imagined themselves to be a Magistrate, tax collector, a police 'Lord', Chief of all the White people. Nols, a young Msutu, was Jesus Christ, magistrate and native commissioner, three personalities in one . . . the delusion of being a white man, and then punishing the whites was very frequent. (712)[12]

At this point we may worry seriously about the human capacity, including our own, to perceive the social world. That criminology was science, that law was justice and that perceptions of persecution and the desire for revenge were madness are by no means peculiarly South African views of a criminal justice system. But they capture in this case the interlocking essences of rationality, rectitude and righteousness. The strength of the legalistic culture of the higher criminal courts has its place within this context.

---

[12] To be fair to Dr Sachs the purpose of his article was to provide refutation of the view that the minds of whites and blacks were essentially different, by showing that they had the same mental illnesses. 'There might be a slight difference in the content of the delusions . . . in the objects of fear' (712–13).

Alcohol and interracial contact

Few matters were debated with more animation in South Africa in this
period than the question of prohibition, and little can be understood
about thinking about crime or the workings of the criminal justice system
without an awareness that this was the area which was its largest single
activity (see in general Crush and Ambler 1992). All the South African
colonies had forbidden or strictly controlled black access to alcohol, and,
after extensive consideration, a Union-wide prohibition law was enacted
in 1928 (the Liquor Act 1928).[13] One of the factors in regard to
prohibition was the effect of alcohol on the productivity of labour, but it
was not the most prominent one. In relation to the debates about crime
the starting point was the effects of drunkenness on blacks whose inherent
savagery was only intermittently repressed when sober. Alcohol *released*
criminal violence from blacks. Many authorities testified to the connections between drink and violent crime among blacks (e.g. Bain 1938:
38–40). And there was an additional element. As the Chief Commissioner
of Police told the Assaults Commission in 1913: 'The effect of excessive
drinking on the Native is deplorable. The already diminished respect
entertained by natives towards the white race disappears entirely under
the influence of liquor' (UG 39 1913: 15). A window sometimes opens
through which we can see the temper in which these things were debated.
Sir Thomas Watt described the National Party leader, General Hertzog, in
parliament: 'He declared *with a scream as if he were struggling for life* that
the drunkenness among the coloured people is a disgrace to us and that he
and his party would, if they had the power, stop drinking by coloured
women' (Watt–Smuts 24/6/24, in Hancock and van der Poel 1962 vol. II:
329; my emphasis).

Yet, while there was consequently a white consensus on the necessity of
prohibition, there was also a lively awareness of the problems of enforcement. Law enforcement efforts were targeted at two groups: black female
brewers; and the marginal white group which lived off liquor sales to
blacks. Black brewers suffered under the heavy hand of police action. But
it was the whites who came under the scrutiny of disciplinary thought.
Once again it was the effect on them, and on blacks, of the contact

---

[13] South Africa was not alone in restricting African access to alcohol by law. The Brussels
Convention of 1890 and the Treaty of St Germaine-en-Laye in 1919 banned spirits from
much of colonial Africa.

involved that was ultimately seen to be of importance. 'From his contact with or observation of the actions of the white criminal classes the Native probably forms an exaggerated and distorted idea of the vices and profligacy of the white man' (Bain 1938: 38–9). But it was possible to categorise more closely those who were responsible for the undermining of white prestige. 'These people [who] are one of the causes of the native losing . . . respect for the white race', the Assaults Commission found, were 'mainly a low class of aliens'. The commission's response was in line with the mainstream South African approach to criminal remedy. Having classified the offenders as ethnically other, the first thoughts were of their excision from the social body, and in this case the recommendation was that the law should be changed to enable the deportation of naturalised foreigners. As was usual too, local poor whites were cast in the role of economic and social victims, always redeemable, if the environment around them was purified (UG 39 1913: 16–17). The division of the population into different racial groups made it possible for all schools of criminology to be simultaneously embraced.

The other side of the criminological debate was that which linked liquor to crime by blacks. The report from the Eastern Districts Supreme Court for 1918 claimed that 'so far as the Native population of South Africa is concerned, they are anxious to uplift themselves'. But liquor was in the way. In the Eastern Cape crime rates were falling. 'Grave assaults and culpable homicide are generally the outcome of over indulgence in kaffir beer, which also in the majority of cases, leads to faction fighting, and if it were possible to apply total prohibition to the Native population, the crimes mentioned will be greatly reduced if not entirely disappear' (UG 36 1918: 5). The urban view from Durban was less one of uplift. Crimes of violence were 'directly traceable' to 'indiscriminate' drinking (12). Payment of workers in the cane areas was made partly in treacle or brown sugar which they transformed into a drink known as *isityimiana*. One Eastern Cape magistrate summed up a general view that total prohibition for Africans 'will prove one of the surest safeguards to the peace and welfare of the country' (46). But many of the white population, especially employers in the Western Cape, where the 'tot system' of part payment of wages in wine had long been in place, and the holders of urban liquor licences, had a direct interest in facilitating the flow of liquor to both coloureds and Africans. However the reports towards the end of the decade reflect a rising tide of increasingly agitated opinion urging the extension of complete prohibition to the coloured population. In many small towns public drunkenness was a part of the struggle for the control of urban space. Weekend drinking in the Western Cape produced a particularly violent reaction from many whites. One typical description will suffice. From Worcester the magistrate wrote in 1912 of labourers coming in from the surrounding farms to get drink: 'they reeled about the streets cursing and swearing indiscriminately . . . The railway station and carriages were thronged for hours with numbers of intoxicated men and women, who converted the locality for the time being into a veritable pandemonium' (UG 44 1913: 28). Sometimes the concern seemed to be less with individual consumption of alcohol than with its uncontrollable social function. Many magistrates objected to rural beer-drinking parties. As one put it 'the trouble comes in' when the reason for drinking was 'hoeing bees, marriages and other celebrations . . . the big beer drinks are a fruitful source of crime and disorganised farm labour' (292).

There were indications that the American adoption of total prohibition was influential and approved (see UG 36 1918: 45/6). Both Cape and Transvaal magistrates called for total prohibition. The Benoni magistrate suggested nationalising the liquor trade as a way of controlling supplies to blacks (97). State control and profit was essentially the solution adopted so far as the supply of 'kaffir beer' to Africans in urban areas was concerned. But the suggestion, which struck at not only white interest but also at economic principles, was not pursued in relation to the rest of the liquor trade. The Transvaal police knew full well that the main sources of supply for the illicit trade were the white-owned liquor stores from which poor whites generally bought in small amounts for resale. There was no control over sales of up to eleven bottles at a time from the stores, and many, the police reported, could not operate profitably without the trade. Similarly they pointed out that the main staple of the trade was Cape-produced liquor. Much of the trade was done into the mine compounds, allegedly, according to the Police Commissioner, with the connivance of the compound police and managers (UG 62 1912: 80).

Union wide between 1911 and 1914 in each year well over one-third of all whites convicted had breached the liquor laws, nearly two-thirds in the case of European women convicted. Total admissions into prison for all races for breaches of the liquor laws made up between 54 and 62 per cent for these four years. The 1918 prisons report notes that 'in all 20,000 persons of all races in round numbers were imprisoned during the year for offences with regard to liquor. Twenty three out of every hundred prisoners in the Union were in durance for liquor offences, and in the case of European female prisoners . . . 64 out of every hundred.' But these figures did not lead towards the conclusion that the effort to control drinking was hopeless and the cost enormous. Instead more total control was increasingly envisaged to combat the drunkenness of non-whites. This report picks up on overseas trends: 'the restrictions on facilities for obtaining liquor in Canada and New Zealand are specially noticeable. Canada is fast tending to total prohibition for all, and New Zealand has simply decided to close all liquor places while it is dark' (UG. 36 1918: 91).

Given the mounting dissatisfaction of the administrators of the liquor laws, the question that needs to be answered is how the restrictions remained in force for so long. The Johannesburg magistrate's report for 1917 reflects the dissatisfaction with the state of the liquor laws. 'The general tendency of public opinion', he wrote, was in favour of allowing the supervised sale of alcoholic drinks to Africans. His experience had shown him that total prohibition was impracticable; 'in fact that the attempt to enforce it has resulted in the corruption of large numbers of Europeans' (UG 36 1918: 52). Act no. 33 of 1919 finally amended the Transvaal Ordinance of 1902, and allowed the court to suspend the sentence of imprisonment which had to be imposed for supplying liquor in the case of first offenders.

When the policies of the state in relation to the supply of liquor to Africans came under total review in 1926, the experts who spoke of and for Africans were against giving them equal access to alcohol. Loram, who favoured total prohibition for Africans, struck all the possible notes. He told the Select Committee on the Liquor Bill that 'the extension of liquor privileges to natives will not only cause them to degenerate as a people, but will interfere very considerably with the supply of labour and the efficiency of that labour' (SC 7 1926: 35). He spoke movingly of the dangers of prostitution, and the threats to the families of lonely farmers. Those who lived in the Western Cape and saw the coloured people on Saturdays, he said, 'dread any possibility of that demoralisation affecting the native people'. His fellow commission member, A. W. Roberts, made the familiar discursive connection between liquor and segregation. The disastrous influence of alcohol on the younger generation of Africans, he said, meant that 'town locations should be placed as far as possible from

European dwellings', at a distance of at least three miles. 'This separation should be made a matter of definite policy for the future' (76). This was also a part of the policing perspective. When Morris Kentridge asked whether segregation would make a difference, the Johannesburg Chief Magistrate, J. Young, told him: 'We are doing that now. The police have been systematically for the last two years clearing the natives out of Johannesburg. It is a slow business but in the matter of another year we shall have the whole of the urban area free from natives' (450).

The nature of enforcement of the laws begins to emerge. Young gave evidence to the effect that it would be relatively easy to enforce total prohibition if the liquor trade was a government monopoly, like Sweden's. As long as it was in private hands, however, it was impossible (SC 7 1926: 448, 457). Major Trigger, the chief of criminal investigations on the Witwatersrand, described the corruption that pervaded the licensing process (402–5). But the white private financial interests which ultimately profited from the sale of illicit liquor were not the subjects of state action. Who then could be policed? Certain white groups were targeted. Syrians ('really Asian') were mentioned by Trigger as the worst offenders: Jews were enquired about by the committee, but largely exonerated (447, 468, 556/7). But the main white group caught in the police net continued to be Afrikaner poor whites. And this was the core of the policing problem. The police had by the 1920s abandoned the trapping system which had been so heavily criticised by white politicians, public and judges (450). Poor whites had become less an object of censure and more one of compassion. Concern focused on white women who were the unintended victims of the conviction of white men (450). Young told the committee that for white offenders the trade was not a moral offence, but an economic question: 'The ordinary person does not look upon supplying liquor to a coloured person as a moral offence like theft.' It was simply a way of making a living. The Transvaal law, with its mandatory sentence of six months in prison, seemed to him inappropriate. He argued for greater discretion and flexibility to allow magistrates to fine for first offences. For ten years, he recalled, the courts could not even impose a suspended sentence on first offenders. As Inspector of Prisons he had found that 'exactly one half' of the European prisoners with sentences over two years had been sentenced under the Transvaal liquor law. 'That struck me at the time very forcibly how this liquor law was degrading a certain type of white people' (457–8). They were just poorer whites, not 'really criminally minded people', who had become recidivists after their first liquor conviction. An interesting division was beginning to emerge. As Trigger affirmed, from a 'national' point of view, in terms of the overall discourses of social control, the illicit liquor traffic was 'an absolute menace' (482). This implied that some drastic action needed to be taken. But, on the other hand, as the Deputy Commissioner of the Criminal Investigation Department for the Union pointed out, 'when the common sense of the individual is against the law it is difficult to administer them [*sic*] properly' (551). He also pointed out that offences related to alcohol were proportionally fewer in South Africa than in the UK, and with regard to drunkenness in South Africa it was 'better than it is in London, and much better than in Australia. It is not too bad' (561).

Hysteria and pragmatism could live side by side because while nominally they were both focused on alcohol, they had different referents: the whole field of social relations between races on the one hand, and petty crime on the other. And while there were two sides to illegal supply, increasingly police action moved from concentrating on suppliers and their intermediaries to targeting consumers. Poor whites, who had been the subject of disciplinary thought and of condemnation in the first decades of the century, were more and more the sympathetic subjects of potential rehabilitation. When the Chief Constable of Pietermaritzburg advocated farm colonies and segregation for white liquor sellers who 'really cannot help themselves, they are weak minded people' (SC 7 1926: 871), he was straddling two worlds of conceptualisation. Soon the element of punitive segregation was to be reserved for black consumers, as police action concentrated on 'clearing the natives out' of urban areas. By the mid-1920s Young was able also to tell the Select Committee that 'native women . . . brewing . . . is the chief aspect of the illicit trade which the courts in Johannesburg have to deal today' (449). In 1925 2,000 whites were convicted in the Transvaal for liquor-related offences, mainly drunkenness. There were 21,000 convictions of Africans, of which 9,400 were of women. Out of 13,000 convictions of Africans for possession of kaffir beer, 8,000 were of women, a threefold increase over the past four years (rounded figures); 445 whites were charged with illicit supply of liquor to Africans, and 375 convicted (438–45). In the Union as a whole in 1925 there were 26,000 convictions for drunkenness. There were another 31,000 convictions for illegal supply, brewing and other offences related to prohibition for Africans: 26,500 of these were for possession of kaffir beer;

and 4,000 for possession of other alcohol. While there were only 560 convictions of whites for illegal supply across the colour line, there were 4,000 of Africans for having been supplied. It can readily be seen that possession of kaffir beer had become the main policing problem and that whites were not the focus of the policing of prohibition. From one policing point of view 'clearing out' seemed to be paramount. The interwoven nature of the concerns of prohibition and segregation was again clearly expressed. Lieutenant Colonel Trew, for example, focused his evidence on liquor on the subject of the failure of the courts to support police action in Cape Town. When he came to the Cape from the Transvaal in 1919, he encountered the difficulty of enforcing the old Cape law 'which compelled a native to live in a location'. With some indignation he recalled: 'The natives were living all over the city and when I started on a campaign to drive them out the magistrates refused to convict because there was no accommodation for them.' Because there were no pass laws in Cape Town, there were fewer police per head of population. The pass law system 'helped the police tremendously in Johannesburg and Pretoria. If a native is drunk in the Transvaal a policeman can approach him and ask for his pass, not for drunkenness, but for being without his pass' (940). (Africans were not the only incipiently deviant subjects. Almost any agenda of control could be linked to that of control of liquor supply. The Chief Constable of Durban wanted to limit the service to white women in bars. 'An absence of sobriety', he said, was 'particularly noticeable in the case of women whose husbands are out of town on business for short periods . . . It might be arranged that liquor would only be supplied to women accompanied by their husbands' (appendices: xxv).)

We may understand the nature of the rule of law in this area in relation to Africans in yet another way if we look at the perspective of the Native Affairs Department. Whether, how much and how far to relax restrictions on liquor supply was the main agenda of the mid-1920s debate. There were clear differences of opinion between those who wanted a continuation of strict, or stricter, control; those who wanted to allow the supply of wine and beer to Africans; and those who pragmatically identified the main 'cost' of prohibition to lie in the restrictions on the supply of kaffir beer, and were prepared to advocate relaxation in this area. When Major Herbst gave evidence to the Select Committee he pursued another agenda. First he objected to the 'widely abused' privilege of the Cape African voters, and demanded that they be subjected to Transvaal restrictions. But he concentrated on the role of the Native Affairs Department in governing Africans. It was the department, he said, and not the Ministry of Justice, that should have power over the administration of drinking laws over Africans in rural areas. Not only that but there should be no 'rigid law with regard to kafir beer by Act of Parliament'. The department should be legislator as well as administrator. 'I say the Native Affairs Department is in the best position to say how far you can make or relax restrictions in connection with the brewing of kaffir beer. This should be done by Proclamation on the initiative of the Native Affairs Department' (930). Even in this area, treated with punctilious legalism in the courts, the ambition was to control administratively. Herbst explained that, because of the changing conditions of African life, 'today you cannot make one uniform law applicable to all natives throughout the country. You need practically different laws for every area' (ibid.). So far as Africans were concerned then, Herbst wanted the liquor law collapsed into administration, rather than a more rigid enforcement of rules by the police. The authority of chiefs was to be supported because 'it is much easier for an agitator to influence a detribalised native than a native under the control of his chief'. The extension of the drinking laws would tamper with the principles commonly accepted as necessary for the good government of Africans. He submitted to the Select Committee the full sections dealing with prohibition for Africans in the 1883–4 Commission on Native Law; the Native Affairs Commission of 1903–5; and the Natal Native Affairs Commission of 1906–7 as an accumulation of knowledge and authority on the matter which brooked little dissent. The problem of drink simply became a part of the Native Administration Department's larger predicament which was the perception of increasing difficulties 'in preserving law and order amongst the whole body of natives' (930–2). The circle had been closed: after a detour through the facts related to policing, discussion was back among the inherent dangers of the African population. The Gold Producers' Committee of the Transvaal Chamber of Mines voiced its objections to going beyond the supply of kaffir beer in terms all the white participants in the debate were comfortable with, the problem of control: 'The conditions of the mines are peculiar, inasmuch as, on all of them, there exists a collection of varying, and sometimes hostile tribes. Faction fights are, in such an atmosphere, easily generated by a comparatively small excess of liquor' (appendix F: ix).

The strange direction of the discussions, and their obsession with race and segregation, did not go entirely unnoticed. The South African Indian Congress told the Select Committee: 'Unfortunately, the trend of legislation in this country, even in matters of temperance, is racial, and seems to be not in consonance with the trend of modern political thought' (appendices: lxxvii).

Dagga

The development of law and policy regarding the control of the use of marijuana exhibits the same compendium of panics about loss of control. While before Union the Cape and the Orange River Colony had acted to restrict the growth of *dagga* as a noxious weed, Natal and the Transvaal had not. In the Transvaal it was sold openly and normally by mine storekeepers to workers in compounds. Mine managers who were canvassed in 1908 had seen no need for its prohibition, and the Minister for Native Affairs advised that it was not used to excess (Union Archives NTS 3/345). In the early years of Union little panic was shown in the magistrates' reports about the use of *dagga*. The huge effort put at this time into the control of the consumption of liquor, and the complex administration of the 'blacklist' of individuals who could not buy alcohol, stands out in sharp contrast to the little attention given to *dagga*. Some references to *dagga* were couched in extreme and apocalyptic terms similar to the debates on alcohol, but other magistrates' reports simply noted it was an 'evil habit' and that controlling it would be very difficult (see Natal reports in UG 36 1918). Prison statistics were gathered about those who admitted to being *dagga* smokers, but it is notable that in the intensive and often bizarre classifications and suggestions about the causes of crime (see below) it was never featured as a major problem.

Between 1908 and 1912 C. J. Bourhill conducted a study of 627 male cases of insanity in the Pretoria Native Asylum and concluded that 18 per cent suffered from 'dagga insanity' (Bourhill 1912).[14] This proportion,

---

[14] See UG 31 1952: 8, 21. His thesis, 'The smoking of dagga among the native races of South Africa and the resultant evils', was awarded an MD by Edinburgh University in 1912. I have found no evidence that it was referred to in any of the discussions of *dagga*, or of crime, at the time or in the subsequent two decades. But it does illustrate the state of scientific and official discourse at the time. The 1952 committee (UG 31 1952) which did refer to his work noted that the corollary to Bourhill's views was that 'if intoxication is dependent on the nervous and mental constitution of the addict, then it must be assumed that it *reveals the real nature of his*

Bourhill said, exceeded any other individual form of insanity, except *dementia praecox*. He did record, however, that the vast majority of those afflicted recovered. But *dagga*, Bourhill wrote, not only produced 'dagga insanity' but was instrumental in producing other types of insanity, such as schizophrenia, dementias and manic depressive and delusional psychoses. It was not the case, he wrote, 'that dagga alone causes any of these insanities, but rather that it merely plays a part in the causal trinity – environment, nidus and vice'. The analysis was similar to that of the effects of alcohol on blacks, in which vice was added to the usual factors, heredity and environment. Again, as in the analysis of alcohol, indulgence in the dangerous substance brought out the inherent vice in the consumer.

Internally it was not until 1921 that there were serious signs of a moral panic focusing around *dagga*. The panic focused on the Western Cape, and cohered around crimes supposedly committed under the influence of *dagga*. Both public debate and bureaucratic discussion were driven by this and not by the infrequently expressed effects on labour efficiency. Not until after the moral panic had reached intense levels were the issues of morality, dangerousness and labour brought together. As one Department of Justice official wrote: 'the evil effects are found principally to concern Public Health and crime; but Agriculture is by no means unaffected since the effect upon farm labourers of the smoking of the herb greatly depreciates the quantity and value of the labour they would otherwise be capable of rendering' (Union Archives MM 2372/22: 24/11/21). However, public ventilation of the issue at the Cape continued to focus on the criminal danger, especially coming from a drug-addicted coloured population, though the *Rand Daily Mail* (6/10/21) did raise the issue of African workers handling explosives while 'dazed' with *dagga* (Union Archives MM 2572/22).

Controlling a substance which grew wild in much of the country was

personality and character' (22; my emphasis).
    Bourhill could find no evidence that *dagga* acted as a sexual stimulant, and none at all that in any court trial 'had an accused Native been proved to be under the influence of dagga when he committed or attempted to commit rape'. But the question was, and remained to white South Africa, more important than the answer. Thirty years later, in spite of there being still no evidence, the committee came 'to the conclusion that dagga does not directly stimulate the sexual desires, [yet] it nevertheless is of the opinion that the question of the relationship between sex and dagga on the one hand, and sex stimulation and sex crime, on the other hand, is so important in the Union with its multi-racial groups that the subject merits further scientific investigation' (UG 31 1952: 22).

not simple. Action could be taken under the noxious weeds legislation to prohibit cultivation, but this would be very difficult to enforce. Medical and public health legislation prohibiting sale, and even possession, might be easier law to use. But how much further should the law go? The Secretary for Native Affairs advised that while his department favoured prohibition of cultivation, placing *dagga* on the list of poisons and prohibiting its sale, it was against making the smoking of *dagga* a criminal offence. The Transkei Chief Magistrate and the Chief Native Commissioner of Natal thought criminalising use would be unenforceable. But, once the drive to prohibit *dagga* got under way, police officers wanted the prohibition. It would be 'useful', it was said, in relation to crimes of violence, and offences against morality. The objections of Native Affairs were responded to by the suggestion that the letter of the law would not be applied in remote localities where 'moderate dagga smoking by some natives is of little importance from the point of view of public order and welfare' (Union Archives MM 2372/22: 22/11/21; 12/12/22).

South Africa was a signatory to three international conventions on narcotic drugs (1912, 1925 and 1931). It was at the 'express wish' of the South African government in 1923 that *dagga* (Indian hemp or marijuana) was included in the list of narcotics covered by the international convention on narcotic drugs which had hitherto been almost entirely limited to opium and its derivatives (UG 31 1952: 1). In 1922 regulations were issued under the Customs and Excise Duties Act (no. 35 of 1922) which criminalised the possession and use of 'habit forming drugs' which included not only *dagga*, but cocaine, morphine, opium and others. Cultivation, possession, sale and use of *dagga* were prohibited under regulation 14. Following the form of the Transvaal legislation (Ordinance 25 of 1906) prohibiting the import and use of opium, the burden of proof of any defence against a charge, for example that possession and use were authorised for medical reasons, lay on the accused (Gardiner and Lansdown 1924 vol II: 1039/42, 1451). The likely offenders against the new law were black, and the onus of proof was reversed: the contrast between this and the treatment of alcohol is clear. (On the onus of proof see further below, chapter 6.)

Between 1924 and 1935 there were about a thousand convictions annually for *dagga* use. (There were 18,000 convictions for drunkenness in 1923.) Among the coloured community this made up 2.55 per cent of criminal convictions. Yet while the numbers remained small, the problem appeared increasingly menacing to administrators. The Cape Coloured Commission warned that *dagga* was harmful 'especially when indulged in simultaneously with alcoholic intoxicants, and that the mental state thus induced makes it a cause of crimes of violence'. They advised that the evidence to this effect given by magistrates and police was scientifically supported. In support they noted the Department of Public Health report for 1935 which deplored allegations in the press that people were being senselessly prosecuted for smoking a harmless substance. 'Public conscience', said the commission, 'should be aroused to a realisation of the evils of dagga . . . more active steps should be taken' to eradicate its use (UG 52 1937: 27).

In 1935 a medical congress urged the Minister of the Interior to conduct investigations into the relationship of *dagga* use and 'the ultimate production of mental degeneration' (UG 52 1937: 23). In pursuance of this experiments were conducted at the Pretoria Mental Hospital. Observations noted a universal 'dulling of the mental faculties', and in some cases 'wild motor excitement'. The conclusions supported Bourhill's view that

> dagga produces different responses in different individuals. Herein lies the potential danger . . . The smoker's behaviour . . . depends on his underlying personality make-up . . . and is for that reason entirely unpredictable. Some addicts become maniacal and are driven by irresistible impulses. A highly intelligent person under the influence of the drug might have varied and brilliant hallucinations, whilst a man of baser type might have savage reactions. (1912: 24)

The danger, therefore, was that violent crime would result from the use of the drug by those with criminal 'traits or tendencies'.

While discussions of alcohol focused on blacks and poor whites, there was a marked tendency to consider *dagga* in relation to the racially marginal Indian and coloured communities. Most complaints about its use related to law enforcement among the coloured community of the Western Cape. The percentage of persons prosecuted for *dagga* offences was higher among coloureds than for any other group. The fear of what blacks might do under the influence of *dagga* was nonetheless a strong strand of the debate. Bryant's *Olden Times in Zululand and Natal* told readers that young warriors were 'especially addicted' and under its influence, capable of 'the most hazardous feats'. They were to be feared, as indulgence could permanently blunt mental faculties, cause 'extreme morousness . . . [and] dangerous and criminal incitement' (1929: 222). Yet even as late as 1949 the number of persons prosecuted for *dagga* offences was small: 12,235 or 1.48 per thousand of the black population (3.8 per thousand for coloureds). But there was fear of the potential. The 'relative insignificance' of the figures for offences, the 1952 committee found, gave no indication of the actual numbers who habitually used the drug (UG 31 1952: 5). And, as in the case of alcohol, the contagion of *dagga* smoking was not simply physical, but undermined the essentials of social structure. The committee noted the 'camaraderie' which led some 'to lay aside race and other prejudices with regard to fellow addicts' (7).

5

Prisons and penology

Penology

In looking at the nature of crime, convictions and remedies it is clear that white and black in South Africa were subject to different kinds of social control, and criminalised as a result of different, but interlocking, agenda. Large numbers of Africans were criminally punished for breaches of the laws of labour discipline and mobilisation, the tax, pass, and masters and servants laws. Large numbers of whites were criminalised by the liquor laws (which of course also affected Africans), and other measures aimed at imposing on them the disciplines of the new segregating society. Most criminal offenders in all racial groups were manufactured by the intensified drive to create a segregated society supported by black labour. The discourses of criminology and penology, which were derived from, and sustained from, outside the country, had to be used to apply, explain and control these local and particular patterns of criminalisation. So too did the discourses and methods of the equally exotic criminal law. Both also had to be rehearsed against a background of the threat to white rule perceived and feared by the state.

The development of a body of criminological thought which stressed the inherent and determined differences between the criminal and others also had important implications for penology. The idea that free will was a delusion undermined the belief in the reformative aspects of imprisonment. This was connected to a fascination with recidivism. Wiener observes that in Britain 'recidivism . . . was the central issue around which criminal policy was re-shaped in the 1890's' (1990: 342). The view that none could be cured never quite took hold, so while some criminals were perceived to be curable, others, marked by their repeated offences, were clearly morally pathological. If reform was impossible by ordinary means, then prevention was necessary for social defence. These ideas, and their institutional corollaries, were a part of the international penological agenda. A form of internal transportation became both a fashionable and a usable idea. As one American text put it, 'an appreciation of the fact that a surprisingly large percentage of the population cannot be reformed' led to the conclusion that they 'should be, figuratively speaking, banished to some kind of colony or institution where they shall remain until definitely cured or transformed. If that be for life, so be it. It is not a punishment, but a kindness' (Henry H. Goddard, introduction to Hoag and Williams 1923: xiii). The renowned criminal lawyer Clarence Darrow wrote that all sentences should be indeterminate, and every prisoner should be placed under competent observation, just as if he were ill in hospital (Hoag and Williams 1923: 199). The ideas of the habitual criminal and the indeterminate sentence, and of the redemptive benefits of work in a work colony, were interconnected.

Cures, it was thought, could best be achieved with the young. Indeed, one of the most prominent of the criminological obsessions of the time revolved around the corruption and salvation of youth. A whole panoply of purported remedies and new institutions were put in place in Britain between 1898 and 1914 (Garland 1985: 20–1). The Inebriates Act of 1898, the Probation of Offenders Act of 1907 and the Childrens Act of 1908, the Prevention of Crime Act of 1908 (which enacted the indeterminate sentence for habitual criminals), the Mental Deficiency Act of 1913 and the Criminal Justice Administration Act of 1914 all provided a legislative framework of additional controls and punishments on which South African measures were based.

Both the international ideological agenda and the British legislative repertoire were incorporated into South African practice. There continued to be an openness to and awareness of international discussions. The report of the Union's Director of Prisons for 1910 contains a long account of the International Prisons Congress held in Washington in that year (UG 35 1911: 96–7). The most important principles affirmed, he wrote, were 'That the scientific principle of the indeterminate sentence is approved. That it should be applied to moral and mental defectives and to criminals, especially juveniles, who require reformation . . . the prevailing conceptions of guilt and punishment are compatible with the principle of the indeterminate sentence' (ibid.). In a spirit of uplift the congress declared that no person should be considered to be incapable of improvement and that it was in society's interests not to impose merely retributive and deterrent sentences but to 'make an earnest effort' to reform the criminal. But this was not a licence for leniency: 'The reformatory system is incompatible with short sentences, and a long period of reformative treatment is more likely to be beneficial than repeated short terms of rigorous imprisonment.' All prisoners, the congress decreed, should be employed at useful labour, whether inside or outside the prison. Congress affirmed 'the right of society to take compulsory measures of social preservation against mendicants and beggars . . . [and] recommended taking severe repressive measures against professional vagrants and establishing institutions to make them work'. On the control of 'criminal inebriates . . . The extension of the principle of detention under State control was recommended, and useless repeated short sentences for drunkenness deprecated.' The Director of Prisons concluded his account with the satisfied observation that 'it is interesting to note that a fair percentage of these matters has been provided for in the new Union Prisons Act'. Indeed they had, and much more of this common world agenda was to be picked up in the South African context. The respectability of long-term administrative detentions and compulsory labour as a way of dealing with a widely definable range of deviants was the background to many South African adaptations.

The Prisons and Reformatories Act of 1911 embodied the latest theories about crime and prevention. But the new discourse did not dominate practice totally. Indeed, with criminological and penological thought, as with law, the role of illusion was central. Institutions were created according to images which themselves could seemingly serve to conceal practice from their creators. As early as 1910 the Director of Prisons noted the gap between ambitions and realities. In the training of prison staff 'much elaboration' would be required before the 'ambitious curricula' of training in Europe could be approached. Colonial recruits who had 'a better knowledge of treating the native owing to life long experience' were preferable, but those with adequate educational qualifications could find far better employment. The alternative was to recruit ex-soldiers, though, it was noted, this had been abandoned in Germany. Nonetheless 'a leaven of trained soldiers tends to supplement the side on which the colonial is not strong, namely, in habits of discipline' (UG 35 1911: 108). The spirit in which the prisons were run was well described later by Justice Krause. He concluded that 'the whole conception and manner of carrying out the sentences imposed breathes a spirit of brutality and savagery' and that 'physical pain and degradation' was the purpose and policy of the prisons, especially as far as the treatment of black prisoners was concerned (Krause 1939: 114, 116). The report of the Penal and Prison Reform Commission of 1947 put the matter well (UG 47 1947: 92). The 1911 Act, they discovered, embodied many of the reforms being advocated in 1947 but 'the spirit underlying the Act has not been adequately applied . . . Militarisation and restraint, while essential to some degree, have been permitted to submerge the farseeing objects of the measure.'

But the Department of Prisons report for 1910 highlighted other things.

> In the Central Prison, Pretoria, lectures on elevating and inspiring subjects are given from time to time to provide convicts with some mental develop-ment, sound pabulum for cogitation. The following lectures were given during the year:-
> The Heavenly Bodies, by Professor Gundry.
> The Formation of the Earth's Crust, by Professor de Villiers.
> Nature Study and the Insect World, by Dr Gunning.
> The Mealie, by Mr Burrtt-Davy.
> Similar lectures have now been inaugurated at other big prisons . . .
> Besides these formal lectures, the Very Reverend Dean Gore-Browne and the Rev Cross take alternate Saturday afternoons in the prison for the practice of singing and conversational lectures. The following were among the subjects lectured on: Palestine, the late King, Colonial Life, Literature, Milton, Tennyson, the English Humorists, and Mark Twain. (UG 35 1911: 111)

My purpose is not to mock, but to draw attention to the degree to which fractured vision is possible – in penology, and, as we shall see, in law. Whether as an antidote to their special evil, or as a recognition of their desperate circumstances, special spiritual provision was made in South Africa's worst prison. 'Only at the Native Indeterminate Sentence Prison at Barberton is there a fixed departmental all-time Chaplain, in whose hands the religious and moral teaching of the inmates had been placed' (UG 36 1918: 125).

For a statement of the objects of the Prisons Act in terms of the prevailing criminological discourse, with its capacity to mask realities, we can do no better than turn to the words of the main progenitor of prison reform in South Africa, J. de Villiers Roos, the former Secretary of the Law Department and Director of Prisons in the Transvaal. The guiding principles of the Union's penal system, he wrote, were

> to rescue the child from the criminal environment and prevent it from becoming a criminal; to build up and supplement in the criminal the elements necessary to prevent a recurrence of crime; and if all else failed, by means of the indeterminate sentence to remove the habitual criminal from society and prevent his remaining as menace to it. (Quoted in Chisholm 1989: 198)

Drawing on the imported repertoire, the Transvaal Criminal Law Amendment Act no. 38 of 1909 enabled courts to declare someone with more than two convictions for 'serious' crimes a habitual criminal, who was to be detained indefinitely with hard labour. During the first year of its operation this system netted twenty-nine victims, two white and twenty-seven black (UG 35 1911: 105). These offerings on the altar of the new criminology were men whose lives had been disrupted by the South African War and the move from rural areas to the fringes of urban life, and who had a series of convictions for petty thefts, alcohol offences, gambling and vagrancy.[1]

The aims of the new penal system were also in theory to be achieved through industrial schools, reformatories, different types of prisons with classifications and divisions within them, and a system of marks for prisoners. The new scientific approach was marked by a positive mania for classifying and counting. The 1910 report of the Department of Justice illustrates the first fruits of the reform of the system of penological statistics to 'bring it into accord with modern ideas' (UG 35 1911: 99–103).[2] 'The most searching statistics are recorded' with regard to criminals 'to enable

---

[1] By the 1920s it was noted by an ex-judge that the indeterminate sentence 'now plays an important part in the administration of the criminal law' (Morice 1920: 135). It was known among criminals as 'the "special life" sentence' and 'regarded with great dread'. Yet these values did not necessarily prevail in the world of the prisons. Seniority and prestige could become associated with 'the large I.S. sign on the prison jacket which distinguished those prisoners serving an indeterminate sentence. This insignia of the underworld elicited its own twisted form of respect in a twisted institution' (van Onselen 1982: 184).

[2] In view of the copious and seemingly exact figures of crimes and convictions printed in this and subsequent reports of the Department of Justice, one might, as a caution, quote a story from the autobiography of a leading South African barrister, H. Morris. He recalls his meeting in a country town with a magistrate who later rose to the head of the service. The magistrate told him how he had put a stop to 'kleptomania' among black women by having them caned. Morris pointed out that the law did not allow this. 'What did your record show?' 'Discharged with a caution' (Morris 1948: 64).

the authorities in tracing the causes and movements of crime'. No fewer than eighteen different categories of statistics from the Transvaal were given, and they delineate with clarity the compounded mental world of overseas science and local preoccupations. The divisions were

> Race and Crime; Age and Crime; Languages of Criminals; Crimes in order of Frequency; Locality of Crime; Recidivism in Serious Crime; Mental Health of Criminals; Physical Health of Criminals; Religions Professed by Criminals; Education among Criminals; Upbringing by Parents or Other- wise; Where Criminals are Born; Marriage Divorce and Legitimacy in Relation to Crime; Criminals' Trades or Callings; In Employment or Workless at Time of Crime; The Haves and the Have Nots in Crime; Drunkenness and Drugs in Relation to Crime; Facts as to Parents.

Equally bizarre were the basic conclusions drawn. In nearly all crimes the majority of criminals were black. But 'in indecency, immorality and illicit liquor selling the European leads the native'. On 'careful examination' the 'proportion of mental degeneracy [is] very large'. Physical health was fine: only four blacks were certified as unfit for labour; 73 per cent were illiterate; nearly 80 per cent were brought up by both their parents. 'Institutional upbringing would therefore appear not to be to blame for much criminality in the Transvaal.' The analysis of marriage supported 'the findings of European criminologists that marriage among Europeans has a steadying influence', but the opposite was true in the case of black women. At the time of their offences 86 per cent of black criminals were employed, but only 45 per cent of white men, and 12 per cent of white women. 'So far as the native at all events is concerned,' the analysis concludes, 'it cannot be said therefore that want drives him to crime.'

What then was it? Another analysis was suggestive. It picked out what it saw as crucial categories which suggested that European criminals were more rational, while others were driven by different instincts. In its analysis of criminal cases for the Transvaal for the year 1915 the Depart- ment of Justice emphasised what it found to be interesting categorisations: 84 per cent of Europeans convicted had committed crimes for gain; 8 per cent crimes of anger or negligence; and 8 per cent crimes of 'lust'. Among non-white criminals, on the other hand, 22 per cent of crimes were motivated by 'lust', 59 per cent by anger or negligence; and only 19 per cent by gain (UG 39 1918: 6). Elaborate efforts were made, by the production of statistics and charts, to map and analyse the causes of crime. But in the end, there was a confession of failure. Having failed the nation in so many ways, criminals also failed as objects of science. 'No explanation is offered as to the fluctuation in crime returns, as illustrated in the Crime Chart. Crime is essentially influenced by the social and economic conditions prevailing at a particular period . . . so that, in a general sense, no authentic reasons can be assigned for the erratic actions of the criminal classes' (UG 69 1912: 71). In similar vein the Transvaal CID report for 1911 found murders by Africans in that year to have 'no particular cases of interest . . . the motive for native murders is principally one of revenge, jealousy, robbery and infanticide. Numerous women have been killed by their husbands, and children by their mothers. There are some cases of savage murders of natives by natives without any apparent reason' (UG 62 1912: 52). African murders also puzzled the magistrates. The Zoutpansburg magistrate wrote in 1913 that people in his area lived 'under the rule of their ancient rules and customs which were characterised by the most callous disregard of human life. Even as to the murders there was none of that malignity of purpose usually characteristic of murder in civilised communities' (UG 44 1913:114).

The demand for segregation in the prisons had also long been an integral part of reformist discourse. Internationally it was common currency that juvenile offenders should be separated from adults, and first offenders from hardened criminals. In the South African context this became assimilated with the drive to protect whites from the most basic pollutant source, contact with other races. In all areas of the South African state in the early years segregation was seen as an essential part of modernising, improving and state building. The prisons were just one part of the drive to create a segregated society by deliberate progressive reforms. This was not just politics but science (e.g. Muirhead 1911). Entire and absolute separation of white from non-white offenders was seen as being a necessary precondition to any hope of reform of white deviants. The single most important reform highlighted by Roos was the segregation of the prisons, and the cessation of the use of coloured warders to guard white prisoners. The segregatory drive in the prisons reached deep into its legal resources for support. The 1910 report noted that the practice of allowing native and coloured warders to guard white prisoners was in breach of the Cape laws of 1670 and 1707 (UG 35 1911: 108). In Cape prisons white prisoners slept apart at night, but were not segregated during labour. The new Union Prisons Act affirmed the principle of separation wherever practicable.

Sentencing

The criminological discussions fed directly into the practice of an insecure society seeking the best 'science' to justify policies. Departmental circulars to magistrates in 1914 reflected current penological science. They were told that it was useless to commit a drunkard to an inebriate reformatory for a matter of months 'when all the best modern opinion is that from one to three years detention must be imposed if it is to be of any avail'. Again, magistrates were told to commit children to prisons, not reformatories, and advised that short sentences in reformatories were useless (UG 28 1915: 9). In Johannesburg in 1914 forty-four indeterminate sentences (10 per cent of the total) were passed on prisoners convicted in the Supreme Court. Five were white.

Over the four years from 1911 to 1914 just under four thousand people per year received cuts or lashes, with an average of over nine strokes per individual sentenced. Much greater use of the lash, and heavier sentences, were a feature of the administration of justice in the former British colonies, the Cape and Natal. The Transvaal courts sentenced fewer convicted persons to corporal punishment and awarded significantly fewer strokes per person than those of the other provinces. The rate of sentences of corporal punishment was between three and four times higher in Natal than elsewhere, and the sentences were more severe. In 1914 nearly half of these sentences in the Union were imposed in Natal, by 1918 more than half (UG 36 1918: 92). The Director of Prisons observed: 'Natal continues to hold the premier place as the lashing Province' (UG 39 1918: 148). The use of the lash fell in the Transvaal in these years and rose in the Cape and in Natal. In these and following years whites who received corporal punishment were given no fewer strokes each than Africans – between seven and ten depending on the province. On the face of it the major reason for the excesses in Natal was that it was the only province in which there was no judicial review of sentences of corporal punishment. While magistrates' reports indicate that many thought prison an insufficient deterrent, judges were less likely to hold this view (see UG 28 1915: 22). The differences in sentencing may also be understood in the light of the different patterns of conviction in the provinces. Union-wide contraventions of the liquor laws made up nearly 17 per cent of all convictions. Common theft was next with 16 per cent; and stock theft, with 12 per cent, outnumbered all other common-law crimes. Masters and servants and other labour offences made up between 5 and 6 per cent. But in the Transvaal 30 per cent of those convicted had breached the liquor laws, with labour and stock theft offences each making up under 4 per cent. The chief crime for which lashes were given in the Transvaal was assault. In the Cape, however, stock theft accounted for over 30 per cent of convictions, and liquor-law convictions only 4 per cent. Stock theft was the main offence for which lashes were given in the Cape. In Natal common theft, masters and servants, and stock theft convictions were all frequent. Theft was the main offence for which sentences of lashing were imposed. Stock theft was also the most common crime in the Free State, which also had more masters and servants convictions. These latter cases attracted the most lashes. Corporal punishment appears, therefore, to have been applied to the major perceived threat in each locality.[3] While the judges reviewing criminal sentences frequently hesitated about lashing and reduced the number of lashes imposed, other parts of the state did not share these compunctions. The demand for the lash intensified not simply among an inflamed rural public but at the highest levels. In 1931 the Director of Prisons complained that because the depression had reduced the demand for prison labour, the sentence of imprisonment with hard labour was losing its deterrent value. More whipping, he said, was the answer: it was less likely than imprisonment to lead to recidivism, and its 'brutalising effect' had been grossly exaggerated (quoted in Simons 1936: 486). There was also public political pressure on the judges from the Minister of Justice. In 1934 Smuts, in parliament, reproved them for interfering with such sentences, and unnecessarily hampering the administration 'because that makes the carrying out of the law in regard to stock theft almost impossible' (Simons 1936: 488).

Also, the 'advances' in sentencing introduced at the instigation of the officials in the Department of Justice, which enabled magistrates to give suspended sentences, and to give time to offenders to pay fines, were not passed on by the magistrates to black offenders. Time and again magis-

---

[3] Over these years the annual number of executions dropped. While fifty-seven people were hanged in 1911, the figure dropped to the low twenties for the next three years. In 1914 three of the twenty-three people executed were whites, one for high treason: thirteen were African. This pattern continued. While rates of imprisonment soared, executions did not. In the six years between 1923 and 1928 one hundred and twenty-four persons were hanged, while in the following six the number dropped to seventy-one. Two hundred and seventy-eight death sentences were commuted between 1923 and 1928, and 385 in the next six years (UG 47 1947: 170).

trates reported that they had no use for the new sections in relation to blacks not simply because they could not, for example, give security in relation to fines, but on the broad grounds that leniency would be interpreted as weakness (e.g. UG 28 1915: 135). From 1912 to 1914 an active prison Board of Visitors dealt with nearly six thousand cases of remission of sentence each year, of which a high proportion were granted. White prisoners were more likely to succeed. In 1914 the Probation Act came into force. Probationers could either be referred by the courts or the Board of Visitors. Those referred were predominantly white. Probation officers struggled with a rhetorical framework of reform, cure and betterment, which appeared to be quite inappropriate to the social structure within which they worked. The Witwatersrand report shows that many probationers were alcoholics living on the illicit liquor trade, with family histories of involvement in alcohol related offences (222). In Johannesburg 46 per cent of the long-sentenced white prisoners were in gaol for selling liquor to Africans (246).

While the statute did not limit the work of probation officers to whites only, this was in effect the case in the Transvaal. As the Johannesburg probation officer noted in his report in 1918: 'Owing to the great pressure of work in European cases I have been reluctantly compelled to leave the great question of Coloured and Native juveniles almost entirely alone' (UG 36 1918: 123). Similarly prisoners' aid work among discharged prisoners was available only to whites. In 1913 the Johannesburg Superintendent of Prisons urged that 'the time has arrived when steps should be taken to extend some sort of help to discharged natives. If it is impossible to assist discharged natives', he went on, suggesting an added punitive measure, 'he considers that all recidivists should be repatriated to their kraals and compelled to keep away from the towns' (UG 44 1913: 272).

As in many countries those who concerned themselves with sentencing found the judiciary to be erratic. In 1914 the prison Board of Visitors for the Transvaal called attention to the disparity in sentences given, especially in the 'very numerous' cases of culpable homicide among Africans (UG 28 1915: 246ff). The Board, they said, 'approach this subject with considerable diffidence', wishing it to be understood not as 'carping criticism, but courteously as a subject for judicial consideration as a whole'. They noted that sentences varied from two and ten years in cases where the 'crime has taken place under Native social conditions such as beer drinks etc.' Significantly they found that earlier expressions of disquiet had met with the response that 'the greater sentence cannot be regarded as too severe, although the smaller one may be too lenient'. In the face of this lack of sympathy the board nonetheless suggested that 'the difficulty might be met by the American form of Indeterminate sentence, i.e. a minimum and maximum limitation e.g. a sentence of not less than three years and not more than six'. This was not taken up.

The following year the Board of Visitors drew attention to the great disparities in sentencing between judges in cases involving violence against white women and children by Africans. Natal, they noted, imposed the longest prison sentences and lashes for rape; the Free State the next longest prison sentences, while they were lowest in the Cape. In prisons men complained to them that they had been more severely punished than their fellow convicts for the same crime. 'Inconsistency of this nature presents itself to the native mind as a serious grievance, and policy dictates for the benefit of the native mind that there should be as far as possible uniformity in the apportionment of sentences.' They suggested a judges' conference to bring this about (UG 39 1918: 150). They continued to remark that 'convicts had constantly pointed out to the Board the great difference in sentences for offences which were apparently alike' (96). They expressed the view that where, in the opinion of the Board, lenient sentences had been given, the Board should grant no remission of sentence. The judge on the Board disagreed. Prison regulations, he argued, provided generally for remission for good conduct, otherwise 'all inducement to men . . . to conduct themselves properly during incarceration would be removed'. The Board, he said, could not practically increase sentences which it deemed too lenient by refusing remission (159–60).

In October 1917 a national conference of Boards of Visitors considered the principles upon which indeterminates should be recommended for release. The type of crime, character, family relations and so on were all to be considered. The principles adopted were far more severe on the socially weak than on the malefactor. 'It was felt that even a convict who started off his sentence badly by kicking against the pricks could redeem himself, but that drunkards, vagrants and convicts who were easily led astray should not be lightly released but rather kept under control' (UG 36 1918: 94–5). The Transvaal Board gave considerable time to the question of indeterminates. It questioned whether the type of warders being used, who 'should be men of education, intelligence, knowledge of human nature and broad sympathies', were of the standard required. As in so many matters in this area the gap between real and ideal was fundamental, so fundamental that questions as to the rationality of those who spoke the language of the ideal must be raised. They objected to the reluctance of judges to impose the indeterminate sentence:

> the kindness of the judge in giving what has been termed another chance was a mistaken one, as the convict regards it as a mark of weakness and there was no incentive to reform. When a man gets the indeterminate sentence he knows very quickly that his sole chance of release is evidence of reformation . . . This is an incentive which does not obtain in a definite sentence . . . release has to take place in due course, and the worst criminal and the greatest danger to society under a definite sentence is always ultimately released. (97)

A definite criminal sentence was meant to avenge the breach in the law, the Board said, deter others, and release the convict reformed. But, said the Board, 'the definite sentence cannot fulfil these objects as well as the indeterminate one, and . . . does not protect society as well as the indeterminate'. They therefore urged that the discretion given to judges to decide whether they would pass the sentence on repeat offenders should be removed, clearly preferring the length of sentence to be one of administrative discretion, and not one for the courts. 'The element of notoriety or heroism or bravado, all so dear to the criminal mind, is altogether eliminated. No prince of criminals cares to be labelled a common habitual criminal.' Another use of the indeterminate administratively controlled sentence was the appeal it had as a possible total solution to difficult crime problems. The Board continued:

> There is also the economic side. If a hundred or so of the European Liquor Law offenders got the indeterminate sentence, for a considerable period the Police on the Reef would have less work and the Courts very much less. The Board submits that the indeterminate sentence can easily be put to greater use for the protection of the community and the benefit of the criminal. (96–7)

Reviewing the experience with indeterminates sentenced 1910 and 1914 the board noted that sixteen out of twenty-five whites and seventy-two out of two hundred and forty-six non-whites had been released. Up to 30 per cent of releases had been 'unsuccessful'. They concluded that 'the number released has not been excessive, and that there are probably quite a number who will never earn their release'. It is not surprising to find that over the years race became the dominant factor in the board's thinking. Roos told parliament when he was minister responsible that 'generally speaking our boards have been a bit pessimistic about the chance of your native indeterminate reforming. They say the percentage is very low. They do not put the percentage very high as far as the Asiatic is concerned. They say that, as far as the European is concerned, there are better chances of reform' (Hansard 26/4/28).

Prisons

The building of the de Beers Convict Prison in Kimberley ushered in an important development in South African penology. Black prison labour was thenceforth frequently to be used to perform ordinary economic tasks and at little cost, or even at a profit, to the state. The mine paid all the running costs, plus a fee to the state (2 pence per day) for the use of convict labour.[4] The flow of African convicts sentenced for minor offences kept up a large labour force which was used for road building and other public works. In 1910 the prisons report put a penological gloss on this: 'These road camps were the means of keeping 16,833 natives sentenced for trivial pass and masters and servants offences out of gaol, and away from the possible risk of contamination by association with hardened criminals' (UG 35 1911: 113). The Prisons Act of 1911 gave power to the Director of Prisons to contract for the use of convict labour, with the proviso that the work should be on public works as far as possible (section 93). Under the regulations developed no female prisoner of any race was to be employed outside a prison and no European prisoner was to be placed to work where he would be seen constantly by the public, for example in road gangs (UG 47 1947: 130). The prisons reports show the emerging differences in approach to criminals which were developing within the penological community, and which were based upon different discourses from those of the lawyers. The 1918 report discusses the 'new tendencies and developments in penology' in America. One was 'the tendency to do away with prison walls and inside work and substitute outdoor farm and road work for convicts. In the Union our policy is: the natives for outside work and the European for inside workshop work' (UG 36 1918: 92). Morris

---

[4] In 1914 the Kimberley diamond mines were closed down after the outbreak of war, and along with them, the large de Beers Convict Prison. But it was to prove useful. After October 1914 it was used to house over four thousand white rebel prisoners (UG 28 1915: 243).

Alexander raised this in parliament in 1918. European prisoners, he noted, were no longer sent to the Breakwater in Cape Town, or to work in the streets, but to industrial prisons where they were taught trades. Why was this not done for coloured and black prisoners? The minister, de Wet, told him that 'the reform of coloured and native prisoners is sought to be attained along somewhat different lines' and in their case 'workshops are not essential to reform' (Hansard 27/3/18). Black prisoners worked on road building, and indeterminate and long-sentence prisoners on some gold mines. There was some objection that the use of convict labour by private corporations was wrong, but when parliament discussed the matter the focus was on diverting more of it to farmers, and reducing the rate that was paid for it. There was little support for the Minister of Labour's policy of favouring free labour. As Roos, the Justice Minister, said, 'certain special types of work would not be done at all unless they were done at the specially low rate paid for convicts' (Hansard 20/8/24). Shorter-term African prisoners were placed in farm work, in some cases the male members of the farming community being sworn in as warders (Morrell 1986: 391–3; UG 47 1947: 131–2). There was no direct Prison Department supervision, and prisoners were dependent on the farmer for food, clothing and conditions of detention. There was evidence that release on the due date was by no means certain (UG 1947: 132). The 1913 report paid attention to the economic advantages of enabling the department 'to work them on the roads in their own clothes during their trifling sentences at a minimum cost to the Government' (UG 44 1913: 268). Both the main road between Pretoria and Johannesburg and most of the Main Reef road were built by these means.

The South African Prisoners Aid Association was a part of the lobby for the use of compulsory labour as a way of dealing with the indigent. In 1914 its annual congress passed a resolution calling for the consolidation of the nation's vagrancy laws 'with a view to the establishment of Labour Colonies for dealing with the Indigency question' (UG 28 1915: 238). The system of apprenticeship in the Cape for coloured youths sent to reformatories placed them straight back into the labour system which so many had tried to avoid. The warden of the Porter Reformatory expressed his ambivalence in 1918. On the one hand, he noted, 'these apprentices are chiefly sought as a source of cheap labour, and their masters were not looking after them as they should'. On the other hand, however, in relation to inspection of apprentices' conditions, he 'warns against making the path of the Coloured juvenile offender too easy. His response to kindness and sympathetic interest was sometimes quite contrary to expectations' (UG 36 1918: 134).

In 1916 the Director of Prisons noted a decrease in the number of white prisoners directly attributable to war and recruiting, but observed that the experience of other wars in South Africa and elsewhere was that the prisons would fill again once the war was over. Black prisoners had increased. He wrote:

> Generally the gaol is far too common an adjunct of social life in the Union
> . . . [it] serves as an 'omnium gatherum' to which we quite cheerfully
> relegated last year, besides people who had to be hanged, lashed or
> imprisoned, 218 persons whose sole fault was that they were lunatics, 482
> paupers because they were sick and we had not provided hospitals for
> them, and 649 persons because they had not paid their civil indebtedness
> to their creditors. In addition we imprisoned thousands of natives for not
> carrying a pass, for breaking contracts of service, and for being in posses-
> sion of liquor for which they had paid . . . In a single Session of the Union
> Parliament viz 1916, 158 new crimes with the ultimate sanction of impri-
> sonment were created, and besides under powers conferred on them the
> Provincial Councils, Municipalities and the Government by virtue of
> regulations created many more offences . . . I do not think I can bring the
> cheapness of gaol in the Union home better than by pointing out that for
> the year ending 31st March 1916, England and Wales with a population of
> 36,960,000 sent 64,160 persons to gaol, where in 1916 the Union with
> under 7,000,000 people sent 95,927 to gaol. (UG 39 1918: 147)

He was especially sensitive to the question of youth in prisons. He noted that nearly fourteen thousand people under twenty-one had been sent to prison without going to a reformatory at all, in the great bulk of cases for theft. He urged that for youth short sentences in prison were disastrous, and that magistrates needed to have brought home to them the 'correct doctrine' that what was required was two years in a reformatory. In 1918 the Director of Prisons was critical of both judges and magistrates for their readiness to sentence young people to prison rather than to send them to reformatories (UG 36 1918: 91).

The international interest in recidivism was duplicated in South Africa, but it merged into discourses which regarded whole racial groups as quasi-criminal. Just over one-fifth of all prisoners sentenced in 1914 were classified as recidivists, and this figure had been more or less steady for four years. The figure for European male repeat offenders was consistent at over 30 per cent, while that for African males was uniform at under 20 per cent (some of the difference may have been due to the admitted problems of identifying African offenders). While a complex set of structures was beginning to be put in place to deal with white recidivists, racial essentialism remained the interpretation for others. From the Cape in 1914 the superintendent of the Tokai prison reported that more than one-third of his admissions had more than three convictions.

> This would tend to show that amongst the coloured classes the rule holds that once a criminal always a criminal. Imprisonment had no deterrent effect . . . There is no disgrace attached . . . Since new regulations came into effect the diet was made more distasteful, and the kit and bedding provided have been made scantier, yet all this had no apparent effect. (UG 28 1915: 244)

The Department of Prisons' own figures showed clearly that there was a higher proportion of repeat offenders among white convicts than blacks in the country as a whole, but no conclusion was drawn as to the inherent criminal propensities of whites. All of the copious statistics broke down offenders, convicts, juveniles, etc. into four racial categories, and broad conclusions were drawn about races far more often than about other classifications of offender, such as age, short or long term, recidivist, violent or non-violent etc. Indeed, racial classifications were thought to be significant even within the broader categories of white and black. White offenders were broken down in the 1915 report into twenty-eight different national groups. From the exercise was drawn the apparently meaningful conclusion that of the main white groups in the Union, 826 of British descent and 618 of Dutch descent had been convicted. Africans were broken down into twelve tribal groups. More Zulus had been sentenced to prison terms than any other group in the Union. More realistic analysis was possible but was not offered often and was crowded out by the focus on race. The same report noted that over the four years the number of illiterates in prison was steady at just over 80 per cent. In all of these years under 1 per cent had received any secondary education. Nearly four-fifths were labourers or domestic servants. Among whites, miners were the most common group in prison. The conclusion reached was that 'a very large proportion of crime in the Union can be attributed to want of employ-ment and poverty' (UG 28 1915: 281). It was a more sober and realistic conclusion than that which was most prominent in public discourses.

The racial focus also made poor whites particular subjects of the penological discourses. They lived on the frontier of the white state's law and order, straddling both sides. They made up a large part of the lower end of the police forces, and of the offenders in the most visible of 'frontier' petty crimes. In the early years of the Union the numbers of white convicted criminals born outside of South Africa exceeded native whites, due, it appears, to the large numbers of immigrants on the Reef, the centre of most white crimes. But soon the new criminals were different. Reformatories for white boys were filled largely with Afrikaner youth with minimal education. They were also not necessarily looked upon unsympathetically by the Afrikaner community. From the Transvaal in 1912 it was reported that there were many absconders but that those sent 'in search up to the present have never been successful in effecting a recapture, owing . . . to the fact that farmers are inclined to sympathise with the absconders' (UG 44 1913: 281). Whatever the reforming ambitions of the more criminologically minded, the realities of the prison system were different. The Inspector of Prisons for the Transvaal summed up in 1918: 'The keynote of the administration was discipline – obedience to orders' (UG 36 1918: 95). A similar spirit pervaded reformatories. The warden of Houtpoort in the Transvaal wrote in 1918: 'The main object was to prepare the pupils in the first instance not to pass an examination test but the stern test of life' (131). Nonetheless, the aesthetics of prisons in the new segregating state were also conceived quite differently for whites and for blacks. The 1913 Department of Justice report notes that 'in the Transvaal the big new Cinderella Prison for 1,000 native convicts . . . built to a great extent of wood and iron, surrounded by a barbed wire fence, was completed . . . At George the picturesquely situated gaol embowered in oaks has been converted . . . into a Government Industrial School (Reformatory) for white boys' (UG 44 1913: 233).

6

Criminal law

We can now turn our attention to the criminal law and to its relationship
with the discourses about crime. Criminal law, as Garland has written
(1985: 103), is limited as a disciplinary mechanism. 'It functions through
the specification and prohibition of definite acts and is thereby limited to
the policing of these acts, rather than the general inspection/control of
individuals themselves.' In South Africa there was perhaps not so great a
tension between the jurisprudential approach to offenders and that of the
new criminology. While the criminal law, like that of England, was built on
the notion of individual responsibility, it was not set within a nominally
liberal political culture into which this notion became naturalised. For, as
Garland observed, in the new criminology there no longer existed a
'universe of free and equal legal subjects, which coincides with the sane
adult population . . . Neither reason nor responsibility can any longer be
simply presumed in the presence of juveniles, vagrants, habituals, inebriates or the feeble minded' (1985: 25). South African politics had little in the
way of a liberal orthodoxy. The state was a creation of the imperial state,
with its overarching ideology of explicit racist hierarchies, exploitative
efficiency and regulation. In South Africa it was the bulk of the population
who were considered to be not wholly adult either culturally or politically,
and who *all* could be consigned to the categories Garland listed. As far as
they were concerned responsibility meant only liability for acts done; there
was no presumption of rationality, rather the reverse. Barbarian free will
was not the same as civilised free will, but a form of determined action in
itself. Barbarian crime was not to be explained by choice, nor excused by
lunacy, but arose from the very nature of the savage.

Criminal responsibility in both Roman-Dutch and English common
law was based on the guilty intention of the offender to commit a specific
proscribed act, and a sentence was related to conviction for that act. But

in South Africa the moral culpability and social dangerousness of all who were not white was predetermined. Convicted persons could routinely be seen to be both morally culpable as individuals and members of a menacing group, and sentences therefore as both particular punishment and general 'social defence' (Radzinowicz 1966: 52–3). The criminal law had a relationship also with the administrative traditions of Southern Africa (and of the British empire as a whole) which relied upon wide-ranging discretionary administrative powers to proscribe behaviours and prescribe punitive remedies among the subject populations. Criminological thought was one way of easing an accommodation between the legal and administrative imperatives in the criminal law area.

In trying to connect the world of thinking about crime to that of the criminal law, should we expect a close and logical connection, with the law itself tailored to accomplish the purposes identified by other discourses, whether 'scientific' or political? The major problem in trying to comprehend the criminal law is in relating the common law, and the approach of the higher courts, to the rest of the mental and actual world of crime control. To a legal realist most of 'law' happens at the bottom of a pyramid of which the high courts represent only the peak. From the point of view of the judges in the high courts the pyramid is inverted, and most law happens at the top, with very little at the bottom. An analysis of legalism has constantly to juggle these two perspectives. As an object of analysis 'the criminal law' itself dissolves into pieces as it is approached. It is made up not only of common law and statutes but also of the way these are interpreted in the higher courts, and the way they are routinely applied in the lower ones. In addition there are the discretions involved in the selection of actions for prosecution, and in sentencing, and there is a world of police coercion which never reaches the courts.

The lower courts present us with less of a problem. Their concerns were not the same as those of the high courts. One magistrate described his world: 'week after week, month after month in the fetid [*sic*] atmosphere of a busy criminal court, listening to almost unbelievable stories of the underworld, of rape, sodomy, bestiality, prostitution, seeing the lowest type of humanity . . . in almost endless procession, and his job to punish, punish, punish' (Corder 1946: 34–5). Another recounted the 'Magisterial mill . . . the same monotonous grind. The same deadly convictions follow similar, sordid stories. Most of our criminal cases have some connections with colour' (Devitt 1934: 126). ('It is a thousand pities', he remarked,

'that we have coloured people in South Africa at all' (205). Prosecutors
preferred to bring charges in these courts where legalism was less punctilious and also because the sentences were usually heavier. A large proportion of the cases arose out of statutory offences. Corder's Cape court
heard cases at the rate of 120–50 cases per day (1946: 94–5). Simons notes
that it was bad for a magistrate to get a reputation for being 'slow'. Over
two hundred cases were handled in a single court in Johannesburg on
Monday mornings (1936: 470). Brookes wrote that a Witwatersrand
magistrate 'was recently held up to public admiration by a Johannesburg
newspaper for having dealt with a record of over 500 cases in one day . . .
It is the European case which tends to be heard and the native case to be
"polished off"' (1930: 384–5).

In overall terms, what were they doing? Again, figures of convictions
are revealing. In 1930, in rounded figures, 52,000 Africans were convicted
of alcohol-related offences, of which 36,000 were for illegal possession;
79,000 were convicted of offences against the pass and municipal laws
controlling movement and residence; 50,000 were convicted of tax offences; 39,000 were convicted of labour-law infractions, including 16,000
against the master and servant laws. There were 31,000 convictions for
common-law criminal offences, less than one-seventh of the number for
statutory offences (UG 22 1932). In 1914, 16.1 per thousand of the African
and coloured population were given prison sentences; in 1924, 19.69; and
in 1934, 26.5. Over the same period the number of whites so sentenced
declined from 3.6 to 2.3. In 1932 nearly six times as many Africans as
whites convicted in the courts were given penal sentences (figures from
Simons 1936: 473). Elsewhere modern states in the making also widened
the reach of regulation and punishment, creating what Wiener has called
'the police-man state' (1990: 262). But nothing could demonstrate better
the connections between the style and content of criminal justice and
democracy than the contrasting paths taken in Britain and South Africa.
In Britain, Wiener writes, democratisation made it harder for the state to
maintain the expansion of criminal sanctions. After 1918, he writes, 'while
the law itself . . . was altered only slowly, major changes took place in its
administration'. In 1934 in Britain the prison population was one-third of
what it had been in 1910, with many fewer short sentence prisoners
(379–80). In South Africa rates of conviction and incarceration for minor
offences by the disenfranchised continued to rise.

In South Africa's criminal law there was another complication. It had, as the major textbook of the period put it, been 'enormously influenced' by English forms and practice, 'especially in matters of procedure' (Gardiner and Lansdown 1924, vol. I: v). The Roman-Dutch common law had been supplemented for over a century in the Cape Colony by English procedures and practice, and a code of criminal procedure based upon the Cape, Queensland and Canada was introduced into the Transvaal as one of the first acts of the imperial government's extensive reform of the statute book after the annexation of the Transvaal. This ordinance (no. 1 of 1903) was to form the basis of the Union-wide Criminal Procedure Act of 1917. By statute there had also been an adoption on a continuing basis of the law of evidence as applied in English courts. Writing in 1924 about the substantive law, Gardiner and Lansdown felt able to say (decades before the determined and ultimately successful effort to produce a purer Roman-Dutch criminal law) that 'our criminal law is much more akin to the law of England than to the Roman Dutch Law' (1924, vol. I: 6), though the kinship was closest in the procedural aspects.

According to English practice South African statutes providing for criminal penalties of any kind were interpreted strictly by the Supreme Courts; in addition they were only taken to alter the common law where that was a necessary inference. The basic doctrine of the common law was the requirement not only of an *actus reus* (a wrongful act) but also of *mens rea* (wrongful intention) as necessary components of a criminal act. This doctrine was applied, except where explicitly excluded by the statute, to statutory crimes as well as common law ones. Apparently sweeping methods of social control became as a result potentially difficult to operate. There was also a careful definition of the limits of vicarious responsibility and, perhaps surprisingly, only a very limited use of the idea of communal responsibility for offences. The few pieces of existing law all pre-dated Union in 1910 and were derived from the British colonial repertoire. The dominance of the notion of individual responsibility also seems to have impeded the usability of communal responsibility in the criminal law. Transvaal Law no. 4 of 1885 and Natal Act no. 47 of 1903 both had provision for fining the male adults of a tribe for impeding the investigation of a serious crime. Natal Act no. 1 of of 1899 and the Cape Act no. 32 of 1909 had provisions for communal responsibility in relation to cattle theft. It may help us to think about the essential nature of the adherence of the South African law to its English 'rule of law' heritage if we note what it did not become. In Germany in the 1930s insistence on crimes pre-defined in law was, in accordance with 'free law' thinking, abandoned. The new section 2 of the German Penal Code, adopted in 1935, read: 'He will be punished, who commits a crime which has been declared punishable by law or which deserves punishment according to the principle of a penal statute and according to the sound feeling of the people. If no penal statute can be directly applied to such crime, the crime is punished according to that statute whose basic idea is best fitted for it' (Neumann [1942] (1963): 114).

Much depended, of course, on where, and by whom, cases were heard. In the eyes of the executive government the primary role of the magistrates was, in these years, a mixture of the political and administrative, not judicial. The magistrates appointed to run the Transvaal after the war, for example, were neither lawyers nor Transvalers. Out of fifty-six, twenty-three were born in the UK; eight in other parts of the empire; and nineteen in the Cape Colony. Only twenty-nine had experience of legal practice, or magistracy, while sixteen had seen active service with British forces in the South African War. The capacity of the Transvaal magistracy was called into question in a most public way by the new Transvaal Chief Justice, Innes, in 1903. Judging from many of the cases that came to the Supreme Court for review, he said, it was evident that some of the magistrates were unacquainted with even the elementary principles of law. As only the most serious cases were sent up it was not unlikely that in many smaller charges injustice was done to the accused (Cd 2027 1904: 4). But there was a wide difference between the judicial view and that of the legal administration. In response to Innes the Transvaal Attorney-General noted that 'in most of the districts of this Colony the Magistrates have had no time to discharge their judicial functions. They are appointed in very abnormal times, and their time has been fully occupied in important administrative work.' Judicial work had been left to the assistant magistrates. In some areas public prosecutors worked as temporary magistrates. In fact, in spite of Innes's dismay, fewer than 5 per cent of sentences in cases reviewed (about 5 per cent of all cases) were either quashed or varied by the Supreme Court. In all there were sixty-nine formal appeals out of a total of over twenty-nine thousand convictions, of which thirty-one were allowed. Even of this small number the Attorney-General's view was that 'many appeals are allowed on technical points, even when real and substantial justice has been done by the conviction of the appellant' (5). In only ninety-three cases were sentences varied on review. While the

Attorney-General took this as evidence of the high quality of the work done by the magistrates, another view might be that the system of appeal and review was not operating effectively. Innes urged that formal legal qualifications should be required of the magisterial bench but in 1904 Milner told the Secretary of State for the Colonies that 'the time has not yet arrived' for such a requirement (3). Though there were special features of the magistracies appointed for the defeated republics, the prioritising of their political and administrative roles remained a feature of the magistrates' role throughout the period of this study.

The competency and reputation of the Transvaal magistracy remained controversial. In 1914 a number of Johannesburg attorneys complained to the Chief Magistrate that there was little observance of a separation of powers between magistrates and prosecutors; that a number of magistrates were financially embarrassed, *habitués* of race courses and bars and in debt to lawyers who had undue influence as a result; and ignorant of the laws of evidence and procedure (Union Archives, Department of Justice 1914). They complained also of the absence of records of court proceedings. In his report to the minister the Chief Magistrate first observed that 'Civil Service training is not a qualification for judicial functions and that these functions would be better performed by Magistrates appointed from the Bar'. The acceptance of the Civil Service Lower Law Examination as the 'standard of legal knowledge' meant that the quality of the courts would never be high. The ways that the court functioned meant that 'neither side has, as a rule, had much opportunity for considering the case' before the brief hearings that followed. Furthermore, 'independence and impartiality are not virtues developed in a civil service training'. But, he concluded, 'inferior courts are not expected to turn out the same class of justice as Superior Courts . . . Inferior Courts are, necessarily, a compromise between justice and economy'. A plausible picture of incompetence and corruption had emerged, perhaps not too remarkable in a new state, but the importance of these misgivings is that they were expressed, and were completely ignored, in the lead up to the great increase in the criminal jurisdiction of the magistrates in 1917.

Magistrates' courts, like lower courts everywhere, delivered a sort of administered law, and were less concerned about the niceties of interpretation than the higher courts were. Magistrates' courts often ignored the procedural requirements that evidence had to be presented that the offence charged had actually been committed, and by the person charged, and simply accepted the guilty pleas of the (usually illiterate and rarely represented) accused (e.g. Simons 1936: 470). One of the most significant features of the legal history of this period is the shift of the bulk of cases down the judicial ladder. In 1917 the jurisdiction of the magistrates' courts was greatly extended (by sections 86 and 87 of the Criminal Procedure Act). The 1917 Act was based on the imperial model Transvaal law of 1903. There were additional features: it introduced majority jury verdicts country wide; judges were given the power to recommend to the Attorney-General that a jury be dispensed with in treason trials; and defendants given the right to request a non-jury trial. Indeed, 'distrust of juries' was one of the reasons for the increase in the jurisdiction of the magistrates (Department of Justice 1914: Buckle–Secretary of Justice 12/9/14), but it was a distrust that had arisen from the difficulties the state had had with juries in prosecutions connected with the white strikes on the Rand, and with illicit gold sales. African complaints about white juries, though vocal, were not directly influential. In May 1918 the African National Congress in the Orange Free State protested that trial by jury was an 'absolute farce . . . in mixed cases'. A public meeting passed a resolution that 'the shooting of natives is not likely to cease until such cases are tried by Supreme Court judges without the aid of juries'. While the Free State Attorney-General acknowledged privately that there had 'perhaps' been miscarriages of justice where juries 'were loath to convict white men where the complainants happened to be natives', the government's public response was a straightforward denial (Union Archives S1/75/98/18). These complaints remained a feature of African commentary on the criminal justice system. Fourteen years later nothing had changed. In 1932 the judges' conference noted that 'the reluctance of juries in some parts of the Union to register a conviction under the insolvency laws, in trapping cases, or to deal faithfully with matters in which colour prejudice is involved, is common knowledge' (Archives GG 70/390 1932). All the judges suggested was raising the qualifications for jurors so that jury duty was not done by 'persons of comparatively low standing in the community'.

The English law of evidence was simply deemed to be the law of evidence in South Africa. But judges, unlike those in England, were given the prerogative of giving their opinion on the facts of the case in their summing up to the jury. The jurisdiction of the courts of the rural justices of the peace was also greatly increased in 1917 and again in 1918, when they were given full magistrates' court jurisdiction in masters and servants cases (Act no. 2 of 1918). This, said a National Party member in parliament, 'would greatly satisfy country districts' (Hansard 27/2/17). The justices, who dealt largely with rural master and servant cases, were given the power to impose ten strokes with the cane. While the increased jurisdiction of the lower courts might have been matched by a comparable increase in higher court supervision, the opposite course was taken. The powers of review of the Supreme Court over the sentencing of both magistrates' and justices' of the peace courts was reduced in this year. Thus while a jurisprudence of strict interpretation flourished in the Supreme Court, it had only an attenuated influence on most cases of the implementation of the common and statutory criminal law. There was also tension between the different levels of the judiciary. The judges frequently criticised the magistrates' proceedings, findings and excessive sentences. The magistrates resented the interference of the judges, especially where local political and economic discipline and the administration of the criminal law were mixed, as, for example, with the Masters and Servants Act. As the magistrate in Estcourt complained to the Secretary for Justice in 1928 in regard to cases arising out of the activities of the Industrial and Commercial Workers' Union, the union was being 'backed up by Quixotic judges obsessed with the idea that they are the God sent protectors of the blacks against imaginatively harsh Magistrates and oppressive farmers' (Bradford 1987: 271). The differences between the magistrates and the judges were canvassed at some length in the debates on how to deal with the other major rural flashpoint, stock theft (see SC 4 1923). Lashes were the focus. Senior officials gave evidence that young magistrates gave 'absolutely brutal' sentences (11). But some magistrates had a different view. As one said, farmers wanted the Magistrates to give deterrent sentences, but the magistrates were 'really between the frying pan and the fire. The judges when reviewing a case will not allow the Magistrates to give a sentence which in his opinion is an effective deterrent so that . . . a very large number of Magistrates were afraid.' Magistrates who followed their experience as to what sentences were effective were 'subjected to somewhat severe remarks' (20–1). Another put the matter succinctly: 'The position now is that the Magistrate is between the judge and the public . . . the Judge knows the law but the Magistrate is best qualified to say what the circumstances in his district demand, and what the best way is to put down crime' (ibid.). Yet while some individuals found a degree of relief through judicial review, the trends in sentencing show, as we have seen, a steady rate in increase in the percentage of non-whites being sent to penal institutions.

The notion that the burden of proof in a criminal charge always lay with the Crown, a doctrine which was inherited from English law, was another fundamentally restricting legal doctrine by which the Supreme Courts were obliged to limit the effectiveness of prosecutions. Yet some fundamental matters were dealt with by statutes which reversed the onus of proof and which, therefore, made the restricting approach of the high courts less effective. The legal origins of these statutory reversals of onus appear to have been in the repertoire of the English Vagrancy Law. Following this model, Cape Act no. 23 of 1879 placed the onus on the apparent vagrant to prove that he was not idle or undesirable, as did Transvaal Law no. 1 of 1881 (Gardiner and Lansdown 1924, vol. II: chapter 40). It was this reversible onus (as well as the repertoire of ideas about idleness and criminality drawn from vagrancy law) that became the crucial feature of the administration of the powers to banish in the Native (Urban Areas) Act (no. 21) of 1923. The willingness of parliament to transform the normal rules with regard to burden of proof in cases concerning blacks is highlighted by section 17 of this Act (see below, part IV). The 'normal' protections offered by the law of criminal procedure were withdrawn precisely in those cases that affected a large number of black rather than white accused.

The second fundamental area where reversal of the onus of proof was introduced was in relation to certain economic crimes. More than any other crime, stock theft marked the struggle between black and white in the rural areas, and it was singled out as being a crime to which reverse onus would apply. There were similar provisions in legislation regarding dealings in diamonds and gold. The criminal law in this area reflects the fierce determination with which the state defended the enormous concentrations of wealth in gold and diamonds against a multiracial netherworld of black and white mine workers, Jewish jewellers and Indian exporters. Whether or not there was a requirement that a person found in possession of goods that had been stolen had to establish that he had come by them innocently had been an area of controversy in English criminal law. While the English courts established in *R v Schama and R v Abramovitz 24 Cox 591* that the onus still lay on the Crown to show that a person in possession of stolen goods had come by them illegally, in South African statutes relating to diamonds, gold and stock the position was enunciated that the onus lay on the accused to show that he had come by them innocently. As one commentator wrote, in South Africa the English statement would normally have been followed, as the rules of evidence and procedure had been so closely assimilated to those of England. But

> Fortunately for those who administer justice in the country districts, in the most important cases that come before them – cases of stock theft – the burden of proof is regulated by Statute. The Stock Theft Act no. 26 of 1923 is fairly drastic in this matter. It creates two new offences, one consisting of being found in possession of stock reasonably suspected of being stolen and being unable to give a satisfactory account of such possession, the other consisting of receiving stock without reasonable cause (proof of which is on the accused) for believing that the person from whom it was received had authority to deal with it. (Morice 1924: 137)

These provisions had been vigorously debated when the stock theft legislation was presented to parliament. Guilt would be placed on 'innocent shoulders', said one Labour member, questioning the meaning of the words 'reasonable suspicion'. Other Labour members opposed the law. Blackwell captured the general arguments when he claimed (inaccurately given the existing gold and diamond laws) that 'the Bill would revolutionise the whole criminal procedure with regards to thefts . . . departing from the whole of our traditional jurisprudence'. There was opposition also to provisions in the Bill giving magistrates the power to impose whipping for a crime that did not involve physical violence. Such concerns were swept contemptuously aside by the Minister of Justice, de Wet. Farmers needed every assistance, he said, and the existing Cape law of 1893 empowered the arrest of persons who could not give a satisfactory account of goods in their possession: 'He failed to understand the sickly sentimentality which had been uttered on behalf of the criminal' (Hansard 16/2/23). Again, we have not a legal invention but the picking up of a usable legal tool for use in cases in which the overwhelming proportion of those accused were African.

I have discussed above the analyses of the effects of alcohol on blacks in relation to crime, with the amalgam of fears of primitive passions, loss of respect, and the undermining effects of the multiracial *demi-monde*. A vast apparatus of enforcement to control the flow of alcohol to blacks was erected, and its operation was one of the main activities of the administration of criminal law. What can one discern from it in relation to the criminal law in the South African state? One of the basic approaches to the question has been to ask how effective the control of alcohol was, and it is not really in dispute that, despite a continual guerrilla warfare between police and populace in relation to this, prohibition failed (the laws were eventually repealed in 1961) (Scharf 1985; Crush and Ambler 1992). But my interest here is in the relation of the concerns of the criminal law to those of the purposes of the state. Law enforcement of prohibition by the police was vigorous, constant and brutal. (It was estimated in 1962 that one-third of the police budget was spent on policing prohibition (Scharf 1985: 55).) Life in the black urban areas in particular was constantly punctuated by raids for liquor. Complicated trapping operations were employed by the police to catch suppliers. These were the subject of a great deal of political controversy. Objections were raised to the use of black police agents to trap whites. Not only politicians disapproved of the reversals involved in the use of black detectives to trap white transgressors. Innes CJ expressed the reluctance of the courts to rely on the evidence of black policemen where whites were involved, urging that a European detective in charge watch all the transactions (*Myers and Misnum v Rex 1907 TS 760* at 761). There were similar objections to the use of trapping by black police agents on the diamond diggings, where the victims caught in the net were poor white diggers.

Police action seized alcohol and produced bodies before the courts. Once there, however, they were subject to a peculiar discourse and set of concerns. The concerns of the criminal law seem curiously unrelated to the fears about alcohol and the policies of prohibition. Many cases concerning alcohol supply found their way to the Supreme Courts. The courts' preoccupations appear to be quite different from those of the criminological discourse. They were worried over definitional matters. What was an intoxicating drink? Who exactly were included in the array of prohibited racial categories? These questions provoked parliament into the typical legislative responses of definitional hyperbole (see below, part V). Then the courts focused on what constituted illegal supply. Mere possession of illegal alcohol was not enough. An act of supply and purchase had to be proved. Was the purchaser an accomplice to an illegal sale? (This was of vital importance to trapping convictions as the evidence of an accomplice had to be corroborated.) Did the state have to prove that the purchaser intended to consume the alcohol? What if there was absence of knowledge, either of the race of the purchaser or the nature of the brew? Were holders of liquor licences liable for the acts of their employees who sold illegally? What if the sale was for medicinal or sacramental purposes? What if the sale had been fraudulently induced, for example by a misrepresentation of racial identity? The courts held that the breach of licensing conditions could not be found unless the issuing of the licence was proved in court; evidence of the names of the recipients of the illegal liquor had to be supplied, as well as proof that they were coloured persons. As Mason said in *Bosch v Rex 1904 TS 55* at 59, 'every fact necessary for conviction must be clearly proved'. This sampling of the courts' concerns will make it clear that they applied to the major state purpose of prohibition all the rigours of the restrictive approach to the interpretation of criminal law. This was not popular with police or politicians. The Native Economic Commission (UG 22 1932: para. 752) complained that, with regard to blacks and alcohol, police were 'bound by the somewhat cumbrous proceeding necessary to obtain a conviction in a European court'. They had considerable success in finding and destroying liquor but much difficulty in proving possession to the satisfaction of the courts. For years magistrates affirmed the impossibility of enforcing the prohibition laws, and urged that it be made a criminal offence for a prohibited person to be found in possession of liquor. They also suggested reversing the onus of proof, to make the accused supplier prove that he did not know the recipient was a prohibited person. Police and magistrates in the Cape wanted total prohibition to be applied to Africans. The failure of the existing restrictions was put down to the trade carried on by registered African voters and coloureds (UG 62 1912: 80 and UG 28 1915: 35/6). Magistrates also complained about the approach of the Supreme Court. 'Unfortunately', wrote one, 'all sorts of technical legal points arising out of certain decided cases' made matters difficult to control (UG 28 1915: 36). Another harked back with nostalgic approval to the recent martial law proclamation in the Northern Cape under which liquor was not available to Africans and noted the marked improvement in the behaviour of labour, and the reduction in crime (37).

Why then did the courts take this attitude to these statutes? Clearly it is difficult to separate some areas of criminal law from others, and one would expect that the techniques evolved to deal with common-law crimes also appeared to lawyers to be those most appropriate for statutory ones. We have seen too that, where really necessary, the legislature was able to present statutes to the courts which nullified most of the protections that the legalist techniques gave to those accused. It is significant,

therefore, that prohibition laws did not reverse the onus of proof. This
was because they caught within their net large numbers of whites charged
with illegal supply, and reverse onus laws appear to have been largely
reserved for criminalising statutes which netted mainly black offenders.
Between 1903 and 1918 fully 3.8 per cent of the white male population of
the Transvaal were convicted of offences against the prohibition laws
(Simons 1936: 449). The Carnegie Commission on the poor-white
'problem' noted in relation to these laws that 'the poor white is not
accustomed to considering its observance a moral obligation' (quoted in
ibid.). In the consolidating statute of 1928, the Liquor Act, a government
sensitive to urban Afrikaner public opinion acted to protect poor whites
by substantially reducing the penalty for a first offence to a fine and
limiting the use of police traps. The criminal law must also be understood
in relation to what happens after conviction. When Roos became the first
National Party Minister of Justice he systematically released prisoners
from his political constituency. After his first year he criticised the
'severity' of the liquor laws, and reported the release of 855 persons
convicted (Hansard 6/7/25).

The point can be underlined when we note that in relation to criminal
law procedural niceties were not always observed. In *Mosala and others v
Native Commissioner 1906 TS 949* the same court that had established the
strict approach to the liquor laws declined to overturn the criminal
convictions for riot of a number of persons by a native commissioner's
court. This was despite the finding of Wessels that there was 'not the
slightest doubt that a great number of irregularities took place in the trial.
Evidence was wrongly admitted, and extracted from the accused. Native
law was not proved in Court' (953). But there may be a further point
related to restrictive legalism in the criminal law area. Legalism may
appear to have made it harder for prohibition to succeed in that many
persons clearly involved in the illegal trade were not convicted. But overall
it is doubtful whether it had much effect at all on the war between police,
suppliers, purchasers and illegal brewers. Interdiction of supply, corruption, destruction of stocks, and refurbishing of stills all took place long
before any of the activities came within the ambit of a court, and most of
them never did. What the supreme courts did was to patrol the boundaries of the state's policing and punitive powers. The purpose of the patrol
was not to protect rights by limiting the reach of the law. Many in the
target population of the law, blacks who wanted to consume alcohol, were

caught by simple police action, or in the lower courts where convictions and punishments were handed out in a routine and administrative style barely encumbered by the Supreme Courts' legalisms. The purpose of the patrol was to ensure that state actions did not spill over and completely engulf the wrong targets, in this case a class of offenders produced by a criminalising statute who were mainly white. The effect of a strict constructionist 'rule of law' in this area of the criminal law appears to have been to act as a targeting mechanism. This argument also applies to analysis of the 'rule of law' in relation to political offences. The courts defined the operation of statutes like the Riotous Assemblies Act, which severely limited freedom of speech, very restrictively. One political purpose of the Act was to limit black political agitation but a wide interpretation of its provisions would have netted many white politicians, i.e. the wrong targets. Similar considerations applied to the strict interpretation of the provisions of the Masters and Servants Act which criminalised enticing workers away from a particular employer. In *R v Jacob 1905 TS 88* the conviction of a black worker who urged other employees to remain on strike was reversed by Innes CJ who urged the necessity for narrow construction. The alternative, of course, would have been to criminalise the activities of an extremely powerful, and enfranchised, white labour movement.

The criminal law, the construction of self and the place of the imaginary

We may now return to the questions of ethnography raised earlier in the quest to understand the roles of legalism, in this case the place of the criminal law as expounded by the superior courts, in the system of control of crime. I have already said that one of its roles was systemic. Police action and the lower courts provided a carpet bombing approach: the higher courts, even where cases did not in each case concern white accused, helped the legislature in more refined targeting. The 'rule of law', far from being colour blind, was in its outcomes an instrument of legal segregation. But there is another aspect to consider. Just as thinking about crime is the rulers' thinking about and description of otherness, so law is the rulers' thinking about and description of self. The more untamed the others, the more correct the selves. The image of legalism, its justice, discernment and restraint, is a counterpoint of the opposing image of savagery, impulse and transgression. Judge President Boshoff told the accused in reluctantly acquitting them of murder in *R v Magundane and others 1915 NAC 64*:

> I want to say that if you had lived in Zululand under the Zulu kings, you know what would have happened to you without my telling you. You are most fortunate (although I do not think you realise and appreciate it) in living under the white authorities . . . We do not judge you according to your laws . . . but . . . according to our laws . . . Our law throws a protection around every subject of His Majesty the King; and our law says that no man shall be deprived of either liberty or life unless the case against them has been established . . . beyond all reasonable doubt. (77)[1]

The courts played an essential role in segregatory processes. They worked with differentiating legislation. And while the lower courts were agencies through which labour and other disciplines could be imposed, the higher courts were refiners of the definitions of self and otherness. That the judicial mind embraced an overall South African segregationist common sense is hardly worth commenting on. The point that I wish to stress, however, is that what is involved is more than 'prejudiced remarks' by judges (Corder 1984: 132).[2] The judgments of courts were an authoritative part of the discourses that divided self and other, ruler and ruled, white and black. While purporting to treat all equally (where statute so allowed), the courts were fundamentally involved in the creation and elaboration of difference and separateness. The judges accepted as a matter of course, for example, the need to prise the races apart, even when not directed specifically to do so, in terms which echo closely those of the

---

[1] Also illuminating as an 'ethnographical' observation is the contemporary scene-setting description of a notional murder trial courtroom by a prominent legal journalist and author.

A red-robed judge is enthroned high above black-gowned, white cuffed counsel. Natives . . . gape like sheep from a pen. Brightly coloured blankets are draped around their shoulders. The men scratch peppered covered heads in bewilderment at the *indaba* directed by Him of the Red Robe. The women, shiny faced and of enormous bust . . . watch unmoved and unmoving . . .

A native is thrust into the dock. The central figure of the stage, he knows nothing of the rules and stage-craft . . . A white man calls it 'wilful murder'. The witchdoctor, with his necklace of tiger's teeth, his bones, magic potions and mystic rites, called it mystification . . . .When the tribal gods demand blood, blood they must have. (Bennett 1934: 5)

[2] Corder does conclude of the Appellate Division that 'the court seems to have identified itself with contemporary social conventions . . . as far as matters of race were concerned' (168) and that judges had 'a close identification with the race policy of the social elite' (215).

government commissions of enquiry noted above (see *Smith v Germiston Municipality 1908 TS 240*; below, part V).

The directly political aspects of control were also a part of the 'ordinary' functioning of the criminal law. Sentences imposed on blacks (often for minor offences) were harsh if one views them as being only punishment for the offence, or deterrence. But punishment and deterrence were also closely involved with the protection of the exercise of white power. What had to be deterred was not simply crime, but defiance and rebelliousness. The courts operated within a context of incipient revolt. This made it more difficult to perceive offenders as individuals separable from a potentially defiant mass. This was not unconnected with the orthodox white views regarding black political institutions and submission to authority. Even under their own institutions Africans were said only to have been controllable by implacable authoritarianism. If whites were overly tender this could only be mistaken for weakness.

Courts accepted also that blacks and whites were inherently different, a matter of crucial importance to the administration of criminal justice where so much depended on interpretation of guilty intention. This kind of thinking is to be found in many judgments and the approach was enshrined at the highest level by the Appellate Division. As Wessels CJ said in 1933: 'In punishing them we must remember that they are not civilised Europeans but kaffirs living more or less in a state of nature and when they act according to their natural and inherited impulses they do not deserve to be punished too severely as if they were civilised Europeans dwelling in a city or village' (*R v Xulu 1933 AD 197* at 200; Corder 1984: 138). This could often be to the advantage of the accused, and indeed, these remarks were generally made in order to find reasons to mitigate sentence or avoid conviction. Different standards of behaviour tended to be accepted in 'black on black' crimes, and in matters involving witchcraft. In *R v Masipula Nxele NAC 1917 17* at 18 Boshoff JP told a man who had, while drunk, beaten his wife to death: 'Strictly speaking it is murder. A white man was hanged at the Cape for thrashing his wife to death, and perhaps if you had been a white man today you would have been sentenced to death.'

Differences taken for granted by the judges were not only mental and cultural, but physical. In *R v Mayana and others 1908 TS 71* the accused had been given two years and twenty-four lashes for the theft of two sheep. In reviewing the sentence Innes CJ noted that twenty-four out of twenty-seven district surgeons in the Transvaal had recently expressed the view in the light of their experience that only fifteen lashes could be administered without the risk of severe injury. 'I am assuming that the lashes were inflicted on natives,' Innes remarked; 'in the case of Europeans and Asiatics the danger is greater still' (72). This was, it must be noted, simply common sense. Close observation by other 'experts' seemed to support this common sense. The Director of Prisons report for 1934 notes that after the effects 'have been closely watched for some time at some of the largest institutions . . . the definite conclusion has been arrived at that the infliction of a lesser number of strokes than six in the case of Europeans and eight in the case of natives is not an effective punishment'.

The 'rule of law' remained embedded within the constant construction of self and difference. This offers an avenue to understanding the adherence to the niceties of procedural and substantive legalism in the context of racial oppression. From one perspective the judges and their law appear to have been a part of this structure of domination. But the judicial selves of the Supreme Courts appear to have evaded this continuum which stretched from the actions of officials and police, through the courts of the justices of the peace and native commissioners, and the magistrates' courts, and then to the Supreme Courts. Instead, they placed themselves within another continuum. In a feat of self-imagining they saw themselves as brothers to Grotius and the Master of the Rolls rather than to the farm foreman and the prison warder. They found their reality and their law by connecting themselves to Renaissance European jurists and to the judges of the House of Lords and the Court of Criminal Appeal. (There was a substantive base to the imagining of self. Half of the judges who held office in this period were graduates of Cambridge or Oxford; many had qualified at the Inns of Court; and others had attended Scottish, Dutch and German universities.)[3] This legal identity not only helped evasion of South African actualities, but constructed a philosophical, juristic, correct and formal self which could be opposed totally to the barbarian other. The process of creation of self broke the continuum with the lower realms of the legal/administrative machinery.

---

[3] The construction of a collective self can be traced through the biographies and tributes in the *South African Law Journal*. Biographical details of all of the judges in this period can be found in Zimmerman and Visser (1996: chapter 3).

I began this section by emphasising perceptions and have shown how the imported and adapted 'sciences' of criminology and law contributed to what appears from current perspectives to be a distancing from reality and a construction of difference. We may return to the question of stock theft, one of the nodal points of the rural rule of law. There was ample opportunity to observe the real context. Every farmer, and every thief, knew what most stock theft was about. Government commissions and contemporary commentaries contain copious descriptions of the processes of rural impoverishment. The nineteenth-century conquests deprived black pastoralists and mixed farmers of land. The Land Act of 1913, the expulsions of black sharecropping tenants and the subsequent squeeze on the access of labour tenants to land for grazing as they were reduced to agricultural proletarians further deprived rural blacks of access to a basic resource of wealth and food. In a vast and thinly policed countryside persistent appropriations appear to require little further explanation. From the point of view of legal administration also it did not seem too mysterious. I have discussed above the adoption of the reverse onus. With this aid to conviction rural magistrates punished heavily, favouring lashes and long or indeterminate sentences. These sentences, especially lashes for first offences, frequently had to be reduced on review by Supreme Court judges, applying a more distant and metropolitan standard of appropriate punishment. But in 'science' other explanations were possible. In his extended discussion Laubscher, who had a senior position in the mental health services, emphasised the infantile state of black culture and consequent 'oral traits' (Laubscher 1937: 302ff.). 'If we appreciate the two needs of this culture, namely sex and food,' he wrote, 'we begin to understand that cattle and horses are complementary to the fulfilment of sex needs, so that we may say that there is an instinctive disposition which can only obtain its goal in an approved manner via the possession of such animals' (302). There was also the 'native's craving for meat . . . whenever meat is available he gorges himself to the utmost. There is something ravenously sadistic in his attitude towards meat . . . the native's general attitude towards food and his stomach is indicative of powerful oral needs, which reflect the infantile nature of his culture' (303). This is one example among many of how scientific expertise on Africans described and understood them. 'Legalism' creates parallel problems with the discernment of reality. It appears necessary to expand our views of 'law' and to add another to the various matter-of-fact understandings of it revolving around morality, rules, social control, practical mechanism, ideology, or simply hypocrisy. If one considers the realm of discourse shared by law and criminology both can be seen as ways of not knowing, of avoidance and of imagination.

7

Criminalising political opposition

In the period from the 1890s onwards, the instability of the South African Republic, the war, the subsequent fragility of the new Union and the continued industrial strife all contributed to a vigorous development of the common law relating to offences against the state, and, especially as African opposition grew, to the development of statute law aimed at controlling and criminalising political opposition. The trial for treason of leading industrialists following the failure of the Jameson Raid in 1896, the rebellion of Afrikaners in the Cape during the South African War and the Zulu rebellion in Natal gave the courts the opportunity to consider the common law relating to high treason. The Cape rebellion, the immediate post-war regime in the conquered Transvaal, the Afrikaner rebellion in 1914, and the strikes of 1913–14 and 1922 were occasions for the proclamation of martial law. These led the courts to consider their role *vis à vis* the state, and also to the emergence of the view among politicians that common law was inadequate and that new statutory law was needed which would cover these situations. This view, and the rise of black political movements, were behind the original architecture of the statutes that were to be so prominent a part of South African legality.

The strong elements of formalism in South African legal culture faced complex challenges in dealing with those who rejected the South African state itself, and these were made more convoluted by the changing political alliances, and by the political necessity of incorporating all whites within the political settlement. In Roman-Dutch law hostile intention towards the state, and an overt act of hostility which endangered the state, constituted treason (see the extended discussion in Gardiner and Lansdown 1924, vol II: 722ff.). While the original Roman-Dutch law, in Lansdown's words 'was not astute, in acts which directly, openly, immediately and as an inevitable consequence, harmed the State, to seek evidence

of expressed intention to that end' (727), South African courts began by
looking closely for the common-law combination of act and intention.
The context in which this restrictive approach was taken was in cases
concerning those Cape Afrikaners who had joined or assisted the Boer
commandos which had invaded the Cape during the war (730). In
particular the courts insisted that expression of hostility towards the state
was insufficient without the proof of a specific act to put the feeling into
execution. Hostile words alone were insufficient to sustain a charge of
treason unless they amounted to conspiracy, or to direct incitement. An
act that endangered the safety of the state, or excited disaffection among
its subjects, but which was not accompanied by the hostile intention of
overthrowing the state, was not treason but could be prosecuted as the
common-law offence of *crimen laesae Majestas*. In the trial following the
Jameson Raid, fifty-nine of the sixty-three accused pleaded guilty to this
lesser charge (*State v Phillips and others 1896 SAR)*. This weakness in the
courts' approach in dealing with white rebels was to be one of the flaws
dealt with by the later statutes.

   The Cape rebellion by whites, and that by blacks in Natal in 1906, were
also occasions for the use of martial law. In the Cape where a significant
part of the white population supported the republics, and which was
invaded by republican commandos, Milner had insisted on martial law
over the bitter opposition of Innes, who was then Cape Attorney-General
(see Wright 1972: 270ff.; Le May 1965). The wartime experience in the
Cape also produced two other precedents which were to be important in
the years that followed. Both were embodied in the Indemnity and Special
Tribunals Act of 1900. This Act indemnified civil and military authorities
for acts done under martial law. It also set up special civilian courts to try
cases of treason (with reduced penalties), routing these trials away not
only from the military, but from the ordinary courts (Wright 1972: 279).
And it was in appeals originating from the Cape that the Privy Council set
out its version of the effects of a proclamation of martial law (*In re Marais
1902 AC 109* and *In re van Reneen 1904 AC 114*). These cases affirmed that
civil courts could not intervene in any way with acts by the military and
that there was no role for the civil courts in reviewing the administration
of martial law as long as war was being waged (See Keith 1916: 271).

   In Natal martial law was proclaimed in February 1906 during the Zulu
rebellion. By using the weapon of resignation the Natal ministry prevailed
over both the Governor and the Colonial Secretary and used courts

martial rather than the High Court of Natal to try and to condemn rebels. In July 1906 the Natal legislature passed an Act which completely suspended the rule of law. It departed from the principle of only indemnifying acts done in good faith by deeming all official acts to have been done in good faith and it indemnified the authorities not only for all actions taken under martial law but also for all future acts 'having reference in any way directly or indirectly' to the rebellion, and also all actions taken by the Governor in his capacity as Supreme Chief. There was some hesitation in the Colonial Office before approval of a law which was without precedent in the empire, and, it was said, made the Governor into a military dictator (see Marks 1970: 237; Keith 1916: 269–82). The complete suspension of ordinary law was followed by the creation of a special court to try Dinizulu on charges of high treason in 1908 (Keith 1916: 273; Walker 1937). The Privy Council refused to consider the validity of the indemnifying legislation, and also reaffirmed that military courts were beyond challenge by the civil courts. In a state of war there was a right 'to repel force with force'. It was sometimes 'convenient and decorous' to use military courts to restrain 'acts of repression' which might otherwise happen 'without sufficient order and regularity'. But to try to make the proceedings of courts martial 'analogous to the proceedings of Courts of Justice is quite illusory' (*R v Tilonko 1907 AC 461*; see Keith 1916: 273).

In the Transvaal Milner armed his new regime with the Peace Preservation Ordinance of 1902 to protect the new colony against sedition. The ordinance was based closely on English law. According to Lansdown's description in 1926 it was

> taken over from Stephen's very precise classification of the crime of sedition, omitting certain references to the Sovereign which did not seem to be necessary . . . for all practical purposes it will be found that this coincides with the English definition. It is particularly noticeable that the English definition includes any act or word which is likely to promote public disorder, to incite people to unlawful associations, insurrections . . . and to excite ill-will between different classes of the King's subjects. (SC 14 1926: 7–8)

Three things should be noted here. First, that seditious words alone constituted the offence. Secondly, that the phrasing relating to the inciting of ill will between 'different classes', which was to be adapted in later Acts, was taken from the English common law of sedition. Thirdly, this law, to which South Africans looked, was close to its repressive peak in the late nineteenth century. Dugard writes that its use against Irish and labour opposition had brought it closer to the law of treason (Dugard 1974: 208). During the periods of martial law in South Africa which were to follow, the regulations were based on the Peace Preservation Ordinance.

The new Union thus had behind it a recent history of martial law, indemnity and special courts, and new statute law. All of these weapons were soon to be deployed. In mid-1913 as a result of strike action the new government lost control of the Reef and had to call upon the British garrison to protect lives and property. This dramatic example of its weakness was humiliating. We need to feel the temper of the times and the anxieties, and vengefulness, of conservative politicians, in order to understand the framing of the laws. The Act of Union had given discretion over prosecutions to the Attorneys-General of the provinces. But there was caution and uncertainty as to how to use the existing legal repertoire. Smuts's pressure upon them to crack down on 'flagrant instances where the limits of free speech have been grossly exceeded in the speeches of . . . labour orators' was not successful (Hancock and van der Poel 1962, vol III: 111; Smuts–Merriman 5/9/13). Merriman focused on what was at stake: 'We may laugh at the ravings of the syndicalists, but the dangerous thing is that they are appealing . . . both to the poorer Dutch and to the Natives . . . Do recollect that the maintenance of law and order is the great question before the country' (Merriman–Smuts, ibid.). In January 1914 he wrote again of the speeches of white labour leaders: 'Surely under the common law of any civilised country these men are liable to arrest for using language calculated (even intended) to provoke a breach of the peace, and arrested they should be unless the law is a farce' (157).

In the same month Smuts, concluding that law had failed, responded to the strike by the entirely extra-legal arrest and deportation of the strike leaders and the declaration of martial law. The dramatic story and atmosphere of Smuts's secret commission to accomplish the deportations is well captured in the arresting officer's account. After the deportees had been taken on board ship 'they demanded to see my warrant. I said "There is no warrant." Then they said "Show me your written authority for this outrage." The reply was "There is no written authority." He explained that they had " . . . no appeal to any power or person" ' (Trew 1938: 266–7).

The reaction, both in South Africa, and in Britain, was intense and angry. There was real perturbation among the judiciary (see Lewsen 1969:

249–50). Innes was outraged. It was, he later wrote, an 'audacious misuse' of martial law in which the executive had 'sabotaged' its own courts. (Rose-Innes 1949: 254–5). Not only was the viability of the new state called into question again, but so too was its commitment to govern through law. Merriman thought it 'astounding . . . a violent unconstitutional action' (Lewsen 1969: 249). Even the apolitical *South African Law Journal* published a critical comment. It was noted that while the Cape episode of martial law had been during war, the January 1914 declaration of martial law in time of peace was without precedent in the empire, where the rule of law was respected, and the continental doctrine of the 'state of siege' unknown. But the journal also referred to the new conditions of class warfare. There is, it said, quoting Sir John Macdonnell, 'industrial warfare as well as warfare proper' and the former could be 'more deadly' (1914: 164). But as the final justification Smuts played the race card, telling parliament that 'people did not know . . . what had been anticipated from the natives'. He conjured up 'the dreadful spectacle of thousands of natives in the compound singing their war song . . . What would have happened if that wild collection of savages had broken loose?' (Hansard 5/2/14).

The theme of industrial warfare was picked up by Smuts when parliament debated the indemnifying bill. He expressed his extreme dissatisfaction both with the common law relating to treason and with the processes in the ordinary courts. The Roman-Dutch law of high treason, he said, had been written in the sixteenth or seventeenth century, 'when Syndicalism had never arisen, and when high treason meant the introduction of an armed force into a country or a conspiracy to upset the King or ruling authority'. The common law did not fit today's 'novel and extraordinary conditions . . . and if you were to indict these people for the crime they have really committed you would never obtain a conviction'. He complained bitterly that Johannesburg juries had acquitted those involved in incitement to public violence. 'I do not think', he said, 'that in matters of this kind the question is really one for the ordinary courts. The question . . . is rather one for the public authority and Government to decide whether these people are political undesirables.' The government were the best 'judges of the public interest . . . far better judges than any judge or jury in a court of law could possibly be' (Hansard 5/2/14). The judges of the Transvaal Provincial Division, he said, had played comedies to which the government would not submit (Hansard 12/2/14). However,

while the Transvaal Supreme court had not acted against speech, it did
support the declaration of martial law. *In re Marais* had left it open for a
Court to decide whether or not war was being waged. But in *Ex parte
Kotze 1914 TPD* the court said that martial law was

> a weapon available for use in cases of emergency and crisis for the
> protection of the State. It is founded on the principle of self preservation
> embodied in the maxim *salus reipublicae suprema lex est.* . . While courts
> had the power to test whether the necessity existed they would be guided
> by the opinion of the executive officers responsible . . . I do not for a
> moment suppose that a Court of Law, or any judge, would interpose his
> own individual opinion as against those responsible for the conduct of
> military operations.

But Smuts's extra-legal action in deporting the strike leaders proved to be
electorally unpopular in the Transvaal, and was followed by a stunning
victory for the Labour Party in the Transvaal. Dismay was also expressed
by Britain whose subjects had been illegally deported. Smuts agreed after
prompting by the imperial government to amend the first draft of the
indemnity law which appeared to cover future actions, and was obliged to
allow the return of the deportees (see Keith 1916: 160ff.). Parliament
passed the Indemnity Act (no. 1 of 1914) but this did not in itself solve the
problem, which was how to deal with such situations in future without
breaching the rule of law. It was Merriman who recalled the Cape
experience with martial law and indemnity and who asked whether the
country was to be governed in the future 'by law . . . or by military
violence'. But his strong advocacy of law, in a situation of bitterly
contested political legitimacy, was bound to be a compromised rule of
law, as his models showed. His essential message was that every form of
restriction desired could be legal, so that resort to extra-legal force was not
again required. He urged the need for a Riot Act. 'Nothing was more
needed in this country so that the officers of the law could deal with these
matters at once as they could in England . . . they [also] wanted a Crimes
Act on the model of the Irish Crimes Act.' He referred also to the British
Act of 1875 which dealt with conspiracy and protection of property,
which punished municipal employees who maliciously broke contracts of
service for the supply of gas and water and he urged similar legislation for
South Africa, which should also extend to railway workers who should be
treated as servants of the state.

The Riotous Assemblies and Criminal Law Amendment Act, which came into force in July 1914, was designed to construct the necessary legal regime. Magistrates were given authority to prohibit public gatherings and to close public places. There were also provisions, modelled on English law, for the dispersal of unlawful gatherings by force. The Act included a statutory addition to the common law by deeming a person to have committed the offence of incitement if he had acted or spoken words such 'that it might reasonably be expected that the natural and probable consequences of his act, conduct or speech . . . would . . . be the commission of public violence' (section 7). There was also a new series of strike-related offences. Intimidation, restraint, picketing, blacklisting and opprobrious epithets designed to prevent people from working were criminalised. It became a criminal offence for employees in light, power, water, sanitary or transportation services to break contracts of service (section 12). Incitement or conspiracy to commit these offences was also punishable. In addition it was provided that special criminal courts, which could hear cases without a jury, could be set up to deal with offences under the Act (section 18). The Act replaced the Transvaal's Peace Preservation Ordinance. The new Union rapidly moved further to take political trials away from juries and place them in the hands of special courts. The trials arising out of the 1914–15 rebellion were heard before a special court, and the position was generalised in the 1917 Criminal Procedure Act which gave the Attorney-General discretion, in a wide range of matters including political offences, to request the constitution of a special criminal court of two or three judges.

The next phase of legal development took place in the following year in the aftermath of the Afrikaner rebellion. Neither the government nor the courts responded with the severity that characterised the actions taken against white strikers or resistance from Asians or Africans. Faced with having at the same time to mount an expeditionary force to German South West Africa, and fearing a full-scale civil war with further division in the army and a collapse of support among Afrikaners, the government entered into negotiations with the rebels. Merriman was aghast at the failure simply to apply the law. '*Is* there no law?' he wrote. 'Are the crimes of robbery, sedition and public violence merely venial eccentricities when committed by a certain section of the community?' Once again he raised the spectre of a lawless society in which 'there will be little respect for the law in the future and . . . the condition of South Africa will be that of Mexico or Peru' (Hancock and van der Poel 1962, vol III: 209; Merriman–

Smuts 8/9/14). He urged Smuts to avoid special measures and special courts, and to bring indictments under the ordinary law in order to avoid political martyrdom (224; Merriman–Smuts 23/12/14). But martial law was again proclaimed, this time in time of war, and again the government relied on an Indemnity and Special Tribunals Act, passed in 1915.

After the rebellion was over two cases concerning sedition found their way on appeal to the full bench of the Transvaal Provincial Division. (It is worth noting that while the crimes alleged were very serious, the sentences imposed in the magistrate's court, which were being appealed against, were light: in Endemann's case a month on two counts; in Malan's, six weeks on three counts.) In *R v Endemann 1915 TPD 142* the accused had been convicted of speaking against the expeditionary force to German South West Africa, urging that Smuts should be shot, and the commandos rebel. Without the Peace Preservation Act which had enacted the English law of sedition that criminalised speech which incited disaffection alone, the state had lost its major weapon. Endemann's actions were not covered by the new clause in the Riotous Assemblies Act, nor, the court said after lengthy deliberation, by the Roman-Dutch law of sedition, which was found to differ from the English law in terms of which the charge had confidently been brought. Sedition in Roman Dutch law, said de Villiers, was *oproer*, which 'takes the form of a gathering or gatherings, in defiance of the lawfully constituted authorities, for some unlawful purpose', and a person who incited to sedition was only guilty of sedition when the crime itself was committed (147). While Curlewis agreed, Gregorowski dissented, rejecting the need for a gathering and preferring the view that 'the main feature of sedition is in the seditious intention'. The correctness of de Villiers' view was doubted by both judges in *R v Malan 1915 TPD 180* but they felt themselves bound to follow it. Mason went to the heart of the matter that perturbed the government, which was that de Villiers had left nothing between high treason and public violence, and that a different view of 'sedition' would fill this gap. Bristowe complained that de Villiers had not given the word sedition its ordinary English dictionary meaning and instead had limited it by the Dutch word *oproer*, meaning insurrection. Thus the Roman-Dutch common law left the state without protection against seditious speech, and it would henceforth be dependent on the development of its statutory repertoire. In any case, even when the courts could, and did, convict, political realities led to leniency towards white political offenders. In 1919 the 158 people convicted of treason and

8,027 convicted of other offences were amnestied and had their full civil rights restored. (See Hansard 20/3/19 for the debate on the Amnesty Bill.)

The next chapter was the Rand rebellion of 1922, which was crushed by the mobilisation of large military force and substantial loss of life. Smuts defended his actions to parliament by emphasising the government's responsibility to maintain law and order. (One Labour Party member, in a comment that could be a coda for the times, remarked that he was 'getting tired of the phrase "Law and order", which he had noticed that the Prime Minister had used no fewer than 22 times in his short speech' (Hansard 7/3/22).) The tactic of the government after the rebellion was not to bring offenders before martial law tribunals as in 1914, nor before a special court, as after 1915. This time, Smuts told parliament, 'we are going to let the ordinary course of justice take its way'. This meant that nearly nine thousand people would face charges against the martial law regulations in the Transvaal courts. But since 1917 the government had had the power to avoid trial by jury and the cases did not go before Rand juries. A Labour member, Arthur Barlow, expressed a preference for martial law as common law was 'more cruel . . . Justice had run amok on the Rand' (Hansard 21/3 and 23/3/22). The Transvaal Strike Legal Defence Committee bitterly attacked the refusal to put those charged of serious crimes before juries, which, they claimed, would never have convicted Long or Stassen, both of whom were hanged. Their rhetoric was infused with race, in this case an attack on the purity of the white credentials of the Afrikaner political elite, many of whom were believed in Labour Party circles to be really coloured. 'One of the most sinister features of South African public life is that trial by jury is openly derided by many politicians and judges, and that attempts are being made to transfer power from the people to a bogus aristocracy partly of coloured blood' (1924: 30).

The law had failed the government in its utility to control dissenting speech without resort to martial law, and this was the subject of one of the findings of the causes of the 'Revolutionary Movement' made by the Martial Law Commission (UG 35 1922). Prior to the proclamation of martial law several leading communists, and some others, had been arrested on charges of incitement to public violence. In a much-criticised decision they had been released on bail after a direction by two judges of the Supreme Court, Wessels JP and Mason. Mason's reasons, quoted by the commission, went to the heart of the failings of the law from the point of view of the government. The real point, he said, was whether the magistrate could refuse bail because he thought that the men would further incite the public. This would amount to preventive detention, and if the legislature had intended to grant this power in the Riotous Assemblies Act it would have done so (UG 35 1922: 33). (It is of note that this power was not one that was to be added by the subsequent statute, though the power of banishment was.)

In relation to treason vast discretions were exercised as to when a charge would be brought. None were brought, for example, for what the Martial Law Commission called a 'treasonous resolution' proposed by the Labour Member of Parliament Bob Waterston during the strike. Addressing a large public gathering he had, accompanied by references to the need for violence, called for the establishment of a republic[1] and the proclamation of a provisional government (UG 35 1922: 34). But where charges were brought the Appellate Division appeared helpful. In *R v Erasmus 1923 AD 73* Innes appeared to have taken on board the points made earlier by Smuts, that the law of treason had to be adapted to deal with class war. While the Roman-Dutch authorities appeared to require intentionally hostile acts against the state with the purpose of overthrowing it, the court now required only 'armed attacks on the State or Government, perpetrated with hostile mind or intent' (88). In *Jolly's* case it affirmed that it was not necessary for there to be proof of intention to overthrow the state, as long as the state was seriously endangered or exposed to risk of destruction (*R v Jolly 1923 AD 176* at 181). In *R v Viljoen and others 1923 AD 90* the appellate bench adapted and broadened de Villiers' judgment in *Endemann*, which had limited the crime of sedition. De Villiers had insisted that hostile intention alone was insufficient and that *oproer* was required. Innes read this to mean that *oproer*, 'a gathering in defiance of the authorities and for an unlawful purpose', was sufficient for sedition without the proof of hostile intent (see Corder 1984: 80–1 for a discussion of these cases). Nonetheless, while the judges were

---

[1] Republican propaganda, and disloyalty to or insult of the King, was a sensitive issue in this area of the law. Only three years before, leading National Party politicians had gone to the Versailles Peace Conference to put the republican case. In 1936 The Appellate Division declined for a number of reasons to convict the editors of a newspaper which had accused King George V of being the figurehead of imperialists who were robbing and exploiting the workers, and had urged them not to kiss the boot that kicked them. Beyers JA, formerly a leading Nationalist and republican, observed that such a conviction would render liable anyone who agitated for a change in the form of government, and would limit the freedom of republican propaganda (*R v Roux and another 1936 AD 271*; discussed in Corder 1984: 53).

bringing their interpretation of the law closer to that favoured by the executive, there was some appreciation of the special problems of political motivation and of sentencing for political offences. De Villiers JA in *Jolly*'s case pointedly endorsed van Leeuwin's remarks on *oproer* (sedition):

> As however the origins of this crime is often found in the different opinions respecting the measures of the Government when the latter has been affected by revolutions having taken place, there is hardly any crime in which greater caution is to be enjoined upon the judge, as on the one hand to preserve the maintenance of peace and good order, and on the other hand not to render anyone the unfortunate victims of political dissensions by excessive severity. (183)

While the Appellate Division had remedied some of the defects that the state had felt in the law relating to the control of political dissent, neither their new version of the law relating to treason and sedition nor the 1914 Riotous Assembly Act were readily adaptable weapons against the rise of the ICU and other black opposition in the early 1920s. An Emergency Powers Bill, which gave the Minister of Defence the power to declare a state of emergency, and provided for subsequent indemnity, effectively a form of statutory martial law, was withdrawn after a first reading in 1925. It did not meet the objective of making new restrictions a part of the ordinary law. The basic problem was that since the repeal of the Transvaal Peace Preservation Ordinance no law simply penalised political *speech*. The evidence given to the Select Committee on the Prevention of Disorders Bill in 1926 provides an illuminating and comprehensive summary of the developments of the law, and the legal needs as perceived by police and law advisers (SC 14 1926). The immediate agenda was twofold. The first related back to 1922 when most of the proceedings against persons advocating the use of violence at public meetings had been taken under the martial law regulations. Trew told the parliamentary committee that 'The object of this Bill is to obviate the use of martial law except in extreme circumstances' (11). The second illustrates the goal of criminalising hostile politics, as well as acts against the state. In 1914 the Riotous Assemblies Act repealed the Transvaal Ordinance, leaving, apart from the new statutory provisions, only the Roman-Dutch common law of sedition. What this was was still not clear. Some Cape and Transvaal judges had considered that sedition in Roman-Dutch and English laws were equivalent, while others found that sedition in Roman-Dutch law was equivalent to *oproer* which denoted the stirring up of a crowd acting in insurrectionary concert, and did not cover words alone.

In *Viljoen*'s case the Appellate Division had affirmed that in order to constitute the crime of sedition there had to be a gathering of persons for a violently unlawful purpose. This, as Lansdown told the Select Committee, meant that unless the prosecution could associate speech with *oproer*, it was 'helpless' (2). He gave as an example a man addressing a meeting of Africans, who had referred to the achievements of American Negroes, and had said that in fifty years the English would be forced back to their own country and 'we are going to rule those that remain here'. Under the current state of the law, Lansdown complained, this 'was not *laesio majestas*; nor was it a direct injury to the State; nor could it be associated with any incitement to public violence, nor could it be connected with any possibility of an uproar'. It could not, therefore, be prosecuted. 'In England, and I suppose in most civilised countries, that would be treated as sedition, because . . . it appears to be a direct attempt to set one class of the community against another and thus add to the perils and difficulties of the State administration' (2). Without a change in the law 'this man would be able to go about the country repeating these utterances with impunity' (3). Lansdown, showing little of the reverence for the sanctity of the old Roman-Dutch authorities that ruled when the civil law was concerned, told the Parliamentary Committee:

> The Common law of the Roman-Dutch writers is notoriously in a vague state, particularly in connection with crimes of state violence. There is a distinct absence of precision. The criminal part of the Roman-Dutch law is notorious for its vagueness and its absence of precision and contradictory authorities dealing with many important aspects of administration. (7)

There needed to be, he urged, an 'extension beyond the mere violence towards persons and property. One can conceive of unlawful acts which are not really violent acts' (ibid.).

In their search for other weapons the police and Attorneys-General had in addition looked to the Holland Placaat of 1754 which laid down penalties for seditious writings, and assumed that it was a part of South African law. But here the Supreme Courts had let them down again. In the offending case two white communists accused had distributed to Africans, who were attending a mass meeting to protest against the massacre at Bulhoek, a pamphlet headed in red letters 'Murder! Murder! Murder!' It had made reference to 'Another of the brutal Empire bleeding picnics'; to the shootings in Johannesburg in 1913 and Port Elizabeth in 1920; and attacked the government 'whose latest debauch is the grossest mutilation of hundreds of native Christians . . . to . . . maintain the position . . . (of) an idle and parasitic class whose arms are ever available to suppress any liberative effort from the oppressive yoke of capitalism' (5). In the Cape Supreme Court Searle, after referring to the value of free speech, ruled the Placaat, under which the prosecution had been brought, to be applicable. But the Appellate Division declared the Placaat never to have applied to South Africa (*R v Harrison and Dryburgh 1922 AD 320*).

There was disagreement among the police about the immediacy of the threat posed by the new black politics. While Major Trigger told the committee that 'a time of crisis is very remote' in spite of the extravagant language being used, Trew thought Clements Kadalie was exceptionally dangerous (SC 14 1926: 8ff.). 'Kadalie is dangerous to the State, not because he is preaching trade unionism. As long as he sticks to that no-one will interfere with him. The moment he talks of driving the white man out of South Africa I say it is time to stop him' (12). Both, however, agreed that legislation aimed at seditious speech was necessary to meet contingencies. Trew considered that it should not be used 'except in times of public excitement'. He went on to point out that laws were not self-enforcing: 'Every law you pass in Parliament depends largely on its administration.' The police, for example, did not enforce the Sunday observance legislation. 'With regard to anything that concerns political matters or labour unrest, we never prosecute without consulting the Attorney-General. In future the Attorney General will be under the Minister of Justice, so that prosecution will be in the hands of the Government' (12). J. F. Herbst, Permanent Secretary of the Native Affairs Department, approached the issue differently. Unlike the police whose concerns were within the parameters of the legalities of political expression and the keeping of order, Herbst was concerned with white authority as a whole, and the consequent necessity of controlling anti-government speech. The possibility of driving movements underground was not, he thought,

> so dangerous as natives being allowed to stand up in public and make speeches of this nature without action being taken. The kraal natives do not understand that . . . it is extraordinary for [them] to see a black man making speeches against the Government and white men, and not being

stopped. It gives the natives the impression that the Government is afraid of them. (14–15)

While there was, therefore, widespread agreement among white politicians and their officials on the need to curb black political expression by law, the major problem was not obstruction by the courts, but how to frame laws which would not at the same time impact on white political freedoms. The situation was rendered all the more sensitive by the fact that the Labour Party was a member of the governing coalition. For one thing Labour Party rhetoric embraced the promotion of hostility between different classes. Tielman Roos, the Minister of Justice, opposed 'actually referring to any particular race or class'. It was pointed out again that everything depended on the administration of the law. As one Member of Parliament observed: 'For some hundreds of years they have had in England a law that it is seditious to excite ill will between different classes of the King's subjects. I suppose that if this were literally obeyed every Conservative, after a meeting, would be prosecuted by a Liberal, or vice versa' (10). Labour had opposed the 1914 Riotous Assemblies Act which had, among other things, criminalised the incitement to breach of contract in relation to any public utility and in 1919 had opposed the addition of a clause which would have prohibited any speech or publication 'wherein members of the aboriginal races of South Africa are exhorted to break lawful contracts of employment' (9). It continued strongly to oppose any attempt to restrict the trade union activities of the ICU as it was fearful of the effect that this might have on trade unions generally. Labour member Arthur Barlow deemed the proposed Bill to be a panic measure resulting from farmers' fears, particularly in Natal (Hansard 29/ 3/26). Roos had to rule the question of incitement in relation to employment contracts out of the new Bill. 'It would be going rather too far in this Bill if you said anybody who incited anybody else to break any contract would be guilty of an offence here' (9/10). The Select Committee had recommended that section 1(1) of the Bill should read: 'Any person who . . . speaks seditious words, does or suggests or justifies seditious acts, publishes a seditious libel or is a party to a seditious conspiracy' should be guilty of an offence. Seditious intention was deemed to be present if the natural and probable consequence of speech was the commission of acts to alter the system of government, alter established law and promote feelings of hostility between races. It was far wider than the definition given by the Transvaal judges in 1915 which required 'conduct directed against the safety of the State by which public peace and order are imperilled'. One member observed in the debate: 'There is not the slightest doubt that it is aimed at the native, but it is so wide that it is not going to stop there' (G. B. van Zyl in Hansard 29/3/26). This wide definition could have covered strikes, which in many circumstances were unlawful, and threatened to bring white trade union activities within its ambit. Thus, while it embodied the consensus that the law and order community had been building over the years, the Labour Party's role in the Pact Government meant that the law could not pass through Parliament.[2]

It is clear that the overall agenda of criminalising opposition to the political order had radically changed. Both National and Labour parties, the white targets of the earlier laws, were now in government. The real problem was now non-white opposition. Hertzog's solution was the ingenious segregation of the law relating to political expression. The provisions related to suppression of political speech were placed instead in the Native Administration Act of 1927. The draft of section 29 prohibited the 'promotion of all doctrines subversive of peace and good order' among Africans. But this was abandoned. In its place there was a return to the formula of the English law of sedition of 'promoting feelings of hostility' but substituting 'races' for 'classes' to meet the South African situation. But still this did not solve the problem. Many prosecutions did not succeed, the most important case being the Supreme Court's decision in *R v Bunting 1929 EDLD 326*. Judge President Graham, while he thought that communism did 'great mischief' as a doctrine, said that the Act did not apply to persons propagating a political doctrine in good faith unless it 'necessarily' (342) had the effect of promoting hostility. Otherwise

---

[2] It is significant, given the numerous references to British models, that there was no reference to British legislation for Ireland, and that South African legislators of this period did not have recourse to a provision like that in the Ulster Special Powers Act of 1922, section 2(4) of which read: 'If any person does any act of such a nature as to be calculated to be prejudicial to the preservation of the peace or maintenance of order in Northern Ireland *and not specifically provided for in these regulations,* he shall be deemed to be guilty of an offence against these regulations' (my emphasis). The police had earlier canvassed the new draft American legislation facilitating the deportation of communists by means of the oath forswearing ambition to overthrow the government; and in 1925 had asked the Dominions Office for advice on statutory anti-communist measures in the UK. They were advised that there were none 'specifically directed' against communism but that the powers in the Aliens Restriction Acts of 1914 and 1919 and the Aliens Order of 1920, and those in the Emergency Powers Act of 1920, were 'sufficient for the purpose' (Union Archives Jus. 4/10/21; 19/10/25).

intention to promote hostility had to be proved.[3] The Supreme Court's decision should not obscure the full legal story of Bunting's campaign for election as a Natives' Representative for the Transkei, during which he and his party were harassed by the police and magistracy and had several convictions recorded against them. The actions of the legal authorities on the lower levels had a greater inhibitory effect on his political activities than could be alleviated by the ultimate Supreme Court decision (see Roux 1948: chapter 18). Nonetheless, in raising the question in parliament in 1929 Smuts urged the government to tighten up the law. The whole country, he asserted, was in a state of agitation 'more dangerous' than the ICU. 'We see indications that a real communist movement is arising among the natives.' Hertzog, who claimed to have been responsible for the drafting of the Act, admitted his disappointment with the court's decision. 'I think', he said, 'it will be very difficult for anyone to do anything by way of legislation which will meet the object.' The Minister of Justice pointed out that if the Act were to be amended to make intention immaterial it would mean that members of the House could contravene it without meaning to or knowing they had done so, in other words, that even in its segregated form it would spread potentially to cover white political debate. The answer was to take the matter out of the legal framework in which courts (restrictively) interpreted a statute to see if the acts of an accused fell within its terms. The Minister suggested instead the use of administrative powers through which agitators could be excluded from African areas, and public meetings controlled. The solution was refined by the Minister for Native Affairs. Action should not be taken through the statute, he said, but through the Governor-General, who already had power in 'native territories', by giving him power to take steps at any time to prevent such crimes (Hansard 8/8/29).

It was not only the politicians who were determined to prevail. Unlike other departments of state, the Ministry of Justice was led by National Party officials with far right political tendencies. Roos, Hertzog and Pirow, as ministers, placed W. H. Bok, Charles Pienaar, Hans van Rensburg and Toon van der Heever in control of the Justice bureaucracy (van Rensburg 1956; Duncan 1995: 191). Van Rensburg, who was later to become

---

[3] Canadian courts during the First World War had also, though under intense pressure, imported intention to provoke ill will into their English-derived law of sedition. See Swainger (1995), who contrasts this with the objective 'clear and present danger' approach applied by the United States Supreme Court in *Schenk v US 249 US 47 (1919)*.

Commandant-General of the proto-fascist *Ossewa Brandwag*, wrote of his response to the courts' attitude towards the law: 'Where the existing law is not demanding enough it would be suicidal not to change the law to meet the growing requirements of the situation. That is how I saw it as Head of Department' (1956: 63). He was focused on the communist challenge: of *Bunting*'s and *Sachs*' cases he wrote that it was 'the irony of our system that, while dangerous men can press for a State which should be unfettered by law, they have every right to run to our law for protection' (63). In 1930 new provisions were introduced into the Riotous Assemblies Act which adopted the administrative solution and gave the discretion to the minister to determine when action to curb political speech should be taken. The new law provided that 'whenever in the opinion of the Minister there is reason to apprehend that feelings of hostility would be engendered between the European inhabitants of the Union on the one hand, and any other section of the inhabitants of the Union on the other hand' any public gathering could be prohibited, and the attendance of any person prevented (Act no. 19 1930: 1(4)). Whenever the Governor-General formed an opinion that the publication of material would engender hostility he could prohibit it (1(7)). Whenever the minister was 'satisfied' that the presence of a person in an area would engender hostility, he could prohibit his presence in the area (1(12)).

This strategy was successful. The Appellate Division considered the 1930 Act in *Sachs v Minister of Justice 1934 AD 11*. The Acting Chief Justice, Stratford, conceded that the law gave to the minister 'discretion of a wide and very drastic kind . . . a serious inroad on the ordinary liberty of the subject'. However, it dealt with circumstances in which 'prompt and unfettered action is manifestly necessary'. Once satisfied that the Act gave the minister

> an unfettered discretion, it is no function of a Court of Law to curtail its scope in the least degree, indeed it would be quite improper to do so . . . the plain principle [was] that Parliament may make any encroachment it chooses upon the life, liberty or property of an individual subject to its sway, and that it is the function of the courts of law to enforce its will. (36–7)

Interference was justified only if the exercise of the power was not honest or the discretionary power was exceeded. The 'only question' of actual fact that concerned the court was whether the minister was actually satisfied.

Parliament was 'free to violate' the maxim *audi alteram partem*, 'sacred' though it was held to be. He embellished his remarks by adding that (in reference to the decision in *Bunting*'s case) 'mere disregard' of a court of law's decision was not itself sufficient to invalidate the exercise of a discretion (38, 39). He concluded that while 'a credulous or over-apprehensive Minister may be satisfied of the existence or imminence of a danger by reasons which would not move another to act' his actions would be valid if these were his true reasons (40). The language of his acquiescence was embarrassingly wide and sweeping, even if it was a logical sequel to other cases on ministerial discretion (see part V) which did not affect basic liberties in this way.

The judges knew well the legal and political history that had brought them to this point. They knew also that the government had not hesitated to abandon law altogether. And there had been high costs for involving the judiciary as the arbiters in the bitter conflicts over the legitimacy of the state. The judges who had been involved were attacked after the 1915 rebellion, particularly those who were English speaking, not Dutch. One National Party member observed that 'so far as the cold letter of the law was concerned', the trials had been in order, but 'it was the soul, the heart of the people, which these judges failed to understand' (Hansard 25/11/15). The Speaker intervened to protest against attacks on the judges' good faith. In the aftermath of the 1922 strike judges were traduced in both the press and parliament. Neither the Labour Party nor the National Party supported the judiciary. It was claimed that out of twenty-eight judges none were Labour, and only two were Nationalists (8/3/23). Walter Madeley called Long's execution 'a judicial murder', and was cut short by the Speaker who would 'not allow . . . any reflection upon a judge who has discharged his duty' (27/1/23). The debate on the report of the Martial Law Commission produced even more bitter attacks on the judges who had served. Smuts specifically blamed 'young lawyers' (who were later to be leading National Party members) and their allegations that judges were 'partisan' for the 'spirit of lawlessness and anarchy' in the country. F. W. Beyers, who was a KC and later to be elevated to the Appeal Bench, responded with a sustained attack on the judiciary. Hertzog was even more openly intimidatory, referring to his 'contempt' and 'disgust'. Judge Lange was dead but 'he hoped his words would be a warning to the Judge who today was still on the Bench ' (8/3/23). While the judiciary may not anyway have been overzealous in their defence of either white or non-white communists, the eagerness to be out of the firing line is comprehensible. The tradition of openly criticising the judiciary in parliament was alive until the coalition years of the Fusion Government when political leaders combined to mute it. In 1935, in response to parliamentary criticism of Wessels CJ for being anti-republican, the Speaker of the House of Assembly ruled that motions criticising or censuring judges could not be introduced unless they concerned actions which might lead to dismissal (*SALT*, March 1935: 47).[4]

[4] For an account of hostile criticisms of judicial appointments see van Blerk (1988: 116ff.).

PART III

South African common law A

8

Roman-Dutch law

South African common law has most frequently been characterised as Roman-Dutch law, and its essential nature has been portrayed in a history which gives it a particular narrative pedigree (see e.g. Hosten 1983; Hahlo and Kahn 1968). This narrative traces the sources of South African law from the Roman law from the earliest period, through the republic and empire to Justinian. It then moves on to the reception of Roman law in Europe in the twelfth century onwards (with a nod towards Germanic tribal law); and discusses the development of the Roman-Dutch law in the feudal Netherlands and the Dutch Republic. There are two important things about the pedigree. First, and this it has in common with the pedigree of the English common law, it is long and *old*. Secondly, it is presented as having its essential roots in Europe, and in two basic European traditions, Roman and German. In this conception the law was both established as a sort of organic heart in the body of the state, and also situated in the external, non-African, European heritage. A by-product of its being so situated was that it is obscure and difficult to master, requiring knowledge of texts and commentaries in Latin and old Dutch. This way of presenting the history of the law had two effects. One was instrumental, in that it was resurrected and developed to combat another narrative and pedigree, that of the English common law. A second was that it drew attention away from the local situations in which the law was developed in response to contemporary needs and conflicts. This study rests on another narrative and pedigree. It looks on the essence of South African common law as neither ancient nor external to South Africa, but as created in the late nineteenth and early twentieth centuries in South Africa in response to local circumstances, and the needs of the developing state, economy, and ruling classes and race. Part of this development was the way in which law was imagined. The Roman and European pedigree was vital to presentation, form and justification, to the language and self-image of South African legal culture, but it may not have been vital to much else.

The survival of the Roman-Dutch law was by no means a matter to be taken for granted. While it was portrayed by the jurists who were responsible for its development in terms of a long seamless history of evolution, my focus will be first on conveying the historical contingencies, and second on considering the reasons for its success, the form that it took and the limitations of the triumph, and third to ask what the effects on the legal system as a whole were. Just what was the significance for legality in South Africa of the survival of a Roman-Dutch private law embedded in English forms and procedures?[1]

It is important to note that while, to take the celebrated example of the law of contract, and the South African rejection of consideration (see below), there were apparently substantial doctrinal differences between English and Roman-Dutch law, there was no essential difference in outcome. The effect was not to develop a law of contract which was essentially different from that of England, or of Australia, which accepted English rules and decisions. While evidence of intention was construed differently, the English and South African laws in this period both rejected the contextualising of contract law, and insisted on a contractual regime in which equity (in the broad sense) played no part. Even in the case of the law of delict all of the thought and controversy that went into the development of the Roman-Dutch law made little substantial difference. The law in this area also evolved in South Africa in ways that accorded with the development of legal thinking elsewhere. As Watermayer, soon to

---

[1] Lest we should assume some automatic connection between local circumstances and differential legal developments we should think briefly about the essential nature of the legal system of another new state, developing contemporaneously in the British empire. In considering the development of Australian law Paton wrote that '*the advantages of uniformity are so obvious that special efforts are made to keep common law decisions uniform with those of England*' (Paton 1952: 11; my emphasis). It was also, he said, 'natural . . . that there should be tendency to turn to English statutory law as a source of inspiration . . . there is an intelligent argument for borrowing – it gives to the Dominions the benefit of English draftsmanship and of the English decisions on interpretation of particular sections' (15). In both contract and tort there was 'little significant departure from the English model' (20).

The Australian story was complex (see in general Kircher 1995). Though, as Finn writes, the common law in Australia was denied the opportunity 'to embody the story of a nation's development', he describes a process in which there was early innovation, later followed by an increasing conformity with and deference to English law. By the end of the nineteenth century, he writes, 'Australia and Australian history were losing their significance for Australian lawyers. Legal colonisation had begun in earnest' (Finn (1987: 166): cf. the similar conclusion on the growth of Australian legalism in Kircher (1995)).

be Chief Justice, wrote in the early 1930s: 'South Africa has witnessed a very remarkable extension and development of the principles of the *Lex Aquila, comparable with and consequent upon the development achieved by the jurists of the Empire.* The result has been to produce a generalised theory of negligence, which is not afraid to leave wide discretion to the tribunals in applying it to particular states of fact' (Watermayer 1936: 872; my emphasis).

The Roman-Dutch law appears in retrospect to have had a solid identity and existence, being a continuation of the common law in force in the Cape at the time of the second British occupation in 1806. But in reality during the nineteenth century it was but a shadow little known to the few judges whose task it was to enforce it. Writing about Natal in 1863 a magistrate posed the question 'What is there in the shape of settled law and practice in the minds of the Judges?' There were, he said, two folio volumes in Latin of Voet which only one judge, Connors, could read, and Grotius and van Leeuwen in Dutch, which were even less accessible. Even if the judges could all read the texts, what role did they really play in the world of colonial Natal?

> Of what avail would be the elaborately qualified and general propositions of Voet and others? . . . or of what use precedents hunted out of English common law? – arising out of a state of things wholly different from that prevailing here, and useful not so much as a guide to a decision, as to account for it when already forgone. (Currey 1968: 93)

In the other colonies as well the law rested on a narrow textual base not very well known to the courts or practitioners to whom the major works were frequently unavailable or incomprehensible. Nathan relates the story of Jorissen, the State Attorney and later a judge in the South African Republic, who was a clergyman who 'bought a couple of Dutch law books which he read in train and coach on his way up North; and by the time he reached Pretoria he was fully qualified to become State Attorney' (1944: 34). The constitution of the South African Republic specifically gave authority to certain texts: van der Linden's *Handbook*, a compilation produced in 1806; and two original authorities – Grotius' *Introduction to Dutch Jurisprudence* (1631) and van Leeuwen's *Censura Forensis* (1662). Roman-Dutch law in its wider sense was only made generally applicable in the Transvaal by the new British regime in 1902. In the Cape de Villiers regarded Voet as the 'touchstone' of the Roman-Dutch law, but even he, as Sampson testified, 'rarely quoted in detail the authorities he had consulted' (Nathan 1944: 174; Sampson 1926: 54). It was a meagre, haphazard and scrappy heritage.

Much of the activity of the Supreme Courts of the provinces before 1910 and the Appellate Division after Union must be understood in the light of their conscious efforts to defend and create a specifically South African common law. The natural dominating tendency of English law – the decisions of the English courts, English constitutional and procedural frameworks, English statutes, English texts and English-trained lawyers – had, as we shall see, an enormous influence. It is not surprising that specific challenges to the Roman-Dutch law were issued. After the defeat of the republics there had been calls for the complete repeal of the Roman-Dutch law which were mounted on two linked grounds. One was that it was 'the law of a bygone age' (Vindex 1901: 153). The other was that it was a fertile and constant source of anti-British feeling. Putting these together Vindex's piece noted the accusation that de Villiers, as Chief Justice of the Cape, had led the anti-British feeling which was reversing the tendency to assimilate the law to that of England. It became useless to quote English law to judges 'who have set their minds against everything English' and who preferred 'flimsy deductions from some Dutch writer of the days when the law was in its infancy' (154). The flimsiness of the deductions is particularly evident if one examines the leading cases of the period, for example in Innes's court, where the narrowness of the scholarly base for the determined development of the law which was carried on is striking.

In the post-war years, the judges of de Villiers' court were moved to the former republics: Wessels and Solomon to the Transvaal; Maasdorp to the Orange River Colony. In the new British administrations they 'found themselves in a society in which to be ultra-English was the fashion and in which everything Dutch was regarded as effete and archaic' (Walker 1925: 407). There was a strong impulse for the anglicisation and codification of the laws of the ex-republics. The new Bar was being filled by men with a scant knowledge of Roman-Dutch law. But the Roman-Dutch law was embraced by sections of the South African profession as a defence. Nathan recalled that in post-war Johannesburg members of the English Bar arrived looking for 'an opening in a new country . . . thinking that English law would be the vogue' and expecting to 'wipe the floor with the local practitioners. They did not foresee that Roman-Dutch law would continue to be administered' (Nathan 1944: 194). In the Cape the situation was similar. Sampson observed that barristers at the Cape Bar who had been admitted in England had 'a strong tendency to consult English authorities rather than Roman Dutch ones' (1926: 77). Wessels wrote in some despair in 1908 that 'the English barrister who attends a South African court must often wonder what we really mean when we say the Roman Dutch law is the common law of South Africa'. The pleadings were the same. The rules of evidence 'are the same as he learnt at his Inn . . . he hears quotations from familiar books such as Addison or Leake on Contract, Addison or Pollock on Torts, and he finds that both Bench and Bar refer to the same Law Reports he is familiar with in England' (quoted in Kennedy and Schlosberg 1935: 387).

In this situation, writes Walker, it was de Villiers, and the other leading judges, who mounted the determined defence of Roman-Dutch law (1925: 407). Much was done by the Transvaal Supreme Court under Innes which set its face firmly against anglicisation. But it is worth noting that this was not necessarily the only response possible. Sampson's view from the Cape Bench underlines that resistance to anglicisation was a political choice, not a legally determined one. In Sampson's view the guidance of the English law was 'generally agreeable to the spirit of the Roman-Dutch commentators' who were themselves guided often by what appeared to be 'the most reasonable and equitable doctrine to follow on general principles gathered from Roman law' (1926: 126). But this syncretism was not favoured by the leading judges. After Union the creation of a Roman-Dutch canon was carried on by the Appellate Division which rolled back the advances that English common-law doctrines had made, particularly in Natal. Paradoxically, however, because the judges were the primary agents, they saved the Roman-Dutch law by English common-law methods, case by case. In doing so they forestalled a more decisive move away from English forms towards a civil-law system, and stifled the demand for codification on the European model.

Sometimes telling the story of an event that did not happen can be as important and revealing as the story of one that did. Why, given the urgent agenda of unification of differing provincial legal systems, and the existence of quite distinct legal traditions in South Africa, was a codification of the Roman-Dutch law never achieved? Why instead was it eventually left to the random process of precedent to establish an accommodation between English and Roman-Dutch common laws, to create a new South African law, as the jurists proudly proclaimed? There are several strands to this story. One concerns the role conceded to the judiciary; another the influence and organisation of the legal profession; another the late development of legal scholarship outside the judiciary; and another the relative weakness of the resources of the state in legal expertise. Nonetheless, as we will see in the next section there *were* two significant nineteenth-century experiments with codification, the Natal Code of Native Law and the Transkei Criminal Code. Codification could be seen as appropriate for the convenient administration of 'native law' by legally unsophisticated Native Commissioners, yet quite unsuited to the complex requirements of white law.

The production of a uniform law for the whole of the country was seen as a priority after 1910. After *Webster v Ellison 1911 AD* had established that the Appellate Division could override long-established provincial law, it was evident that some areas of law would never be clear at the provincial level unless and until cases were appealed. But relying on the unifying effect of judgments from the new Appellate Division would be a slow process. There were early signs of real anxiety in the legal profession on this point. In 1913 the *South African Law Journal* criticised the government for lack of movement in ironing out the divergent legal systems and called for codification of magistrate's court procedures (454). Most significantly too the new editor, S. B. Kitchin, wrote that unification of the common law by the Appellate Division's random processes could not be seen as the court's proper function. Was it the legislature's? Kitchin pointed out that this too would be a prolonged operation. Even the process of producing consolidating statutes was estimated by the Minister of Justice in 1912 to be a task requiring ten years. It did, of course, take far longer. The legislature was active in passing major consolidating statutes for the new Union. In the first session of the Union parliament statutes in relation to Crown liability, stock diseases, explosives, mines and works, mining taxation, native labour, naturalisation, and prisons and reformatories were passed. The following year the police and public service, and railways, were legislated for nationally, as were fencing and land bank loans. The next two years saw consolidating statutes passed on children's protection, customs, immigration, and workmen's compensation. But in addition to those there were further pressures for action from the legal profession in relation to commercial law. In September 1913 a meeting of the Associated Chambers of Commerce called for the earliest possible codification of the Union's laws in relation to insolvency, companies, weights and measures, registration of deeds, patents, trademarks and copyright (*SALJ* 1913: 454).

This would not touch, necessarily, on the common law. Perhaps, Kitchin suggested, a special codifying commission was necessary. Over a decade later these concerns among the profession with the protracted process of developing the Roman-Dutch law by the judges were still active. The obscurantist creativeness of the Appellate Division and its expanding invocation of Roman-Dutch textual authorities meant a condition of flux and uncertainty in the law. While this appealed to the new segment of scholars, it was not as popular with practitioners. In 1926 the president of the Cape Law Society raised a matter that, he said, many might feel 'too delicate'. Cases were simply taking too long. The existence of the Appellate Division and the lower judges' fear of reversal at the hands of appellate judges invoking hard-to-come-by texts meant that judgments were too frequently reserved and delivered much later. But the public desired judgments as soon as possible (*SALJ* 1926: 478). In 1934 the *South African Law Times* repeated the criticism that judgments were taking far too long. Lawyers and litigants, it said, wanted to know decisions, not how they were arrived at. And there was criticism too of the appellate courts' habit of handing down several judgments, concurring and dissenting, which, the paper said, caused confusion and encouraged further litigation (January 1934).

In spite of the direction taken by the judiciary, the feeling among some of the leaders of the renaissance in Roman-Dutch law was one of insecurity. In 1918 Melius de Villiers, former Chief Justice of the Orange Free State and professor of Roman-Dutch Law at the University of Leiden, raised the question of the need for a university law faculty in South Africa, and connected it with the questions of the future of the South African profession and of a distinctively South African law (*SALJ* 1918: 155 *et seq*.). Judges, he pointed out, relied heavily on the Bar in civil litigation for the presentation of the law. This being so there was a great need for the 'scientific teaching' of law in order to neutralise the anomalies in the current rules of admission to the Bar. It was possible to be called to the Bar in London, without any knowledge of South African law, and then be admitted at once in the Cape. The consequence was that Roman-Dutch law was being 'almost ignored' and English law 'almost exclusively relied upon'. There was, he urged, a need to check the tendency to mix English law and South African common law by instilling the idea that there were 'fundamental principles' not to be ignored into the minds of local law students.

Two years later de Villiers' concerns were taken up by Sir John Wessels, then the Judge President of the Transvaal (*SALJ* 1920: 265). Most significantly, from the perspective of a Supreme Court judge, he saw that the question of the anglicisation of South African law was not simply a matter of the common law, but had to be linked to the effect of the wave of new statutes on South African legal culture. Legislation, Wessels observed of the process of re-making the statute book since Union, was often taken ready made from England or the Dominions. As he pointed out, it was not parliament that was the author of these laws, but civil servants, who, in his view, could not rest until they had a law identical with the one in England. It was not only ideas that were copied, but exact words. The Company Acts, workmen's compensation laws and most of the taxation and financial laws had been so produced. (Indeed, it was the practice of the draughtsmen to draft all legislation in English first, and then translate it into Dutch: Hansard 3/6/21.) It would, he went on,

> be easily seen that this method of making laws must have a profound effect
> on the common law and its interpretation . . . If a statute is copied from
> the English statute book and questions arise as to its interpretation our law
> courts do not always apply for its interpretation the canons of interpret-
> ation adopted by the civilians, but they naturally place upon this statute
> the same interpretation that it has received in the English courts. In a long
> series of cases this has led to a method of interpreting statutes which is
> often not quite the method that an old Roman Dutch lawyer or even a
> French lawyer would adopt. From interpreting the statute laws in accord-
> ance with English ideas other laws have also come to be so interpreted and
> in this way English case law has come to modify our law far more than
> most lawyers realise. (*SALJ* 1920: 265)

While the South African common law was, wrote Wessels, in harmony like a stately cathedral, the new edifice of statutes was 'like some botched building raised in a hurry' (276–7).

Wessels' response was not simply a conservative defence of the Roman-Dutch law. He pointed out that the conflicts between social reformers and conservative lawyers that were taking place in England were coming to South Africa, and 'when the new ideas are copied in South Africa, the Roman Dutch law will probably undergo a great trial'. There was much in this law that was obsolete and if it was to survive it would have to adapt itself while maintaining its distinct features. To do this South African lawyers needed to have a larger and wider knowledge of the civil law, and its history and development in Europe, beyond that of textbook rules and recent decisions (279–81). To cap these wider intellectual defences of the civil-law culture Wessels urged a codification of the Roman-Dutch law (282–4). A code 'would be a great boon to future generations of lawyers and it would save the Roman-Dutch law from being corrupted out of existence'. It would also make it possible, following continental models, for far simpler diction to be used in statutes. He concluded: 'A code will, therefore, besides crystallising our common law and bringing it into a manageable compass, help us to do away with our heritage of statutory English.'

The condition of legal flux and contest was noted by Lee (1923). Unlike Wessels he saw a process that was being driven by the courts, with the Appellate Division 'leaning . . . away' (446) from anglicisation. 'Seldom have the courts of any country enjoyed the opportunity which the courts of South Africa now enjoy, of moulding the laws to their will . . . though the Union Parliament has not been inactive in consolidating . . . the task of directing the course of legal development has principally rested with the courts of justice' (443). His diagnosis saw less conflict than Wessels'. The South African courts, Lee wrote, were 'administering a system of law which is neither pure common nor pure civil law . . . it is heir to two great traditions, inspired by each, enslaved to neither' (446). A year later Lee reported again on the outcome of the clash between the two legal traditions in South Africa (1924). From his perspective it seemed that the expectations of rampant anglicisation had been unrealised. The 'influence of English law is not what it was,' Lee wrote. The Appellate Division had 'revived interest in the original sources of the Roman Dutch Law' (297). Lee thought that while the court had not shown an 'undue kindness' to obsolete rules of law, its renewed interest in the Roman-Dutch law 'coupled with a sense of nationality exhibiting itself in the field of law' may 'create a certain atmosphere in favour of ancient institutions' (306). He stressed the uniqueness of the fluid state of South African law. While the settled judicial system with established rules of procedure and 'a considerable accumulation of judicial decisions' might suggest a state of things in which law was firmly established, the Appellate Division was not only harmonising existing laws but submitting them to 'question and review' (302). This being the case, Lee concluded, even assuming the correctness of Wessels' strictures on the influence of English law, he doubted whether codification would be timely. It would be better to wait, he thought, until the civil law had been more completely covered by the decisions of the Appellate Division.

In 1928 Wessels returned to the debate as the lone advocate of codification (1928: 5). He complained of the use of English authorities by practitioners in the courts. The real reason, he wrote,

> why English authorities bulk so largely in our courts is because it is far easier for a practitioner to find out the English law on a subject than to go back to the principles of the civil law and starting with these work up to the reception of these principles in Holland . . . and so to ascertain upon what principles a Dutch Court in the 18th century would have decided the case. (11)

If, he warned, 'the influence of English law increases in the proportion in which it has increased during the last 50 years the Roman Dutch law will inevitably be pushed back' (11). Codification was the answer.

The breadth of the difference between South African legal culture and the civil-law culture of Europe can be seen when one considers the nature of the small role played by academic legal faculties in these developments. Lee thought that the 'activity of our Schools of Law' would prepare the way for codification (1915: 25), but this did not happen. There was no academic participation in these codification pressures. Nonetheless there was a connection between the establishment of academic law faculties, with chairs in Roman and Roman-Dutch law, and the entrenchment of the latter. In the English-speaking faculties at Cape Town and the University of the Witwatersrand the development of Roman-Dutch law was seen as a matter for the judges, just as in England the common law was expounded by the judiciary. Thus while the teaching of Roman-Dutch law had been introduced (in Cape Town in 1916) it was based on *stare decisis* and the judiciary's antiquarian wielding of Roman-Dutch texts. Authors of academic texts like R. J. McKerron, who was professor of law at the University of the Witwatersrand and who published *The Law of Delict in South Africa*, thought that the law schools should be focusing on teaching the decisions of the courts. Gardiner and Lansdown (themselves judges, and compilers of the monumental text on criminal law) were firmly of the view that the decisions of the courts should take precedence over the 'unprofitable, confusing and superfluous' Roman-Dutch authorities. When the University of Cape Town began formal law teaching its syllabus was a combination of Roman, Roman-Dutch and English law. Significantly the jurisprudence taught was English positivism; Austin, Salmond and Pollock dominated the jurisprudence syllabus. And while practising lawyers rarely recall their course in jurisprudence, the confining concepts of English positivism underlay all of the assumptions of South African lawyers in this period (see Zimmerman and Visser 1996: 23). The emphasis at Stellenbosch and later the University of Pretoria was different and academic writing was to focus far more on the systematic exposition of the principles of the Roman-Dutch law and was to give to principle, system and logic precedence over the decisions of judges (van Blerk 1984: 255–6). None of the approaches gave attention to the considerations of legal policy that were increasingly finding their way into English and American writings and judicial decisions.

Writing in the early 1930s Watermayer noted that given the widespread 'assault upon it by the English system' it might appear a matter for surprise that the Roman-Dutch law had survived at all. He gave the major credit to Lord de Villiers and the judges on the Transvaal Bench influenced by Cape practices (1936: 867–8). It was 'the Bench devoted to the maintenance of Roman-Dutch law' that had led to the translations of the older authorities and the production of South African textbooks. But just as the civilian lawyers were beginning to flex their muscles in the universities, he appeared to feel that things might be going too far.

> Perhaps there is an inclination today to delve too deeply into the past and in the decision of a case to place reliance on the opinion of some medieval writer on Roman law . . . The task of interpreting an ancient code in the light of modern conditions is no easy one, and is made more difficult in South Africa by the rarity of some of the early legal works and the obscurity of many of their writers.

He felt that the Appellate Division had 'achieved a remarkable degree of success avoiding the perpetuation of ancient subtleties merely because they are ancient' and the 'abandonment of sound principles merely because they are not shared by other codes'. The tone of self-congratulation was a common one. Yet Watermayer sounded a clear note of caution: 'The process, however, has still a long way to go. It is still possible for an apparently solid line of modern cases to be upset by reference to a 17th century civilian, and for a doctrine which has been thought dead for a hundred years to rear its anachronistic head in the midst of affairs today' (870).

Kennedy and Schlosberg were less reverent about the role of original sources. 'These dead men's books', they wrote, 'are the only living witnesses of what the Roman-Dutch law of Holland was.' Judges could 'declare what the author has stated to be the law . . . a preponderance of opinion is usually conclusive' (1935: 351, 384). We must ask why should this have been acceptable and why the trend, warned against by Watermayer, should have strengthened not weakened? Lee also had anticipated incorrectly that as the Appellate Division developed 'the old folios and quartos will be less and less consulted' (1915: 25). It is at least illustrative of the difficulties of drawing any inherent connection between the decision of cases, and the arguments that they entertained, and conditions beyond the courts. But it is not obvious why anachronism was embraced by the judiciary, under the influence of a few leading figures. It was not attachment to language, as the curial language of this crucial period of the development of Roman-Dutch law was exclusively English. Not until the early 1930s when Beyers (to the dismay of the other judges) was appointed to the Appellate Division was a judgment given in Afrikaans. It did give to the judges in the new state a peculiarly important and pivotal role, one which they were keen to emphasise, especially as their political prestige and influence was small, and both their political and judicial performance often slighted. And, of course, it was a way of emphasising difference, cultural and political, from England. Indeed, finally it cannot be understood outside of the manufacturing of difference. For the style of the Roman-Dutch law was, perhaps, more important than its substance. Its practice required exposition of a complex tradition, a knowledge of Latin, some of Dutch and a familiarity with ancient texts. In South Africa this was wedded to the English common-law style of judgment which required a lengthy exegesis, not a brisk conclusion. Learned disquisitions flourished in the Appellate courts. Nothing could be more demonstrably different from the customs of savages. In a sense the Roman-Dutch law embodied the capacity to be civilised. One should realise also the important political dimensions of the elaboration of a separate Roman-Dutch law. Without it South African courts would have adopted English law, and been obliged to follow English precedents. With appeal to the Privy Council in place, the Appellate Division would always have been subject to reversal on the basis of English court decisions. The effect of developing a separate body of Roman-Dutch legal principles in nearly all areas was to establish independence from the English courts.

The declaration of a law of contract, for example, which differed from English law, had important effects in relation to political matters like the law of sedition and treason. For in establishing incontrovertibly that the common law of South Africa was Roman-Dutch law, it obliged the Privy Council to follow Roman-Dutch law in appeals from South Africa, and it also meant that all South African courts had to follow the Appellate Division and not English precedents.

As I have emphasised, the Roman-Dutch law was by no means there as a finished artefact, waiting to be found. As Eduard Fagan points out, it was 'not easily defined', its 'boundaries undefined in terms of time and space' (1996: 41); it had to be made by choices. Yet it is precisely this process of choices that the judges constantly denied which was ever present in their finding of what authorities bound their decisions. I have noted that the display of authorities, preferably with copious quotations in Latin and Dutch, was a vital part of the South African judicial style. But it remained a contentious matter which authorities were binding. One basic issue was the identity and limits of the law to be applied. Was it simply the law of Holland as it existed in the seventeenth century, or was it the common law of Western Europe, of which the law of Holland was just a piece? De Villiers and Innes in the Cape and Transvaal respectively espoused the narrower view which conveniently limited the sources (42). But they were criticised for their lack of scholarship and a very much wider range of authorities was called upon by other judges who were demonstrating their superiority as masters of the Roman-Dutch law. Indeed the uncertainty as to what constituted the very law being applied points to the elements of symbolism in its invocation and use. The greater the range of civilian texts that could be marshalled on a particular point, the more adamantly could English precedents (and extraneous contextual or policy concerns) be excluded. As Fagan points out the 'Roman-Dutch law's claim to pre-eminence rests, historically, on a fragile base' (61). Securing that base was an enduring preoccupation. That the South African judgments show so much less concern for some of the broader issues about contractual relationships and delictual liability which began to feature in some of the common-law judgments in England and America in this period can be explained by the dual concern of establishing that Roman-Dutch and not English law applied, and then debating about which texts contained the Roman-Dutch law to be applied. The consequence – a doctrinal discourse overwhelmed by the search for authorities, a willed belief that the law was dictated from elsewhere, even in the area of the law's greatest creativity – was congruent with the authoritarian positivism that dominated all the discourses about South African law. As if to emphasise the given nature of the law the courts adopted, in supernumerary addition, the English doctrine of precedent, another device to invoke the binding nature of authority and the absence of substantively influenced choices. (The third part of this approach was the deferential method of statutory interpretation – see below.)

The dominant narrative in the history of South African private law – of contract and delict (or tort) – has clearly been the triumph of the Roman-Dutch law over English common law. This story was both experienced and written as a nationalist triumph over foreign domination. This is *prima facie* ironic given that at the same time the Roman-Dutch lawyers celebrated and gloried in the Roman and European origins of the South African law they were creating. It was a double act, but one that was a part of more fundamental exclusions. The first was that the master narrative occluded the African: one of two European traditions was identified as the indigenous South African legal tradition. The second was that the dominant concerns of this narrative took attention away from the substantive issues in the history of private law. In the narrative histories of the development of the law of delict focus was on issues such as the correct meaning of the *actio legis aquiliae* in Roman-Dutch law and 'on the nature, extent, and desirability of English influence on the development of South African law' (Zimmerman and Visser 1996: 561). The story of the clash of English and Roman-Dutch law has been told in terms which strike an outsider as unusually intense. The conflict, referred to as a *bellum juridicum*, is portrayed as a 'struggle for the soul of South African law'; an 'acrimonious battle' (24–5; 524). It was this very intensity that absorbed those in the judiciary and academic commentators, who tried to bend legal doctrinal development in particular directions. The contests over the role of English law in delict following the publication in 1933 of R. G. McKerron's *Law of Delict in South Africa* is referred to in Zimmerman and Visser as an 'unpleasant war' (537). There is little sign in the scholarship on the law of delict of consideration of the policy issues relating to liability and compensation, or of the utility of the law in the society in which it operated. The same absences are marked in studies of the law of contract. A third exclusion is that, caught up in doctrinal struggle between common and civil law, there was little awareness of contemporary legal developments elsewhere. My approach in this section is not to rewrite the stories, so very skilfully told already, of the developments and disputes about doctrine in the major areas of South African private law. It is, rather, to consider what has been excluded by the privileging of those narratives.

Contract

The preoccupations of South African jurists in our period can be well illustrated in the fierce controversies that waged over contract, an area which illustrates the intellectual appeal and strength of Roman-Dutch law. For the first two decades of the century much attention was given to the issue of whether the English law requirement of consideration was necessary for the formation of a valid contract and whether the civil law concepts *justa causa* and *redelijke oorzaak* were the equivalents of consideration. Alternatively, if consideration and a civilian equivalent were not necessary, the Roman-Dutch law could be developed on the basis of a purely consensual concept of contract, in which parties were bound by promises alone (see the discussion in Zimmerman and Visser 1996: 165–73). The controversy was extremely heated, both doctrinally and personally, but the outcome, both nationalistically and logically appealing, which cast off consideration, was not of great significance once the whole framework of the law of contract formation and validity is taken into account. What is important is the attention that the controversy absorbed, both then and subsequently. What did this obscure? To answer this question I shall focus not on the doctrinal triumph of pure consensualism, but on the opposite elements of compulsion at the core of contract law.

One of the matters obscured from the sight of legal scholars was the wider use of the concept of contract as a master tool of discipline and rule within the society as a whole. Cornish and Clark write that by the middle of the eighteenth century 'contract was advancing as one of the great organising categories of liberal thought' (1989: 200). Along with property it was far more than a legal doctrine, carrying the weight of the justification of inequality and crucial to the conceptualising of the fair yet unequal society. The values which contract embodied 'buttressed freedom of dealing and sanctity of bargain, the economic superiority of market place pricing over government regulation, the moral righteousness of self-sufficiency and self improvement' (201). There was little difference in the overarching framework of contractual discourse between England and

South Africa. And doctrinal developments in England and in South Africa were not, in spite of the narrative of difference and divergence that the Roman-Dutch jurists developed, markedly different. In both countries, as Cornish and Clark wrote of England, the law 'gives up its earlier willingness to rectify elements of unfairness in bargains and instead insists on enforcing whatever terms have been agreed' (201–2). In both countries the development of the law of contract in the courts left their courts only with the role of ensuring that the contract had been agreed to and to enforcing its terms. This was, in the eyes of the times, an essential state function. As Lord Melbourne had said, the only purposes of the state were the prevention of crime and the preservation of contracts. Indeed as Wiener has indicated, these were not unconnected, both were a part of the 'central myth of the responsible individual' (1990: 48). He quotes Atiyah to the effect that contract was far more than a practical tool, but that faithfulness to engagements was 'the most important rule of behaviour' in nineteenth-century European life (62). The observance of promises was a part of the ethic of self-discipline (see above). Wiener writes that 'central to reasonable behaviour were foresight, self-discipline, reliability' on which both civil and criminal law insisted (91). The historical controversy about the doctrinal aspects of the formation of contract has also obscured certain key features about the internal discourses in South Africa. The Roman-Dutch law developed on the basis of subjective intention in contractual relations, in relation both to formation and interpretation. (Though the practicalities of commercial life did mean that, in the absence of ambiguity or alleged fraud, the written contract would stand as objective evidence of intention: *South African Railways and Harbours v National Bank of South Africa 1924 AD 704.*) But there were obvious problems in resting contractual validity purely and simply on a subjective 'will to be bound'. The Renaissance European jurists such as Grotius and Voet had clearly raised and canvassed the issue of the 'free exercise of will' and the influence of 'fear', 'duress' or other undue influences on the will of a contractor, in vitiating the promise made (Zimmerman and Visser 1996: 181; 286ff.). In the South African context, with its racial oppression, vast differences in wealth and power and atmosphere of personal violence, an elaborated jurisprudence relating to oppressive contractual relations could well have been developed. But the judges quickly took the law in the opposite direction, firmly casting aside the problematical and equitable issues relating to the enforcement of unfair contracts.

The complexities of the evolving law in relation to contract can also be traced in the attitude taken to the doctrine of *laesio enormis*. In the Roman-Dutch law a certain equity in commercial transactions had been protected by the rule that relief could be sought by a buyer who had paid more than double the true value, or a seller who had received less than half the true value. This was, of course, a legal remedy out of touch with modern economic doctrine in which value could only be gauged by the market price, which was that agreed upon between buyer and seller. In *McGee v Mignon 1903 TS 89* the court ruled that *laesio enormis* was still a part of the common law 'however much it may be considered that the doctrine is hardly one in conformity with the altered conditions of modern times'. But this was an unusual decision. The Transvaal Supreme Court's decision in *McGee*'s case indicated a willingness to defend the Roman-Dutch law against the triumph of freedom of contract. In *Rood v Wallach* the court again showed a determination to apply a pure Roman-Dutch law, in this case upholding an unhindered contractualism.[2] The literal view of contractual intention was strengthened by the Transvaal court's insistence on enforcing the written words of a contract, regardless of equitable considerations. Innes said in *Rood v Wallach* that the 'signatory to a written document must be held to mean what the document says, whether the result be hard or not' (193). Solomon reinforced the message: 'That the defendant himself may not have realised the full effect of his undertaking is quite possible; but a man who puts his name to a written undertaking is bound by its terms, and cannot be heard to say that he did not intend to enter into any such engagement' (205). The Transvaal court, under Innes, further determinedly distanced itself from equitable considerations. As he put it:

> This court has again and again had occasion to point out that it does not administer a system of equity, as distinct from a system of law . . . We are always desirous to administer equity; but we can only do so in accordance

[2] In *Rood*'s case Innes CJ sharply distinguished his view from that of the Cape Supreme Court and ruled that consideration was not a necessary part of a valid contract. Consideration, he said, was an English doctrine, only adopted by the Cape court in 1874 under pervasive English influences and the lack of Roman-Dutch texts. But since Kotze's 'masterly' translation of van Leeuwen's *Commentaries* in 1886 it was clear that consideration was not a part of Roman-Dutch law. Therefore, he ruled, a court administering Roman-Dutch law 'is precluded from adopting a doctrine peculiar to English law and in conflict with the principles of our own'. Furthermore, he said, it was not advisable, and he observed that European and Scottish courts had found other ways of testing the intention of parties to a contract to bind themselves (*Rood v Wallach 1904 TS 188* at 195, 196, 201).

with the principles of Roman-Dutch law. If we cannot do so in accordance
with those principles, we cannot do so at all. (*Kent v Transvaalsche Bank
1907 TS 765* at 769 and 774)

I am not arguing that South African judges were uniquely severe in this,
only that given the range of civilian authorities which could have been
employed, and the inherent and obvious susceptibilities in the society to
non-consensual contracts, it is not beyond imagining that different
doctrines could have been emphasised and developed. Indeed it is argu-
able that a very large proportion of the contracts entered into between
Africans and whites, and enforced by the law, were, in terms of the
consensualism celebrated in the sophisticated end of civilian jurisprudence, not contracts at all. A consensus-based doctrine of contract was
bound to be, for many South African contracts, fictional. A subjective
meeting of minds was frequently not present.

   Before we embark on a closer look at contracting in society some
thought therefore needs to be given not only to the broader role of
contract as a political, social and economic doctrine in industrialising
societies in this period, but specifically to how the ideology of contract
operated in colonial and racially stratified societies. The history of the
South African law of contract cannot be written as if the society were
made up of white businessmen contracting among their peers. In South
Africa, which was both an industrialising and a colonial society, the
broader and the specific colonial aspects of contractual ideology, and its
consequent legal applications, intersected and interacted in ways that
made the idea of contract a central tool in the enforcement of a range of
social and economic discipline. Contracting in South African society was
more complex than the formalist doctrines of the Roman-Dutch lawyers
reveal. Two features of the discourses on contract in South Africa are
important here. One was the claim to, and the denial of, contractual
capacity for a range of people and purposes, which served as a marker of
racial difference. As was often the case, this was supported by the best
scientific authority. A. R. Radcliffe-Brown, then professor of anthropology
at the University of Cape Town, told the Economic and Wages Commission: 'The native does not know what a contract means. Debt is to the
native one of the most sacred things. To the native a debt can never be
abolished . . . but contract does not exist.' To these irrational beings, to
whom debt was 'sacred' but who knew nothing about voluntary promises,
there could be no stigma attached to imprisonment for breach of contract.

'That was one of the great difficulties in our inducing in the native . . . any conception of what we mean by "legality" and "illegality".' Indeed the matter was beyond rationality. Radcliffe-Brown continued: 'After all the most important thing about law is its prestige. The native has the very highest respect for his own law. It is a thing absolutely and entirely sacred to him.' He regarded kings and chiefs as 'sacred persons' because they were 'the repository of the law'. It was therefore dangerous 'to teach him that law is a thing which need not be regarded as sacred, that it is a profane thing . . . it seems desirable to transfer to our law that sacredness with which he regards his own' (UG 14 1926: 329).

Alongside this formulation which put Africans insofar as contract was concerned into the realm of the irrational and the sacred was the connected claim that contract was not only an economic but a moral imperative, something which the inferior civilisation had to learn. Africans (see below) were treated as minors for the purposes of some contracts; denied capacity in others; but deemed to have full capacity in the circumstances in which they were most vulnerable. In the latter circumstance it was the combination of the claim that parties had freedom to enter into their contracts, with the right of enforcement[3] that was of absolute importance, and this was reinforced by the moral claim that the idea of contract and contractual capacity was a central component of the advanced status of white civilisation. It was a singular ideological instrument combining both moral and practical power.

At the risk of labouring this point I would like to look closely at exemplars of the minutiae of mutual consent.[4] In the single contract that affected more people in the country than any other, the one workers

---

[3] On enforcement it may also be relevant to note the 'chasm' between Roman-Dutch law and English law on specific performance. While by this time English law allowed only damages for breach of contract, in the Roman-Dutch law of this period suits for specific performance were 'of daily occurrence' and in 1912 the Appellate Division affirmed that it was 'beyond all doubt' that the claim existed 'as of right', although a court had the discretion to say that it was not an appropriate remedy (*Farmers Co-operative Society v Berry 1912 AD*). Only in 1926 did the Appellate Division say that South African practice followed the English rule of not ordering specific performance of an employment contract (*Schierhout v Minister of Justice 1926 AD*). This did not, of course, apply to the law of master and servant. (This note is drawn from the discussion in Cockrell 1996.)

[4] It is not as if thinking about the inequalities involved in contract was a later development in legal thought. As Horwitz writes, Roscoe Pound's article on 'Liberty of Contract', which was published in 1909, pointed out that a 'conception of "equal rights" between employers and employees . . . could only be called a fallacy to everyone acquainted at first hand with actual industrial conditions' (Horwitz 1992: 34).

signed to work on the gold mines, the mine at which work was to be done was not specified, nor was the range of duties, and nor were the wages to be paid, which, in the standard contract, were to be 'at the ruling current rate'. The question as to whether this actually was a valid contract at all was raised in *Gegingana v Rex 1912 EDL 377* when it was argued *unsuccessfully* that a recruitment contract which the worker did not understand was void as there was no *consensus ad idem*. In *Tetyana v Rex 1912 EDL 295* the court said that section 12 of the Native Labour Regulation Act required the attesting officer to be satisfied that the contract was understood so that the persons recruited 'might be fully acquainted with the nature of the contract into which they had entered, so that, having that knowledge, they were bound to fulfil their part of the contract, and failing to do so, they became liable for the penalties provided' (297). The realities were better portrayed by Buckle, in his Native Grievances Enquiry Report. While he accepted the rationale of a 'wholesale' labour recruiting system, he observed that he was 'not aware of any other case in which an employee binds himself to work for a long period without stipulating for a fixed wage' (UG 37 1914: 57). He observed that a Native Affairs Department official was supposed to explain the terms of the contract but 'a large number of men are constantly going through a routine business' and it was to be doubted whether an official who had always been stationed in a 'native district himself sufficiently understands the effect of all the conditions of a mining contract' (75). Further to the question of consent and contract, Buckle commented on the sub-contracting system on the mines whereby white miners were responsible for the payment of the wages of African workers: 'The usual contract system really amounts to this, that if the miner chooses to pay the native, he does so; if not he simply pockets a part of [*sic*] the whole of the native's wages. Certainly no contract on these terms has ever been agreed to by any servant' (41). Behind the recruitment contract lay another network of unequal colonial contracts. The recruitment system, and, indeed, the economic system of the rural areas more broadly, was underpinned by advances and loans, often made in order to secure labour well in advance of the time at which the labour period was to begin. While some employers complained loudly and bitterly that it was they who were most exploited by this system (which better off and better organised employers, such as the mines, could use at the expense of others), its result was that large numbers of workers were bound to work to pay off debts and loans which could be almost impossible to discharge. These circumstances were related to the larger question as to whether and when Africans could be treated by the law as having full contractual capacity. Usury legislation in the Cape and Natal (see below) was introduced to place a limit on loans to Africans. And there was constant pressure from certain employers to place a limit on the amount that could be advanced on a labour contract. Buckle recorded that traders and recruiters argued that 'if they like to lend the money, and the native to borrow it, that is their business, and the Government is in no way concerned'. However, in these circumstances, the premises behind the subordinate position of Africans in the country as a whole were invoked into the civil law. 'The principle that the native must, in many respects, be treated as a minor', he wrote, 'is . . . too well established to be open to discussion at this time of day' (79). Nonetheless in relation to labour contracts African workers (many of whom were in fact minors when contracting) were treated as majors by the law. (Masters and servants law and its peculiarities in relation to the idea of contract are dealt with below in part V.)

Contracts relating to the right to use land are often accompanied by a high degree of legal formalism, and might be thought to fall well within the paradigm of the Roman-Dutch law's view of contractual formation and obligation. Yet perhaps the next most important contract in South African life in this period was that between white landlord and African tenant farmer, and again the realities seem to escape the conceptual world of the civil law. Of the sharecropping agreements, Macmillan wrote that 'perhaps the main characteristic of the system is the absence of any formal written agreement or contract, this being also its greatest defect' (1930: 90). Formal legal contracts were not common, he pointed out, in any circumstances in South African rural life. The Carnegie Commission observed the business habits of whites in rural areas regarding the absence of contracts and the 'unbusinesslike ways' which 'provided the unscrupulous trader or attorney with many opportunities to deceive and fleece him' (1932: vol. II: 42). Formal contracts were even less common between whites and Africans. There was an almost endless variation of conditions and, as Macmillan observed, 'any system based on verbal agreement is liable to be so complicated, [and] open to very grave abuses' (1930: 98). In relation to this we may also consider the annual *akkoord* (contract) between farmers and tenants. The *akkoord* was 'more than just a paper signifying agreement', it embodied 'the sum total of all the terms' under which the labour tenant or sharecropper would work. It was a wide-ranging negotiation of a whole working relationship, rather than a narrow set of 'terms', and included much that was customary and understood between the parties (Matsetela 1982: 221–35). Customary arrangements of this sort did not fit easily into the narrower and more technical concepts of contract applied by the courts. Part of the problem posed was that the contracts were oral, and that conflicts arose over what they contained. Magistrates testified to the Native Economic Commission that 'misunderstanding of the terms of the contract' accounted for a consider-able proportion of masters and servants cases (UG 22 1932: 363).

But there was a more basic issue. The theory and nature of contract in Roman-Dutch law implied the willing making of a bargain between the parties. But the power to bargain, even an unequal power, subverted racial superiority where contracts were across the colour line containing as it did the possibility that a part of the will of a white would be accommodated to that of a black (see below). This led to the demand not just for written contracts but for standard form contracts. Africans as freely contracting and bargaining agents unregulated by imposed and legislated terms were, outside of the fictions of the common law, not acceptable. Commonly too rural tenancy contracts were made between a landlord and a family head contracting on behalf of his extended family, who could bind adults both male and female over whom customary law gave him legal authority.

Credit and debt

Our understanding of the meaning of contract law in South African society can be illustrated by a consideration of the politics of credit law. This is a crucial topic in understanding the evolution of South African legalism. It should not be thought that the politics of law ends with a discussion of public law, and that there was a realm of private and commercial law which developed in a manner insulated from political struggle in South African society. Major commercial interests urged from the beginning of British hegemony that there be developed an effective country-wide legal regime to give creditors security. Even before the Transvaal Colony had been established Milner was being urged by lawyers in the Transvaal to get the new Supreme Court operating as people were simply refusing to pay debts in the absence of a mechanism to make them do so. The effort to establish effective means of debt collection, and a uniform insolvency law, absorbed a great deal of attention. Reflecting the creditors' interests the editorial in the first *Union Law Review* claimed that 'taken as a whole, the law of South Africa is more favourable to the debtor than to the creditor' (1910: 8). More than a decade of reform was to be devoted to changing this balance. It becomes plain that running through this struggle was both a racial and an urban–rural divide, with the inevitable consequences that positions would be taken according to the major divisions of South African politics. Urban lenders supplied credit to (among others) rural borrowers. Afrikaners (among others) borrowed from non-Afrikaners. White lenders advanced money and goods on credit to black borrowers.

Dealing with credit law also enables us to look at some of the issues surrounding law and race in a different light; in particular it provides another angle of approach to the claim that the system of private law was colour blind. Private law in this area protected some interests and discriminated against others. It was (and is) also a vital reservoir of symbols about the nature of people in general, and particular kinds of people. And there is a further point. One of the features of Western private law of this period, particularly contractual law, was its formalism, its reluctance to look beyond, for instance, the forms of contract to the real positions of the parties. We might observe, therefore, that, doctrinally, private law had to be colour blind. If it was not, it would have to take account of the real circumstances of the parties, and relinquish all the advantages that accrued by not doing so. While in some areas of law formalism might have been usable as a defence against racism, in others formalism was a way of escaping from the realities of economic differences based on race as well as class. Much of the discourse, and practice, of credit law was specifically race based. We can see this if we consider the collection of small debts, an area which does not find its way into Supreme Court reports where the lack of overt racism should not be taken as its absence from contractual law. Concerns about the operation of credit laws, and a general climate of feeling among creditors' interests that debt enforcement mechanisms needed improving, surfaced in the enquiry into the system of garnisheeing wages (SC 10 1913). In England these matters were dealt with by a lower court which, in making an order for payment of debt out of a future wage, had to leave a fixed minimum for the debtor to live on. Legislation passed in the Transvaal in 1908 placed these matters in the Supreme Court giving it power to make orders against a person's salary without any limit on the amount or proportion of the wages garnished. The Transvaal Federation of Trade Unions urged the abolition of the system, arguing that as tradesmen could not be sued on future profits, it should not be possible to sue 'craftsmen' for future earnings. They described the system as follows:

> The law has created a system of credit in the Transvaal [in] which . . . the only people who appear to benefit are the solicitors . . . Workmen are pressed to incur liabilities which otherwise they would not do owing to the facility with which the creditor can obtain a garnishee order . . . and thus obtain a lien on the workman's future wages, which causes him to . . . incur further debts. (SC 10 1913: viii)

There were a number of ways of enabling the recovery of debt from wage earners who had no assets. One was civil imprisonment, which could only be ordered in cases where the debtor was believed to have the capacity to pay, but was denying it. But as the Government law adviser, E. L. Matthews, pointed out, civil imprisonment operated only for a certain length of time and a debtor prepared to sit it out could escape liability (8). The solution advocated by Matthews was to abandon the garnisheeing of wages in favour of orders for payment by instalment to be made against the debtor only, not the employer. This may well have restricted the availability of credit to wage earners. The third possibility was to retain the garnishee system but to set a limit on amounts or proportions. But here the issue of race entered the considerations. The Witwatersrand Trades Hall Council asked that a minimum of £20 per month be left. But this was seen as creating a problem, because such a limit would exempt virtually all the earnings of non-whites. Matthews rejected a limit on these grounds. Could different limits be set for different racial groups? The Johannesburg Chief Magistrate, H. O. Buckle, told the committee that action for debt against Africans was 'hardly known'. Africans were simply outside the operation of the law altogether. An African wanting credit submitted to an informal garnishee system in which the employer agreed to pay over his wages (26). It was Indians who were the problem. Sir David Harris told the select committee: 'You know the Indian can live on a very small sum. *It would be impossible to fix a minimum wage below which garnishee orders would not be allowed*' (26; my emphasis). He was supported by the Chief Magistrate, who had, he said, made orders against a good many Indians 'on the assumption that the Indian can live upon £3 or £4 a month'. Far better then to maintain a formal law which did not recognise real racial differences in levels of wages, and which did not set a minimum which might benefit white workers but would also exclude Africans or Indians. For the element of discrimination could always come in the court's order, depending on its view of the minimum living income required by different races.

The remedies that were appropriate to use against wage-earning debtors were not so easily applicable to traders and farmers. And it is in relation to these areas, most particularly rural debt, that concern was growing. One can get an understanding of the ways in which the issues were perceived from the magistrates' reports which showed a similar set of concerns across the country. Many small shopkeepers had gone insolvent (UG 44 1913: 11). In 1913 the reports of the Masters of the Supreme Courts indicated different types of insolvencies in the different provinces. (It seems apposite to recall that the law of insolvency was racialised in that insolvency was not normally available to Africans in debt; see below.) Major features were the paucity of assets in the insolvent estate and a reduction in rehabilitations, owing to 'the misconduct of the applicants'. In the Free State, on the other hand, it was not retail traders but farmers who were the main class of insolvents and estates had a relatively high proportion of assets to liabilities. The problems of access to credit in rural communities were considerable. The major imperial banks, the Standard and the National, concentrated their activities elsewhere. While the rural areas were starved of money the banks kept large surplus funds in the London money market (Kantor 1972: 61). The Land Bank Act, in spite of criticism on this point, would only allow the advance of money against a first mortgage, which most farmers already had. Farmers therefore depended on small traders for extended credit. The borrowers easily saw themselves as victims, and were sometimes portrayed as such by politicians and magistrates. One local magistrate urged that 'the long credit system with its pernicious effects should be prevented . . . the buyer never really knew his position until he was so deeply in debt that mere inability to pay suggested the idea of defrauding his creditors' (UG 44 1913: 44, report of the magistrate for Aberdeen). In 1914 the magistrate at Barkly West outlined the position of debtors on the diamond diggings. They lived a hand-to-mouth existence, supported and financed by shopkeepers: 'As a result they get deep in the storekeeper's debt and, when they do find stones, the proceeds are used up in the liquidating of these debts. Their condition thus becomes one of virtual slavery' (UG 28 1915: 70).

It was plain to many, however, that one of the prime purposes of moving towards Union was to create a more secure field for business, not relief for debtors. This was a broad agenda which included a common patents and trade-mark law; a new national companies law; and uniformity on the matter of prescription for debt. As early as 1906 the *South African Law Journal* campaigned on the 'pressing need' for improvement in insolvency administration and the development of national uniformity (345). In 1910 Carl Jeppe argued the case again for the urgent need for a Union-wide insolvency statute. 'How serious the perils to which [current law] exposes commercial transactions and business credit, can hardly be realised at first sight' (Jeppe 1910: 566). In the years between 1910 and 1914 all provinces reported a steady rise in insolvencies (UG 1915: 23–4). The Transvaal situation prompted the recommendation that the insolvency law was 'urgently in need of amendment'. Magistrates picked on the weaknesses from the creditors' point of view. One Transvaal magistrate pointed out that section 55 of Law 13 of 1895, the insolvency law in force in the Transvaal, did not give the trustee any *locus standi* to examine the insolvent. It also confined the right of examination, unlike the Cape law, to matters relating to secret alienation or concealment, rather than the more general power in the Cape law to cover any matter. A Natal magistrate identified another weakness. Under the Natal law, he said, 'the debtor almost invariably escaped his obligations'. He urged that 'the burden of proof in cases of undue preference should rest with the defendant and not with the plaintiff as at present'. Calls for a Union-wide insolvency law included urgings that there be more stringent provisions as to the keeping of books (UG 44 1913: 122). These provisions, once enacted, were to create great difficulties for farmers, many of whom were chronically in breach of the law, and liable, once insolvent, to criminal penalties.

The new insolvency law, which aimed at rectifying the weaknesses identified and considerably shortening the proceedings necessary, was introduced into parliament in 1916 (Hansard 15/2/16). Unlike many other major statutory initiatives of this time the wording of the Act was not imperial in derivation but was based on the Transvaal republican law no. 13 of 1895 (UG 39 1918: 2). The Bill was subjected to bitter attack by Hertzog. It was, he said, a 'measure entirely in favour of people connected with trade. Far-reaching privileges were being given to one particular section of the people.' It was by no means, he said, simply a consolidating measure, but one that enacted new policy, giving merchants security at the expense of wives and children, and creating hardship for farmers and 'the small man'. Some of the essence of the objections, and of the debate, might be captured by considering the exchange about the proposed clause 76, providing for the sale of a debtor's property, and the exemption of such household goods and tools 'as the creditors determine'. Some members objected that this went too far, and proposed that the exemption should take into account 'reasonable requirement'. The minister refused. Parliament, he said, 'must be just before it was generous'. To the objection that other provisions made it more difficult for farmers to get credit, de Wet replied that the 'great danger lay in the fact that too much credit was given'. The leader of the Unionists, Sir Thomas Smartt, pronounced that farmers borrowed far more than the value of their property warranted. The matter was summed up by Hertzog: 'The fact was that the interest of the farmer had come into conflict with the interest of the dealer' (Hansard 5/5/16).

The new law did not suddenly change the relationships between creditors and debtors in the countryside. In 1918 the Carnarvon magistrate called for the abolition of the 'long credit' system which encouraged dishonesty on the part of both creditors and debtors (UG 36 1918: 48). In 1919 another Cape magistrate referred to 'landowners who were in the grip of debt . . . Debts were run up at the stores, and things were allowed to drift till the time came when there was no alternative but to join the poor white society' (UG 35 1920: 55). Another familiar note also crept into the debate about insolvency. The Master of the Supreme Court at the Cape commented that 'a sad feature was that the respectable middle class small European shopkeeper was going to the wall. He could not compete with the Asiatic who had little else but himself to support and sent the money he made, or owed, out of the country' (UG 39 1918: 11).

There continued to be division along political lines about the insolvency laws. After his first year in office the National Party Minister of Justice, Tielman Roos, rendered the provisions requiring farmers to keep proper books a dead letter by releasing from jail one convicted for such an offence and announcing that the Attorneys-General had decided that there would be no further prosecutions (Hansard 6/7/25). Yet the National Party in power found itself obliged to further protect the creditors' interest. In 1926 an apparently reluctant Roos, as Minister of Justice, introduced amendments to the insolvency laws which he blamed upon the commercial community's 'neglect' in giving 'too great credit'. But he told the House nonetheless that they must make the 'penalties large for going insolvent, and thus give the traders of this country a better status, not only inside South Africa, but outside, and thereby increase the credit of our own country' (Hansard 10/2/26). Labour member Morris Alexander told Parliament that the laws were 'so drastic that very few persons accused of insolvency offences escaped punishment'. The insolvent, he added, 'has a very thin time of it'. On the contrary, claimed R. Stuttaford, one of the country's leading retailers, it was the view of the commercial community that criminal insolvency was 'rarely' punished and that the 'dice are loaded against the trustee' (Hansard 3/3/26).

The legislature, and the courts, struggled to adapt the law to the prevailing commercial conditions in South Africa. On the one hand there was a sympathy in both towards a relatively unregulated market economy in the realm of commercial transactions. Yet there were significant elements of the Roman-Dutch law which reflected a more equitable approach to economic transactions, and also, as I have outlined, political and class divisions about the appropriate regime of commercial law. While it was clear that the Roman-Dutch law had prohibited the charging of usurious interest, the courts after 1902 were cautious about appearing to set legitimate rates of interest. In the South African Republic, Kotze, as Chief Justice, in *Taylor v Holland 2 SAR 78* had refused to enforce a contract to pay £14,000 plus interest at 8 per cent per annum on a loan of £7,000. The court, he said, would not countenance 'excessive and exorbitant interest, upon the grounds that this would be contrary to good morals and public policy, not merely on the grounds that protection should be afforded to the promisor'. Predictably the Cape court had taken a somewhat narrower view. In *Dyason v Ruthven 3 SC 282* it had ruled that for 'usury to be a good defence to an action founded on an agreement to pay interest, [it] must under Roman-Dutch law involve extortion amounting to fraud'. In *Reuter v Yates 1904 TS 855* Innes followed the Cape approach, ruling that the test was whether the lender has taken such an undue advantage of the borrower, and had so practised extortion and oppression, that the conduct was 'akin to fraud' (858). Excessive and exorbitant interest, he said, was not merely high interest but a rate 'contrary to good morals, the interests of our citizens and the policy of our laws'. The court would not, for example, enforce a contract for double the amount advanced, plus interest. But interest well above current rates was not necessarily excessive. In 1911 the Supreme Court in the Transvaal allowed a rate of interest of 120 per cent. Wessels ruled that there was no statutory or customary rate of interest, and that the rate 'varies with the nature of the financial transactions carried on in the country'. The aggrieved party was 'an ordinary farmer who knows perfectly well what he is doing' (*South African Securities Ltd v Greyling 1911 TPD 352* at 355).

But beyond the business transactions dealt with in the supreme courts lay an unregulated world of small borrowing and lending which was producing problems for administrators as well as for borrowers. Control of interest rates was unfashionable during the era of *laissez-faire*. In England in 1854 all legislation against usury had been repealed. But by 1900 law to control moneylenders (though not banks) was introduced. In 1908 the Cape Usury Act was introduced as a result of representation from the magistrates of the Transkei that Africans were being charged ruinously high rates of interest. But control of interest rates was not easy. There were complaints that white traders were being forced out of business by unfair limitations on lending, and that others were unable to recover money lent. Unsurprisingly too, indignant attention was drawn to the creation of a usurious 'underground' by African lenders. Before the election of a parliament more sympathetic to the interests of white debtors, unsuccessful demands had been made for a Union-wide regulation on the rates of interest. In 1916 the Natal Chief Magistrate drew attention to the need for a usury law in that province, referring to the practice of charging interest at the rate of 120 per cent per annum (UG 39 1918: 102). In his report for 1918 the Chief Magistrate of Durban called for 'a Usury and Money-lenders Act to be placed on the Statute book, as there was a real necessity for it to prevent the bleeding of natives' (UG 36 1918: 79).

In 1921 in response to a member's plea that moneylenders were charging rates of between 60 per cent and 200 per cent, the Minister of Justice said that the government could not interfere with private contracts and pointed to the common law protection that a creditor could not demand more in interest than the original debt (Hansard 18/5/21). In 1926 the National–Labour Party government, responding to a poorer white constituency, introduced new legislation primarily to give relief to white borrowers. Country members told of the 'heartbreaking' plight of persons commonly paying interest at rates of 60 per cent and 'remaining year in year out under the millstone of the money lender'. It was claimed that there were over 20,000 moneylenders active on the Reef, lending to those who could not get bank credit. Labour members asked the minister to ensure that no debtors were civilly imprisoned for failure to repay money borrowed (Hansard 8/1/26). In controlling the market for money the government had a balancing act to perform. On the one hand there was the political pressure to give relief to private, and especially to rural, borrowers, and on the other no desire to compromise commercial operations by appearing to weaken the obligations of creditors. The general manager of the Standard Bank complained bitterly that the law interfered with everyday commercial and banking business, especially the banks' transactions with farmers (SC 4 1926: 26). There were also external considerations: the new Bill exempted foreign bills of exchange so as not to affect foreign commerce.

Succession

In the development of the law of succession we can see again the force of the drive to rationalise the common law and bring it into line with market principles. It is worth spending some time on this issue because it shows how readily basic principles of the Roman-Dutch common law were discarded when they appeared to obstruct economically rational use of land. Indeed it might suggest that Roman-Dutch law was acceptable only as long as it worked basically like English law. In the Roman-Dutch law that had applied at the Cape a child could not be entirely disinherited by a parent, but freedom of testation was introduced by statute in the Cape, and the English forms of will introduced in 1873/4. However this anglicisation did not apply to intestacy. There was no primogeniture (Watermayer 1936: 866, 871), and it also remained possible for a testator to impose *fidei commissa* binding upon beneficiaries up to the fourth generation, and it was common to leave land with restrictions preventing further alienation.

The uses made of this law of succession were of great significance. During this period the increasing capitalisation of agriculture, and the growth of class divisions among rural whites as the poorer whites struggled to maintain a hold on the land, challenged a cultural legacy of notions of equitable shares of farming land. It was a common practice to leave farms in undivided shares which, under the terms of the existing laws of inheritance, could not be realised separately. As successive generations clung to the land the farms could not support the numbers of people living on them. Magistrates urged the need to change the laws allowing

> the constant splitting up of farms into undivided parts. This was one of the causes of the ever increasing numbers of poor whites. The farm which supported a whole family in comfort while under single control became inadequate for the family on the father's death owing to the divided control. One retrogressive member among many progressive co-owners had a disastrous influence on all. On the other hand if there was no room for them all on the land they had better understand it at once. (UG 44 1913: 124)

A visiting Australian journalist, A. Pratt, recorded that he was told that the Roman-Dutch law, which permitted entail and undivided ownership, was partly to blame for rural backwardness. Traditionally each child was entitled to a legitimate portion, and undivided ownership made the land unsaleable unless all agreed, and thus land was in effect withdrawn from the market. The existing law, he wrote, 'is a deadly enemy of progress' (Pratt 1913: 86–7).

The Botha–Smuts government was responsive to the 'progressive' agenda. Accordingly the subject was addressed by a parliamentary committee in 1914 (SC 6 1914). The modernisers argued that it had become plain that the original intention of the law, which was to ensure that succeeding generations were catered for, was not necessarily being met. Sir Henry Juta, then Judge-President of the Cape, gave evidence before the committee to point to 'the fallacy of the sentimental idea' that leaving land with these restrictions 'means that your descendants are going to occupy it' (10). For one thing life interests could be sold by the original legatee or successors. Sometimes the legatees were too poor to occupy the farms left to them successfully and the share left could not support them. Juta told the committee that there were 'cases where the whole farm has deteriorated so much' that life interests were sold 'for a song'. Many poor whites 'had the home feeling and they lingered around the old homestead', yet the farm became worthless 'because nobody had control and nobody could improve or do anything' (35). The Land Bank would not lend money on farms in which large numbers of people had an interest, and private providers of finance were equally cautious because courts would not allow such properties to be sold to satisfy creditors (64 *et seq.*). While many committee members and witnesses shared the view that a will was 'the most sacred kind of a document that one can conceive' (39) sympathetic attention was paid to the 'struggle' of English law to put land 'into the market' (61). It was noted that changing the law would tip the balance in favour of 'moneyed' heirs who would be able to use the courts to force poor ones to relinquish their rights (39), but the interests of the poor attempting to cling to a vestige of land rights was overridden. Because farms were 'going to wrack and ruin', the committee thought, they had to be bequeathed 'in such a way that it becomes of benefit to the country at large' (13). As in the case of the credit regime, private-law developments were not solicitous of the interests of poorer whites. These would have to be catered for in the realm of politics.

While the 1914 committee looked favourably on legislation to prohibit entail of land it was felt that sentiment against this would be so strong that it could not be carried through parliament. It opted, in spite of the reluctance of judges to be given the duty to make such determinations, for a law which gave the courts power to alter wills where no beneficial value accrued to the legatees. In 1916 parliament passed the Removal or Modification of Restrictions on Immovable Property Act. This allowed the overriding of testamentary dispositions in the case of fidei commissary or entailed estates to relieve beneficiaries of unforeseen burdens.

Company law

Important areas of commercial law were not included in the Roman-Dutch narrative. In 1906 the *South African Law Journal* referred to the urgent need for company law reform to stop the 'reckless over promotion and over capitalisation of Companies' which was in vogue in the Transvaal. The English Companies Act of 1900, which set out requirements as to statements made in prospectuses, had been evaded by the non-issue of prospectuses. Both the Cape and the Transvaal had been conspicuous for 'wild cat' schemes: 'At present almost unlimited licence is allowed to the promoters of Companies.' What was required was legislation which would protect the public from fraud, and increase revenue by the taxation of capital: 'The legislature will have to pay special attention to the question of prospectuses, the rights of vendors and promoters, the proportion of working to subscribed capital, the payment of duty on capital other than working capital.' Those who had suffered in the recent smashes had reason to lament the lack of protection of the confiding investor (428).

In 1907 the United Kingdom Board of Trade had put before the Imperial Conference a memorandum on company law in the British empire to prod it to consider the desirability of securing greater uniformity of mercantile law throughout the empire (Cd 5684 1907). In 1908 the nineteen British Acts relating to companies were consolidated into a single statute which was to serve as an empire-wide model. This was to have an immediate impact on South African law. In the words of the Board of Trade memorandum of 1911 the Transvaal Act of 1909, which was to be the basis of the later Union Act, 'is founded upon the Imperial Consolidation Act, and great care has been taken by the draughtsman to adopt the exact wording of the Imperial Consolidation Act so that the decisions of the Courts of this country will be of service to and assist the Courts of the Transvaal. By the passing of the above named act a real advance has been made towards the unification of company law throughout the Empire' (Company Laws of the British Empire. Memorandum prepared for the Imperial Conference, 1911 by the direction of the Board of Trade: 34–5). In the same way, the wording of an imperial or a dominion statute gave a *de facto* if not *de jure* control over the evolution of the dominion law to English courts, which would have to interpret the Act far more frequently and whose interpretations would tend to be followed by other courts interpreting the same section.

As in the case of the management of debt, South African governments were caught between felt lack of power and a reluctance to intervene too aggressively in the operations of the economy, and the all too obvious local needs for regulation. The desire was to establish a respectable commercial regime, an atmosphere of mercantile integrity in order to give confidence to investors. In 1915 the Registrar of Companies called for a Union-wide Act to 'mitigate the evils resulting from the registration of bogus Companies' (UG 28 1915: 25). In 1923 the Minister of Justice told parliament that there was a greater need in South Africa than in Britain for control over companies because of the possibility of their use for fraudulent purposes. He introduced a new provision by which companies would be required to state their main object specifically in their memorandum of association, rather than listing anything and everything. But this step away from the British model of giving wide-ranging powers to companies at formation was as far from the British law as he was prepared to go. Opening up too wide a gap between the British and South African laws appeared undesirable, perhaps because of the discouraging inhibition it would place on companies incorporating in South Africa. The government would not extend the liability for written statements in prospectuses in the direction of the American model where the registrar of companies could investigate statements made in the prospectus. This, said the minister, would be 'unadvisable' in South Africa (Hansard 3/1/23). Labour Members of Parliament also pressed for a different style of company law. They drew attention to the powerful grip of international finance on local communities and urged that government directors be appointed to the boards of mining companies, with rights of disclosure to the public in order to protect the public interest (Hansard 25/2/26).

This was not the direction taken. The consolidation of company law in 1926 was based on the 1908 British Act, and the later consolidation on the British Act of 1929 (also used in Canada and New Zealand). It was desirable, the Company Law Commission reported, that there should be consistency with British law because for the courts 'the advantage is secured of British judicial decisions of high authority and precedential value', while for businessmen 'much assistance' was derived from being able to follow British practice (UG 45 1936: 6). Furthermore, there was the constant eye on external credibility. It was, the commission said, 'of the greatest importance to the Union generally, and to its commercial interests in particular, that South Africa's fair name and credit shall not be tarnished by any suspicion of manipulations by unscrupulous Company promotions or unsound Company administration' (7).

Similar problems were evident with the regulation of insurance where a poorly regulated industry had led to widespread fraud. When statutory regulation of insurance on a Union-wide basis came, an approach similar to that taken for regulation of companies was adopted. In 1923 de Wet introduced to parliament an insurance Bill based on the English Act of 1909 and the Australian federal legislation of 1912. He explained that there were two models for controlling insurance. The American and Canadian way was one of 'detailed interference' with the internal concerns of the companies, and restrictive supervision, including the fixing of premium rates. The other model was a minimum of interference with freedom of contract or internal management, and simply relying on full publicity of results, and the lodging of security with the government. 'The Bill', he explained, 'is framed on the principle that "freedom and publicity" is a better basis for legislation than "supervision and restriction"' and had the advantage that the government could 'administer the Act effectively with a much smaller and less expensive staff' (Hansard 12/4/23). Again one might usefully compare the government's enthusiastic creation of bureaucracies, boards, inspectorates, and other detailed apparatuses of control in other areas of life with its hands-off attitude towards major economic institutions which controlled large concentrations of capital. The National Party opposition objected to foreign insurance companies draining the country of premiums and asked for local reserves to be held. The Labour Party's call for state insurance companies was rejected.

Delict and compensation

In 1911 Merriman observed that the African mine worker 'does not know how he has contracted, and he may be selling his very life away' (SC 3 1911: 32). This comment on a situation in which hundreds of thousands entered into contracts without knowing the terms, and which exposed them to extremely high risk, provides a bridge between the discussions of the law of contract, and of delict (tort). I have noted the absence of the obvious from the dominant narrative of the law of contract. There is a similar absence in the heart of the history of the South African law of delict. This story has usually been written in terms of undeniable self-congratulation, as a story of the progressive development of principles of compensation for harm caused negligently which was conceptually well in advance of the English common law.[5] But there is another story of terrible failure. The mining industry underpinned South Africa's economy and state. Its horrific record of injury to its workforce has been copiously documented. Yet however conceptually advanced the doctrines of the Roman-Dutch law were, most of the victims of negligence in South Africa were not the beneficiaries of tort law, which offered them no compensation and no protection.[6] The carnage caused by the mines has not been the focus of lawyers' writings about the South African law of

---

[5] See for example the good and detailed discussion by Hutchison (1996) which celebrates the importance of Innes's 'wisdom, learning and vigilance' in protecting the principled basis of the Roman-Dutch law as opposed to the 'detailed' and 'rigid' approach of English law (600).

[6] Visser (1989: 5, note 39) draws attention to Horwitz's (1977) discussion of the American debate as to whether tort law provided a 'subsidy' for entrepreneurs. This has not been a focus of interest among South African studies of the law of delict.

negligence and compensation. Both contract law and the law of delict, therefore, were developed by the South African Supreme Courts towards a purity of doctrine: in the case of contract, towards subjective consensus; in the case of delict towards the right to recover damages for all loss negligently and wrongfully caused. This purity of doctrine coexisted with a state of affairs which mocked the jurisprudence developed, which systemically denied compensation for the major areas of wrongful damage, and in which contracts were focused on the disciplining of racial subordinates. To point this out, in a form of realist exposé, does not reduce the juristic achievements of the makers of the Roman-Dutch law. For I argue in this book that we must go beyond a simple comparison of formal doctrine with 'social reality' or 'law in practice'. What concerns me here are the relationships of knowing and not knowing that can contemporaneously exist between the two.

I shall approach the question of this relationship by considering the areas in which different legal discourses overlap, in which we can, as it were, look through a window at both doctrine and legal practices. While the oppressive uses of contract were sidelined in the development of doctrine, societal and political concern with issues of debt (which affected both white and black) and debt recovery and usury ensured that these issues were alive social foci. As illustrated in the development of African law, the capacity, or lack thereof, to contract, was a part of the discourses of otherness. In the major area of contracts across the colour line, the rural contracts on land use and sharecropping, and the labour contract between master and servant, the use of concepts of contract and contract law were crucial mechanisms of white rule. Likewise while the issue of adequate industrial compensation was very rarely put before the judges in the courts, it was a legal issue which was extensively discussed between officials, industry, politicians and legislators. (The judiciary's contribution was an adamant maintaining of the boundary between common-law and statutory claims for compensation which essentially ensured that no common-law claims could be made (see Corder 1984: 109–12).)

An alternative focus of an historical understanding of the South African law of compensation for negligence could, then, be not on the *actio legis aquiliae* but on the Witwatersrand, where, as it was pointed out in 1910, after a comparison of death-rates in the British army in the South African War between 1899 and 1902 and that on the mines, that 'Mining is more dangerous than war' (Katz 1994: 3). In relation to silicosis alone a doctor observed in *The Lancet* in 1911 that 'such a death rate from a single occupational disease must be unparalleled in the whole industrial world. It can only be compared with King Leopold's Congo Free State' (quoted by Katz 1994: 213). The abolition of the inquest courts in the Transvaal in 1909 meant that there was no judicial enquiry into mining related deaths. A second foundational point must be made. It is that in this central area, the one of greatest concern to the largest number of negligently injured persons, the essence of South African law relating to negligently caused harm was based on English, New Zealand (and later on German) statutory models, and owes nothing to the Roman-Dutch law. South African workers' compensation legislation, not surprisingly, used the same conceptual framework and language as the British Acts of 1897 and 1906. Under the 1907 Act, however, an injured worker was still required to prove the negligence of the employer, or a fellow worker. This requirement was abandoned under heavy trade union pressure in the 1914 law.[7]

As Atiyah has pointed out the question of the compensation of workers for industrial accidents is essentially a part of the law of delict and grew from its deficiencies (1970: 341ff.). Victims of accidents in industry had been frustrated by the doctrines of common employment and contributory negligence and *volenti non fit injuria*, all of which made the legal attribution of fault to employers difficult in the extreme. Following the serious breach made in the employers' defences by *Smith and Baker 1891 AC 325* in England, the first Workmen's Compensation Act was passed in 1897. The Act infringed upon the principle that liability had to be based on fault, but the legal framework remained problematic. The adversary procedures of the common-law tort system were retained, which meant that accident victims were put in a position of having to accept the lump sums offered in compensation because neither they nor their unions could afford the delays or costs of litigation. And, of vital importance to the South African story, while it was usually relatively simple to show the connections between physical injuries and work, the probative issues raised by industrially caused diseases were far more complex, contentious and elusive (see Katz 1994). In South Africa miners' phthisis compensation

---

[7] An injury had to be consequent on a risk incidental to the employment. An insight into the acknowledged working conditions of the mines can be gleaned from *McQueen v Village Deep 1914 TPD*, when the court ruled that being attacked by African workers under his command was a risk 'incidental to the employment of a man in charge of a gang of uncivilised natives underground in a mine' (349).

was eventually separately provided for in the Miners' Phthisis Act of 1911 after the damning report in 1910 of the Transvaal Mining Regulations Commission on the failure of the mines to apply the existing regulatory apparatus designed to increase safety.[8]

One of the accepted precepts of South African private law is that it has paid no attention to race, but this aspect of the law of delict was premised on racial discrimination. The original Transvaal Act of 1907 completely excluded African workers from its provisions. They were similarly excluded from compensation under the Union Act, no. 29 of 1914. In 1903 the Native Affairs Department in the Transvaal and the Chamber of Mines did negotiate a schedule of payments (£35 for death or permanent total disablement and £17 for permanent partial disablement), in compensation for injury and death of African workers. However the agreement was not accepted by the industry at large and the sums were substantially reduced – to £10 and £5 respectively. No compensation was payable at all for 'minor' accidents. This was an entirely *ex gratia* scheme, and was not made obligatory by the workmen's compensation legislation of 1907 (SC 3 1911: 14ff.). It was the very high rate of accidents, fatal and otherwise, on the mines that was given as the justification for denying legal rights of compensation for victims. When asked why the Workmen's Compensation Act should not be applied to Africans, S. A. Pritchard, the Director of the Native Labour Bureau, answered: 'I admit the principle, but the accident rate on the mines has been so terribly high' (18). 'I do not dare to think about what is happening among the Kafirs', whose work is 'far more dangerous' than that of the whites, a mining engineer said to the Phthisis Commission (SC 4 1914: 275). Concerns with cost were central in the thoughts of those engaged in devising legal remedies, and were linked consciously to issues such as the demands to protect the position of white labour on the mines. One witness to the report of the Select Committee on European Employment and Labour Conditions noted explicitly that

---

[8] The English workmen's compensation legislation of 1906 had included industrial diseases on the basis that the injury had been incurred during work from a risk created by the employer. This was not the case in South Africa where the phthisis legislation required workers and employers to contribute to a fund from which compensation was paid. The mining industry (with state support) continued to deny any liability. The Chamber of Mines claimed that treating occupational disease as accidental under workers' compensation law would 'lead to interminable litigation' as 'you cannot fix the liability on the employer . . . the government, the mine owners and the miners are to blame . . . the responsibility can be laid on many shoulders . . .' (SC 10 1912: 118, 166, 168).

the 'fact remains' that if more whites worked underground 'we shall be having more claims for compensation under the Miners' Phthisis Act' (SC 9 1913: 179).

Section 22 of the Native Labour Regulation Act of 1911 provided for compensation for African workers injured in the course of employment, though the original draft of the Bill contained no such provision, and it was altered on the recommendation of the select committee (SC 3 1911). The Transkei Chief Magistrate, A. H. Stanford, began his evidence to the Select Committee on the Native Labour Regulation Bill by drawing attention to the fact that there was no provision for compensation for injuries or death. The Transkei, he said, 'had a large number of maimed people', dependent on the government. The amounts which seemed appropriate to him were £100 for permanent disablement, and £50 for death (SC 3 1911: 237–9). When provision for compensation was included in the Native Labour Regulation Act it was for between £30 and £35 for total incapacitation; £1 to £20 if incapacitation were partial (the amount being at the discretion of an official); and £10 for death. There was an overt connection between these rates and what was believed about and legislated for African family systems. Africans were not compensated on the same principle as whites – rates fixed with regard to their probable future earning power – because they were deemed to be supported by kinship and social obligations. In his (generally unsympathetic) report for the Native Grievances Enquiry in 1914 H. O. Buckle wrote that calculations showed that compensation for total incapacity was the equivalent of two to three-and-a-half years' earnings, which, given the comparative youth of the typical labourer was not a real equivalent of the loss he had suffered. The lack of fairness applied even more to the death benefit, and to the 'obviously inadequate' amounts for partial disablement. If, as he pointed out, an unskilled labourer lost his capacity to do unskilled labouring work, the loss amounted to total incapacitation. In comparing the amounts receivable by African workers with those of white workers under the Workers' Compensation Law he showed that a totally incapacitated African worker was eligible for twelve to twenty months' pay, while a white worker could get three years' worth. The maximum for an African was £50, that for a European £750. African workers' maximum compensation, whether expressed in terms of time, or wage equivalent, was half that given to whites. In terms of partial disablement the African maximum of £20 was compared with a European one of £375. In terms of working days the whites' rate of compensation was three to four times higher. And while the European death payment was two-thirds of the total incapacitation rate, the African rate was below half of this (UG 37 14: 49–50). The purpose of compensation was to make up for loss of capacity to earn wages, but until 1934 no provision was made for temporary loss of this sort.

The processes that determined liability were worlds away from the careful reasoning of common law delict. Whether or not an African worker received compensation for phthisis depended on the mine medical officers: 'The decision as to whether the mine is to pay compensation is virtually in the hands of a nominee of the mine' (51). 'Mine doctors', Buckle observed, 'have not invariably shown themselves sufficient guardians of the native's interests.' Under section 30 of the Miners' Phthisis Act, no. 19 of 1912, doctors were required to report 'forthwith' on cases. If a man were to qualify for total incapacitation he was 'usually very near death'. If assessed while he was alive, he received between £30 and £50. If he died, £10 was payable to his dependants, if he had any. 'It is therefore in the interests of the native that the word "forthwith" . . . should be strictly obeyed; the interest of the mine is the other way' (52). His observations did not alter practices. Packard notes on the basis of evidence from the end of the decade that prior to the 1925 Act there was a similar 'financial disincentive' to the early detection of tuberculosis among African mine workers. African workers could only be compensated if they were diagnosed and certified before either death or discharge. Thus discharge and repatriation without certification, and the practice of holding TB sufferers in hospital for long periods before forwarding the case for certification, were adopted. 'If the unfortunate worker died while in the hospital, as so frequently happened, no compensation would be paid' (1994: 181). The failure of compensation law to cover workers who had been discharged and the desire to limit the compensation payments, he writes, explains the cursory nature of discharge examinations, after which 'many . . . simply returned home to die'. The Native Affairs Department recommended that a central depot be established for discharge examination at which medical officers 'would not be confronted with the question as to how much it was going to cost the Company in the event of compensation being awarded' (NAD memo of 1919, quoted in ibid. at 182). The mines rejected this proposal. The position of white workers, while bad, was different in that they qualified for compensation even if they were diagnosed and certified after discharge from service, and they received more thorough interim and termination examinations. After 1925 African workers became eligible for compensation if diagnosed within six months of discharge. This Act, Packard writes, eliminated the financial advantages in delayed diagnosis and led to more frequent examinations. However scant manpower and technical resources were put into this area (182ff.).

As was openly acknowledged, although the phthisis compensation legislation applied to Africans the effect was nominal as no steps were taken to inform Africans of their rights (SC 4 1914: xii). They did not present themselves for diagnosis as they usually did not know that they could be compensated (321). While white workers, who were supported by trade unions, knew their rights and how to act on them, in the case of Africans phthisis was diagnosed in a large number of cases 'by autopsy' (338–9). The Director of Native Labour defended this state of affairs. When asked why the regulations were not published in African languages he said:

> It is a serious thing when a law of this nature comes into force and regulations are published, to go among upwards of 200,000 natives, address them all and tell them what their rights are under the Act . . . Unfortunately along the reef and in Johannesburg we have a class of Agent who does a lot of very shady business with the native population . . . There are a good many sea lawyers among the natives, and others who act as touts to agents who, as has previously been our experience might be anticipated to cause considerable trouble in connection with the presentation of the native's claims . . .
>
> Experience has taught me that when you make public to Natives what their rights may be under any Act . . . you have to see that that assurance is capable of being carried out to the letter.

This experience had been gained, he added, through his administration of the pass laws, and of compensation under the Native Labour Regulation Act. Keeping Africans away from lawyers and the legal system in pursuit of their claims was fundamental. As he complained, 'from time to time natives have had resort to lawyers to assist them in obtaining compensation in cases which had already been dealt with by the Department' (328, 333–4).

When a sick African worker succeeded in seeing a doctor and was actually diagnosed with phthisis, access to compensation was by no means automatic. Companies, Pritchard testified, 'consistently refused' to pay compensation for 'permanent total incapacitation' if the applicant was not fit to return home. It was, they contended, 'not the intention of the Act to compensate a native who might be on his deathbed in a sum of £30–50 for total incapacitation' (334). The doctor's certificate of diagnosis clearly stated the anticipated life expectancy and companies preferred to wait for death if it was a matter of a 'few months'. In 45 out of the 106 cases known to Pritchard the employer had limited its liability in this way (358, 336). The prominent Unionist Member of Parliament, Drummond Chaplin, did not find this unreasonable. If the man died, he said, there would be no cost of upkeep of a 'cripple', and if compensation were to be paid it would go to the heir, who under customary law need not have been a dependant. The £10 payment on death was adequate because 'it does not in the least follow in the case of the native family as in the European he would have dependants in the ordinary acceptation of the term, as it may be that his wife is remarried' (359–60). Any payments were made to the Director of Native Labour, who was the representative of the interests of the mine worker and thus any 'rights' given to African workers were also subject to administrative discretions. The statutory law preserved the common-law right to sue, provided compensation had not been accepted. But, Pritchard testified, he had been advised not to take this course because if the man died while the case was proceeding the expenses would be charged to his estate. There was no real bridge out of the statutory system into the common law. The provisions remained when the Act was revised in 1934. While African workers now came under the workers' compensation statute there was a separate process for their claims. It was the Native Affairs Department, Duncan writes, that sought to gain credit among Africans by being the conduit through which their payments passed, and which fought against provisions in the law that would give lawyers an avenue for intervention (1995: 68–9). Under sections 67 and 68 compensation was assessed by an official appointed by the Native Affairs Department and paid to a native commissioner and then 'the form and manner' in which payment was made was 'in the discretion of the officer'. In case of death, in contrast to the specific and complex provisions for whites, a sum was paid which 'the officer deems equitable in each case' having regard to the number of dependants and the degree of dependancy (section 71).

9

Marriage and race

Marriage: whiteness and the poor whites

It is hard to exaggerate the importance placed on the distinction between European and African marriage, and the insistence on a legal separation between the two forms. A basic way of expressing the difference was to emphasise the incompatibility between Christianity and paganism. As in many colonial situations the focus was on the gulf between monogamy and polygamy. We may gather some of the tone set for our period from the report of the major South African Native Affairs Commission of 1903–5. The 'one great element for the civilisation of the Natives', they wrote, 'is to be found in Christianity' (Cd 2399 1905: 41). 'Christianity', they averred, 'teaches that marriage is the sacred union of one man and one woman for life, and that fidelity to a single love is as much the duty of the man as the woman.' But polygamy was a central feature of African life. While it was an obstacle to the advance of Christianity, it was nonetheless better than the 'state of licentious confusion' that would have been the alternative. 'On analysis', they pronounced, 'the objections resolve themselves into the undeniable charge that the custom is essentially material and unchristian. The Commission has no wish to defend it and looks forward to the time when it shall have passed into oblivion. But no attempt to Christianise the heathen by compulsory legislation can be advised.' But if African marriage had to remain, it clearly had to be legally separated and distinguished from Christian marriage. The commission resolved that African marriage 'should not be accorded the same status as Christian marriage', but that it should be registered, and be the legal source of inheritance rights for children (41–2).

The view taken by the Native Affairs Commission that African marriage was not to be treated equally with European marriage was endorsed judicially by the Transvaal Supreme Court two years later in *Nalana v Rex 1907 TS 407*. While many of the decisions of Innes's court were to go back self-consciously to Roman-Dutch law, this was not one. The Chief Justice drew his justification from the English Chancery court decision *In re Bethell*, in which, said Innes, it had been ruled that a union formed in a foreign country was not a marriage 'unless it is formed on the same basis as marriages throughout Christendom' i.e. that it was monogamous. Africans in the Transvaal appeared to him to live legally in a foreign country. He continued: 'No union would be regarded as a marriage in this country, even though it were called, and might be recognised as a marriage elsewhere, if it were allowable for the parties to legally marry a second time during its existence.' The republican law of 1885 had recognised 'native laws and customs' as long as they were not 'inconsistent with the general principles of civilisation recognised in the civilised world'. Innes concluded, without citing further authority: '*To my mind* a polygamous marriage is inconsistent with the general principles of civilisation recognised in the civilised world' (408, 9; my emphasis). The consequences were far more than symbolic. The following year in *White v Pretoria Municipal Council 1908 TS 128* the court ruled that the African wife of an Asian was not entitled to live with him in the Asian area because, as their Islamic marriage was potentially polygamous, it was not a legal marriage, and she was not legally a wife.[1] We should note that this was a step away from the position taken in the republic's own courts in which Chief Justice Kotze had held that a man married to a woman by native law and custom was not a compellable witness, and that the onus was on the state to prove that such a marriage was in conflict with natural justice (*Marroko v State* quoted in *Kaba v Ntela 1910 TPD 964* at 968). As Innes said, again citing no authority, in *R v Mboko 1910 TPD, 445* at 448, Marroko's case

> seems to have held that the first wife of a man who was allowed to have more than one wife was his lawful wife. But it appears to me *the better principle* that when a man marries under a system which allows polygamy, his marriage is polygamous, and therefore is not recognised by this Court, whether he married one wife or two. (my emphasis)

Innes's determination to separate monogamous and polygamous marriages was capped in his Appellate Division pronouncement in *Seedat's*

---

[1] See also its decision in *Mashia Ebrahim v Mahomed Essop 1905 TS 59* when it ruled that polygamous Islamic marriages had no legal validity.

Executor v The Master (Natal) 1917 AD 302. It is hard to find any other case in the period covered by this study with a more racist outcome. It discriminated against most of the population of the country and cannot even be explained as being a part of maintaining white rule. Seedat was survived by two wives, both of whom he had married in India. His counsel, C. G. Mackeurton, argued that in the case of South Africa polygamous marriages could not be so entirely repellent or immoral as to render them not recognisable in law because African polygamy had been recognised by statute in the Natal code, and the Orange Free State law book. But Innes was determined. The South African statutes which recognised polygamy, he said,

> represent special concessions in favour of native tribes with whose laws and customs it was at the time undesirable to interfere. They do not in any way infringe upon the fundamental principles of the common law. And their existence does not indicate a tolerance of polygamy as part of the general South African system any more than the special recognition of Moham- medan marriages in India proves that polygamy is not repugnant to the common law of India. (308)

As in *Nalana*'s case Africans were defined as foreigners in relation to South African common law. Innes ruled that neither of Seedat's widows was a surviving spouse in South African law, and that even a monogamous union which contemplated the possibility of polygamy was invalid. Using strong language, and, characteristically, citing no authority, Innes wrote: 'No country is under an obligation to recognise a legal relation which is repugnant to the moral principles of its people. Polygamy vitally affects the nature of the most important relationship into which human beings can enter. It is reprobated by the majority of civilised peoples on the grounds of morality and religion' (307).

This decision excluded most of the marriages in the country. As Corder comments: 'There can be no disputing the fact that the vast majority of the Union's citizens both recognised and practised polygamy at that time' (Corder 1984: 133). In considering this decision we must also place it in the context of the long struggle against Asian immigration which had specifically targeted the spouses and children of Asian men by denying their legitimacy as family members. As a result of the intervention of the government of India and the imperial government, a settlement had been reached on a wide range of issues, and the Indian Relief Act of 1913 had

specifically allowed for the entry of the wife and child of a lawful monogamous marriage. The issue of what a monogamous marriage was was
therefore crucial to the fierce conflict over immigration. All of this was
well known to Innes who had been a member of appeal courts in the
Transvaal and the Union which had dealt with immigration cases. His
decision was a direct challenge to the settlement and the Act and it is in
this sense that it was understood by those affected. Keith wrote of the
right of entry given in the 1913 Act that 'there is no doubt that this clause
was intended to permit the entry of the wives of Indians who in fact were
monogamous' (1929: 207–8).

But the importance Innes had attached to white marriage was by no
means reflected in practice, nor, indeed, in the development of the
Roman-Dutch law. In *Green v Fitzgerald 1914 AD 88* the Appellate
Division removed some of the symbolic protection of Christian marriage
by declaring that the criminal sanctions for adultery had fallen into
desuetude. In the years immediately following on Union, magistrates'
reports noted the steady increase in the number of matrimonial cases.
Innes's high-flown pronouncements were far removed from what the cour
knew about actual marital practice. Desertion seemed to be the main
problem. In spite of the tenor of Innes's pronouncements South Africa
was an 'easy divorce' country (Hahlo and Kahn 1960: 425). No minimum
period was required for desertion by a spouse to be grounds for divorce. It
was therefore far easier to sue for divorce on these grounds than that of
adultery. An apparently increasing divorce rate appeared to many observers to be a sign of white society fraying at its edges. In 1912 the Cape
Supreme Court reported that members of the 'lower white' classes were
predominant in divorce cases (UG 44 1913: 10). One report said: 'In the
desertion cases the married life had invariably been of exceedingly short
duration, and in almost every case the husband had been the delinquent.
The desertions were deliberate and the deserters' whereabouts were
seldom traced. Paupers or *pro deo* petitions had increased . . . the majority
being from deserted wives' (11). By 1916 it was noted that the number of
divorces sought on the grounds of adultery were falling off, while those
citing desertion were rising. The 'question which involuntarily arises is in
how far collusion plays a part in changing the cause of action from
adultery to desertion?' (UG 39 1918: 6). Throughout the period magistrates continued to express concern at the increase in deserted spouses
and the rising divorce rates. The Appellate Division's elevated view of

Christian marriage also went along with a relaxed view of violence in white marriages. In *Oberholzer v Oberholzer 1921 AD 272* it found a serious assault which had caused a 'fearful' wife to leave her husband insufficient to establish cruelty. Innes remarked: 'Great sacrifices are made by women for their children . . . the Courts of Law should encourage rather than discourage attempts by spouses to forget the past' (273). (See too *Wentzel v Wentzel 1913 AD 55* at 59 where Solomon ruled that 'cruelty' alone was insufficient as a grounds for divorce unless it was 'of such a nature and so persistent as to make cohabitation . . . impossible'.)

In all of the public and legal discourses on marriage remarkably little attention was given to the complete legal subordination of white women married according to Roman-Dutch law. A white married woman was under the tutelage of her husband, was a legal minor and had no independent contractual capacity. The joint marital estate was administered by the husband, who had unfettered control over it. While these powers could be varied or excluded by a pre-nuptial contract, even such contracts had a limit, in that the law could not imagine a contract under which the husband was placed under the tutelage of the wife, even if he was insane. The husband's sole guardianship of the children could not be varied by pre-nuptial agreement. The first substantial account of women's legal position was given by I. A. Geffen (1928) who was the first woman barrister in South Africa. She averred that apart from tutelage in marriage and exclusion from the franchise women were 'in a favourable position under South African law' (xxxix), emphasising equal rights to divorce; the statutory suppression of immorality; and protection of health in industry. Her book was not concerned with African women at all. But it did not entirely escape notice that exclusion from the franchise, which until 1931, in addition to legal subjugation to their husbands, was another factor white and non-white women had in common, was of relevance to white women's legal disabilities. One witness before the Select Committee on the Enfranchisement of Women (SC 12 1926: 73) observed that there was a link between exclusion from the franchise and the inability of women to influence the marriage laws where their voice was 'absolutely ignored'.[2]

It was not the inequality of women but two other basic issues, both focused on race, that dominated the discourses in relation to the develop-

---

[2] The debate on women's franchise was conducted almost entirely in terms of how to exclude coloured and African women from the vote should it be extended to white women.

ment of family law, and related welfare and children's law. One, as we have seen, was the clear distinction that was to be drawn between European and other forms of marriage. The other was the 'health' of the white population as a whole, in the sense of its reproductive vigour, and the strength of its family life. These were constant matters of concern against a background of frequently expressed fears about the balance of population between whites and others. Magistrates' reports reflect the conscious anxious eye that was kept on population figures and on comparative birth and death rates. One Free State Magistrate's remark captures the atmosphere of many: 'As every native adult female was married the native population was increasing at a greater rate than the white. The native wars and famines which in the olden days had reduced the native population were now a thing of the past and the native continued growing in numbers to an alarming extent' (UG 44 1913: 219).

Consternation about family-law issues was blended with worries about the poor-white question, as it was poor whites who were seen as the weak point in the white race, and these concerns fused with the issue of the demarcation of civilisation itself. Merriman wrote to the former President of the Orange Free State, Marthinus Steyn, in 1912: 'It is the crumbling away of the lower fringe of our white population that makes the great danger – not the slow but still evident, gradual elevation of the non-Europeans' (Lewsen 1969: 226). The Supreme Court's insistence on a most elevated view of Christian marriage was, as we shall see, by no means a reflection of the facts of family life in the white community. We must, therefore, try to understand the relationship between the Supreme Court's emphasis on the sanctity of monogamy, which was somewhat different from the more relaxed view of the sanctity of marriage taken by the Roman-Dutch law itself, and the facts of poor-white life.

In the years after Union the poor whites attracted strong disapproval from state officials for their improvidence, thriftlessness, unwillingness to work and failure to support their families. In 1912 the magistrate in Port Elizabeth reported 'a noticeably increasing tendency on the part of people of the poorer class to disregard their family obligations and throw the burden of the support of their relations on the public funds' (UG 44 1913: 73). The education of poor-white children was being neglected. Many were taken from school and put to work in unskilled occupations by their parents, and thus rendered permanently unfit for the struggle against blacks in the labour market (74).

There was some indication too of concern that children of poor whites were marrying too young, and calls for the raising of the marriage age. (With parental consent, a boy could under Roman-Dutch law marry at fourteen, and a girl at twelve.) A Free State magistrate wrote in 1916: 'How the majority of them live is a mystery yet to be unfolded. Many young men earn enough to support themselves, but their first thought is to get married, for which their means are totally inadequate . . . before long the Government will have to provide medical attendance for wives and children' (UG 36 1918: 44). We have seen in the development of the commercial law a drive towards a market model, excluding equity, favouring lenders over borrowers, and intent on providing only a minimum of state regulation of the commercial economy. But the pressures of the facts of poor-white life, many of whom suffered indirectly under this regime, especially in relation to credit and debt, provided a counter-movement in the law and a drive for greater state intervention. We shall see also that the proclamations of the benefits of a minimum of state intervention did not apply to the labour market. Nonetheless the provision of welfare in place of family support was slow in coming. It ran counter not only to the material interests of the dominant among South Africa's whites, but it was against the ideological grain of the social Darwinist civil religion of the imperial ruling classes, as well as the ruling tenets of the Calvinist religion of the poor themselves. The demoralisation and unwillingness to work of poor whites was frequently commented on, but gradually there emerged the view that it was the next generation that had to be saved. 'They marry and inter-marry,' wrote the magistrate for Steynsburg in 1914, 'and bring into the world big families and these children grow up uneducated and very soon become a burden on the State. They are slothful and indolent.' 'Redemption' through education had to be sought, 'the education which teaches men to hanker after truth, thrift, honesty, cleanliness, etc., and which brings with it quicker understanding of the duty of man to man and to the state' (UG 28 1915: 75).

The shortcomings of the white rural population attracted much comment. Frequent reports testified to their failure to educate their children adequately, and compared this with the threatening willingness of blacks to take advantage of education. One Cape magistrate commented that the 'figleaf of not being able to find servants, is but too often made use of as an excuse for keeping children from schools' (UG 36 1918: 50). Another wrote of the 'remschoen [homemade hide shoes] element' of parents who were totally unable to provide for their children but refused to send them to free church-run boarding houses, preventing them from getting an education and 'causing them to become poor whites'. The remedy seemed clear: compulsory education for white children. Another magistrate found the poor whites 'thriftless and wanting in energy'; another that they were 'lazy, ambitionless, exceedingly prolific and eking out a parasitical livelihood'. Another wrote that the 'poor white class have two inherent characteristics, indolence and false pride'. Not surprisingly one reported: 'The poor whites in this district appear to have a dread of the Magistrate.' There was more than one hint of low sexual morals, and the possibility of prostitution. 'Judging from the complaints made at his office', one magistrate had 'reason to think that illicit intercourse is carried on somewhat extensively but whether this is directly attributable to poverty, he finds difficult to say' (UG 36 1918: 67). It is important to grasp the tone of the comments and the strength and depth of the adverse moral judgements that were made. There is little trace in the state's voice at this time of sympathy or generosity. The fault belonged to the poor whites, theirs was the deficiency and theirs the true failure to be the kind of white men they ought to be. For what was seen to be imperilled by their failings was the status and future of whites as a whole. Magistrates were alarmed by the tendency of poor whites to live among non-whites, even to work for them (67). Without the intervention of the state, the rural social formation made no necessary distinction between landless whites and landless blacks. Many tended to be in the same economic position, either as labour tenants or tenants sowing on shares. Farmers often found whites working on shares as unsatisfactory a use for their land as having black tenants, and ejected *bywoners* (white tenants) who then drifted into the towns in a state of pauperism (UG 35 1920: 103).

In both urban and rural areas it was necessary for the state to take action to prise poor whites and blacks apart. The poor whites would not, as another magistrate wrote, 'take up any regular work or submit them-selves to any sort of restraint or discipline' (UG 36 1918: 68). And, as another said, helping poor-white families did not necessarily improve matters as 'the more charitable persons do for these children the less their parents bother about them, and the more they expect from other people' (ibid.). The hostility and contempt felt led towards thinking in terms of the kind of solutions so frequently suggested in relation to blacks, the combination of a wish to exclude and compulsion to work.

In 1913 the Report of the Select Committee on European Employment and Labour Conditions (SC 9 1913) noted how poor whites sank into 'a demoralising and corrupt intercourse with non-Europeans'. Its remedy was harsh. There should be for poor whites, it said, 'a strengthening and enforcement of the vagrancy law, under which anyone found guilty of repeated begging or who should have no lawful means of subsistence, should be liable to deportation to, and detention in, a labour colony for a fixed term' (xvi). To this end, it suggested, labour colonies on the model of those in Belgium, Holland, Germany and Denmark should be studied. 'The labour colonies would in fact be adult reformatories or houses of detention' (ibid.). Magistrates around the Union continued to urge compulsion as the means of getting poor whites to work, though their advice was sometimes sceptically treated by central government. The magistrate for Zeerust reported in the war years that the poorer classes were without ambition or responsibility, and lived from hand to mouth. 'The Magistrate was rather drastic in his suggestions how [*sic*] these people were to be treated in future; he thought they should be put on the land and made to work with overseers appointed by the Government, reminding one of the Egyptians with their whips' (UG 36 1918: 60). These were precisely the terms in which unemployed black urban dwellers were discussed, and in which they were legislated for in 1923. Different remedies were eventually sought for whites.[3]

Running through the approach to family and welfare was a constant view that people needed to be more self-sufficient, and look to family ties for support rather than to the state. Roman-Dutch law recognised reciprocal duties of support between husband and wife and between ascendants and descendants according to need and ability to pay. It also recognised a duty of support to brothers and sisters. But its precise extent was unclear as regards the age up to which support of children was mandatory, and in relation to the duties owed to illegitimate and stepchildren, half-siblings and spousal relatives (Hahlo and Kahn 1960: 349). These common-law duties were supplemented by a series of virtually identical Deserted Wives and Children Protection statutes in the Cape and

---

[3] One might also note that interference in the market as between white and white in rural land holding was not a solution adopted to deal with poor-white landlessness. One Cape magistrate's report in 1920 said: 'Rich men were getting richer and buying up more land, so that young farmers were unable to obtain land. The Magistrate thinks that the Government might well consider whether the time has not come to limit the extent of ground that might be held by one man' (UG 35 1920: 31).

Natal in the 1890s, and the conquered colonies in 1903 (351 note 39; UG 38 1937: 46). These reaffirmed the common-law duties and gave jurisdiction to magistrates' courts to enforce them through criminal proceedings in the case of failure to support a wife or children under fifteen. But in the absence of broader welfare provisions the magistracy found that this did not go far enough. In 1912 the Johannesburg magistrate suggested that the provisions in the Deserted Wives and Children Ordinance of 1903 should be extended to provide for the support of parents by children. He commented that he

> was constantly meeting with cases of old couples quite past work, who gave a long list of sons and daughters scattered over the country, none of whom were contributing to their support. While there was no doubt of their legal liability to do so, such liability could only be enforced by civil action and the parents did not generally have the necessary means for the purpose. (UG 44 1913: 121)

The principles of the Roman-Dutch law were perceived to be of little use in these situations. The failure of the poor to look after themselves and their relatives became a generalised complaint. The magistrate for Elliot reported in 1914 that his district was 'saddled with a considerable number of poor whites, improvident and thriftless persons who show a marked disposition to disregard their family obligations and responsibilities and throw the burden of the support of their relatives on the public funds' (UG 28 1915: 72). In 1919 the magistrate for the Cape district of Montagu 'drew attention to the growing impression among the public that when the poorer class of person became old and decrepit they had simply to be taken by their relatives to the Magistrate and handed over to him for the Government account' (UG 35 1920: 55). From Oudtshoorn the magistrate wrote: 'On the one side there were people living in affluent circumstances, and on the other, others living in extreme poverty, even among blood relations, and the affluent seemed to feel no obligation to assist the poor. An ugly feature was the number of cases met with in which parental or filial obligations were entirely ignored' (ibid.).

In 1921, the increasing problem of desertion and non-maintenance by fathers led to the institution of pensions payable to supporting mothers as preferable to the removal of destitute children to institutions. But the general strategy of emphasising family networks as the prime means of support remained. As late as 1937 a committee of enquiry affirmed the spousal duty to support not only a spouse and children under nineteen, but also indigent ascendants and spouse's ascendants, as well as adoptive parents, and full and half-siblings (UG 38 1937: 46ff.).

The marriage patterns of the poor whites also caused concerns of a special kind, which reflected the overall anxieties about racial matters. In 1919 one of the Transvaal magistrates called for the prohibition of marriage between first cousins on the grounds that the greater number of children born were defective (UG 36 1918: 97). A Transvaal magistrate reported that among the poor whites there were 'families in which a large percentage of the children were blind, deformed, or otherwise incapable of earning a livelihood, and such sooner or later became a burden on the State' (UG 35 1920: 103). Behind this was a fear of the effects on the quality of the white race. The magistrate from Willowmore in the Cape reported of the poor whites in his district that 'on account of want of intercourse with the outside world, a system of close relationship through intermarriage had reduced the mental status of many'. The resulting 'degeneration' left many 'worse off than the coloured people' (57).

The image of coloured degradation was, in fact, one of the most powerful available to white South African eyes. Coloureds were described by the 1937 commission as a 'socially submerged population'. Popular belief put this down to inherent racial inadequacies, though the Commission was non-committal. They said that 'limited scientific knowledge of the relative importance of heredity and environment makes it impossible to state, with any exactness, to what extent their position is due to innate tendencies' and to what extent to conditions (UG 35 1937: 18). The commission dwelt on the instability of coloured family life; the relative infrequency of marriage; the frequent desertions; the loose relations between parent and child; and the absence of family discipline. There was a high percentage of illegitimate births, and an 'atmosphere of drunkenness and crime' (19–20). In the case of urban Africans similar observations of conditions could be contrasted with a moral tribal state the laws of which could be forced upon Africans, but for coloureds there was no traditional legal regime for the state to fall back on. In the Cape particularly the coloured population represented an immediate moral threat and moral opposite. But remedies for these circumstances were not the prime concern: they were invoked in official discourses as an example of the degeneracy into which whites might fall and from which they must be protected.

Defence of the white family, and that of the 'race' as a whole, were connected. Illegitimate births placed white babies at risk; broken families put the futures of white children in jeopardy. There were some institutional lines of defence, like the Infant Life Protection Act. But there were considerable difficulties in practice. The provisions of the welfare Acts, like those of the labour regulation and other laws, often required a far greater administrative apparatus than that which actually existed. Following the English model there was reliance on a voluntary organisation. Much depended on the Society for the Protection of Child Life. It was the society that had to take care of children removed from their parents or guardians, as there was no state-run 'place of safety' as provided for in the Act.

The disruption in urbanising societies and the perceived failings of family in respect of children made legislative provision to deal with children 'in need of care' a common feature of this period. The Union 1913 Children's Protection Act, which consolidated and extended the previous laws, was based on the British statute of 1908, and incorporated the definitions of neglected children and those in need of care which were common parlance in statutes throughout the empire. But what is significant about the South African legislation was the ways in which these definitions were to work. Those children who were identified as being in need of care were those who inhabited the racial borderlands. The placing of white children with non-white foster parents and the mixing of children of different colours in city streets and rural kraals were identified as the prime situations requiring protective intervention. There were also many reports over the years (UG 35 1920: 74) of white illegitimate children having been placed in the care of coloured women, and having to be 'rescued' and placed in suitable institutions. Once again state action had to be taken to maintain the boundaries of whiteness. Magistrates commented on the uncontrolled mixing of poor-white rural children with blacks, but it was the urban situation that attracted most attention. As in other areas separation of the races was seen to be the foremost means of remedy. Those concerned with child welfare earnestly called for residential segregation. Otherwise, as the Secretary of the Children's Aid Society wrote, whites 'assumed the colour of their surroundings . . . and became submerged' (Chisholm 1989: 118). The Act provided both for the placing of children in institutions such as industrial schools and for their apprenticeship. While the aim was to prepare children in general for the rigours of labour, the statute in operation provided a built-in mechanism of differentiation and segregation, as compulsory apprenticeship to white employers became the major way of redirecting non-white children.

In 1934 the government began a process of review of children's law (UG 38 1937). Among the subjects it considered was whether it was desirable to change the judicial model for consideration of cases involving children, 'to dispense with criminal procedure in dealing with . . . delinquents, and instead to deal with them paternally' (5). It based its discussion of possible children's court procedures on an informed review of international practices starting with the International Penal and Penitentiary Commission in 1910, and taking into consideration the English Children and Young Persons Act of 1933, and a 1935 League of Nations survey of special children's courts. This discussion is worth noting precisely because of its careful and informed discussion of appropriate legal procedures as embodied in legal reforms in countries such as Denmark, the USA and the UK. It points to the coexistence of different pockets of legality in the South African legal system. The commission noted the difference in principle between those countries that operated less rigid forms of criminal procedure for children's cases, but in which the 'underlying principle of criminal justice remains unchanged', and those, like the United States, where the jurisdiction exercised over children was 'generally chancery or equity and not criminal in nature'. In the latter emphasis was not laid on the particular act of which the young offender was accused, but on 'the social facts and circumstances'. The purpose of the proceedings was not punishment but 'correction of conditions, care and protection' (13). (The commission also embarked on careful dissections of the age of legal responsibility, and of the problems involved in holding parents responsible for the acts of their children (16; 22).)

The extended and jurisprudentially sophisticated discussion also draws our attention to the gap between theory and practice in children's law, as noted by the commission itself. In 1935 in South Africa nearly one-third of the children dealt with by the courts were whipped, and just over 2 per cent benefited from 'educational treatment' (27). On page 52 of their fifty-four-page report the commission got around to 'Non-European aspects of the problem'. The draft bills, they pointed out, made no distinctions on racial grounds, but were to be administered with discretion because of 'special social circumstances' affecting non-Europeans. In the matter of general principle the commission reflected the prevailing view. 'There is a tendency to require the State to assume more and more responsibility for social work and to relieve private effort of its share,' they wrote. 'This tendency should . . . be resisted. Child welfare and other forms of social work should represent a joint enterprise between the State and private agencies' (10). Among 'non-Europeans' the 'large proportion . . . lives in extreme poverty' and were subject to 'social, legislative, educational and vocational restrictions . . . These factors account to a considerable extent for the inadequacy of the measures taken by non-European communities for the upliftment of their own members' (52). There was a 'striking insufficiency' of children's institutions for non-Europeans, a need which could only be met by the state. Furthermore the probation service was barely operative for these groups.

> It is evident that the dearth of non-European child welfare services, the inadequacy of probation services for non-Europeans and the very restricted provision of certified institutions greatly limit the extent to which the provisions relating to children 'in need of care' can be applied. It is not surprising, therefore, that a very high percentage of non-European juvenile cases are dealt with according to criminal procedure and are disposed of by sentences such as whipping, imprisonment and reformatory treatment. Apprenticeship to farmers is used very extensively in the case of Coloured children in the Cape. (53)

Marriage, race and racial definition

In his consideration in 1927 of the 'five fears' of South Africa, Lord Olivier listed as third that white South Africans 'fear that white civilisation may be infected, or the morale of its European stocks deteriorated by the mere induction of the proximity of increasing numbers of natives . . . White people in contact with backward races are demoralised and deteriorated' (1927: 213). The fourth fear was the fear of miscegenation. He wrote:

> The trekking Boers, isolated from opportunity, and by universal juvenile marriages, avoided such relations; but the early marriages and very large families of the Boers have resulted in a progeny of Poor Whites which is a more undesirable element in the South African population than are the coloured people begotten by their own progenitors before they quitted the Cape. Many white men cannot, and will not, marry into such prospects. (220)

It is in the context of the concerns about poor-white degeneration, a double degeneration of physical inbreeding and sinking below the colour line, both of which were seen to pose threats to the 'white race', that we can consider the question of miscegenation and mixed marriages. In the years following Union there was no quick consolidation of marriage laws. An attempt was promptly made, as might have been expected, in 1911. The government introduced a Marriage Bill to parliament which contained no racial barriers, but withdrew it after it proved to be an issue on which there were basic dissents. In the Transvaal interracial marriage was not possible, but, even there, was recognised as valid if entered into elsewhere. Many Transvaal members were reluctant to relinquish the racial barrier, and some wanted it extended. The matter was promptly dropped, and a Union-wide ban on interracial marriage was not imposed until nearly forty years later.

Interracial sexual relations, outside marriage, were, however, subject to wider prohibitions. During the South African War the growth in the number of white prostitutes and their use by black men created concern 'that the white women of the country should not . . . be brought into contempt in the estimation of native or coloured males' (UG 30 1939: 14; see too Matthews 1921). This concern led to new legislation in all four colonies rendering both white women and black men liable for severe penalties in these circumstances. The Natal Native Commission of 1906/7 gave its attention to the issue of interracial sexual relations. Concubinage and indiscriminate intercourse between white and black, they said, 'most urgently require to be forbidden by law'. They warned first of further black unrest if sexual relations between white men and black women continued to be allowed. 'No nation', they wrote, 'can tolerate members of an alien race tampering with their women and nothing is more calculated than the debauchment of girls to stretch the endurance of even the most submissive people to the breaking point.' On the white side, they found that 'we are distinctly losing in moral reputation and at the same time producing a harvest of legal, social and political problems by an ever increasing number of bastards'. There was a 'positive duty' on the government to 'excise this evil, which like a canker is insidiously destroying our reputation' (quoted in UG 39 1913: 8). Adding to the alarm the Natal Police Commissioner reported gloomily in 1911 that there was an increase in the number of white women cohabiting with black men (UG 62 1912: 18). Neither the existing marriage legislation nor the new laws on interracial prostitution addressed the far more common situation in which white men lived with black women out of wedlock. This was often associated by the authorities with life in the criminal underworld (59). The whole question was considered at some length in the context of the Assaults Commission in 1913 which took an apocalyptic view of the subject. 'The gravity of the matter', they wrote, 'cannot be over-estimated . . . circumstances such as these must in the end have disastrous results as regards the influence of the white race.' Not only interracial sex outside marriage, but interracial marriage, ought, they thought, to be forbidden. (Only the chairman, Melius de Villiers, dissented.) It was 'imperative that steps should be taken to terminate a condition of things . . . [that] perpetuates and increases the dimensions of grave political and social problems' (UG 39 1913: 8–9).

Yet despite their firm view there was no legislative action on the matter of intercourse between white men and black women until 1927, and none forbidding intermarriage until 1949. In 1926 the Minister of Justice, Tielman Roos, introduced an Immorality Bill into parliament which introduced an important new principle into existing law on the subject.[4] While existing provincial laws punished black men for sexual acts with white women, the new law would punish white men for sexual acts with black women. While the debate was dominated by the expression of views about the need for racial purity there were also strong objections to the effects on 'our own sons' (Hansard 3/3/26 and 23/3/26). Members pointed out the potential severity of punishment for young white men, the effect on their futures and the possibility of blackmail. Boys, it was said, should be able to plead enticement by black women as a defence, and there was strong objection taken to the idea of the evidence of black women convicting white men.

In 1927 parliament passed the Immorality Act. During the debate there were calls for bans on interracial marriage which Roos answered by suggesting that the new law would help move public opinion in this direction. In the meantime, it was said, the new law created the undesirable situation in which persons could escape punishment by marrying (Hansard 2/2/27). It does not appear that the new law was easily enforceable. J. T. Jabavu noted in his evidence to the Mixed Marriages Commis-

---

[4] An understanding of mood can again be instructive. One National Party member recalling the minister's laughter at criticism of the new law wrote that 'in some things Mr Roos was inclined to be rather frivolous' (Reitz 1946: 116).

sion that the Act was 'unworkable: no one gets arrested, though there are . . . many instances of illegitimate births among native women due to white men' (UG 30 1939: 20). Public controversy on the issue of mixed marriage continued against the background of anxiety about the poor whites, and a new determination among the white ruling class to uplift them. In 1936 and 1937 non-government members attempted to introduce legislation prohibiting interracial marriage into parliament. In 1937 the major government enquiry into the Cape coloured population was published (UG 54 1937). The commissioners were concerned with racial mixing, and noted an 'increasing tendency' for coloureds to 'pass over the line'. By this means 'an infusion of coloured blood into the European group is being brought about' (30–1). But they thought that the claim in Findlay's booklet, *Miscegenation* (1936), that one-third of the 'alleged' white population had 'some degree of non-European strain' was exaggerated. Responding to the political pressure for the legal prohibition of intermarriage they noted that in the period 1931 to 1935 under half of 1 per cent of European marriages crossed the colour line. Prohibition would therefore have no significant effect and there would be 'insuperable difficulties' with regard to 'borderline cases'. They recommended against a legal prohibition.

In 1938 a government Commission of Enquiry into Mixed Marriages was established. Its report (UG 30 1939) was to recommend legislation prohibiting such marriages. The concern was not as a result of a rising incidence of such marriages. While figures were not available as to their numbers before 1923, when legislation first required information about race to be recorded on marriage registers, the figures for the second half of the 1920s and early 1930s show a low and falling incidence of interracial marriage (between 1925 and 1931 the numbers declined from 133 to 85; from .9 per cent to .5 per cent; in 1937 there were 101 such marriages, or .4 per cent: UG 30 1939: 26). Nonetheless, the commission, in the course of both a historical and contemporary survey, reported that 'a very large portion of the white population not only deprecates, but condemns, mixed marriages and that, with many, the feeling has transcended the bounds of what is ordinarily known as public opinion and has become an article of faith' (32). Given the alleged strength of white public opinion, which itself acted as a deterrent to such marriages, was a legal prohibition necessary? The commission fortified itself with detailed references to the thirty American states which had found such legislation necessary in spite of strong public opinion, and on the failure of public opinion alone to eliminate it in the Union. It was 'probably for the reason that a sentiment of that kind tends to operate feebly, if at all, among the lower strata of the community' (ibid.). This was the core of the question. The absence of effect of the growing strength of public opinion in South Africa was the result of severe economic depression which forced poor whites to turn '*blindly* for the larger cities' (my emphasis). Having no means they were forced to

> the cheaper quarters of the town. Considerable numbers came to live in this way among people of colour. Living with the coloured classes in their areas and associating with them in the same work establishes a species of equality which soon eliminates the differences formerly recognised and increases the likelihood of intermarriage . . . Similar results may be expected as the consequence of Europeans and non-Europeans of opposite sexes working together in factories and other undertakings. (Ibid.)

The commission proposed 'segregation by means of housing schemes and separation of the sexes of different races at their places of work' as one means of dealing with the problem (34).

The family life of poor whites was not only a social and potentially political weak link but also a biological one. Mixed marriages, said the majority of the commission, can 'assist in producing people who can pass as Europeans. They lead in this way to the infiltration of non-European blood into the European population . . . There are risks attached to the continuation of this process of infiltration, both with regard to racial and social heredity' (33). The commission noted the extensive American legislation forbidding mixed marriages (which it documented at length) and observed that 'far from becoming obsolete, it is constantly being added to and amended' (37). It recommended adoption Union wide of the 'wisely conceived and simply planned' (35) two old Transvaal laws which did not expressly prohibit mixed marriages but had simply provided separately for marriages between whites, and between non-whites, and had contained no legal possibility of conducting a valid interracial marriage.

Laws prohibiting interracial sex and marriage required consideration of how to test and prove that a person was not white. It is of importance that the South African legislation did not adopt the pattern of American state legislation in which the general pattern was to specify descent to the third generation or one-eighth or more of non-white blood as defining the prohibited categories. Legislative definition of 'Native' had varied from colony to colony, and, within colonies, from act to act (see the discussion in Cd 2399 1903–5: 9–10). The Cape definitions aimed at indigenous inhabitants. The Glen Grey Act proffered 'Kafirs, Fingoes, Basutos, Zulus, Hottentots, Bushmen and the like'. The Liquor Law of 1898 said 'any Kafir, Fingo, Basuto, Damara, Hottentot, Bushman or Koranna', though this definition, lacking a supplementary catch-all, was taken by the courts to exclude all those not mentioned. Cape Act no. 40 of 1902 had a longer list, and a catch-all: 'any Kafir, Fingo, Zulu, Mosuto, Damara, Hottentot, Bushman, Bechuana, Koranna or any other aboriginal Native of South or Central Africa'. But it also indicated a political rather than a racial preoccupation by excluding 'any Native while serving in any of His Majesty's ships and while in uniform'. The Natal law of 1888 distinguished different 'Natives' for different purposes. For being subject to the operation of Native law 'the word Native shall mean all members of the aboriginal races or tribes of Africa south of the Equator' but not including Griquas or Hottentots. However, for the purposes of the liquor law, Griquas and Hottentots were 'Natives'. While neither the Cape nor Natal definitions of 'Native' included coloureds or Asians, the Transvaal laws were simpler and more inclusive. In 1895 Law no. 28 the definition was in terms of racial descent: 'any person of any kind belonging to or being a descendant of any Native races of South Africa whatever'. The aim of the Transvaal law was to discriminate between whites and all persons of colour. To make matters even more explicit the following year it clarified that coloured person signified 'any African or Asiatic Native or "coloured Americans" or St Helena person, Coolie or Chinaman'. The following year it affirmed that the word 'Native' applied to all 'coloured people' and 'coloured races of South Africa'. Even though the inclusion of coloureds in the definition had been one of the overt differences between Britain and the Republic in the period leading to War in 1899, the first British proclamation on the matter, the pass laws for the conquered colony, took the same position. The definition was persons 'belonging to any of the aboriginal tribes or races of Africa south of the Equator and every . . . person, one of whose parents belongs to any such race or tribe as aforesaid'. After political pressure from London this was amended to provide that both parents must be of an aboriginal race. In the Orange Free State, and the Orange River Colony, 'Native' explicitly included 'all coloured persons, and all who, in accordance with law or custom are called coloured persons, or are treated as such, of whatever race or nationality they may be'.

Surveying these differences the Lagden Commission preferred the view taken by the former Republics, and they urged a broad definition for future adoption. It was, they found, 'a most perplexing problem'. It was 'notorious' that there had been much racial mixing; that 'many of the so-called coloured people' had by their 'industry and intelligence and self respect, raised themselves to a high standard'. They recommended 'that the word "Native" shall be taken to mean an aboriginal inhabitant of Africa, south of the Equator, and to include half-castes and their descendants by Natives'. This would appear to indicate that 50 per cent or more of African blood made a person a 'Native', but that 25 per cent or less did not. There remained the problem of the special meaning given to the word 'native'. The Witwatersrand division of the Supreme Court ruled soon after Union that white Syrians were natives of Asia and therefore subject to the same restrictions that were placed on Asians in the Transvaal. But the Appellate Division adopted colour not birthplace as the test and said that Syrians were not Asians in the South African sense. The word 'native', they ruled, had acquired a secondary meaning in South Africa and was confined to the coloured races. In construing vague expressions the court had to ascertain their popular sense. Otherwise, said Innes, Jews would be relegated to locations and compelled to carry permits (*Moses Gandur v Rand Townships Registrar 1913 AD 250*).[5]

The courts, even when given statutory definitions, had to decide whether they applied to the people who came before them, and they did not opt for descent tests, but for a test of physical appearance. Innes CJ confronted the issue robustly when faced with a statute in the Transvaal limiting the municipal franchise to white British subjects. Though the law contained no definition, he said 'white' meant of unmixed European descent. How to go about proof? 'We all know in this country what an admixture of coloured blood means, and the appearances which prove the presence of such blood; and when we find one in whom these appearances are present, then unless it is clearly proved that his ancestors were of European descent we would usually be guided by his appearance' (*Swarts and Appel v Pretoria Town Council 1905 TS 621* at 622). This was the

---

[5] There could be complications. The Transvaal Supreme Court ruled both that Asians were 'coloureds' and therefore forbidden to walk on the pavements, and that 'coloureds' were not Asians and could therefore not live in Asian 'bazaars'.

approach taken by the new Appellate Division in 1911 when it supported the exclusion of coloured children from Cape schools. The phrase 'of European parentage and extraction' meant, said the Chief Justice, Lord de Villiers, unmixed European extraction. It was however 'fortunately, unnecessary to decide how far back in a person's pedigree it would be allowable to go in order to decide whether his European extraction is unmixed . . . if it is not obvious from the appearance of the child that he or she is of other than European descent' (*Moller v Kiemoes School Committee 1911 AD 635*). Subsequently courts refined their methods of observation of appearance, to include 'the particular observation of certain physical characteristics such as facial features, hair, fingernails, stature, and pigmentation' as well as 'enquiry into the habits, associations and mode of living'. Only if all this was inconclusive was there investigation into descent (UG 30 1939: 36 and *R v Sonnefeld 1926 TPD 597*; *Anderson v Green 1932 NPD 241*).[6]

Disputes about racial identity could arise in a number of circumstances. In the Transvaal after the war cases arose concerning the racial status of persons as they tried to avoid discriminatory legislation about residence, trade and political status. Other circumstances were in the application of native law, or the punishment of persons by a chief, when it was often of advantage to a person to get the court to declare that he was not a native. In *Strydom v Sisila NHC 26/2/01* the court held that the son of a European and an African woman was not an African. What is of particular interest is the range of issues canvassed in arriving at the decision, which went beyond the appearance test that Innes applied in the Transvaal. If, it was argued, Roman-Dutch law applied, then, because the child was illegitimate, he took the status of his mother, and was therefore an African. Justinian was quoted to the effect that the illegitimate issue of slaves were slaves. Another argument put forward that the person was obviously not African as he lived in a square house. To one judge the

---

[6] Racial determinations were not, of course, usually made by the courts, but by informal administrative decisions. We may consider the process on the Witwatersrand described by the Director of Native Labour. Whenever there was doubt the matter was referred by the police or an employer to a committee consisting of the pass officer, his assistant and the police fingerprint expert. They took into account appearance, descent and manner of living: 'The decisions of this Committee, *which has no statutory authority*, are usually accepted by the parties' (UG 3 1934: 31; my emphasis). Similarly Nelson Mandela has recalled a case in which a magistrate determined a man's race by an observation of the slope of his shoulders (Mandela 1994: 141). It is in such extra-legal processes, involving curious 'expertise', as much as in the elaborate statutory definitions, that we must situate our understanding of the legal culture.

question of legitimacy was crucial. But while social criteria were raised, in the end the court concluded that to say that an illegitimate child was of the same race as its mother was to strain the meaning of the rules about illegitimacy.

South African statutes after Union continued to have differing definitions according to the administrative purposes of the Act. The Land Act of 1913 and the Urban Areas Act of 1923 defined 'Native' as any person who was a member of an aboriginal race or tribe of Africa. The Native Taxation Act used this definition but also included coloured persons living in African areas under the same conditions as Africans, that is, a socio-economic test including habits of life and associations rather than a racial test. Similarly the Native Administration Act included in the definition of 'Native' any person residing in 'Native Areas' under the same condition as a 'Native'. The Native Appeal Court held, in effect, in 1930 that the Act had intended a social not a racial definition (*Tshongwe v Tshongwe NAC 1930*; cited in Stafford 1935: 11). The presiding judge, Stubbs, ruled that an extended interpretation must be given, declaring an illegitimate child of a white and African, who was living as an African, to be one. In several other decisions it was affirmed that legitimacy affected racial status (12). The Representation of Natives Act of 1936, the purpose of which was to remove the African voters in the Cape from the voters' roll, contained sweeping definitions of a socio-economic kind. These included, after a definition by descent, any person 'desirous of being regarded' as a native; anyone 'by general recognition and repute a native'; anyone who 'follows in his ordinary daily mode of life the habits of a native'; anyone who used a native language as his 'customary and natural mode of expression' and anyone who 'associates generally with natives under native conditions'.

But defining a coloured was more difficult. In a supreme example of political pragmatism in Hertzog's Coloured Persons Rights Bill of 1926 (which was not enacted) whether people with one African parent were coloured or African depended on whether they had been born before or after the law was enacted. In the case of coloureds what was needed was a definition that distinguished coloureds from both whites and Africans. One comprehensive effort was made in the Pensions Act of 1925 which tried to define a coloured as someone who was not anyone else. This was quite complicated. A coloured person was any person who is neither white nor . . .

a) a Turk or a member of a race or tribe whose national or ethnical home is Asia, nor
b) a member of an Aboriginal race or tribe of Africa nor
c) a Hottentot, Bushman or Korana,
d) a person residing in a native location under the same conditions as a native
e) an American negro

and includes 'a member of the race or class commonly called Cape Malays' or 'Griquas'. But three out of the six members of the Cape Coloured Commission felt the need to provide a positive definition of a coloured, one in terms other than 'exclusion'. A coloured was, they suggested, a person who was not a member of an aboriginal race but one 'in whom the presence of coloured blood can be established with at least reasonable certainty'. But how? First 'from knowledge of the genealogy of the person during the last three or four generations'. Secondly, 'by ordinary direct recognition of characteristic physical features (such as colour of skin, nature of hair, and facial and bodily form), by an observer familiar with these characteristics'. A footnote qualified the word 'recognition'. 'Exact anthropological measurements would no doubt be far more satisfactory theoretically, but would, in the main, be far too cumbersome for ordinary use' (UG 35 1937: 10).

Scientific racism was certainly present in South African discourses (see Dubow 1995). Leading scientists linked racial mixing with degeneration, feeble-mindedness, decay and hereditary disease (131–40). Perhaps the questions to be asked should not be why the laws were enacted but why it took so long for laws forbidding interracial marriage, and also why the tests of race remained the pragmatic ones of appearance and way of life? For there were other examples before South African legislators. There were the American laws embodying racial tests. And closer to home the far more drastic example of German South West Africa. In 1908, after the rise of the eugenic movement in Germany and the formation of the Society of Race Hygiene, not only was racial intermarriage forbidden in that territory, but all such existing marriages were annulled and the Germans involved deprived of their civil rights. In the 1930s the Nuremburg laws forbade not only sexual relations between Jews and Germans, but intermarriage as well. Racial testing for these purposes was the responsibility of a major scientific institute. The elaborate system of 'Health Courts' is described in Lifton's *Nazi Doctors* (1986). In 1937 it was decided that all mixed-race children in Germany were to be sterilised (Muller-Hill 1988). South African law used different mechanisms, and for different ends: legal definitions of race remained haphazard and pragmatic; political rather than scientific.

The alleged strength of feeling about race mixing took a long time to affect the law. In his relatively restrained, erudite and in the context of the times liberal account of policies towards Africans, Brookes wrote of those who had

> committed high treason against their colour and white prestige by having immoral relations with Native women. It is not only a question of morality. Supposing we concede the Epicurean rule of life, yet, what is the paltry animal pleasure of a few individuals against the whole future of white and black South Africa? . . . It should be punishable by imprisonment and lashes. (1924: 167)

Yet, as he noted, 'public opinion often condones the offence'. As in other areas of the construction of South African segregation, here too we appear to have a demand for separation driven from the top, and imposed upon a society in which it was by no means inherent.

10

The legal profession

While the concept of the legal profession summons up a vision of a learned profession with a powerful social and economic position, it is difficult to recognise the South African profession of this period in this image. A colonial profession has to struggle to establish for itself a place that befits the image bestowed from the metropolis. The number of lawyers in South Africa was small. In 1920 there were approximately a hundred and fifty barristers and two thousand solicitors in practice (Nathan 1919: 411). Socially the background of lawyers ranged from established colonial families, to recently arrived and not very successful members of the profession in England and Ireland, to upwardly mobile Jewish immigrants, and Afrikaner rural practitioners whose legal practices were often an adjunct to a range of other commercial activities. Perhaps the most obvious place to begin a description of the South African profession is with its divisions. In all provinces but Natal there was, on English lines, a division between Bar and Side-Bar, in South African terminology between advocates, who had the right to appear in the Supreme Courts, and attorneys. The lawyers were also divided most importantly between English and Afrikaner, whose mutual political hostility and social separateness came to dominate social and professional interactions. For the first half of the century the language of courtrooms and judges was overwhelmingly English, and this was increasingly resented by Afrikaans practitioners. In major centres, particularly Johannesburg, a large Jewish presence complicated professional interactions and self-images, as did the powerful challenge to self-image posed by the very few African and Asian practitioners. The paths to admission were varied. Some came straight from the English Bar, or universities in England or the Netherlands; others (in the case of attorneys) had served local articles of clerkship and passed professional examinations; and, during this period, local university training became available as the normal pathway to the Bar. Given the disparities in social status and education, it took some time for the profession to establish for itself the image its leading members idealised. Indeed, as we shall see, this had to be imposed upon it from above. It was also by no means clearly established what kinds of activities it was legitimate for lawyers to be involved in, nor what their relationship with non-lawyers could correctly be.

Status and competition: propriety

The status accorded to the profession was a particularly important aspect of those British colonial legal cultures where the judiciary, like that of Britain, was recruited from the Bar. In the years about which I am writing there was a very large gulf between the judiciary and the bulk of the practitioners, socially and economically. However the profession's elite tried hard to impose its standards in the drive for a more aloof professionalisation. The most important time and place was after 1902 in Johannesburg, which had become the commercial centre of the country. After the end of the South African War, the reconstruction of the Transvaal was driven by a regime which actively remade the public and legal institutions of the state. In the minds of the new British rulers was a powerful generalised image that the state which they had just defeated had been corrupt in all of its public practices. A new Supreme Court Bench replaced the former judiciary and it presided over an energetic policing of the limits of professionalism in the free-wheeling commercial life of the Rand.

One of the first cases reversed the established practice which permitted partnerships between attorneys and local land agents and auctioneers, an arrangement which was particularly important to rural lawyers. But the new Supreme Court held that it was conduct 'inconsistent with proper professional practices' (*Pienaar and Versfeld v Incorporated Law Society 1902 TS 11*). Once they had begun, the Law Society and the Supreme Court together moved further in defining the limits of conduct becoming to a member of the legal profession. The court accepted as unbecoming but not unprofessional that an attorney could act on a retainer from a company. While recognising the facts of practice, and the reliance of many of the leading firms on retainers from leading mining houses and other corporations, Innes CJ likened the relationship to employer and employee (*Incorporated Law Society v Hubbard 1904 TS 169* at 171).

However, while the court protected this important interest of the richer metropolitan attorneys, it was far less sympathetic to the interests of lesser members of the profession in both country and city. A good deal of legal work, especially in relation to land sales and mineral rights, originated in rural areas where often no qualified attorney was available. These transactions had to be concluded in the city where courts and registries were situated. A most common practice was for a local agent to refer work to a city attorney who received a share of the fees. In 1904 the Supreme Court ruled that this widespread practice was unprofessional. Both Innes and Wessels feared domination by the agent: unqualified agents in effect practising through 'weak' attorneys (*Incorporated Law Society v de Jong 1904 TS 283*).

In the other major centre, Cape Town, where there was less of a drive to re-make public culture and institutional practices, the Supreme Court did not take this view. However, in the face of the court's apparent indifference to this version of professional nicety the Cape Law Society itself attempted to secure the same position by legislation (see SC 6 1912: 75–6). Yet when it came to explaining its request to parliament, the society's position was based not on propriety but competition, an indication that these considerations were hard to separate. It explained that 'in the old days the allowance did not matter . . . competition was not nearly so keen at that time'. Young attorneys now had to be protected from agents' competition, and from the auctioning which had led 'interloping' practitioners to offer up to one half of their fees to agents. But while the Transvaal court had assisted the profession, the legislature, which had a broader view of the public interests involved, did not act.

Professional exclusiveness was but one aspect of the push for 'standards' in professional conduct. In 1904 the Transvaal Law Society successfully brought to the court a case in which a debt collection agency had advertised the use of a named firm of solicitors. Innes CJ thought this different from acting on a retainer. To him it was a matter of 'grave importance' that 'the standard of the profession of an attorney should be maintained at the highest possible level'. He would not treat with 'indifference' attorneys 'struggling by unworthy means to secure the work which would not otherwise fall to their share' (*Incorporated Law Society v Tottenham and Longinotho 1904 TS 304* at 310). The maintaining of professional standards could, of course, be at the expense of access to legal services by those who needed them. In *de Jong*'s case the court had cut off a ready avenue of access to those in country areas. In 1907, in defence of its image of professional status, it was to limit black access to legal services also. Every day the lower courts in Johannesburg were crowded with people charged with pass-law offences and masters and servants offences. It was a common practice for attorneys to employ black agents to take those who wanted representation to a lawyer. This was a practice with both drawbacks and advantages for the clients so recruited (see Basner 1993: 17–18 and the discussion below). But these were not considered at all by the court. In suspending a practitioner, at the instance of the Law Society, for eighteen months Innes CJ said 'I look upon *this class* of touting as extremely objectionable' (*Incorporated Law Society v Zimmerman 1907 TS 637* at 641; my emphasis). Touting of a different kind came under attack in Cape Town. The Immigration Department reported 'tremendous trouble' caused by attorneys' representatives at the docks 'trying to get hold of immigration cases'. One or two persons, it was said, dominated immigration work, and the Law Society urged an end to the practice (SC 6 1912: 90). What we can see here was a sensitivity about the kind of work that was proper for an attorney to do, and actively looking for clients among those who were (Africans and immigrants) objects of administrative discretion rather than subjects of law was to be actively discouraged.

I have related some of the disbarment cases because they cast light on the divisions in the legal profession as well as the ideological stance of its elite members. The judges saw themselves as divided by a wide gulf from the attorneys with their grubby search for clients and money. This was well put by Hathorn J when, in 1932, the perennial question of dividing the undivided Bar of Natal was being discussed. The Bar, he said, 'is the proper school for judges. The members of the Bar . . . belong to the same brotherhood as the judges . . . the idea of brotherhood is necessarily destroyed when every attorney has the right of audience because judges and attorneys belong to professions which are essentially different' (Union Archives GG 70/390 1932). However much the status of attorneys needed to be raised it could not, as far as their professional betters were concerned, be raised to fraternity with the Bench or Bar. Yet the Bar was also dissatisfied with its status. Complaints were made that while the legal procedures of South Africa were based on those of England the position of members of the South African Bar was 'radically different'. In England 'practically all judicial functions are exercised by officers who have been appointed from among the practising barristers . . . here the very great preponderance of judicial work is done by officers who by training and experience are quite unsuited to the discharge of such functions' (ibid.). To remedy this they wanted a basic change in the magistracy, and they also attacked the increase in the magistrates' jurisdiction which allowed attorneys a greater share of court work. On their part attorneys resented the expansion of the Bar's sphere of practice as the number of advocates grew. The president of the Cape Law Society observed in the following year that while in earlier years counsel had seen neither clients nor witnesses, nowadays clients were familiar with counsel and 'look upon solicitors as something quite unnecessary'. The remedy was for attorneys to take more responsibility and 'go to counsel only as a last resort' (*SALT*, July 1933: 156). Neither side identified the restrictive practices involved in the division of the profession as the primary problem.

Status and competition: membership

This period saw in South Africa, as elsewhere, a struggle over the admission of women to legal practice. In 1909 the Transvaal Supreme Court refused to register articles of clerkship for Sonja Schlesin, who had been an active participant in the Indian Satyagraha campaigns in the Transvaal and Natal.[1] The judges agreed that section 10 of the Interpretation of Laws Proclamation of 1902 said that 'words of the masculine gender shall include female', unless a contrary intention appeared. The contrary intention in this case had to be inferred from 'universal practice' (*Schlesin v Incorporated Law Society 1909 TS 363* at 364–5). In 1912 the Women's Enfranchisement League in the Cape supported a woman's application for admission as an attorney. When the application came before the Cape Provincial Division, Maasdorp J ruled that, because at the time when the legislation relating to the admission of attorneys was passed there had been no law disqualifying women, the word 'person' in the Acts had to embrace both men and women. The Law Society's appeal was upheld by the Appellate Division. Innes CJ, now translated to the new Appellate Court for the Union, said that as the common law at the time of the passing of the statute prohibited women from practising as lawyers,

---

[1] See Gandhi 1928: 164–6. Gandhi attested to 'her ability, her mastery over the strategy of the movement and the hold she had acquired over the Satyagrahis' (166). This could have endeared her neither to the Law Society nor to the court.

'person' had to be interpreted as meaning only 'man'[2] (*Incorporated Law Society v Wookey 1912 AD 623*).

The South African Law Societies in 1917 supported the English House of Lords in its decision not to allow women into the profession. It would be, it was observed, unfair to ask a man to plead before a woman judge (*SALJ* 1917: 343). In a strange illustration of the ingrained South African tendency to leap towards segregation as the answer to all problems it was suggested that 'separate courts for women's cases . . . in the end may be the correct solution of a very difficult problem'. Segregation and race could permeate consideration of any problem. A year later, Melius de Villiers wrote, in an argument based upon 'the perpetuation of the race', that admitting women to the profession would be 'a revolt against nature . . . In this country especially, with a black population increasing at an alarming rate, is it desirable that there should be checks in the normal increase of the white population?' (1918b: 289–91). Women were finally admitted without opposition from the law societies in 1923.

The organised profession in the Transvaal also opposed African entry. In 1910 the Transvaal Law Society told the Supreme Court that

> in the present state of society in the Transvaal there was no possibility of a native finding work as an attorney among white people, and . . . he would have to make a practice among the natives; . . . the policy of the Government was to discourage litigation among them, and to encourage them to have their grievances settled by the native affairs department or by means of native courts; . . . it would not be in the interests of the natives of the Transvaal to create among them a class of native practitioner and . . . such a practitioner would be beyond the control of the Law Society, which would find it difficult to exercise discipline over him. (*Mangena v Law Society 1910 TPD 649*)

But in this case the court did not agree. Smith ruled that there could be no advance assumption that the applicant would encourage litigation or be guilty of unprofessional conduct.

The Transvaal Bar, however, maintained its refusal to admit non-whites to membership, which meant that they could not have chambers, and that no other advocate could appear with them, crippling their ability

---

[2] This interpretation of the word 'person' was not limited to this case, and could have beneficial effects for women. The same court later stunned the government by ruling that the 'person' who was subject to the pass laws could not be applied to black women because it had been universal practice not to apply those laws to women. See *R v Detody 1926 AD 198* (see below).

to practice (Blackwell 1962: 15). When *Mangena*'s case was noted in the *Union Law Review* the fear was not that there would be no work for such a practitioner, but that African practitioners would soon come in large numbers and crowd whites out of the lucrative practice which existed among African clients (*Union Law Review* 1910). Yet there were few African attorneys, and this made it difficult for other African aspirants to serve articles and enter the profession. And because there were few African attorneys, there were few African barristers. When Z. K. Matthews graduated with his LLB in 1930 he considered that practice as a barrister offered him little because as African attorneys 'could be counted on the fingers of one hand' he would not get briefs. He felt that, unlike African doctors, none of the African barristers 'have had a particularly distinguished career' (Matthews 1981: 91).

In addition to these attempts to exclude specifically by gender and race, there were broader efforts to make qualification more difficult. As early as 1908 a contributor to the *South African Law Journal* raised concern about the 'obvious' overcrowding of the profession due to its 'reckless' increase in numbers. A number of limitations were proposed: higher educational qualifications; a 200 guinea payment for articles and no salaries for work as a clerk for the first four years of a seven-year period; and harder examinations (Lex 1908: 154–5). All of these, as will be immediately apparent, would have increased the expense of, and limited access to, qualification. As I have said, anxieties about status are hard to separate from fears about competition. In 1910 the *South African Law Journal* again reflected the concern in the profession at overcrowding. Both the Bar and the Side-Bar, it was suggested, were 'grievously overstocked' and there was 'emphatically no room for any more aspirants'. In all cities and towns, it was said, surplus practitioners vied with one another to 'eke out a living' (350). In 1912 the profession staked out various claims to exclusiveness before parliament, in an effort to get a Union-wide law society with powers over admission and conditions of practice. Practitioners, it was claimed, were in competition with unadmitted law agents, particularly in rural areas, who conducted a wide range of work, especially in relation to land sales and debt collection. It urged a five-year period of articles for all aspirant attorneys, and asked for legislation embodying the principle that attorneys should not be allowed to enter into partnerships or share fees with non-attorneys, and to limit the right to practise as a conveyancer to admitted attorneys (SC 6 1912). After failing in 1912, the

Cape Law Society came back to parliament in 1916. It asked for membership of the society in the Cape (only half of the 600 admitted practitioners
were members) to be required of attorneys, as it was in other provinces, so
that the society could exercise 'proper discipline, control and supervision'
(SC 1 1916: 1).

The Law Society complained that there was no legal definition of
'unprofessional conduct', which would have given it greater powers of
control. But there were limits to what it would define as unprofessional
behaviour. It resisted the suggestion that the lucrative practice of lending
money on behalf of clients, even the advertising of money available for
loan, was unprofessional. It demanded the right to control the commissions offered by city attorneys to country attorneys for work referred (SC
1 1916: 3) and it strongly opposed a competitive market in fees. A man
'who sells cheaper clothing', it told the committee, may benefit the public,
but a man who offered cheaper legal fees was a 'danger', because he
induced people to come to him regardless of the quality of his advice, and
tended to 'rush into litigation' to compensate for his lower charges (18).
In addition it added its voice to the demands that the period of articles be
lengthened, and that fees for admission be increased and urged other
means to reduce the pool of aspirants. Legislation in 1916 and 1923
established most of these demands. In 1921 the Appellate Division dealt
the final blow to the tendency towards the merging of legal practice, and
trustee, auctioneering and land agency business in the rural areas. An
attorney 'who is in any way party to a movement which tends to undermine his own profession', said Solomon, 'is guilty of unprofessional
conduct' (*de Villiers v McIntyre 1921 AD 425* at 435).

The formalist voice

The role of the South African profession in politics has long been a
fraught question, and it is clear that the development of a professional
ethos of detachment from politics was, in these years, a crucial part of the
creation of the meaning of being a lawyer. There appeared early a feeling
that the profession should distance itself from political involvements. This
is noteworthy because these years were ones of intense political conflict
involving many figures who were appointed to the judiciary, and in which
public criticism of the judiciary, and comment on legal matters, was
extremely vigorous. Most of the early appellate judges (and some other

judges) had been active in politics before appointment to the Bench, and appointment from political careers was not uncommon, nor was the reassumption of such careers after stepping down from the Bench. Lawyers were also, as elsewhere, well represented in parliament and political leadership generally. Cultivating a non-political image of lawyers was therefore a considerable task, and involved both censorship and self-censorship in professional journals. In the furious atmosphere of political controversy that prevailed after the war, the *South African Law Journal* was seen as a medium which would only contain 'such criticisms and suggestions as are not out of place in the serene atmosphere of a legal journal' (*SALJ* 1904: 124). Early in the years after Union the *South African Law Journal* proclaimed that it had 'no political colour or leanings' (1913: 308). When a rival voice, the *South African Law Times*, appeared, it too announced that it was 'not a critical journal. And we decidedly resent being classed as negrophilist' (July 1932: 141).

As the legal profession grew in numbers and confidence so did its concern with establishing greater attention to legal formalities, a concern which was linked to its attempt to establish its status, and dominance over the magistracy, in the lower courts. As we have seen the magistrates in South Africa at this time were, on the colonial model, both administrative and judicial officials. Their appointments had usually been made with a prime eye on their administrative abilities, some had no legal qualifications, while some had passed the Civil Service law examinations (the attorney's examination without the Roman law which provided for the attorneys a snobbish intellectual content). Tension between the profession and the magistracy was evident early in these years. An article published in the *South African Law Journal* in 1908 ('Lex' 1908: 152) complained that any young clerk who passed the Civil Service law examinations could sit on the lower-court Bench. There was concern about the standards in the courts, especially in rural areas. In 1913 an attorney from the Orange Free State drew attention to the resident magistrate's courts, where, he reported, business was 'conducted in a very slip-shod manner' and 'proceedings are hurried through without any form of procedure' (*SALJ* 1913: 337–9). A letter from a Transvaal practitioner pleaded for greater attention to formalities in that province's magistrates' courts (*SALJ* 1913: 466). In the following year there were further complaints about the lack of reform of the lower-court system, raising concerns about lack of formality, appropriate attention to procedures and incompetence (*SALJ* 1914: 51–2). In

1915 the weakness of the magistrates' courts was attacked again. While, it was pointed out, for most litigants the magistrates' courts were the final courts, the magistrates did not have access to superior-court reports, and were often ignorant of their rulings. Sometimes these rulings were simply disregarded (*SALJ* 1915: 374–5). In 1916 the journal wrote: 'It is an undoubted fact that . . . the magisterial bench of the Union is not conspicuous for its number of magistrates with high legal qualifications.' People were promoted to the bench 'without any idea' of litigation. During the past year, it was pointed out, more than half the appeals against magistrates' decisions in civil matters had succeeded. It is hardly surprising then that there was opposition from the urban legal profession to the proposals for the great widening of the jurisdiction and powers of both magistrates and justices of the peace in 1917 which was seen as an attack on legal standards and a serious threat to the relevance of the superior courts (*SALJ* 1916: 411–12).[3] While the professional representations in relation to the changes were not successful, the profession continued to advocate greater formality in the magistrates' courts (requests for compulsory robing were turned down) and longer periods of qualification (*SALJ* 1918 217: 433–4).

In addition to the objections made by the legal profession to the reforms of the lower courts, which had been inspired by the administrative agenda of the state, it expressed serious disquiet about the changing form of legislation. In 1916 the country's law societies noted that for the last two years there had been an increasing tendency to legislate not by statute but by regulations. This posed, they pointed out, great difficulties to practitioners as it was difficult to answer simple questions about the state of the law: 'these regulations are not as the law of the Medes and Persians: they are continually altering, as the inclination of the Minister or his subordinates dictate.' They did not object, however, only on these grounds. There were broader issues.

> in times to come a real danger to the State will occur . . . our children may
> wonder why in these times we set the example of allowing legislatures to
> frame laws in such a way that the actual procedure and practice of those
> laws should be formulated at a later date by officials and persons of whom
> those legislators had no knowledge whatsoever. (*SALJ* 1917: 70).

---

[3] There was also much critical comment about attorneys from the magistracy, their reports containing complaints about their encouragement of litigation and their high fees (see the annual reports of the Department of Justice).

This unease continued. In 1924 the Cape Law Society observed that the 'enormous' growth of government by regulation 'was a real danger to the State'. While the focus of most commentators was on the struggle between English and Roman-Dutch law, and the revival of Roman-Dutch law by the Appellate Division, this may not have been the most significant story of legal development in these years and this was picked up by those concerned with the difficulties of daily practice. The Law Society observed that the eleven volumes of regulations produced between 1910 and 1921 had a thousand pages each, and pointed again to the difficulty of answering simple questions about the state of the law. Even if a regulation was found one could not 'be sure he has got hold of the latest regulation on the point, because the regulations are continually being altered as the inclination of the Minister may determine' (*SALJ* 1924: 490).

The profession and the public

There were clear signs of political hostility towards lawyers, and of a lack of that respect which the profession so prized. In 1916 the Law Society (Cape of Good Hope) Bill, which aimed at defining unprofessional conduct and excluding unauthorised practitioners, was attacked in parliament. The member for Port Elizabeth represented the professional projects 'as if the attorneys were in a sort of sacrosanct position, with a barbed wire fence around them, as if it was a sort of apostolic succession' (Hansard 6/4/16). While anxiety was being expressed by members of the Bar that their status would be reduced if the preliminary BA degree was dispensed with, 'angry' contributors to *Farmers' Weekly* were complaining about being 'ruled by lawyers' (Hiscock 1924: 262, 266). In 1926 the House of Assembly debated the Admission of Attorneys Bill which extended articles of clerkship from three to five years. It was attacked as favouring lawyers' sons and excluding others who could not afford the extended period, and a 'lawyers bill for lawyers' and a 'great burden on the farming population' (*SALJ* 1926: 154ff.).

We can see something of a conundrum in relation to the 'prestige' of law in South African society. Lawyers were not popular, yet 'law' came to be a central and eventually revered part of the composition of whiteness. In terms of numbers the private profession was not large, but their political role was important. They played a prominent part in rural life. Nathan wrote that country lawyers were typically valuators, auctioneers, trustees, executors, accountants, and secretaries of government and voluntary bodies. 'In this way he often attains great influence, being regarded as one of the most important, and often succeeding in becoming one of the wealthiest men in the district' (1919: 411). The historian W. M. Macmillan put this in another way. In his slashing attack on land policies in rural South Africa he was particularly hostile to the political and economic role played by lawyers. All over South Africa, he wrote, mortgages were collapsing and land was passing into the hands of 'stronger farmers, more often of the chief agricultural bankers – country storekeepers and "law agents" of one kind or another . . . cute lawyers' (1930: 76). The political leadership of the Afrikaners, he wrote, was made up of '. . . the relatively successful farmers, or the law-agents, a considerable host themselves waxed fat on lapsed or lapsing mortgages. Since even the lawyers are usually quite large landholders they are supposed to know what the country needs' (86). He implicated these lawyers in the failure of national policies: 'Big farmers, and little lawyers, are the poorest guides to a landless class of people . . . full of irrelevant national ideas' (112). More recently Murray (1992: 142–3) has written of the ways in which lawyers were active agents in the dispossession of weak landholders in the area which he studied: 'local attorneys who were spiders at the heart of the web' (142).[4]

The Carnegie Commission also targeted lawyers in its descriptions of the ills of rural South Africa. Lawyers were responsible, in its view, both for cheating farmers and for leading them into dishonesty. The 'unbusinesslike ways' of farmers gave 'unscrupulous' attorneys many opportunities to deceive or fleece him' (1932, vol. II: 42). And even when lawyers were acting for farmers the commission thought that lawyers were harming them. The farming population, the commissioners wrote, 'still has a strong sense of honour' but there were 'reasons for believing that some attorneys exercise a bad influence on their clients and are partly responsible for the increase in dishonest insolvencies, even among farmers' (1932, vol. I: 94). In the early 1930s the *South African Law Times* reflected the profession's concern about the low status of attorneys which

---

[4] See also the appendix (289–94) entitled 'A landowner, three lawyers and a liberal' which describes the methods by which 'the local lawyers [were] actively implicated in the creeping dispossession of Barolong landowners'. Murray claims that there was 'professional sharp practice by which law agents of one kind or another directly profited, without necessarily behaving illegally, from the financial discomfiture of landowners, both black and white' (289).

was added to by the publicity given to the removal or suspension from practice of thirteen attorneys in the Transvaal. This the journal put down to the depression in general, but in particular to the 'illegitimate competition' on which they continually harped: 'overcrowding' of the profession; competition from debt-collection agencies and trustees; and the charging of low fees by some lawyers (*SALT* September 1933: 244).

The high status at which the Supreme Court and the profession aimed was, therefore, by no means unquestioned. In 1927 a concerned article by S. B. Kitchin KC addressed 'The Lawyer's Place in the Commonwealth' (*SALJ* 1927 140 ff.). He objected that the profession was 'excessively overcrowded', that hostility to lawyers was frequently expressed in parliament, and that lawyers were, in general, the 'butt of uninformed and prejudiced criticism'. He also brought together a number of more significant concerns. He detected a serious disrespect of the superior courts by parliament. There was

> so great a tendency to make laws by means of regulations, and to appoint non-judicial tribunals and boards, with very wide powers . . . civil juries in the Cape Province and Natal abolished without a murmur, the quorum of the Appellate Division reduced . . . a growing tendency to abolish trial by jury altogether . . . [The] jurisdiction of the Magistrate's Courts has been increased, and if it is increased much more there will be little need for a Bar or for Superior Courts. (142)

In the same year another article discussed the growth in commercial arbitration (*SALJ* 1927: 168). The state, it noted, provided courts for the settlement of disputes. 'Why is it, then, that lawyers with this State assistance cannot retain the settlement of disputes in their hands?' Businessmen seemed to prefer arbitrators 'who are often totally unskilled in the law' and the result was that 'it is quite certain that in this country the majority of legal practitioners make little more than a bare living' (169). Why was it that 'practitioners specially trained to deal with disputes are in danger of being ousted by other expedients?' (170). One reason was delay and expense. The other was that businessmen preferred to avoid the strict rules of law. The article declared: 'If this is a ground for the desire for arbitration then it is a very serious matter. Nothing could be more harmful to the State than a contempt for or a dislike of the law in force. It aims at the very root of respect for law which is the foundation of the social system' (169).

A second article by Kitchin raised the concerns caused by the growth of alternative state tribunals (Kitchin 1927). He referred to Innes's concern expressed in *Shidiack v Union Government 1912 AD 642* at 653 about the 'growing tendency in modern legislation to clothe with finality the decisions of public officials' and to 'practically oust the jurisdiction of the Courts'. Kitchin went on to warn that it must be recognised that there was a growing body of opinion 'irreconcilably opposed to the judicial method of doing justice' (193, 195).

It is apparent that there was, both in the community and in the government and parliament, a less than total commitment to and admiration of the values of legalism, and a lower degree of respect for the courts than they desired. How did this sit with the often-proclaimed virtue of and value of law? And how important a part was it in the atmosphere in which the assertions of the value of legalism were made by the profession and the courts? An impatient administrative state, and an indifferent public, were not the ideal soil for attachment to even the symbolic values of law.

Matters left unsaid: lawyers and Africans

The profession's focus and its preoccupations were clear. But they cannot be understood without considering what was not made an issue. Attorneys and advocates practised within a system which, as they witnessed day by day, discriminated against Africans and made it difficult for them to gain access to legal representation. Indeed it was a debated topic among those who made 'native policy' whether Africans should have access to legal services at all. Those who were closest to the administration of justice to those living in the African reserves and who were under African customary law, were mostly of the view that lawyers simply served to undermine the prestige of the courts and the magistrates, and that their activities were contrary to the inherent African belief in unchallenged despotic power. Trials and appeals in which lawyers took part were considered to be puzzling and confusing to Africans. As one senior magistrate put it, anyone who 'knows the people can do better justice without lawyers in a Court than with them' (Cd 2399 1903–5: appendix: Evidence, vol 3: 245). In particular senior state officials objected to attorneys giving advice to Africans 'against the Government in matters that are between the native and the Government' (ibid., vol. 2: 410). Even when access to legal advice for Africans was defended by a member of the profession, R. W. Rose-Innes, he exempted 'the very unhelpful class of attorneys' who specialised in African cases, as well as any advice on 'administrative' matters (ibid., vol. 3: 638). Many administrators felt, with justification, that those lawyers who practised in tribal areas did not know a great deal about customary law, and involved their clients in expensive and inappropriate litigation. Most likely to be criticised were those practitioners who acted for the small *évolué* class who claimed the right to marry as Christians, make wills and to be economically emancipated from their heads of family. Lawyers practising in these border areas between the Roman-Dutch and the customary law were deeply distrusted by the judicial officials in whose courts they appeared, and also often by their clients and other litigants.[5] The Native Disputes Bill which was introduced into parliament in 1912 would have given magistrates the power to decide whether lawyers should be allowed to appear on a case by case basis but the Bill was withdrawn for other reasons.[6]

In the urban areas, however, a different set of circumstances applied. African customary law was not administered by the magistrates' and native commissioners' courts, which were essentially factories for the processing of Africans accused of committing offences against the vast range of pass laws, municipal laws, tax laws and against the masters and servants law. Improving lawyering on behalf of these people was not a concern of the profession's leaders. Those attorneys who did appear for Africans were either from the tout-employing class which were targeted by the law societies, or those who did so largely (though not entirely) for

---

[5] Much was made by those commissioners and witnesses hostile to practitioners in African areas of the Xhosa word *igwetu*, said to mean perverter of the truth, which was the noun used to translate 'lawyer' in the Eastern Cape. In the best piece of writing on South African legal practice, Jeff Peires tells us why lawyers should have been seen in this way (Peires 1987). This account should be read together with Colin Murray's (1992). Debt and the importance of physical control of deeds and documents features in both stories. Peires concludes: 'The Xhosa word for lawyer is *igqwetha*, from a verb meaning to "pervert, to turn upside down" . . . while the folk image of the country lawyer to the rural Afrikaner is that of the *boere-verneuker* (cheater of farmers)' (89).

[6] The view that Africans should not really be litigants at all persisted in government. In 1916 a government circular prohibited magistrates from funding interpretation into languages other than English and Dutch. Of all the law societies only Natal objected. The minister told the protesting law society that 'it is not a sound policy to encourage the Native to embark on litigation, in which, if anything, he is already too prone'. The prohibition was declared *ultra vires* by both the Natal Provincial Division and the Appellate Division. (See *SALJ* 1916: 504–5; 1917: 73/4 and 223.)

reasons of political conviction and sympathy. As Basner described the situation:

> Magistrates' Courts were intolerable by the meanest standards. Most lawyers in those days would not bother to appear for an African client unless pressed to do so as a favour by his employer, a clergyman, or some philanthropic body. The fees were not the problem as much as the loss of prestige, the unpleasantness of having blacks in the waiting room, or the possibility of having to contradict (or even impugn the veracity of) a white policeman or white witness giving evidence against a black.
>
> This situation led to the evolution of a group of solicitors who for a variety of reasons were unable to earn an ordinary living in their profession, and therefore specialised in appearing for African clients. (Basner 1993: 17)

He wrote graphically that 'hundreds of hard working black women drudging in kitchens and fathers in the countryside who sold their cattle to find fees were robbed by these pests each year' (ibid.).

The lower courts where petty offenders are processed are not the best of arenas in which to showcase the claims of a learned profession anywhere. However, to pursue Basner's account of the Johannesburg courts further: 'in South Africa there was an added dimension of colour-obsessed officials, special offences, specifically racial victims and switches to loud bullying or quiet, cruel indifference when the accused was black and obviously in a state of confusion and pathetic fear' (19). As we have seen, the professional bodies found fault with the courts, but not in these terms or for these reasons. The organised Bar did not complain about conditions relating to legal services to Africans either. They were uninterested in African cases. As Miriam Basner noted, when accused of serious crimes which had to go before the Supreme Courts, 'Africans could rarely raise the large sums required by the barristers, whose society refused to fix smaller minimum fees for them'. As a result of this ruling 'based entirely on a blinkered class attitude on the part of the higher tier of the profession . . . dozens of young advocates remained idle and inexperienced, whilst Africans and other poor people were deprived of a proper defence in serious cases' (44). In January 1932 in a unique instance of attention to the subject the attorneys' voice, the *South African Law Times*, published Julius Lewin's opinion that the absence of legal aid in South Africa prevented most of the population 'from attaining legal redress for the wrongs done to them'. It was accompanied by an (again unique) editorial disclaimer that the journal was not responsible for the contributor's opinion (July 1932: 153).

The lawyers who practised among Africans for reasons of political conviction included Percy Bunting, a founder of the South African Communist Party, and Hyman Basner, who later became the senator representing the interests of Africans in the two northern provinces. It might well have been the case that Bunting 'gave up music to study law, not to earn a better living but because he confused law with justice' (Basner 1993: 33). But Basner's practice was more complex. He opposed Bunting's 'often sentimental reluctance to charge proper fees' (36) and his practice was a profitable one. His speciality became the representation of ' "pirate" taxi drivers and slum landlords, burglars and dealers in stolen goods and liquor sellers and *dagga* (marijuana) smugglers . . . These were clients who had the money to pay good fees, and were also constantly in trouble' (45). Ironically, after Bunting's expulsion from the Communist Party in 1931, Basner also became the lawyer to whom the party turned as its primary source of legal assistance. As the lawyer for *Ikaka laba Sebenzi* (Workers' Defence) Basner developed a new political style of practice which took off after municipalities began in earnest to try to enforce the segregation provisions of the Urban Areas Act of 1923 (see chapter 7). Other attorneys joined in as the number of test cases grew. Basner commented:

> For every instance of racial discrimination and injustice the remedy had become a 'test case', and a test case, even when victorious was as much use as a mustard plaster on a raging bout of sciatica. As he had earlier become aware, if a regulation, ordinance or by-law was upset as unreasonable or *ultra vires*, all the lawmakers had to do was change the wording or add a phrase or two. (49)

He 'became all the more convinced that political soldiering rather than legal sparring was the means of redress' (ibid.). But other lawyers did not take this to be the lesson and this was a growing area of practice (even if one unmentioned in the discourses of the leaders of the profession) and one which others entered. Miriam Basner wrote that Basner had set out to 'defeat the touts and the drunken, dishonest crew of broken down lawyers' who had dominated practice among Africans. But things were 'scarcely better' even though there was later 'no lack of a new breed of young, intelligent, and in some instances, idealistic' practitioners. There came to be 'rich rewards for a non-white practice'. A 'new kind of tout', the leaders of all kinds of African communal and political associations, acted as 'collectors who worked on commission; legal work was handled by responsible attorneys who charged legitimate fees and ultra respectable advocates who had no personal contact with their clients' (49–50).

'Africans needed lawyers, not as citizens, but as outlaws,' Miriam Basner wrote (48). Among those who catered specifically to these needs, and who, like Basner, found profit in it, were the attorneys employed by the Industrial and Commercial Workers' Union. They won, like Basner, many significant victories in individual cases, though they could not prevail in a broader political sense. As the union leader A. W. G. Champion boasted: 'We had a lawyer in Durban, we had a lawyer in Pietermaritzburg, we had a lawyer in Ladysmith, we had a lawyer in Dundee, we had a lawyer in Vryheid, we had a lawyer in Stanger, we had a lawyer in every big town' (quoted in Bradford 1987: 132–3). Bradford claims that 'the costs of lawsuits were astronomical' and that the Union's main attorney, Cecil Cowley, 'extorted' large sums in fees. 'Funds poured out in an endless stream of individual cases' (134). Extortion is not necessarily the best way to describe legal charges, which are rarely welcomed, but the point that much money was made out of lawyering for the ICU's struggle is a valid one. Cowley had many successes, and, like Basner (though to his right politically), a reputation as a fierce fighter on behalf of his African clients. 'They had a lawyer, Cowley and Cowley of Durban and he fought! Eh, that man did fight for the African people' remembered one ICU member (Bradford 1987: 136). Lawyers like Basner and Cowley were a part of the South African profession which was not highly regarded by the leaders of the profession of the time. Nor were they necessarily appreciated by others engaged in political struggle. The ICU's own adviser, the English trade unionist William Ballinger, complained that the ICU had become 'nothing more nor less than conscious or unconscious touts for the legal profession'[7] (quoted by Menachemson 1985: 13).

---

[7] For a more comprehensive account and analysis of the ambiguities involved in the legal battles and strategies of the ICU see Bradford 1987: 132–8.

Another model

The model of the British legal profession was central to the imagining and understanding of the lawyer in South Africa in this early period of state making. And there were other features to the role of the profession which are recognisable from any study of lawyers. One was the ideological and professional attachment to formalism. In a colonial state which had just become constitutionally autonomous and had still to build regular institutional practices, the espousal of formalism, even in a version adjusted to racial rule, was a distinctive voice in South African discourses of the time. The struggle to establish professional status is also a continuous theme in histories of the legal profession and there was also little to distinguish the South African profession's distaste for women, and non-whites, from the attitudes of legal professions elsewhere. So too was the ambiguity of the status established, which has frequently been combined with public scepticism about both the activities and the voice of the legal profession. Lawyers and dealings in land are very commonly linked and it is not surprising that the South African profession was deeply involved, both as agents and principals, in the concentration of rural land ownership which was, along with growth of the mining industry, perhaps the most important structural economic change during this time. And common too was the ignoring by the profession's leaders of the legal needs of the most disadvantaged, as well as the growth of a sub-class of lawyers who could profit from this.

It was, however, possible to rise above the struggle for status and income, and on rare but notable occasions, lawyers did bring another quality to local political and institutional behaviours. This can be illustrated by the story of William Schreiner's defence of the Zulu king, Dinizulu. Schreiner, like Smuts, was educated in law at Cambridge. As a leading Cape lawyer and politician he was expected to play a prominent part in the convention in 1909 which was to decide on the form of association of the four Southern African colonies. Yet he dramatically renounced his place in history and resigned from the Cape delegation in order to undertake the defence of Dinizulu, who, in one of the earliest uses in South Africa of the criminal law as an instrument of political revenge, was arraigned in Natal on charges of treason arising out of the Bambata rebellion of 1906. The story of Schreiner and Dinizulu and the immense ordeal of the trial can be found elsewhere (Walker 1937). We may observe here his beliefs about what was at stake. 'The occasion is historic', he wrote, 'and the consequences of distrust in the absolute impartiality of the "white man's justice" might be most serious and permanent . . . If the Natives throughout South Africa feel that injustice is done, the evils following will be terrible and long lasting' (288, 300). He became, in his own words '*obsessed* with this huge case and its great issues' (292). The 'persecuting political trial' (293) became for him not simply a matter of the highest political importance for the future of all of South Africa, but one of divine inspiration (300). He had a partial victory. Dinizulu was convicted of lesser offences, and gaoled, later to be released soon after the formation of the Union. Schreiner's Christian-based liberalism, the belief in the justice that should and could be delivered by white law and the trust of Africans which it could deserve, was worlds away from both Basner's criminal and political practice, or from the determined efforts made by the law societies to impose 'standards' and secure a monopoly over land transfers. There were, in other words, many ways of being a South African lawyer in this period, and many ways of imagining what that might mean. Yet it is of interest that Schreiner declined when offered a seat on the Appellate Division on the death of Lord de Villiers, the first Chief Justice. Even so astute a liberal politician and lawyer, an outspoken opponent of the colour bar in the Act of Union, and a vigorous defender of African interests in the Senate did not, apparently, think that the political composition of the Appellate Bench was crucial (or at least it was secondary to his concerns about travel and accommodation allowances) (362).

PART IV

South African common law B

11

Creating the discourse: customary law and colonial rule in South Africa

This part is in four sections. The first (chapter 11) describes the unfolding parameters of white discourses about Native Law after the conquest of Natal and the Eastern Cape and the extension of colonial administration over large African populations. The second (chapter 12) considers how these discourses developed after Union in the context of the search for the 'solution to the Native Question' and the movement towards segregation. The third (chapter 13) turns towards the ways in which African Law was actually developed in the state's Native Courts in Natal and the Transkei during these years, and illustrates the interplay between the broader discourses on Native Law; the Roman-Dutch law; and the development of the legal doctrines of the Native Law. Finally (chapter 14) I consider the position after 1927, bringing together the politics of segregation and the doctrinal development of Native Law in the New Native Appeal Courts. The account is a temporal narrative, rather than an analytic treatment of legal categories, in order to place the unfolding doctrines of this law within its intellectual, political and institutional contexts.

Creating the discourse

In the years covered in this book two new bodies of systematised common law were developed in South Africa. While the Roman-Dutch and African systems of law have been treated as separate and different their history was closely connected, and neither can be fully understood without the other (see Chanock 1995). There is no mention at all of African Law in Hahlo and Kahn's history *The South African Legal System* (1968), yet the creation of a specialised field of knowledge of 'native law' was a crucial part of the building of both the white and black systems of law. As I shall show 'native law' became an arcane expertise considered to be understood only by those who were experts, not just in 'native law', but in 'native affairs' and the 'native mind'. It was also virtually ignored by white lawyers, though images and ideas about 'native law' were vigorously canvassed in the wider white public debates about 'native affairs'. Both elements of this discourse, the expert and the popular, drew upon an extensive and ever-expanding series of public documents. In this process a powerful and discrete discourse about 'native law' was created, and if the history of the development of the body of systematised 'customary law' is to be understood, it must be placed first within a narrative understanding of the unfolding of this discourse. In this section my prime concern is neither what African law might have been prior to conquest, nor the rules developed by the white state, but the way in which this law was 'known' within a legal culture which could know ancient Rome as itself but contemporary Africans only as others.

While the court systems were increasingly separated, at the appellate level there was a mixing of laws. White judges, as I will show, used a promiscuous and unsystematic amalgam of legal ideas in dealing with the African civil cases that came before them. There were also fundamental problems in the nature of legal rights in a polity which was simultaneously a democracy and a despotism. Occasionally judicial dicta which were generated for the white part of the system strayed into the consideration of matters concerning Africans. But Africans were neither political nor legal subjects in the same sense as whites: in Rhodes' terms, citizens but not altogether citizens. Similarly they were in some senses bearers of rights, and subjects of duties, under the Roman-Dutch common law, and in other ways their rights in law were constituted differently.

I begin consideration of the constitution of the system of common law for Africans with the different trajectories apparently followed in Natal and in the Cape Colony. The ways in which problems were conceived and discussed in the twentieth century were fundamentally shaped by the development of a discourse of enduring vitality during the second half of the nineteenth century. My interest in looking at nineteenth-century developments will not be, therefore, in the specifics that gave rise to it, but in illustrating the parameters of knowledge which were inherited by the twentieth-century commentators and policy makers. One striking feature is how the terms of the debate about African law remained fixed. The dramatically changing conditions of the period between the mid-nineteenth century and the 1920s had only a marginal effect on the conceptualisation of the problems. Like the forms of the Roman-Dutch law, the discourse on customary law was useable in a variety of circumstances. Various themes and interests make repeated and interwoven appearances. Fundamental was the search for the most effective mechanism of control of conquered people, and debate as to whether this was done best by taking over the powers of existing leaders, and changing existing rules, or by using and adapting them. In nineteenth-century South Africa the answers to this depended on a number of circumstances, such as the degree and effectiveness of local white power; the degree of cohesion, after conquest, of African polities; what would be allowed by London; and changing discourses about the nature of African civilisation and African government. The second prominent theme was the sexual economy of African societies: polygamy; bride-wealth marriage; the status of women. Also scrutinised by white judgement were African systems of land-holding, the nature of African judicial systems, and the content of legal rules. In particular, witchcraft provided a nodal point around which debates about the inherent irrationality of Africans could gyrate.

Natal

The administration of law in Natal took place in a continuing atmosphere of rebellion, war, fear and hysteria. It was unique in producing a sub-stantive codification of African law that was developed over a period which saw a major war which ended in the defeat of the Zulu by the British in 1879; the upheavals and insecurities of the South African War; and the Zulu rebellion of 1906. Legal forms, processes and the atmosphere in which the codified law was propounded and administered were pro-foundly influenced by these events. The earlier confrontation between the Trekkers and the Zulu kingdom; the death of Piet Retief, and the battle of Blood River in 1838, left a legacy which was to dominate subsequent South African history. Part of this was the image of the Zulu king embodied in Shaka and Dingane (see Hamilton 1998). This became basic to discussion of the 'problem' of African law in white South Africa. In 1847 a Natal commission adverted to the problems of control of the conquered Africans. The 'universal character' of the conquered was described as 'at once superstitious and warlike . . . they can be restrained only by the strong arm of power' (see Welsh 1971: 14ff.). However the early impulse was aggressively assimilationist. Chiefs and African law were to be disregarded. Judicial and administrative powers were to be vested in a European officer. Family law was to be reformed. (It was recognised, however, even by the 1847 commission, that African law which was not incompatible with Roman-Dutch law would have to be used for the time being, and that reform of polygamy, bride wealth and divorce would take a period of time.) In the following year, however, instructions from London reversed this approach by applying to Natal the basic British Imperial principle of recognition of local laws, subject to the repugnancy principle. Nonetheless in both analyses it was the issue of control that was uppermost. Welsh remarks that it was thought to be of vital importance to white government that 'the executive and judicial arms of government should not display any outward signs of disunity' (17). This was to remain a basic theme. Africans, it was emphasised continually, did not distinguish between executive and judicial functions.

The model of an autocratic African chieftaincy came to be crucial to the mechanism of white government of Africans. This was because the happy device by which the white head of government was declared to be supreme chief of the black population was taken to confer the same supposed autocratic powers on him. The astonishing farce of the trial of the Natal chief, Langalibalele in 1874 (see Welsh 1971: chapter 8), however, underlined certain consequences of this for whites as well as Africans. The claim that the white head of state was automatically a supreme and autocratic African chief placed the greater part of the population beyond the rule of law. Not only was there no certain or written knowledge of the 'native law' according to which the white supreme chief claimed to govern, but he could also declare the law at will. This proved to be unacceptable to the imperial authorities. There were two important consequences. One was the confirmation of what was to become a fundamental feature of South African law, in spite of the continuing entrenchment of legal pluralism, of the principle that criminal offences were not to be dealt with by African law. The second was to give great strength to the demand for a codification of customary civil law. These developments underlined the difference between the development and use of African law in South Africa and those in other British African colonies. Fundamental to the South African situation was the existence of a white population and legal system which adhered in ordinary civil and criminal law to the canons of a rule of law. Coexistence with a completely discretionary unwritten system was full of tensions and problems. The solution attempted in Natal was codification. The later history of British colonisation in Africa did not produce similar codifications, nor were they adopted in other parts of South Africa. But in the second half of the nineteenth century, both in relation to India and domestically, codification was fashionable legally (see Smith 1988: Chapter 4).

If some sort of customary law was to be recognised, the next question was who were to be the judges, and how were they to operate? Should chiefs be replaced; should white officials hear cases only on appeal? And should they hear cases as chiefs would, or as magistrates would? Under Ordinance 3 of 1849 the chiefs continued to hear cases, and had to be the first resort for civil cases, with white magistrates hearing appeals. But this raised complex problems for a rule of law. Should the white courts which used African law adhere to white procedures, and should they create a system of legal precedent by a rigid application of rules? One missionary claimed that the effect had been to 'cafferise the subordinate officials, and made them like so many petty white chiefs'. Theophilus Shepstone diagnosed the process in a way that anticipated much of twentieth-century anthropological insight into dispute settlement.

> The Administrator of Native Law . . . sits as a patriarch required by the members of the family to . . . decide upon the circumstances of a difference between individuals, rather than to try a specific case; it is not competent for him to give judgment, except on the full merits of such difference, and this may involve enquiry into a series of cases . . . This patriarch Administrator cannot . . . be the mere passive recipient of such information as may be laid before him according to certain inflexible rules, about a difference between two individuals of whom he knows nothing.

He had to make an 'adjustment . . . [to] enable them to renew their intercourse with a clear future' (quoted in Welsh 1971: 117–18). As we will see this form of idealism did not prevail in the development of the bureaucratised and legalised the white administration of African law.

Complex problems were also posed in Natal by settler and missionary attacks on African law, and by the increasing demands from the new class of African Christian converts for exemption from it. The problem of exemption was one fraught with difficulties for white South African governments. For if more than lip service was given to the civilising mission, it seemed obvious and desirable that those who were adjudged to meet the new standards should be treated in the same way as whites. But the recognition of a large class of such persons raised clear political problems. Were they to be exempt from the customary regime only in such matters as marriage? Did exemption extend to a wider range of legal disabilities, such as the colour bars and pass laws? And, most contentious of all, what political rights might it imply?

The parameters of the struggle in Natal, between the native administrators, many of whom wanted to preserve an uncodified native law controlled by their expertise, and the white colonists, lawyers and politicians who favoured a law-like administration of native law, answerable to the white polity, run right through the conflicts over African native law until the Union 'solution' of 1927. It was the desire to control the native law that fuelled the assimilationist rhetoric which attacked polygamous marriage and barbarism and the chieftaincy, not a commitment to a common set of social and legal institutions for white and black. Those who pressed for the code believed that it was a step towards legal assimilation. But for the experts in native administration the reduction of native law and custom to writing was essentially the price that was paid for the concession of the principle that Africans would continue to be governed by a different set of legal principles. The preface to the 1875 code stated these clearly: 'The main elements of native law hinge upon a few leading principles. The subjection of the female sex to the male, and of children to their father or other head of their family. Primogeniture among males as the general rule for succession – the incapacity, generally speaking, of women to own property' (Welsh 1971: 166). In spite of this apparent clarity the framing of the code was evidently fraught with problems caused by the insistence of local variations. Welsh quotes the Attorney-General's explanation in 1884 that 'the great difficulty the Board had to contend with in reducing the Native Law to writing was to reconcile the conflicting opinions expressed by the skilled members as to the various Native law doctrines and canons' (166). The administrative 'experts' in native law, as we will see, always insisted on their specialist knowledge of differences, while the lawyers tried to establish principles. The lawyers also radically systematised legal doctrine. In 1918 Chadwick, who had been secretary to the board that had formulated the first code, gave a description of how the code was originally drafted. The *modus operandi* had been to frame a series of questions to all magistrates and administrators of native law, some of the old missionaries and other old colonists. From these answers Sir Henry Connor, the colony's Chief Justice, drafted the code of 1878. Chadwick explained the way in which complex detail was turned into the principles which were to be implacably applied by the Natal courts.

> I may say that the answers to some of the questions specially dealing with the Native law of inheritance were very voluminous . . . The Chairman boiled down all these voluminous answers into a few leading principles shown in the Code as it now stands. All that was said about ancestral kraals . . . [was] swept away by him as only calculated to trouble and confuse the Courts. He confined himself to declaring the supremacy of the kraal head, who had complete control so long as he lived over all the inmates of his kraal, and all the property of all the houses, but he gave a clear definition of house property and simply declared that all property which was not house property was kraal property. (*Ntukwini v Miso 1918 NHC 216* at 223)

The special expertise was closely guarded from legislators. When the first code went to the Natal legislature it was passed as a whole, and not considered clause by clause. When reissued in 1932 it was by proclamation. At no time was it considered in any detail by a white legislature.

The effect of codification was to shift control of African law away from Africans and place it in the hands of white administrators and magistrates. Sir James Hulett summed up in 1904:

> The tendency naturally would be to keep the Magistrates on more uniform lines. Before the Code was made the Administrator of Native Law used practically to be guided . . . to a great extent by the *Induna* of the Court . . . the Magistrate was compelled to rely for his knowledge of Native customs, Native habits, and Native Law upon old men, the Chiefs and Headmen, and men about the Court . . . Consequently that led very frequently to diversity of action and conduct by the Magistrates. (Cd 2399 1903–5: Evidence, vol 3: 190–1)

Until the code was passed, Judge Finnemore told the commission, 'all was chaos. Each Magistrate administered Native Law according to his own ideas, or the views of the *"indunas"*' (393).

Codification thus reduced the African input into the state's version of the customary law, and made it more uniform in application. As Hulett said, 'Directly you reduce a traditional law, which varies according to the tribes and customs in different parts of the country, if you bring it down to one level, then, of course, you interfere with the rights and opinions of other portions of the community' (180–1). And with rare insight Harriet Colenso pointed to another problem. It was, she said, 'difficult . . . for them to understand our imperfect rendering of their own language and intentions' (404). One of the results of these effects, as noted by the Transkei Chief Magistrate, was that a civil code could be rather difficult to apply. 'If the people do not choose to accept it they keep out of court, and you cannot compel them to take a civil case into court' (192: Sir Henry Elliot).

The Cape Colony

The relationship between white and African law, and the control of the content of African law, were treated differently in the Cape Colony. Following on Ordinance 50 of 1828, which purported to declare equal rights in law regardless of colour, and the abolition of slavery in 1834, virtually all official opinion in the nineteenth-century Cape Colony paid lip service to the principle of assimilation, but wide differences were possible as to its consequences and to the time scale on which it would be feasible. Few adopted a logic which encompassed both legal and political assimilation, and most of those who advocated legal assimilation saw it only as a long-term evolutionary goal, which was subordinate to immediate needs to adapt to existing African systems. Specific settler and missionary interests had an impact on these formulations, and both groups were particularly concerned to mount an offensive on African marriage systems with a fervour which was not matched by governments. Both marriage and land tenure were depicted as being obstacles in the way of African males acquiring habits of industry, and both also had important places in a differentiating and evolutionary discourse. Laws relating to other forms of contract, sale and debt had less symbolic importance but also raised vital issues as economic integration proceeded.

Before the large-scale annexations of conquered territories densely populated by Africans in the east the assumption behind the Cape system was that there was only one kind of common law operative in the colony. This remained the assumption in the colony itself, but in the new territories to the east adjustments began to be made. In 1855 the Chief Commissioner, John Maclean, began a haphazard process of enquiries into the 'general and correct view of Kafir jurisprudence' because, as he put it, 'without some insight into the nature of Kafir law, the newly appointed magistrates might feel some difficulty' (1858 (1968): 58, 57). A collection of opinions was put together and published in 1858. This odd and insubstantial book was to be a major source on which the field of knowledge of Cape African law was built, and, in 1874 during the Colonial Office's disputes with Natal, Maclean's *Compendium* was identified by the Colonial Office as 'the only independent Record we possess of what is Kafir Law' (Welsh 1971: 143). Significant parts of the collection concerned the system of political succession, a crucial focus for a new overruling power. The Reverend Dugmore noted, nonetheless, that 'it is common to talk of the *despotism* of Kafir Chiefs. If by the use of the term it is intended to be implied that the will of the Chief is the sole law of the nation, it is incorrect' (Maclean [1858] 1968: 24). He willingly ascribed despotism to both Mosheshe and Shaka, but in the Cape 'the government of the Amaxosa and Abatembu tribes is a sort of mixture of Patriarchism And Feudalism'. Much of the rest of the volume was devoted to descriptions of marriage and circumcision ceremonies and to ruminations on the subject of witchcraft and superstition. As was characteristic of analyses of African customs a very long-term evolutionary framework underlay the descriptions of the present: Reverend Dugmore noted that the history of the tribes 'exhibits, on a small scale, an exemplification of the periodical *swarming* by which, from the ancient *hives* of nations, the earth was overspread. In this point of view it will form an interesting illustration of some branches of the study of *Man* to those who can free their minds from the influence of temporary circumstances' (23).

As always in these discussions, the state of the law was indicative of the peoples' place in history: the postulate of a correspondence between law and stage of historical evolution being an essential component in the construction of the 'other' system. Warner observed that the system was 'very defective in many respects; yet on the whole it is well suited to the present state and circumstances of the Kafir Tribes' (62). While much was made of the age-old continuity of custom and the immutability of ceremonies and beliefs, Dugmore complained of 'incessant fluctuation', and the lack of solid precedent, in a system 'destitute' of 'fixed principles . . . It affords no guarantee for the uniform administration of justice. – There is no *letter* of the law' (34). Even in the system of 'marriage price', which Dugmore noted was a 'usage which has the sanction of patriarchal antiquity, and is mentioned, without prohibition, in the Old Testament . . . as existing amongst the Kafir tribes [it] partake[s] of the grossness to be expected in a barbarous state of society' (55). But convenient principles could still be found. Warner advised that 'the grand principle of Kafir Law is *collective responsibility* . . . Do away with this, while the Kafirs still continue in their present clannish and barbarous state, and they would immediately become unmanageable.' Another of Warner's principles was that 'females can inherit nothing, but are themselves property' (74).

In 1880 the government of the Cape Colony set up a commission to enquire into the native laws and customs in the annexed territories to the east of the Cape Colony (G 4 1883). The commissioners were instructed to frame suitable codes of civil and criminal law; to consider the questions arising out of African marriage and inheritance laws; and to make suggestions regarding the individualisation of land tenure. While the commission worked under difficult political circumstances because of the war in neighbouring Basutoland, it committed itself to a thorough field investigation (Burman 1981). Direct evidence was gathered from the usual range of experts, 'officials, missionaries and professional and other gentlemen' with knowledge and experience of 'native tribes', and also, secondarily, from chiefs and headmen. In addition printed circulars were sent to 'various individuals who by lengthened residence among native races in different parts of South Africa were known to be more or less conversant with their laws and customs' (14).

It is important to consider the nature of the knowledge gathered, and the range of experts. As we shall see, over the next few decades the range of experts changed, with residents and missionaries slowly yielding ground to anthropologists and others scientifically interested in comparative racial and cultural differences, though administrative officials throughout remained the most authoritative source. Africans did not have expert status regarding their own cultures. White expert opinion about African cultures did not exist, it must be stressed, in a disinterested scientific environment, but in a highly politicised one, in which it competed with, while being linked to, white settler opinion, for the title of giving the most accurate portrayal of the true nature of black societies. Expertise on the 'native question', and on customary law, came to be built upon familiarity with the ever-growing body of government reports. The new sciences, therefore, drew upon the common images and details in these reports in the process of creating a supportive and pedigreed apparatus of knowledge. There were important differences in the kind of knowledge that supported expertise in white law and that which was usable in black law. The former was based on a knowledge of and an ability to construe Roman and Roman-Dutch texts, the latter on personal knowledge and experience, mediated by knowledge of the established discourse. This had some consequences for judicial methodology, allowing a wider scope for common knowledge, as well as for the expertise of privileged witnesses, in cases concerning points of African law. Yet once enshrined in government reports, and through them, court decisions, the nineteenth-century observations became the governing texts of the customary legal system, a documentary resource comparable, in the way in which they were used as authorities, to the legal texts of the Roman-Dutch system.

The Cape commission which reported in 1883 (G 4 1883) characterised the existing African system of law as being one embodying customary precedents from 'bye-gone days, handed down by oral tradition and treasured in the memories of the people' (14). It was 'not unlike that which prevailed amongst our Saxon ancestors in the early days of civilisation' (ibid.). Nonetheless it contained 'a number of pernicious and degrading usages and superstitious beliefs' for example with relation to sorcery and witchcraft, which were 'utterly subversive of justice, and repugnant to the general principles of humanity' (15). Over the previous half century Cape policy had grappled with the question of how to maintain the useful, while eliminating the objectionable features, and the problem of what the ultimate goal of legal policy should be. The questions that were asked in Natal also surfaced in the Cape. Witchcraft, bridewealth payments and polygamy were the prime targets of objection. How far should they be allowed: should special provision be made to exempt Christians from the operation of the marriage laws? Who should be charged with responsibility for enforcement of law among tribal Africans – chiefs or white magistrates? Should the aim eventually be to bring all under a single system of British law? In general before 1880 the answers that had been developed in the Cape's African territories were those of British colonialism elsewhere. Local rulers became administrators of their own law and keepers of law and order on behalf of the colonial state, aspects of customary law were modified, and an ultimate merging of African law with the law of the Cape Colony was envisaged (18).

Yet the commission noted that while this assimilationist goal had been proclaimed, there was little evidence of a coming together of black and white law, and it sounded a cautionary retreat from earlier assimilationist optimism. 'Kafir laws and customs', they wrote, 'are so interwoven with the social conditions and ordinary institutions of the native population . . . that any premature or violent attempt to break them down or sweep them away would be mischievous and dangerous in the highest degree.' It would be, they concluded, 'inexpedient wholly to supercede the native system by the application of Colonial Law in its entirety' (19, 20). In spite of this movement towards an acceptance of legal pluralism, the outcome was apparently quite different to Natal's. Codification of the customary civil law was rejected, as this would have interfered with the ultimate Cape aim of assimilation. But the impulse to codify found its outlet in the production of a special code of criminal law for the new Cape territories. The major necessity identified was to secure the administration of justice along uniform and 'civilised' lines. All the 'experts' agreed that, while premature codification of civil law would freeze its development, or, if too far ahead, be ignored, this did not apply to a criminal code. This conclusion came out of an examination of the basis of customary law. The Cape commission took pains to refute the dominant and popular settler 'inexpert' view of a despotic African chieftaincy, unrestrained by law, and ruling by caprice (20–1). The will of the chief, they found, was not law, the power of making law did not reside in him, and he was subject to existing laws. Yet this was not so much because he was like a modern constitutional monarch, as later anthropological theorists were to proclaim (e.g. Schapera 1943), as because 'so conservative are the natives' that laws were not made but have 'all grown up among the people', and 'embody the national will' (21). Because of this view that customary laws were based on 'ancient native usages' which were in 'sympathy with national feeling', the commissioners were reluctant to impose any code. But they found that there was no systematic idea of criminal law in existence, in that customary law did not adequately distinguish between civil and criminal law.

The new criminal code was a full statement of English criminal law and was based on the Indian code and the draft English code which failed to pass through parliament in London. It contained only a few special features related to conditions in the territories. Chapter XI on 'Pretended Witchcraft' criminalised the imputation of witchcraft and provided for up to five years imprisonment for anyone who was proved by habit or repute to be a witch finder. Employment of a witch finder and the use and supply of medicines were also criminalised. In addition the 'spoor law' imposed a communal responsibility on the inhabitants of a kraal to which the spoor of stolen stock was traced.

Provision was made for the magistrates to use African assessors, and there was no racial barrier in selection of jurors.[1] There were some procedural innovations. The commissioners noted that 'we have also given effect to the native mode of trial, allowing the examination of the accused – a mode which, although hitherto absent from our method of criminal procedure, is familiar to some European codes; and proposed to be recommended for adoption in England, as well as by the Indian code' (28). They also proposed departing from the English rule which allowed no civil claim to arise out of a felony (27). The code as a whole, according to the Native Affairs Commission of 1905, embodied 'in a convenient form the spirit of the statute and common law of the Colony, from which it differs only in providing for the punishment of criminal offences arising peculiarly from local aboriginal conditions and in the adoption of certain principles of the Native spoor law' (3).

The commission also subscribed to the conventional wisdom regarding African views of government, and this had implications for the nature of law and its administration. The fault, it seemed, lay not in the fact of conquest, but in the ideas of the defeated about government. 'Anything in the nature of an abstract idea like "Government" is to him next to if not altogether impossible' (43). The chief was regarded as 'at once their father and leader, the source of honour and the dispenser of justice'. How could such an idea of personalised rule be combined with a rule of law? A bureaucratic magistracy could not 'take that place in the Kafir imagination which has from time immemorial been filled by their Chiefs' (44). This was the basis of the development of the mystique of the Transkeian magistracy, as expert and suitable administrators of Africans. Essentially they were to be a special corps, not of ordinary state servants, but white chiefs. The self-imagining included not just superior character, but also 'virtue, strict justice, and good faith, as well as . . . unvarying accessibility, patience, kindness, friendly consideration, and earnest desire to promote their interests' (53). The commissioners thought that, in the existing political circumstances, it would be undesirable to take from chiefs their power of hearing cases. But they did hope to encourage the practice of bringing cases to the magistrates. It was pointed out that a right of appeal

---

[1] Questioned on this by the South African Native Affairs Commission in 1904, Sir Henry Elliot, the ex-Chief Magistrate of the Transkei, avowing the principle that a man ought to be tried by his peers, said: 'It is hard to exclude them in Native cases . . . But we do not follow it out.' He could only recall one case. And, he excused himself: 'I was not present' (Cd 2399 1903–5: Evidence, vol 3: 208). Sampson (1926: 72/3) also notes that white jurors would not sit with African ones.

lay to the magistrates who then re-heard the case in full, and that this 'practically reduces a Chief's position to that of an arbitrator' (25). The Cape, like Natal, had to struggle with the idea of exemption. The issue was more directly political than in Natal in that it involved the question of what status was to be given to African voters, rather than African converts to Christianity. Could voters have an 'advanced' political status and at the same time be subject to African law? The answer given in 1887 appeared to be no. The Native Registered Voters Relief Act excluded voters, unless they chose otherwise, from the customary law of succession (31), and there was therefore no prolonged elite African struggle for exemption from native law as in Natal. However for most Africans the policy of legal assimilation did not survive the annexations of the 1870s. After the annexations, Cape policy began to move closer towards the Natal model. As Simons observed, 'an inequality of political status went hand in hand with the dualism of personal law' (1968: 31).

The caution expressed by the commission in relation to the proclaimed goal of assimilation was not sufficient for Jonathan Ayliff MLA, who submitted a minority report. He interpreted policy as being rightly the search for 'a system of law less artificial in its form and more elastic in its working' than that prevailing in the colony proper (G4 1883 Annexure V: para. 14). Government should maintain the tribal system, the basis of which was 'monarchy, but by no means an irresponsible despotism' (para. 21). Under this monarchy there flourished, in all the tribes of South Africa, a more or less uniform system of laws and customs. He invoked the authority of Shepstone who had told the commission that 'Native law is purely a law of equity'. Accordingly, 'you want laws as general as possible, giving you the power of filling up'. While the object of assimilation could be kept in mind, 'the danger lies in going too fast . . . The main object in keeping Natives under their own laws is to ensure control of them. You cannot control savages by civilised law . . . It would be best at first to have a mere skeleton . . . I have a fear of laws being too rigid at first' (para. 23–6). This way of thinking sharply distinguished between the two legal cultures appropriate for South Africa and was to be frequently revived. The law proper for whites was detailed, written, formal, that fitting for blacks, simple, elastic and personal. This being the case Ayliff rejected the highly detailed code proposed by the other commissioners, it 'being the very thing that the more learned of the English lawyers desire to see provided for the Mother Country', and an 'admirable specimen of high class law' but not suitable for the 'suspicious and excitable people' in the annexed territories who were 'absurdly conservative' (para. 28–32).

The Transvaal

Consideration of these issues was not a preoccupation of government in the South African Republic. Its own provisions were swept away during the first British occupation of 1877–81, and replaced in 1881 and 1885 by a 'replica' of the Natal legislation of 1849 and 1875. The Transvaal version, however, was without the provision for codification, and the Native Appeal Court. The spirit of the enactment is indicated by the preamble to the *Volksraad*'s version of 1885 which read:

> Whereas the ignorance and the habits and customs of the native population of this Republic render them unfit for the duties and responsibility of civilised life;
>
> And, further, whereas it is necessary and desirable to provide for their better treatment and management by placing them under special supervision and for the proper administration of justice among them until they shall be able to understand and appreciate such duties and responsibilities as they may reasonably be deemed capable of undertaking in obedience to the general law of the Republic. (Law 4 1885)

As was the case in Natal the jurisdiction of the 'white' Supreme Court was excluded, except in the case of common-law crime. In 1902, however, when the Transvaal Supreme Court was re-established by Milner, jurisdiction over the native commissioners' courts and their law was not excluded, and the segregationist Transvaal entered the period of legal assimilation.

The Native Affairs Commission: 1903–5

The 1905 report of the Native Affairs Commission was built upon half a century of debate about the relationship between white and black law. Appointed in 1903, the commission's task was to arrive at recommendations for a 'common understanding on questions of native policy' in view of the anticipated federation of the British colonies in South Africa. The preferred political solution to the 'native problem' was, as always, to be fortified by facts, and to this end commissioners were instructed 'to gather accurate information' on a range of matters including African law, marriage, polygamy and land tenure (Cd 2399 1903–5: 1). Formulating a single policy was not easy. The commission, like earlier enquiries, tried searching among the recondite ethnologies and digests of native law for 'uniform principles' of customary law. But there were the differences in colonial policies, and the complexities posed by the contrast between 'Natives comparatively advanced in the scale of civilisation, holding land in their own right, and . . . the . . . masses who still cling to the tribal system and communal occupation of land' (8). Unlike earlier enquiries the commission did not begin with the shortcomings of despotic chiefs, or of polygamy, but declared that land tenure 'dominates and pervades every other question' (10). (The commission's views on land are discussed fully in part V.)

The commission's discussion of land emphasised communalism rather than individualism as the defining feature of African life. With this to the fore the commissioners turned their attention to African law and the question of how far a different legal regime should in general apply to Africans. Past legislation, they said,

> has recognised the principle that the application of certain special laws to Natives is necessary and the Commission does not advise a change of policy in this respect. At the same time it is recognised that the protection of the law should be extended impartially to all alike . . . Many of the existing Native laws and customs are so interwoven with the social conditions and ordinary institutions of the Native population that any premature attempt to break them down or sweep them away would be inadvisable. At the same time the object of improvement and, so far as may be, assimilation with the ordinary Colonial law should be kept in view as an ultimate goal. (32)

But this was a fading impulse of assimilationism: difference was recognised and elaborated, the goal of similarity deferred. The commissioners themselves emphasised a major difference between the legal regimes applying to whites and blacks. In an echo of their insistence on the communal nature of African land law, the first characteristic the commissioners ascribed to African law, after the chieftainship, was the 'principle of communal or collective responsibility' (32).

The commissioners rejected the Natal approach of enacting a statutory code of customary civil law, preferring the production of descriptive handbooks for administrative convenience. The difference was important. A code would have had the effect of restricting administrators' application of African law by requiring the principles of statutory interpretation, and consequently strengthening the supervisory authority of the courts. Handbooks, on the other hand, were not laws which could be construed by the courts, but resources that served to reinforce the administrators' claim to expertise. They heard extensive evidence regarding the code from Natal. By the early twentieth century many of the judicial officials in Natal were opposed to the concept of the code continuing to provide a separate system of civil law for Africans. Some remained loyal to the code, like Judge Beaumont of the Natal Native High Court, who thought that 'the Native Civil Code is a beautiful thing of itself: it is perfect' (Cd 2399 1903–5: Evidence, vol 3: 20). But others were sceptical. His colleague Boshoff called the code 'defective in many ways' (348).

> The hardships which were imposed upon Natives by their own law might in some instances be removed; for instance in regard to the earnings of a son; he should not be obliged to give his earnings to the father . . . That would guard against unscrupulous fathers availing themselves of the earnings of honest and energetic sons . . . [We] might also improve the status of Native women. At present Native women have no status at all . . . There are cases where women have by their own energy acquired property, and some provision should be made to protect them . . .'[2] Lobolo' seems to have degenerated into a matter of commerce. It has lost its old beauty . . . I may say at once that I am in favour of the abolition of Native law, I think there should be only one system of law; but . . . not . . . immediate abolition. I think that every Act of Parliament which is passed should tend in that direction, that there should be a gradual tendency to abolish Native law as a system. (350)

The object ought to be, said another Native High Court judge, Finnemore, 'to gradually bring them under our own laws' (393). In his evidence to the Native Affairs Commission, Robert Samuelson, who had practised as a solicitor in Natal for over twenty years, told them that 'the Code . . . has a bad effect, for the reason that it is not his Native law nor our law . . . it is a mongrel law . . . It neither gives the Natives a chance at their law nor of our law' (501). The resilience of the rhetorical fiction of the native administrators that the code was 'their' law was all the more remarkable

---

[2] 'You recognise', it was put to him, 'that it would be a very serious thing to make it general?' Boshoff did. 'It is not so with us,' he pointed out, 'and therefore the Native woman can hardly expect it. Every married woman with us is a minor by reason of her marriage, and she can do nothing without the consent and assistance of her husband' (358).

considering the weight of expert legal advice as to its non-indigenous character.

One white voice was less directive. Harriet Colenso's answer to the question of whether it would be better to bring Zulus under the common law of the Colony is instructive.

> In many respects it would not be emancipation for them, it would be upsetting them. They have not even got the books to study it out of, to find out what the change amounts to, but they have to pick that up from word of mouth and from finding the changes let loose amongst them. No, wait until they ask themselves. Take them into council on the matter. Wait until there is a general request from them to have some particular law altered. (413)

The suggestion that there should be an African voice, that policy should not simply be commanded, was very rare. Colenso's hints at the powerlessness of being shut out of the processes were affirmed more directly by African witnesses. M. R. Radebe told the commissioners that when Africans heard of proposals, 'the only idea that they have got is that they are getting a lot of fresh laws again . . . they always hear that there is a law out, and they do not know who is the maker of the law, and when any assembly assembles they only think it is fresh laws coming out' (521). It is, as he said, 'simply the suddenness of the law that makes all the mischief' (526). Radebe spoke strongly in favour of a single common law for Natal. While enforcement was an oppressive burden, customs, such as bride wealth, would continue without legal sanction as people wanted them to (531). 'They dislike the compulsion,' he said. 'They do not like to be compelled' (523).

In matters of process also there was ambivalence about legal assimilation. Africans, the commissioners said, should not be discouraged from pleading their own cases in courts of any kind and lawyers should be excluded from cases between Africans which were tried under customary law (33). Even in 'cases in which Natives only are interested' it recommended that it would be neither advisable nor right for Africans to serve as jurors (36). But it is significant to note that while there was acceptance that different laws and procedures could apply to Africans, there was a reluctance to separate entirely an African system of justice from the white one. The right of appeal from the courts of chiefs, native commissioners and magistrates who heard cases under customary law was seen as important, 'affecting as it does the contentment of the Natives' (35). Yet who were they to appeal to? The commissioners approved of the Native Appeal Court in the Transkei because its proceedings were subject to Supreme Court review. They did not like the model of the Native High Court in Natal because it was independent of jurisdiction of the Supreme Court. In this there lay the 'risk, indeed the certainty' (35–6) of different courts giving inconsistent decisions, and this went against the crucial principle that the state should only speak with one voice to the African population. The commission resolved that 'whilst . . . attaching much value to the necessity of not undermining the influence of those who preside over Native Courts, and deprecating that any ideas be created in the ignorant Native mind suggestive of appeals being made easy' there should be a right of appeal or review to the Supreme Court in all native cases, civil or criminal, tried under statutory or common law. They expressly disapproved of the creation and existence of separate and independent courts of appeal to deal with cases concerning Africans. Where civil cases concerned Africans alone, however, and were tried according to African law, they conceded that the existing Native Courts of Appeal should continue to hear cases, but that all should be subject to the powers of review of the Supreme Court (36).

Marriage

Natal

We can now consider the creation of the official discourse on African marriage, which was at the core of the construction of segregation of the common law. While it remained the ostensible goal of the Natal government to abolish polygamy and bride-wealth marriage, imperial policy, force of circumstance and the influence of Sir Theophilus Shepstone, the architect of the Natal system, led to their continuing legal recognition. Shepstone argued, and he was to be influential in relation to Cape policy as well, that polygamy could not be abolished without 'great and severe coercion' and that even this would affect only the form of marriage and not the practice (Welsh 1971: 71). Once this was recognised, he argued, it could not be ignored by the law because to do so would be unjust to large numbers of African women who would be left without legal rights. Nonetheless, Shepstone supported a legislative intervention in Natal which aimed at modifying African marriage law, with the aim of limiting polygamy by means of registration and taxation of marriage, and placing a limit on the amount of bride wealth payable (ibid: chapter 5). While this was supposed to raise the status of women, there was a price to pay in new legal support for 'morality'. Dissolution of marriage was to become more difficult and the transfer of women deemed to be more permanent. In addition far harsher and criminalised treatment of adultery and seduction would protect the legal rights of husbands and fathers.

The Natal code accordingly entered aggressively into the regulation of marriage. The ambition to abolish polygamy was abandoned, but its incidence, and the payment of bride wealth, were to be strictly regulated. In order to prevent what was considered to be endless petty litigation about bride-wealth claims which continued throughout the lifetime of marriages, the code required the bride wealth to be paid in full at the time of the marriage, and purported to place upper limits on the amounts that could be asked for. The model was legally and bureaucratically rational, and also an unworkable alteration of pre-existing law and practice. Yet the fiction that the _lobola_ system of the code was African customary law continued despite objections. Martin Lutuli was explicit.

> _Lobolo_ at the present time is not the same as the '_lobolo_' of the older times . . . One head of cattle was enough and then the marriage would take place . . . afterwards, if the father in law was in need of a beast or anything he would go to his son in law and ask for a gift, and, if the son in law had got something . . . he would give the father something. They never took these matters into the courts. (Cd 2399 1903–5: Evidence, vol. 3: 864)

M. S. Radebe described the situation, in which the upper limit of ten head of cattle had become the standard 'price' demanded by fathers:

> The law provides that on the day of the marriage the party who marries the girl must have finished the _lobolo_. Now, it is often . . . the case goes to law simply to get a kind of bridge over the law, and they say 'We are finished' when they are not finished, and the fact remains that the father of the girl wants the cattle.

Both parties were in effect forced by circumstances to represent that the whole amount had been paid when it had not because it was a great deal for a man to pay, but great ill feeling and enmity was created. The law of previous times, on the other hand, 'was not a forced thing . . . if a man had only five cattle to pay at the time they would . . . lend him his wife, and afterwards he would complete the payment. Now he has to pay on the spot and they part on the spot' (523). Labour contractor John Mackenzie gave a similar picture of the way the law worked.

> In Zululand *lobolo* was a form of marriage, but at present it is a trade transaction under the direction of the Government, at a stated price, and the man must pay the dowry before he is married, and the result is that eight out of ten young girls have children before they are married. That is caused by the Code prohibiting marriage until the dowry is paid . . . the father or guardian will not allow the marriage until the *lobolo* is paid up . . . the father says 'You can keep the girl in the meantime, and all the children she has in the meantime belong to me.' That has been the great curse of the Native Code. (545)

Much of the reason for the breakdown of the system was attributed to the huge cost of bride wealth under the code. Monetisation of customary payments, and inflation, changed the balance in bride wealth. Harriet Colenso said that ten to twelve years of steady work might not be sufficient to accumulate the necessary wealth (407–8), an estimate supported by Mackenzie's calculation (547–8). There was general agreement that the valuation of cattle at £3 a head was now far too low (in the Transkei £5 per head was held to be acceptable (*Mbali v Badizo 1913 NAC*)). One African witness estimated that a year's earnings would purchase two head of cattle (497), so twenty years would be needed to accumulate bride wealth (see also McGlendon 1995).

The Cape Colony

The commissioners in 1883 had baulked at the task of proposing a civil code. The ordinary civil law of the Cape would be used, except in the areas of marriage and succession. White experts and Africans agreed that the 'great essential of marriage' in customary law was the payment of bride wealth (G 4 1883: 29). But there were fundamentally competing inter-pretations about the meaning of this practice. The commissioners noted that there were those who saw it as a contract under which a woman was, without her consent, 'bartered away for cattle to the highest bidder, and that polygamy is the inevitable and actual outcome of this system, which reduces the woman to a condition of slavery' (ibid.). But they preferred an alternative benign version. They were impressed by the evolutionary scholarship of the Reverend Kropf, and gave much credence to his paper which was to become a perennial classic in discussions of customary marriage. It indicated to them that bride wealth was not simply unique to African barbarism and that similar practices existed among orientals, Hebrews, Greeks and 'early German monogamists'. In the benign version the practice was for the benefit of all, and arose out of the duties of the head of the family to provide for his children. It supported the 'service and obedience' of sons to fathers, and was an essential guarantee of the good and proper conduct of daughters, once married (29–30). They disputed in particular the imputation that the compulsory marriage of girls was involved, and the idea that women were slaves. Abolition would

> directly touch material interests, or lessen or destroy what was considered, however rightly or wrongly, a right and lawful source of individual wealth. Individual interests and national customs and feeling are all thus attacked at the same time . . . with . . . at the present moment, an irritable and suspicious mood among the whole native people within and beyond the colony. (31)

Nonetheless the commissioners bravely remarked that their task was to attempt to 'mould native law into some shape that would conform more closely to civilised law and to secure the sanctity of marriage and the rightful place of women'. But, given the entrenched nature of the marriage system, how were they to do more good than harm? They proposed that the law should ensure the 'perfectly free consent' of women to marriage; and that there should be no legal recognition of suits arising out of polygamous marriages. The 'caprice and connivance' of women would, however, be guarded against by the recognition in the courts of claims for the return of bride wealth on the breakup of marriage. Bride-wealth payments would not, however, be essential for a marriage to be recognised in law. Where 'just cause is shewn' (32) the commission proposed that a woman could be given custody and control of children by a court, with maintenance for them paid out of the restored bride wealth.

Apart from these measures, the commission said, they could not recommend the suppression of bride-wealth marriage, 'even though strong statements are sometimes made as to its connection with stock-stealing'. This hesitation, which was to be the rock on which the Cape drive towards legal assimilation would founder, was explained as follows:

> The time is inopportune; the custom is of very old standing; is deeply rooted in the native feeling and habit; is regarded, however mistakenly, by

the native people as not only not unlawful but as just and right; and from the native woman's point of view, and as concerns her marriage, it imparts to it something which is best expressed by the English word 'proper' or 'respectable'. (32)

It was a means for binding families together, and 'acts among heathen parents to take greater care and oversight of their daughters at marriage-able age'. An 'absolute prohibition', they concluded, 'would be perfectly futile' (33).

On the touchy question of polygamy the commission also concluded that there was neither sufficient acceptance among the population nor sufficient force in the hands of the government to effect the most desirable end of suppression (33ff.). Only indirect measures were possible while the influence of magistrates and missionaries would gradually spread a more enlightened view. The commissioners pointed out that polygamy, while repugnant to 'Christian law and feeling', was not repugnant to 'humanity and justice'. Among those practices that were so repugnant they listed 'suttee, or the immolation of widows; infanticide and the exposure of female children, and the self-immolation of religious devotees in India; and the practice of witchcraft and smelling out among some native tribes in this country'. In these cases absolute prohibition was necessarily consequent on the state's duty to protect life. The same view could not be taken of polygamy which, while it fell short of the Christian marriage, 'the truest and purest idea', was practised by two-thirds of the population of the world. Its direct suppression had been attempted nowhere in the empire.

Nonetheless they inclined towards a programme of limitation of the legitimacy of polygamous marriages. The commissioners noted the Natal system under which the amount of bride wealth payable had been limited and in which all marriages had to be validated by an official 'native witness', and registered by a magistrate. This system, they said, 'multiplies husbands, and introduces a habit of looking to Government sanction as indispensable to marriage' (35). It might in future be used to suppress polygamy 'which has been sapped by the slow process thus set in operation'. But it was felt that in the Cape territories such a degree of compulsory control and registration was not yet possible, and would simply be evaded. They proposed to work towards compulsory registra-tion in stages. All marriages existing would be recognised. All future Christian marriages would be registered. At some time in the future all customary marriages, polygamous or not, would be registered. And, finally, when it became possible, only monogamous marriages would be registered and recognised. Informal dissolutions would continue to be recognised. Registration, rather than suppression of polygamy, became the immediate goal. Registration would be the 'means of securing certainty as to the rights of husbands, wives and children, and so preventing that utter confusion into which rights to property of deceased persons will, as the wealth of natives increases, be brought' (36).

The moral excitement raised by questions of African marriage obscured much of the concern about how customary law was to adapt to the new conditions of acquiring and holding wealth. The commission proposed to wean Africans from polygamy by eventually withdrawing legal recognition, which would mean withdrawing legal recognition of rights of succession. The commission found that only one system of inheritance existed among all Africans in South Africa, primogeniture, under which the eldest son of each house or wife succeeded to all property (38). They noted that in India Hindu and Muslim laws of inheritance existed successfully side by side with British ones, and proposed that pluralism should continue in South Africa. But, in a dutiful nod towards the rights of women, they were to be given the rights to property earned and acquired, and to testamentary disposition. The power of making a will was to be given to all over the age of twenty-one (39).

In his minority report Ayliff also contended with the majority of the commission on the subject of the recognition of African marriage. While against substituting white law for African law generally, he was also against giving legal recognition to bride-wealth transactions in white courts. He scorned 'the ideal character which it has become the fashion to give' to bride wealth, and the 'euphemism' by which it was compared to scriptural and classical institutions. It was, he said, in its practical working, 'a sheer transaction of bargain and sale, by which a father disposes of his daughter, without due regard to her own feelings, to the man who will give the most cattle for her' (para. 56). Drawing upon reported Natal experience, and opposition from missionaries and African converts, he argued that bride-wealth transactions had 'been growing worse and worse' since becoming legalised. The recent Natal commission had, he pointed out, recommended the re-tracing of steps, and proposed that the courts should in future refuse to recognise suits arising out of bride-wealth claims. Similarly he argued that no recognition should be given to polygamous marriages. If customary marriages were recognised, he claimed, 'we shall be under the necessity of giving facilities for dissolving them as freely as they are contracted. We shall be bound to spread divorce courts all over the country, and . . . we shall have to bring them down to the level of the lower courts' (para. 69).

The 1905 commission

It was clearly in relation to marriage, and its easy association with morality in general, that the most important real and symbolic differences between white and African law existed, and the 1905 commissioners characteristically devoted considerable time to these. Their views on the processes of culture contact reflected the orthodoxies of white discourse of the time. 'It must apparently be accepted as axiomatic', they wrote, 'that contact with what we are accustomed to regard as civilisation has a demoralising tendency as its first effect on primitive races. It is clear that the Native year by year is becoming familiar with new forms of sexual immorality, intemperance and dishonesty' (Cd 2399 1903–5: 40). In general, they believed, 'the restraints of the law furnish an inadequate check upon this tendency towards demoralisation' (40). African family life, they observed, was undergoing great changes as a result of contact with civilisation and Christianity. 'There has been and there continues a great struggle between the powers of good and evil, of light and darkness, of enlightenment and ignorance' (38). The results were mixed. 'Wholesome patriarchal control' had been undermined, and 'lax morality', especially among women, set loose (ibid.). In view of the demoralisation the commission recommended 'the adoption of any measure calculated to preserve the inviolability of the marriage tie, the support of the authority of parents and guardians over minors, the enforcement of laws against immorality and drink' (39). Polygamy, as we have seen, had long been the lightning rod that attracted white moral condemnation. By the early twentieth century, however, it seemed that other forms of African moral failings were taking its place, and that, on the matter of polygamy itself, the commission found that 'the end is gradually drawing near' (41). This they attributed to the increased cost of living; the widespread loss of cattle due to recent epidemics of stock disease and the consequent difficulties in finding bride wealth; and the increase in the proportion of men marrying (42). In common with previous white prescriptions, at the same time as African marriage was condemned, it was considered unwise to move towards suppression. Bride wealth they found to be not a contract of purchase and sale but 'in the heathenish state a salutary check on both husband and wife' (43). But the majority were firm in their resolve that a degree of recognition, even of registration, of polygamous and potentially polygamous marriages should not accord to them the same status as marriage under Roman-Dutch law. A very clear distinction was made, therefore, between African and European marriage forms, due, said the commission, to 'the lack in marriages under Native custom of the essential condition in Christian marriage, that it is the union of one man and one woman for life' (44). The Natal representatives, however, thought that as long as polygamy was allowed 'the Native form of marriage should be recognised as valid and binding in law in the same degree and manner as marriages under common law' (42). But the majority of commissioners were prepared to go no further than a limited legal provision for hearing and determination of claims for return of bride wealth arising out of marriage breakdown 'as may be determined equitable where a husband is deserted without sufficient cause by his wife' (44).

There remained the question of what legal regime was to be applied to the marriages of African Christians. In all the colonies but Natal a marriage under Roman-Dutch common law, or by Christian rites, brought the property regime affecting the couple at once under the operation of Roman-Dutch law. This regulated the matrimonial estate and succession. In Natal, however, African marriages and their consequences were legislated for under the Code of Native Law, and the property and succession regimes of married persons was not affected by their entering into a Christian marriage. As the commissioners put it:

> The tendency there has been to level up in certain respects the Native marriage to the Christian marriage, and the status and permanence of Native marriages has been recognised and strengthened by legislation . . . Further, in Natal, differing again from other Colonies, Christian marriage, unless the husband be exempted from Native law, does not improve the status of himself or his wife and does not remove his property from the Native law of succession . . . so that, failing sons, his property in the event of his death goes to the male next-of-kin on whom devolves the guardianship of the widow and daughters. Except in Natal, the intestate estate of a Native who has contracted a Christian or civil marriage is administered according to the Roman-Dutch law, the principle of which in this respect is

the division of the property in prescribed shares to the widow and children of the deceased. This is distinctly opposed to Native law, which recognises the principle of primogeniture . . . The effect of Christian marriage under such circumstances is, therefore, to alter the distribution of the intestate estate very much in favour of the widow and minor children but to the disadvantage of the eldest son or other male heir. (45)

The commissioners were unhappy about any blurring of the lines between the two kinds of marriage, and urged that stronger support be given to Christian married women who should be 'thereby exempted from the tribal law and custom of guardianship, and in the event of widowhood . . . be personally free and independent' (ibid.). But if encouragement was to be given to Christian marriage, there should be, they found, strict controls on the rights to conduct such ceremonies. No minister of religion should, they said, perform a marriage without being licensed as a marriage officer, and the granting of such licences to African ministers of religion in Native Churches should be strictly controlled (46).

The commission also considered a number of other issues in relation to family and property. They noted that in the Cape and Natal, except in relation to land held under individual tenure, Africans could not make wills. There was, they said, 'no good reason' for withholding the power to make wills. Even more contentious and far reaching was the question of the legal age of majority. Only in the Cape did African women attain the age of majority at twenty-one. This, the commission noted, conferred on them legal powers not contemplated by customary law. Reflecting on this issue a nineteenth-century proclivity towards emancipating African women, rather than a twentieth-century one towards keeping them under control, the Commissioners supported the country wide introduction of an age of majority at twenty-one for both African men and women. Emancipation of women would not, they said, have 'disastrous results' for family life. And there would be other advantages as increasing numbers of 'self respecting' African women, would, as 'free agents', find their way on to the labour market (33). However this element of emancipation, unlike most of the other recommendations, did not become a part of the ensuing administrative agenda.

The concept of an age of majority was, as we shall see, vital for the assimilation of Africans into the common law of the country as a whole. The patriarchal family involved not simply powers of control over marriage, but a common economic estate. Integration into a market economy posed questions about liability for debt, and for delicts. The commission firmly supported the individualist view in a far more explicit way than the courts would.

> In this connection there arises the question of how far the principle of family responsibility should be maintained in respect of the head of a family being liable for the payment of the debts of his adult children or *vice versa*. Already the tendency is to leave each man to answer alone for his own debts or torts. Much injustice is wrought by exacting payments from individuals no longer able, in view of changed conditions, to control the actions of those related to them, and the granting of independence to young Native men and women as recommended above should be accompanied by sole responsibility being placed on them for their own debts and torts. Nor should sons be liable for debts incurred by their fathers except to the extent of the property inherited by them from their fathers. (33)

The Transvaal

The legal systems of the two northern Republics had given less recognition to African law. The Free State gave none apart from a limited recognition of the customary law of inheritance (36). In the 1870s the Transvaal went further and actually legislated against any recognition of polygamous bride-wealth marriages. After the first British annexation in 1877 policy was guided towards recognition of customary law, including bride-wealth marriage. Henrique Shepstone, brought up from Natal to sort out native administration, told the Transvaal government in 1879 that 'the government of the Natives cannot be carried on under the common law of the country'. Some recognition of their own customs was necessary (Brookes 1924: 125). This was a necessary step if Africans were to be weaned from their own courts, and brought into those of the government. But once the occupation had ended the republican government and its courts still refused to recognise the legal validity of any polygamous marriages.[3] Only in 1897 did the Republic make any legal provision for the marriage of any but whites, providing for a separate form of monogamous marriage. Transvaal parliamentarians argued that allowing Africans to marry under

---

[3] The result was that no marriage litigation was heard (at least officially) by the native commissioners' courts in the Transvaal, whereas these cases formed the bulk of litigation in the Transkei and in Natal. In 1922 Transvaal native commissioners were to urge the government to recognise African marriage.

the same laws as whites would have the effect of promoting the equalisation of status of the races.

In the absence of a clear legal pluralism in the Transvaal, the republic's High Court had had to evolve its own approach towards polygamous African marriages. Pragmatically Chief Justice Kotze rejected complete non-recognition, arguing that a marriage was only against public morals, or civilised practice, if it was actually polygamous. In *Marroko v the State Hertzog 110*, he held that a man married to a woman under African law was not a compellable witness, which implied that the marriage was not invalid. After the British conquest and annexation in 1902, however, Innes took an absolutist position, insisting on a radical distinction between the two kinds of marriage. In an important decision, which he was to reaffirm after Union, Innes adopted the 1905 commission's agenda of refusing equality of status between African and European forms of marriage. In *Nalana v Rex 1907 TS 407*, the Transvaal court held that not only could African marriages not be recognised, but that the consequence was, and here it followed the line of decisions from the Eastern Cape, that children of such marriages were illegitimate, and that bride-wealth payments were 'a consideration given for future immoral cohabitation, and therefore, being illegal, cannot be recovered in a Court of Law' (969).

This logic was, however, to place the Transvaal courts in an uncomfortable assimilationist position. A policy of non-recognition, born out of the view that the customs of savages could in no way be treated as law, implied that these very savages had to be treated as subjects of the general law of the land. In *Meesadoosa v Links 1915 TPD 357*, an African widow claimed a substantial amount of stock from the brother and customary heir of her husband. Was the woman a perpetual minor, unable to sue or own property? Yes, said the magistrate, this was customary law, as was borne out by the Natal code. The Supreme Court judges did not agree. If native customs were to be recognised, de Villiers said, 'we must go to the fountainhead of their customs, which is the constitution of the family' (358). The first and principal custom was that the father, like the Roman *pater familias*, had control and management of the property of the family, of male children up to a certain age, and all females, by direct descent or agnation. This all arose from the system of marriage, with bride wealth and polygamy. But the Transvaal courts had decided not to accord recognition to this system.

> When we have rejected these customs we have so undermined the funda-
> mental native customs that there is very little left as to their customs as to
> marriage and status. I also ask myself whether it is a principle of civilisation
> recognised by the civilised world that a woman shall always remain under
> the tutelage of some man?

This was the case under early Roman law, but it was not a part of modern law. He conceded that a woman was a minor 'for some purposes' while married in community of property, but overall, he declared, constructing a clear contrast between white and African law, 'a woman is in every respect the legal equal of a man according to our civilised customs' (359).

Mason confirmed that the necessary result of the decisions that polygamous marriage was invalid in law in the Transvaal was that African women had the same 'general rights' as European women. Those native customs that depended on marriage had disappeared in law in the Transvaal. Curlewis confirmed that this was the 'logical conclusion'. And he could see the difficulty that had been created. Stepping easily over the boundary between policy and law he urged that it was 'desirable that the Legislature take some steps to put this uncertainty on a more definite and certain footing, and either adopt a Code of Native Law, such as that in force in Natal, or once and for all determine that all questions between natives have to be decided according to the ordinary law of the land' (361–2). This appeared to a lawyer to be the clear and obvious choice. As we shall see the administrative and political agenda was to find a solution which would reinstate legal segregation without committing the state to a code that would weaken administrative discretion.

12

After Union: the segregationist tide

Codification

In 1910, as we have seen, the government of the new Union inherited a diversity of approaches. There was a formal assimilation in much of the Cape, subject to a recognition of an uncodified colonial version of African law in its African territories. In Natal a codified African law had priority in cases concerning Africans. In the republics there had been virtually no effective legal recognition of African personal law. Three questions became perennial in the debate about African law. One was whether it was to be recognised Union wide. This was answered in the affirmative in 1927 by the Native Administration Act. Another was the complex set of issues that arose as to its relationship, where and if it was recognised, with the dominant system, and when, and to whom, African law was to apply. The third, closely related to the debates about the others, was how to determine what it was. In particular, did recognition admit of a need for certainty, and did the latter mean codification? As early as 1835 the Governor of the Cape had proposed the codification of a law for the conquered African subjects. Brookes prints the reply of Lord Glenelg, the Secretary of State for the Colonies. It would not be possible, wrote Glenelg, for

> the legislature of a civilised country to devise and promulgate a Code fit for the government of a barbarous people. If not accommodated to their habits of thought and action, it would be at once unjust and inefficient: and if so accommodated, it must involve a compromise of many principles which we justly regard as sacred. (1924: 212)

This logic gave no answers to the problems of administrators.

Codification of the customary civil law was specifically rejected in 1883 by the commission that produced the Transkeian penal code. But this code was not a code of African law, but of British criminal law. There was a great difference between this penal code, which embodied British legal ideas, and applied to all in the Transkei, and a codification of African customary law. Only Natal had attempted this. But this was rejected in principle by the Native Affairs Commission of 1903–5. The battle lines were essentially drawn between the Natal approach and that of the Transkei. Brookes suggested that because they could not emerge naturally from a non-literate society 'Native Codes today are not natural but artificial: they are imposed from without, not evolved from within' (1924: 223). Codification of Bantu law was 'premature'. The major problem he perceived was that a code would require constant modification. But in the Union legislatures 'have had neither the time, the inclination nor the expert knowledge to revise the existing Codes adequately'. If, he went on, parliament could be persuaded to delegate its power to those expert in native law, such as the Native High Court judges, or Transkeian magistrates, much objection to codification would fall away. But these 'would be the very people who would administer and mould the unwritten Native Law, [so] why create so artificial a thing as a Code?' (225).

For many years, as Brookes noted, Transkei magistrates had been uneasy about the fact that they were, as one put it, 'law unto ourselves'. Each magistrate, as one said, 'acts as he may think best', and conflicting rules of law governed in different districts. (A. R. Welsh, quoted ibid.). It was clear, as Brookes observed, that one danger of the native law was uncertainty; another was 'the intrusion of personal caprice' and ignorance. Many of the magistrates had called for a code, notably the Chief Magistrate of the Transkei, Sir Henry Elliot, who feared that without one the Supreme Court would upset decisions based on native law (226). But Brookes, fortified by the strong opinions expressed by Sir Theophilus Shepstone before the 1883 commission, argued that codification would bring rigidity to 'an archaic and imperfectly developed system' (ibid.). The solution was the middle way of issuing a descriptive handbook or compendium, which would guide the magistrates towards uniformity. A committee of 'qualified persons' would revise it every five to ten years to bring it 'into line with practice' (228). This should be combined with an Act requiring the Supreme Courts to recognise customary law.

Towards the 'solution'

Two years after Union the government introduced into parliament a Native Disputes Bill which indicated the direction to be taken in the 'solution to the Native problem'. The Minister for Native Affairs described it in the House of Assembly as an 'innocent little bantling' (Hansard 8/5/12). It was unfair, he said, that while Africans in Natal had the benefit of the code, those in the Cape (outside the Native Territories), and the Transvaal, had to have their civil cases settled on European lines. Based on the report of the Cape Native Affairs Commission of 1909, the Bill placed large powers in the hands of magistrates. They were given the power to decide whether a case concerned 'purely' African questions, and, if it did, to apply African law and exclude attorneys. The Bill would have placed African civil disputes throughout the country beyond the legalism of the common-law system. Magistrates were given the power to 'dispense with the procedure, including the manner and form of proceeding and rules of evidence, governing the trial of the dispute by ordinary action at law, and substitute such procedure and rules as may, in his opinion, best assist the determination of the matter in dispute' (section 3D; see Brookes 1924: 206). Appeals beyond magistrates' courts would be done away with. Magistrates would also have taken over the existing jurisdiction of the chiefs. The substitution of discretion for law went to substantive as well as procedural rules. Under section 6, the Governor-General, after consultation with the Chief Justice, was to have the power to make rules as to 'the custom or usages to be observed in the determination . . . of any particular class of disputes' (209). Both of the contending approaches – codification and the expertise of magistrates in the native courts – would have been replaced by the complete power to make law by proclamation.

The Bill would have embodied a sharp move towards legal segregation in both substance and procedure. Most significantly, as one member said, the government had listened to the 'official mind', not to the 'native mind'. The debate canvassed the usual parameters of civilisation versus barbarism, and assimilation versus segregation, but there was little political interest. The Bill was introduced into the lower House late at night, only two cabinet members were present, and the quorum failed in mid-debate. It was a decade and a half until the lower House again turned its mind to the question of the private-law regime affecting most of the country's inhabitants.

In the interim several steps were taken which indicated that the administrative mind continued to move towards segregationist solutions. The senate select committee of 1913, under the influence of Senator Stanford (a former Chief Magistrate of the Transkei, a Cape member of the 1903–5 Native Affairs Commission, and a senator representing African interests), urged recognition of African marriage law in the country as a whole. Stanford tried to provide for all sections of the African population. He wanted both to do justice to those who entered into customary-law marriages and to give to those who were deemed civilised relief from disabilities imposed in African law. The senate, which had in the previous year passed the Native Disputes Bill, also passed Stanford's Natives Relief Bill, even though the latter had far more assimilationist implications, most immediately in relation to disputes about property. It would have relieved women of the minority status imposed by customary law, and given to magistrates the discretion to decide whether parties were of sufficiently civilised status to have European law applied to their cases (Simons 1968: 47). Once again the House of Assembly did not proceed.

The evidence given to the senate committee in 1913 returned to several of the major themes, and cast light on the gap between debate and reality. While disagreement raged among white administrators and jurists about the merits of the Cape and Natal approaches to emancipating African women, the committee concluded that the nominal rights conferred on unmarried women at the age of twenty-one 'are generally not known', and that the influences of custom were 'too strong to permit of women asserting themselves' (SC 6 1913). The Union Secretary for Native Affairs, Edward Dower, testified that African women had little choice as to whom to marry, and that the provisions in the Natal code for witnesses to their consent were not followed (28). The Tembu Paramount, Dalinyebo, gave evidence that women did not know of their right to choose husbands. The proclamation to that effect had simply not been spread among them. The procedure was that magistrates stated the law to the assembled chiefs, who were then supposed in turn to announce it to their people. 'Even where such law is stated to the Chiefs', said Dalinyebo, 'they seldom take notice or go back and spread it among their people' (87).

Clifford Harries, a native sub-commissioner from the Transvaal, told the senators that although he had in law no authority to apply African law nor to act as a court, he did so without legal sanction 'by judicious bluff' (52). Africans in the Transvaal, he said, did not understand the legal position resulting from the Supreme Court's decisions relating to their marriage laws, but simply assumed their laws to be in force. As to the age of majority he said that African women did not know what it meant, and that it caused no 'difficulty' (53). If, he reported, women went to towns on their own, the government assisted their guardians by recovering and returning them. 'Then in that sense the law is inoperative?', asked a senator. 'In that sense it is,' affirmed Harries, asserting an administrative prerogative to ignore the law, 'because we regard it as an undesirable thing to allow these girls to remain at large about towns. They must be under control' (ibid.). Another senator returned to the theme of administrative lawlessness, commenting that it was 'odd' that officers who had to administer the law that gave women majority at the age of twenty-one in the Transvaal should 'not apply the law in that respect'. Harries answered simply: 'If they thought they were as free as the men, the Native social fabric would be shattered, and there would be nothing but chaos' (57).

Dalinyebo told the senators that all his people strongly wished for the Natal principle of perpetual minority for women (89). One Natal chief, when asked whether women should be emancipated at twenty-one, replied intractably: 'It would be considered that the authorities were killing us if they passed such a law' (46). Northern Transvaal chiefs who gave evidence defended the forced marriages of women. One said that the women had frequently been consulted when younger, but tried later to refuse when the bride wealth had been paid. 'We cannot allow them to change their minds' (65). Marcus Masibi stated directly, 'I am not satisfied that the Christian laws should go up and that ours should go down' (70). Some African Christians too were not happy with the implications of conversion in the area of marriage law. As one witness said, 'I do not think the Christians of today have quite the enthusiasm of the earlier converts . . . In those days *lobola* ceased to be practised among the Christianised people and now it is being revived amongst them' (Charlie Veldtman, 87). Walter Rubusana, a leading Cape *évolué*, who was a clergyman of the Congregational Church and a Member of the Cape Provincial Council, gave evidence which reflected this view. He opposed an age of majority for African women, and urged that the Transkei recognition of African law should apply in the Cape as a whole. The payment of bride wealth was, he said, 'a national custom'. Even Christian women had 'higher status' if it had been paid (14–15). He also rejected the idea that a Christian woman for whom bride wealth had been paid should, if divorced or widowed, have a right to claim custody of her children. His view was traditional in that he did not see the wife as claimant at all: 'I do not think that it would be right that the parents of the wife should keep the children and the *lobola* cattle' (17). One Zulu Christian witness told the committee that he had wanted Christian women completely freed from African laws, but had not been aware that European law gave majority to women at the age of twenty-one. This he opposed (47). African Christians also rejected the idea of community of property in marriage (which was a principle of the Roman-Dutch law). Again it was bride wealth that was at the core of the objection. Most Christian men paid bride wealth. A husband objected to being told that his wife owned half his property even though he had paid for her (56).

Along with the support for bride wealth there was also dissatisfaction expressed with its modern legalised administration. Rubusana opposed fixing the amount payable in law. 'The Xhosa are very considerate', he said, and demands varied according to circumstances. 'They do not expect him to give up the last hoof to get that wife' (15). He also pointed out that bride wealth was often only paid in part at the time of a marriage, with the remainder not being claimed, if ever, until it ended. A legal insistence on drawing a time line under the claims would make customary practice difficult (16). One Natal chief expressed his preference for the existing Cape system which left the amount and timing of bride-wealth payments to the families. In Natal now, he said, '. . . it is just like buying a blanket in a store. It has broken down all family relationship' (46).

Most importantly, however, what the select committee revealed was the direction of the administrative and expert agenda. Support for customary law and legal segregation was firming, and at the same time support for wider administrative powers in relation to a segregated civil law was growing. The committee recommended legislation to give Union-wide application to customary law. Its ideal model was not that of Natal, where a fixed native law had to be applied in African cases, but the Transkei system where the magistrates had discretion as to what law they would apply (iv). As Edward Dower said, native custom should not be 'crystal-lised into law' (27). African women should have their position changed not by Act of Parliament, nor uniform administrative measures, but by leaving the discretion to the magistrates in individual cases as to what law to apply to them. The concept of rights in law was clearly not appropriate for African women: for those at the bottom of the South African social order the state's attachment to legalism evaporated. Dower specifically rejected both the idea of bringing African marriages under the Roman-Dutch law and the enactment of an African code for the whole country. He preferred, he told the senators, 'the elastic system' (ibid.) contemplated under the Cape Colony's Native Succession Act under which power was given to the Governor-General to proclaim what customs should and should not be observed.

We might ask at this point why there was a growing resistance to legalisation in relation to law affecting Africans. One reason was that it was too hard for a state with limited resources – intellectually, administratively and politically. Extended legalisation would have implied a commitment to compulsory registration of marriage, and legal control of divorce, and neither of these was possible within the range of existing administrative priorities or resources. Another was that experts in native administration both feared and resented the prospect of losing power over Africans to the courts. And there was another vital dimension. At the core of the discussions was the marriage law. Dower, and others, wanted the Union-wide recognition of African marriage, but without law – an 'elastic power . . . to meet the needs in different parts of the Union' (27). What he did not want to concede was anything that implied an equalising of status between white and African marriage. Recognition was necessary. 'The position is', Dower conceded, 'that we must *tolerate* the Native marriage.' But, he said, 'I do not like taking any action, legislative or otherwise, by which a Native marriage can be *exalted* to a Christian marriage' (28, my emphasis). The elevation and dignity of white judges and courts were also involved. They should not be mired in African domestic squabbles. 'There is a feeling', said another witness, 'that we do not want our high courts to deal with *lobola*' (72).

Stanford, the Transkei Chief Magistrate, affirmed the magistrates' sole possession of the necessary expertise with which neither the customary knowledge of Africans themselves nor a codified law could compete. On the one hand, he said, African assessors were always available, 'but we do not often refer to them, as we are so well acquainted with the customs ourselves' (77). On the other hand codification would not be helpful because custom 'varies so much' and 'our people are in a state of evolution' (78). But this evolution needed strong control. Administrators and politicians were, like African male elders, increasingly concerned that evolution should not mean a widening of women's powers and liberties.

On the important issue of whether African Christian marriage under Roman-Dutch law should extend to African women even the limited property rights of a marital community of property, the committee found that this would be 'entirely foreign' to African ideas (iv). Richard Addison, Natal's Chief Native Commissioner, warned forcefully that women would abuse any extra legal status given to them (28). Senator Schreiner raised the lurid prospect of a 'flood of evil' in the country caused by a 'large class of lawless women who would lead immoral lives' (6).

The public discussion of an appropriate regime of personal and property law for Africans was swallowed in the years that followed by the segregation debate. It was the overall politics of segregation that governed the direction taken, rather than any close look at the pressures on African law resulting from loss of land, industrialisation and urbanisation, and migrant labour. For this reason legal reforms ran increasingly against the current of social and economic realities rather than adjusting to them. Yet it was precisely these realities that produced a reaction, not only among the white administrators and politicians who had the final say what place African law was to have, but among African male elders. Segregationist administrators leaned heavily on their support.

In 1917 Botha placed before parliament a Native Affairs Administration Bill intended as a solution to the 'native problem' (see Chanock 1977). Among its various provisions were the recommendations of the 1913 select committee for provision for separate African courts, and legislation by proclamation for African areas. While this Bill foundered in parliament over the land issue, and was withdrawn, these principles remained alive. Legislation by proclamation for Africans, placing them outside the constitutional doctrine of the separation of powers that was applicable to whites, meant that law making for them was to be done by the executive, not the legislature. Both, it is true, were under white control. But parliaments did contain dissenting voices, and issues and laws were publicly debated. A long tradition of South African government, dating from the Cape Colony, found this element of debate and dissent, of different public white voices to which Africans could listen, to be undesirable. The justification was that law making for Africans should be out of the hands of partisan white legislatures, and in those of an executive, speaking with one authoritative voice, which could take a long-term view of African

interests. Cape rule in the Transkei was already based on direct proclamation of laws specific to that territory. In addition laws passed by the
Cape parliament had not applied there unless they were specifically
applied by proclamation. 'In practice', Brookes wrote, 'the Administration actually superseded Parliament as law making authority for the
Territories; and Proclamations were numerous, frequent, and important'
(1924: 298). After Union, parliament's laws applied automatically to all
territories, but could be withdrawn or amended by proclamation. The
1917 Native Affairs Administration Bill would have reverted to the
stronger Cape principle of legislative separation, and given the Governor-
General full power to amend statutes, and to enact new laws, for all
African areas. Brookes urged that matters be taken yet further. 'Past
schemes of legislation by proclamation have based themselves on territorial lines. It would be quite necessary, today, to give the Administration
power to legislate not only for all matters regarding Native Areas, but
also for all matters regarding Native Affairs even outside Native Areas'
(303). In 1923 Proclamation 145 introduced into the Transkei the
principle that had been embodied in the failed Native Disputes Bill,
giving to magistrates the discretion to apply African law to civil cases
concerning Africans (Simons 1968: 53). Four years later this system was
extended to the country as a whole by the 1927 Act which put together
the materials of the previous half century's debate. Objections voiced in
the parliamentary debate to the revival of chieftaincy and the acceptance
of polygamy and bride wealth were drowned in the wash of approval for
a measure which would shore up conservative institutions and leaders
against the growing strength of African radical movements. Government
by proclamation under the Governor-General as supreme chief, which
finally placed Africans beyond the 'rule of law' in the constitutional
sense, was the crucial feature of the Act, from which the establishment of
separate courts, and the acceptance, Union wide, of separate private law
followed. E. L. Mathews, the government law adviser, treated the draft
bill with contempt, refusing to believe that parliament would grant such
wide powers to deal with so wide a range of matters by regulation and
proclamation. He was wrong (see Dubow 1989: 92). In parliament little
hesitation was expressed about the principle of legislating for Africans by
proclamation. When Hertzog was asked why all laws were not passed in
this way, the following exchange was recorded in Hansard. It was,

hereplied, 'a point of the very greatest speculative interest and the question is whether we have not already outlived the time of parliamentary legislation. An Hon Member. Mussolini' (Hansard 28/4/1927). But the parliamentary debate on the Act was dominated by the political concerns: the fear of Bolshevism; the rise of the ICU; and the desire for stronger legislation against sedition. One National Party member captured the mood, remarking that the rise of Clements Kadalie and others 'reminds me of the Dragon of the Apocalypse whose tail sweeps the third part of heaven'.

Defining the chieftaincy

As we have seen the undefined powers of the chief had been found to be particularly useful to white government. There was by now a long-established habit of justifying autocratic rule over Africans as being justified by their own methods. The despotism that was attributed to Shaka was invoked as appropriate not only for the Zulus but eventually for Africans as a whole. This attribution was within a wider imperial discourse about the government of others. Cohn (1996: 64–5) gives an account of the development of the 'Despotic model' of pre-British Indian government – a vision of arbitrary and tyrannical rule in which law was simply the 'pleasure' of the Mughal. This model of 'absolute and arbitrary power, unchecked by any institution', Cohn writes, was a part of the 'ideological infrastructure of British rule in India' (see also Hamilton 1998). The Natal Native Affairs Commission of 1852–3 had purported to find that 'the powers, authorities and functions of Kafir Chiefs are great and varied; in their nature they are despotic; in their extent they are only limited by the talents and energy of the individuals who wield them' (see Welsh 1971: 33–4). Maclean's *Compendium* stated authoritatively that 'the Paramount Chief of each tribe is above all law in his own tribe: he has the power of life and death and is supposed to do no wrong' ([1858] 1968: 78). In accordance with these definitions, the statutory position in Natal was that 'the Queen's representative has as Supreme Chief of the Natives absolute legislative authority over them' (see Garthorne 1924: 28). In Natal in 1850, the Governor, and in the Transvaal in 1885 as a by-product of the first British occupation, the State President, had been made Paramount Chief over all Africans. The nature of the powers given to this invented figure varied, but they were extensive, and essentially subjected all Africans, in the name of their own tribal system, to a government by executive power.

The 1905 commission concluded that experience had shown that special powers were required 'in respect of the large masses of Natives', and that the system should be continued, with the adaptation that the supreme chief should, in self-governing colonies, be responsible to the ministry of the day, and the local legislature (Cd 2399 1903–5: 31). It defined as central to African life 'tribal organisation' under the 'control and leadership' of the chief, who was 'as the father is to the family'. The chief ruled and exercised authority, and, while it was considered that he was not an untempered despot, the commission noted that the chiefly form of government 'required implicit obedience to authority' (30). However, while the chiefs continued to be recognised as a means of government, their jurisdiction in criminal matters had been increasingly transferred to white magistrates, as part of an evolutionary process, largely 'being left to time', which would lead to the end of the tribal system (31).

But this relatively soft version of African despotism and the broadly evolutionary approach were not sufficient for the courts which were frequently presented with the need to decide more exactly what a chief's powers really were. Drawing upon the prevailing images in white South African society, both courts and legislatures in the early twentieth century fashioned an African institution to fit not only the administrative needs of the state, but also the symbolic needs of white discourses, legal and general, about the nature of African political institutions. The definition of the chief's powers in the courts was part of the process by which Africans were placed, justly and reasonably, and according to their own ways, beyond the scope of association with political democracy and the rule of law. The construct of the chieftaincy could be extended beyond a traditionalist justification of sweeping authoritarian powers over Africans, and adapted to more of the functions of the modern state. Shaka, by 1935, was not simply a despot, but a lawgiver. As H. C. Lugg, the Chief Native Commissioner Natal, wrote: 'Shaka, the South African Attila, was not only a military genius but, like Napoleon, a law maker . . . he effected much uniformity in tribal law, so that when the European later made the attempt to codify indigenous law his task was greatly simplified' (foreword to Stafford 1935: v).

The Transvaal Supreme Court under Innes had several opportunities to consider the nature of the chieftaincy. Section 13 of Law 4 of 1885, which had been drafted during the British occupation, and which the court still administered, gave to the State President 'all power and authority which in accordance with native laws, habits and customs are given to any paramount chief'. These bare outlines remained to be filled in. In *Hermansburg Mission Society v the Commissioner for Native Affairs and Darius Mogalie 1906 TS 135*, the court had to decide what power a chief had to sell his people's land. The council of *indunas* (elder councillors) had agreed to past sales, but the current chief urged that this was insufficient, and that the consent of the full tribe, in a *pitso* (assembly) had been needed. H. M. Taberer, the Assistant Secretary for Native Affairs, and Sir Theophilus Shepstone gave expert evidence to the effect that only the councillors' consent was needed. Innes preferred their views, 'the result of their long experience' (143), over those of the African evidence.[1]

A pattern was being created. In *Mathibe v Lieutenant-Governor 1907 TS 557*, the court had to consider the extent of the powers of the Lieutenant-Governor in his capacity as a paramount chief to depose a lesser chief for drunkenness. Solomon rejected the African evidence as not 'satisfactory as to the powers which can be exercised by the paramount chief of such a tribe as, for example, the Zulu or the Pondos or the Basutos or any other of the large tribes that are known in this country' (569). Contending once again were competing visions of the African polity. African witnesses, themselves often *évolués* powerfully influenced by a desire to present indigenous institutions in a light which would fit them into an order of representative institutions, described a chieftaincy of limited powers. European experts, clinging to the image of Zulu absolutism generated in the nineteenth century, rejected this, and generalised autocracy. Solomon accepted the evidence of Marwick and Taberer as justifying the conclusion that according to native custom a paramount chief had 'arbitrary power' to dismiss sub-chiefs. He might consult his council but he was not bound by its advice. 'Practically his power over his sub-chiefs is a despotic power, a power which he can exercise of his own free will.' Unlike some other African laws which could not be enforced by the court because they were contrary to civilised principles, Solomon considered that arbitrary power

---

[1] This case was to be the authority on which the Privy Council later rested its opinion in *In re Southern Rhodesia 1919 AC*, which validated the land concessions allegedly made by Lobengula in Rhodesia (see Chanock 1977). For the importance of the case in the construction of the customary law of African land tenure see Chanock 1991 and Klug 1995.

of this sort was not inconsistent with the general principles of the civilised world. because there were civilised countries 'where autocracy still exists' (570–1.) Bristowe also tied the people of the Northern Transvaal into the ruling white version of African history. Those small tribes, he said, did not have paramount chiefs, and therefore the witnesses from them did not 'really have any knowledge of what the power of a Paramount Chief is'. But the people in question had, at 'some time or other', been 'detached' from the Zulu race. Despite this, they continued to carry with them Zulu laws and customs. 'To ascertain what are the powers of a paramount chief . . . we have to go not to the customs of those scattered northern tribes as they now exist, but we have to go to the Zulu nation and find out what powers were possessed by the great chiefs who ruled them.' He invoked Shaka, Dingane and Cetshwayo. 'It is hardly disputed', he declared, 'that the powers exercised by Chiefs of that kind were of a despotic character.' The Voortrekkers had taken those powers by right of conquest (573–6). Curlewis summed up. The Paramount Chief was 'a ruler whose power is limited only by his will and by the means of enforcing his will'. He was 'a despot'. The State President of the South African Republic had had, and the Governor now had, those same powers (576).

It was not possible to debate with the uni-vocal pronouncement of a court, but there had been a nice exchange when Shaka was invoked by Stanford during J. T. Jabavu's evidence to the Native Affairs Commission of 1903–5. Stanford described the chiefs as 'despotic'. Jabavu responded that they had been limited by 'the Council'. 'What restraint could there be on the will of a man like Tshaka or Lobengula?' asked Stanford. Jabavu responded that Shaka was 'an exception . . . You have had your Charles and your James, and knew how to deal with them: the same with the Natives' (Cd 2399 1903–5: Evidence, vol. 2: 745). But this was not a voice heard by the judges. The extent of a chief's arbitrary powers was confirmed by the Transvaal court in another context in *Mogale v Mogale 1912 TPD 92*. An appeal had been brought against a chief who had decided a case in which he had an interest of his own. Wessels J pronounced that 'however unusual the procedure might be . . . the Court cannot scrutinise too narrowly the procedure followed by a native chief . . . we must rather uphold his decisions' (95–6). This dictum was quoted with approval in *Makapan v Khopa 1923 AD 551* which confirmed that a chief had power to punish for contempt of his court.

But there was a limit, and it related to property rights. In 1920 the

Transvaal court heard a case in which a chief had imposed a compulsory
levy to pay for the expenses of tribal litigation, and had seized property of
a man who had refused to pay – *Molusi v Matlaba 1920 TPD 389*. The
power to levy, said Wessels JP, was 'an extraordinarily large power'. 'How
can we maintain in this Court', he asked, 'that a native custom is
according to natural justice or the principles that are used by civilised
people when it gives a chief autocratic power to seize any asset that he
may please?' (392). (Chiefs could also not enter into labour-recruiting
agreements on behalf of their subjects. See Transvaal Proclamation 38 of
1901 and *Eastwood v Shepstone 1902 TS 294*.)

In the mid-1920s the Appellate Division had two opportunities to
consider the extent of a chief's powers. They did so in ways that
corresponded with the executive's growing need to control disaffection in
African areas.[2] In *Mokhatle and others v Union Government 1926 AD 71*,
the judges decided that according to native law and custom a chief had
power to banish a 'recalcitrant and rebellious' person from his tribe and
home. The power to banish had a long pedigree in white authorities. It
had been affirmed in Maclean's *Compendium*; by the Cape Native Laws
Commission of 1883; and the Natal code, though these were not referred
to. This power, the court said, as it was not an exercise of criminal
jurisdiction, could be exercised without an investigation or trial, and was
not in conflict with the general principles of civilisation. Kotze JA accepted
the evidence given by a missionary, and an 'aged headman', and explicitly
rejected that of the appellants' star witness, the African intellectual Sol
Plaatje. Plaatje's education, said Kotze, 'has evidently influenced him in
the forming of his opinions, which incline towards the introduction of
modern civilised principles in the government of native tribes by their
chiefs' (76–7).

In *Rathibe v Reid 1927 AD 74*, a case from the Western Transvaal, the
court had to consider the extent of a chief's powers to sell land. The court
of first instance had rejected any notion of tribal democracy. De Waal
insisted that

[2] See Simpson (1986) for a particularly acute analysis of the struggles between chiefs and
subjects over the extent of the chiefs' authority over land distribution and sales, the right to
tribute, and the control of migrant workers' cash earnings. While the Native Administration
Department firmly supported the chiefs against what was seen as a rising tide of individualism,
people tried to invoke the authority of the white courts to escape from the chiefs' jurisdiction.
But this door was to be firmly closed.

even in respect of tribes where democratic influences have been the longest
at work, the Chief's authority is still supreme in the sense . . . that there is
no obligation on him, in carrying out governmental functions – judicial,
legislative and executive – to consult his people assembled in *pitso*
(assembly). At most he consults his *legothle* (council) . . . Whether,
however, he is obliged to act on that advice is doubtful. (76–7)[3]

In the Appeal Court de Villiers 'noted the strong conflict' between the
witnesses as to the nature of a chief's powers. Before the court there were
several proponents of each view, the absolutist version and the version in
which 'under the democratic influences of the age the powers of the chief
have greatly diminished'. In favour of the latter view were experienced
officials, like Stubbs, the Rustenburg magistrate, Harries, the Native
Commissioner, and 'educated natives', Dr Modiri Molema and Solomon
Plaatje. Stubbs told the court that the powers of the chief might once have
been greater, but since 'civilised ordered government' he had had to
consult both *legothle* and *pitso*. This was due 'very largely to the disintegrating influences which are abroad today and steadily weakening the
form of tribal government and the authority of the chief' (78–9). The
missionary, Behrens, also attributed the practice of consultation to recent
outside influences. This was slightly but significantly different from the
account in Dr Molema's book, *The Ethnology of the Bantu Peoples*,
published in 1921. In it the need for consultation and consent of a tribal
majority was set out as a tribal norm, for without such consent the only
respite was force and civil war. Plaatje agreed. In no new policy, big or
small, such as the purchase and sale of land, could a chief act without the
consent of councillors and assembly. The Native Commissioners, Harries
and Keys, who also gave evidence for the plaintiffs, supported the view
that such consultation was necessary, but for different reasons. It was not
disintegrating influences or a tribal norm, but the recent policy and
requirements of the Native Affairs Department regarding land transactions (80–1).

A determined de Villiers picked his way easily through the inconsist-
encies. His remarks are worth setting out at some length as they embody

---

[3] De Waal and Tindall complained specifically about the 'unsatisfactory' need to involve 'native
evidence' to prove 'native custom'. They wanted a 'hard and fast law' as in Natal. The
suggestion that the *legothle* was paramount was interpreted politically: it was attributed by one
magistrate to 'a Bolshevik spirit, or a spirit of insubordination . . . They want their little
Parliament' (see Simpson 1986: 307–9).

the mixture of historicism and policy that were the elements of the construction of the chieftaincy.

> The weakness of the evidence for the plaintiffs lies in the fact that most of the witnesses fail to distinguish with sufficient care at what stage conduct of a certain kind on the part of a chief can be said to have crystallised into native law and custom. Throughout the evidence the witnesses confuse the actions of the chief in consulting his *legothle* or his tribe based on expediency or convenience or on instructions of the native commissioners with what he is bound to do under native law and custom. Now whatever may have been the reasons for the autocratic powers possessed by the chief when he first came into contact with our civilisation, it is clear that at that time he was an autocrat . . . No doubt contact with the white man has not made the task of the chief easier. The mere neighbourhood of the white man is in itself a disintegrating factor. So also are unfortunately some of our laws such as the failure to recognise the system of *Lobola*. Moreover, every educated native becomes practically emancipated and is himself a further source of disintegration. Small wonder then that a chief should be anxious to carry his people with him in every important transaction. But it does not follow that because a chief pursues a certain line of policy from motives of expediency or acting on instructions from the Native Affairs Department that that necessarily implies that native law and custom have been modified. (81)

A witness such as Plaatje, he said, 'quite unconsciously' told of what he thought 'ought to be' native law and custom.

He accepted instead the evidence of the defendants' witnesses, again a mixture of Native Affairs officials, missionaries and Africans. Long 'experience' of 'natives' was the main criterion for expertise. One official affirmed that a chief could conduct any important transaction without reference to anyone else. 'He would have the first word and the last word. He can do as he thinks fit' (83). Other evidence accepted by the court declared, and this was important, that powers and customs were essentially the same among all tribes, and that this included the right to act without consultation or consent (84). Furthermore all members of a tribe were part of a single entity recognised by law and all were therefore bound by a chief's actions (85–7).

The courts' definitions of the powers of the chieftaincy were to be matched by the legislative developments. The 'solution' arrived at in the form of the Native Administration Act in 1927 gave to the Governor-General all the powers said to be possessed by a supreme chief in Natal, and these were extended to the Transvaal and Orange Free State in 1929. These powers were absolute, and subjected all Africans to an extensive, localised and legal arbitrary rule. They included authority to punish disobedience to his orders as supreme chief by both fine and imprisonment. In 1928 a government notice delegated the powers of the supreme chief to native commissioners (see Stafford 1935: 24). Disregard of 'any reasonable order' given by such officials became an offence summarily punishable by a fine of up to £10 or two months imprisonment. These punishments, being administrative acts, were not reviewable by courts. Chiefs and headmen could also 'require compliance by the people under their jurisdiction with their duties under native law and may give orders for that purpose. The enforcement of obedience to authority, of the duty of children to their parents and of the obligations of inmates of kraals towards their kraal heads shall in particular fall within the scope of their authority.' A fine of £2 could be imposed 'for any defiance or disregard of their orders' (Natal code: section 18). Orders and fines under this section could not be reviewed by a court.

There were inroads too into the principle of an 'assimilated' criminal law. While the common law relating to criminal liability required the proof of both *actus reus* and *mens rea* in relation to offences, the Natal code's provisions, reaffirmed in 1932, provided for collective punishment of a sort which ran entirely contrary to the common law precepts. Section 6(1) provided that in any case of major crime if it was shown 'to the satisfaction of the Supreme Chief' that there was 'reason to believe' that members of a tribe or community had acted in concert, any or all of the male members of the community could be fined up to £20. The supreme chief could also detain for up to three months any African he was 'satisfied' was dangerous to public peace (sec. 8). The Supreme Court was excluded from considering any punishment given in the capacity of supreme chief, though the court took the view, as in relation to other statutory exclusions of jurisdiction, that it could still consider whether an act was within the scope of the authority given (Stafford 1935: 27).

In exercising the powers delegated to them by the supreme chief, the native commissioners were also encouraged to use persuasion to block the access of Africans to the civil law. In the instructions issued to them under the Native Administration Act they were enjoined that in the settlement of civil suits they should 'encourage natives to avail themselves of . . . the simplified form of procedure in Courts of Native Commissioner' (28). As all Africans in the reserves were deemed by the code to be members of the tribe in whose area they resided, all were subject to a chief. Their residence was fixed according to tribal boundaries, and they could not move without the permission of a native commissioner (33). In 1928 it became an offence to be found in a chief's area and to be 'unable to give a satisfactory account' of oneself (37).

13

The native appeal courts and customary law

We are now in a position to consider how those higher courts in Natal and in the Transkei that were entrusted with the administration of 'native law' operated within the context of the administrative and political agenda, and contributed to the formation of the discourses on African law. In a society dominated by racist politics, and racially inspired public policy and legislation, the private law and the high courts have often been seen as essentially only racist when explicitly forced to be by a sovereign legislature. However both the supreme courts and those special higher courts that dealt with African cases were crucial to the elaboration of a differentiated and segregated law, and contributed both to the crushing of an assimilative legal liberalism and to the elaboration of a restrictive and authoritarian style of customary law based on differential racial capacities. In using the records of these courts my aim is not to illustrate the making of customary law and the management of social relations by African people. I am here trying to show how the dominating legal culture thought and worked; it is primarily an ethnography of the rulers' law, rather than one of the ruled. The leading studies of African law have been positivist, written for use within the system, and concerned with establishing the rules of law, and have therefore treated the reasoning and the decisions of the courts as sources of law established by precedent and *stare decisis*, developing a picture of increasing systemisation. Or, like Simons' *African Women* (1968) the interest has been on the real-life position of women, and how this was created and defined by law, realist studies that focused on the effects of decisions of courts more than their reasoning. Both kinds of study, positivist and realist, make the processes appear to have been systematic, and iron out both the real eccentricities, and the actual processes of intellectual creativity.

The great outburst of legal creativity, in which two new systems of law were fashioned, was marked by a concealing of creativity behind an elaborate subservience to authority. As the Roman-Dutch law was built on attachment to European texts and authorities, so the native law was elaborated with its attachment to the 'unwritten' immemorial customs of Africans. South Africa not only failed in this period to develop a unified common law, but deliberately failed. It succeeded instead in developing two new legal systems living uneasily together as white and African lives interconnected, yet were increasingly separated in law. Yet despite the institutional separation, and the drive towards doctrinal separation, it is impossible to understand the reasoning that made the content of the African law in isolation from its white legal counterpart. White judges drew of necessity on their own jurisprudential stock of concepts and these concepts turn up over and over again in reasoning about 'native law and custom'. Sometimes the white legal authorities are used to confirm a line of reasoning, and sometimes to provide a desired contrast with the doctrine of 'native law' being expounded. We should bear in mind also the *ad hoc* nature of much of this development. Those who developed 'native law' were not South Africa's leading jurists and they relied, as noted above, on the major administrators' handbooks, a rough-and-ready knowledge of the common law, and remembered principles. The Transkei court, for example, frequently cited the brutally brief dicta of Maclean's *Compendium* as authority (for example for the principles that there was no legal process for divorce and that a man might repudiate his wife at will). Some of the *ad hoc* flavour of the judgments, with their appeal to a few texts, general principles, wide-ranging historical and ethnographic authorities and, often, personal knowledge of 'native life', can be explained by the realities of the conditions under which the native courts worked. As Boshoff JP remarked in *Manqatsha v Rex 1910 NHC 122* at 130, 'It is quite impossible for the judges of this Court to carry a library with them on Circuit.' In the Transkei this tendency of magistrates to revert to first principles, as well as the limitations imposed upon them by the realities of their situation, may be similarly explained to some extent by the remark by Warner in *Nkonqa v Bipu Jada 1919 NAC 258*: 'The Court with the extremely limited law library at its disposal has laboured under the disadvantage of not having access to most of the authorities' (259).

In the creation of the system of native law there was also the creation of a complex system of theorising about the nature of Africans and African societies. This vast edifice of theorising about primitive societies was often based upon the adjudication of disputes about small numbers of stock circulating from kraal to kraal. The judges and magistrates delighted in their mastery of the technical difficulties of great houses, right-hand houses, and left-hand houses, and in the details of wives' ranking, and primogeniture, producing a mirror image of the Supreme Court judges and their displays of Latin learning and obscure technical exegesis. While the monopoly of judicial decision making by whites was to a large extent the result of the politics of conquest and white rule, it is nonetheless worth underlining that for all the lip service paid to the principle of governing Africans by their own law, and while African assessors were sometimes used in the Cape native courts, the obvious resort of using African magistrates was never adopted. The 'expertise' the African assessors held about native law was clearly deficient in the eyes of white lawyers, and could not be expressed in the arcane manner the courts had embraced. In all of this one must wonder who the magistrates and judges of the native courts imagined their audience was. It was neither the litigants for whom they gave judgment nor was it the bulk of the white judiciary, or legal profession, who had no interest in the mysteries of native law, but rather the more limited cohort of 'experts' in native affairs.[1]

The native appeal courts

Before embarking on an account of the ways in which a body of law was developed in the judgments of these courts some consideration needs to be given to the circumstances of their production. In using the courts' records one sees that in many cases concerning debts, particularly for bride wealth, but also arising out of other transactions, claims had not been acted on for decades. There were frequently very long delays in the bringing of cases in which a series of debts and promises were involved. The Natal code and the native courts could be manipulated by parties.

[1] It was more widely common for anyone who claimed authority over African lives to claim expert knowledge of their laws. There was another level of administration of native law of which we should be aware. An informant interviewed by the University of the Witwatersrand's oral history project told of the white farmer for whom he worked:

> Even when my son had perhaps seduced your daughter, you did not have to worry. He would personally come and tell me that according to Bantu Law and Custom I am supposed to pay six head of cattle . . . and would tell me 'Man, I know your laws, I am not going to allow you to come and spoil my farm here' . . . he would tell you that Native Law is at his fingertips. (Interview with N. Makume, 8/10/82)

People frequently ignored the technicalities required of them by the code, for example in relation to marriage consents and formalities. But later they would come to court insisting that as the formalities had not been followed, the marriage was not valid. Eventually, however, one of the parties had resort to the white courts to compel the observance of 'custom', by deliberately bringing their claim within a more determined network of regulation. It could be that these reports could be used to analyse the use made of the state's native law by litigants, and that the court's records could provide a window through which to peer at African society in Natal. But my concern here has been with the ways in which the judges imagined that society. Thus their broad reflections are at times more important than either the facts or the decisions in a particular case.

The Natal Native High Court was not accorded the respect routinely proclaimed for other judicial bodies precisely because it dealt with African law. J. W. Mackenzie put it with vigorous contempt: 'You have three judges there and they cannot make use of their legal knowledge; they have to go on what old Kafir women tell them is Native law. They spend their time in valuing second hand Kafir women, and the ownership of illegitimate children, from one year's end to another' (Cd 2399 1903–5: Evidence, vol. 3: 568). Its judges did not have prestige: 'A judge of the Native High Court is, after all, only a Magistrate raised' (941 G. Hulett). Unbelievers could not understand why the Code of Native Law required a separate Court to administer. As Hulett said, 'At present you have the Native law codified, and why cannot it be administered? If the Code, as it exists, is so complex that it really cannot be understood, the sooner that it is put right the better. . . . so that it can be understood by the superior European Courts' (939).

At times the Natal court seemed confused about what it was doing. Was its mission to apply the 'letter' of native law, as found in the code or some other evidence of custom, or to do what seemed fair? It did think that its role was to shield Africans from the complexities of the common law. As Boshoff put it: 'The Natives of this Province do not understand the intricacies and should not . . . be dragged through the niceties of the system of European Law' (117). In *Sidunge v Nkomokaze 1913 NHC 114* the court allowed the admission of verbal evidence to vary a written agreement, though this was contrary to common law. Boshoff said: 'This Court is . . . not only a Court of Law, but also a Court of Equity' (115–16). But it was far less likely to refer to equity when applying native law. While we have seen that in the administrative and political discourses there was an emphasis on the avoidance of technical legalisms in native law, the Natal court, which administered the only codified system, was highly technical in its approach. None of the simple justice for Africans that affected the approach of other courts was operative there. The Court tried to distinguish for itself the difference between its legal authority and the despotic Zulu chieftaincy it both imagined and validated. It both restrained and supported the exercise of customary rights and authority. In Boshoff's words:

> While we quite realise the importance in all cases where the Supreme Chief gives an order that that order should be implicitly obeyed . . . we owe a duty to the Natives of this country, and it is our duty to see that they receive justice as British subjects. *It is right that they should obey an order, but it is also right that that order should be given to them in a proper manner.* (*Nkantolo v Msuluze 1910 NHC 69* at 73; my emphasis)

Among the uses of the fiction that African law was being applied was that it could excuse any hint of oppression as long as legalistic forms were adhered to. The Judge President of the court characterised the position as he saw it when he referred to 'Native rule as formerly observed among tribes governed by autocratic . . . and paramount Chiefs . . . and whose laws, in a modified and more stable form, are being administered in our Courts' (*Sipongomana v Nkuku NHC 20/6/01*). 'In Zululand', he said of the case before him, 'such an action would be met by the Chief rectifying the wrong: he would wipe out the offender' (27–8). But things had changed. As Boshoff put it, 'these days of horror and darkness have passed' (30).

The court also gave itself considerable leeway in administering the code, which it did not regard as a complete statement of native law. There remained scope for creativity in the name of applying 'original' native law. Campbell JP was not prepared to limit himself to the confines of a code. As a common lawyer, to him the code was like another statute simply set within a larger body of customary law.

> The Code created, altered or modified but little of Native Law, as known and administered by the Courts. Its main purpose was to define, and it must therefore be regarded as mainly affirmative and declaratory. Neither does it embrace all the juristic practices of the natives. There remains still a large body of unwritten and uncodified law behind it. (*Tekeka v Ciyana. NHC 25/2/02 18*)

Lawyers

The development of a dual system of law, with different courts, posed questions about the role of legal practitioners. Were those who practised in the white courts to be accorded the same role in courts that administered African law? Did they impede the state's administration of law? Were they of use to their clients? It was certainly not accepted without question that there was a role for lawyers in African cases. The role of attorneys in the courts was frequently criticised by both politicians and administrators, and attempts made to limit their power to appear (Zulu-land Proc. 2, 1887 and the Native Disputes Bill). While this might in part have reflected a desire to limit the aggressive pursuit of rights at law by Africans, and a paternalist desire to save them from the clutches of expensive lawyers, it indicated more the desire of administrators, that decisions about Africans should as far as possible be administrative rather than judicial. If courts and judicial decisions could not be avoided entirely, then courts without lawyers would at least leave the administrators free to define the procedures and the law, in a way that maximised administrative control. The issue is important because of the light that it throws on the ways in which the 'rule of law' for Africans was conceived. The objection to the appearance of lawyers was linked to ideas about the authority of law, and the view that argument, appeals and the changing of decisions undermined African faith and obedience. The 'despotic powers' of the supreme chief for punishing without trial, were, as Hulett put it,

> in consonance with the Native idea. The Natives in their natural condition recognise supreme power. Directly a decision is given promptly . . . they fall in with it . . . [even] if it has gone against them they immediately salute a sentence by a salute to the Chief. They understand that sort of thing very much better than the uncertainties of law . . . [now] it is a puzzling matter to them to know where finality comes in. (Cd 2399 1903–5: Evidence vol. 3: 182)

Hulett, though he did not agree with the view that lawyers be prohibited, thought that 'Natives have been to a considerable extent plundered' (182). Sir Henry Elliot testified that lawyers led Africans into litigation in which 'in many instances they are absolutely ruined'. Legal costs often bore no relation to the sums originally in contention (209). F. R. Moor put the objections together. Africans 'appreciate summary justice' he thought, and also incurred 'ruinous expenses' (223). Elliot also blamed lawyers for the evils of the use of testamentary succession by Africans in the Transkei. Old men, he said, 'very often' 'fall into the hands of law agents and others, and were induced to make wills, that otherwise they would not have contemplated' (207). Africans too could blame lawyers for encouraging non-traditional behaviours. M. S. Radebe thought them responsible for the difficulties in enforcing the moral aspects of the code. Control of women was made difficult by the intervention of lawyers in seduction cases. 'Every Native boasts about a lawyer. He says, "I can do this and go to a lawyer." ' (545).

C. J. Saunders, the Chief Magistrate of Zululand, where lawyers were not permitted to appear, combined the full complex of reasons for being opposed to the appearance of lawyers in African cases. Legal practitioners, he said, were simply out to 'fleece' Africans, and, furthermore their 'practice tends to set aside the authority of the Magistrates, and everyone else in authority' (755). Worse still, some of the lawyers before the Native High Court were Indian. But the core of his objection related to the links between allowing lawyers into the courts and the obligation of officials who dealt with Africans to follow legal forms. 'You cannot very well deal with these people within the four corners of a Code . . . Lawyers are allowed to appear in cases, and they get the Magistrates' decisions upset . . . because [a man] has not been charged under a particular section of the Code, he is discharged' (756). Better than the constraints imposed by legalism were the powers of the Supreme Chief. 'I could mention several cases where you could not get at a man without going to a most elaborate process through the law Courts, but should one recommend that action be taken by the Governor as Supreme Chief, he issues an order and that order is carried out' (767). Another senior Natal magistrate told the Native Affairs Commission that government of Africans in the South African Republic had worked well without a formal code and it could be done in Natal 'if they are not too much tied by the law, and there are not too many lawyers knocking about' (Evidence: 601).[2]

Not only magistrates chafed against too much legalism for Africans.

---

[2] Natal legislators had, in fact, attempted to rule out the 'technical' application of the law to Africans under the code by providing that no case should be dismissed 'merely by reason of exceptions or objections founded upon irregularity or defect of procedure or the like, unless the Court shall be of the opinion that a failure of substantial justice will result' (Law 49 of 1898: see also Natal Code, section 82).

Judge Beaumont of the Natal court decried the mounting public calls for magistrates to be better versed in law. Criticism from the Bar and the press and 'constant appeals by lawyers on technical points' had 'brought about an opinion that the magistrates are not legally fit for the positions they hold; and that, therefore, there should be a test in every case before a Magistrate is appointed that he has got some legal qualifications . . . [however] the chief and main object is an administrative faculty and the *power of governing men*' (my emphasis). The law, he said, should be 'a secondary thing' (722). Others formulated a kind of command theory of law for Africans which illustrated the undesirability of lawyers and appeals. When Harriet Colenso suggested that there should be fewer prohibitory laws for Africans she was met with the question 'Do you happen to remember whether the majority of the Ten Commandments is "Thou shalt" or "Thou shalt not"?' (416).

Status and capacity

As I have stressed, the supposed contrast between African communalism and European individualism was central to the script in which legal segregation was discussed. The courts administering 'native law' discouraged the emergence of individualism. In relation to succession there was much distrust of an individual right to alter and ignore the strict rules of primogeniture. Further, contracts entered into by individuals which went against native law were inhibited by the courts. People were held strictly either to the code or to custom for apparently contradictory reasons. In some cases it was because they were suspected of backtracking to a dissolution and barbarism even lower than the provisions of native law, in others because they were inappropriately foreshadowing individualist assimilation, which the system of native law prevented.

The court had doubts as to whether Africans in Natal had any right to individual property. In Chadwick's view there was no individual property recognised under the code. 'There are only two kinds of property known under Native Law, (a) Kraal property, (b) House property' (*Tsho v Qointaba 1908 NHC 19* at 25). However it was clear that some had greater powers to deal with property than others. The difficulties were evident in cases concerning the common estate. In *Mona v Mzanya NHC 12/6/01* the appellant had handed over his earnings to his kraal head for over eight years, but was denied cattle for bride wealth. He claimed return of his property. The court refused, adhering strictly to section 138 of the code which said that the kraal head was entitled to receive all the earnings of the inmates. Boshoff alone expressed a doubt. 'It was', he said, 'a very serious thing to deprive a young man of all his earnings' (20). But the new situation where cash wages were being earned meant that a new property relationship, one of permanent tribute from the young to the old, was being created by the native court's administration of the code. In *Mbumane v Nkulukundhlini 2/10/02* the issue arose again. Campbell stated the idealised view. 'The family, and not the individual, being the unit of the Native social system, mutuality of interest requires that all members of the kraal should combine for the common good.' The duty to hand over earnings, and the duty to provide bride-wealth cattle were reciprocal. But was the latter a legal duty? The use that the kraal head made of the contributions 'is left more to individual feeling and public sentiment than to law . . . with the observance of a custom rather than a rule of law, the assistance rendered by one to the other, and the property which voluntarily passed from one to the other are not reclaimable by an action at law' (40). This was, in one sense, sensible pragmatism, as any attempt to impose exact liabilities on kraal heads in relation to bride wealth would have involved the courts and the administration in endless interference in marriage negotiations. But it also left intact a very one-sided property law.

In the cases concerning status and capacity one can see how easily the Natal court moved between and used the ideas of legal systems other than the native law they were supposedly applying. Frequently, in order to define concepts, resort was had to Roman-Dutch writers. In addition the cases seem to show the strong influence of the Roman-Dutch law of marriage, with its emphasis on marital power, and the complete control of the husband over the joint estate, on the Native Court's definition of an acceptable African property regime. In *Macabangwana v Nompola NHC 23/10/02* the court held that a woman was incapable of holding property independently (a ruling it later confirmed in a number of cases). The code was not explicit on the point. Campbell found that the code did, in relation to women, 'confirm the condition of tutelage in which, by their own immemorial laws and customs, they have been placed'. He cast his discursive net widely.

> The dependent position of women in early law is proved by the evidence of most of the ancient systems, which in whole or in part, have descended to our times. The tutelage of women is by no means peculiar to our natives,

and their law may take its place with others as an ancient system, which has come down to us, with many of its essential features unaltered, at least in so far as the position of women is concerned in relation to property. As bearing upon the question of status, it is sufficient to say that in early times women were subject to many disabilities, and among some races were under perpetual tutelage, whether married or not. Emancipation from her position of subordination has been very gradual, even amongst the most civilised nations. It required special legislation in England, as late as our own times, to bestow the property rights of men upon unmarried women and widows, and to enable married women to acquire, hold and dispose . . . of property . . .

It must be remembered that our natives are still in the early stages of social development, as observed among mankind.

The independent holding of property was not one of the changes made by the legislature to improve the status of women. Therefore, he concluded, women remained in their ancient state, 'one of tutelage'.

The question of whether emancipation should be 'further extended' to African women was, said Campbell, 'not a judicial question'. But he did not avail himself of this opportunity to evade the question. The temptation to enter into the questions of policy was too great. It was possible, he noted, to strike a blow at polygamy and increase the supply of labour 'by securing to married women and their houses the fruits of their own work and earnings'. But he did not propose to go down this path. To Campbell it was clear that a 'woman's interest in property is domestic, and personal only, in a relative sense, as an inmate or member of her house. Her acquisitions are on behalf of her house and not for herself, and to admit that property becomes her own . . . would lead to a conflict of authority.' No definition of her rights was possible, because the property regime under which she lived was discretionary.

> The native kraal household, now composed mainly of blood relations, is undoubtedly a relic and modification of the ancient patriarchal system, with its wider core of consanguinity. A ruler with large discretionary powers is essential to the continuance of such a system, and, as the Code recognises the existence of such communities, so it also recognises the necessity for their domestic government, and provides for the same through the head of the family.

The strength of his argument, and his model, swayed even Boshoff, although he continued to show his concern for fostering protection of rights to private property. 'I confess', he said, to trying to find 'some way of escape for the unfortunate woman . . . To hold that a woman . . . is little better than a mere machine (strictly speaking, that is what it amounts to) is so revolting to ones feelings . . . and yet I am unable to differ.'

Many interesting themes arise out of Campbell's judgment, but the one that I would like to comment on is that related to the invocation of the authority of age by judges in the South African courts. In this case African law is validated by reference to its age. It is a part of the ancient institutions of all mankind, old and therefore venerable. But it is also distinguished from white law in that, while old, it has remained in its early, original state. Age is therefore at the same time a marker of worth and a measure of difference, and lesser value. As we have seen, one of the main discursive strategies of the judges in elaborating the Roman-Dutch law was also a celebration of its age. The most characteristic feature of common-law judgments was their exhumation of late medieval and early Renaissance texts, as well as reference to Roman law, from the first republic to Justinian. But here, authentication by age serves a different purpose. For the antiquity is not that of an unchanged human childhood, but part of the developing tradition of an elaborate civilisation. Thus the age of the African system was a sign of the continuing infancy of African law, while the age of the white system indicated its long and complex maturation.

The common estate idealised by the Natal code could not continue to have the same meaning once families began to be separated by forces that they did not control. Many of the cases show how little control over their own destinies people had as they were forced from farm to farm, or to migrate to earn a living. Prolonged absence from the common homestead was a feature of many of the cases that came to the court involving marital, property and support claims. Customs that depended on co-residence and co-operation became unworkable even where people clung to the outer husks and the symbolic meanings. People found themselves in conflict over the duty to pay over earnings, and the right to assistance with bride wealth, feeling the strong presence of obligations and rights, even though the circumstances of their lives had rendered them economic strangers. For the judges this created dilemmas. Too rigid an application of the common estate model would create hardship for those living independently of control of the family head, yet to deny the letter of the code was a fundamentally dangerous departure from the whole model of governing through native law. And, in any case, it was not something that the courts wanted to do. In *Uzimongo and Mdata v Nkomozake 1913 NHC 88* the court found that two men aged twenty-six and thirty, who were unmarried and living in the kraal of their older brother, the kraal head, were minors in law and could not claim from him the transfer of disputed immovable property. Boshoff said: 'A native kraal head somewhat resembles the old Roman *pater familias*; he is vested with certain powers and authorities; he has complete command and control of his kraal; he has the right to exact obedience etc; and the inmates of his kraal are subordinate to him' (89). The analogy is important. It was one that would have been familiar to all South African lawyers, coming from the static textbook images of Roman society to be found in texts on Roman law. Its presence in the minds of the judges enabled them to categorise in legal terms the powers of the Zulu kraal head. It is but one example of how the pressure of common-law categories and concepts was crucial in the forming by the judges of the native law. Boshoff was not happy with the situation he had found to exist. 'Wisdom, no doubt, demands an alteration of this state of affairs,' he said, 'but this is a matter for the Legislature and not for us.' But the legislature was accustomed to seeing Africans in subordinate positions, and from a broader South African perspective, there was little anomalous in the civil law treating grown African men as children and rarely quite fully adult.

The absence of men caused by migrant labour also had implications for property relations, because it sometimes left women necessarily managing property, and responsible, through its use, for the upkeep of dependants. The law of complete male control and ownership did not always coincide with realities. The Natal court recognised the right of a wife to act as the husband's agent in securing necessities for the family (*Silwane v Cetshwayo 1909 NHC 26*). However even though women might in some circumstances live relatively emancipated lives away from their kraals, the kraal members persisted in their claims to control them and their property. Few of these cases could ever have come to court, but those that did give a clue to the prevailing attitudes. *Lubuya v Sala 1913 NHC 48* concerned a claim made by a man that his dead brother's widow should live in his kraal and hand over her property. She had left Natal thirty years before, had worked as a washerwoman in Johannesburg, had invested her earnings in livestock and had also 'purchased a hut with an iron roof which had previously been occupied by a European'. She was 'a woman of considerable property' (51). While the court declined to endorse the claim on the grounds that she had been self-supporting, and had received no assistance from the heir, the fact that it was confidently brought, and plausibly argued as far as the full appeal court, was significant.

Property rights needed to be defined not simply because of the claims made by Africans against each other, but because of the increasing number of claims made by whites against Africans. The common estate and delayed majority clearly had in many circumstances economic benefits for whites. In *Marala v Mbilinana 1917 NHC 32* a father had bound his adult son to supply labour to the farmer on whose land they lived. The son did not do so, and the father was successfully sued for £12. He paid the debt with stock in his son's possession. The court held both that he could bind his son to the labour contract and that he could pay the damages in this way. In *Kanyile v Zinyongo 1917 NHC 128* the court had to decide whether an heir in Zulu law was liable to meet the debts of the deceased even where they exceeded the estate's assets. It said yes. The evidence of four chiefs was taken, and they affirmed the heir's liability even if he inherited nothing, though they added the rider that 'if such a case came before them they would use their discretion and not compel the heir to pay'. Boshoff held that the heir's liability was 'no doubt good law in the days of the Zulu kings' but that he would be 'very sorry' if it was good law still. Gibson wanted to distinguish between a claim against an estate, made by a European, in which liability would be limited to assets, and a claim against the heir, made by an African (*Mhlengwa v Mhlawuli 1920 NHC 30* at 30–2). In the following year the Appellate Division without any of these hesitations confirmed that in Zululand, where it held that section 41 of the 1878 law was still in force, heirs were liable in respect of debts of the inheritance even where it was beyond the amount they had received. 'The law is certainly a hard one,' said Solomon, 'but that is no ground for not enforcing it' (281). While a kraal head had power to use property of the members, such property could not be seized by creditors to satisfy a kraal head's debt, though the fact that cases of this kind came to court suggests that this might frequently have been done (*Cwelembu v Makuza 1908 NHC 87*). Separation of property was further recognised when it was held that kraal heads could not be responsible for the non-compliance with court orders on debts made against their wards (*Nkomo v Siqova 1909 NHC 44*).

The Transkei native appeal courts also supported the patriarchal control of property. It was, they said, 'very clearly laid down by all authorities upon Native Law that no female can inherit property' (*Madolo v Nomawu 1896 NAC 12*). The family estate remained under the control of the kraal head. 'A Native marrying more than one wife establishes them in separate houses and apportions property as he sees fit for the support of each house but during his lifetime he does not lose control of this property' (*Mfenqu v Tshali 1900 NAC 31* at 32). In *Nomlota v Mbiti 1910 NAC 4* Stanford ruled that the earnings of a man's wife were his property and could not be disposed of except by himself, or with his consent (5). The expectations of sons in respect of their mothers' property may be garnered from a case in which a son sued his widowed mother for property she had earned since her husband had died. Elliot found that section 38 of Proclamation 140 of 1885 had made widows over twenty-one majors, free of all control and entitled to retain their earnings. 'The Court is aware', he said, 'that this is in conflict with Native custom' (*Nolanti v Sintenteni 1901 NAC 43* at 44). Unlike Natal, there was in the Transkei no common estate in property between father and sons after the age of twenty-one, and the courts established that, contrary to native custom, the property of a son could not be attached to meet the debts of the father (*Mfanekiso v Mpakana 1905 NAC 85*). In *Maziwayo v Mrapu-kana 1911 NAC 172* the Transkei court confirmed that a widow had the rights to use the property of her deceased husband, and that she could not be compelled to move to the residence of the heir. The frequency of this type of litigation indicates, however, that pressure on women to surrender control must have been considerable.

Succession created many problems in relating European and African law. In the case of land tenure, for example, what law would apply to surveyed plots held under individual tenure? While land held under customary tenure was not heritable, land held under the new form of tenure was. The solution adopted was roughly the same as for Christian marriage. While the legal status and rights of the parties might be assimilated to the common law while they were alive, after death the native law of succession in the male line would apply.[3] But, as Brownlee

---

[3] The effect of Proclamation 142 of 1910 was that no greater property rights were conferred on women entering a Christian marriage than they would have had, had they been parties to a customary union (*Tukuta and Ndela v Panyeko 1927 NAC 195*). Nonetheless although the property of a Christian marriage descended according to the customary law of succession, a Christian widow, unlike a customary-law widow, was held to be the guardian of her minor child (*Ntoyi v Ntoyi 1920 NAC 172*).

said in *Magaqana v Sukulwa 1915 NAC 148* at 149, 'this law of succession in many instances imposed great disabilities upon widows, many of whom were ejected from their fields by the heir upon the death of their husbands'. Consequently Proclamation 16 of 1905 had provided that a widow should have the use and occupation of the immovable property as long as she did not remarry. But the protective impulse could still be trumped by the native law. Brownlee found that not all widows were protected. The proclamation had to be read, he found, in the light not of common law, but native law, 'and it must be borne in mind that in all this matter of succession to rights in land the Native rule of succession has been carefully adopted' (149). If the Great Wife had left a son, his rights prevailed over that of a lesser widow.

Thus while the rhetoric of the assimilators in the Cape had had much to say about the rights of widows to freedom from forced remarriage, and had been concerned to give property rights to some African women, the administration of law by the native courts held widows effectively to the former regime in which they were tied to their husbands' families. While the court held that widows could live where they pleased, if they did they could retain the use of none of the husband's property (*Guluse v Zuka 1918 NAC 156*, Kokstad; Moffat). For many this rendered the choice meaningless. It is notable that while Moffat found that the case 'is undoubtedly a hard one', the principle was not hard enough to declare it to be no longer part of native law (see too the decision of Warner CM in the Umtata court in *Damoyi v Matshiki 1918 NAC 158*).

The expounding of the law relating to succession also shows clearly the differences in legal capacity attributed to whites and Africans. Under section 97 of the Natal code an African could not make a will. Natal Act 7 of 1895 made it possible for immovable property to be bequeathed by will. That will had to be read over and explained by an administrator of native law in the presence of two witnesses. Section 140 of the code laid down that in order for a man to disinherit his heir he had to have sufficient cause, have the consent of the chief, give prior notice to the son, and register the fact. How was an heir to the kraal head chosen in this system? It was normally the male heir of the first married wife. Many of the claims about succession took a very long time to come to fruition, because the value of an estate could not easily be ascertained at death. Much of an estate normally consisted of rights to the bride wealth of women and girls which would not be realised for many years. Thus disputes about succession arose frequently not at the time of death, but long afterwards. It was the judges rather than the litigants who stood up firmly for the principle of primogeniture, and the principle that kraal property could not be assigned away from the general heir. 'Under native law', said Chadwick, 'succession to property on the death of a kraal head is governed, not by the will or caprice of a kraal head on his death bed or elsewhere, but by the position of his sons derived from the rank or status of their mothers' (*Upimi v Francis 1918 NHC 56* at 58–9). We may contrast the great hostility among the practitioners of native law to the idea that an African should be able to make a will with the tone of the debates about testamentary succession among whites. White testators' ability to leave their property was taken to be semi-sacred, courts were most reluctant to intervene with testators' wishes, and the legislature very hesitant about interfering with testators' powers. But African individuals were not accorded such powers over property.

The issue of the undivided estate also affected the extent of the liability of a kraal head for damages for the torts of inmates. In *Mbaso v Mtimkulu 1915 NHC 124* a man was found liable to pay damages for an assault committed by his wife. In an earlier case the Natal Supreme Court had declined to find a man liable for the conduct of his son, committed when he was away from his father. The court had been confronted, said Boshoff, with 'the monstrosity of compelling a man to pay for something which he did not know and which was not under his control' (126). But where a man's wife had committed an assault in his presence, the court was ready to find him liable. Jackson added that

> it may be observed that although the liability imposed on kraal heads under native law may be regarded as inequitable under Colonial Law, it must be remembered that the inmates of a kraal are a source of wealth to the kraal head, and it is for that reason they are held to be largely responsible for the misdeeds of those under their control. (128)

It may, he observed, be 'too great a strain' to hold them responsible for 'remote acts' but it was 'a liability which is hard to get away from'.

While the Transkei courts did not, because of the age of majority legislation in the Cape territories (sec. 38 of Proc. 110 of 1879), uphold the principle of the single estate when it came to questions of contract and property ownership, they supported the unadulterated principles of patri-archy and the unity of the common estate so far as they could when it came to questions of delict. While it accepted that a kraal head was liable for the torts of his sons, and, indeed, of all kraal inmates, it held that 'Native custom . . . does not hold a father liable for his son's debts in matters of contract' (*Qukwana v Makubalo 1920 NAC 177*). Under native law, it said, the head of a kraal was liable for any of the torts committed by kraal members, not as a wrongdoer, but as a 'surety responsible for the good behaviour of the members of his kraal' (*Macebo v Mham 1915 NAC 139* at 141). Commenting in the *Union Law Review* Truro similarly found an administrative rationale for supporting the customary law in this instance, noting that the 'great principle which runs through the native law of torts' was responsibility of the head of the kraal. He applauded it as 'salutary . . . It makes for control and discipline, *besides obviating the necessity of too strict proof as to the identity of the person who is alleged to be the wrongdoer*' (1910: 352; my emphasis). They also held that, in reverse, a father could claim for the damages done to his dependants, for 'if the Court will refuse to relieve a Native parent of responsibilities involved by a peculiar provision of Native custom much more will it refuse to deprive a Native father of a privilege conferred upon him by the same custom'. This was particularly so in relation to damages for seduction, where the 'real injury', in Brownlee's view, had been done to the father not the daughter.

> While among Europeans, the injury is more to the outraged sense of propriety and morality, yet in Native cases the injury is real and material, for the father looks to his daughters to build up the fortunes of his house by means of their dowries, and the deflowering of any of his daughters has the immediate effect of depreciating her marriageable value. (*Mbongwana v Ngolozela and Gila 1912 NAC 256* at 257)

Making the kraal head liable for all torts was certainly convenient for plaintiffs, and provided a remedy against the person most likely to be able to pay. But continuing to recognise a single estate, and subordinate contractual capacities for most persons, made economic assimilation more difficult. While the idea of a single estate might have helped some litigants, the necessary concomitant, minor status in law in contractual matters, though it was adapted to the needs of rural white employers who contracted for labour with family heads, would not have made life easy for other employers or for traders. Transkei courts also took the view that Proclamation 140 of 1885 gave to them the discretion not to apply Native law even to cases between Africans. In several reported cases parties sought to evade the application of native law. In relation to the responsibility of the father for the torts of a son, for example, it was successfully claimed that this did not apply to a 'civilised' person. Attributes of civilisation included Christian marriage, the type of house (square) and furnishings (e.g. *Tumana v Smayile 1908 NAC 207*). In holding that the magistrates had a discretion on a case by case basis, the Transkei courts were far freer than those in Natal, where only officially exempted Africans could be freed from customary obligations.

The readiness to support customary law was more strained where rights in property and rights in persons appeared to the courts to be confused. In *Silwane v Bobotshe 11/2/03 NHC* Boshoff objected to the practice of promising the bride-wealth cattle eventually to be paid for a young girl as security for a loan. 'You want to attach a servitude in a human being', he said (17). In *Nsizwana v Vovo 12/6/03* the court declared this practice of pledging a girl or, strictly speaking, her future bride-wealth cattle, in security for, or satisfaction of a debt, to be illegal. But it soon stepped away from this disapproval. In *Matshuba v Fogoti 1908 NHC 12* the court distinguished between the allocation of the property rights in a girl, and dealing with a girl as a chattel. Campbell dissented: the girl, he said, was dealt with in a manner 'resembling property', allocation of rights was a 'euphemism' for the 'predominant idea' of possession. But Boshoff had relaxed his view. 'It must be clear to anyone accustomed to dealing with natives that these cases cannot always be decided on the same lines as a case between two Europeans. Knowing that natives look not so much at the children as children, but rather to the property rights which such children represent' (*Bunyolo v Gimba and Mtongana 1911 NHC 201*). The new analysis was that what had passed in the transaction was not the girl, but the potential bride wealth. Chadwick also found the transaction legal, reasoning by analogy. 'In my judgement', he wrote, 'a girl so assigned or allocated is very much in the position of a promissory note given in satisfaction of a debt, which only extinguishes the debt on being honoured at maturity' (18). The Cape Native Court also took this view. In 1918 while it rejected the pledging of the girl herself, it declared that 'the Native Custom by which the anticipated dowry of a girl is pledged to meet a lawful claim is quite distinct' (*Ndabankulu v Pennington 1919 NAC 171*). A note on the judgment reads, as if to clear up the complex issue: 'The underlying principle appears to be that a contract whereby a man acquires rights in the *dowry* of a girl is *not* immoral; but where the rights are acquired in the *girl herself* then the contract *is* immoral' (172). The issue continued to cause unease. To prevent the courts backsliding to a more interventionist position the Natal code of 1932 (section 146 (1) and (2)) provided that women were not to be treated in any way as property 'notwithstanding any property rights which might be connected with them'. However, 'the mere indication of a woman or girl as the source from which, through her *lobolo* a debt or obligation is to be met shall not invalidate a contract based purely on native law and custom, but this shall not apply to any other contract'.

The customary law of contract was thought by all commentators to be 'imperfectly developed' (Truro 1910: 351). 'They are not', Truro observed, 'a great trading or bartering people, and therefore we do not find anything of importance relating to the law of contract, such as purchase and sale, or bailment' (341). In considering what kind of property transactions between Africans could be dealt with under native law, and what had to be dealt with under the common law, the courts tried to decide whether the transaction was one that was known to native law and custom. In *Nyongwana v Xolo 1912 NHC 46* the court ruled that the purchase and sale of a beast was known to native law. This meant that the technicalities of the Roman-Dutch law, with its insistence on delivery before ownership passed, did not have to be applied to cases of this sort. 'Our law of delivery', said Boshoff, 'is quite incomprehensible to the uneducated Zulu' (52). Boshoff however was not prepared to generalise to the position that any purchase and sale could be thus categorised. 'It all depends . . . on the thing being sold. The purchase and sale of land, or of a motor car by one native to another would undoubtedly be a trade transaction unknown to Native law' (51).

A serious contract could not, in the Natal court's view of customary law, be made with a woman. In *Ugwabu v Masoye 1916 NHC 224* at 226 Jackson had to consider whether or not a contract to loan stock had been entered into. 'The contract of *sisa*', he said, 'must be made with some responsible person, the head of a kraal. In this case the plaintiff contends that it was made with a woman . . . No contract such as this would be made with a woman' (226). In 1921 the court rejected the idea that a married woman had contractual capacity to bind her husband for anything but household necessities. The case concerned a woman who had sold a cow while her husband was away working in Pretoria, and applied the proceeds to the medical treatment of the husband's sister. Fifteen years later the husband sought to have the sale declared void. Even given the circumstances surrounding the sale, and the long acquiescence in it, the court declared it void (*Mzwendayi v Busobengwe 1921 NHC 62*).

Marriage and divorce

As we have seen, determination to keep white and African marriage legally apart was fundamental to the formation of South African private law. Dealing with the marriages of African Christians, therefore, posed difficult problems for the native courts. Assimilative behaviour was often frowned on and impeded, but sometimes the courts were determined to enforce its obligations, to exact a price, as it were, for the ambition to assimilate. In some cases the elevated status of Christian marriage was endorsed. In *Elisabeth v Lazarus 1909 NHC 17* Campbell tried to unravel some of the problems caused by Christian marriages in Natal, which left the parties' property subject to native law. The wife had left her husband on the grounds of his adultery, and had claimed support from him. Could this claim be supported? Clearly it did not exist in native law, but did that apply to the case? In native law, he pointed out, her father, who had received the bride price, would be liable to keep her if she separated from her husband. Did the Christian marriage introduce a new element into the situation? 'Uncultured Native feeling is not outraged' by adultery, said Campbell. Even though the code had introduced it as a ground for divorce in 1891 it was rarely relied on. But, he said, in the case of a Christian marriage 'an effort has been made to rise to a higher social and moral plane'. Polygamous and monogamous marriages should, he thought, be viewed from different standpoints, and courts administering Native law should exercise their authority to protect women, married according to Christian rites, from being 'compelled to live with unfaithful husbands' (19). One of the markers of difference between whites and Africans perceived by the white courts was adultery. For white marriage it was perceived as the most serious offence, causing unbearable moral outrage. But for Africans it was considered to be a relative trifle, easily compensatible, and no grounds for divorce. Magistrates in the Transkei found support for this in *Conana v Dungulu 1907 NAC 135* at 136 where the native assessors advised the court that the wife's adultery was not a sufficient cause for the dissolution of a marriage, and that a husband was not entitled to a return of the bride wealth if he repudiated her. In another case, *Mtembu v Rex 1912 NHC 50*, the appellant, who had married by

Christian rites, and subsequently entered into a customary union, had been convicted of bigamy. The court was divided. The majority found that bigamy was not a crime in native law, and that prohibitory laws had not been extended to Zululand when the marriages took place (57).

The determination to keep the marriage laws separate had consequences with regard to bride wealth which people marrying may not have foreseen. It was common for people to marry as Christians under Roman-Dutch law, but also to exchange bride wealth. The Transkei court held, however, that 'payment of dowry is purely a Native Custom and the fact that dowry is paid in connection with a Christian or civil marriage does not make it any the less Native custom'. A divorce in a Christian marriage had no implications for bride wealth. Customary unions, said the Transkei court, entailed

> much that is opposed to the ideas underlying Civil marriage. A native may repudiate his wife for no cause at all provided that he does not ask for the return of his dowry and a Native wife may dissolve her marriage simply by having the dowry paid for her restored to her husband. Payment of dowry makes, and restoration of dowry dissolves, a marriage according to Native custom. It has neither effect in a Civil marriage. While Native custom is allowed to run parallel with common law – and undoubtedly people are not ripe for its discontinuation, nor is it at present desirable that it should be discontinued – the only sound rule to follow is to apply Native law to the settlement of matters of Native custom. Any attempt to reconcile common law with Native law is bound to fail. The two systems are diverse, and opposed in principle is many respects. (*Somzana v Banshi NAC (Umtata) 1921 86*)

Thus while a divorce was available on the grounds of adultery to those who used the white law to marry, neither guilt nor innocence in this regard affected the liability to hold or return bride wealth.

In *Guma v Guma 1919 NAC 220* Warner elaborated (in a disquisition which included references to Voet on deflowering and the canon-law position on the marriage of Henry VIII) on the differences between white and African marriage. (The question before the court was whether a man could marry, under common law, his brother's customary law widow. While such a marriage had been a duty under customary law, marriage with a brother's widow was forbidden by the white common-law, indeed was criminal incest. If a customary law marriage was really a marriage, a subsequent common-law union with the husband's brother would be incestuous.) Warner held that a customary union was not a marriage. It was, he said,

> necessary to guard against the assumption that, because the single term 'marriage' is used to describe the conjugal relationships established under both the common law of the country and Native law, they are one and the same thing. They have, indeed, so much in common, that each form regularises sexual unions and the status of offspring, but in other respects the two institutions are fundamentally different in nature and the law governing them. While a common law marriage implies a contract on both sides of exclusive cohabitation terminable only on death or the decree of the Courts, a Native marriage is essentially casual and one sided, allows polygyny, and may be dissolved on the action of either party; it is moreover subject to the doctrine of 'no cattle no wife' which was reaffirmed by this Court . . .
>
> The simple fact is that the Native customary relationship can be identi- fied as a marriage only by reference to its surroundings: its recognition is strictly limited and local: and to separate the custom from its associations; universalise its recognition, and judge of its significance in every issue of South African law by the test of a civil marriage must inevitably lead to confusion and chaos. Whatever it may be, a marriage under Native Law is not equivalent to a marriage by common law. (223/4)[4]

The strict application of the code on which the Natal court insisted was a part of a framework in which all African actions were looked on with suspicion as being either backsliding to barbarism, which the code had superceded, or foreshadowing assimilation, which the code prevented. Native law had to hold a fixed, narrow position between the two. The code, said Campbell, 'attempts to elevate the standard of morality among the natives' (*Tshiliza v Ntshongweni 1908 NHC 10* at 11). But it was still their own, different, and lower, standard of morality. The more 'liberal' the attitude towards the 'recognition' of customs, the easier it was to maintain the essential differences between white and black. This is especially evident in the area of marriage and sexuality. Endorsing the right to be different in these areas reinforced a fundamental moral differentiation. The tensions around this issue remained acute, though we can trace a weakening of the moralism that accompanied the Cape liberal

---

[4] The separation of the two systems of marriage was confirmed again by the court which ruled that it was not possible for a European to marry an African under customary law. Africans, we might note, could marry under the European law, but Europeans could not use the African one (*Dana v Pambaniso 1924 NAC 94*).

tradition and its replacement by an endorsement of difference. We may consider two such examples. In *Lusinga v Pulugudhlu 1914 NHC 163* the court had to deal with the question of the morality of using a man to 'raise seed' on behalf of another. Boshoff and Bennett thought it clearly contrary to good morals, and unrecognisable. But Chadwick urged that the court had to look at it 'from a purely native point of view', from which viewpoint there was nothing immoral or irregular in the practice (165). In the second, while the Transkei courts had the power, according to section 297 of Proclamation 140 of 1885, to give relief to women who had been forced into a repugnant marriage, they decided that the practice of *twala* or the forcible seizure and kidnapping of a girl, with a view to subsequent marriage, was not a custom contrary to civilised practice. Transkei courts continued to validate the practice, and to hear suits arising out of it, partly because it was seen as a tactic to force the hand of an unwilling guardian, and a step in the negotiation of bride wealth. The imposition of an unwanted marriage by the guardian was not necessarily easy to prove to white magistrates sympathetic to male claims. In *Nomatusi v Nompetu 1915 NAC 165* a woman alleged that she had been forced into marriage with an older man, and assaulted when she ran away. Brownlee said:

> In accordance with Native custom it is not unusual for a father to use force on his reluctant daughter to induce her to accept a bridegroom whom she does not desire and . . . in many cases the bride gives way to such force . . . The father is often influenced by the hope . . . that when once the girl has given birth to a child she may out of love for her child consent to remain with an unloved husband rather than be separated from her child . . . and then again it is customary for a bride, even should she be a willing bride, to exhibit the most lively signs of grief upon being taken from the familiar home of her father to that of a stranger. (165)

The philosophy of the court in relation to women, and customary law in general, came under challenge in the case of *Sipoxo and Delayi v Rwex-wana 1919 NAC 205*. The Chief Magistrate, Warner, and W. T. Welsh, another senior magistrate, in the spirit of adhering closely to native law, in a cursory judgment, applied the rule that as payment of dowry was an essential of the marriage, the return of the dowry by the father, regardless of the daughter's actions, dissolved the marriage. The native assessors affirmed that 'there can be no marriage if there are no dowry cattle in the kraal of the woman's father' (206). The third member of the court, W. Carmichael, dissented vigorously to what he called 'the essentially slave law of parental divorce' (208). His judgment captures the discourse of an era of administration that was waning in favour of a rule-bound application of native law. The application of native custom had, he insisted, always been subject to modification when it 'conflicted with the common rights of all subjects of the Empire or outraged deep-seated instincts of humanity'. In particular, the great tradition of the Cape courts had been 'to permit the gradual rise in the status of women' (207). How could this be compatible with a situation in which the continuance of their marriage depended on the will of their father? Carmichael ranged through Sir Henry Maine, the Digest and Justinian's code to show how the original powers of a father had included the right to divorce his children, but noted that these powers had been effaced by social develop-ments. Similar developments, enlarging the scope of women's freedom, were to be found in the judgment of the Cape courts, relating to the freedom of movement of widows (208). It was, he urged, going back on the 'best traditions' of the Cape courts not to acknowledge that 'a Native marriage should be regarded as dissoluble in life only by the will and act of the party thereto' (209).

While the native appeal courts struggled over the problems of the chattel-like position of women in customary law they did not favour making things easy for them. In 1910 the Natal court considered the question of whether divorce was known to the native law operative in Zululand. 'From our own knowledge of Zulu laws and customs, and from what we have been able to gather', it said, 'it is clear that in pre-annexation days a woman in Zululand had no rights; she was simply the property of her husband and guardian; but in cases where she had been grossly ill-treated by her husband her cause could be taken up by her father' (*Ugijima v Mapumana 1910 NHC 3*). In 1922 the Natal High Court produced a particularly spirited defence of the marriage system, scotching any impression that the full provisions of the code were being laxly enforced by the court. The judgment was a vigorous affirmation of the rights of the guardian to refuse consent to a marriage on the basis of his material interest in the woman under guardianship (*Mfanobama v Fana 1922 NHC 26*). In the case the widow of the guardian's brother had lived with a man for fifteen years and they had had three children. The guardian refused consent to the marriage because the full bride wealth demanded had not been paid. The court noted 'a number of decisions in this Court in which the tendency has been to recognise as *de facto* marriages mere cohabitation of two persons for a number of years' in spite of the provisions of chapter 10 of the code (28). It was the policy of the province to regulate marriage contracts among Africans and require proof of them. In this case the guardian's consent had not been unreasonably withheld, nor had his refusal been challenged in the way provided by law. Recognising the marriage would be

> to say that something which the law has declared to be essential to a marriage is not essential. It is the strict duty of this Court to be guided by the law and the provisions of Section 148 cannot be lightly brushed aside; otherwise chaos will result from what is at present a well established and regulated system of marriage according to native custom . . . and the work of over fifty years will be undone. (30)

The Transkei courts did not make it easy for an African woman to take the initiative in securing a divorce. The magistrates continued to uphold the principle that a customary union could be dissolved without court sanction, by a return of the dowry. This, however, meant that a woman could not divorce herself without the co-operation of her male relatives. But if she came to court the principle that a customary union was dissolvable by an act of the parties evaporated. To obtain relief from a court a woman had to prove good and sufficient cause. This was not easy where a degree of force and pressure were a part of the marriage culture, and where male witnesses had a material interest in denying accusations. Brownlee confirmed in *Nomatusi v Nompetu 1915 NAC 165* that while parties to a customary marriage could divorce themselves if they did this in the proper manner, if either came to court 'then due cause must be alleged and proved' (166).[5]

---

[5] The recognition of divorce, as McGlendon has noted (1995), even in circumstances in which courts moved towards a view defensive of male claims to control women, nonetheless gave a public forum to women, even though it was one that they could not easily afford. Litigation about divorce, as he shows, involved 'strategising by the two lineages . . . to control the *lobola* cattle' (543). Such litigation was expensive. On his calculation the costs for someone who lost involved fifteen months' wages for a rural woman, to which were to be added the costs of the victorious party (548 note 98).

In Natal, unlike the Transkei, bride wealth was not a necessary legal ingredient of a marriage, but consent of the guardian was. In Natal a determined effort had been made to keep litigation about bride wealth out of the upper levels of the court system. Section 182 of the 1891 code barred all such claims from the state's courts. In 1910 it became possible to appeal from the chief's court as far as a magistrate's court, but no further. Lawyers of all sorts were specifically prohibited from appearing in bride-wealth cases. In *Hlungwane v Mapumulo 1929 NAC* Stubbs held that the Native Administration Act had impliedly repealed the Natal restrictions.

Administration and courts lent their criminal and administrative authority, as well as the authority of the civil law, to the power of guardians to control the marriages, courtships and movements of unmarried women. In approving a magistrate's sentence of two months imprisonment imposed on a woman for wandering from her kraal without the consent of her father Chadwick said that 'the subordination of girls and women to their parents and guardians is a matter which has been recognised in Zululand from time immemorial' (*Mhlongo v Rex 1915 NHC 60* at 61). Women found wandering from their kraals and unable to give a good account of themselves committed an offence under section 289 of the code. It appears that husbands and magistrates used this to harass women who left home expressing their intention not to return to their husbands (see e.g. *Nomasotsha v Rex 1912 NHC 31*). The position in which married women could find themselves is well illustrated in the case of *Mabaso v Ndabankulu 1915 NHC 147*. If a woman left her husband, she could be brought by him before the magistrate and criminally charged with wandering. She might be driven off by the husband who was determined to recover his bride wealth by alleging that she had deserted him. And her guardian, who might be determined not to part with the bride wealth, might not receive her back even if she had a legitimate reason to leave her husband. In one case the criminal law which penalised harbouring for immoral purposes was used against the brother of a woman who had come to him on leaving her husband (*Njakabana v Rex 1917 NHC 267*).

Segregating

As we have seen, the assimilating impulse was fading, but the problems of keeping the systems of law separate in these years when ideological lines were unclear, and lives increasingly crossed the systemic divide, were complex. The Eastern Districts division of the Cape Supreme Court often had to deal with cases that arose out of the increasing commercial contact between whites and Africans. What law would apply to a white creditor's claim against the heir of an African debtor for debts in excess of assets left? The native appeal courts had accepted that under African law the heir would be liable to another African for such a debt. But Roman-Dutch law was supposed to apply to all cases between whites and Africans, and this would exclude white creditors' claims. Nonetheless under the Cape's Native Succession Act of 1864 the heir was made liable in the Cape

Colony. But in the various native territories beyond the colony, as Roman-Dutch law applied, the heir was not liable to a white claimant (see *Lloyd v Nkokele 1907 EDC 127* and *Mbila v Spaulding 1907 EDC 181*). Some more complex difficulties arose in *Mfuleni v Mills 1906 EDC 93* which illustrated the problem of juggling the different concepts and doctrines that had been expounded for the two systems of law, and the kinds of pressures that affected the definition of African law. *Lobola* cattle handed over to the father of a woman in anticipation of a marriage were seized to satisfy a judgment debt against the husband-to-be. When this was challenged on the grounds that the cattle were now the property of the father, the issue was approached by the court in terms of the Roman-Dutch law concept of *dominium*. When had *dominium* in the cattle passed? Did it pass before the marriage took place? It was argued that if it was said to pass on delivery of the cattle, debtors would be able to shelter behind alleged intended marriages. Transkei magistrates and the Cape Supreme Court had taken the view earlier that *dominium* did not pass until the marriage took place. But was *dominium* an appropriate concept? It was now argued that the cattle could not be reclaimed if the intended husband broke off the marriage, but could be if the woman or her father were at fault. Kotze decided that the cattle could not be taken to satisfy a debt owed by the intended husband, even before the marriage. But he could only do so by invoking another Roman-Dutch concept. The situation was, he said, analogous to a pledge of movables accompanied by delivery, and these could not be taken by a judgment creditor.

While most attention has been paid to questions of marriage in relation to customary law, perhaps greater insight into the relationship between South Africa's legal systems can be gleaned by paying closer attention to questions of 'economic' law. There was no assumption at all that Africans would be subject to the same law as whites. In relation to insolvency, for example, there was great doubt as to whether it would be appropriate to allow Africans to take 'advantage' of the insolvency laws which applied to whites in order to 'evade' their debts (Cd 2399 1903–5: Evidence, vol. 1: 209–10). According to African law, the argument was, not only would a man be liable for his debts all his life, but so would his relatives, and the heir would remain so after his death. In these circumstances, insolvency was clearly 'evasion'. Together with the legal recognition of the common estate in Natal, this had clear advantages for creditors. As one local solicitor remarked, 'If a native owes you money you can go to the father for it, and if the father owes you money and dies, his heir is responsible, and that really keeps the Native in subjection' (25). Section 152 (1) of the Natal code of 1932 laid down that 'no Native may avail himself or be brought under the operation of any insolvency law or regulation, to the prejudice of claims against him by any other Native, unless he is a trader'.

Another example is the issue of which law to apply to a claim for money lent between Africans. This came before Warner in 1920 (*Tango v Ngqongo 1920 NAC 306*). Proclamation no. 140 of 1885 said that the court 'may' apply native law to cases between Africans. Did this mean 'shall'? Should customary law be applied to economic transactions, like loans, which were universal? Two answers were possible. One was to say that as everyone lent money, a loan was not specifically an African custom, and could not, therefore, be dealt with by customary law. Another was to say that as everyone lent money, such transactions were known to customary law, and should therefore be governed by it. There was clearly no legal way of choosing between these two options. The answer depended on policy and the overall ideological framework. In 1918 the Cape Supreme Court had held that claims between Africans for cash lent were to be decided by native law (*Makalima v Gubanxa 1918 CPD 58*), though the Transkei court thought otherwise. In a number of cases also it was held that the charging of interest on a loan was unknown in native law.

In an apparent nod towards recognition of assimilation section 104 of the Magistrate's Court Proclamation of 1923 limited the application of native law to suits involving questions of custom between Africans. But there was still a wide discretion as to what fell within this rubric. In a case concerning the question of whether an illegitimate son of a widowed first wife born after her husband's death, succeeded to the father's estate ahead of his legitimate sons by later wives, Welsh ruled that any issue of the first wife prevailed over issue of other wives. By 1927 the Transkei court was far less likely to strike down a custom than in earlier years. This was a matter of policy, not law. As Welsh said, the court 'should not interfere in matters of broad policy which is the prerogative of the executive and . . . would . . . not be justified in setting aside a custom which had long since become crystallised into law' (*Dumalitshone v Mraji 1927 NAC 168* at 169–70). To this view Whitefield entered a strong assimilationist dissent, opposing 'the continued recognition of a Native Custom opposed to public policy and natural justice and which is based on immorality and unchastity . . . The custom is manifestly immoral and repugnant to

Christian principles and is thus opposed to public policy' (170). But this was now outdated rhetoric. The courts were moving, before the 1927 Act, from the Cape policy of giving priority to Roman-Dutch law towards giving priority to African law. In 1926 the Transkei court rejected the view that customary law which conflicted with Roman-Dutch law must be rejected. Both were valid in their spheres (*Ludidi v Msikelwa 1926 NAC 28*). Two systems were now being evolved, parallel to each other, each with its 'genius' and distinctiveness and with discrete applicability to group race and culture.

Criminal law in the Natal Native Court

The principle of applying native law and custom to conquered African populations was not as clear cut in relation to the criminal law. In Natal Ordinance 5 of 1849 it was laid down that crimes amongst 'natives' should be judged by 'native law', subject to the repugnancy principle: 'except so far as the same may be repugnant to the general principles of humanity recognised throughout the whole civilised world'. However in 1875 the jurisdiction of native chiefs and administrators under native law was limited to civil matters, and criminal matters were to be heard in the colonial courts applying the common law of the colony, with the exception that the Native High Court would hear appeals in crimes arising out of native law, such as faction fights and witchcraft. The principle that had been established in the Natal code of 1875 (which was re-enacted in the Transvaal in 1881) was that there was no distinctive 'native' criminal law. This was a rare victory for the original Cape principle of assimilation. As Boshoff said in *Msilawemfene v Rex 1908 NHC 36* at 38–9, 'We have nothing to do with the native views in criminal cases, we are here to administer the criminal law which is the same for all classes.'

But there was one important difference. Judicial control over the administration of Africans proceeded along different principles from that related to whites. The administrative powers and discretions given to officials, and to chiefs, were wider, and the court-imposed limitations fewer. Disregard of an administrative order, or disrespect towards an officer or chief, was commonly made a criminal offence. Punishment for disobedience of an administrative order, said Jackson, 'is no new principle and has long been recognised as a necessary provision in the government of the Natives' (*Manqatsha v Rex 1910 NHC 122* at 125). Jackson ruled that the imposition of criminal punishment under this section, either a fine or imprisonment, was done under administrative and not judicial powers. The powers given to officers of state to punish for disregard or defiance of orders was not, however, without limit. Jackson said that they were

> not intended to supersede judicial procedure, or there might be no limit to the extent . . . it is rather the legalising for supplementary authority for effective administration under circumstances which require prompt and perhaps arbitrary action to be taken administratively in preference to a judicial procedure which might not be effective or which might cause undue delay. (*Zita v Rex 1915 NHC 56* at 59)

The distinction that the courts made between administrative and judicial decisions enabled them to place large areas of decisions affecting Africans beyond their responsibility.

Household heads also had considerable personal powers. The Natal code laid down what was recognised elsewhere as a general principle, that inmates owed 'obedience' to him. He could summarily arrest any person defying his authority, and 'inflict reasonable but not excessive corporal punishment upon the inmates of his kraal for the purpose of correction and to maintain peace and order therein' (sec. 38, 40). The distinctions between criminal and civil liabilities, so jealously guarded by the Roman-Dutch law, were not a part of the state's law as applied to Africans. Section 167 of the Natal code read: 'Any Native who disregards or fails to comply with any duty, obligation, direction or prohibition imposed on him by this Code shall be guilty of an offence.' This brought into the realm of criminal sanction all duties imposed by the code, such as those of support. I do not know whether many were prosecuted under this section, but it is an indication of the difference in legal regime deemed appropriate.

Yet in the criminal law technicalities were upheld in the Native Appeal Court. The role of the courts was to defend the integrity of the state's administrative processes, not to impede them. The occasional objection to the caprice of subordinates was a part of this defence. Magistrates' findings were overruled where the charges did not follow the wording in penal statutes. In *Tela v Rex 1915 NHC 107*, for example, a charge was brought under section 271 of the code which criminalised 'insulting gestures' and 'offensive and disparaging language' at 'any feast, dance or gathering', intended to provoke a breach of the peace. The accused were charged with using 'threatening and insulting' language. Jackson ruled (109) that the exact wording must be used 'otherwise an offence might be created which was not contemplated by law'.

The Natal court heard criminal appeals in a specific range of 'native' cases, and it is of interest to consider how this aspect of their jurisdiction contributed to their analyses of African society, and to the colonial view of African behaviour and the role of law in constraining it. Horrific murders involving witchcraft; the use of human flesh; the killing of white women; and drunken brawls and faction fighting were a part of the context in which statements about civilisation and barbarism were made by the court. They confirmed the images of barbarism for the judges and they illustrate the process whereby each extreme case tended to be taken as signifying a general pattern of behaviour among the subject people as a whole. In the case of *R v Msweli and others 1911 NHC 64*, a poor-white farmer's wife was battered to death. The principal accused was a chief's heir, whose father was buried on the farmer's land and who had avenged himself after the trees surrounding the grave had been cut down. The case arose out of colonial conquest, confiscation of land, outraged feelings and revenge. Boshoff began his judgment by saying:

> In spite of the most earnest missionary and educational effort, the native population of this Province still continues to contribute largely to the criminology of this country. One feels irresistibly driven to ask oneself the question: What can be done, if not to obliterate, certainly to mitigate these terrible evils? The case . . . discloses one of the most shocking, . . . diabolical murders that can be found in the annals of crime. (64)

Witchcraft

No class of cases was as significant in the creation of a characterisation of Africans as those dealing with witchcraft. The 'subject of witchcraft' was, Hailey wrote, 'the outstanding problem of the lawgiver in Africa' (1938: 295; see also Chanock 1985: chapter 5). It was problematic not only in practical terms, but also produced in South Africa, as it did elsewhere in Africa, huge problems for a discourse about legal rule, and was a node around which opposing images of African and white societies were created. The Natal Native High Court heard a series of cases in the decade after the crushing of the Zulu rebellion which caused significant concern to whites involved with legal administration. In 1910 the court heard the case of *R v Butelezi and others 1910 NHC 84* in which eleven persons were convicted of a murder in which there was detailed evidence concerning the ritual use of the body parts of the victim. In the following year it heard a case in which a suspected witch was murdered. In *R v Magabeni and others 1911 NHC 107* the accused were convicted of stabbing and burning to death a man suspected of causing sickness in their kraal. Boshoff said: 'From the natives' point of view he was looked upon as an *umtagati* [witch] . . . There is no evidence that . . . any of . . . the prisoners consulted a diviner: but our knowledge of the Native, and his superstitions and customs and character, leaves no doubt whatever in our minds that a diviner must have been consulted' (109). He rejected the argument that belief in witchcraft should be a defence against the crime of murder. 'We are asked to say that these persons are innocent of that crime . . . I do not think we . . . are prepared to excuse them on the ground of the Native superstitions . . . When is it to come that these Natives are to learn that consulting diviners and committing murders will not be tolerated' (111)? In *R v Qoqa and others 1911 NHC 112* the court dealt with a gruesome killing by eight persons, to the prosecution otherwise motiveless, in which body parts had been cut off for ritual purposes. Nine were charged and convicted in *R v Usiyeka and others 1912 NHC 98* in which a diviner had pointed out a widow and she had been beaten to death. Chadwick said: 'In this remote corner of the Colony [they] may . . . have considered that they were at liberty to resort to their old customs of smelling out and wiping out' (100–1). In *R v Radebe 1914 NHC 194* the defendant's plea that he had committed the murder in the belief that the dead woman had by witchcraft killed two of his children and would kill a third was rejected by Boshoff.

The judges were puzzled because the murders seemed to be not individually motivated but appeared often to be the result of obedience to others and to custom. Many of the murder cases featured large numbers of accused who had acted in concert with little attempt at concealment of their crime from witnesses, which confounded the court and contributed to the air of implacable irrationality and brutality involved. In the face of this judges liked to be correct. In *R v Magebe and others 1916 NHC 167*, another case in which body parts were cut from the victim, two of the accused were acquitted of murder. Boshoff told them: 'You have escaped by reason of the fact of living under the white man's rule . . . the white man's law requires that the evidence of a [co-accused] witness . . . should be corroborated before either the liberty or life of a subject can be taken' (177). But they were also bewildered. Jackson said in *Fayedwa v Rex 1915*

NHC 44 at 47: 'The native is brought up in an atmosphere of superstition, and superstition is engendered by every unusual circumstance. Especially is this so in cases of illness or disease, the origin of or cure for which it is hoped will be revealed by divination.' The appellant in this case was charged with acting as a diviner. Boshoff pointed out that for similar offences he had already spent ten years in prison and received between eighty and one hundred lashes, and that he had a *bona fide* belief that he communicated with the spirits. He was nonetheless convicted. In *R v Sitendeni Dimba 1913 NHC 45* the murdered man had been pointed out as a witch by a diviner. The motive for the crime was, therefore, 'so obvious'. The opportunity was taken of 'meting out to him that form of reprisal and punishment which centuries of barbarism have recognised as just, and which is ingrained in the native mind' (48). Boshoff described the African way of thinking in a passage that could as well have been written by Rider Haggard:

> In a previous case we found it necessary to remark upon the tenacity with which the native holds to the idea that the diviner is possessed of superhuman powers, and to the implicit submission with which the decision of the diviner is accepted. When the Zulus were a distinct nation ruled by their Kings, once a man was pointed out as the culprit by the Diviner, he would in all probability not witness the setting of the sun . . . That night his kraal would be surrounded by an Impi, and he, the inmates of his kraal . . . would be done to death . . . His cattle would be confiscated and become the property of the King. So strong is this belief in the Diviner instilled in the native mind, that the culprit's own people, no matter how near and dear they may be to him, would turn against him . . . they would join in the chorus with others, namely 'Away with him . . .' (57–8)

We can follow this process at the highest level of government. The Natal cases, and the high number of death sentences handed out by the court, gave rise to an outburst of interest and concern from Lord Gladstone, the Governor-General and High Commissioner, whose responsibility it was to confirm the sentence or exercise the prerogative of mercy. In October 1911 he wrote to the Minister of Native Affairs, Henry Burton: 'The Zulus are a fine race; perhaps the finest in South Africa' (Union Archives HC 6871/F1079, Gladstone–Burton 28/10/11). He had been shocked, therefore, by the number of murder cases involving witchcraft, ten cases which had called for the execution of twenty-five men and twelve other long terms of imprisonment, which had since May 1910 involved Zulus. (The total number of executions carried out in the Union in this period was sixty-five. Executions for witchcraft were, therefore, close to 40 per cent of the total.)

Within the High Commission much thought had been done as Gladstone had sought for advice in dealing with the sentences. As the Governor-General's secretary wrote: 'In the cases brought before Your Excellency . . . we get many hard facts but little insight into the native mind' (ibid., Beresford–Gladstone, memo 13). The High Commissioner's advisers sought out expertise on the nature of witch-related beliefs and practices. Attention was given to Henri Junod's *The Life of a South African Tribe* (1912, vol. II: 460ff.) which was, however, singularly unhelpful as regards the ways in which the legal questions of guilty intention and degrees of culpability were framed. Junod had written of the confusion commonly made between witches and witch-doctors, between black and white magic: the criminal magical practice and that which fought evil influences. While he appeared to have no doubt that there were practitioners of black magic he was not certain whether they were 'conscious of their doings as witches'. 'They are murderers', he wrote, all the more to be feared as they 'act unconsciously, without being seen or known. Two motives inspire their crimes – hatred and jealousy.' What he called white magicians, on the other hand, were 'the helpers and upholders of the social order, and not criminals . . . and are regularly consulted by the Native Court in order to detect wizards'. As was the case elsewhere in Africa, South African laws made no distinction between the two kinds of practitioner. Junod documented the methods of witch-finding – the divination; the 'smelling out ecstasy', conducted at the behest of a chief before a large assembly; and the poison ordeal. Witchcraft, Junod wrote, was one of the 'greatest curses of Native Life'. He attributed it to 'animistic beliefs'; to the previous practice of cannibalism, which had left a feeling of 'disgust and horror'; and to '*The terrible hatred* of which the Native mind is capable. If some people dare to accuse members of tribes of such awful acts as those of killing and eating human flesh it is because they know that a Native who hates would not shrink to satisfy his desire of vengeance' (his emphasis). Junod nonetheless reminded his readers that 'the witchcraft superstition has been universally spread amongst our own forefathers, and that there have been epidemics of it in the 14th, 15th and even the 16th centuries, hundreds of wizards having been tortured and burnt in most of the European countries, after having been tried before the regular courts'. The invocation of comparative history had great appeal. On the one hand it appeared to close the gap between savages and civilised by reminding the audience of white South Africans that they too had a past of comparable social practices. But on the other hand, to stress common humanity and cultural flaws was also to emphasise the distance between the advanced and the uncivilised, and the responsibility of those who had opened up an evolutionary lead to impose their standards.

Junod's belief that witchcraft was on the increase also found its echoes throughout the administrative and legal analyses of the period. Some put this down to the decline in the authority of the chiefs (e.g. Union Archives HC 6871/F1079, Beresford memo to Gladstone). Other more common analyses saw the powerful chiefs of old as having relied upon belief in witchcraft for their power and having been the main fomenters and users of witchcraft accusation. As Theophilus Shepstone had advised in 1892:

> Prohibit absolutely accusations of witchcraft. 'Witch dances' as they are called, such accusations being their purpose, are the great political engine of the hereditary chief . . . they make it easy to strike down, without trial or defence, the most formidable rival . . . Take away this engine and nothing will be left to lean upon but the power of the government. (Quoted in Welsh 1971: 113)

Shepstone seems to have drawn on Warner's notes in Maclean's *Compendium* which contained several pages of the most lurid description of public witch-finding ([1858] 1968: 91–5) and noted that chiefs made use of the ceremonies

> as a political engine, to get rid of some influential but troublesome individual; for once a person has been legally charged with this crime, it matters not how popular or respected he might have been before . . . The chiefs there find this a very convenient and powerful state engine to support their power, and enable them to remove individuals who they would otherwise find great difficulty in getting rid of. (95)

What gave the ceremonies their power was that there was 'not the slightest doubt that Kafirs do frequently attempt to bewitch each other . . . there is no wonder at their superstitious fears having invented some kind of scheme to detect and punish individuals, whom they believe to be guilty of these crimes' (ibid.). The existence of witchcraft beliefs, then, reinforced the view that Africans were not only superstitious and violent, but were legally irrational in crucial aspects, and that their administration of justice was all too often premised on manipulative and terrifying irrational despotism. As Warner concluded, 'what a melancholy state of society this is' (ibid.).

The common legal response in British African territories was to follow the model of the English Acts of 1736 and 1824 and treat all forms of witchcraft as a pretence, prohibiting both its practice and its detection. The penal code drawn up by the Cape commission contained sections 'imported . . . solely with the view to suppressing the native witch-doctor' (para. 46). Chapter XI penalised the imputation that anyone had used non-natural means to cause injury or damage; forbade the employment of a witch-doctor or witch-finder; 'professing to a knowledge of so-called witchcraft' and supply of 'the pretended means of witchcraft'; and using the 'pretended knowledge' to use processes calculated to injure; and provided the heaviest penalty for anyone 'proved to be by habit and repute a witch-doctor or witch finder' (secs. 177–81).

The difficulties of dealing with the irrationalities of witchcraft can be illustrated by the concerns put before the Governor-General in relation to the commutation of death sentences. Was it a sufficient ground to commute if the plea was that the killer had acted because of superstitious belief in witchcraft and had killed after a witch had been pointed out? If this was accepted what would the effect be on the overall effort to eradicate witchcraft beliefs? Should there be some special evidence of primitiveness to justify such a plea? One adviser urged that hanging before assembled headmen from the offender's kraal would be a deterrent. Gladstone tended towards commutation of death sentences on the grounds that he did not think that 'by hanging them, we shall impress them to such an extent that they will disregard the decrees and statements of the witch doctors'. He wrote, calling on his experience as Home Secretary in Britain:

> In considering death sentences the most perplexing problem in 'civilised' countries is in determining when guilt is proved whether the prisoner is so far responsible for his actions that the extreme penalty can be executed. I have had to decide many very difficult cases when it was argued that because of epileptic tendencies, or weak mindedness, or low physical development, or gross ignorance and depravity resulting from surround-ings over which the prisoner had no control, the prisoner could not be held fully responsible. (Union Archives HC 1832/12, minute)

He was against automatically ruling out the death penalty. If, he said, it was now laid down that when murder followed 'smelling out' hanging should be excluded, a precedent would be created which would make it very difficult to impose the death penalty when the time had come 'when the natives could not plead ignorance'. However, he pointed out, the death penalty was only applied to a proportion of murder convictions – in England about 30 per cent. It should not be assumed, therefore, that it should apply as a matter of course in witchcraft murders. But it would be suitable where the 'smelling out' was a pretext for a killing, and where 'the practice is catching, and sometimes especially infests a district. It may take a resemblance to a Vendetta. In such cases the severest penalties may be necessary.'

It is of considerable significance that this complex of concerns, which had for decades concerned administrators and anthropologists, and now the Governor-General and his advisers, relating to the difficult dilemmas in witchcraft cases, were not felt at all by the judges of the Appellate Division. In 1915 when the court had an opportunity to think through what Hailey had called 'the outstanding problem for the law-giver in Africa' it abruptly dismissed the question in the briefest of judgments (*R v Radebe 1915 AD 97*). Innes, not even calling on the Crown to argue, turned down leave to appeal from a decision of the Natal Native High Court. The court was asked, he said baldly, 'to say that the condemned man suffered from a delusion which relieved him from legal responsibility – in other words that the *deliberate belief* in witchcraft is equivalent to insanity. I do not see how we could assent to such a proposition' (97; my emphasis). The executive remained more sensitive than the appellate court on these matters. In 1917 the law adviser summed up: 'The death penalty is usually a) carried *into effect* when the witchdoctor himself is the murderer b) commuted when the prisoner has slain the wizard (or witch) indicated by the witchdoctor.' There were two cases of murder for the purposes of obtaining medicine from the body of the victim. In both the witch-doctors were executed 'while mercy was shown to their dupes who had actively assisted'. There were two cases in which the person accused of witchcraft had 'retaliated' by killing his accuser. 'Here mercy was shewn' (Union Archives 1/67/22; Minute 13/11/17).[6]

---

[6] There was a second round of government concern regarding the prevalence of witchcraft accusations, resulting in homicides and serious assaults in the wake of the influenza epidemic that followed the end of the war in 1918. Legal authorities in the Transkei, perceiving a threat to the maintenance of law and order, and knowing the difficulties in obtaining evidence that an accused was 'by habit and repute' a witch-finder, pressed for more severe penalties for the allegation of witchcraft and the extension of the power of the magistrates to deal with the cases.

14

Customary law, courts and code after 1927

This chapter has two parts: the first is a reprise of the major themes in the state's relationship with African law, while the second illustrates briefly the doctrinal directions taken by the native courts after the passing of the Native Administration Act in 1927. In creating a separate court system for Africans, the 1927 Act adopted the Transkei formula which gave to magistrates in the native courts discretion as to whether to apply African law. Section 11(1) of the Act provided that

> it shall be in the discretion of the Courts of Native Commissioners in all suits or proceedings between Natives involving questions of customs followed by Natives, to decide such questions according to the Native law applying to such custom . . . Provided that such Native law shall not be opposed to the principles of public policy or natural justice: Provided further that it shall not be lawful for any court to declare that the custom of *lobola* or *bogadi* or any other similar custom is repugnant to such principles.

But the Act did not make clear how this discretion was to be exercised. Did it mean that the Roman-Dutch common law was to be considered to be the law that usually applied to African civil cases, except in matters peculiar to tribal life and custom, for which there was no common-law provision? Or was it to be taken to mean that African law would usually apply to civil cases between Africans, the only exceptions being those circumstances in which it was impossible to apply the concepts of African law? Unsurprisingly the different divisions of the new native courts initially took different views. The Cape court initially applied the Transkeian view which was to limit African law to traditional transactions related to personal law for which there was no Roman-Dutch law that could be applied, and to apply the Roman-Dutch law to commercial exchanges between Africans. The Northern court, under the leadership of

328

McLoughlin P, endorsed the Natal view that African law must be assumed to apply to all transactions between Africans (see Simons 1968: 62; Lewin, 1947). This had the effect of subjecting Africans to two different sets of law relating to economic exchanges. The Roman-Dutch law applied to their increasing economic contacts with Europeans, but African law to their dealings among themselves.

Giving priority to African law also indicated the spirit in which the new Act was to be applied to personal law. The way in which the South African law developed was contrary to the expectation of Hailey's *African Survey* (1938) where it was predicted that it was 'unlikely' that native law not contained in statutes would extend its field (268). It also appeared to run counter to the ways in which many lives were lived. By the time the Native Administration Act came into operation in 1929 marriages under Roman-Dutch law may have made up between one-fifth and one-quarter of all African marriages (no figures were kept for customary marriages; Simons 1968: 68). While common-law marriage did imply a break with bride wealth and customary succession laws, it did not necessarily affect the lives of those involved in this way. Even those who did not marry under customary law were often reluctant to abandon bride wealth, and widows of these marriages, as we have seen, were not necessarily in a position to assert the rights of inheritance which the white law nominally gave to them. It was not the spread of Roman-Dutch law marriage, but the changes resulting from migrant labour, land shortage and the increased rate of urbanisation and its lopsided pattern that had far greater real effects on family behaviour. In 1911 there were just over half a million Africans resident in towns, with men outnumbering women by four to one. In 1921 there were around six hundred thousand, and the ratio was three to one. By 1936 there were over a million, with just over two men to every woman. In the period as a whole the black urban population more than doubled, with the female population growing considerably faster than the male. The mid-point, 1921, shows the beginning of the great migration of African women to the towns. Between 1911 and 1921 the male African urban population increased by 7.1 per cent; and between 1921 and 1936 by 78.4 per cent to around 785,000. In the same periods the female urban population increased by 50.3 per cent and 142.3 per cent; from under a hundred thousand to close to three hundred and sixty thousand. To a white population already alarmed by black migration to the cities, the huge increases in the number of urban black women seemed pathological. One of the responses of government was to try to extend the pass laws to African women, an attempt which was frustrated by widespread resistance and by the Appellate Division in *R v Detody* (see below). In the early 1920s the Urban Areas Act authorised a greater means of administrative control over population movement to white government, but it was years before it was administratively operative. In this context we can see that the ultimate white endorsement of African patriarchy after its initial rejection in nineteenth-century liberal discourse is related to territorial segregation as well as cultural differentiation. The reversion to and strengthening of patriarchal controls over black women was part of the context of attempting to control their movement into urban areas by enlisting the help of African men. Brookes put the two concerns together when he wrote: 'Needless to say, parental power over minor sons and over daughters is one of the most marked features in Native Law. The flight of girls from farm or location homes into towns and villages is one of the gravest dangers to Native morality at the present time' (1924: 170).

The policy and legislative measures of the time, as well as the prevailing discourse on corruption and degradation, reflect these fundamental changes which must be remembered when trying to make sense of the government's efforts to endorse African marriage systems in a situation of increasing instability, dislocation and economic stress.

State and marriage

African polygamy was, as we have seen, also a fundamental cultural symbol, both for Africans and for whites, for whom it was a crucial marker of both difference and moral debasement. Yet while during this period the courts insisted on its prominence as a fundamental feature of African marriage, it was on the decline. Population pressure in the limited areas left available for Africans in rural areas, and urbanisation, undermined the economic base of polygamy. Fewer than 15 per cent of those counted in the 1921 census were polygamists, perhaps one-third of the rate fifty years earlier (Simons, 1969: 78). While, as we have seen, governments had not attempted to confront polygamy through the marriage laws, it was attacked directly by both tax and land policies. Taxes were levied on each hut. More importantly, as land shortage became acute, land allocation made no allowance for more than one wife (79).

One of the most important developments in African marriage law in this period was the changing power over the decision to marry, and the choice of partner. African law had not emphasised the free consent of parties to a marriage, women in particular being constrained by the wishes of their male guardians. The perceived limitations on the freedom of African women provoked a complex response from whites. There were complaints about African women being reduced to the position of slaves, and sold in marriage. As apprehension developed about social dislocation there were multiplying complaints about the reduced control exercised over African women. Between these two rhetorical poles the law had to manoeuvre, constructing a changing regime of status and freedoms for African women. It was not only the growing tendency to support traditional authority that limited any drive towards establishing legal equality between men and women. For any such urge was limited by the fact that the mirror of judgement held up to African institutions, the Roman-Dutch law, did not give women such equality. White public and family law relegated women to secondary status, excluding them until 1931 from political life, and subjecting most married women to the power of their husbands. It is hardly surprising that the white state did not concede to African women a status equal to that of men. In any case, freedom and equality were not, in white discourse, favoured as answers to any African problems. In the overall context of political domination, personal and family laws were easily called in service as justifications for control and limitation of African freedoms.

It was a common belief of white observers that African marriage was increasingly unstable, and that this was a part of a general crisis in morality, represented by an increasing and uncontrolled licentiousness among women, and a threat to the fabric of life and social stability in general, in particular in urban areas. While instability might be thought to be an expected consequence of social and economic disruption, we know very little about marital stability in rural tribal societies. The view that marriage became less stable over this period cannot be supported by any statistical evidence, but this is perhaps less important than the belief, which was held by judicial officers, as well as policy makers and the white public.

The spread of legalisation to African marriage was uneven. Its effect was to increase rigidity and to move towards the lawyers' goal of 'certainty', not to promote emancipation and equality. Only in Natal was a formal ceremony necessary. But the influence of white courts, lawyers and judges pushed the law towards a definition of essentials and criteria of validity. In customary law divorce was not a matter for public courts. In a polygamous system husbands rarely sought formal dissolutions, and wives could not do so without the concurrence of the male elder who had received her bride-wealth payment. As Simons shows, one of the ways in which increasing support was given to patriarchal authority was the rejection as 'misplaced sentiment' by the Native Court of Appeal in the North at the end of the 1930s, of the Cape view that a woman could sue unaided for divorce (1968: 129–30). The spread of legal forms would seem to have demanded that an official court-granted divorce was necessary to determine precisely the status of the parties. But it appeared to white courts administering African law outside Natal that there was no legal justification for this. Without formal requirements for forming and dissolving marriage, marital disputes therefore tended to focus on bride wealth, which became for white courts the 'keystone' of the existence or otherwise of a marriage (127).

Simons quotes the missionary H. A. Junod's remark that *lobola* 'poisoned the whole of native life' (88). It might be better to say that the debates among whites about *lobola* poisoned the whole of African law. The prominence of this institution in discussions of how to deal with African law has already been noted. On the one hand it was condemned as the sale of women, on the other lauded as the cement of African marriage, and a guarantee of the status and protection of women and children. White jurisprudence came increasingly to classify bride wealth as a contract. This was partly a classificatory problem, but partly too a logical reflection of the fact that bride wealth increasingly operated in a money economy, and became payable and expressable in financial terms. But a strict contractual view could not begin to capture the nature of the relationships involved. The institution of bride wealth affected relations between the generations throughout the life-cycle of the family. It was for most their principal economic transaction. Sons' earnings accrued to family heads, who were liable to pay bride wealth on their behalf. Long-term borrowing, and long-term unfulfilled obligations, characterised the economic history of families. It is hardly surprising that disputes were frequent and complex. Even those who were married under Roman-Dutch law preferred to fulfil bride-wealth obligations, though they were not legally necessary. Indeed it became for many an important symbol, and an answer to white condemnation of African marriage. 'In the last resort', Simons reports of reasons for adhering to bride wealth, 'they say that the custom is good because it is theirs and not the White man's' (94).

The Natal code, in contrast with those of the other provinces, asserted state control over the formation and dissolution of marriage. It provided for a public ceremony, the presence of a state official, and dissolution by court order. In Natal also, Africans could only contract a marriage outside customary law in a ceremony conducted by a Christian minister licensed by the state. The state jealously guarded the right to conduct such ceremonies and there was much reluctance to concede to African clergy, especially those in African churches, the right to conduct Christian weddings. An uncontrolled spreading of African Christian marriages would have blurred the line between African and white marriage, which the law sought to delineate so clearly. The safeguards against coercion into marriage were not necessarily effective. Formalisation and registration of bride-wealth payments caused some difficulties, but the changes made did not interfere with patriarchal powers and interests. The direction was that which may have been expected from a state aiming at bureaucratising marriage. A limit on the amount of payments was set; as well as a period within which payment had to be finalised. In Natal lifelong negotiations and claims were replaced in law by a single, final transaction which conclusively transferred a woman to her husband's family. The Natal law also provided for state-controlled divorce which could only be given by a court. Again the legal system kept the divorces under white and African law quite separate, African divorces only being granted by native commissioners' courts. On divorce the wife reverted to the guardianship of her family head, while the children remained under the guardianship of their father.

The Cape, on the other hand, had tried at first to use registration as a weapon against African marriage, and failed. In 1910 in the Transkei it abandoned its attempts to turn African marriage into white marriage. But in the Cape Colony itself, where assimilation was the official goal, the Cape courts, like those of the Transvaal, refused to recognise African marriages at all. As Innes was to do, de Villiers purported to follow English precedent in declaring polygamy inconsistent with and abhorrent to the state's idea of marriage (*In re Bethall 188 (38) Chd 220; Ngqubela v Sibele, 1893 (10) SC 346*). The consequence of the limited and confused form of recognition given to African marriages was that they were always inferior in law to Roman-Dutch law marriages, and gave way to them. This relationship was of great importance to the large and growing number of African Christians who entered into Christian and not into customary marriages. In one of the first cases heard by the new Native Appeal Court after 1927 Stubbs was able to pronounce on the relationship between customary unions and marriage in the Transvaal. The court held that it was not possible for a legal customary union to follow on an existing Christian marriage. In 1927 a customary union had been defined in the Native Administration Act as 'a marriage according to Native law and custom' (sec. 35). To avoid confusing white and African marriage the definition was altered by proclamation in 1929 to 'Customary union means the association of a man and a woman in a conjugal relationship according to Native law and custom, where neither the man nor the woman is party to a subsisting marriage.' A person who was a party to a marriage could not at the same time have a legally recognised customary union. This, of course, caused great difficulties where a 'marriage' was contracted by a man who already had one or more wives in 'customary unions'. While the administrators of African law tried hard to find compromises which would preserve some form of rights, especially to house property, for customary-law wives, supreme courts were more implacable in their logic which told them that the Roman-Dutch law marriage carried all before it.

A variety of institutions contributed towards the 'construction' of the legal regimes governing African marriage during the first quarter of the century. The colonial governments, the various commissions of enquiry, the native commissioners' courts and appeal courts and the practices and 'resistances' of Africans were all part of the creation of the system, and they all exhibited a degree of flexibility and realism. At the top of the legal pinnacle, however, the supreme courts were the least flexible of the operators in the legal system, continuing to insist on a rigidity of principle in the name of the supremacy of monogamous Christian marriage. Yet there were many men who had entered into marriages of different types. Natal tried to separate the systems entirely in law by prohibiting the 'reversion' to customary marriage by the widows or children of Christian marriages. This was a failure. The attempt to prohibit backsliding by Christian families, under pain of criminal penalty, was strongly resented by those whose civilised status was thus to be protected. John Dube wrote that 'some . . . feel that the prohibition interferes with the free rights of people in choosing life partners' (quoted in Shropshire 1941: 10). In the Cape it was suggested that a Christian marriage should not be valid unless there had been an actual divorce in the customary-law marriage. This was not adopted. One reason was that it would have placed the two forms of marriage on a conceptually equal footing, and this the common law did not recognise. And it would also have required the administrative effort and interference necessary to require a state-controlled divorce process for customary-law marriages, and this effort the Cape did not make.

It is significant that while Africans in the Cape who contracted Roman-Dutch, Christian marriages did so under the same law as Europeans, in Natal and the Transvaal special separating statutes governed these African marriages. In Natal religious marriage ceremonies were required to mark the transition from paganism to Christianity, of which the different marriage was seen as an essential part. Transvaal law, ever alive to the symbolic aspects of difference, after resisting provision for Christian African marriage under Roman-Dutch law, finally provided for it under a separate statute, so as to ensure that there was no identity in marriage, in spite of the fact that the legal consequences would be the same. The Transvaal principle of segregation and differentiation of otherwise like marriage forms was affirmed Union wide in 1929 when parliament laid down that divorce suits between Africans married under Roman-Dutch law were to be heard not by the Supreme Court, but by the specially created native divorce courts.

Once an African couple had contracted a monogamous Christian marriage, what were to be its legal consequences? Was it to be a marriage in community of property? What succession laws would apply? Once again the assimilationist assumptions of the Cape approach gave way to differentiation. African male opinion objected strongly, and successfully, to community of property on the grounds that it gave unfair preference to women who had already been paid for (see above SC 6 1913: Evidence). It was conceded in the Transkei in 1910 that it would not apply to them unless specially opted for, and in 1927 this was enacted for the whole country in the Native Administration Act. This meant that African women, even when married under Roman-Dutch law, had no claim to a share of their husbands' property. On death, also, it was established that the estate was distributed according to customary law, and widows, therefore, did not receive the shares guaranteed to white widows under the Roman-Dutch law of succession, and later under the Succession Act.

And, while an African wife married under Roman-Dutch law received none of the benefits of community of property, she was subject to the Roman-Dutch law disadvantage of being under the husband's marital power, which made her a minor in law during her marriage. Monogamous marriage, therefore, did very little to improve the status of African women, which had been the aim of the earlier liberal reformers. As Simons later wrote, 'The patriarchal principle of tribal marriage, its property relations and *lobola* contract are allowed to recur in a monogamous marriage' (1968: 174).

Status and capacity

Even greater problems about legal segregation arose once African patriarchs, women, and minor sons and daughters became increasingly active participants in the money economy. While white public opinion endorsed the existence of status inequalities in African personal life, white traders and employers were greatly concerned about the legal capacities of the people they dealt with. Who could contract? Who was responsible for unpaid debt? Whose assets could be seized? Who could bind whom in a contract of employment? All these were increasingly important practical questions to which the answers lay in African personal law, as interpreted and reconstructed by the white state's judicial and legislative institutions. How the family was defined, and the extent of the father's powers over children, had great importance in relation to rural labour contracts, and to the right to live in urban areas. The nature of the common household estate, administered by the father, and his rights to the assets and earnings of his major children, were of importance in relation to debt.

One part of these problems was the varying directions taken with regard to whether women could achieve the status of legal majority. The Cape had given majority status to African women at the age of twenty-one in the 1880s, though this law was largely ineffective. In Natal, however, an African woman could never be a legal major, falling under the guardianship of her father or other household head, husband or husband's successor. After 1927 the Northern Appeal Court endorsed the Natal approach, claiming that the Native Administration Act enjoined the giving of priority to African ideas in this regard (Simons 1968: 189) Arising out of the desperate efforts to control the movement of African women to the towns, the Secretary of Native Affairs, E. R. Garthorne, had proposed that the Governor-General, in his capacity as Paramount Chief, should be given the powers of legal guardianship over all unattached girls and women. The Department of Justice demurred, on the grounds that 'native guardianship of women [was] not in accordance with the principles of civilisation' (see Eales 1991: 93, note 200). In 1943 the legal capacity of both African men and women was declared by parliament to be the same as that of whites except in the case of married women in customary marriages, who were deemed to be minors (Simons 1968: 190). The new law did not apply, however, to matters arising out of customary law. This meant that African women could still not sue on their own in any matter arising out of customary law.

In all matters related to legal capacity, however, much depended on the interpretations of white judicial officials administering customary law. For it is clear that in making judgements about the capacity, for example, to own property as an individual, or to earn wages, or even to move to town, they were considering situations for which there were no real precedents in customary law. It was thus a matter of choice whether the institutions of patriarchal power would be held to be relevant to new situations. In exercising these crucial choices, white lawyers and administrators were not much constrained by black public opinion. They could choose which black interests, if any, to give priority to. And they were influenced by a legal style which applied to both black and white law, and was dominated by the practice of 'finding' principles of law in old and obscure authorities. Just as white courts did not acknowledge the choices they were making in constructing the Roman-Dutch law, neither did the judges in the native courts acknowledge the way in which they were making new law out of old. They also found it difficult, and in the end impossible, to think without the civil law concepts of *locus standi*, *dominium*, contract, majority and so on, and all these shaped and transformed the customary law that emerged. Legal education also contributed towards the prism through which African law was understood. In September 1932 the *South African Law Times* commented on the new Natal code

> To a lawyer trained in the Roman-Dutch system, the new Code is interesting as containing a combination of many of the principles of our law – which possibly existed in Native custom as well – and also showing the survival of many of the principles of primitive Roman law, which we learned from our student days in Maine's *Ancient Law* and *Early History of Institutions*. Among these principles there can clearly be seen the perpetual

minority of women . . . the conception of *patria potestas*, and the principle
that property belongs primarily to the family.

The possibilities of dealing with subordinations within a subordinate legal
system are many. One is to reject specific legal disabilities in the name of
an overall equality of status in law embodied in the ruling system. This
assimilationist approach was not followed in South Africa. There the
approach was pluralist, but pluralism can be liberatory, or confining and
demeaning. If the latter, the inequalities can be rejected, and at the same
time this rejection used as a justification for judging adversely all the
values of the subordinate culture. This was the basis of the pure Cape
approach to customary law, which it repudiated as part of a contrast
between civilisation and barbarism. But the distinction between civilisation and barbarism can also be usefully drawn by accepting the inequalities in the subordinate system, and declaring them to be particularly
suited to those people. It was this approach that characterised the way in
which South African law dealt with the legal status of Africans after 1927.
Natal law codified the approach to status. Everyone was declared to be
either a household head or subject to the head of a household (sec. 25).
The household head was 'entitled to the earnings of his minor children
and to a reasonable share of the earnings of the other members of his
family and of any other kraal inmates'. He was 'the owner of all kraal
property in his kraal' and had 'charge custody and control' of the property
of his wives, which he could 'in his discretion use . . . for his personal
wants and necessities' (secs. 35–6). Until 1932 all men were minors and
subject to the legal powers of the household head until marriage. After
1932 the code conceded legal majority to men at twenty-one to bring
them into line with the position in other provinces. But women in Natal
remained perpetual minors in law. Those African adults who were minors
in law could nonetheless bring actions in delict under the Roman-Dutch
law. But delictual actions under customary law, like seduction and
adultery, could only be brought by the male guardian, who was deemed to
be the injured party.

    In a society in which both men and women were becoming increasingly
engaged in a capitalist system of economic relationships, many questions
arose in relation to the confining of large numbers of people to a property
regime in which they did not have full rights to own and to dispose of
property. Were they better off being protected from a regime of individu-

ally held property? Would their interests necessarily have been better served by equality of status, and, concomitantly, responsibility? These are questions that cannot be answered in retrospect. I mention them in order to point to the chorus of justification and support for the inequality of status. From the point of view of African males and household heads the interests involved were clear enough. But why should white administrators have supported these interests? In South Africa, unlike other parts of British Africa, this support did not rest on a necessary alliance between whites and African male elders, as African interests were rejected swiftly and summarily enough in other areas, though it was no doubt convenient in local administration to rule through family heads. Nor was it a matter in which political government took much interest. The support came rather from within the discourses of 'Native Affairs', 'Native Law' and 'Law', where the contrasting regimes of status were basic to the justification of separation.

Africans were also differently placed in relation to the major areas of common law. Where it was deemed that native law on the subject existed, this applied. In relation to the general law of delict, Stafford wrote: 'There is no native law governing negligence generally' (1935: 252). Common law therefore applied. But the new Native Appeal Court decided that it did not apply to the right of a girl to sue for seduction, as this was 'known' to native law (*Kambula v Kunene NAC (N and T) 1932*). The complainant was a school teacher and the native commissioner had heard the case under common law. When her father appealed the court endorsed the view that native law, under which he had the right to sue and claim the damages, should apply. The field of contract and commercial law was also full of confusions. Native law was held to have recognised, and therefore to apply to, contracts of sale and purchase, though how far it did so remained in dispute. But while native law applied to purchase and sale, so did white statutory law on these matters. Also some contracts of sale, for example sale on instalments, were considered not to be known to customary law. While the 1932 version of the Natal code made loans between Africans recoverable, it laid down that interest and prescription were 'unknown in native law' and that parties claiming interest had to point to specific contractual arrangements (secs. 151(2); 152(2)).

Succession

We noted earlier that there was great reluctance to change the Roman-Dutch law of inheritance, and that debate about it focused on the sanctity of succession laws and the need to respect the wishes of testators. Yet in the case of African succession, the solution adopted was one that left much to the discretion of officials. Priority was given to the customary law of succession, which meant that the male heirs of men married under customary law succeeded to the exclusion of widows, who had only a personal claim to support by the heir. Stafford wrote in relation to succession that

> we must realise that we are dealing with a family system totally different from that which prevails among Europeans. With us, the passage from the stage of minority brings us to full manhood . . . independent of any parental or family control . . . When we die our estates . . . are distributed according to our will or . . . the laws of intestate succession. With the natives, on the contrary, the *kraal* system prevails. The *kraal* head is the *paterfamilias*. He may have numerous wives . . . When he dies the eldest son of the chief house takes over his position, and no liquidation of the estate takes place. (1935: 107)

This conceptual framework, however unsuited to the new conditions of urban and migrant life, accounted for most estates. Where there had been a non-customary marriage complications set in. The customary law of succession applied, by statute, where no will had been made. But the partners to such marriages could leave their property by will, though this did not apply to land held under customary tenure. Very few Africans made wills. Where such a person did not leave a will, however, the minister was given the power to decide whether all, or some, of the assets should descend by Roman-Dutch or customary law. In practice this meant that he apportioned the estate between the widow and the male heir under customary law. Simons commented: 'It is unusual, to say the least, to equip a government department with such wide powers of disposal over a deceased's estate' (1968: 241). While there were very few applications of this sort it is significant that this relatively relaxed attitude was taken to the variance of the property interests of Africans. It contrasts markedly with the attitude taken to white property rights under the Roman-Dutch law of succession.

The laws relating to succession were largely irrelevant to land, because most of the rights of occupation were under a regime of administrative discretion rather than legal rights. Most rural Africans lived in the reserves where trust land was allocated, depending on the district, by chiefs, headmen or native commissioners. It reverted for reallocation on the death of the holder. No one could claim land as of right. The competing claims of widows, the male heir and other dependants were subject to the discretion of the administering official. His decision, being an administrative act, could not be challenged in court. In conditions of prevailing scarcity, where officials could allocate land according to 'personal tastes', it is not surprising that preference was given to male claims (Simons 1968: 264). The emphasis on exactness in dealing with the private-property rights under the common law can again be contrasted with the discretions considered to be appropriate in dealing with these rights in relation to African claims to property under the customary regime. Administrative limitations could also be placed on the extent of African propertyholding within the customary system. Upper limits could be placed on the number of stock held by Africans in reserves if, in the opinion of the Native Commissioner, they were excessive or prejudicial to the interests of others (see Stafford 1935: 186). Similarly an upper limit could be placed on land holdings, and the amount allotted reduced by the Native Commissioner (180).

There were other ways too in which the law of succession was an important marker of difference between black and white. African women, as we have seen, could not succeed on intestacy, but became the responsibility of the male heir. The estate was succeeded to as a whole, and originally this meant that the heir was liable for all debts, even those exceeding the assets inherited. The idea of a *damnosa hereditas* was not a part of Roman-Dutch law, but the state was slow to decide that it was inappropriate for Africans. The original Natal code had affirmed liability, the later versions limited it, but courts continued to uphold extended liability into the 1920s (Stafford 1935: 112–13; *Ntulizwe v Kombe 1921 NHC*). In 1929 a regime of succession was laid down by Proclamation no. 1664 (printed in Stafford 1935: 114–17). Exempted persons, and those who had contracted civil marriages, were subject to the Roman-Dutch law, under which women could inherit.

Exemption

The increasing swell of official opinion that African law should be recognised and applied throughout the country had to be reconciled with the emergence of a large class of people no longer living in tribal conditions, whose way of life was recognised, even by the least sympathetic official observers, as being inappropriate for the application of a tribally based law. Hailey thought that 'the most urgent need' was defining the field of exemption (1938: 269). Prior to the segregationist wave, the growth in numbers of these people was regarded as a positive sign of the beginnings of the Christianising and civilising of Africans. It seemed appropriate in some way to exempt them from the provisions of African law. But the concept of exemption was fraught with potential dangers for white politicians. Was the status of an exempt person to be the same as that of a European? If it was to be different, what would the exempt person be exempt from? Would it be simply the customary laws relating to marriage, guardianship, and inheritance? Would they be free from the authority of the chiefs and native commissioners? Would they be free from the operation of discriminatory statutes, such as the pass laws, and laws relating to the consumption of alcohol? And how, above all, could the state prevent a blurring of the line between exempt status and the demands for equal political rights for all 'civilised' persons?

While the Cape Colony proper had been prepared to consider the emergence of a class of *évolués* in all senses including political citizenship, other schemes of exemption drew the line clearly between political and legal status. The Cape scheme, embodied in the Native Registered Voters Relief Act of 1887, started from those who had political status, and exempted all voters from native law, and from other differentiating legislation. It also offered a partial exemption, from the operation of the African laws of marriage and succession alone, to ministers of the gospel, university graduates or students, elementary teachers and those who had achieved at least the fourth standard of education. The administration had no discretion enabling it to refuse a certificate of exemption to a qualified person. The status was not inheritable. (Brookes 1924: 196–7). Of this system Brookes commented: 'The first point that strikes one in the Transkeian exemption law is the extreme lowness of the standard set for exemption. But even apart from this it cannot furnish us with any assistance regarding a Union Exemption Act, for full exemption is only obtained as a result of the possession of the franchise' (197).

The Natal law was much less generous in that exemption depended both on the recommendation of a white resident and on the exercise of discretion by the Governor. Monogamy and literacy were the basic requirements. The exemption of a married man carried with it that of his present wife and children. The effect was limited, in that it gave exemption only from African law, and not from other discriminatory laws. Crusaders against the perceived immorality of bride-wealth marriage urged the extension of exemptions; white colonists their restriction. Few applications were granted. African Christians, seeking to protect themselves against patriarchal authority, and their wives against reverting on widowhood to tribal control, complained with great bitterness of the difficulties of the procedures. Between 1865 and 1891 only 851 letters of exemption were issued (Brookes 1924: 242). About 7,500 were estimated to be living a 'detribalised' life, out of an African population of 375,000. By 1904, 5,000 had been exempted, but delays were long, and refusals common (197). In addition to the limiting of the numbers exempted, White colonists succeeded in limiting the meaning of exemption in Natal to exemption from Native law alone, and not from other disabilities. One African witness complained to the 1906–7 Native Affairs Commission that 'exempted natives resembled a bucket filled with water, the water representing the privileges extended to them. But there was a hole in the bucket, and, as time went on, more holes were pierced in it, and the water gradually vanished' (Brookes 1924: 297; see in general Welsh 1971: chapter 7). White politicians explicitly warned of the potential link between the demand for exemption and for the franchise, and as a result the policy in the years before Union was 'strictly to discourage it' (Brookes 1924: 197).

The Natal Native High Court was also not sympathetic to exemption, seeing it as a matter that assailed its jurisdiction. In *Ephraim Mahludi v Rex 1904 NHC 101* it narrowed its scope by ruling that exemption was personal to the exemptee, and was not transmitted to children unborn at the time exemption was granted, thus ensuring a limitation on the numbers exempted. It dismissed arguments based on the uniformity of the family as concerning 'the sociologist rather than the jurist' (102), even though it admitted that striking anomalies could be created in family relations. Every African, it said, was on birth subject to native law, and could only be freed from it by the Governor-in-Council's discretion exercised in each and every case.

There were further status issues which muddied the waters. Section 28 of the Natal code of 1932 created the possibility that an unmarried, widowed or divorced woman 'who is the owner of immovable property or who by virtue of good character, education, thrifty habits or any other good and sufficient reason; is deemed fit to be emancipated' could be freed from the control of her male guardian and vested with full legal status including the right to own property, and to control the property of her minor children. This possibility spoke to the situation of a Christian widow who was subject to the guardianship of the 'pagan' head of her former husband's family, and who, under customary law, lost control of property left by her husband to his male heirs. Application had to be made to a native commissioner in whose sole discretion the decision lay. However, as Shropshire wrote (1941: 37–8), it was 'abundantly clear that this law of emancipation is not generally known, especially in the rural areas', and that native commissioners could be 'over-exacting' and 'rigorist'. Even church and missionary opinion, which had once been behind the drive for exemption of Christians from pagan law, was by the 1930s not wholly supportive of emancipation of Christian widows. Fear of family disintegration reigned supreme. The Bishop of Zululand's view was not untypical: 'Any breakup of native family life, which would seem to be the inevitable result of a large number of exemptions, is to be deprecated' (Shropshire 1941: 14). His Archdeacon wrote that 'the tremendous increase in divorces in the last few years points to the undesirability of tampering' with Native Law (16). The Christian widows who might seek emancipation under the Natal code were a part of a so-called 'intermediate class' of persons, who while not qualifying for the restrictively administered full exemption, were, in Hailey's words, 'rapidly passing under Europeanised conditions, but is not so fully Europeanised as to come easily under European civil law . . . No conscious effort seems yet to have been made to adjust the judicial system to the needs of this class' (1938: 283). Political and legal opinion in the post-1927 era tended to oppose any suggestion of moving towards the ultimate assimilation of these people (see e.g. Shropshire 1941). The 1927 Act, which repealed all of the pre-existing laws relating to exemption, gave discretion to the Governor-General to exempt a person from as much of the laws affecting Africans as he saw fit (with the exclusion of land, tax and liquor laws). In the two decades that followed there were no full exemptions granted. Nonetheless exemption did develop, in addition to the possibility of emancipation for widows, some different forms. Shropshire says that while between 1936 and 1940 only 119 Natal exemptions (from native law as a whole) were issued, in the Transvaal and Free State between 1934 and 1940, around ten thousand exemption certificates, which exempted the holders from pass laws, municipal curfews and the requirements of the registration of employment contracts in urban areas, were issued. The two concepts of exemption were quite different. One was based on an admission that the exempt person was in status in civil law effectively a 'European'. In the other an exempt person remained securely 'native', but freed from some of the statutory restrictions on pass holders.

In the context of the government's search for an overall 'solution' to the 'Native Problem' exemption was a thorny matter. Brookes argued the administrative view that the status of exemption should be more easily attainable, but that it should be clear that it was a question of legal convenience, and not linked in any way to political status. 'The political use of Letters of Exemption to form Natives into a separate and widely distinct class should be discouraged, though their use as a convenient measure of distinction between tribal and de-tribalised Natives is permissible and right' (1924: 201). It should flow to all those who had a Christian marriage or Cape-type educational qualifications but should be revocable on conviction of a criminal offence or 'reversion to Native habits' (ibid.). Originally the idea of exemption had been premised on allowing the civilised to 'escape' from native law, prefiguring the gradual disappearance of that law and its eventual assimilation with Roman-Dutch law, as envisaged by the 1905 commission. By the 1920s however, the base assumptions were changing. Brookes was able to envisage a time when African law progressed in its own way, towards its own, but separate, perfection, a time in which advanced Africans would cease to apply for exemption from it so that they could come under European law.

> Just as, in discussing administration, we saw the advantage of a special administration and judiciary for Natives, so now we have seen the advantage of a *permanently* separate system of law. Practically and theoretically we can see the expediency and the justice of preserving, within the unity of humanity, the spiritual lines of demarcation between race and race laid down by the Great Lawgiver Himself. (205; my emphasis)

The New Courts

The legislation of 1927 was meant as a departure not only in the substantive law, by recognising native law, but also in the area of procedure, where it purported to recognise African ideas about the machinery of justice. In his opening address Stubbs, president of one of the new native appeal courts, said in 1929 that the court would provide for Africans 'the great open road' by which they could seek redress for civil wrongs 'with comparatively little expense' (Stubbs 1929: 4). It brought 'a system of judicature embodying simple and convenient forms of procedure, stripped as far as possible of legal niceties and technicalities' (Stubbs, quoted by Lewin 1947: 15). In the following year Stubbs heard an appeal from the Native Commissioner's Court in Johannesburg in which it appeared that the Commissioner had announced his intentions as to judgment prior to hearing evidence. Stubbs noted that he had, the year before, already criticised the Johannesburg court for 'the entire absence of any attempt on the part of the Native Commissioner to observe the rules of procedure'. The Appeal Court would, then, ensure procedural integrity, but what did this mean? In Act 38 of 1927, Stubbs said,

> the Legislature sought to bring into being forums – Courts of Native Chief, Native Commissioner and Appeal – designed to suit the psychology, habits and usages of the Bantu, creating as nearly as possible the atmosphere of the *lekgotla*, to the arbitrament of which they have from time immemorial been accustomed to submit their disputes. While the attempt has been made to create forums and forms of practice and procedure approximating to Bantu conceptions of legal jurisprudence, the machine has been made sufficiently flexible to meet the needs of the native who has emerged from the tribal state . . . It is nevertheless a moot point whether the Bantu in the latter category is more at home and in happier frame of mind in an environment which imposes upon him a system differing from his own.
> (*April Motaung v Philemon Dube 1930 NAC 12–13*)

This may have been anthropologically admirable, but in practice the effect was rougher justice in some areas, and a more technical justice in others. As Lewin wrote, 'As soon as we enter the realm of the court itself, the influence of anthropology flies out of the window while the lawyers . . . come in at the door' (1947: 16). The increasing use of lawyers led to a situation in which, according to Lewin's calculations, half of the cases heard in the native appeal courts involved procedural issues. The 'culture' of the ruling system, in other words, pulled the subordinate one towards the dominant law in the realm of procedure, as it did in substantive law. White officials and lawyers, with their manuals of native law, could not reproduce an anthropological vision of a consensual justice. Indeed, in spite of the rhetoric of some, this was not the aim of those who drove the agenda of native affairs, which was speed, the elimination of lawyers, and a freer hand for judicial officials to invent native law.

Once lawyers arrived on the scene they brought with them, Lewin wrote, 'a whole apparatus of procedures, appeals, precedents and rules of interpretation' (1947: 20). This is nowhere more evident than in the workings of the Natal Native High Court, hearing cases under the Natal code. Indeed the litigation brought by Africans was bound to be very complex, arising as it did out of the increasing integration of Africans with a money economy and an industrialising society, and raising complicated points which inevitably spread across both African and white legal ideas and rules. Stubbs proclaimed at the opening of his court that the 'background of all Native law is the tribal system'. Lewin commented that it was rather 'the vastly more complicated social and economic system' in which Africans now lived (21). Simple lawyerless procedures were not what they needed, yet they remained the administrative ideal.

At the opening of the first session of the new Native Appeal Court for the Transvaal and Natal in 1929, Stubbs made an extensive statement of the policy which was to inform his approach. It is important to note his conception of African law, because he was the only permanent member of the court, and as such was dominant in making its legal policies for over three million people. He opened by referring to the unsatisfactory position in which Africans had found themselves in the Transvaal because of the Transvaal Supreme Court's interpretation of Law 4 of 1885. He quoted the Under Secretary of Native Affairs, Garthorne, to the effect that the court had 'bastardised almost the entire Native Population of the Transvaal' by its decision in *R v Mboko 1910 TS 445* which 'deprived practically every native father of guardianship or other rights to his children' (1). In *Kaba v Netaba 1910 TPD 964* and *Meesadoosa v Links 1915 TPD 357* the court had 'destroyed any equitable claim in property, the passing of which to the Native mind alone differentiates marriage and prostitution', and had left 'very little as regards status'. But a new era had come. By Act 38 of 1927, proclaimed Stubbs, 'the position has been considerably retrieved in favour of the Natives.'

Stubbs devoted considerable time to discussing the changed regime in relation to bride wealth. No longer would it be recognised by courts in some parts of the country but not in others. He dug deep into the available scholarly resources, among them Reverend Kropf's 1873 paper, to justify the changes. Kropf's attempt to show that bride wealth was a common human institution, and not a barbarous anti-Christian invention of black tribes, had an extraordinary intellectual life in South African discussions of native law. It was quoted extensively by the Cape commission of 1883, by subsequent commissions, and by experts, such as Brookes. It appealed partly because of the obscurantist nature of its learning, which lent a broad philosophical and historical dimension to what might otherwise have appeared to be a debate about savages, and because it placed bride wealth well back in the evolution of mankind, and so proved that African institutions were comparable to others in humanity's infancy. Bride wealth was, Stubbs said, 'unquestionably an integral part of the foundation on which the whole fabric of native family life and society rests' (4). He quoted extensively from Brookes to prove that it was not a contract of purchase and sale. Then he invoked further authority. 'I do not think there can be any doubt', he said, basing his view on quotations from Genesis and Deuteronomy, 'that *ukulobola* has the sanction of the scriptures.' Even Homer's *Iliad* was quoted at the opening of the Native Appeal Court to validate the policy of the Native Administration Act in 'breaking down [the] invidious distinctions in the judicial recognition of this ancient and honourable custom' (6).

The case of *Nsele v Sikakane 1929 NAC 123*, of which the court said that 'the issue involved in this case ranks as one of the most important for many years' (125), illustrates the interplay between ideology, policy and law finding in the Native Appeal Court. The case involved a seventeen-year-old girl who been a pupil of a fifty-year-old Dutch Reformed Church preacher. She had been seduced by him, a child had been born, damages for seduction and then *lobola* cattle had been paid, but the girl had died before any further marriage ceremony. Had a marriage taken place? If not, should the cattle be returned? Section 2 of the Natal code of 1878 had laid down that, for a woman marrying for the first time, the consent of her father, the right to claim *lobolo* and the holding of a marriage feast were essentials of a marriage. As the code had not been enforced in Zululand, the court held that it was thrown back on 'purely native law', in which a ceremony was necessary (126). Lugg's judgment noted that the native courts of Natal and the Transkei had differed on their approach to the validity of unions which did not embody all the formalities recognised to be a part of native law. While in Natal there had been a tendency to recognise *de facto* unions, this had been cut back by the Natal Native Court in 1922. In the Transkei, on the other hand, it had been recognised that all that was necessary was the payment of bride wealth and the handing over of the girl. But Natal, he said, was different. 'Ever since the promulgation of the Natal Native marriages regulations in 1869, which were re-enacted in the Codes of 1878 and 1891, the policy had been to tighten up the marriage laws and to put them on a proper footing' (127). Apart from the question of policy, it was, he claimed, also customary law that demanded a ceremony. Such a ceremony was not 'empty ritual but is imposed as a social sanction as a check against immorality, and as an inducement for women to remain chaste. The whole purpose of a wedding is to sanctify the union. We should be careful . . . that such rules of custom are not lightly interfered with' (128). 'Loosely formed unions', he went on, 'should be discouraged. This has been the policy since 1869 in Natal, and there is no reason why the Natives of Zululand should not *be required to adhere more strictly to their more ordered customs in matters of this kind*' (129; my emphasis).

Stubbs also found a happy coincidence between pure customary law and desirable policy. It was clear there was to be no 'modern native law' allowed here, and that whatever flexibility there appeared to be developing in the customary system was treated as degeneration.[1] He acknowledged that there were large numbers of African women who had 'contracted unions without regard to the essentials of marriage as laid down in the Code or as recognised in Native Common law' (130). However, he said, the court could not contemplate 'with equanimity' the legitimisation of marriages in which a girl had covertly left home to live with her lover, or those in which only bride wealth had passed. The spectre of the uncontrollable urbanisation of African women, which was so prominent in the

---

[1] See also McGlendon (1997) who recounts the court's findings that it was a 'dangerous doctrine' to upset 'a law which has its genesis in the ancient polity of the founders of the race' (132): in this case varying primogeniture to allow inheritance by twins.

    This is a point at which one might draw attention to the sharp contrast between the way in which legal change was conceived for whites and Africans. In a 'living system of law', Innes had said in *Blower v van Noorden 1905 TS 890* at 905, old practices must be modified to keep in touch with the 'expansion of legal ideas' and changing conditions.

minds of politicians and administrators, found its way into the court. There were, Stubbs said,

> the implications of an analogous situation brought about by the modern habit, largely the outcome of contact with Europeans and the influences abroad in the industrial centres, of loose relationships that spring up and subsist between men and women in those centres producing an outlook wholly different from that of fifty years ago, which all goes to show the tendency of modern times to look with complacency upon the steady whittling away of orthodox forms which made the institution . . . into being something more than a mere convenience to be lightly set aside at the whim and caprice of a couple desirous of living together in illicit intercourse, and these tendencies we should resolutely combat. (131)

With somewhat strained eagerness Stubbs found that a marriage that had not gone through all the formalities found to be part of Zulu common law was not valid. Whatever native law was, then, it was not any more to be held to be common practice, for the court admitted that informality was widespread.

It must be emphasised that the judgments of the new native courts, with their insistence on the legal technicalities of traditional marriage, developed in counterpoint with the increased pace of urbanisation and the rapid changes taking place in African marriage practices. As Brookes wrote in 1933 the 'majority of sex unions in our urban locations are marriages neither in the Bantu nor in the European sense'. A high proportion of children were illegitimate: 'even when the intention is to create an absolutely permanent union, new and strange ways are creeping in' (quoted in Phillips 1938: 90). Because of irregular unions and the non-payment of bride wealth many children, Phillips wrote, 'have no father' with social or legal responsibility (96). The township regulations in force in most urban locations effectively outlawed the patriarchal household so beloved of the native court judges. As one of Phillips's informants told him, because of 'loss of parental control, liberty from tribal law and customs . . . the urban native is *decaying morally*' (94; his emphasis). The judges' approach, to fall back on a legalism designed to reinforce traditionalism and turn back the tide of change, echoed other official and public discourses. The Native Economic Commission observed in 1932 that there was a 'spiritual decline' among urban Africans who were ignoring native law in relation to the family and adopting 'European marriage rites, usually for the purpose of evading the *lobola* custom' and were 'forsaking tribal moral law, leading to moral straying and collapse' (UG 22 1932: para. 716). The language of moral decay and collapse was everywhere, strong not only among officials but in missionary and welfare circles, and among the African clergy (see Phillips 1938: 94–5). And the native court judges were closely reflecting the anthropology of the times with its emphases on the damaging losses to African cultures caused by urbanisation, individualism and acculturation, and the desirability of fostering, not assimilation, but, in the words of the government anthropologist, a 'Bantu future' (see Chanock 1994: 310).

Stubbs also addressed himself to the question of what the court was going to administer when it claimed to administer native law. 'Is there such a thing as pure native law? The answer to the latter is, of course there is' (1929: 6). It was, he said, 'as pure, rational, and logical a system of law as many of our systems of contemporary jurisprudence of Western civilisation'. But having stated this article of faith he was torn between different approaches. Brookes had laid down that while there were 'many differences of detail from tribe to tribe' the 'broad principles of law involved are the same'. But G. P. Lestrade, the government ethnologist, emphasised variations between tribes and, within tribes, between regions (6–7). While the insistence on the importance of differences appeared to undermine the lawyers' claim that there was a systematised jurisprudence, it was useful in supporting the claim of all who administered native law to be operating as specialists in a complex area of expertise. Stubbs tried to put the two together. He recognised variety but said that 'the various Bantu tribal systems are very much closer than the systems of common law of those countries which build on the Code of Justinian' (7). He worked through a by now familiar litany. The 'background of all native law is the tribal system. The individual is absorbed in the commonwealth, the man is lost in the citizen. The Chief is the embodiment of the tribe, the head and centre of the whole fabric.' But, lest it appear that the way was open to the systematisation of native law, Stubbs also stated the claims of *ad hoc* and specialised expertise. He quoted Dundas to the effect that African law was 'evolved by custom', and known by old men who had learned it by 'the experience of age'. This definition, said Stubbs, would no doubt make a more immediate appeal to native administrators, 'the majority of whom have graduated in the hard school of experience' (8). This led him to refer sceptically to the Natal experience of codification. It was, he said, 'a moot point whether in the process of codification which after all is the product of a foreign mentality and environment, native law may not be the poorer in ethical, moral and logical quality' (ibid.).

The ingredients of the motives that went into the framing of the 1927 Act, and section 11 (see above), were complex and contradictory, encompassing both the worst and best ideas of segregation and appropriate law. The idea that section 11 meant that customary law should apply in cases between Africans became dominant just at the time that an increasing number of African cases arose out of disputes about ordinary contracts and debts. But Stubbs determined that while economic transactions between Africans might appear to be the same, they could also be different. In *Ndimande v Ndimande 1930 NAC 114* Stubbs took the opportunity to assert the authority and expertise of the Native Appeal Court in its area. The Native Appeal Court had responsibility to administer law to a different kind of people.

> The Courts constituted under Act 38 of 1927 have in Natal jurisdiction in civil matters over a Native population of approximately one and a half millions. A large proportion of these people live under tribal forms of government subject to Native law and custom. They are without education and live the life of the kraal and the open veld. From the beginning of Bantu history it has been the custom among them to accommodate one another in the matter of loans in kind, e.g. cattle with which to *lobola* a wife, goats to pay a medicine man . . . Never . . . were loans either in kind or in money made with interest which is unknown amongst the Natives. (120)

There could, in other words, be no general assumption that the character of economic transactions among Africans was the same as those among whites, and no reason for the legal system to assimilate them automatically. While the 1927 Act itself had not indicated a general policy, towards the end of the 1930s it had become quite clear that preference would be given to Native law in all the suits between Africans where it could afford a remedy, including most contracts and delicts (see Lewin 1947: chapter 5). Thus the courts tried to solve the problems caused by the fact that Africans no longer confined themselves to the transactions of tribal life, but insisted on living conceptually messy lives in the new society and economy, by applying customary law to them. But the confusions were not simply in the lives of the litigants. Just as they crossed the boundaries between systems in their daily activities, so did the judges in their legal conceptualising. Stubbs indicated his determination to keep the systems of law apart. In *Ntsabelle v Poolo 1930 NAC 13*, he urged the necessity of native commissioners making it quite clear which system of law they were applying and 'to avoid in the future a confusion of the two systems of law'. This was, as we have seen, a fiction. It proved impossible for white judges to separate the different legal cultures in their own minds and reasoning. It is of great significance that the very concept of 'custom' deployed was based on English and Roman-Dutch law, as made clear by the Native Appeal Court's definition in 1932 which was based on van der Linden, and Holland's *Jurisprudence* (McGlendon 1997: 132). As I have suggested this was a necessary part of the formation of the native law, by a process of continuing refinement by opposition. Importantly also legal maxims, especially Roman-law maxims, were invariably invoked as part of common human wisdom, and Roman-Dutch texts could also be invoked as an aid to the refinement of concepts. As an example we might note the 1939 case of *Mbani v Mbani* discussed by Lewin (1947: 123ff.). At issue was whether a refusal to pay bride wealth in a customary-law marriage could be held to amount to constructive desertion, and therefore be grounds for divorce. To answer this question, itself framed in a way that mixed the systems and invoked Roman-Dutch concepts, the court had extensive resort to a text published in 1664, Hendrik Brouwer's *De Jure Connubiorum*, illuminating the parties by extensive quotations in Latin. Remarks about *lobola*; references to Appellate Division cases about white marriage; Dutch legal terms; all were a part of the judgment based on native law.

To add to these complexities were those caused, as we have seen, by the conceptualisation that there were many different systems of tribal law in the country. It was a central part of administrative expertise, based as it initially was on local administrators' knowledge, that it revelled in the existence of many different 'tribes', which accordingly had their own systems of law. The differing details of each were lovingly elaborated both by whites and by Africans. This meant that specialised knowledge of many regions had to be staked out, and also that a way had to be found to deal with the problems caused by the increasing interactions of those deemed to live under the different systems. The obvious reaction of the lawyers was to bring to bear the whole apparatus of conflict of laws, the intricate system of rules developed for international transactions. To try to simplify matters section 11(2) of the Native Administration Act laid down that where different native laws were involved, the law to be applied would be that 'prevailing in the place of residence of the defendant'. But there were problems. Was native law territorial in application or personal? What was the law of a Zulu living in a Sotho area? What applied between two Xhosa living among Swazi? In one sense it can be seen that the logic of applying 'their own law' to Africans was that it was personal law, and carried wherever they went. But increasing travel, urbanisation and integration rendered the continuation of a system of personal laws obsolete. What, in any case, did 'resident' mean? Was it different from the international-law concept of domicile? Once again one can see that the administration of native law could not be done without resort, by the courts, and the legislature, to legal ideas, concepts and precedents from outside native law, in ways that shaped fundamentally the outcome of cases purporting to be settled by native law.

Stubbs also affirmed the backbone of the new system which had been emphasised in the parliamentary debates. He proclaimed in his opening address that new and simplified procedures now operated and a new system of appeals from chiefs' courts to native commissioners to the Native Appeal Court gave 'the great open road' by which Africans could now seek redress for civil wrongs with 'comparatively little expense' (1929: 4). But in the new dispensation, whatever the strategies of litigants, the existence of a new system of courts, and the 'great open road', was not to be allowed to weaken the chiefs. As Stubbs said a year later, 'It is as well to draw attention to the strengthened position of the chiefs by the recent statutory enactment by which their judicial authority is definitely en-trenched and defined and any ill-founded attempt to flout their authority will be resolutely discountenanced' (*Sikoane v Likoane 1930 NAC 26* at 28).

It is in this last remark that we can see the tensions between Stubbs' new legalism and other ways of understanding what was occurring. Of the Natal code, from which the definition of the powers of the Governor-General as Supreme Chief was drawn, Kennedy and Schlosberg simply said: 'Nowhere else in the British Empire does such an arbitrary code exist' (1935: 462). Beyond this cold realism lay the new texts developed for Stubbs' new jurisprudence (Seymour [1913] 1960; Whitfield 1930; Blaine 1931; Rogers 1933).[2] They inevitably took the direction of the new native

---

[2] The Prime Minister, Herzog, himself contributed a reflective introduction to one of these texts. Recent events in Europe had shown the 'futility' of applying the democratic form of government to all. It was for that reason that in South Africa the principle of 'personal law', which had made life possible for 'youthful states' in Europe with heterogeneous populations, had been developed. The book, he said, 'marks merely the beginning of a process of development of native law' which the authors 'as representatives of the ruling class' had undertaken (Blaine 1931: 1).

law in the direction of greater systemisation and towards a mimicking of the common-law methods of case citation and *stare decisis*. Nonetheless for them native law still existed in a realm somewhere between law and philosophical anthropology. As G. F. Burchell was to write in a foreword to a later edition of Seymour, 'temptations' were ever present 'not only to describe minutely the investigated sources from which the particular rules of law have sprung but also . . . the questions . . . which in this case might trespass on the field of the anthropologist or of the philosophical anti-quarian' (Seymour 1960: 1). If even the writers of pragmatic handbooks could slide into anthropologising, how much easier it was for Brookes to whom the conflicts and problems ordinary people brought before the native courts were illustrative of fundamental issues in social evolution and were rooted in another place in time. It is important to remind ourselves of the flavour of his work. The 'whole system of Native Law and custom', he wrote, 'is strikingly illustrative of Maine and Vinodograff's contention that status is the determining factor in all systems of archaic law.' That there was 'no law of contract at all . . . suggests to us that, as a legal system, native law is more archaic than the oldest extant Roman law, and a detailed study of it is therefore a matter of intense interest to the scientific investigator of jurisprudence'. Furthermore, he concluded, the absence of a law of contract, while there was a 'distinct and effective government', and 'admirable' personal law, 'is a very convincing disproof of the suggestion that government is based on contract and a clear indication that the State has evolved from the family, and is to be explained ultimately by sex, the divine sacrament of society' (quoted in Kennedy and Schlosberg 1935: 402–3).

While, then, there were differences between the various brands of white practitioners of the arcane art of native law, they were united in seeing it as quite distinct from the ordinary law of the country. But there were other voices which were looking for a role for African law which was not that of a tribalised, segregated and subordinated part of a dual system. At the Pretoria Native Conference of 1930 several delegates called for a national codification to control the discretions exercised by both chiefs and native commissioners. One delegate said that 'there was a widespread movement among the Bantu to regard themselves as one race and it was necessary that they should have one system of law'. Herbst, the Secretary for Native Affairs, countered this legal nationalism with a strangely assimilationist argument. He 'did not think there would ever be uniformity in Native Law: when each tribe would be willing to surrender some of their customs and be prepared to adopt the customs of other people, then he thought tribes would adopt European law.' This was really an argument for continued segregation and administrative control of an expertly known and diverse system. A code of 'each tribe separately' could be developed by decisions of the Native Appeal Court, he said, 'That was the English way.' But, as another speaker, T. S. Mpatheng, pointed out, diversity of customs and unity of law could both be achieved. While each tribe might want its 'customs', 'the principles of Native Law were almost the same throughout the Union'. But once African law was distinguished from African customs in this way, the basis for treating it as a lesser form of law was undermined. Indeed, as Mpatheng said, the Native Appeal Court was doing the same work as the Supreme Court, and its president should be judge, and its members should wear robes. 'There was no reason why the Native Court of Appeal should be less dignified than that of Europeans' (UG 26 1932).

Z. K. Matthews also thought along these lines. His perspective was quite distinct not only from the segregationists but also from those African *évolués* who sought to escape from a law they saw as primitive: and it was different too from the assimilationists who would have preferred native law to disappear. In 1934 he submitted a dissertation to Yale University on Bantu law (Matthews 1934) which of necessity reflected the academic approaches of the time, and which showed the contamination of the ways in which after colonisation a Western-educated African could know customary law. His authorities were Aristotle, Salmond's *Jurisprudence*, Hobhouse's *Morals in Evolution*, Radcliffe-Brown on *Primitive Law*, Holland's *Jurisprudence*, Maine's *Ancient Law*, and also local authorities: Brookes, Whitfield and A. T. Bryant (chapter 1). From these he drew fairly conventional conclusions about the 'aggressive individualism' that confronted the Bantu whose 'high degree of development of collective responsibility' and 'group solidarity' were the foundations of their 'moral code' (3, 74–5). But while to Brookes these differences made the Bantu law 'archaic', to Matthews this law was a normal part of the present, and something that ought to have a future. He feared that *ubuntu* would be lost (3). But he anticipated also a development of the law which would be brought about by the greater systemisation and unity that the new Native Courts would introduce, aided by the increasing contacts between people of different tribes and the growth of 'race-consciousness'

(86–7). What set him apart from the other commentators was that from his perspective he could not understand why Bantu law should not now develop as a part of the common law of the country. He observed that the study of African law was not placed in law faculties in South African universities (219). (Indeed he was soon to become head of a department of anthropology and law at Fort Hare University College.) In particular he criticised the exclusion of Africans from the development and administration of what was purported to be their own law. The Transvaal Native Appeal Court had rationalised this on the grounds that it was 'well known that educated natives are apt to fall away from the customs of their fellow tribesmen and . . . frequently view matters rather from the European standpoint'. This was, Matthews wrote, an 'invidious attempt to discourage the use of educated Natives in a field in which they ought to render signal service to their country' (308–9). In his concluding thoughts on the future of African law he suggested that it might have a 'bright future' as a separate system of law on the analogy of the development of Roman-Dutch law, but the difficulties were threefold. One was that white law had the 'prestige' of the 'dominant'. The second was that all cases between the races had white law applied to them, and these cases would increase in time. The third was that the character of cases between Africans was changing: here were more contract-based cases and more wills; and this would lead to a 'greater clamour' from Africans for the abolition of a separate law. There could, on the other hand, be a greater assimilation of African and Roman-Dutch law into a 'South African Law' (351, 354). He envisaged 'the development of one system of South African law to which Native Law may contribute, as well as Roman-Dutch law' (Matthews 1981: 98). Specifically Matthews rejected the separation, and different order of rationality attributed to native law. There was no reason, he wrote in 1945, why the ordinary supreme courts should not administer customary law because there was 'after all . . . nothing mysterious about native law' (quoted in Simons 1987: 6).

PART V

Law and government

15

Land

In 1905 the Transvaal Supreme Court handed down an emblematic decision. *Tsewu v Registrar of Deeds 1905 TS 130* overturned the refusal of the registrar to register land title in the name of an African purchaser. The court affirmed his right under the common law to be registered as the owner. This short-lived and contentious assertion of a liberal law of property rights in accordance with which Africans were viewed in law as bearers of ordinary economic rights under common law, and not as bearers of differentiated rights, provides us with a starting point for a consideration of land law. *Tsewu's* case had been brought in the context of mounting pressure from Africans for the right to buy land and register it in their own names. 'We must of course presume', said Solomon, 'that all the inhabitants of this country enjoy equal civil rights under the law.' Specific legislative authority, he said, was needed to override these rights (135). In early republican law Africans had not been allowed to buy land. In 1881, in the Pretoria Convention which ended the first British occupation, the British forced upon the Transvaal provision for Africans to buy land, but transfer of land was to be to the Superintendent of Natives who held it in trust. There was immediate political reaction to the court's departure from the existing Transvaal law. As Milner's apologist was to write, the decision 'subverted' the policy of the administration (Worsfold 1913: 203). All white political parties united in supporting an ordinance which would have reversed the decision had it not been vetoed in London by the Secretary of State (Denoon 1973: 116–24). After the grant of Responsible Government the new government of the Transvaal introduced an Occupation of Lands Bill which would have achieved the purpose of putting an end to most African freehold purchase by prohibiting the communal purchase of land by more than five buyers, but it was withdrawn after objection by the High Commissioner to the restriction on African landholding rights. The Transvaal court's decision stands out as a distinctive moment that was out of kilter with the historical trajectory of South African land law and policy. The Land Act of 1913, one of the first fruits of Union, capped the political efforts to reverse the decision in *Tsewu*'s case.

The Land Act

Solomon Plaatje entitled the chapter with which he began his contemporary account of the 1913 Land Act 'The grim struggle between right and wrong and the latter carries the day' (Plaatje 1916: chapter 2), and it is with this characterisation in mind that we can approach this story. The Act froze the pattern of landholding on racial lines, and it made new sharecropping tenancies illegal. The narrative in relation to the latter concerns the process of reducing those still relatively independent African peasant producers to the status of labour tenants and wage labourers on white farms.[1] But there are other stories to be told. One concerns the politics of segregation and the eventual swap, in 1936, of the African vote at the Cape for the release of the extra land implicitly promised in 1913 (see Tatz 1962). The stories of labour and politics have often been told, and this account will build on those sources (see Keegan 1986; Wilson 1971; Wickins 1981). However its main focus will be on other aspects, the themes of law, the market, and property rights and the intersections between statute, customary and common law. Underlying the common law was the market model in which persons were the bearers of equal rights and duties and actors and contractors in a market which determined their fate in the light of their own decisions. On one level of discourse this market model was constantly reaffirmed in South Africa. Yet the market had, of course, disturbing features in that it might operate without regard to race. It is hardly surprising that a market-based common law had constantly to be challenged by a political process which was continually intervening in the market, not simply in the usual sense of structuring market advantage and price, but also by the differential

---

[1] See Wilson 1971: 127–8. Contemporary evidence on agitation for the legislation, he writes, suggests far more concern with the problem of labour supply than anything else. Keegan writes that 'recently the significance of the act has been seen more centrally in terms of its decisive role in the emergence of a white dominated capitalist agriculture at the expense of the black peasantry' (1986: xv–xvi).

definition of rights and duties on racial lines. The Land Act will also be considered then as an episode in the story of the relation between law and market. In relation to the customary law, the Land Act story also enables us to consider the ways in which African tenures were developed by the state, and the abandoning of the pursuit of the individualisation of African land tenure.

The Land Act froze land transactions between 'Natives and other Persons' pending the report of a promised commission.[2] All agreements to the contrary were void. In addition section 5 made any such attempted purchase, sale or lease criminally punishable by a fine of £100 or six months imprisonment. Sharecropping arrangements fell within the definition of leasing and hiring of land which was defined as not only paying a rent in money, but rendering 'to any person a share of the produce of that land, or any valuable consideration of any kind . . . other than his own labour services or services of his family' (secs. 7 (3) and 10).[3] But labour tenancies did not fall within the definition of leasing. Such arrangements were included in the definition of 'farm labourer'.[4] Section 7 (2) applied the masters and servants law to all such labour tenants in the Orange Free

[2] 'Native' included any company or body, corporate or incorporate, if a controlling interest was held by natives (sec. 10). It was the absence of specific provision of this sort that enabled the Appellate Division to allow Asian-owned companies to evade the prohibitions on Asian land acquisitions (see chapter 18).

Succession retained its sacral status by being excluded from the effects of the Act (8 (c)). The law relating to mineral rights was also unaffected (8 (f)).

[3] Also included in the definition of henceforth illegal interest(s) in land were the interests of mortgagees. This meant that white bondholders could no longer register mortgages over African land, and this cut off this source of credit. Plaatje notes, with some irony, that while Tengo Jabavu stood apart from other African leaders, and supported the Land Act, he fell foul of its prohibition of further mortgages. Jabavu wrote: 'There is only one flaw in this otherwise useful Act . . . and that is the provision relating to lending money' (Plaatje 1916: 170). There were several complaints on this point by African witnesses to the subsequent Beaumont Commission. A meeting of Africans in Queenstown in 1914 complained that the effect of the Act was to bring down the value of land held by Africans. Existing mortgages were not affected by the Act as such, but the land values of African-held farms began to fall once it was anticipated that they might fall within the African-scheduled areas. White mortgage holders looked to call in their bonds and farms were lost, selling well below their previous market price, as would-be African purchasers were now without access to finance. The provision was seen as effectively cutting Africans off from access to finance. E. H. Chaka told the commission that it would be 'useless to hold an individual title as you are debarred from making use of your title deed because no bank would advance money. I must go to a native to get an advance but the native has got no bank' (UG 22 1916: 286).

[4] A farm labourer was defined as an African who lived on a farm and was 'bona fide, but not necessarily continuously' employed in domestic service or farming. *Bona fide* employment required that such a person rendered at least ninety days service per year, and that 'no rent is paid or valuable consideration of any kind, other than service' was given (sec. 10).

State. This was not the position in Natal and the Transvaal until 1926. In accordance with section 2 a commission was to report within two years, with recommendations, including boundaries and maps, concerning areas in which Africans should not be allowed to purchase or lease land, and as to areas to be set aside for Africans. Astonishing as it seems in the light of the protracted history of the dividing of the land of South Africa along racial grounds, the expectation on the face of the law was that the task could be substantially achieved by the new state in two years. But this time limit was offered only as a sop to those opponents who urged that the work of demarcation should precede the freezing of African purchase and the displacing of African tenants. The section said nothing about any action the government was obliged to take after receiving the commission's report. As the Under Secretary for Native Affairs was to note in 1921 the words 'until Parliament shall have made other provision' had no time constraints but 'the naked prohibition of the law remains; and what was admittedly adopted and openly proclaimed to the natives as a temporary expedient becomes a permanent rule' (Memorandum: Native Occupation of Land, in Davenport and Hunt 1974: 43).

The Act had a curious legislative history. While its provisions reflect longstanding 'solutions', they were brought on suddenly by a political crisis for the Botha government (see Wickins 1981). In 1911 a Native Settlement and Squatters Registration Bill would have extended the principle of the Cape Location Acts to the whole country as recommended by the 1905 commission (Wickins 1981: 117ff.). This Bill distinguished between labour tenants (those giving six months service) and squatters. For these a landowner, especially an absentee, would be heavily taxed. The idea behind the law was that African squatters would be ejected, or leave because of higher rents, and (on the level of rhetoric at least) that this would open land for poor whites. But the Bill was withdrawn, magistrates warning of the difficulties in differentiating between labour tenants and squatters and of classifying family members, as people frequently changed status over the years (these difficulties did not go away after 1913). Yet the new government was under pressure to deliver the fruits of Dominion status by enacting measures which had previously been rejected by the imperial authorities. In Plaatje's words, 'when the South African Parliament was at the noontide of its "mad career"' it passed both the Land Act and a law 'imposing the most humiliating limitations of British Indians'. In the immediate aftermath of the political crisis faced by the government following on the departure of Hertzog from the ministry, the Land Act, embodying all the demands of those rural constituencies to whom Hertzog had most appeal, was rushed through parliament. The apparati of Royal Commission, Select Committee, and the Native Affairs Committee were all bypassed. The Bill originally introduced at the second reading was amended by the government itself to make it far more stringent. The first version (see Wickins 1981: 124–5) would have made provision for the allocation of individual lots to Africans on Crown land, but this provision was dropped. Only in the third version was the Free State demand for the application of the masters and servants laws to tenants included. As Merriman said in his speech, the Bill 'fell upon them like a bolt from the blue' (Hansard ibid.). The fundamental demand behind the legislation was simply expressed by one Free State member, J. G. Keyter. The African had to be told 'that it was a white man's country, that he was not going to be allowed to buy land there or to hire there, and that if he wanted to be there he must be in service'. This point was acutely understood by Plaatje who correctly anticipated that once the Land Act had made it illegal for Africans to live on farms except as servants, it would be followed by a 'Natives Urban Act', which would only allow them to live in towns as servants in European employment (1916: 53).

Before Union both the Transvaal and the Free State had enacted squatters laws to deal with the continuing residence of Africans on land taken by whites, and their utilisation as farm labour. In order to distribute labour among farms there was a notional legal limit of five families per farm; in the Free State this could be increased to fifteen. In neither Republic were these laws enforced. Sharecropping was widespread (in general see van Onselen 1996). White farmers were dependent on their tenants not only for labour, but also on their capital resources. In the typical sharecropping arrangement, the African tenant provided the oxen for the ploughing, and often the seeds and plough, as well as labour. In the case of sharecropping tenants labour was not supplied directly to the farmer. Tenants were able to establish an independent livelihood in return for crop share. Objections were often made precisely to this independence. According to one opponent some white farm owners 'have farms in their own names but allow the well to do natives to make use of the farm and in fact become servants of the native . . . the white man is kept on simply for the sake of appearance . . . This system is having a most demoralising effect' (Murray 1992: 75). Another observer described how the poor-white farmer 'hires a piece of ground rent of which is paid by the native and the farmer lives with the native as *Bywoner* [tenant]' (Keegan 1986: 70).

Equality in bargaining power was not unusually seen as subverting proper race relations and contractual agreement between white and black as implying the subordination of white to black. If labour service was not required by legislation, one Free State farmer said in 1911, farmers would have to go 'hat in hand', to Africans to beg for services (Wilson 1971: 128–9). Dower, the Secretary for Native Affairs, put it in another way when explaining the Land Act to an angry African protest meeting. Parliament had decided on the abolition of the contract of sowing on the halves, he said, as it 'amounted to a partnership between a white man and a black man' (Plaatje 1916: 115). And partnership so perverted the proper relationship that of itself it implied something more than equality. In the words of Keyter, the Member of Parliament for Ficksburg, 'when the boy had his whole piece of ground to sow and be given half the crops, he was not a servant but a partner – a master' (UG 22 1916: 51; quoted in Davenport and Hunt 1974: 59).

The 1913 Act, though it gave statutory voice to those farmers who could make the break with sharecropping, did not change rural practices at once. One of the differences between the republican squatters laws and those of the Union was that the new British model state had a far more effective bureaucracy. Even so it took some time before legal forms triumphed over local practices. Many farmers could not manage their farms without the 'capital reserves of their black tenants' (Murray 1992: 90). The main significance of the Act, Murray writes, 'was that it subverted the bargaining position of black share-croppers' (91). It was a decisive moment in the struggle between owners and workers of the land, over shares of crop, the amount of labour the owner could command, and tenants' access to arable and grazing land (ibid.). Sharecroppers were 'gradually squeezed out' as white agriculture developed 'rather than suddenly squeezed out by a single piece of discriminatory legislation' (ibid.). After the passing of the Land Act, as Keegan points out, whites could legally lease land, and Africans could not. Poor whites were able to act as the nominal lessees of farms which continued to be worked by black sharecroppers (1986: 36, 68–72).

The Act was difficult to enforce against those farmers who evaded its provisions. Even where white farmers used the Act to break with share-cropping, they could not usually afford to make the transition to wage labour. Continued access to land for black workers, now labour tenants, was necessary in the cash-starved countryside. As the Wynberg magistrate pointed out, confirming the difficulties anticipated earlier, magistrates had no power to compel either farmers or tenants to reveal what the terms of their contract were (UG 22 1916: 2). The Native Affairs Department issued a circular which appeared to invite a measure of circumvention in that it pointed out that while sharecropping as such was illegal, it was permissible for the farmer to make available land for the tenant to plough for his own benefit (31). Giving the labour of only one member of a family satisfied the law, while others could, if they could find such a landlord, continue to farm on their own account. As Plaatje admitted, 'no police officers scoured the country in search of law breakers to prosecute them under this law' (18). Enforcement of section 5 was not vigorous. The Native Affairs Department had initially asked the Attorney-General's Department to consult before prosecutions because 'it was feared that an upheaval might result'. This request was later withdrawn after the Transvaal Attorney-General protested (evidence of L. de Villiers Roos in SC 1 1914; quoted in Plaatje 1916: 210). Existing agreements were automatically terminated by the Act only in the Free State. They were renewable in the Transvaal and Natal (Brookes 1926: 337).

Nonetheless it seems plain from Plaatje's account that for significant numbers the law did have immediate and disastrous effects. In some areas tenants were given only the option of labour tenancy or leaving. In particular many who sought places to stay had to sell or surrender their accumulated wealth – their stock. Chaos reigned in the immediate aftermath. The administration of the new state, in this as in much else, did not live up to its ambitions. Local officials did not have copies of the new law and 'people went around and . . . everybody had his own version' (evidence of the Kroonstad magistrate: UG 22 1916: 9). In any case, as Keegan points out, for Free State farmers what the Act precisely said was not the issue. What it did was provide 'an affirmation from the highest authority of the legitimacy of their cause' (1986: 189). Like all legislation the Act was a flexible resource in the hands of its beneficiaries and the state. Protest delegations were brushed aside. The Minister for Native Affairs, having heard representations about the 'real physical suffering' replied that 'this Act was the law of the land, which must be obeyed'. The delegation to England met with no success. Harcourt, the Secretary of State for the Colonies, defended the Act in the House of Commons, representing it as the logical outcome of long-established imperial policies. The different attitude of the imperial government to the legislation affecting Asians and to the Natives Land Act did not escape comment. While significant amendments to the former resulted from imperial pressure, the British government refused to give any response or comfort to African representations on the Land Act (see Plaatje 1916; Chanock 1977).

It is noteworthy that in the course of all of these discussions about land rights, virtually nothing was said about mineral rights, and there was no serious suggestion that anyone other than whites should benefit from these. The form in which the state recognised title to minerals had always been devised in response to political considerations. The basic concept of the Roman-Dutch law of property gave ownership over minerals to the owner of the land. But this simple solution did not take into account the other economic and political interests involved. The South African Republic had had to juggle the interests of the state in revenue; the farmers who owned the surface; and the diggers, who entered the Republic in increasing numbers during the 1880s, staking claims in accordance in forms developed in the USA and Australia, and at the Kimberley diamond diggings. How could all of these interests be resolved within the basic common-law framework? Some form of separation of rights to minerals from rights to the surface would have to develop. Republican law gave to the farmers, i.e. the surface owners, rights to minerals which they could dispose of separately from title to their land, thus enabling them to profit out of mineral prospecting. After the discovery of gold, the republican government, to attract capital investment, offered exclusive mineral concessions over large areas. Increasingly the law recognised that although the holders of surface rights had a right to profit from their sale, the rights of the prospector, developer and miner, once he held the mineral rights, took precedence over the rights of the surface owner. But after the war the view grew that these practices yielded insufficient state revenue or control over mining activity. The Transvaal Precious and Base Metals Act, no. 35 of 1908 (the Gold Law) gave to the state the right of control over mining and disposing of precious metals. Ownership still rested in the surface owner, until disposed of to the miner. But a third party, the state, now controlled this transaction. After 'proclamation' of an area, the state licensed the miner, and shared the proceeds with the surface owner. No African, coloured or Asian could own or occupy land proclaimed under the Gold Law. Nor could they participate in gold or diamond rushes or alluvial diggings as stakers or holders of claims for which one had to be over eighteen, and in all other respects qualified as a voter (see Union Government Yearbook 1923; Kaplan 1984: chapter 8, 553ff.; Hepple 1960; Milner 1996).

While the Beaumont report had envisaged the extension of African-owned land, this was to apply to the surface only. Where, he advised the Minister for Native Affairs, mineral rights of land to be acquired by Africans belonged to the owner, the transfer 'might be effected exclusive of the mineral rights' (UG 25 1916: 13). But this did not apply to whites acquiring mineral rights in African-held land. 'The possibility of minerals being discovered in land in Native occupation was a disturbing element . . . From an economic point of view,' he wrote. 'The locking up of highly mineralised land appears unwise.' Acquisition by Europeans of mineral rights in 'Native areas' should continue (13–4, 18). Some African landholders were alive to this issue. Jona Ntsiki told the commission on the behalf of the people of the Tsolo district that they 'desire to receive all benefits which accrue to the inhabitants of a land whenever and wherever precious stones and minerals shall be found' (UG 22 1916: 96). The Precious Stones Act of 1927 restricted claims to such stones to whites.

Land and the market

The market had not been the source of white acquisition of land. Conquest, colonisation and the granting of land by colonial governments had provided the foundations for land ownership. But once the foundations had been laid, land could be bought and sold. These processes did not necessarily protect the interests of white settler farmers, nor did they provide for the wants of the entire white rural population. In the South African Republic, under Boer administration, the market led to a situation in which land companies and absentee landlords, whose interest was speculation on the possible value of mineral rights, owned nearly a fifth of the land. In Natal likewise companies held huge tracts of land, much of it as labour reserves. Large-scale dispossession by foreign capital interested in mining, and local dispossession by local capital gathering pace in commercial farming, constantly threatened occupation of the land by whites. It is hardly surprising that there were constant cries from those threatened for intervention in the land market. The ruinous effects of the war, and the displacement of large numbers of Boers from land in the Free State and Transvaal increased this pressure.

Political interventions in the processes of 'land settlement' were a feature of the post-war years. Partly they were in fulfilment of Milner's aim to settle a loyal English farming population in the former Republics and partly to resettle displaced Boers (see Murray 1992). Prosperous and successful farmers were to be encouraged, others were not. It was a matter of continuous contestation as to which of the diverse white rural interests state policy would give succour and support. Legal history, with its concentration on the picture from the top down and its use of the texts of the central government, tends to give a picture of uniformity in developments and interests. But it is important to remember both that neither white nor African interests were homogeneous in a country with wide regional economic differences and rapidly growing differential class patterns in relation to land, and also that the implementation of apparently uniform laws differed from locality to locality. The Land Bank created in the Orange River Colony, which would lend land to non-landowners, was more solicitous of the poorer white farmers than that created in the Transvaal, or that created for the whole of the Union.

The political preoccupation with 'land settlement' schemes as the solution to the poor-white problem remained powerful in the early years of Union. Land law was therefore at an intersection of a number of different legal regimes. There was persistent political and statutory intervention in land entitlements. These concerned both the distribution of land among whites and the distribution of land between whites and non-whites. These two contexts must be considered together, because cutting down non-white access to land was one way of seeming to ensure white access. It could be done this way without sacrificing any of the ideological attachment to the rights of ownership, and raising ugly debates about the distribution of ownership within the white community. The separation of white and African regimes of land law was a part of this context also. It provided a justification for the dealing with African rights in a way in which 'true' rights of ownership could not be dealt with, and for exclusion of Africans from an undivided market. And while the statutory and political interventions provided the framework, it was the common law of property, mortgage, tenancy, credit and debt that determined on an individual basis who would hold land and who would lose it. Common law also constituted an irreducible set of concepts beyond which politicians would not readily venture. And both the statutory regime and the common law operated within a structure of struggle not simply over ownership but also over occupation. Large numbers of people continued to occupy land, which the political processes had allocated to whites, in ways to which the common-law concepts of ownership and lease had little application. The terms of this continuing occupation provide yet another point of intersection, in this case between land law and labour law. Political intervention, as we shall see, was far more easily accommodated into the reigning legal discourses in the area of labour than into those in the law of property.

The strength of attachment to the sanctity of property and the reluctance to interfere with the market and with common-law property rights of landowners becomes clearer when one considers the reluctance to use the power of the state to intervene in the land market and redistribute land as between whites. In a political atmosphere saturated with mounting agonising among whites about the poor-white problem, the Union senate in its first year established a select committee to consider closer land settlement. In the face of the rising demand for land from landless whites several witnesses urged the commission to recommend the expropriation of lands not in beneficial occupation, especially the speculatively held lands in the Transvaal (SC 6 1910–11: 56–8, 82–3). But few witnesses had a favourable view of poor-white capabilities, and even the most sympathetic, Senator Jacobus de le Rey, thought expropriation 'very drastic' (86). The committee thought that the future of the poor whites lay in the creation of demand for their employment, not in land settlement, and rejected expropriation and redistribution.[5] It concluded, in the mildest terms, that only if sufficient lands were not available, and land was not beneficially occupied, then it 'may be desirable' to supplement the government's powers (vii).

Before the Land Act was passed both Botha and Hertzog had campaigned in the rural areas for farmers to replace blacks resident on farms with poor whites. But they were advocating the utilisation of poor whites

---

[5] Massive statutory interventions in the existing rights of large property owners were not beyond the imagination of contemporary law in the British empire. Visser draws attention to the programme of land reform enacted by legislation in Ireland between 1881 and 1903, which, while not immediately redistributory, in that it gave rights to those already occupying, eventually provided for the compulsory transfer of title away from the owners (Visser 1989: 23–5).

as labour, not redistributing land to them. And these exhortations made neither economic nor social sense. In 1916 the Beaumont Commission raised the question of poor whites with rural witnesses. While one magistrate thought that white labour could be used, it would happen only once 'the native element is eliminated'. Until then farmers would operate on 'semi-partnership' with Africans, which was 'easiest'. The difficulties were made specific by the Heidelberg magistrate:

> I have spoken to farmers and asked them for their objections to trying white labour and they tell us they do not understand how to handle it. They know exactly how to handle a native and order him about but they do not understand how to order white men about. There has been too much equality with the whites. (UG 22 1916: 290)

Many white landholders were also marginal and insecure. The economic enterprise of white farmers was dominated by the search for cheaper capital and for secured labour. They were in competition with the mines for labour, and antagonistic towards the financial system which so severely priced and rationed credit. Black landowners suffered from the lack of credit and access to cash which plagued white farmers. Both sets of rural landowners were heavily mortgaged, and the loss of land to richer farmers, local land agents, lawyers, local merchants and finance companies was a common feature of rural economic life in this period (Murray 1992: 142). The rising value of land made bonds easy to raise, but agricultural productivity was not sufficient to pay the interest. Plaatje remarked of a farm: 'nor could we say whether the present owner was a Dutchman, his lawyer, or a Hebrew merchant' (1916: 63). Rural indebtedness was, therefore, a significant part of the context of white insecurity over land as it was a major cause of loss of land, and changing patterns of land ownership. The Bloemfontein magistrate wrote with feeling of the 'exorbitant terms of the local money-lender and the horrible tenacity of his grasp once it has fastened on the land' (Keegan, 1986: 46).

The political process, however, through the Land Bank Act, gave access to credit to white farmers at 2 to 4 per cent lower than the market rates (in this period 6 to 8 per cent; Murray 1992: 144). This discriminatory access to credit was, as Murray points out, a factor in African dispossession. Here, the forces of market and common law were let loose, to run against African owners. Black farmers, without Land Bank assistance, bore an increasingly heavy burden of debt on their land, often having to rent it to white occupiers in order to service their mortgages, as neither cash rentals nor the duties of labour tenants could be demanded of kin who might otherwise occupy the land (75).

The Land Act brought to an end the acquisition of farm land by Africans in some areas, and this, together with its outlawing of share-cropping, reversed the development of an independent African farming population. In some areas of the country Africans had bought considerable land with freehold title, acting not as individual purchasers, but as tribal communities. But the market was not, in popular representations, a neutral economic realm. It was an arena of conflict, conquest and defeat. This process of African purchase led to sharp white reaction in which it was represented that land conquered from Africans would be 'lost' through the unchecked operation of the market (see Wilson 1971).[6] Africans were represented in evidence to the Beaumont Commission as having an unfair advantage in the market. Whites, one witness said, had been ruined by the war, forced to borrow money which they could not repay, and consequently had to sell to Africans, from whom they got better prices. 'It is so much easier for natives to acquire land than for Europeans. The chief brings the order for each man to bring up so much money. If he has a thousand natives and each brings a couple of pounds it soon makes up the purchase price. It is seldom that the individual native buys' (UG 22 1916: 333; Davenport and Hunt 1974: 41).

The purchase of lands by communities on whose behalf title was held by the chief provided complex problems at the intersection of two different regimes of ownership. The issue of transformation of the supposed communal title, over which the chief had the right to allocate land, to a private title, registered in the hands of the chief, was contemporaneously being faced elsewhere in British Colonial Africa where considerable wariness had developed over the expansion of chiefs' property rights (Chanock 1991). In some cases chiefs, as registered owners of land purchased by communities, managed to transform their position into private ownership. In others private owners found themselves treated by others as trustees of a communal resource. However purchase in the

---

[6] Though note the observation of Morrell that in the Middelberg district of the Transvaal the supply of land was greater than white demand for it, and this allowed the emergence of African buyers after the war (1986: 388).
   At the time of hysteria about African purchase when the Land Act froze landholdings, African and coloured privately owned land amounted to around one million morgen, or .70 per cent of the Union. Whites owned 106 million morgen (UG 19–1916: 4–5).

private land market, utilising the mobilised resources of a group, was an important way by which, before 1913, African landholdings had been increased. The process also imposed continuing heavy indebtedness of many purchasing communities. While in the nineteenth century purchases had usually been made with a one-off payment in cash or cattle, the development of the financial and banking systems made loans and mortgages readily available.

While some wealthy Africans had been able to buy farms as individuals before 1913, forms of purchase by combining resources had been more common. In some cases this was done by individuals, in others through chiefs. But, as Beinart and Delius point out, 'Whatever the method of purchase, the tendency was for African landholders to let their lands to tenants and claim rent, rather than to farm extensive tracts for themselves. In some districts land purchase was effectively a means for chiefs to extend the reserves; African owned land seems frequently to have been effectively re-communalised' (1986: 45–4). Farms bought on behalf of communities by chiefs would fall under their authority for allocation of sites as if they were communal lands. J. F. Herbst told the Beaumont Commission that on lands which had been communally purchased by chiefs on behalf of communities, and with their contributions, people who offended chiefs were in 'many instances' ordered to leave. Chiefs allotted land, and deprived people, without even being subject to the controls which existed on the 'real' communal reserves (UG 22 1916: 34). Owners of privately owned land, with some encouragement from the administrative authorities, might try to transform themselves into headmen. Beinart writes that such African landowners tried to 'change the basis of their authority so that they would become more akin to headmen in communal tenure locations' (1986: 300). In the Umzimkulu area described by Beinart, farms bought communally, and those bought by individuals, became densely populated. On the latter land was let, and also parcelled out into unregistered 'undivided shares', which were sometimes sold to raise money for mortgage repayments (284). What is plain is that the nature of land use and dealings, though nominally within the paradigm of the common-law system of individual ownership and use and registered deeds, took little account of either its forms or its substance.

As Venable shows, the segregated market created after 1913 hugely increased the prices at which such land became available. As he writes, the Act did not create a system of territorial segregation, as Africans remained a majority population even in so-called white areas, rather 'it created a system of segregated markets for property and contractual rights' (n.d.: 16). Restricted supply and high demand in the segregated African land market forced prices well beyond the levels prevailing for similar land in the wider market in which European farmers purchased and sold. Venable traces the process, in the Western Transvaal, of the increased and desperate indebtedness of African communities who had purchased land during the boom years before 1921, and who had to service the debts during the depression that followed. Communities were forced into dependence on migrant labour to meet the debt. Chiefs, who were the nominal purchasers, had to enforce these financial obligations. Increasingly the Native Administration bureaucracy became drawn into supervising the contracts made by chiefs to ensure that they had tribal consent, and then to supporting their powers to raise financial levies. This market, far from the common-law model of individual decision making and contracting, was communalised and bureaucratised. In it African tribesmen could become bound by their chiefs to contracts to which they had never consented and from which they had no escape even by refusing payment.

In the end what it came down to was who could use the law to protect themselves against the market, and who could use the market and its law as a weapon against others. Control of the political process was vital. However when Africans lost in the market place their loss was seen as a combination of the working of inevitable market laws, bringing in their train inevitable consequences in common law, with the inherent incapacity of Africans to operate as fully competent persons in market systems. As Mason put it in *Emdin and Carelinsky v Matlapeng and Others 1922 TPD 523*:

> One knows from one's experience with natives that they are improvident, that they will always hope to be able to pay in the future enormous sums, which when the time comes, they never can pay, and the result is that they are landed in litigation, and enormous losses such as these, which will unfortunately fall upon these unlucky defendants. (528)

Tenure

It is plain that the actual pattern of land occupation in South Africa at this time was one in which numbers of people asserted different types of rights over the same pieces of land. But in Roman-Dutch law concepts of ownership were developed by the courts in a way which placed emphasis on the total and exclusive rights of ownership. Visser has observed that the idea of individualist, absolute ownership was only weakly developed in the Roman-Dutch law. During the Middle Ages, he writes, ideas of split ownership, 'inspired by socio-political reality', of the claims of lords and tenants to the same lands, prevailed (Visser 1985: 39–40). Yet the redeployment of Roman-law ideas of ownership which took place within the social formation of early twentieth-century South Africa, at a time in which property rights were fiercely disputed, recognised a reality of a different sort and 'discovered' the pure doctrine of absolute ownership. In the Transvaal of the time whites had been given title by the republican state over huge areas entirely inhabited by Africans. In the urban areas Asians were trying to find ways to own property in areas in which it was forbidden by republican law. In this most basic area of law, more, perhaps, than in any other, the displacement of focus and of discourse was complete and significant. The concept of the rights of ownership, which was expounded by the Transvaal Supreme Court under Innes, and accepted as South African common law, was not the only possibility available in the repertoire of the Roman-Dutch law (see van der Walt and Kleyn 1989).[7]

In *Lucas' Trustee v Ismail and Amod 1905 TS 239* the court rejected the plaintiff's contention that *dominium* could be divisible into bare ownership and beneficial ownership. It is important to pause over the facts of the case as they are just one example of a series of attempts by Indians to avoid the ban on Asian land ownership. Ismail and Amod had paid for the property and used it to conduct their business. Lucas had paid nothing,

---

[7] It is striking how recent sophisticated jurisprudential discussions of possible different meanings of the rights involved in ownership have taken place in complete separation from the questions of African 'communal ownership', or other rights of African occupation. Van der Walt and Kleyn in their excellent analysis, for example, discuss the choice made for absolute ownership in terms of a narrative rooted in Roman law, Germanic law, and the Renaissance, but not in the context of the intense struggle to establish, hold and exercise rights over land in South Africa.

They discuss the development of the Germanist school of law in the nineteenth century, and the 'discovery' by the Germanist scholars of the concept that, while Roman law emphasised absolute and individual rights, Germanic law recognised rather 'the more socially oriented right to use and enjoy'. They comment acutely that the 'so called principles' of German law '*were for the most part invented by 19th century authors of the Germanist school simply by stating them to be the exact opposite of what they perceived Roman law to be*' (1989: 238). This insight can also be applied to the relationship of the conceptualisation of Roman-Dutch and African laws of property.

and had never used or occupied it. Nonetheless, because of law 3 of 1885, Lucas had been registered as owner. It was claimed that he was simply a trustee, holding on behalf of the beneficial owners. The court ruled that he was the sole owner. To find that Lucas had only a 'bare *dominium*' would be, it said,

> subversive of the well established principle of our law regarding the owner-
> ship of immovable property; it would recognise that *dominium* in immo-
> vable property could be separated into two parts, into a legal estate, as it is
> called in England, and an equitable or a beneficial estate. Now I do not see
> how, consistently with the principles of our law, we can support such a
> contention, because it appears to me that it is one of the essential
> differences between the English law regarding the ownership of immovable
> property and our law. (247)

A tendency in the Cape Supreme Court to explore a less absolutist view of ownership did not take hold (see van der Walt and Kleyn 1989: 248–9). As they conclude, 'The rejection of the one and the acceptance of the other was, therefore, a choice between alternatives within the same legal tradition' (249). They relate the choice not to a context of racial competition over land but to one of 'individualism and liberal capitalism', yet English law, even more entangled with these, could, as the court in *Lucas*'s case acknowledged, accommodate in practice the less absolutist view.[8]

A further irony can be noted. The legal doctrine, and the contrasts made between individual and communal ownership, did not even reflect the way in which rural Afrikaners held property. Under the Roman-Dutch law of succession (see above) testators provided for all family members and farms were treated as family resources rather than as individual property. Though this law was abrogated in the Transvaal in 1902 both habits of mind and practice lived longer. Most Afrikaners in the rural Transvaal, as Denoon has pointed out, were concentrated on approxi-mately six thousand farms, owned in undivided shares by families rather than by individuals (Denoon 1973: 61).

---

[8] The point was driven home, legally, in *Johannesburg Municipality v Rand Townships Registrar 1910 TPD 1314*. Here the argument was put forward that a long lease involved a transfer of *dominium*. Wessels thought not. He adopted Savigny's view (expressed in 1840) that *dominium* comprised 'unrestricted and inclusive control' (1319). The roots of the absolutism, Visser pointed out, were in nineteenth-century Germany (1985: 47).

Communal tenure

The exposition of the principle of the absolute *dominium* of the individual owner under Roman-Dutch law can be contrasted with the development of what was regarded as appropriate in the way of rights for Africans. Here an adaptation of the 'unacceptable' English idea of the trust came to dominate. The idea that land held by Africans should not be held by them directly, but in trust for them by a government agency, was adopted first in Natal and then in the Transvaal. The Natal Native Trust was created in 1864 to acquire and dispose of African land, notionally acting only in African interests. In the Transvaal, where Africans had under original republican law not been allowed to own land, the British forced the trust concept on the republic in 1881 (Davenport and Hunt 1974: 31).

The Native Affairs Commission of 1903–5, unlike earlier enquiries into native affairs, did not begin with the shortcomings of despotic chiefs, or of polygamy, but declared that land tenure 'dominates and pervades every other question' (Cd 2399 1903–5: 10). Cape policy had accepted and utilised the existing 'communal system of occupation', while at the same time aiming at a gradual introduction of individual tenure. Land tenure was closely linked to the continued authority of the chieftaincy as chiefs and headmen continued to be given responsibility by the Cape government for the allocation of land. This power was a vital part of the continuance of their role as judges in customary law. The Glen Grey Act, no. 25 of 1894, had introduced in the Cape a form of individual tenure, but one which was insulated from market forces in that land was not alienable and could not be sublet, and was also subject to the customary law of inheritance. While holders could not, therefore, try to benefit in the market through the use of their land, they could be penalised by it, as the land was subject to execution for debt. It was also liable to forfeiture for rebellion, theft and non-beneficial occupation. There was no general legal bar to Africans buying land in the colony. Nor was there in Natal, where there had been purchases of Crown land not only by individuals, but by syndicates of African buyers. In the Orange River Colony the general principle was that Africans could not become private owners of land. In the Transvaal there had been some private acquisition of land under the terms of the Pretoria Convention of 1881, but these lands had been acquired by tribal groups, and continued to be occupied communally by them (10–17).

Nonetheless, of course, very few Africans lived on land they held privately. Most either continued to occupy communally those tribal lands that had survived white conquest and appropriation, or to live on white-owned farms under a variety of sharecropping and tenancy arrangements. The commission tried to make recommendations for the legal regime of the future, which involved thinking about the balance between the three types of occupancy. Several of the *évolué* witnesses who had appeared before them eloquently urged the advantages of individual tenure. As one said, under tribal tenure people 'will never see anything in front of them'. 'We want to . . . go forward,' said another, adopting the evolutionary narrative. Other nations had progressed because they had individual tenure: 'Our system . . . tends to draw us back' (Cd 2399 1903–5: Evidence, vol. 2: 289). The commissioners were less concerned with these aspirations than with the structures of authority. They asked one of the African witnesses, 'Does not the possession of individual titles remove natives from effectual control?' (408). In their report the commissioners concluded that communal occupation was 'admirably suited' to the needs of 'aboriginal races'. Most Africans, they wrote, 'instinctively cling to and cherish the communal system' (19). But there were those who wanted to 'gain independence and assert individualism'. The tension between the strand of evolutionism that held that promoting individualism in property holding would be 'conducive to greater industry, enterprise and pro-duction' (20) and the political caution that was strongly aware of the advantages of maintaining traditional structures of authority was evident in the recommendations. These were that while greater provision should be made for individual holding in existing tribal areas, there should be no 'undue pressure for its acceptance' (22). Commissioner Hamilton had earlier wondered about promoting individual tenure and

> Tying up forever a large territory for the use of Kafirs in small bits each big enough to support a man and his family . . . to tie up the man whose labour is worth more elsewhere . . . Does it not strike you as rather a waste of both the man and the ground . . . Why give him legal title? *And how will you dispossess him afterwards?* (Evidence, vol. 2: 1078: my emphasis)

J. T. Jabavu focused precisely on this issue, in his clear perception that individual title could be a defence against administrative dispossession, if not against the market. 'The Europeans do not consider that the Natives occupying land under Native tenure . . . are fixed to the land in the sense that the individual tenure man is; that is the only difference . . . The

Natives however consider that they are fixed sufficiently under their own system of tenure' (724). Other considerations were canvassed: Sandili, the Gaika chief, pointed out that surveyed individual holdings would be of no use to polygamists unless there was to be a separate one for each wife (948). Other whites thought that one of the advantages of individualising tenure would be a reduction of polygamy and 'a check on the abnormal increase of the Native' (950).

But there was also a far greater political question in the minds of the commissioners. If individual tenure were to be encouraged, were Africans to be free to enter the market in the country generally? The position, they argued, had to be approached in the light of the 'special protection' afforded to African landholdings in the reserves and of the growing capacity of Africans to purchase land, either individually or collectively. They anticipated a large and to them quite undesirable extension of African land purchases, which would put at risk the principles of segregation, and the political system as a whole. It would be 'difficult to preserve the absolutely necessary political and social distinctions' if a mixed rural population of landowners 'owning the land of the country equally' were allowed to develop (Cd 2399 1903–5: 25). They recommended therefore that African land purchase be limited to particular areas and that the purchase of land which would lead to collective possession or occupation be not permitted (26). One of the Cape representatives and the two Natal representatives dissented. The Natal members pointed out that the recommendation 'limits the right of free trade possessed by every other subject of the British Empire, a right which is enjoyed by the Natives of South Africa in every other sphere of business' (27).

The commissioners also made recommendations on the subject of Africans living on Crown land or private property who were neither servants nor labour tenants (22–4). It had been profitable, they remarked, for speculators to purchase Crown land and let it to African tenants. This, they said, 'restricts the supply of labour . . . fills up with Natives much land which would be otherwise better utilised and developed, and . . . leads to an absence of due control over them' (22). The commission noted that all South African colonies had enacted legislation to control the number of Africans living in this way on white-owned land, though in some cases the laws had not been enforced. They suggested adopting the principle of the Cape's Location Act, no. 30 of 1899, which was that none other than the servants, and their families, of an owner or occupier be allowed to live on private lands. (Families in their view would not include adult sons.) The effect of this would be that privately owned land could not be leased to Africans.

The concern about the conditions on which land was held had wider ramifications. After extensive analysis the commissioners found that 'the British South African aboriginal Native has not fully met the labour requirements of the country'. Their labour had had to be supplemented by the importation of Indians, Chinese, and Africans from other parts of Africa. In relation to the latter, they wrote, 'the serious annual loss to British South Africa by the withdrawal of the large sums in wages paid to these foreigners is manifest' (57). A prime cause was the terms upon which Africans occupied land, the bulk of them 'communally or free of charge, except hut or poll tax'. Among the measures recommended 'to stimulate industry among the Natives' were 'a strict enforcement of the laws designed to check the practice of unrestricted squatting and to regulate and control private locations' (59).

The received white view of African tenure was, as we have seen, that it was 'communal'. This meant that, in Shepstone's formulation, 'the land belongs to the tribe'. The right to use it derived from the hierarchical political structure. The chief 'has the right of giving occupation to it as between members of the tribe, and the headmen again have the right of subdividing . . . Land is, however, always spoken of as the property of the chief' (Shepstone's evidence to the Cape Native Laws Commission, 1883, quoted in Davenport and Hunt 1974: 34–5). As elsewhere in Africa the idea of communal tenure owed more to the need to oppose African and European concepts and to render easier the seizing of African lands than to description of actual use (Chanock 1991). All observers agreed for over half a century that farming land was divided and used individually, and was inheritable, but the facts of this usage was not cognisable by the legal and political formulations. The supreme courts rarely dealt with the definition of communal tenure, and, when they did, relied on the received version of the 'experts'. In *Khonou v Minister for Native Affairs and Mokhatle 1908 TS 260* the court held that neither individuals nor sections of a tribe could hold land separately from the tribe. It defended a version based on communalism and chiefs' power. The law, said Solomon, recognised the tribe as an entity separate from the individual members, and all land held under tribal tenure belonged to the tribe (265). Smith thought that land could not be held apart from a tribe by anyone wanting to remain an integral part of it as this would be 'an absolute negation of the tribal system' (267). Bristowe tried to base this view on some general theorising, a mixture of ideas about primitive communalism, and Hobbes, made into customary law.

> Probably most of the aboriginal laws and customs of the native tribes may be referred back to the principles of self preservation. A tribe apparently consisted of a group of families with community of property. The existence of these bodies depended on how far they were strong enough to resist the aggression of other similar tribes . . . It seems necessary for this purpose that the chief should be an autocrat, that his will should be law. (270–1)

The importance of the final part of the formulation was that, though land could not be owned separately, portions of it could be sold by a chief. The judgment in this respect supported Innes's earlier ruling in *Hermansburg Mission Society v the Commissioner for Native Affairs and Darius Mogalie 1906 TS 135.* Though land was said to be held in common, and though at the time of the disputed transactions Africans could not acquire freehold land in the Transvaal, Innes (who accepted the evidence on custom of the white experts T. Shepstone and H. M. Taberer rather than that of the current chief) found that a chief could sell tribal land.

The powers recognised as belonging to the chiefs stretched of course beyond the right to sell, to the more basic task of land allocation. As Sir William Beaumont observed,

> Communal occupation has tended to preserve the tribal system and the powers of the Chiefs. These powers are considerable, and the Chiefs are prone to exercise the authority with self-interest and partiality. It is the Chief who, practically, allows or refuses permission to Natives to enter his location; it is he who allots garden lands and building sites. (Minute to the Minister of Native Affairs. UG 25 1916: 5)

The opposition between the ideas of communal and individual tenure allowed the tenure issue to become a part of the evolutionary narratives in which the pace, appropriateness and direction of the civilising mission were framed. Within the Cape story of assimilation it was logical that the goal of policy should be individualisation of title, but this was usually expressed in a way that allowed emphasis on difference in concepts, and the consequent postponement of assimilation. The Native Laws Commission of 1883 found that land belonged to the tribe and that the chief held it in trust. People used the land 'in subordination' to the chief 'on communistic principles'. Africans had 'a deep and ingrained prejudice' in favour of this system (G 4 1883: 40; Davenport and Hunt 1974: 36). Having described the radical difference in conception between white and black, and the unreasonable attachment of Africans to their ideas, the commission recommended that the goal of 'dividing native lands and securing rights of individuals by separate title deeds' should remain the ultimate goal of government policy, but that in the shorter term the government should insert itself into the system of trusteeship and allocation.

Shepstone and the Cape commissioners also linked the idea of individualisation of land to detribalisation. While Shepstone admitted to the commission that Africans in Natal readily accepted the idea of exchange in land as was evidenced by their increasing purchases of land from white farmers, the development was portrayed as unnatural, common among Christians 'whose cupidity has been excited'. 'This individual tenure', the commissioners prompted him, 'is in the hands of men who have broken away from their tribes for the purposes of gain' (Davenport and Hunt 1974: 38–9). And, it appeared, it was not even real individual title, as some purchasers had clubbed together to buy land in common. This latter feeling of disquiet was reflected as we have seen in the recommendations of the Lagden Commission. Like the 1883 Native Laws Commission, it adhered to the idea that ultimately individual tenure should be the goal for Africans. But, in the meantime, the market should be segregated. Land purchase by Africans should be limited by legislation to particular areas. And there was to be no mixing of the two systems. The 'purchase of land which may lead to tribal, communal or collective possession or occupation by Natives should not be permitted' (para. 193). In 1916 Beaumont urged the re-affirmation of this principle. While he said there should not be a 'bar to joint ownership of a piece of land in the defined areas by a limited number of natives, the object of the Commission, which is unanimous in this respect, . . . [is] to prevent large numbers of Natives . . . by acquiring and holding land in undivided interests, and thereby, in effect, extending tribal or communal occupation' (UG 25 1916: 6).

While Beaumont paid lip service to the idea of individual tenure for Africans who were 'growing out of' the tribal system, he observed that for many African purchasers it had not been a success. They bought more land than they could pay for, were heavily mortgaged, and many of the transactions were 'hopelessly irredeemable' (8–9). To meet the purchase price it had, especially in Natal, become a common practice to form syndicates in which the members became owners of undivided shares. This, he wrote, 'has led to the utmost confusion owing to the difficulty of ascertaining the rights of individual members or their lawful successors and the difficulties in effecting transfers'. The effect, he claimed, even where Africans had been buying in the private market, nominally under individual tenure, was to defeat the objects aimed at by individual tenure (9). Even where joint purchase of this sort had not taken place, African individual owners, to meet costs, brought large numbers of tenants on to the farms they were supposed to own as individuals, which then became 'small Kaffir locations'. Beaumont also urged that there be other restrictions on market access even for those Africans allowed to participate as purchasers in the market. It was essential, he urged, to prevent Africans buying speculatively, and to allow purchase only by those 'who are really fitted' for individual tenure (15).

Joint purchase could be put in a less negative way. Matheus Legoati, describing land purchases in the Northern Transvaal, told of 200 families living on five farms he 'owned'. 'A certain sum will be paid by each and each will have an equal share. The land will not be cut up . . . Each farm occupies a portion and we have free grazing. If anyone wants to have more land he just has to speak and he shall have it. Each man can have the same amount of land' (UG 22 1916: 276). It was not, of course, simply a matter of a cultural proclivity to share. As Plaatje had pointed out in his evidence to the Beaumont Commission, the 'average pay of the native population would be a shilling a day, and at that rate it would take a lot of saving to buy even one area of ground'. The tendency was, therefore, to combine to buy land. They could not do 'otherwise with their small earnings than to buy on the communal system'. It would, he thought, be better if they could buy smaller surveyed and subdivided land, but without a new government initiative such land was not available. Furthermore he could see disadvantages in such tenure. Individual subdivisions could lead, as he had seen, in the Cape to shocking overcrowding (93).

Plaatje was correct in his linking of division of lots into individual tenure holdings and land shortage. In such settlements, once the subdivision had been made, there was no further room for outsiders, even though there was constant demand from the sons of plot holders. The magistrate of the Glen Grey district observed to the Beaumont Commission that there were considerable numbers of squatters who were sons and relatives of allotment holders: 'All these men are waiting for land and there is no land at present to give them. It is, of course, from this class largely that the supply of native labour comes, and from this point of view it is very desirable that such a class should exist' (UG 22 1916, appendix XI: 11). From another such area the magistrate reported that survey and the grant of allotments 'has the effect of creating a surplus population' (29–30). As Brookes wrote, 'undoubtedly the Glen Grey system involved recognition of the fact that only a certain number of the Natives . . . could own land' (1924: 329). Indeed one of the major limitations on the acceptability of individual tenure by those affected was that it was appreciated that only very limited areas were available, while the experience of communal tenure was that space could always be found. This rationality was none-theless presented in governing discourses as irrational, as part of a culture too backward to appreciate the advantages of individual tenure. But to those in charge of actually administering the schemes the point, even if perceived from a reverse point of view, was obvious. In the words of the Herschel magistrate, 'where you have got a surveyed location and want to put natives in it, it is extremely difficult to do so. I mean that land held under communal tenure will support more natives than land held under individual tenure. My point is . . . if your allotments are surveyed you cannot get hold of land to allot other applicants' (UG 22 1916: 120). From an administrative point of view individual tenure obstructed the capacity to cram people into limited areas. At the same time African pressure for individual tenure was fuelled by precisely the conditions of overcrowding that caused the administrators to resist. Robertson noted in 1934 that it was both the young men who could not get communal land from the chiefs who had exhausted their space and those who held communal land but were looking for protection from encroachment who could see advantages in an alternative form of title (1934: 424). Much of the African evidence given to the Beaumont Commission concerned land shortage and overcrowding. Beaumont fundamentally rejected this view. In his address to headmen in the Herschel district he told them firmly, 'You do not know what over population means,' and advised them to keep less stock and cultivate more intensively (UG 22 1916: 124). He told the Minister for Native Affairs that a 'crux of the Native land question' was a shift from pastoralism to agriculture (UG 25 1916: 6).

The representatives of the Cape tradition who appeared before

Beaumont were still arguing the case for the ultimate goal of widespread individual tenure. T. L. and W. P. Schreiner both argued for extended individual tenure, with acquisition financed by payments extending over a long period. Dower, the Secretary for Native Affairs, urged that provision be made for individual ownership of property within the reserves. Furthermore, he pointed out, the land available so far for African purchase had been in large blocs. This was beyond the means of individual purchasers unless they 'combined with a number of others, and in that way the tendency was to extend the communal system . . . The native himself has put it to me, "Why cannot this land which we at present use be cut up into portions and why cannot we be given the opportunity of acquiring those portions?" ' (UG 22 1916: 213–31).

Both Natal and Transvaal Africans, he said, were asking for the right of purchase within existing African areas. The characteristic drawback of the individual tenure schemes of the past, Dower said, was that 'land has been subdivided for the purpose ostensibly of native settlement, but in almost all of these schemes perhaps the most important aspect is that of exploitation of the native'. But he adhered to the Cape evolutionary view: a move towards the Transkei scheme of individual title for the whole country was not only desirable, but inevitable, 'only a question of time' (232).

Dower and Schreiner had a different vision of Africans' future in the South African economy, in which they were subjected to the same market forces as whites, but had the same opportunities to respond to them. We need to pause to consider their visions; they underline how much the debate about tenure (and the Land Act in general) was linked to the broader question of what role Africans would have in the market, and how far law and policy would be constructed unequally to structure, and to limit, their market participation. To Schreiner the policy of segregation behind the Act was bound to fail because of 'the exigencies of a law that operates outside the laws of Parliament – the law of supply and demand'. The question of labour supply, which dominated much of discussion of land, should, he said, be left to 'solve itself on economic lines. Bills, Commissions, regulations, can never fight successfully against the economic aspect of the situation' (213). Dower envisaged a future in which Africans would be able to purchase on individual tenure in both reserves and the towns. Far from wishing to hold back African urbanisation, he saw it as a natural consequence of increase in population in the rural areas. In towns individual ownership was vital in the construction of townships to which people could bring families. These town dwellers would 'by their thrift' accumulate enough to purchase land at home among people 'of their own tribe'. It was an image of a far freer participation in economic life than any policy was to grant.

Apart from constantly opposing the ideas of communal and individual tenure, official administrative, legal and political discourses, as was the case in the rest of colonial Africa, contained little in the way of interest in or description of how communal tenure really worked. The most basic problem was the confusion of the practices that had grown up in the circumstances of conquest, the creation of reserves and European admin-istration with a pre-existing 'system' of land allocation and tenure (Chanock 1991). Justifications for what was convenient to governments were drawn from the model of 'primitive law'. In Brookes's description

> As usual in a primitive legal system, the conceptions of jurisdiction and ownership (*dominium*) were confused. The tribe – or the Chief – a Native would not draw the distinction between the two that we would – was sovereign over the land which it occupied: therefore it owned the land. The individual in Native Law never held on any other tenure than occupation at the tribe's (Chief's) pleasure . . .
>
> The individual tribesman had only the right to occupy a piece of land; and this right was neither transferable or heritable, save at the Chief's good pleasure.
>
> This is virtually the present form of tenure substituting 'Government' more or less for 'Chief'. (1924: 353)

The substitution of the government for the chief had bureaucratising consequences. Over most of the African areas of the Union, at the time that Brookes wrote, chiefs were under a legal duty to allocate land to male heads of household sufficient for the support of the household. The land had to be cultivated by the person to whom it had been allotted, or a relative if the holder was absent as a migrant worker. It could not be assigned by the holder to anyone else, and fell free to be reallocated if not used. Not only did individual households have no secure 'title', but neither did the 'tribes' who all occupied what was either legally Crown land, or land held by the Native Trust – after 1912 effectively the Minister for Native Affairs – as trustee (Act 1 of 1912). Such 'titles' were to become even less secure. After the passing of the Native Administration Act of 1927 any individual tribe, or portion thereof, could by moved at will by the Governor-General, i.e. by the Minister of Native Affairs.

Brookes was an admirer of Glen Grey tenure because land could not be mortgaged, and therefore the peasantry was protected against the money-lender, and because of the one man one lot principle, which preserved the rough equality of status of native custom (1924: 366–7). In an important departure from native law the widow could be granted a usufruct on the land, which could not be willed, but passed according to the rules of intestate succession. Among the questions to be faced was whether the existing reserves should be surveyed, as a first step towards a wider introduction of Glen Grey-type tenure (369). No one would argue, Brookes wrote, that Glen Grey tenure revert to occupation at pleasure under tribal conditions. But survey, the next step, was politically unpopular, as well as administratively complex. It was opposed by the peasantry, who feared that it presaged further confiscations. And it was opposed by both the chiefs and the native commissioners for fear that it would substantially diminish their discretionary powers. And, while the discourse on the 'problem' of African land tenure still focused on the rural areas, a new and urgent question for which there were no answers in a 'customary' regime, however constructed, was emerging. As Brookes also noted, the insecurity of tenure in urban locations was 'one of the greatest practical grievances of present day Natives' (375).

Expression of scepticism about the fairness of the administration of the 'communal' system did surface. Brookes noted evidence from the Transkei and Tembuland of the 'capricious interference' by chiefs which 'fell heavily on the progressive Native, whose activities are regarded by the Chiefs as indications of undue individual claims to the land' (381). Other evidence came from Natal where land was distributed by chiefs without the supervision of magistrates that the Cape had imposed. The chiefs were stigmatised as 'absolutely unfair' by one senatorial witness (UG 22 1916: 414–5). Another, F. R. Moor, the former Natal Secretary for Native Affairs, observed that friends of the chiefs accumulated land unfairly (429–30). Another witness suggested that people lost their land for appealing against chiefs' court decisions (508). Even with government administrative oversight, communal tenure gave rise to many disputes. J. F. Herbst, then magistrate of the St Marks district in the Eastern Cape, advised that in the system he administered allotment was done by the headmen, subject to magisterial approval. Without this certificate of approval it was a criminal offence to cultivate. There was only a very vague description of the land. The question is becoming more vexed as time goes on, while the difficulties of finding land for new applicants are increasing daily. Many of the original residents of the locations have more land than they can cultivate . . . [Lands were] all huddled together, with boundaries zigzagging in all directions, and little to indicate where such boundaries are. The result is that there are endless disputes. (Appendix XI: 31).

Young married men had no suitable ground, while that of the older residents was seldom available for redistribution (32). The magistrate at Umzimkulu portrayed similar conditions. 'The best ground was . . . taken up years ago, and it would seem that the Chiefs and Headmen were at that time extremely liberal in regard to the acreage allotted to their followers, especially the favourites, relatives and those who paid them well.' Similar allegations were made about the Zoutpansberg, that families which were not favoured by chiefs were 'gradually squeezed out', and that, because of milching by chiefs, people would prefer to buy their own plots (266).

While some thought that the remedy for maladministration by chiefs was to increase the right to individual tenure within the reserves, the clamour is better understood in relation to the desire to assert more control over the processes of communal allocation as a means of increasing the density of settlement in the reserves. Many witnesses told the Beaumont Commission that there was no scarcity of African land, simply an inefficient use of it. There was, said one Natal senator, still room 'for these natives provided they get closer together' (UG 22 1916: 419). The Members of Parliament for Zululand and Umlazi both asserted that 'waste' characterised communal land use and that 'a lot more natives' could be put into existing reserves. The lack of African enthusiasm for a Glen Grey-type tenure had less to do with attachment to traditionalism than with an emerging understanding of the connections between such schemes and increased control by officials, and landlessness. Landless people, as well as administrators and politicians, understood that it was easier to insert people into the reserves than into surveyed areas, and that this flexibility would be diminished if survey was extended. The report of the Beaumont Commission, the furore created among whites by its recommendations to increase areas of land which should be reserved for African occupation, and the subsequent appointment and reports of the local committees created a stalemate. As Garthorne, the Secretary for

Native Affairs, admitted, it would have been impossible to put before parliament proposals that did 'justice' to Africans, and 'honoured the pledges' given without evoking 'inconvenient or dangerous antagonism' among members of the parliament. In 1921 the choice was made to sacrifice African interests and to adopt the local committees' far more restrictive recommendations (Davenport and Hunt 1974: 43). At the same time as this hardening of the limitations placed on African acquisition of land in the market, a turn towards emphasising 'communal' and not individual tenure was taken. The Prime Minister, Garthorne reported, 'was impressed with the importance of providing for community occupation, which seemed to be better adapted than individual tenure to the needs of the native at his present stage of development' (ibid.).

Edgar Brookes's dissertation, which was written in 1922, still reflected the older official wisdom and assumed that the survey of the existing reserves was still on the agenda (Brookes 1924: 369–70). On the basis of a sort of 'Merrie Africa' view he favoured one man one lot as 'maintaining the primitive principles of equality among residents of a Location . . . Why impose our individualistic system of "grab" on a people who are less grasping and more contented than we are?' (374). But policy was to take a different turn. In 1922 M. C. Vos, a former Secretary for Native Affairs, submitted a report on the survey of African allotments for individual tenure which, in Davenport's words, 'had considerable influence in undermining official confidence in the merits of individual tenure for Africans' (Davenport and Hunt 1974: 49). It provided further impetus towards the abandonment of the goal of assimilating the systems of tenure. The Glen Grey system, Vos reported, 'has not been such a success as must have been anticipated'. Initially this was because of the 'deep seated aversion of the chiefs to individual tenure, as it would gradually and surely sap their control over the people', the dislike of people to being 'tied down to definite and permanent sites' for houses and cultivation, the high costs of survey and title, and 'surveyors not consulting the interests of the future occupants so much as their own convenience in the survey', and the consequent 'unwillingness to take up title and . . . the large numbers which had to be cancelled owing to the lots being utterly unsuitable for tillage' (UG 42 1923: 1). Vos recounted the confused history of attempts to survey individual lots in African locations. Reports showed that in some cases titles were not taken up, in others boundaries were not respected and common land was cultivated, in others substantial proportions of the allotments were in the possession of the wrong persons. Summing up his general tale in the history of these schemes, Vos wrote that they 'entailed no less than three Select Committees and two Acts of Parliament to rectify the grants of freehold title to natives. This . . . could only be done at considerable cost to the Government' (1). Schemes like the Glen Grey settlement were, in any case, not solutions to the broader problem. It designedly made 'no provision for the natural increase of the population', who were expected to 'find work elsewhere'. Even there it was found in 1919 that '40 per cent of all allotments were in possession of the wrong people', that is neither the registered owners nor their caretakers. Transfer of title was not being passed on change of ownership. The magistrate had recommended that title to nearly 1,300 out of some 8,000 lots be cancelled for non-payment of quitrent or lack of beneficial occupation. When the scheme had been applied to the Tsomo district of the Transkei the result had been the same. There were around 1,250 'faulty occupations' out of 6,450 (5–7). One conclusion that could have been drawn was that the schemes, in which the lots could not support full-time agriculture for families and on which lot holders were under enormous pressure from those excluded, required better administration and more land. But Vos deemed that there had been a social evolutionary failure by Africans as a whole. In 1883, he pointed out, the Tembuland Commission report had said that 'as the natives see the advantages of individual tenure they will gradually fall into European ideas as to the ownership of land'. But 'after 40 years the natives are no further advanced in their views on land tenure' (10).

A meeting of the Prime Minister, the Minister for Native Affairs and senior Native Affairs officials took place in November 1922 (see Davenport and Hunt 1974: 50–1). Vos's doubts were confirmed. The Transkei Chief Magistrate, Welsh, urged halting the survey of districts for individual tenure as it was 'in advance of the people'. The Chief Native Commissioner for the Ciskei thought there should be 'reversion to a system in conformity with native ideas'. But what were 'native' ideas? The Minister, F. S. Malan, in summing up the discussion, seemed to have progressed beyond the dichotomy between individual and communal title. There were at issue, he said, 'four species of individual tenure. 1. With record of title on European lines; 2. With security of rights according to . . . [a] simpler system . . . ; 3. On allotment after inspection and official demarcation; 4. On allotment by Chief and Council according to tribal usage.' Unsurprisingly it was decided that emphasis should be not on either of the first two, but on the two alternatives which left African holdings without security and at the discretion of officials. Accordingly the meeting concluded that there was 'no need to disturb the practice of allotment by Superintendents and Headmen or Chiefs and Councils'.

Hertzog's Bills and land tenure

Hertzog's 1926 Native Land Act Amendment Bill proposed to meet the commitment to make more land available for Africans by adding not areas for African purchase or occupation alone, but so-called neutral areas which would be open to all. Greeted by some as an apparent backdown from the principle of possessory segregation, the proposal had a basic logic. It had become clear that Hertzog's supporters were strongly opposed to the addition of lands reserved for African purchase. Both the areas proposed by the Beaumont Commission and the more limited areas which had been recommended instead by the local land committees had proved too much for the political process to swallow. The neutral-area proposal, relaxing as it did the harshness of the absolute ban in the 1913 Act, would have notionally made more land available for Africans without having much practical effect. The area proposed was smaller than the areas suggested for African purchase by either of the earlier sets of recommendations, and in them Africans would no longer be the only purchasers. But the proposal failed because it had been made dependent on the package of measures involving the removal of African voters from the common roll, which the government did not have the necessary two-thirds majority to pass. In any case Smuts fervidly opposed the principle of allowing mixed purchase in the areas previously set aside for Africans on the grounds that it was a reversal of the policy of the 1913 Act, which was to 'prevent promiscuous buying of land as between whites and Natives' leading to all the 'evils' of 'piebald' landholding. In addition to the application of the metaphors of miscegenation to a free market in land, Smuts used those of disease. White owners near areas where African purchase expanded 'would be subject to the fear of creeping paralysis which will sooner or later overwhelm them' (quoted in Hancock and van der Poel 1962 vol. III: 307–9; 322).

In November 1926 the government convened a 'Native Conference' to discuss the proposed Land Bill. The final resolution comprehensively rejected the entire land policy. It asked first for the repeal of the Land Act. Failing that it demanded the implementation of the Beaumont report. It took issue with the growing emphasis on tribalism by denouncing the Bill's allocation of areas according to tribe. Finally it demanded that the restrictions on land purchase by associations of Africans be lifted and that 'a Native Land Bank be established on the basis of the European Land Bank' (UG 17 1927; Davenport and Hunt 1974: 44).

The issues were further ventilated when the Bills were referred to a select committee. Members of the Native Affairs Commission and African witnesses were put under heavy pressure to concede that more people could be settled on existing African lands, and that communal tenure was the ideal instrument to ensure dense settlement, even if more land had to be acquired. More than one white witness opined that both Europe and Asia were more densely populated than the reserves. But an alternative critique and policy did emerge in the evidence before the committee which is important to consider because it helps to underline the choices made by the government. Loram and Roberts did not challenge the notion that Africans could only be smallholders, apparently accepting the conventional wisdom that four morgen of arable land and fourteen and a quarter of pasturage was what was needed for a family of five. 'If you give them 1000 acres they will only cultivate 100,' said Roberts (SC 10 1927: 21, 23, 49). However, as Roberts pointed out, people in the reserves were already living 'on the edge of starvation'. If population increased, and the reserves were more intensively farmed, 'the conditions will be just the same as now' (23). More space was needed. But 'under a system of individual tenure we will have to give the native more land. This system will always demand that' (ibid.).

While the government's solution was to pursue tribal occupation on communal tenure, there were other ways without reopening the ban on the growth of African individual purchase enacted in 1913. The suggestions that were made were linked back to the labour agenda of the land legislation. As we have seen the prohibition of squatting was one of the major aims of segregatory land legislation. The road taken, as Loram pointed out, was one of 'bringing about progression from squatter, to labour tenant to servant' (72). There must be, he said, a way of getting rid of the squatter 'in some way other than by compelling him to become a labour tenant or servant . . . or by trying to force him into the reserves'. The African demand for more land, and the abolition of squatting, could

be resolved by allowing Africans to enter the market as tenants, to lease
land from whites. Pim and Macmillan, appearing on behalf of the Joint
Council of Europeans and Natives, also urged the leasehold solution.
Squatting could be eliminated, Pim said, by a combination of definite
contracts of lease of arable land for a cash rent, and wage-paid labour with
cash wages for all family members. Macmillan argued that a 'new step'
was needed in developing African tenure, and that a beginning needed to
be made in getting people used to leasehold. The right to lease, he
suggested, could be a *quid pro quo* for the abolition of the right to buy if
leases long enough to give security, say five years, were adopted. Characteristically he presented his argument in terms of non-racial economic
solutions. Both the *bywoner* and the black squatter needed to be given
access to the 'rent paying lease properly negotiated, and exposed to
market forces . . . If he does not pay his rent out he goes' (149–55). The
suggestion was taken up by the principal of Lovedale College, Reverend
James Henderson. Exhausted and overpopulated lands in the Eastern
Cape were leading to a 'crisis of a desperate nature'. Land purchase, even
if allowed, was not affordable. Provision had therefore to be 'in the form
of tenancy under lease with security of tenure' (Appendix A: vii).

In addition to canvassing leasehold, these and other African witnesses
returned to the question of co-operative purchase. Macmillan objected to
the restrictions on purchase by associations of Africans. (Government
practice allowed no more than six buyers to club together.) Without this
facility, he said, purchase by Africans was 'simply impossible'. Representatives of the Transkei Bunga said the same. They brushed aside the usual
objections that such purchases led to inevitable complications when one
or more buyers wanted subdivision. 'We think', they responded, 'it may
be possible to evolve some simplified scheme of survey under which they
can be allocated a residential site and arable ground, and have grazing
ground left in common to all of them' (SC 10 1927: 58–9). So it would
have been. In other words collective purchase could have been, as they
clearly envisaged, adapted to reflect communal practices while at the same
time giving security of tenure. But the suggestion fell on stony ground.
Ideologically whites continued to insist on the incompatibility and diame-
trical opposition of communal and individual tenure, while in the realm
of practice there was the danger that combinations of buyers would
actually be able to afford to buy farms. 'We as farmers', said the
spokesman of the Free State Agricultural Union, 'have learned what power

there is through co-operation, and the natives, by combining, will buy *any* land' (217; my emphasis).

Macmillan and others, in their discussion of leasehold, brought out another of the major continuing features of the discourse concerning land and law, which was the domination of the idea of the final solution. Talking in terms of 'solving the native problem' created a logic in which it was easier to proclaim bans and limitations for all time on African landholding. 'I think we are trying to look too far ahead,' Macmillan warned. 'And trying to meet troubles too far in advance. This "Native Question" is not to be solved by one or two Bills or Acts of Parliament' (185). Any system, he said, 'must be sufficiently elastic to deal with questions that will arise from time to time in the course of a long future' (159). 'We are opposed', said Pim, 'to the idea of once and for all limiting the areas; we want elasticity' (164). But the formulation of policy and law marched to another tune. There was, said the Transvaal Agricultural Union, a 'paramount necessity of settling the Native Land Areas once and for all'. A Member of Parliament told the committee that its task was 'settling the land question for all time' (193). This kind of thinking cannot be overlooked in considering both the content and temper of the legislation of this period.

One of the major strands in the tenure discourse had been that communal tenure was 'backward' in the economic sense as it gave little incentive for the land user to invest in land, and individual tenure was economically 'progressive' and led to increased agricultural production. In order for the official move away from individual tenure for Africans to prevail finally this package of ideas would have to be confronted. The Native Economic Commission in 1932 drew from prevailing discourses the necessary analysis of the reasons for African backwardness, providing further reasons for separating Africans from land-market participation. African culture, pre-eminently the attachment to cattle, and their 'social communism', provided major 'anti-economic inheritances' (UG 22 1932: 50, 34). This reflected the continuing discourse on the 'expert' level which was still expressed in terms of fundamental and opposing differences, and which remained available for deployment by politicians, judges and administrators. The government anthropologist, Professor G. P. Lestrade, was still insisting in 1934, in the face of the prolonged clamour for the right to purchase, that Africans suffered 'bewilderment' when they found that under the European regime they were not entitled to land for nothing and had a 'total inability to understand land transactions involving selling and buying, letting and hiring'. It was this lack of comprehension that caused 'dumb and inarticulate resentment' (Lestrade 1934: 430, 442). The Native Economic Commission admitted that an African area 'can be distinguished at sight by its bareness', but this was because Africans were insufficiently conservationist, not because the areas were too small for their populations (even though they also observed that in the Transkei alone there were about eleven thousand married hut owners who had no arable plot allocated to them under communal tenure; UG 22 1932: 21). There were weaknesses in the 'attitude towards their environment' and an absence of the use of fertiliser was 'connected with the universal cry of Natives for more land' (54, 61). Among the weaknesses of unsupervised communal tenure, the commissioners said, was that lands were 'wastefully dispersed . . . Instead of land adjoining land in an orderly way they lie scattered over the countryside higgledy-piggledy, as if a giant gambler had thrown them out of a pot of dice' (24). Not pausing to consider whether this might have reflected the careful choice of sites by cultivators, the commissioners used it to affirm that 'much idle land could be brought into use' (24). Because they were anxious to slow the flow to the urban areas they were committed to the idea of developing the reserves. But how? One way was to give more scope in them to 'Advanced Natives'. The present system of one man, one lot, they pointed out, meant that all were considered to be peasants, and this hindered development. Some should get more, and some less. Land was being allocated under communal tenure to families who did not farm it, and others could not work it. But simple individual tenure under something like the Glen Grey system was not the answer. The commission found, after 'careful inquiries' about individual tenure, that 'while the possession of a title gives the Native a large measure of personal satisfaction, there is very little difference to be noticed in the way in which land is worked . . . There is no magic in individual title to overcome the inertia of custom' (23; Davenport and Hunt 1974: 51). They noted that all title was insecure. Under communal tenure while some had 'a reasonably secure right to the arable plots allocated' others 'may be at the mercy of a grasping Chief or Headman'. They found 'numerous instances' in which 'enlightened Natives' had had plots seized. Even Glen Grey-type title had its weaknesses. In the first place it was subject to alteration by proclamation. And, under the 1927 Native Administration Act, customary law now governed succession. This, the commission claimed, 'has the same effect as an insecure title in the mind of Native owners', as if they had no sons, the improved land would pass on their death to a male heir who 'may be a "red" Native or a total stranger' (140–59).

The commission therefore concluded that the problem was not with deficiencies in title, but with the size of the holdings which 'were not big enough to make agriculture a full time job'.[9] But the conclusion that was drawn was not that holdings should be made bigger. The 'one man one lot' principle, they said, meant that there was no scope for people of 'wider ability . . . advanced natives'. It was of 'outstanding importance' to improve 'differentiation of functions'. Limitations on size could be relaxed, with an upper limit of 50 morgen to prevent 'speculation' (21–2). The transition from pastoralism to agriculture should be intensified, and more land ploughed. Credit could be made easier for some. They observed that 'the principle of segregation in landholding excludes European private capital'. The prohibition against mortgages on Glen Grey-type titles 'excludes what little Native capital there is'. They suggested the formation of a native agricultural bank, which would get no state aid, but in which Africans could invest, instead of stock. From this source loans could be made, though, they observed, credit alone would not solve the problems 'as long as the one man one lot principle continues' (166–70). The problem was not solvable, in other words, by terms of giving Africans more land, more secure titles or more credit. It lay in intensified development of what land there was. This in turn would allow the absorption of the 'surplus' Africans currently finding their way to the towns.

With the analytical nexus between individual tenure and progressive farming finally broken, the Natal system of trust tenure for Africans became the Union-wide model created by the Native Trust and Land Act, no. 18 of 1936, as part of Hertzog's 'solution' to the 'Native Problem'. In the commission's focus on title and tenure the issue of the prohibition on the leasing of land, so cogently raised by Macmillan and Pim in 1927, was ignored. Only Brookes revived the suggestion that 'a great reversal of policy with regard to leasehold rights' was needed (Brookes 1933: 76). But

[9] Land continued to be allotted on the basis of 'one man one lot', which meant that holdings continued to get smaller. Government policies were opposed to the consolidation of larger holdings. In 1949 a survey found that while agricultural experts in the Native Affairs Department were 'keenly aware' of the problems caused by excessive subdivision 'they are required to enforce the principle of one man one lot which perpetuates the migratory system' (Davenport and Hunt 1974: 52).

as the policy statement issued in 1937 showed, an entirely different future was envisaged for African landholders. New land would henceforth 'in accordance with the policy of the Government be made available to the natives on a tribal as distinct from an individual basis'. And furthermore, it was a tribal tenure which would be left under the control of the chiefs. Land would be settled 'under strict supervision' and occupied 'under supervision and control' (*Statement of Policy* 1937: 6). The statement accepted that it was 'notorious that the existing native locations and reserves are congested, denuded, overstocked, eroded' and that there was a need for remedial action before 'they should be entirely ruined' (4). New land to be acquired for African occupation was to provide relief for this deterioration. It would provide not new scope for African economic freedom, but greater and more intensified control. The statement listed a wide range of measures: compulsory crop rotation; the demarcation of land which could not be ploughed or grazed; fencing; and above all limits on stock holdings. 'Undoubtedly', it said, 'the crux of the whole matter lies in the limitation upon the number of stock carried by the Native population in the Native areas' (5). It concluded:

> Detailed and close supervision will have to be exercised to ensure compliance by the people . . . They must be prevented . . . from ploughing in residential areas, from constantly breaking up fresh patches of land for cultivation . . . from depasturing their cattle on reserved areas; from destroying fences, cutting down timber, burning veld and from the malpractices of a similar nature.

The problem of the reserves, in other words, was to be solved not by more space but by extra policing. The outcome of twenty years of discussion of sufficiency tenure and title was not more African farmers with security of tenure expanding their activities either independently or with state assistance, but people without title under closer control.

Land, labour and contract

We can now return briefly to the interlinked labour legislation and the trajectory of turning tenants into labour tenants into farm servants.[10] In 1926 the Masters and Servants Law (Transvaal and Natal) Amendment

---

[10] See in particular the account in Lacey 1981: chapter 4. Both this and other chapters in this work discuss the competition for labour between mines and farms, and the relation of land and labour laws to this competition, questions which are not pursued here.

Act made labour tenancy more uniform, doubling the period of a labour tenant's service from three to six months in some provinces and bringing others into line with the Free State provision which applied the masters and servants laws to labour tenancies. Renewed emphasis on contract as an instrument for binding farm labour was a feature of the post-1926 discussions. As we have seen the common-law idea of freedom of contract coexisted in South Africa with constant limitations on what contracts blacks, whites and Asians could make with each other in relation to land, employment and marriage, and also gave very different contractual powers to white men, white women, black men, black women and chiefs. In relation to farm labour, contract did have some appeal to liberals to whom it could appear as offering some form of security and protection for those caught in the net of unknowable and changing demands which characterised the lives of labour tenants and their families. But both farmers and state officials looked to contract as a better means of controlling their labour. Magistrates had often urged the development of an officially registered contract. The Native Economic Commission noted that such contracts were rare, and that the magistrates' evidence was to the effect that a misunderstanding as to the terms of the contract was responsible for many of the masters and servants cases that they heard (UG 22 1932: 363). Many other witnesses advocated written contracts for farm tenants (393 *et seq.*). The commission recommended that legislation be passed to make the completion of a written contract between farmer and tenant obligatory. But, as Lacey points out, Africans knew they would have no part in drawing up the terms (1981: 139). Indeed as the commission envisaged it, 'An official form of contract allowing for latitude for variations in the detail of remuneration to the labourer, should be available, farmers' organisations being consulted in its drafting'. The contract was thus not to be a private arrangement between the parties, although the courts would treat it as such. It was understood as an officially mediated act, executed before an official, or advised to a magistrate. (The Native's Trust and Land Act of 1936 was to allow magistrates to double the period of labour which tenants were obliged to render in return for residence from 90 to 180 days a year.)

Much of the earlier debate, as we have seen, concerned the question of the contractual powers of African household heads living on farms. Farmers became increasingly vocal in their demands that a 'customary' law that supposedly gave to household heads the power to contract for household members be made explicit. For otherwise, as represented to the Economic Commission, 'The farmer takes on a labour tenant in order to obtain the labour of his children; the children abscond or do not come back when it is their turn to put in their period of labour; the farmer, finding that he does not get the labour he requires, ejects the head of the family' (UG 22 1932: 384). The tightening of labour controls by the Native Administration Act and the amendments to the Urban Areas Act made it far more difficult for labour tenants to leave a farmer against his will. The screws were finally tightened by the Native Service Contract Act, first introduced into parliament in 1929, and eventually passed in 1932. It gave statutory effect to the idea that the household head contracted on behalf of his whole household, adults and juveniles, who could all now be bound by him to six months service each year. Breach by any household member could result in the eviction of all. Lashes could be imposed for any breach of the contract. Notionally using the instrument of contract, with its aura of freedom of choice, the statute intensified coercion.[11] Walter Madeley asked during the parliamentary debate: 'Why turn him off his land, why thrash him into submission, why force a contract on him, why allow a guardian to enter into a contract of service for an indefinite number of years on behalf of a minor native?' (see Lacey 1981: 179). Edgar Brookes wrote in 1933: 'When we realise that the 1913 Act has forced the gradual substitution of labour tenancy for squatting it means that the Union legislation has introduced a system that can only be called indirect forced labour.' Of the 1932 Act he concluded: 'All is lost, even hypocrisy' (1933: 60).

Tenure in urban areas

The ownership of land in urban areas posed a different set of problems. The conceptual differentiation between individual and communal ownership which was applied to rural lands could not apply to urban lots which were to be occupied on a 'non-traditional' basis. All of the major urban areas were, of course, in 'white areas', that is outside the African reserves. But there was a fundamental problem. As policy discourses increasingly focused around the concept of segregation, of both political rights and

[11] Dubow has concluded, however, that in practice the Native Service Contract Act was 'almost certainly a dead letter' because the Native Affairs Department would not administer its provisions (1989: 64, 120–1).

institutions, and of land, 'there must and will remain many points at which race contact will be maintained, and it is in the towns and industrial centres, if the economic advantage of cheap labour is not to be forgone, that the contact will continue to present its most important and disquieting features' (Department of Native Affairs in UG 7 1919; quoted in Davenport and Hunt 1974: 70). If Africans were to be in the towns, what were the legal implications? How could this be achieved without endangering political segregation? Could African urban land ownership be reconciled with the maintenance of separate 'traditional' institutions? Davenport prints an exchange during the gathering of evidence by the 1903–5 Native Affairs Commission. When the Reverend Mdolomba gave evidence envisaging the sale of surveyed freehold plots in African townships a commissioner said to him: 'You are agreed in desiring individual tenure . . . at the same time retaining Chiefs. Do you think one is inconsistent with the other; or do you think it is possible to retain Chiefs and at the same time to own the land individually?' (Davenport and Hunt 1974: 70). While the witness thought that the chief could assume the role of the mayor, to most whites there was a sinister potential connection between urban freehold tenure and the demand for unsegregated political rights. The Stallard Commission explicitly raised the spectre in 1922. If Africans were to be regarded as permanent town dwellers, it wrote, if some were possessed of property, and could establish themselves permanently, 'there could be no justification for basing [their] exclusion from the franchise on the simple ground of colour' (see Davenport and Hunt 1974: 71).

Since the mid-nineteenth century consideration had been given to the terms of settlement of non-whites in the white towns of the Cape Colony. Visions of urban order were as much the issue as rights to property. The Grahamstown town clerk had envisaged in 1843 the establishment of wards for Fingoes and other 'coloured tribes' to prevent 'promiscuous settling upon and occupying' lands close to the town. In these areas 'not more than one family shall reside upon the same piece of ground' and dwellings would be 'so constructed as to form regular streets at right angles (if practicable)' (reproduced in Davenport and Hunt 1974: 65). In the Fingo village created freehold titles were issued. In the period before Union the different colonies had all put in place legislation providing for the establishment of separate African 'locations' adjoining the white towns. The early image of progressive order had not been realised. The locations were, rather, a nightmare world in which the opposite of social order prevailed (see above part II). They were also feared as the sources of physical pollution. The view that had taken hold was that African urban populations were essentially not permanent residents but an available source of labour units whose true residence, and rights to land, were rural. In the new locations tenure was extremely insecure. Residents were usually on short-term tenancies with few rights against the local authority and subject to removal in a wide range of circumstances, including being out of work. One government inquiry in 1914 gave a general description which underlines the failure to achieve the vision of 1843.

> The location is usually placed in the outskirts of the town . . . but the site is in many cases ill-chosen, generally on some *donga* [eroded ditch] and in the vicinity of, or not far from the town sanitary tip, the refuse dump, and the slaughter poles . . . The ground is frequently stony and irregular and fit for no purpose . . .
>
> Rarely has any attempt been made to systematically lay out the site. Huts are dumped anywhere; no proper streets are laid out . . . The plots allotted . . . are often irregular in size and not clearly marked off. (UG 34 1914: 237–8; printed in Davenport and Hunt 1974: 69)

It was also noted, with strong disapproval, that many major white towns actually profited from the running of the locations, which subsidised the general municipal revenues expended on white areas (Davenport and Hunt: 70). The largest urban area, Johannesburg, had placed one of its two major 'locations' on an area which had been used for dumping sewage. Maud observed that 'for some years . . . the annual estimate of expenditure on Natives and on the zoo had roughly coincided'. Both were governed by the same committee (Maud 1938: 100–1). The 1923 Act for the first time put municipalities under an obligation to provide basic services for Africans. Councils were also subject to audit by the Native Affairs Department to prevent them profiting from these services.

The draft Urban Areas Bill which was released in 1918 envisaged that Africans would be able to buy and lease land in the segregated urban areas (Davenport 1971: 8ff.). But this was abandoned. While in 1922 the Native Affairs bureaucracy affirmed the aim of 'fixity of tenure' for urban areas, their vision of a desirable development of African towns was obliterated by the doctrine that towns were white areas in which Africans were only labouring strangers. The issue of urban freehold for Africans came to a head in 1923, when the comprehensive Natives (Urban Areas) Bill was introduced. As had happened in the case of the 1913 Land Act the Bill was drastically altered in the parliamentary process. As introduced the Bill gave to local authorities the discretion to set aside areas in locations in which Africans could buy land and build houses. The National Party objected. Hertzog, Davenport wrote, 'went almost straight to the issue of urban tenure, and scarcely moved off it' (16). As Hertzog pointed out, this would be giving land to Africans which, according to the Land Act of 1913, was reserved for whites, and would be saying to an African purchaser that 'he and his children could remain for all time'. The Bill went to a select committee. Before it Free State municipalities objected on the basis that the right to own land would be 'the thin end of the wedge and might result in Natives becoming owners of property not only in towns but throughout the country'. They also raised the possibility that 'if natives are given a right to own property they will also have the right to vote'. Transvaal municipalities raised the objections that the owners of urban property would let it and become absentee landlords, and also that a right of freehold would make urban settlement attractive and towns would be 'swamped'. Furthermore, if there were African vested interests in the towns the municipalities would lose their control over who could come and who could stay (SC 3A 1923: 100). C. M. de Vries, speaking for the Transvaal Municipal Association, also recounted his experience with the failure of African freehold in the Lady Selborne township in Pretoria. The account compares with the official view taken of the failure of freehold for Africans in rural areas (see above). Plots were sold frequently, passing from hand to hand, without registration of transfer, and rate collection became impossible.

There were other, and perhaps stronger, objections. The representative of the Eastern Cape Municipalities observed from experience that 'It is difficult for the Municipality to retain control of these areas once you give them title deed. The native is more amenable to discipline if he is merely a leasehold proprietor . . . Once he has a title deed there is no shifting him without trouble' (quoted in Davenport and Hunt 1974: 16). The manager of the Durban Non-European Affairs Department agreed that if freehold lots were established 'the natives will cease to recognise that they are in the urban area primarily for employment, and once they become owners in freehold the stimulus to good behaviour which is maintained by the possibility of their leasehold tenure being forfeited will cease to operate, either upon the owners or their descendants' (ibid.). The emphasis on employment and control also meant that 'in urban locations the general rule is that a municipal house will not be let to a woman' (UG 22 1932: para. 965).

Far from being an early beacon of success, the Grahamstown experiment featured in the exchanges as a disastrous example and a warning, as 'trouble' (ibid.). This was partly because it had prevented the extension of the white area of the town. But more sadly, for Loram, a member of the Native Affairs Commission and labelled as a 'friend' of Africans, the Grahamstown experience was an 'object lesson' which 'very much complicated' the administration of Africans in the area. 'The conditions that can be imposed on the location as a whole do not apply to the freehold, so that in questions of discipline and supervision, this freehold strip is a very great sore from the municipal point of view.' He urged a sort of Glen Grey tenure of leasehold subject to good behaviour, with the issue of ejection to be decided by a magistrate (SC 3A 1923; quoted in Davenport and Hunt 1974: 74–5). Members of the committee were moved by these considerations, not by the plea made by D. D. T. Jabavu that Africans were 'clamouring for better and greater opportunities and facilities for acquiring landed property' (SC 3A 1923: 16–17). A. R. Ngcayica pointed out the problems. In townships land was owned by the municipalities and stands were leased to African residents. People built houses on the land at their own expense. If they could not keep up with the lease payments to the municipality, that body took possession of the plot, and the house, for a nominal sum. Africans who built houses, Ngcayica said, 'suffered much' from this state of affairs. 'If the land were sold to the native outright it would belong to him and his house could not again be bought by the municipality' (32). (Even this was not sufficient for some white administrators. The mayor of Cape Town suggested that non-payment of rent also be made a criminal offence: 46–7.) The government preferred Hertzog's view. Smuts said that he 'did not attach too much importance to the native objection to leasehold title as freehold individual title to land was not a native system' (18).

In the Act that emerged from parliament the provision for freehold had been removed. Sites were simply to be allocated, and forfeited, administratively. Section 4 of the Urban Affairs Act also prohibited the acquisition by whites of any interest in lots or buildings in the African areas. This exclusion of private capital was, according to the Department of Native Affairs, 'designed to prevent non-native landlordism in locations' (UG 22

1932: annexure 5). In their consideration the Native Economic Commission noted that the exclusion placed the financial burden on local authorities (412). It also insulated the area from the operation of the rest of the market, and Africans from access to capital. The denial of freehold in the 1923 Act did not affect already existing rights. In the western areas of Johannesburg in townships not proclaimed under the Gold Law, there were African freeholders. As Cobbey explains the eventual application of the Act to these townships was 'held up' as the government was 'torn between the two pillars of South Africa's capitalist system – the rights of property and the imperatives of the racist political settlement' (Cobbey 1990: 21).

16

Law and labour

The issues surrounding labour, which comprise not simply the usual questions of the legal regulation of conditions of work, the labour contract, unions and wage levels, but also the ways in which this was done in a racially divided workforce, are perhaps the hardest to draw a 'legal' boundary around. They go to the heart of the nature of South African society, state and politics, and the legal discourses cannot be separated from the political. The problems of control of wages, the right to strike and the legal position of trade unions have in all industrial countries produced complex attempts at solution. In South Africa these have to be considered in a wider context – that of the use of law in these fields to impose an industrial colour bar. Labour issues were, in the years after 1902, the most violent and contentious in white politics. An account of the development of the divided regime of labour law is necessarily an account of this political struggle.[1] Labour questions were central to the formation of the new South African state. The Milner regime in the Transvaal put the resources of the state behind the mobilisation of labour for the Rand mines. Unable to coerce African labour fast enough, his government imported Chinese labour for the mines. This fuelled the rise of the white Labour Party dedicated to the protection of white workers. The oppressive recruitment of black labour and the tightening of the pass laws prefigured the Union-wide application of the Transvaal system which was accomplished by the Native Labour Regulation Act of 1911, one of the earliest fruits of white independence. While black workers had no political voice, the Labour Party, and white trade unions, both deploying

---

[1] The historiography of labour in these years is particularly rich (see Davies 1979; Johnstone 1976; Simons and Simons 1969). Much of it has focused around the question of whether the 'real' issue was race or class. I do not address this here. The best treatment of labour issues in the context of the years of state making is Yudelman 1984.

406

an international socialist rhetoric, embarked on a struggle to protect white workers against both white capital and black labour. Several major strikes, accompanied by widespread violence and the intervention of both Imperial and South African troops, followed.

The politics of industrial law were dominated by the atmosphere of violence and by the existence and influence of the Labour Party. Controlling and satisfying the enfranchised white labour constituency was a prime political necessity which drove legal developments. In relation to the law that governed African labour, the interests of white mining and farming were completely dominant. These political interests were woven into legal discourses with other foci. The broad context was the unfolding consideration of legal regulation of the economy – of the relationship between contractual and regulatory approaches. In the highly regulated and racially stratified South African society the place of the labour contract was pivotal. Could it be a mutually agreed 'free' contract? If so what was the role of the state in the regulation of wages, and in the control of breaches of contract such as strike and desertions? And in what senses, and how far, could the livelihood and well-being of white workers, and with it the economic position of whites as a whole, be left to the workings of a market in which they had to compete with workers of other races? It is clear that a determination to entrench white power and a purely market- and contract-based model of employment law could not have lived together. In the area of economic regulation in general the new state was unashamedly capitalist, and all of the other major attempts to interfere with the freedom and power of capital failed. Employment law was the exception. The construction of a highly regulated labour market based on a colour bar made politically possible the continued dominance of market ideology in other sectors.

The intellectual capital and subsequent statutory enactments of the legal debates were derived first from the developments in nineteenth-century Britain, and later from other parts of the empire. The Conspiracy and Protection of Property Act of 1875 (also a source for the Riotous Assemblies Act of 1914) had been a watershed in the legal regime of labour in England, and marked the shift from the dominance of the 'legal imagery' of master and servant, which was henceforth 'increasingly subordinated to the ideas of contract' (Creighton et al. 1983). Before the triumph of the idea of contract in the nineteenth century, Holdsworth wrote, it was not considered that wages were settled by individual bargain, 'or that the contract between employer and workman could be regarded as precisely similar to any other contract' (quoted in ibid.: 20). Contract is premised on the free choice of the parties. Once it became the core rationale of the acceptance of the obligation to work, there were two primary effects. One is that labour was set 'free' to accept or refuse terms, and, as contract was 'civil' law, a worker could no longer be criminally prosecuted for breach of an employment contract. The second was to place a powerful new symbolic weapon in the hands of employers. In South Africa the rising 'master symbol' (ibid.) of contract was used hand in hand with that of the older regime of master-and-servant to strengthen and enhance the latter. As the law developed, the emphasis in relation to the master and servant regime which governed black workers was on their 'choice' in accepting the terms of their employment, and their consequent obligation to be completely bound by it. In relation to white workers the development of contract in relation to employment was different. For them the coercive subordination of the whole person of the servant (supported by criminal sanction) gave way to the idea of the contractual bargain for the sale of labour alone as a commodity which was the product of a voluntary exchange. But the realities of employment of industrial society did not fit a simple construct of a freely entered into contractual bargain. How could workers bargain about wages and conditions against capital? How, without criminal sanction, would the breaking of employment contracts be dealt with, especially in circumstances of organised mass action? In all countries the pure contractual regime had to be diluted by statutory interventions to regulate relations between capital and labour.

Because of the highly politicised context, one which was at the heart of racial rule, my focus is on how the laws were talked about, and what roles the representations of categories such as labour and contract served. The major discourses surrounding the labour law were not legal and rule focused, emanating from lawyers or judges; but bureaucratic, political, value oriented and instrumental. The white industrial labour force exercised considerable (and growing) electoral power. In addition, the state was forced by three periods of violent confrontation with white trade unions (in 1907, 1913–14 and 1922) to reconstruct the system of labour law affecting white workers. This was reinforced by a process in which the judges limited the application of the common and statutory law of master and servant so as to exclude industrial occupations. The models of industrial conciliation for white workers were drawn from other white Dominions, Canada and Australia. The other side of the coin was a labour regime for African workers based on confinement in the mining compound; migrant labour extracted from rural areas by taxation and the seizure of land; prison and the extensive use of prison labour in public works and agriculture; whipping (judicially imposed and otherwise); strict control of movement and residence; rural labour extracted as 'rent' from men, women and children; and the denial of a legal capacity to organise and withhold labour. For both legal regimes the idiom of contract was crucial.

In this chapter I shall consider the pass and master and servant laws as part of a larger ecology of labour law. The largest number of workers were within the parameters of a system of unfree labour which originated first in the means adopted to control labour after the abolition of slavery. By the early twentieth century masters and servants laws were tied in with the development and elaboration of a pass system for African workers and the policies of influx control for urban areas which were designed to limit the numbers of Africans permanently resident in towns and cities and which eventually linked the right to urban residence to the existence of a labour contract. These were both connected to the efforts to abolish sharecropping, to extract labour from a family-oriented peasantry and to tie labour tenants to farms in a phase of rising African urbanisation. Competition between white farmers and mines for labour and a shared interest in forcing down its cost lay behind the policies of labour law for Africans. The mining industry developed on the basis of large labour-recruitment schemes, the institutionalisation of migrant labour and the confinement of workers in compounds. The masters and servants laws were a part of the development of a racially bifurcated industrial law in which they were eventually to exist side by side with a system of industrial conciliation which came to regulate much of the conditions of white labour contracts.

There was a significant legal heritage of control of the movement of 'masterless men' in Europe, and of the defence of urban areas against migration of the poor. The English vagrancy laws and the complex of continental controls such as labour passes, movement passes and service books were a part of the history of industrialisation (see Torpey 2000). South African controls were borrowed in this area, as in others, though the major legal inspiration remained the Vagrancy Law. Black labour in South Africa was neither 'tied' nor 'free' and in its borderline status subject to extensive documentation and policing. Also, in contrast to the situation of whites, the South African state did not really bureaucratically know individual Africans until they entered into labour contracts. This made the control of movement through the pass a central part of the legal culture, a crucial marker of the status of unfreedom.

Passes

There was a considerable difference between the pass-law regimes in the different colonies before Union. In accordance with Cape Act 22 of 1867 passes were required for Africans entering the colony from beyond its borders, and for those moving stock. They were not required for ordinary movement about the colony. But the Vagrancy Act passed in 1879 had far-reaching implications for freedom of movement, and resulted in the growth of the 'practice' of Africans carrying passes from their employer, or the owner of the land on which they lived. Under the Act the owner of a property or his representative could apprehend any idle or disorderly person, or anyone found wandering or loitering. The onus of proving *bona fides* was placed on the person arrested. A Parliamentary Inquiry claimed in 1914 that this informal practice of requiring passes was

> a convenience to the Native as it provides him with what is practically a passport and frees him from being prosecuted under the Vagrancy Acts . . . The Vagrancy Acts comprise a very stringent system of vagrancy regulations, and without some identificatory pass . . . a Native travelling by road in the colony is in danger of being arrested . . . and brought before the Resident Magistrate . . . and required to give an account of himself. (SC 8A 1914: iii)

In 1895 this informal system, by which pass carrying became a part of life, was supplemented for urban areas by the giving of power to local authorities to make regulations preventing Africans from being in streets or public places at night without a pass. But it was only on the diamond fields in Griqualand West that the essential legal linkage between the pass and the labour contract was made. There, under Act 14 of 1872 contracts of service had to be registered, and those without evidence of contract and registration were subject to arrest (see Worger 1987). But for the Cape Colony as a whole this did not apply, and apart from the night curfew in some towns, and the possibility of arrest as a vagrant while travelling, the carrying of a pass was not legally required. Nonetheless the 1920 committee was able to note that while it was usually stated that no pass control over movement operated within the Cape the provisions of the vagrancy laws 'to a large extent fulfil the same purposes as the pass regulations of the Transvaal' (UG 41 1922: 2).

In Natal also before 1901 passes were required for travel into and out of the colony, and for moving stock. In 1901 a system of identification passes linked to registered employment contracts was introduced, with the object of regulating employment. Every African in employment had to carry a pass with the terms and length of the contract on it, and produce it when required. This was extended to farm residents in 1904 by a law requiring their terms of service to be registered. In the Orange Free State chapter 133 of the Law Book made all persons of colour moving about the country without a pass liable to arrest as vagrants, and they could be bound in employment by magistrates.

It was in the Transvaal, however, that the most detailed and comprehensive system of control had been developed and by examining the foundations laid in the Transvaal we can gain a clear picture of the fundamentals of the pass laws, and an idea of what was acceptable to the new state as it faced the task of post-war reconstruction. As British government established itself in the Transvaal in 1901 before the end of the war, the Colonial Office in London came under pressure in parliament concerning the harshness of the former Republic's laws in relation to Africans and other non-whites. Under particular attack were sections 150 and 151 of the Gold Law of 1898 which made provision for passes, under pain of ten lashes for default, and which provided for twenty-five lashes for other breaches of the labour law and for criminal sanctions for breach of labour contract, or 'misbehaving in service'. Only after considerable agitation and pressure did the new British administration in the Transvaal agree to do without lashes, but it adhered to the essence (and indeed the wording) of much of the existing law.

Milner wrote a despatch to Chamberlain in 1901 to accompany the new laws which were the fruits of the 'reform' of the Republic's pass laws and explaining the position taken, and enclosing a statement by Sir Godfrey Lagden, the Commissioner for Native Affairs (Cd 714 1901: 29/ 11/01). Lagden's initial point was that many of the laws and regulations of the former Republic 'were sound in principle'. There was, he urged, 'more to be gained by effective administration than by violent legislative changes, which are calculated always to confuse the native mind and to disturb the general community'. The black population had seen the Boers 'divested of governing power. They are aware that the abuse of the lash has been removed, are under the impression that its use is prohibited and are displaying contempt for other forms of punishment.' They were quick to 'presume upon the prospect of administrative leniency'. It was necessary to correct this impression, and the first occasion was the reform and amplification of the pass laws, and the affirmation of the necessity of compelling blacks to carry passes. The first point, therefore, was that the pass law was a part of the basic framework of 'sound relations' to be established between black and white. Milner went on to affirm the basic acceptability of the existing republican laws.

> It was not so much bad laws which were to blame . . . as very bad administration. If aboriginal natives are to come and go in large numbers in search of labour, and to reside for considerable periods in the midst of a white community, there must be some passport system, else the place will be a pandemonium . . . it is absolutely essential to have some reasonable arrangements by which the incoming native can be identified, and his movements traced. (ibid.)

In the realm of native affairs he had resort to the imperial wisdom that 'sound and honest administration' was more basic than law.

Milner laid great emphasis on the new measures to ensure that Africans entered voluntarily into labour contracts by means of the control of labour recruiting agents, and government oversight of contracts before the issuing of labour passes. This was a crucial claim, because once an African was deemed to have voluntarily entered into a contract he was to be locked into it. There were two sets of villains identified with regard to the breaking of labour contracts, the labourers themselves, and competing employers. Both of these were subjected to new controls. In case a competitive labour market should develop through what Milner called 'nefarious traffic' – by which he meant an employer offering work to someone already employed – the new laws subjected to criminal penalties employers who engaged an African worker knowing him to be bound by a contract of service to another (General Pass Regulations, sec. 12). While African workers were no longer to be flogged for desertion, a person leaving service before the expiry of the term of the contract would be liable to a £10 fine or three months imprisonment, and, after serving the sentence, would have to return to complete the term of the contract (General Pass Regulations, sec. 13). Milner concluded by defining the role of government in relation to labour. It was not the government's concern or intention, he wrote, to 'procure labourers . . . by compulsion, and arbitrarily to reduce the rate of wages'. But, he said, if employers 'by combination among themselves . . . can prevent wages from being forced up to a preposterous pitch' it would be beneficial.

> But in any case it is no business of the Government's to interfere in the matter, nor have the mine owners suggested that it should be. What they *do* ask is that the Government should do what it can to prevent the natives, whom they have obtained at great cost, and whose interests are safeguarded by the law in so many ways, from breaking away from their contracts in a mere access of childish levity or being tempted away by unprincipled labour thieves. And this surely is a reasonable demand. (Cd 714 1901: 28; Milner–Chamberlain, 6/12/01)

With these principles in mind we can look at some of the other details of the new laws to get an idea as to what met the standards of the new British colonial state. Proclamation no. 37 of 1901, the Native Passes Proclamation, divided the colony into labour districts, for each of which there was to be an inspector of natives. To this official were delegated powers to act in a judicial capacity in relation to labour and other disputes, one of many interesting examples of the delegation of judicial matters concerning Africans away from the courts, to special administrative officials. The inspector was to enquire into and redress 'grievances' of Africans in mining employment; to enquire into and determine all breaches of discipline; and to 'hear and determine any matter or dispute of a civil nature . . . between any such Natives'. An inspector could examine witnesses on oath, punish for perjury, and impose fines on African employers for breaches of regulations (secs. 5 and 6). In addition at every pass office 'guard rooms of an adequate size' could be established to hold workers suspected of desertion for up to six days (sec. 10). This was taken directly, as were most of the provisions, from the Republican law. 'In order to prevent vagrancy and habitual idling' any African 'found wandering abroad' without the appropriate pass could be arrested, not just by an authorised officer, but by any person on whose property they were found (sec. 6). No person could employ an African not in possession of a pass, which was to be retained by the employer (sec. 7). Africans entering a labour district in search of work were to be given six days in which to find it, and, if they remained longer, without work, could be imprisoned for a month with hard labour (Labour District Regulations, sec. 4).

In explaining Milner's reconstruction of the defeated republics, Worsfold accurately placed the pass law at the centre of black–white relations. The pass, he wrote, 'is the basis upon which rests the entire fabric of the legal relations between the native and the European'. No one could leave their village without one, and it served as 'a record of good or bad conduct and a certificate of identity'. It had to be produced for policemen, Native Affairs Department officials and employers.

> The control of the employer is now substituted for that of the chief. The native cannot leave the quarters assigned to him for a single night without the written permission of his employer. He must return to his quarters before sundown every day. To enable him to return to his 'kraal' or to seek fresh employment, he must have a proper discharge from his first employer, which includes a record of his behaviour.

He concluded that the pass system 'rightly administered . . . is a means of putting into effect an industrial partnership between the white and the black races' (Worsfold 1913 vol. II: 175). The Transvaal division of the Supreme Court was to sum up twenty years later, confirming the objective of labour control and enforcement. 'The policy of the pass laws and regulations is to compel every native (except in special cases) to carry or be in possession of a pass . . . The object of the Legislature is to prevent vagrancy or idleness' (*R v Tsheleza 1931 TPD 1*).

There were also general pass regulations under which all Africans travelling in the Transvaal had to carry passes. Railway tickets could not be issued without production of a pass, and a person was liable to arrest if travelling in a direction not specified on the pass. A person without a pass was also subject to arrest as a vagrant. In addition to the general identification pass there were the laws relating to proclaimed labour districts. On entering such a district an African 'requires in addition to his travelling pass an "identification labour passport". This passport must contain a complete record of the individual, and must contain the history of his movements until his return home' (SC 8A 1914). In 1909 this system was applied to all urban areas of the Transvaal. These laws applied to those both of whose parents were members of 'some aboriginal race or tribe of Southern Africa'. The third set of laws applied to urban curfews.

Under the Night Pass ordinance of 1902 a 9 p.m. to 4 a.m. curfew was imposed on all persons of colour, including those with one 'aboriginal' parent.

The broader framework of the labour 'problem' was set out by the Transvaal Labour Commission of 1903 and by the Lagden Commission two years later in a way that reinforced Milner's agenda. The Transvaal commission found that demand was far in excess of supply, and that the needs of the mining industry in particular could not be satisfied from local resources. The 1903–5 Native Affairs Commission considered how to ensure a greater mobilisation of labour. They repudiated direct compulsion and indirect compulsion in the form of a labour tax. They also rejected measures to raise wages, taking refuge in the market principle. 'Any recommendation as to higher wages is quite out of place . . . any departure from the principle that the rate of wages must be a matter of free contract between employer and employee is unsound, nor is any relief from present difficulties to be found in such a measure' (Cd 2399 1903–5: 58). Instead 'administrative measures' were desirable. The basis of the measures proposed was to close off the spaces in which idleness was possible. Fundamental to this was to control unregulated squatting on private land and to charge rents for occupation of Crown land. But this left another area to be closed off, the possibility of living in the towns without making the desired labour contribution. For this reason the pass laws, in the form of the labour pass, were vital. The commission recommended 'the enforcement of laws against vagrancy in municipal areas and Native labour locations, whereby idle persons should be expelled' (59).

The scale of the administrative and legal enterprise was to be simply enormous, involving as it did the resources of a new and administratively weak state in a bizarre system of total control of movement of the great bulk of its population.[2] Under the circumstances it is hardly surprising that huge strains were to be put upon legal niceties and that both statutes and administrative practices gave priority to convenience of control rather than legal principles. One of the obvious agendas for the new Union was the unification and rationalisation of the pass and masters and servants

---

[2] The absurdity of such an effort is underlined by the responses to the parallel proposals to control the movement of far smaller numbers of unemployed poor whites into the cities. The Johannesburg Chief Magistrate put it well: 'As far as stopping them is concerned you cannot have an immigration law inside the country, or a fence in a municipality.' There was 'no way of getting rid of them when they were there'. If expelled they would simply return (SC 3 1911: 374). Control of white movement was politically and administratively unimaginable.

laws. The Native Labour Regulation Act of 1911 essentially made it possible to apply Milner's system to any proclaimed labour area, though this was not actually done for the whole country. In 1914 parliament looked briefly at the problem of unification of the pass laws and declared it too difficult, seizing upon the excuse that it would have to wait until the forthcoming report of the Natives Land Commission.

But the 1914 war interrupted the process of devising a country-wide pass regime. In the meantime Natal magistrates cast a jealous eye on the comprehensive Transvaal system of controls. One drew attention to the comparative disadvantages in Natal in which there was 'no provision for character supplied by the last employer, rate of wages received in last situation, nature of work, date of last employment, and discharge . . . The employer takes a considerable risk when employing a strange native . . . If these suggestions were adopted there would be considerable encourage-ment for a native to behave himself' (UG 39 1918 103). Another com-plained that Natal laws did not require an African not in white employment to carry a pass when away from his home. He could not, therefore, be identified unless he already had fingerprints on record. 'We require a system under which identification may be established before the commission of a crime.' He also complained that under the 1901 Natal law an employer could only keep the employee's pass with the latter's consent. This meant that 'a native in service almost invariably retains his pass, and in the event of his deserting he is free to produce it to another employer, enter service and escape detection' (ibid.). There were calls also from Cape magistrates for the extension of the Transvaal system (e.g. UG 36 1918: 27). Yet significantly there were signs that the magistrates in the Transvaal were having considerable difficulties with their own system of total control. As one complained in 1914, the pass laws 'are contained in Proclamations, Ordinances and Acts, and overlap. This leads to confusion to a large number of officials, especially Special Justices of the Peace and Police Officers, who are not usually in possession of properly annotated law books' (UG 28 1915: 106). Another urged the unification of the web of laws controlling movement and employment – the masters and servants law, the native recruiting laws, the urban areas law and the pass laws – but this task continued to be beyond the resources of the government and under-lines the incredible nature of the ambitions it had (UG 36 1918: 97). In 1920 an inter-departmental committee of officials conducted an examin-ation of the pass laws. It began with a justificatory narrative. The pass laws

had been considered necessary to 'secure control' over the African population and to 'safeguard against crimes such as stock theft' (UG 41 1922: 2).
In the early days they had been directed against a 'barbarian' influx.

> As the country became more settled they were utilised for enforcing
> contractual obligations between natives and Europeans, and for detecting
> deserters. Later, when the natives began to seek employment in the large
> European urban and mining centres – more particularly on the Witwaters-
> rand – these laws, amplified and extended, have been used to maintain
> order, to detect desertion, to identify on behalf of their relatives natives
> who have become lost. (Ibid.)

The 1920 committee took considerable note of the longstanding opposition to pass laws. It noted the agitation in the Transvaal and in Britain
after 1902 and Milner's rejection of it. After that, it observed, the centre of
struggle against the laws moved to the Free State where it had been
focused on municipal regulations requiring women to carry passes.
Following on the mass petitions of 1912 and 1913 a campaign of passive
resistance was organised leading to the imprisonment of resisting women
(see Wells 1982). The Free State municipalities did not have national
support on this issue. The Native Affairs Department unsuccessfully asked
for the relaxation of the Free State laws, and the select committee of 1914
also called for relaxation. Finally in 1917 the Union government asked the
police not to administer the Free State pass laws against women, and the
resistance ceased.

The 1920 committee was acutely aware of the potential of the pass laws
to become a focus of political opposition and noted broader aspects of the
anti-pass campaign, which it presented as having far wider aims than the
presentation of grievances about passes. In the meantime, the committee
observed, the South African Native National Congress had been 'extending its influence', especially among Africans with education, and it
was trying to become the body that spoke for the African population as a
whole, bypassing government communication through the tribal chiefs.
'To such a body the pass laws offered an excellent line of attack against the
Government' (UG 41 1922: 5). In June 1918, following the European
strikes, African municipal workers went on strike in Johannesburg. The
effort was

> abortive . . . and the result was attributed to the existence of the pass laws
> and the system of registration of contracts under which they were unable

lawfully to leave work at a day's notice. The avowed object of the Congress from that time has been to abolish passes and contracts with a view to giving natives freedom of action to paralyse the industrial world by strikes. By this means it was hoped to secure the objects they had in view, which were not to be limited to the abolition of passes. (Ibid.)

The reaction of the court to the strike was explicit. In passing sentence on the strikers convicted under the master and servant law the Johannesburg Chief Magistrate, Macfie, told the strikers that

> While in gaol they would have to do the same work as they had been doing, and would carry out that employment under an armed escort . . . if it were necessary they would be shot down. If they refused to obey orders they would receive lashes as often as might be necessary to make them understand they had to do what they were told. (See Roux 1948: 138–9)

In relation to the right to strike the masters and servants and pass laws placed African workers in an entirely different position from whites. As they had to enter into monthly or six-monthly contracts of service they were not free to strike without punishment. White workers were perceived to be different. The same magistrate wrote in 1918 that there could be no law against white workers striking 'except on the absurd basis that the workman should be practically a serf'. In any case, as he pointed out, trade unionists outside and inside South Africa had realised that they 'must contract only on an hourly basis, so that all the men affected may be free to end their contracts immediately and simultaneously without fear of legal consequences' (UG 36 1918: 108).

In October 1918 Smuts and the Secretary for Native Affairs had met a Congress delegation and told them that while the government agreed that there should be exemption for some, there was no question of abolition of the pass-law system. But further attempts were made to organise resistance and to collect passes and return them to the government. Congress continued to maintain that no greater system of identification was needed for Africans than for Europeans, and opposed the registration of urban labour contracts. In its report the committee regretted that Congress had maintained its 'uncompromising attitude' (UG 41 1922: 7). It noted that the Assaults Commission had said that the pass laws were now 'so intricate' that it was doubtful that anyone could know when an offence was being committed. It recommended that there should be one single Union-wide pass, with a left thumbprint for identification, which should be available for production whenever an African went beyond the ward in which he was ordinarily resident. Connection with the control of urban labour would remain central. Registration of urban contracts, the committee said, should continue, and it should become an offence for an employer to engage anyone without the requisite labour pass. A record of the movement of Africans throughout the Union must be held at a central bureau (11). They did not, however, recommend the compulsory registration of rural contracts of service, indeed their minds were far more firmly focused on problems in urban areas (and they assumed that labour tenancies were covered by the masters and servants law). If an African remained in a town while unemployed, they wrote, 'he becomes a ready victim to unscrupulous persons of all nationalities and colour', and was subsequently criminalised. To protect the unsophisticated from drifting into criminality there must be definite limits on their remaining in urban areas without work. To make this administratively possible, all Africans had, therefore, to report their arrival. Juveniles, in particular, were 'living out of control' (13). It was, they concluded, 'beyond question that the vagrancy laws have entirely failed to deal with native undesirables and loafers. The accepted definition of vagrant is frequently inapplicable' (14). This failure meant that new mechanisms had to be found. They recommended that for urban areas a court be constituted of an 'experienced official', with two native assessors. These courts would have the right to call on all those *prima facie* leading an 'idle, dissolute or vicious life' to show why they should not be repatriated, committed to a labour colony or indentured. In these recommendations we can see the bases of the provisions for deportation from the towns and the bypassing of ordinary legal processes which were to be in the Urban Areas Act.

The Urban Areas Act of 1923 accordingly contained provision for the registration of 'every contract of service entered into by a male native' in proclaimed areas, and for compulsory reporting of the termination of contracts (12 (1) a). It reaffirmed the requirement that an African male had, on entering an urban area, to report arrival and obtain a pass allowing him to stay and seek work. This permission could be refused 'whenever there is a surplus of native labour available within the proclaimed area' (12 (1) c). Urban local authorities were to be required to render statistical returns on the numbers of work seekers, the numbers employed and the likely demand for labour (16). If such returns showed a population 'in excess of the reasonable labour requirements of that area' a local authority could compile a list of persons already in the area and persons for compulsory removal (16). In the Transvaal and Natal, after the passing of the Native Service Contract Act of 1932, a person could be refused permission to remain if he did not possess a pass showing that he had been 'released from the obligation of rendering service' to the owner of the land on which he was domiciled (12 (1) c (ii)). A woman could not be admitted to urban areas without the multiple permissions of the local authority; the native commissioner or magistrate in her district of origin; and the consent of her guardian (12 (1) d). A person whose job came to an end had between seven and fourteen days to find another, or leave the urban area (though this did not apply to those born and permanently residing in urban areas).

It was section 17 and its encoding and development of the repertoire of the vagrancy law that caused some of the greatest problems for the courts, and illustrates how legal and judicial niceties could be overcome by legislation that had no apparent implications for the civil rights of whites or for vested property rights. It provided that where a police officer had 'reason to believe or suspect' that a person was 'habitually unemployed' or had 'no sufficient honest means of livelihood', or was 'leading an idle, dissolute or disorderly life', or had criminal or liquor-law convictions, that person could be arrested and brought before a magistrate or native commissioner 'who shall require the native to give a good and satisfactory account of himself '. If he failed to do so he could be adjudged 'an idle and disorderly person' and either removed to his rural 'home' or 'be sent to and detained for a period not exceeding two years in a farm colony, work colony . . . or similar institution'.

What attitude did the courts take towards the powers given to officials to impose up to two years deprivation of liberty, as well as removal from the area? In *R v Joe 1924 TPD 696* Curlewis treated the powers given to officials as administrative and not judicial and ruled that the section did not 'contemplate an ordinary judicial trial of the native' and that an order for detention could not be regarded as a sentence in a criminal case. The superior courts could not therefore impose procedures or consider the reasonableness of such orders under their powers to review criminal sentences. The Cape Provincial Division decided otherwise – that the powers exercised under section 17 were judicial and not administrative.

When this decision was appealed the Appellate Division came down firmly on the side of the Transvaal. In *Hashe and others v Cape Town Municipality 1927 AD 380* Solomon (supported by Innes, among others) ruled that the magistrate dealing with a case under section 17 sat in an administrative capacity and that he was not, therefore, bound by the rules of evidence, that evidence of previous convictions could be admitted, and that a decision to remove a person from an urban area to 'the place to which he belongs' could not be reviewed. Hashe's counsel relied on the obvious similarities between the concepts and wording of section 17 and the provisions of the Cape Vagrancy Act of 1879. Solomon took upon himself the far more difficult task of finding differences between the provisions. He emphasised that the proceedings under section 17 were not conducted by a prosecutor and pointed out that no evidence against a man need be led, because the onus was on the accused to account for himself satisfactorily. Finally he distinguished between the penalty of fine and imprisonment for a crime, and detention in a work colony. Trial, conviction and sentence were not mentioned in the Act. The proceedings were therefore 'not a trial but an investigation'. He concluded with the customary expression of regret, associating himself with the remarks of the Judge President of the Cape Court on the 'grave dangers that may arise to the liberty of the subject if persons can be dealt with in this informal manner, and sent to long periods of detention in penal institutions' (384–8). But remedy, Solomon said, was a matter for the legislature. The Act was amended in 1930 to provide for judicial review of such decisions.

Yet despite the drastic nature of the legislation and the complaisant attitude of the courts the urbanisation of the African population continued. The apprehension about the growth of the African urban population increased among both administrators and politicians throughout the first twenty years of Union. The Native Economic Commission was to sum up in 1932: 'The rate of increase of the native (urban) population has exceeded and sometimes considerably exceeded that of the European . . . When it is remembered that during this period there has been a marked urbanisation of the European population, this fact is striking' (UG 22 1932: 407; figures 402). The continued energetic administration of the pass laws, the Native Urban Areas Act and the increased coerciveness of masters and servants legislation in the rural areas were responses to this population movement, which was perceived to have implications not only for labour supply but also for the total social order (see above, Part II). Feelings of apprehension about the menace of the cities were supported by economic arguments for a rational sharing out of and control of the labour of Africans. By stabilising a small and permanently employed African urban population, and by cutting off the flow of others, the redistribution of 'surplus' Africans to mining and farming could be assured (558). The absorption of this surplus would mop up those who at present created the dangerous conditions resulting from the growing urban slums. The apparatus of control recognised that there would be a permanent African urban population. 'It is perfectly clear', the Economic Commission concluded in 1932, 'that a considerable number of natives have become permanent town dwellers. No good purpose is served by disregarding this fact . . . In the interests of the efficiency of urban industries it is better to have a fixed native urban population to the extent to which such population is necessary than the present casual drifting population' (500).

The agenda of control of movement and residence produced ever-increasing numbers of pass-law convictions. By the end of the 1920s they were by far the highest category of criminal convictions in the Transvaal, running at around 40,000 per year (39,000 out of 42,000 convictions Union wide were in the Transvaal: UG 22 1932: 359; see also Simons 1936). The cost to the state, the Native Economic Commission noted, 'is heavy' (UG 22 1932: 722). But, they thought, identifications were 'necessary'. The law prevented 'absconding from farms and other forms of employment . . . in general it prevents crime . . . [it was] a means of stopping wholesale entry into towns'. There were two basic questions, they said. How far could the European social order allow free intermixture of Africans, and 'in the cases of farms, is the Native too irresponsible, too untied to his employment by his living requirements, to be allowed complete freedom of movement without economic disorganisation of agriculture resulting from it?' (725). In answering these questions the commission did not doubt that the cost, though heavy, was justified, and they had visions of an even more far-reaching system of control. The carrying of passes should be compulsory if an African moved beyond his residence. To administer a system in which it would be compulsory to carry a pass and compulsory for an employer to require one they thought that a central bureau should be established

in order that there may be a record of movement of Natives throughout the
Union . . . By these means we consider that a record of all Natives moving
about the country would be built up at the Central Bureau and in the event
of a Native not being at his home or recorded at the local registration office
. . . an enquiry at the Central Bureau should establish his whereabouts.
(My emphasis)

All contracts of service over three months should be registered. Together
with the bureau this would 'go far to check desertion', by making it
possible to trace offenders (735–7). We should remind ourselves that
these fantastic administrative totalities were being envisaged by the officials of a small post-colonial state in the 1930s (which had been forced to
reduce its spending over a decade of economic difficulties) so that we can
gauge the flavour of the impact on law and administration. The severity of
the fines was also extraordinary: roughly calculated the standard fine for a
pass offence was about three to four months wages (translated to contemporary middle-class terms this would be $12,000 to $17,000 on an
annual salary of $50,000).

The huge mass of detailed pass laws which controlled the daily lives of
Africans, and the conditions of their participation in the labour market,
were not passed by parliament, but by proclamation by the Governor-
General. Section 28 of the Urban Areas Act of 1923 gave the Governor-
General power to repeal any of the existing laws, and to proclaim new
ones 'for the control and prohibition of the movement of natives into,
within or from any . . . areas'. Section 28(1) of the Native Administration
Act of 1927 replicated this power. The comprehensive proclamation
issued in 1934 defined pass areas throughout the country. Africans within
a pass area could only travel in that area with a pass from an employer,
chief or headman, which stated the purpose of the journey, and was valid
for only thirty days. A person travelling without a pass 'or travelling
otherwise than in the direction of his destination as indicated in his pass'
could be arrested by an authorised officer or by the owner or occupier of
any private property on which he was found. No African without a pass
could be employed and the employer was required to demand the pass
and retain it in his possession until the end of the period of service, when
it would be returned with the date of discharge. Anyone seeking a pass
had to certify under pain of criminal penalty that he was not 'under an
unexpired contract of service', and no pass could be issued if he was. A
small category of persons was exempted from the pass laws, but had to

carry and produce a document certifying exemption (Proclamation 150, 1934).

Master and servant

Master and servant legislation in South Africa dated back to the Cape in 1841. The Cape legislation 'which studiously avoided all reference to colour' was found by the Crown to be a 'comprehensive safeguard of the equality of treatment of all races' (Mandelbrote 1936: 374). There is a fundamental irony in the origins of the law in South Africa. Introduced to bring all labour, including coloureds and ex-slaves, under the same law, it was to develop into one of the cornerstones of a differential labour regime. Cape legislation, in the form enacted in 1856, was to be the basis of the laws passed in the other South African colonies as well as in other parts of Africa. The different provincial laws were not unified and remained in force throughout the period under discussion, though after Union they were supplemented with a battery of refining and extending legislation on labour, which is discussed below. The basic thrust of the law was to make breach of a contract of service criminally punishable. The term 'servant' was defined as 'any person employed for hire, wages, or other remuneration, to perform any handicraft or other bodily labour in agriculture or manufacture, or in domestic service . . . or other occu-pation of a like nature'. Failure to start work, desertion, negligence, insolence, refusal to obey commands, and the withholding of wages became criminal offences rather than being the subject of civil remedies (Hepple 1960: 774). There were variations in the laws as to the definition of servant (whether, for example, it included industrial workers, or agricultural and domestic workers) and as to the type and length of contract covered by the law (written or unwritten, daily, monthly or annual). It will readily be seen that without any reference to race the laws could be adapted to a racially segregated labour market. It is basically this process that can be traced in the history of the laws in South Africa.

The process of narrowing the definition of a servant was assisted by Innes's decision in *Clay v Rex 1903 TS 482* in which he ruled that a railway navvy, not mentioned in the Act as there were no railways in South Africa when it was passed, did not come under the law. As it 'attached criminal consequences to the breach of what is essentially a civil contract, the Masters and Servants Law must . . . be very strictly construed'. The narrowing process must be understood in the context of increasing complexity in the manufacturing workforce and the fact that the legislation made no mention of race. Many categories of predominantly white workers, such as printers, salesmen, foremen and so on were excluded from the definition (Gardiner and Lansdown 1924 vol. II: 1414–15). But it would be wrong to see this as all of the story. For the close definition of 'servant' was to have important implications for black rural workers as well. For a person to be a servant the courts developed the view that not only did the work have to fall within the definitions in the Act but that there had to be a contract of service for continuous employment over a definite period. There were rulings that persons who did piecework did not come under the Acts, nor did those who were employed by the day, or who might or might not come to work on any particular day (ibid.: 1413). For a criminal conviction a contract had to have come into force, and still be in force. All of these cases concerned rural work practices: itinerant sheep-shearers were not covered, nor tenants with undefined duties, nor tenants who had never before been called on to work. Farmer employers were also restricted by rulings that held that contracts could not be for longer than the statutory period, which excluded those whose workers were working off loans. Most importantly, after a long period in which the accepted law and practice in the rural areas had been that squatters came under the provisions of the Acts the Transvaal Supreme Court ruled in 1921 that they did not, in *Maynard v Chasana 1921 TPD 243*.[3] The white rural outcry led to a swift statutory response. The courts also developed a narrow view, which was in the interest of employers, of the offence of withholding wages. It was necessary to prove criminal intent. A reasonable

---

[3] The court found that the squatting agreement by which a right of residence on white farms was granted in return for ninety days labour a year, and under which large numbers of Africans in the Transvaal lived, was not a contract under the Masters and Servants Act. The position taken under republican law, and subsequently enforced by the British, had been that a squatting agreement was a contract for the purposes of the masters and servants law, and that all members of a squatter family were parties to the contract entered into by the family head. The relief was short lived as new legislation was passed in 1926 to give farmers the right to enforce the labour service provisions of squatters agreements by making the Masters and Servants Acts applicable to them.

Section 49 of Act no. 18 of 1936 eventually defined a labour tenant 'as meaning, in relation to land or the owner thereof, a native male adult (other than a servant) the services of whom or of whose family are actually . . . required by the owner for domestic services or in . . . farming operations . . . or in any other industry . . . carried on . . . on the land where such labour tenant resides, and who, or any member of whose family is dependent on him, is obliged to serve the owner in terms of a contract'.

belief that wages were not due, or a *bona fide* dispute as to amount, or insufficiency of funds, would all be defences (Gardiner and Lansdown 1924 vol. II: 1416). The Cape and Transvaal laws made distinctions between the penalties applicable to those working in agriculture and those in other areas of bodily labour. Only the former could be sentenced to hard labour, spare diet or solitary confinement (ibid.: 1418). Only agricultural employees could commit the crime of desertion, which was leaving employment with intent not to return. Negligence with the Master's property, or its loss by breach of duty, were offences. Rural workers were additionally made liable for the offence of failing to report the loss of stock at the earliest opportunity, and failing to preserve for inspection parts of animals alleged to have died (loss of one animal out of several hundred was sufficient to sustain a conviction: ibid.: 1412–22).

A period of imprisonment was added to the stipulated contract period. It was an offence also not to return to the service of a master after serving a period of imprisonment for conviction under the Acts. A maximum of six periods of continuous one-month sentences could be imposed (1424). The Acts were careful to protect the distinctions in status between masters and servants. Not obeying a lawful command of the employer was a criminal offence, as was the use of abusive language to an employer, employer's wife or any other person placed in authority (1420). Prosecution for offences was at public charge (1428).

While the masters and servants law purported to describe and control legal forms of hiring and firing, the actual employment practices and customs in the countryside did not fit easily into its provisions. As the Worcester magistrate wrote in 1912 of the Western Cape:

> Magistrates were greatly exercised when administering the Masters and Servants Acts owing to the loose contracts entered into, which were generally of such a nature that they could only be described as invalid when compared with the construction of a legal contract under the said Acts as laid down by the superior Courts. The universal agreement was a hiring by the day which has been held did not bring the servant under the provisions of the law. Custom seemed to be the principle which both masters and servants acted upon and they had periodical settlements *(afrekeningen)*. Engagements were entered into for ploughing and harvesting, but no definite dates were mentioned for the commencement or finishing thereof ... Most frequently contracts for further service were made regardless of the provision in law that servants must enter into service within one

month from the date of making the oral contract which was the local mode of contracting farm labourers. He suggested that if a labourer hired himself for any *bona fide* period he should be subject to the penalties provided for any offence committed. (UG 44 1913: 49–50)

The picture is one of established and negotiated local practices which did not fit in easily with a legalised administration. Customary practices that did not fall within the state's legal prescriptions did not enable employers to use the courts effectively to punish and to discipline. Before the state could exercise its power, it had to shape and to regulate rural practices. The Wolmaransstad magistrate wrote in 1912 that the 1880 law should be repealed and

a new law introduced whereby farmers should be required to register their service contracts with natives and heavier penalties should be enacted against natives who deserted . . . The present law was unsatisfactory as farmers often had no proper contracts with their servants, only a sort of tacit understanding which had been running for years and was in conflict with sections 8, 9 and 10 of the Law . . . As the registration of contracts of service was laid down for urban areas under act 18 of 1909 he saw no reason why it could not also apply to rural parts.

One Natal magistrate approached the problem with the more simple suggestion that oral contracts be put on the same footing as written ones 'as natives had a great objection to signing contracts of service' (167). The Kranskop magistrate urged that there should be 'uniformity in farm contracts'. Numerous disputes arose from the condition 'requiring natives to lend a hand as the occasion demanded' (ibid.).

Other suggestions for amendment were made. The Middelburg magistrate suggested that 'the age of contractual liability in respect of natives doing farm work could be fixed as commencing with the age of puberty' (122). He and other magistrates urgently advocated the increase of penalties for breach of the masters and servants law. In the words of the Klerksdorp magistrate, the maximum fine of £1 was 'ridiculously low'. He thought £25 appropriate, and also advised that magistrates be given the power to order imprisonment without the option of a fine. This was because 'cases occurred when a fine was imposed and, on the master refusing to pay the fine, all his other servants gave him notice to leave saying that his refusal showed that he did not care for them. The consequence was that the master nearly always had to pay his servants' fines although he had complained against them' (123). While this magistrate discerned the blackmailing of employers by employees, a Natal magistrate, also recommending prison without the option of a fine, observed another side of the process. Workers were, he wrote, 'being prosecuted under the Act with the object of getting them to borrow the money for the fine and to agree to a further period of service at a reduced rate of wage' (167). Not only could the magistrates' perception of the equities involved in the masters and servants law lead them to see fining the worker as punishment for the employer, but imprisonment also could be seen as a penalty for the master. The magistrate of Hoopstad wrote in 1912 that Africans did not mind serving the twenty-one-day term and 'in the mean time the master was deprived of his services which he could ill afford. On the other hand if the master paid the fine he was generally rewarded by unsatisfactory service.' Wider use of whipping as a punishment seemed to him to be the answer (23).

Two features are apparent from the magistrates' reports. One is the drive to increase the range of legalised administrative control over all walks of life. There is a strong impression of a state in the making, partly eagerly, partly anxiously extending its control over areas of life that seem to escape it. And the most anxiety was expended on areas in which there was contact between and dealings between the races. In a society with an endowment from the previous rulers of judicial institutions, officials could not act without law. They needed law to carry out their functions and ambitions and to authorise the enlargement of their sphere of control. Without it there could not be the detailed control of the social order that they wanted. Law did not so much control the administrators as authorise and empower them. The magistracy, which did the bulk of the judicial work in the country, were, as has been noted, both administrative and judicial officials. Their reports are full of complaints about the excessive legalism of others in the legal system – lawyers, judges and the framers of statutes. They were impatient with the aspects of law that restrained rather than empowered officials. This may seem obvious but it has implications for the conception of what the legal order was. In the process of state building it was, for the officials, not a restraining but an empowering mechanism. There was also a constant pressure in all areas for an increase of penalties for infraction of statutes. Virtually all problems were approached with this remedy ready on the lips of politicians and legal officials. This was accompanied by constant diagnosis of the attitude of Africans to authority. All the law, however minor the area, had to be enforced in its entirety, and strictly. To do otherwise would be to call the state into question and to undermine black attitudes towards its authority. We might note the Winburg magistrate's analysis of the need for the strict enforcement of the law requiring that all non-white persons between the ages of sixteen and sixty in urban areas be in employment. The difficulties with ascertainment of age, and the numerous exemptions available, made it a hard law to administer, but it was urged that it must be strictly applied because 'as things are at present the natives are under the impression that the Government is afraid of carrying out the laws, and accordingly take up a defiant attitude' (UG 36 1918: 24).

The importance of the masters and servants law in the control of labour was highlighted by the magistrate in the border district of Ficksburg in 1912. As he wrote in relation to those Africans who lived on white-owned farms:

> The squatting agreements with farmers were purely civil contracts which did not fall within the Masters and Servants Act. The native was nominally the white man's servant but actually his own master . . . the fact that the farmer was bound by the laws of the land enabled the native to treat him with an easy contempt . . . the whole system was . . . demoralising to the entire labour supply. (UG 44 1913: 208–9)

Indeed squatting made for particular problems with regard to the meshing of customary contracts with the masters and servants law. Many living on white farms had complex arrangements with the farmer which might include wages, or the provision of stock and food, or this and the right to keep stock and to have land ploughed, or ploughing 'on the half' with the owner. It was a complex matter to sort out complaints arising from these circumstances under the masters and servants law. There was strong pressure to bring all farm workers under the masters and servants law, and one way was to outlaw farming on shares. The Member of Parliament P. J. Theron put it simply: 'It would drive the kaffir into the position which most people would like to see him in, and instead of having loose men in our employment, we should have men who were fixed in our service . . . you can get twice as much labour out of him' (SC 9 1913: 583). These powers of control perceived in the masters and servants law worked against the interest of some poor whites. It made it far harder for those who did seek to work for white farmers. A Transvaal magistrate noted that the greatest obstacle to the employment of white unskilled labour is not so much the cheapness or efficiency of native labour, but the greater power of control which the employer exercises over the latter. In the case of the native, the pass regulations and Masters and Servants laws give the employer the necessary control of his labourers which is lacking in the case of the white man. (UG 36 1918: 107)

'The cry as to the scarcity of native unskilled labour was very nearly universal' (UG 44 1913: 80). The masters and servants law was a means of restraining the operation of a market in labour in the rural areas. Where there was competition for labour there was a rise in the number of masters and servants prosecutions (UG 28 1915: 28). Shortage of labour also meant that employers had to pay wages in advance to secure workers, and this practice was closely enmeshed with the administration of the masters and servants laws. As was noted in 1911, much of the recruiting in the Transkei of labour for the gold mines was in the hands of traders who made advances and who then contracted labourers who were heavily in debt. The perception of the Transkei's Chief Magistrate was that the practice advantaged those who took the advances. There were 'hundreds' who took the money and did not go to work, he wrote, and the judges had held that unless a man took money from more than one recruiter he could not be prosecuted for fraud. His solution was that the terms of the Masters and Servants Act should apply from the time at which the advance was taken (SC 3 1911: 243–4). Enoch Mamba saw things differently. Traders, he testified, gave credit in order to force people to go to work. 'I want the native to be free,' he said, 'I do not want the trader to coerce him.' It was put to him that a trader who had given an advance could not legally force the man to work. Mamba's reply reflects the lives of those who did not experience the relationship as being ruled by law at all: 'No, there is no law . . . there is too much coercion' (318–19).

Credit and debt became a problem for farmers and state which the masters and servants law alone could not control. In relation to this too we can again see the difficulties those who would administer the masters and servants law faced in relation to established and negotiated practices. One Natal magistrate reported in 1915 that there had been a huge number of cases of desertion before the courts, and that this did not represent the number of offences because masters condoned the offence to avoid the trouble and time involved in going to court. The reason was due entirely to the pernicious custom which has arisen throughout the Division of making cash advances against labour. To such an extent has this custom grown that it is almost impossible to obtain the services of a Native unless a substantial advance in cash is made. In very many cases once an advance is received great difficulty is experienced in getting the servant to fulfil his obligations and many instances have occurred where a native has obtained such an advance from no less than four Europeans for the same period. (UG 28 1915: 156)

The cash-advance system was widespread in Natal, and caused the magistrates great anxiety (UG 36 1918: 76). Another called for a law which would deprive any person who advanced money to an African against labour of any remedy (78). While nearly all the hostility to the advance system was based on the perceived disadvantages to the employer, the magistrate for Richmond urged its abolition because it was 'one of the worst forms of usury in many cases'. This was an almost lone indication that the system could work not against farmers, but against workers, allowing the exploitation of the desperate need for cash, which forced many to enter into such arrangements. The Bergville magistrate attributed to cash advances the large number of desertions (86–7). The Alexandria magistrate noted that the practice of making advances against labour was a 'curse . . . as under it the rich man and the large concerns have a pull over the smaller ones' (UG 36 1919: 79). The New Hanover magistrate wrote: 'The cash advance system was demoralising the natives.' A case had revealed a company in which the bulk of the workforce was working out loans. 'The Company continued to make advances whether the first debt had been worked off or not. In another case . . . [a debtor] had practically 3 years to work before he had satisfied the loan. The result was desertion' (UG 36 1918: 87).

In 1921 the Native Advances Regulation Act (18 of 1921) gave to the Governor-General power to regulate advances. But the problems of indebted labourers continued to worsen. The Native Economic Commission noted in 1932 that 'the Native does not generally allow himself to be recruited until he is in a position when he must immediately have money to pay his General Tax or to provide for some other urgent need' (UG 22 1932: para. 924). In spite of the regulating legislation the magistrates in many districts reported that it was common for farmers to make advances which employees 'would not be able to repay for a considerable time' (para. 925). In his dissenting addendum to the commission's report Lucas found that in Natal in particular most rural labourers were heavily indebted to employers. He quoted the Heilbron magistrate:

> Some natives owe accounts . . . which at their average wage of 10s per month they can never repay. The result is that the native is nothing less than a slave to the . . . employer until the debt is repaid. There are many of these cases. The result is Natives . . . desert from service and risk years of imprisonment so long as they can get away from the place they are at . . . Persons who for some reason or other cannot keep servants gladly lend them £2 or £3 to hire them knowing that on the wages paid the Native has no hope of ever refunding the money. (148, 155)

He wrote: 'Many employers contend that a servant to whom a loan has been made is subject to the Masters and Servants law in respect of that loan until it has been repaid' (270). This law was 'a cause of very great dissatisfaction among the Natives. Some Natives describe the law as one for legalising slavery.' The Standerton magistrate affirmed that 'many Natives consider the Act, as worked, reduces them to a state bordering on serfdom owing to the creation of conditions which have the effect of tying them down for years to one farm and one master'.

The role of masters and servants law in the rule of law in the countryside was central. The Newcastle magistrate's view was that one-quarter of the police force could be dispensed with if the Act was not enforced. 'Several Magistrates', wrote Lucas, 'stated that their popularity among Europeans in their areas was in proportion to the severity with which they punished Native servants under the Act' (UG 22 1932: 273, 275). The Cape magistrates' reports for 1917 reflect the constant pressure for the extension of the laws and the increase of penalties (UG 36 1918: 27). It was suggested that weekly servants be brought within the laws; and that all contracts of employment should be made before a magistrate, JP or policeman. Masters and servants cases were heard at the lowest rung of the judicial ladder, the courts of the rural justices of the peace, and, where higher sentences were possible, for example in repeat offences, by the magistrates. In 1918 they were pushed further down the ladder by the increase in jurisdiction of the justices of the peace 'for the convenience of the rural population' (UG 36 1918: 1) and the granting of power to them to impose sentences of whipping (Act 2 of 1918).

In the Transvaal, the Free State and the Cape most of the Africans living on white farms were doing so in return for the provision of ninety days labour per year, often spread over the year as two days a week. The tenant in return got land to plough and graze, and rations on days worked. The heads of families did not always work, and, according to the Native Economic Commission, did so 'only exceptionally' if they had grown-up children. The principal source of labour to the farmers were the sons of the kraal head, while women were available for housework. Therefore the flight of young men from the farms to the towns had given rise to considerable friction between farmers and tenants (UG 22 1932: 359). This form of labour tenancy, wrote the Commission, was showing signs of 'disintegration'. The farmers wanted longer terms of continuous labour, and there had been a 'decline of the kraalhead's authority and power over his family' (362). They noted that the tenants were in a perilous position if their crops failed as they were without cash income. Grain was lent by farmers, sometimes at 'usurious' rates, and tenants were trapped in debt (386). Farmers also imposed their own fines, bypassing the courts. In his addendum to the commission report Lucas noted a case which had recently been tried by the Transvaal Supreme Court in which evidence was led by a European farmer to prove that in his district it was customary for farmers to impose money fines on their African employees for various alleged breaches of contract (96–7).

The Commission echoed the evidence of many witnesses that 'the time has come for legislation to be passed to make the completion of a written contract between farmer and tenant obligatory'. This move to extend the administration of legalised relations in the countryside had an economic rationale enunciated by the commission. A nominal cash wage should be stipulated and then deductions for use of land made. This would enable the farmer to have an idea of the cost of labour and would assist tenants 'to a purely economic outlook in cattle' (396–400).

African mineworkers were subject to different controls, in particular to the compound system, though it is far from clear what the legal basis for this was. Indeed it affords an interesting way of making the point that the realities of the exercise of power, even power pretending to be clothed in legal form, were not the same as those apparently portrayed in written law. The powers exercised to keep workers in closed compounds were exercised without question over a long period without legal justification. The contracts of workers (17,000 in 1911) in Kimberley where the compound system had originated nowhere indicated that they would be kept on closed compounds. But to the de Beers general manager it was 'purely a question of the Masters and Servants Act' that they submit to orders. If they left the compound they would be charged with desertion. (SC 3 1911: 280). (African workers only were also detained without pay as a matter of course for several days after their contracts had ended to ensure that they had no stolen diamonds.) In 1913 Percival Ross-Frames, a lawyer who was managing director of the Premier diamond mine and a member of the Assaults Commission, was interrogated by the Labour Party leader, Cresswell, on the subject of the compounds (SC 9 1913: 141ff.). Cresswell put it to him that the Minister of Native Affairs had assured parliament that there was no law preventing African workers from freely leaving their compounds. 'Of course there is no law,' Frames answered, 'but we should have a civil remedy against them under the general law for refusing to carry out his contract.' There was no question of the gatekeepers allowing anyone out, even for a 'walk'. 'I would not tell the natives what their civil remedies are,' Frames said, 'but they have never expressed any desire to go out.' Cresswell asked why the inspector appointed under the Native Labour Regulation Act to protect African workers had not advised them that they were at liberty to go out whenever they pleased. 'The inspectors', Frames answered, 'are not there to induce these people to break their contracts.' It was then established that the contracts made no mention of closed compounds. Was it the case, asked Cresswell, that workers were left by both company and inspectors in entire ignorance of their legal rights? 'Even lawyers are ignorant of the law, sometimes,' retorted Frames. The illegal detention of huge numbers of workers was not hidden, nor hindered, but flippantly justified.

Until after the Native Labour Regulation Act of 1911 the 200,000 mine workers on the Rand were not in closed compounds. Over the years there was an overwhelming rhetorical longing among politicians to close these compounds, but there were obstacles. Senior police were not necessarily supportive. Transvaal CID head, Mavrogodato, thought that compound administration, which was privately policed, was 'morally slack', with 'too much licence' being given to illicit liquor. But also, he told the select committee, 'I do not think they should be treated as prisoners'. The nominally liberal Merriman, who shared the common obsession with urban crime, helpfully provided him with a rationale for the exercise of total control. 'Is it not the same with a man who ships on board a vessel?' (SC 3 1911: 246). But while an extension of total control was imaginable and justifiable in terms of existing legal implements, it was recognised that it would 'ruin the traders'. The Minister for Native Affairs lamented that because of 'vested interests' on the Rand, 'shops, property and so on, the perpetual demoralisation of the natives must go on more than it need otherwise' (258).

While Mavrogodato felt that the compounds were too slack, the Manager of the gold mine Simmer and Jack told the select committee that 'the mine has absolute control of the boy all the time he is at the mine, from the time he goes down to the time he comes up and also when he is in the compound, and I think if you have absolute control over a boy you will probably get better work out of him' (79). The link between control and 'better work' was crucial. The Native Labour Regulation Act created an in-compound system for enforcing the masters and servants law, thereby articulating the criminal justice system with that of labour control.[4] District inspectors of natives were given powers to impose penalties for refusal to work, being absent from work, neglect of work and other offences. The Chamber of Mines testified that the district inspector 'holds a small court very often around the compounds' dealing with 'little batches' of men. One Member of Parliament asked whether the law 'is really an infringement on the ordinary law, that a breach of a civil contract should be rectified by a civil court'. But he was answered by mine and state officials pointing to the usefulness of the law. One said that it prevented physical maltreatment of workers. The Protector of Natives for Germiston said that it was better than taking offenders to magistrates who tended to send them to prison. But in the compounds a fine was imposed: 'The fine is deducted from his wages. This is found to work out very well.' It saved the mines both time and money (169–70). S. A. M. Pritchard, then director of the Native Labour Bureau in Johannesburg, affirmed that productivity had priority over legal niceties. The 'primary reason', he said, for giving judicial powers to inspectors of native labour was to save the mines trouble: a court 'may necessitate the attendance of three white men as witnesses', and a 'large number of natives' might be charged. 'The whole day's work would be lost.' When it was put to him that this was 'unfair' he answered: 'Summary jurisdiction is a very good thing for the native' (20–1). Misgivings were expressed by the only African witness before the select committee, Enoch Mamba. 'I consider that Inspectors would not necessarily make good judicial officers,' he told the committee.

---

[4] This was a widespread practice, even where there was no statutory jurisdiction. For an account of the 'informal' private imprisonment of farm labour see Morrell (1986: 391–3).

'Men are chosen as Inspectors without regard being had to their judicial ability' (320).

Under the Native Labour Regulation Act those recruited and employed on any mine or works became the subject of regulations under section 23 which gave powers to make regulations for 'proper housing, feeding and treatment' and for the 'regulation and control of compounds'. When regulations were finally promulgated forbidding absence from the compound without permission, they were upheld by the Transvaal Supreme Court as being within the powers conferred by the Act. In *R v. Sokkies 1916 TPD 482* the court upheld a regulation forbidding absence from the compound without written permission. Bristowe said, incorporating a rationale of political control and public safety which was not at all apparent from the actual wording of the enabling Act:

> The pass system, involving very considerable restriction of the free movements of natives has been for years in universal vogue in this country. Along the Reef large bodies of natives are congregated in compounds, who might easily become a source of danger if not carefully watched and guarded. Whether it would be possible to invent some other form of regulation less drastic and not less efficacious than the present I do not know. But if I try it by the test whether it is so oppressive as to find no justification in the minds of reasonable men, then I can only say that in my opinion it is not. That it seriously restricts a labourer's liberty is of course clear. But that it restricts it more than is reasonably required by the necessities of the case I am not prepared to say. (88)

The new province for law and order: struggles on the racial frontier

Industrial conciliation law

The labour contract was governed quite differently for white workers. I shall examine it in two legal contexts: the first is the development of the legal regime of industrial conciliation law covering strikes and trade unions; the second the legal regulation of wages. The broader discursive universe did not clearly separate these and both were approached within the context of debates about the role of the state in regulating the 'market' in labour, and the urgent politics of protecting the position of white workers. The first of several major statutes in this period was the Transvaal's Industrial Disputes Prevention Act of 1909, which was to be the model for aborted national legislation in 1914 and 1919. In the Act an employee was defined as 'any white person engaged' in the industries covered by the Act – the mines and public services. This exclusion of Africans from the mechanism of industrial dispute settlement was the subject of debate in the Transvaal legislative assembly in 1909 (see Lever 1978: 85–6). Some Labour members objected, but it was on the grounds that the exclusion made Africans more attractive to hire because of their legally subordinate position. However Smuts stated the central rationale, which was that it was unthinkable that a legislative means of regulating strikes should apply to African workers because it was unthinkable that black workers should take part in legitimate concerted labour actions like strikes. The exclusion of Africans from the definition of 'employee' in the Act also negated the ability of an industrially based trade union to organise black workers. When the national Industrial Conciliation Act was finally passed in 1923, the word 'white' was dropped, and instead the Act excluded all pass bearers whose contracts of service were affected by the Native Labour Regulation Act, the master and servant laws or the Urban Areas Act.[1]

As in most of the cases discussed in this book the South African industrial conciliation legislation was, in other respects, closely based in form and substance – conception, architecture and wording – on overseas models. While the history and particular configurations of power in Britain itself were not as closely applicable, the problems faced by the 'new' states of Canada, Australia and New Zealand were similar, and they groped towards what appeared on one level to be similar solutions. Following the suppression of the strike of 1907 the Transvaal government sent commissioners to Canada and New Zealand to examine their labour legislation. The Commissioners reported that industrial legislation aimed at preventing 'industrial war' could be grouped into those laws that were based on strikes followed by voluntary conciliation, and those that made strikes illegal, and in which disputes were settled by industrial courts whose decisions were binding (Yudelman 1984: 85–7, 118, 198ff.; see also Davies 1979). While the Labour Party preferred New Zealand's voluntary conciliation and arbitration court, the mining employers preferred the Canadian law which combined the principles of voluntarism and compulsion in a different way. Its essential principles involved the establishment of state conciliation boards, and the suspension of the right to strike while a compulsory, but unbinding, conciliation process took place. In 1908 the Railway Regulation Act in the Transvaal prohibited strikes and established a procedure for compulsory arbitration. But neither labour nor capital would accept this framework for the mines. The outcome was the Industrial Disputes Prevention Act in which 'most of the operative clauses . . . were reproduced verbatim from the Canadian Act' (Davies 1979: 118).

The 1909 Act was not effective in preventing the devastating strikes of 1913 and 1914. The increase in membership of white trade unions, and their increasing militancy and effectiveness, necessitated a reconsideration of the issue of the recognition of trade unions which had no role in the processes created by the 1909 legislation. The 1914 Economic Commission argued that unions should have 'the fullest possible status on conciliation boards'. Whether it was recognised or not 'labour organisation will

---

[1] This meant that coloured and Indian workers were not excluded. After years of uncertainty the Supreme Court in the Transvaal ruled in 1944 that African women, not being pass bearers, were also not excluded (Sachs 1952: 162).

continue among white men' and could become (as had been evidenced) extreme or revolutionary if ignored (UG 12 1914: 47–8; see Davies 1979: 122). They argued that instead of extreme opposition, unions could be co-opted into the processes of conciliation and that 'the organisation of labour is an aid to the authority of a conciliation board' (UG 12 1914: 47–8). In line with the existing Transvaal law they recommended that voluntary conciliation boards, which would represent both employers and recognised organised workers, should make recommendations which would not be enforceable at law except where the parties had agreed to accept the outcome of a binding arbitration. (This was also the approach of the British conciliation boards.) But while the 1914 Bill would have provided for the legal recognition of, and given a role to, registered trade unions, its overriding purpose was to contain the use of the strike as an industrial weapon. The minister could establish a conciliation board (or an investigation board, or appoint an arbitrator) without the consent of the parties when there was an industrial dispute. Any strike action was illegal as long as the investigations were taking place. The Bill was opposed by the Labour Party because of the limitations on the right to strike, and also because of the exclusion of African labour on the grounds that this gave it an economic advantage in the eyes of employers. Yet labour leaders were by no means opposed to state regulation as such. The influence of the Australian labour movement was very strong and there was support for the Australian system of arbitration (with its recognition of the role of unions) and binding awards (Katz 1974; Davies 1979: 116). The Bill did not pass through the Senate before the end of the 1914 session, and legislation on the subject was abandoned during the war. This was also because while the industrial disputes legislation did not pass, the Riotous Assemblies Act had done. It contained a series of prohibitions which were aimed at disabling the use by unions of the strike weapon. Picketing was virtually prohibited as it became an offence to make threats against the person or property of a person in relation to their conduct with regard to employment. Similarly outlawed were blacklisting, the enforced joining of unions, and trespass on work premises.

The 1914 Economic Commission had favoured a voluntary approach to wages and conditions, in which boards might mediate but 'should not make decisions enforceable at law' (UG 12 1914: 46). Conciliation, not arbitration, was to be the ruling principle, though the latter could be done with the consent of the parties. 'Market forces', they reasoned, 'make their own equilibrium, but in doing so they generate friction. The problem is to allay this friction rather than to take the settlement of wages questions out of the hands of the parties primarily interested' (41). In short, in relation to the creation of a uniform system for the settlement of wages, they concluded that 'it is generally good policy to let well alone' (49). The insistence of the 1914 commissioners on the limitations of the role of the state in this realm of relations between workers and employers contrasted sharply with the role the state played in the organisation of the African workforce for the mines. By 1910 over two hundred thousand African workers were being delivered annually to the Rand (Jeeves 1985: 3). As Jeeves notes, this required 'an enormous legislative and administrative effort' (10).

The atmosphere of wartime, and the experience both nationally and internationally of the mobilisation of industries, did have its effect on the ways in which the place of the state in economic regulation was discussed. During the war alternatives to the dominance of mining capital in South Africa were envisaged, and though they were ultimately rejected the debate was an important part of the development of the politics of labour regulation. We can contrast the approach of the 1914 commission to economic regulation with the views canvassed by the commission appointed to investigate the advisability of state mining which reported in 1917 (UG 19 1917). The commission canvassed the German experience with state-run coal mines, and the rejection of nationalisation by Asquith in England, as well as the experience in the Transvaal, where the South African Republic had managed gold mines during the South African War. The suppression of the strikes of 1913 and 1914 had washed a powerful and active legacy of anti-capitalist rhetoric across a wide spectrum of South African politics and the war seemed to many to offer an opportunity to confront mining capital (see generally Roux 1948). This discourse found its way into the official arena, largely through the Labour Party, but also by way of some in the National Party, who resented foreign dominance of the economy. The commission's report noted:

> It was frequently asserted in evidence that the exigencies of warfare had settled once and for all the question as to the respective advantages and disadvantages of public and private enterprise. The measures adopted by Governments in industrial organisation . . . for military purposes were accepted as marking the close of the era of industrial organisation under the control of the private firm or the public company. (UG 19 1917: 33)

Within the general environment of the assault on international capital and its concentration of power over the South African economy in the mining industry, the main agenda of the proponents of nationalisation was the promotion of white labour. It was suggested that the government should even run unprofitable mines thereby providing the 'indirect profits' of white jobs and increased markets (12). And, as H. W. Sampson said for the Labour Party, 'a state mine should be run by white labour, otherwise half its utility to the white race . . . would be destroyed' (31). (The party's statement to the commission did, however, say that the state could 'utilise native convicts at the cost of keep' (31).)

These were not, however, the dominant notes of the majority report. The commission had canvassed the issue of a state monopoly over diamond mining in order to control the supply. But here it felt the constraints over the freedom of action open to a state in South Africa's position. Most witnesses, it said, 'seemed to be appalled at the magnitude of the sum that would be required to take over diamond mining' (8). And, as the general manager of the National Bank of South Africa said, a country that already had a large national debt could not borrow for the risky venture of any kind of state mining without affecting its credit. This would lead to a fall in the value of government stocks and a rise in interest rates and a driving away of foreign capital (22). In relation to using nationalisation to support the cause of white labour, the commission's majority took the view that the far greater expense of white labour meant that the state would 'have no alternative' but to support present practices (29–30). Furthermore, it was precisely fear about the powerful position labour and unions would have if the state was the employer that reinforced the rejection of state mining. The commission was preoccupied by the pre-war strikes: a 'period of acute friction between capital and labour' (33). The 1914 railway strike had meant that capital had been 'personified' in the government. The trade union movement would soon 'demand the attention of the state' and 'so long as there is a contest between wages and profits, there will be a need of a strong and vigilant state organisation to maintain order and justice' (41). The state as employer would not be able to arbitrate between the 'contesting interests' of capital and labour, and therefore higher wages and better hours would be 'more easily obtained' (40).

It was the dependence of the country on a wider economic system and its inability to influence its own economic fortunes in that regard that led to the intense conflict which arose, and its damaging consequences. Having no control over an internationally set gold price which had been steadily falling in relation to costs, the 'solution' open to the mines was to attack local costs. By the 1920s the battle lines between capital and labour in the mining industry had become clearly drawn. Regulations issued under the Mines and Works Act of 1911 had reserved skilled occupations for white miners. The mines now claimed that the end of this colour bar, and the consequent reduction in the cost of labour, was essential to the future profitability of the industry. White labour believed that this was based on a desire to exploit black labour more intensively at the expense of the position of whites, and eventually would drive them out of employment in the country's largest industry. The rebellion on the Rand in 1922 was focused around this issue. When new industrial conciliation legislation was finally put before parliament in 1923 it was in the aftermath of the labour rebellion's defeat. The legislation passed went beyond that of 1909 in the limitations it placed on the right to strike. It created permanent industrial councils with the power to make legally enforceable agreements binding on whole industries. While the agreements were in force, strikes in the industry so regulated were illegal. Trade unions received full legal recognition and became an essential part of the regulatory machinery, but to the miners' union this was defeat.

In 1926 the Pact government's wage commissioners, Mills, Clay and Martin, accepted with approval the framework provided by the Industrial Conciliation Act. For this purpose, they noted, effective trade unions must exist, and they had to be unions with an industrial purpose, which did not subordinate the wage-bargaining process to an outside political interest. The 'motive force' behind the Act, they said, had been the failure of the law to deal with issues prior to the 1922 strike. It subjected unions to tight controls in return for accepting their role in the wage-bargaining process. Registered unions had to be representative, and hold ballots before strike action. And while collective bargaining might be voluntary, the agreed outcome could be made compulsory. None of these processes applied to African workers. Mills, Clay and Martin observed that 'so far as the natives are concerned the only method of settling wage rates appears to be that employers determine what they will pay' (UG 14 1926: 50).

But voluntary collective bargaining had its limits. The commissioners were firm on preserving the common-law right to hire and fire. 'No policy should be followed', they warned, 'which would undermine the rights of managers to deal with the engagement, suspension, discharge etc of individuals' (44–5). They also supported the policy of the existing law which made no provision for compulsory arbitration. They rejected the Australian example, warning that there should be no possibility of compulsion if agreement were not reached (55). They noted that it had been argued that

> The device of compelling resort to a Court of Arbitration as a substitute for a stoppage is naturally suggested by the parallel of judicial procedure in settling other disputes. But the parallel is incomplete. The essence of judicial procedure is the application of an accepted rule to a particular case; industrial disputes arise from and lead to . . . obstinate and inconvenient trial (s) of strength . . . just because there is no rule or principle accepted by both parties that can be applied in judgement of their differences. (174–5)

It followed therefore that the function of an industrial arbitration body was different from that of a court of law. An arbitration court had no body of common law and statutes to apply, 'no definite legal principles which no one calls into question'. (Here they noted 'one exception' and quoted Higgins and the Australian search for a definition of the 'living wage': ibid.) An arbitrator's power to act on uniform and definite principles was 'strictly circumscribed'. It was, they thought, unfortunate that the term 'court' was often used to describe an arbitration board 'since the function of the latter is entirely alien to that of a Court of Law'. The second report, signed by Andrews, Lucas and Rood, also quoted extensively and more sympathetically from Higgins' 'New Province for Law and Order' (1915/16). They maintained that characteristically an arbitration court had to deal not with isolated disputes, but with a series of similar and related ones. Awards had to be consistent one with another or industrial trouble would be provoked. Parties therefore had to know in advance the firm lines on which the court would act. Their conception of the desirable process was far more legalist than that contemplated in the South African legislation, resorting to Higgins as an authority for the proposition that wage regulation should be divorced from political influence, and arrived at on the basis of judicial regulation (UG 14 1926: 295).

The colour bar

While Smuts's government had passed the Industrial Conciliation Act, it was the new Nationalist–Labour Pact government that came to power two years after the defeat of the 1922 rebellion, which put into place the other two parts of the triad upon which the regulation of white labour and wages were based. One was the statutory colour bar in employment in the mines: the other a system of wage regulation which created a *de facto* segregation of the workforce. The Masters and Servants Acts, though they did not explicitly differentiate between white and black, created a primary colour bar. As we have seen the questions of who was a servant had on occasion come before the courts which had gradually interpreted the laws so as to keep whites out of the range of the definition of servant, and, in any case administratively, as the first report of the Wage Commission noted, proceedings were not usually taken under the Acts against white employees (UG 14 1926: 39). The burning question of the time, however, in the labour-law field, was whether the statute law should continue to be so coy about a colour bar. Many government commissions had addressed themselves to the issue. The Transvaal Indigency Commission of 1908 had deployed an argument based on 'economic law': 'no attempt to determine the respective positions of the two races in the industrial world which ignores economic law can be successful', they warned, because this 'would have the effect of ensuring the white man higher wages than would be economically justified' (quoted in UG 14 1926: 122). This was hardly a definition of failure that would persuade the advocates of a colour bar. The commission took a broad imperial view of the economic world: 'The cost of production with white labour should not be artificially maintained above that which obtains in other new countries.' In any case, they said, radical alteration of the labour system 'cannot be effected . . . by means of direct or drastic Government action'. Discussion of a legislated industrial colour bar focused on the main employer, the mines. The Mining Industry Commission from the same late colonial period also referred to 'natural laws and economic forces' which would render a colour bar ineffective. After Union the Relief and Grants in Aid Commission of 1916 was of the opinion that the colour bar would be an 'artificial method' which would 'interfere with the operation of economic principles'. This commission also thought that white wages should be comparable to those in other countries, and that the white worker 'will require to adopt a standard of living lower than is now recognised as his minimum standard' (quoted in UG 14 1926: 127–8). Marshalling these authorities, Mills, Clay and Martin said that while 'many witnesses were obviously of the opinion that the scope of employment for Europeans could be increased by the legislative exclusion of natives from specified occupations' such a policy would be economically 'unsound'.

Nonetheless a colour bar had long been an industrial reality. The Native Economic Commission traced it back to the Transvaal Labour Importation Ordinance, no. 17 of 1904, which had set out in its first schedule a list of occupations in which the Chinese workers would not be employed. These, they said, had 'continued to be claimed as belonging exclusively to Europeans' (UG 22 1932: para. 842). The regulations issued under the Mines and Works Act of 1911 had embodied these. This Act permitted the Governor-General to issue regulations requiring in the interests of safety competency certificates for various categories of work (sec. 4 (1)). The regulations said that such competency certificates were not to be issued to 'coloured persons' in the Transvaal and the Free State. In the Cape and Natal, a colour bar had existed in practice. In the words of the Low Grade Mines Commission of 1919–20:

> Custom, public opinion, and Trade Unions are . . . at least as powerful as
> . . . legal provision in establishing and maintaining an effective colour bar.
> This is corroborated by evidence given before us of the position at the De
> Beers mines, Kimberley. Although no legal restrictions are in force here,
> the colour bar is vigorously and effectively maintained as on the Witwa-
> tersrand mines, and any infringements upon it would be as strongly
> opposed by the white workmen. (cited in van der Horst 1971: 226 note 1)

As early as 1913 the Chamber of Mines told the Economic Commission that 'the opinion is held by many that these regulations are *ultra vires*, though the matter has not been tested'. The growing aversion of white miners to manual work, they told the commission, meant that now much of this work was done by Africans and had led to 'the curious and unsatisfactory position . . . of underground supervisors supervising the work of natives who are frequently more skilled than themselves' (quoted by Doxey 1961: 159). There could also be other reasons for finding black workers efficient. Ross-Frames, the managing director of Premier Mines, told the 1913 enquiry into employment and labour conditions that black machinists were 'better than a white man because his brain is free from socialistic and democratic problems' (SC 9 1913: 140–1). Some fifty-one occupations, involving, in 1920, 11,097 workers, were affected by the colour bar regulations (ibid.). The regulations were eventually held to be *ultra vires* in *R v Hildick Smith 1924 TPD 69*,[2] but there was no change in practice. Nonetheless the government had by statute authorised the return of the colour bar to the mining industry in 1926. In the words of its Mining Regulations Commission this went 'some way towards effecting . . . not only safety and health generally but also of counteracting the force of the economic advantages at present enjoyed by the native' (quoted by Doxey 1961: 160). The Native Economic Commission concluded that the colour bar could not be removed 'safely . . . at the present juncture' because state policy could not allow free competition 'between peoples living on such widely different levels of civilisation' (UG 22 1932: para. 845). This in itself was a safety issue to the 1930 Native Economic Commission. They reported the view of the Mines Department which accepted that an African could be technically competent but 'because he is at present a social inferior . . . he has not the influence over the actions of either whites or of other natives that the white man has and for that reason cannot enforce the due observance of the regulations' (para. 844).

Wage regulation

The role of the state in the regulation of wages not only opened up a whole new area for the operation of law, but is relevant to our understanding of the development of discourses around the idea of contract. The dilemma was clear. In capitalist theory the state did not regulate wages, which were left to contractual arrangements made in the market. But, as the Economic and Wages Commission noted in 1914, 'in the present century every English speaking country following the precedent of the Australasian states, has passed legislation providing in certain circumstances for the fixing of wages under statute' (quoted in UG 14 1926: 35).

---

[2] The judgment in *Hildick Smith* was given by Tindall with Morice and Krause concurring. The Governor-General had powers under the statute to make regulations, so the issue, Tindall said, was whether the specification of whiteness was so unreasonable as to amount to excess of the power conferred. Several previous decisions of the Transvaal Provincial Division had already ruled that unless such power was specifically conferred in the enabling legislation, there was no competence to discriminate on the basis of race. He drew support too from Mason's ruling in *Swart v Pretoria Municipality 1920 TPD 187* at 190 where he said that the rule in *Kruse v Johnson*, which said that a municipality could not, unless empowered specifically, discriminate against different classes of inhabitants, had been adopted in the South African courts.

The aims, it noted, had been twofold: the prevention of industrial disputes and strikes, and the elimination of excessively low wages. Nonetheless, they observed, the settlement of wages by 'voluntary contract', after individual bargaining, was still the usual procedure.

The problem of legally fixing minimum wages, itself a complex issue in the contemporary political economy of all industrialised and industrialising states, was made more complex by the racially divided workforce. The developing debate in South Africa contains the characteristic mix of contemporary thought, in this case concerning the relationship between economic laws and legal regulation, with the ever-pressing demand to secure the position of whites. The idea of legal minimum wages, and the question of wage regulation generally, was canvassed by the Economic Commission in 1914, against the background of the strikes and in a period in which the Labour Party, with its demands for the protection of white labour, had reached new political strength (UG 12 1914). Nonetheless at this point white labour's agenda received little sympathy. The 1914 commissioners had not been enthusiastic about wage regulation. Among whites in skilled work, they noted, 'a constant fear of displacement is prevalent, which is comprehensible particularly as the non-white workman usually gets a lower wage' (41). They pointed out that there was a 'sharp dividing line' between proposals for a subsistence wage for the lowest class of labour and proposals for minimum wages above subsistence levels for other classes of labour. In South Africa, it said, this discussion was divided between proposals for a subsistence wage for all and proposals for a minimum wage for whites only. The white workers' demand for a minimum wage fixed to white standards, which would apply to all races and exclude their competition, could, the commissioners thought, lead to an economic collapse. They hastened to add, in case the conclusion be drawn that the high level of white wages depended on the exploitation of black labour, that the differentials did not result 'from exploitation of the non-white', but arose simply because in the market there was an abundant supply of unskilled whites and a scarcity of 'skilled and supervisory' whites (42). A colour-blind minimum wage would not only raise the cost of production but would exclude most non-whites 'under the appearance of giving them equal economic rights'. This, they thought, would be both 'wholly inequitable' and 'impolitic in the extreme' (45). In any case, they urged, there should be no suppression of non-white participation in paid labour because the greater the productivity of non-whites, the greater would be profitability and the demand for white labour. The commission then wondered whether a minimum wage should be introduced for whites alone, to deal with the low living standards of poor whites, and to secure for them a life away from slums and an existence 'recognised as commonly decent for the white population' (42). While some all-white countries had minimum-wage legislation, they said, none were like South Africa. Though the raising of wages in this way would be appealing, the commissioners thought that it would have the effect of reducing employment among poor whites and throwing the lower end of work 'into the hands of black and coloured workers' (43).

With both a colour-blind and a 'white' minimum wage excluded, the next question was whether standard minimum earnings could be introduced for skilled and semi-skilled trades. This would give whites, and a few coloureds, a monopoly and raise their wages, but would, the commissioners said, reduce overall employment because the cost of labour would rise. Such a strategy, they pointed out, involved not only a conflict with the laws of economics but a fraught entry into the problematic area of legal regulation of economic matters. The commissioners thought that it would be difficult to work as well as wrong in principle.

> The penalising of breaches of awards which is easy in the case of employers, is in the case of employees a matter sufficiently awkward to deter the most ardent believers in the wisdom and efficacy of State action. Moreover . . . the best solutions for difficulties are far more likely to be reached in most cases as a result of negotiation than by the arbitrary award of a board . . . In the matter of the relations between employers and employed, the power of the State . . . should be used only when other means fail. (45)

The commissioners were prepared to see an extension of state regulation into another area of the labour market. Having argued against the enforcement of a national minimum wage by law, they rejected the argument that the same principle should apply to the idea of a maximum working day (62–3). But having made this concession, they were far from generous in its application. 'Study of the phenomena of fatigue', they said, 'has shown that pauses are economical, but it is not for the State to go beyond prohibiting what is actually harmful or distressing' (63). They recommended a fifty-hour week, exclusive of mealtimes, as a maximum in all factories and workshops. But they argued against limiting the hours of black labour. Africans were, they said, 'seldom capable of the intense application of a white man at his best'. Furthermore, an African worker 'with his inferior education, meaning a lower appreciation of leisure, is more indifferent than the white man to the hours of labour' (65).

The new National Party–Labour government took immediate steps first to introduce its 'civilised labour' policy, and then to appoint an economic and wages commission to investigate the larger question of how this might work. These commissioners grappled with the fact that there were different regimes of contract in South Africa, and they were divided as to how to deal with them. The position of white workers was affected by the existence of trade unions, and to a lesser extent by protective legislation like the Regulation of Wages Act of 1918. The position of black workers was seen to be different. From one angle the commissioners thought it was stronger than that of whites. The latter were completely dependent on wages, while Africans had the reserves to fall back on. Yet this perception apart, commissioners Mills, Clay and Martin, who penned a report supportive of the market, accepted that African workers were 'subject to certain restrictions of law and custom' which affected their bargaining power, such as the Masters and Servants Acts and the Native Labour Regulation Act. This framework provided penal provisions for breach of contract, permitted or required long periods for contracted service, usually six to nine months, and was underpinned by the recruiting and compound systems (UG 14 1926: 37). These commissioners were told, they wrote, by 'witnesses of great authority' that the penal clauses for breach of contract were a 'necessary means of punishing breaches of contract by the native, who generally has no assets which it is practicable to seize by civil action; that it imposes no greater hardship upon the native than the corresponding civil action imposes on a white man, and that in any case it affects only those who break their contracts'. Long contracts were needed to secure economic input from Africans who were said not to be dependent on wage labour (38). Even those who espoused the market over regulation accepted, therefore, that the punitive regulation of African labour contracts was necessary, and pointed to the complexity of other regulation (written contracts, regulations prohibiting advance payment, remittances to relatives) for the 'well being' of African workers, as a further justification. They came to the conclusion that for most black labour there was much to be said for the masters and servants laws, though, they observed piously, 'as with all Acts affecting natives, a great deal depends upon the fairness and common sense of those who have to administer them' (40). But 'some differential treatment is inevitable when dealing with labour that is mainly illiterate or of inferior race'.

Thus while Mills, Clay and Martin found that the regime of masters and servants, and other labour regulations laws was discriminatory, they nonetheless accepted that it should continue. The report by Andrews, Lucas and Rood, which presented the Labour and National Party viewpoints, differed on both points. They concluded both that the laws gave advantages to black workers and that they should be swept away. Their analysis is important because it highlights the nature of the 'common sense' that dismissed the market approach to labour law and wage regulation, and that underpinned the policies which were to be (without the abolition of the discriminatory labour regime) followed. South African industry, they began, was based on the employment of low-paid African labour. But there had never been enough, and this had led to a strategy of importation – of Indians, Chinese and Africans from Mozambique. The migrant-labour system and low pay had produced impoverished reserves, and detribalised men who, not receiving the necessities of life, were 'driven to extreme measures such as crime or revolution'. White Labour politicians and activists had long been more sensitive than other whites to the thin boundaries between legislative oppression of black labour and the status and freedom of white workers. They argued that the Native Labour Regulation Act and the masters and servants laws had 'the social result of dulling public conscience against interference with the freedom of the individual not only for natives but for whites as well, so that a feeling tends to be established that the manual worker – whatever his colour – belongs to a different species of animal'. The greater powers that employers had over Africans made them preferable as employees. Farmers who had given evidence admitted that even though they rarely used the legislation, it had to be continued 'because of its moral effect on their labourers' (UG 14 1926: 323–5).

Commissioners Mills, Clay and Martin took a broad view of the economic world, arguing, as we have seen, against the maintenance of a high level of white wages by political means. But there was a huge gap between its version of reality and the realities in the political spectrum. Legislation on wage regulation had not proceeded during the war. As the legislative agenda began to be revisited after the war, the subject was approached by the Smuts government in 1918 with a preliminary Wages Act and again in 1921 with a Wages Board Bill. This Bill would have introduced a system of wages boards made up of employer and employee representatives which would negotiate legally enforceable minimum wages. It was condemned by the Chamber of Industries as 'too previous . . . idealistic legislation' which was the result of 'sentimental leanings' (SC 9 1921: 18). The Bill was abandoned in the aftermath of the strike in 1922. The post-war economic situation leading to the strike of 1922 raised the issues both of occupational colour bars and of rates of pay. These were clearly linked in the issue that provoked the strike itself, the aim of the Chamber of Mines to reduce the number of white workers in relation to Africans, who were paid far less, and thereby reduce the cost of labour. Logically it might be said that there were two possible responses to this. One was to restore the statutory colour bar by legislation over-ruling *Hildick Smith*'s case, which was done. The second was to insist not only on occupational colour bars but on regulated wages, a rate for the job which ignored colour but would nonetheless have the effect of a colour bar because it would nullify any wage cost benefit to employers in replacing white with Africans. This was the strategy to be pursued in the Wages Act. Both strategies presented problems for aspects of legal ideology, as both interfered with 'freedom of contract' in substantial ways.

It was left to the Pact government to introduce its version of a Wages Act in the context of the 'civilised labour' policy. The full story of the drive to reduce the reliance on black labour in South Africa's mines and industries and to build an industrial workforce based on white labour cannot be told here. But it formed an important part of the rhetoric of the Labour Party, and was ever present in this period as a straw man in political and regulatory debates. While Cresswell's attempts to establish a mining industry in the Transvaal based on white labour failed, even before 1910 the railways and other state departments had begun preferential employment of unskilled whites. These policies were carried on by the Union government and its railways after 1910 (van der Horst 1971: 249). Thus it was not so much a matter of new principle introduced in 1924; the difference was one of scale and numbers. In the first decade of the new regime of 'civilised labour' the proportion of European labourers employed by the railways and harbours had risen from around 10 per cent to around 40 per cent, while Africans had dropped from 75 per cent to 50 per cent (251). Other government departments now followed the same policy (251). In its implementation of the civilised labour policy the government itself hired an extra 14,000 white workers between 1924 and 1931 while African numbers fell by 18,000 (Davies 1979: 225).

South African politicians had to hand the Australian formulation of the 'living wage'. The context within which Higgins wrote, that of the white Australia policy, with its determined protection of the living standards of white workers, was not dissimilar to the aims of South African labour policies. As Higgins himself had said, the first task he had to face as president of the Australian Court for Conciliation was to define what was meant by 'fair and reasonable remuneration'. 'I decided', he wrote, 'to adopt a standard based on the normal needs of the average employee regarded as a human being *living in a civilised community*' (Higgins 1915/ 16; my emphasis). This was an Australian code for white men, taken up by the Pact government in 1924 with its civilised labour policy. 'Civilised labour' was defined by the government in Cabinet circular no. 5, 31/10/24 as

> the labour rendered by persons whose standard of living conforms to the standard of living generally recognised as tolerable from the usual European standpoint. Uncivilised labour is to be regarded as the labour rendered by persons whose *aim is restricted* to the bare requirements of the necessities of life as understood among barbarous and undeveloped peoples. (my emphasis)

This definition, which was central to the construction of work opportunities and wages in the years that followed, was not a matter of law, nor was it ever legally defined, or tested in the courts. But it served to give meaning to the use of the word 'civilised' in section 3 (3) of the new Wages Act, and it did, of course, have real effects.[3] Nonetheless it was inevitably not wholly clear what the definition meant. This issue was raised particularly sharply in relation to the coloured population. This was

---

[3] Another part of the framework of the 'civilised labour' policy of labour legislation was the use of tariff protection. Soon after Union a foundational commission reported on policies for trade and industry in the new Union (UG 10 1912). Among its recommendations for extended protection for the new state's agriculture and industry was that one of the conditions for granting protection should be the utilisation of white labour in a 'fair proportion' (13). The Customs Tariff Act of 1914 rewarded the use of a 'fair amount' of white labour (Davies 1979: 107). The Board of Trade and Industry established in 1922 was a part of a response to white unemployment and a policy of relating tariff protection to employment of whites (162). In 1925 this mechanism became a part of the Pact government's civilised labour policies through the Customs Act. The Board of Trade and Industry, responsible for the implementation of tariff policy, explained in 1925 that it would be used 'as a means of encouraging the employment of civilised labour' (see van der Horst 1971: 265; Kaplan 1976).

crucial for, as the commission of enquiry into the coloured population (UG 35 1937) later claimed, it was 'clear from the wording of the Government circular that the distinction aimed at is not determined by the nature of the work but the class of person performing it' (37). Their comments illustrate well the complexities of the overlapping discourses of race, economics and law. The commission found that the practice had been to interpret 'civilised labour' as meaning white labour and to exclude coloureds, and it urged that the government issue instructions explaining explicitly that the term civilised labour 'has no reference to any particular race or colour' (41).

In its report in 1932 the Native Economic Commission rehearsed the 1925 definition.

> The term 'civilised' would appear to be a variant of 'living' or 'reasonable' as applied to a European in South Africa . . . the standard represented by the highest wage earned by a skilled artisan in one of the higher wage centres of the country. If this be its meaning, it is obviously a misnomer; for the level of real wages in such countries as Belgium, Germany and Italy is only half that of the white artisans in South Africa. (UG 22 1932: para. 332)

But while the government could introduce a civilised labour policy in state employment without legal sanction or challenge, its application to private industry, with its greater sensitivity to costs, was another matter, and for this legislation was needed. This was the Wages Act which was also a supplement to the Conciliation Act passed by the previous government. While the latter Act assumed trade union organisation, the Wages Act, in the words of its sponsors in parliament, aimed at protecting workers in lower paid and sweated industries where there was little labour organisa-tion. The Department of Labour had told the commission that the purpose of the Wages Act was to provide safeguards for the wages and conditions of lower paid and unorganised workers, and Labour Party leaders like Cresswell and Boydell affirmed this. All were referring only to white workers. The mechanism of the Wages Act derived from Australian law, but the South African Wage Board was required under the Act to recommend a wage rate 'upon which . . . employees may be able to support themselves in accordance with civilised habits of life' (sec. 3 (3)). But unlike the Industrial Conciliation Act the definition of 'employee' did not exclude pass-bearing Africans. In theory, therefore, the board could radically raise the wages of black workers. But agriculture and domestic service, two of the largest arenas of African labour, were excluded from the Act. So too was state employment. In addition the Act provided that in situations where industries depended on the work of low-paid non-white workers the board could take into account the ability of such employers to carry on business and could report to the minister that a civilised wage could not be fixed. If the minister accepted this, he could direct the board to disregard the civilised habits standard and make an award 'suited to the conditions'. Furthermore wage boards could only hear cases referred to them by the minister, and the minister could reject any determination that they had made. This, the commissioners observed prissily in 1926, 'will expose disputants to the risk that their affairs may be settled on the grounds of political advantage rather than economic necessity' (64). It would not ameliorate the 'customary rates' of pay for Africans which were based on the 'quasi-servile tradition . . . of native employment in agriculture' (84).

When it was introduced into parliament the Bill had been opposed by the spokesmen of both the mines and industry generally. As Davies notes it was treated by the opposition as 'drastic' anti-capitalist legislation (see the evidence given before the SC 14 1925 and Davies 1979: 211–12). The objection was expressed that an apparently race-free wage-determination system would have the result of raising African wages, and would be the mechanism through which the Labour Party would achieve its long-stated objective of a minimum wage which would price non-white labour out of the market (Davies 1979: 210–12). Smuts, who had vigorously opposed the Mines and Works Act when it legislated the industrial colour bar, said in relation to the absence of such a legislative bar in the wages legislation: 'It is not only in industry but in employment of all kinds that the essential racial and social difference is recognised. This Bill is going to make a vast change and introduce equality where there has so far been difference . . . you cannot . . . pay the black man a wage which will be a subsistence wage for the white man' (quoted by Davies 1979: 212).

The politicians' idea that wages policy and determinations could be used to establish what was effectively a colour bar without statutory exclusions on the basis of race was also criticised by Mills, Clay and Martin. South African industry, they observed, 'offers a unique field for experiments in wage regulation by law – a field also in which experiments have special dangers'. Wage regulation could modify the distribution of wages and secure increases of wealth to one class rather than another (UG

14 1926: 91). They noted that the Wages Board could fix minimum rates for an occupation so high that no non-white would be employed. Partly this would be because they did not have the skills that would command such a rate of pay, and partly because the exceptionally skilled would in any case 'be excluded by force of public opinion from what is seen as a white occupation' (124). Fixing high minimum rates for an occupation would, therefore, exclude non-whites, while a lower determination would have a different effect. High legal rates for unskilled work would restrict the fields of African employment, crowd them into restricted areas at depressed wages, and widen the gap between skilled and unskilled rates. 'The injustice of this to the native will be apparent; *less obvious is the injury to the white workers*' (124–5).

This was of course the political problem. The commissioners attempted to expound the economic argument. Industry, they said, depended on African labour; only one-third of workers were white. They argued that any restriction on the employment of Africans would curtail the development of industry and, therefore, white employment. The pattern of wage determinations would force down the wages of the least efficient whites who could only do unskilled work. And, finally, the purchasing power of Africans would be reduced, and this would restrict industrial growth and white employment (125). It would force up the cost of industrial production at the expense of the consumer, and would require increased protection against imports. The cost of financing white employment at high rates would, therefore, fall on mining and agriculture which produced for export. They concluded that 'the governing consideration in any wage regulation should be to encourage the use to its fullest capacity of every class of labour . . . the public regulation of wages, therefore, should be first directed to those occupations in which the lowest rates are now being paid' (127–8). 'We are of the opinion', they wrote, 'that the first and chief object of public wage regulation in the Union should be, not the raising of the higher rates of wages still higher, but the raising of the lowest levels of wages, so that the gap between the levels of skilled and unskilled labour is reduced' (63). Nonetheless African wage rates should not be improved precipitately. They thought that 'a sudden increase in pay would be merely demoralising to natives where actions are determined so much more by custom and tradition than by ordinary economic considerations' (92). The inherent, yet apparently fragile, conservatism of Africans had already been relied on to bolster the arguments for retention of the migrant-labour and labour-recruiting systems. Mills, Clay and Martin quoted at length from A. R. Radcliffe-Brown, then professor of anthropology at the University of Cape Town. 'In the case of a primitive people', he told them, morality was dependent on external support and was not 'rational and reflective' as among civilised people. 'Any sudden disturbance, therefore, of the established economic system . . . tends to demoralise them.' It was therefore necessary to preserve the 'traditional social and economic system' during transition to civilised conditions, which would be 'a trying and hazardous experience'. This would be eased 'if it is made gradually by limiting contact as much as possible to intermittent periods of employment under sheltered conditions' while most of life 'is still passed in the nursery of his own tribal community' (156–7).

It is hardly surprising that the repeated invocation of economic laws which required a fall in white wages did not persuade the political representatives of white workers. Nor did arguments based on forecasts of what, ultimately, might be the results of immediate advantages grabbed now. They knew what the Federated Chamber of Industries had readily admitted, that 'white wages have been paid, and are being paid, largely at the expense of the native worker' (86). The Economic and Wages Commission passed on the whole 'native question' in relation to wages to others for further enquiry. It was taken up by the Native Economic Commission which took a different view. Its majority report thought that the low wages suffered by urbanised Africans were brought about by the 'competition of his tribal brethren subsidised as they are by the income from their tribal holdings'. This being the case they could not 'agree that an extension of the laws relating to the regulation of wages represents a suitable way of dealing with this problem' (UG 22 1932 para. 994). Wage regulation for Africans, they said, would always be influenced by 'the subversive factor' of large numbers of casual migrant labourers. In addition to these obstacles, they also identified a need for 'elasticity' in wages, in a time of falling prices. Regulation as an idea, they said, had succeeded *laissez faire* because the latter had been seen as inadequate for social justice. But it was now being pursued as a lever for the redistribution of wealth rather than as an instrument 'for furthering economic health'. When economic rationalism was invoked by this commission it was for the purpose of keeping black wages low. 'The avowed object of those who desire wage regulation for the Natives is to increase their nominal wages. When their real wages are rising, and the fall in prices is inflicting a very heavy burden on those whose duty it is to keep the wheels of industry in motion there should be no further rises' (para. 996–8). As was clear their view was underpinned by their general endorsement of segregation. Regulation leading to improved pay in the towns would increase the rate of African urbanisation, impede 'reclamation' of the slums, and imperil the profitability of mining and agriculture (para. 1000–5). It was possible to see things another way. The minority commissioners Anderson, Lucas and Roberts argued that the cause of the drift to the towns was economic distress and the need for money to pay tax, and that it would be alleviated by higher wages (para. 1049). They also pointed out that the wide gap between African and white wages meant that whites could not 'fall back' on unskilled work. Furthermore appropriate use of the Wages Act (from which they excluded mining and farming) might stop African political agitation and discontent.

Later, after several years of experience as Wage Board chairman, Lucas summed up. 'Wage regulation is far more complicated in South Africa than it is in civilised countries with a homogeneous population. There is here the complicating factor of the different standards of living of the different races' (Lucas 1933: 54). While there was no colour bar in the Act it was 'obvious that different standards of living cannot be ignored in classifying different kinds of work'. Unskilled work was performed (except for subsidised schemes) by Africans and 'that fact must operate to keep the wage for it down at a level which bears some reasonable relation to the level for native wages'. While he saw that a 'serious problem' was presented by the gap between skilled and unskilled wages, it seemed to him to be a problem for white workers. The gap, he said, 'plays a very definite part in preventing the training and employment of Europeans, and in leaving them to look for work at a wage fixed in relation to the low standard of living of the Natives' (ibid.). When the problem of wage regulation was considered again it was in the context of an even greater urbanisation of both whites and blacks, and the intensification of conflict for employment at the lower levels of industry. The question of low wages, the Industrial Legislation Commission reported, was no longer 'merely the concern of non-Europeans . . . A drastic alteration of the wage policy of the country is demanded if for no other reason than the fact that the grounds on which the unusual disparity was tolerated in the past have passed' (UG 37 1935: 39). The wisdom of the Native Economic

Commission had established that the fault was really that of the low paid: 'At the root of the evil of low native wages . . . lies the economic outlook of a primitive people' (quoted at 40). The remedy now emerging from the economists was to cut off the connection with the reserves to stem this flow, and to stabilise the African urban working class. The 1935 commission noted that there were disparities 'several times as great' between skilled and unskilled wages in South Africa than in any other country (17). It strongly urged against 'the imposition of further barriers and restrictions, in creating a more artificial state, in providing for further rigidity, but rather . . . elasticity and a greater equalisation of opportunities and positive efforts to raise the lower wage levels' (20). The extraordinary unanimity of expert recommendations only underlines the vastly greater influence of a determined polity. This was an area in which political and not expert discourses dominated.

The 1935 commissioners therefore had to face again the question of whether minimum wages should be fixed by law (41ff.). Representations were made to the commission that there should be a national minimum wage (10 shillings per day). Opinion both expert and political was that it should exclude domestic, mining and farm work – i.e. the major occupations employing Africans under the provisions of the masters and servants laws. But the commission had to mobilise all its resources of expertise to argue against legislative fixing of a minimum wage. Expert economic discourses did not persuade and for this reason were rehearsed vehemently each time the issue was raised. As a matter of economics, they said, a minimum wage would lead to a decline in employment. Furthermore it would have to include black workers or they would be able to undercut whites. Differential wage fixing on the grounds of colour had been rejected by every previous commission. Wage fixing on the grounds of colour would undermine white employment, said the commission. Evidence given to the commission tended to show that the effect of the workings of the wage boards had, in effect, been a *de facto* fixing of wages by colour even though the Wages Board had in 1926 laid down the principle that the wage rate fixed for an occupation applied to all workers. There was, said Rheinhalt-Jones in his evidence to the 1935 commission, 'a very profound conviction' among Africans that the Wages and Industrial Conciliation Acts had been used to exclude them from employment (69). Between 1929 and 1933 there had been a 4 per cent rise in the European composition of the manufacturing workforce, and a 4 per cent drop in

Africans. The commissioners preferred to think that this might be due to the increased migration of whites from rural to urban areas. Nonetheless they urged that the European 'must prove his superiority. Competition with other races will be a stimulant, but artificial protection may ultimately lead to self destruction' (52).

But if the law should not fix a minimum wage, or provide for differential wage rates on the basis of race, there were other ways, in the commission's view, that the state could help white workers. This could be done by 'subsidising European labour by means of extended social services'. The solution to the white labour problem should be sought in improving living conditions through education and 'constructive social work' and by state aid in connection with housing and health – 'helping them to fend for themselves'. In addition there could be 'the provision of consumptive credit facilities' on reasonable terms with government help (59).

The effect on the labour market of the determinations of the Wages Board was analysed in 1935 by the Industrial Legislation Commission. The statutory wage scales, they said, created impediments to the free movements of labour. 'These barriers block the overflow from the large reservoir of unskilled labour into channels where skill and training is a necessary factor' (UG 37 1935: para. 23). In South Africa, they concluded, industrial legislation served to maintain the structure of wage rates which had arisen because of the scarcity of skilled workers by exclusive devices 'which . . . prevented the adjustment of wage-rates to the potential supply of labour' (257). As van der Horst commented, the 'importance of this type of wage regulation in the market for Native Labour lies in its effect not so much upon the privileged few whose wages may be raised or protected . . . as upon the many to whom opportunities for employment are thereby closed' (1971: 259). This official debate was virtually exclusively framed around the contradiction between regulation and a free market in labour and wages and the issue of economic efficiency. In a sense this excluded a specifically 'legal' discourse centred upon common-law rights to contract freely. In any case while the common-law discursive framework was revolved around 'contract' and its 'freedoms', the area of labour was one in which, as we have seen, this language was fraught with contradictions.

Women's wages

In the regulation of white wages in the context of the 'civilised labour' policy men and women were treated differently. Higgins' 'New Province' had contended that the 'principle of the living wage applied to women, but with a difference, as women are not usually legally responsible for the maintenance of a family. A woman's minimum is based on the average cost of her own living to one who supports herself by her own exertions' (quoted in Berger 1992: 20). This was part of South African orthodoxy also.[4] In 1916 a report on industrial education noted that 'the case of the girl differs in one very important step from that of the boy: the noble vocation of home making is marked out for the great majority of women . . . If she enters on some other occupation it is unlikely to provide her with her life work' (quoted in ibid.: 26). Lucas explained the Wages Board's approach to the 'civilised wage' for women.

> Such a wage for a female employee is taken as one upon which she can maintain herself without having to look to her parents or anyone else for support. Where a different wage is laid down for male and female employees, the civilised wage for a man must not be taken to mean a wage on which he can merely exist but one on which he can . . . maintain not only himself but also a wife and family with a reasonable degree of comfort according to European standards. (1933: 55)

In its determinations, Wage Board policy was to take two-thirds of the man's rate as the standard for women's wages (Lewis 1984: 54). (In the twenty years following Union the wages of white women were roughly between 40 and 45 per cent of those of white men, while the wages of black men were similar in proportion to those of white women (Berger 1992: 35).)

While the earlier commissions had passed over the question, there continued to be an increasing movement of white women to the industrial centres and a growth in their participation in employment. The 1935 commission gave some detailed consideration to this question. The place of women in the labour market was seen to lie in the subordinate and service spheres, in positions of low skills and low pay. This was made clear by the commissioners' opening remarks on the subject. The sphere of

---

[4] Pollak found that a third of the white women working in industry on the Witwatersrand were contributing to the support of dependants (1933: 67).

women's employment, it wrote, was limited by the presence of natives, coloureds and Indians. Women's wages, the commission said, were between 50 and 60 per cent of those of men, which it said was comparable to that of other countries. It explained the wage differential in the same way as it had been done twenty years before. 'The supply of female labour is . . . of a character totally different from that of men. For women, employment is largely a stepping stone to marriage or better times . . . There is reason to assume, therefore, that women are prepared to offer their labour generally at a lower price than men' (UG 37 1935: 23). The issue to which the commission primarily addressed itself in relation to gender was not the low pay and lack of opportunities for women, but the outcry against the displacement of men in jobs by women because they could undercut men in the wage market. As in the case of blacks, this led to demands from white unions for segregation to keep women out of certain occupations. But the commission urged that it would be better for men to seek higher-grade work than to try to compete with women, for example in offices and retail trade where they had come to predominate. To a large extent, they urged, men and women 'constitute non-competing groups'. Indeed female labour was seen to be less skilled and more 'robot' like. (Women were also 'better at sitting'.) White women, however exalted and protected they were in other discourses, were, when considered as workers, rather like non-whites. White women, in the commission's view, were, like black men, suited to less skilled work than white men. They reacted to economic incentives in the 'wrong' way like black men did. If wages were raised for women, the commission was told, they would not want to marry, and the economic need to do so would be reduced. Equal pay for equal work would not be in the interests of white women because, it was said, it would deprive many of them of work. The commission concluded that women should be given equality of opportunity, but that only men would gain if they were given equal pay. (They quoted as authority the rejection of equal pay for women by Beatrice Webb (24–9).) Indeed the Industrial Conciliation Act was amended in 1937 to give to industrial councils specific authorisation for 'any . . . differentiation or discrimination based on . . . sex' (Act 36 of 1937 sec. 24 (2); cited in van der Horst 1971: 245 note 7). (These councils could not discriminate on the basis of race or colour.) In the government's eyes the relief of poor-white poverty depended on ensuring that white men had jobs, not on increasing the workforce participation of white women. Indeed the latter was seen to be a pathology, a result of poverty and a sign of desperation rather than a cure. The increasing migration of young Afrikaner women to the towns was a focus for much anxiety about de-nationalisation and fear of the alien ideologies of trade unionism, and provoked renewed calls for segregation.

The major paid occupation among all South African women was domestic service, and black women were increasingly seen as the resource to be mobilised for this purpose. The Native Affairs Commission of 1905 wrote that 'one branch of the Native Labour question is the employment of women and . . . it is highly desirable that every measure should be adopted which would encourage the employment of Native women in domestic work . . . [which would] release large numbers of men and boys for employment in occupations more suited to them' (quoted by Berger 1992: 26). Because domestic work was seen to be black women's proper sphere they were invisible to industrial law.

Industrial legislation in practice

As we have seen, most of the discourses surrounding the issues of the legal regulation of employment were economic and political, and were not essentially concerned with the common law of contract. But from the point of view of the courts significant challenges were present in the huge new wave of regulation of employment, and the large complex structures of councils and boards, with their agreements and determinations which had legal effect, subjecting employers and employees to criminal penalties. Would these, for example, be approached as contracts, or as regulations? How closely would the courts scrutinise and how strictly would they interpret the complex and wide-ranging determinations, particularly as once a wage determination had been made it was a criminal offence to pay lower wages? The operating principle in the courts was that such bureaucratic regulation was a departure from the 'normal' pattern of contractual wage bargaining between free agents, and could thus only operate within the strict limits authorised by statute. After the first five years of the new regime criticisms of the role played by the courts in relation to the provisions of the Industrial Conciliation Act were widespread. The legalism of the courts, their lack of expertise in the area of industrial relations, the desirability of the creation of special industrial courts and the appropriateness of a regime of legal precedent were all canvassed during the inquiry into the working of the Industrial Conciliation Act (SC 9 1930). Given the extreme political sensitivity that had characterised industrial issues one might have expected the courts to approach the sphere with caution, and to temper legalism with a recognition of the difficulties that such an approach might create. But this was not the case. No such 'lesson' was learned from *Hildick Smith's* case. The Minister of Labour was critical of the interpretations that the court had placed on the labour statutes, 'which seem to us, as plain individuals, to be entirely outside the meaning of the English language' (SC 9 1930: 7). The South African Federated Chamber of Industries wanted industrial councils to be able to settle disputes 'without being tied by previous judgments' (11). The Cape Federation of Labour complained that 'the irritating consequences of legal decisions' were frustrating 'the lawful intentions of parliament to the classes it set out to benefit', and it called for greater administrative powers or special courts or specially selected magistrates (20–1). W. H. Andrews preferred the administrative route. 'We fear that a magistrate might give us law,' he said, 'but under conciliation boards we should get justice' (31). Prominent union activist E. S. Sachs attacked the courts for their ignorance of the technical details involved in various industries, and for the many conciliation agreements 'upset on a very fine point of law'. The Conciliation Act, he said, should be amended to make conciliation agreements 'lawyer proof' (40–1). And with regard to the Wages Act he complained that it had been 'considerably nullified by the Court decisions in regard to Wage Board determinations' (53). To all the major players in the industrial relations arena the methods and approach of the courts were, therefore, seen as inappropriate to the regime of labour relations and wage fixing which the statutes had tried to put into place.

There were other issues in relation to putting the laws into effect. As was the case in so much of South Africa's legislation in practice, there was a wide gap between the state's ambitions, and its capacities. In the 1930 enquiry there was some reference to the evasion of the Industrial Conciliation and Wage Acts, and this was repeated in 1935. The commission noted that the Department of Labour's policy was to secure compliance with the Acts without resort to prosecutions which were only used as a last resort if the opportunities given to comply were not taken. In 1933–4 there were 403 prosecutions and 247 convictions under the Industrial Conciliation Act and 202 prosecutions and 165 convictions under the

Wages Act (130). The maximum penalty for failing to observe the provisions of an industrial award under the former act was a £500 fine or two years imprisonment. Under the Wages Act the maximum penalty was £100 or six months. The commission reported that 'the consensus of opinion was that the penalties are so inadequate that they do not serve as a deterrent'. More tellingly, their analysis of the actual fines imposed shows them to have been very low, often lower than the fines imposed on pass offenders (131). In this environment, they reported, employers ran 'small risks' as inspections were not frequent. As one witness said, 'It pays to evade' (131). There was, they pointed out, no authority in law for the department's policy, and they thought that more prosecutions might have a far-reaching effect (UG 37 1935: 130). Even so, there were 'many undetected evasions'. But enforcement was only part of the larger problem of ambivalence about the role of law, especially penal provisions, in this part of labour law. As one magistrate told the commission there was a 'want of common acceptance of the penological principle'. Professor W. H. Hutt wrote in 1933 that it was

> commonly asserted in casual conversation that evasion takes place on so large a scale that inspectors and other officials are unable to cope with it and are in a position to prosecute only in exceptional cases . . . If this should be so the final result must undoubtedly be a declining respect for law and the growth of suspicions of corruption. Increased penalties would almost certainly add to this danger.

Successful evasion, he noted, had to be based on collusion between employer and employees. The law lacked moral sanction, he claimed, because much public opinion felt that it drove small firms out of business and stopped people from getting work (Hutt 1933: 40–1). In a review of the 1935 report in the *South African Journal of Economics* Reedman commented that, given that the report showed serious evasions of the Acts, it was 'surprising' to find only 'a mild reference to the inadequacy of the inspectorate'. British experience, he said, had shown that an adequate inspectorate was a *sine qua non* of the successful administration of industrial legislation. But the problem was not just one of inadequate state capacity, for, as he pointed out, successful evasion depended on collusion and the prevalence of that indicated that the laws ran counter to economic forces (Reedman 1936: 228–9).

And it was inconvenient. Cases took a long time to prepare, and witnesses were often those who had been involved in collusion, or ignorant of their rights, or subject to economic pressures: and all of this meant that they did not offer evidence in Wage Act cases. Nonetheless the commission strongly opposed on principle the idea that Department of Labour inspectors should be able to impose punishments. 'Only the courts', it said, should have that power (UG 37 1935: 131). Furthermore employers who ignored the wages determination could escape not only without any or any serious penalties but also were not liable for wages in arrears. One decision may illustrate the difficulty which the appellate court had in dealing with the tensions between the law of contract and the new industrial regime. In *Manoim v Veneered Furniture Manufacturers 1934 AD 237* the employer had been convicted for underpayment of wages under the relevant award. Though the statutes gave power to the original court to order payment of the shortfall it had not done so. The appellate court took refuge in the law of contract and denied the right to sue civilly for recovery, a decision which meant that an underpaid worker had no remedy. The contract under which the worker had accepted the lower wages, the court said, was void. 'Dishonest and fraudulent' workers could not enter into a contract for a lower than award wage, and then sue civilly for the difference (246).[5]

But could the courts be the vehicle for the government's labour policies? It was not only ineffective sanctioning that was bitterly attacked. As the commission reported, 'What can be referred to as the "sins of omission" of the courts occupied the attention of a large number of witnesses. The Courts were often severely criticised as being hostile to industrial legislation, unsympathetic . . . little attempt made to understand industrial conditions . . . too easily influenced by technicalities' (UG 37 1935: 135). Evidence was given that agreements reached by industrial councils after weeks of negotiations were invalidated because of technicalities, such as the improper appointment of union representatives (136). As one magistrate told the commission, in defences against charges under the industrial laws, 'the real issues are hidden in a maze of technicalities' (ibid.). Unscrupulous employers flouted the law because they believed that no wage regulatory instrument could withstand attack in the courts (ibid.). In *Ex parte Minister of Justice in re R v Cohen 1934 AD* the court had invalidated thirty-one wage determinations, a decision

---

[5] See the discussion in Corder (1984: 123–4), which cites the scathing criticism of the decision by van der Heever, himself later an appellate judge.

reversed by parliament the following year. The commission thought the evasions of the Wage Act serious (one common method was the formation of fake partnerships between employer and employees, against which a legislative remedy had been sought in 1930) and the cause of a loss of confidence in the law and the courts of the country (121).

'Only the courts', the commission had said, should have powers to impose compliance under the Act. But which courts? In 1932 the government had prepared a Bill providing for the establishment of an industrial division of the Supreme Court. A judge and two assessors, one employer and one employee representative would have had final determination without right of appeal to the Supreme Court. The legislation was withdrawn after employer opposition. But the issue did not die. The accusations levelled against the performance of the ordinary courts in administering the acts tested their control over the area. One suggestion made to the 1935 commission was that once an industrial agreement made under the Conciliation Act had been published it should not be subject to legal challenge and only the Appellate Division should be able to rule on its validity (UG 37 1935: 136). The Wages Board called for the establishment of an industrial court with the status of a superior court at provincial division level. It argued that there was a need to co-ordinate decisions on industrial legislation and that a court was needed which would have the experience and ability to obtain quickly knowledge of the functioning of particular industries. A special court, it argued, was the only effective way of preventing 'disastrous' consequences of delay, such as strikes (138). An industrial court, it urged, would be able to review the validity of agreements and determinations before they were brought into operation, and review all magistrates' court decisions in industrial cases. It thought that industrial court decisions should not be appealable except on the grounds of grave procedural irregularity. In its ambition to free the industrial system from the ordinary courts it had its eyes on the Australian example. In relation to procedure it urged that the court be able to sit as an arbiter and should not be bound to observe the strict rules of evidence, but should act according to the Australian standard of determination 'in accordance with equity and good conscience' (138). But the 1935 commission was unwilling to establish a special court (140).

Trade unions and the Ministry of Labour presented different pictures of the workings of the industrial conciliation machinery. The union evidence expressed dislike of compulsory arbitration when voluntary agreement failed, and objected to the types of person appointed by the minister as arbitrators (80). There was evidence of intimidation and victimisation of union members. Most importantly the new laws had changed the ways in which unions worked. The Industrial Conciliation Act, Davies writes, 'effectively prohibited strikes not by formally pro-scribing them, but by creating so many pre-conditions that, in the words of one experienced participant [W. H. Andrews] "a successful legal strike" became "almost an impossibility"' (Davies 1979: 193). Another impor-tant aspect noted by Davies was the 'tendency towards bureaucratisation', the 'complex, esoteric and centralised' procedures required by the Act which changed the character of union activities, involving them in complex interactions with state officials rather than with their rank and file (196).

The function of the new Department of Labour, as described by its Secretary in 1927, was 'to use all the opportunities afforded by legislation and by administrative methods to further the interests of the white population and to widen the opportunities for white labour in the Union' (Wickins 1978: 137). But it found that this could not be done by completely ignoring the presence of black workers. White trade unions were to find the same. As long as African workers were not covered by the industrial legislation they could, in an industrial labour force, where the conditions were not the same as agriculture or mining, be exploited in a way that was injurious and not beneficial to white interests. The result was, the Department of Labour told the Native Economic Com-mission, that their employers took advantage of the law to employ Africans whose wages were unregulated. In some industries, like engi-neering, they said, 'with advanced division of labour . . . it is possible to conduct work almost entirely with unskilled and semi-skilled workers, and in this way . . . the Act was evaded by the employment of uncivilised labour at low wages' (quoted in van der Horst 1971: 246). In 1930 the Industrial Conciliation Act was amended to allow white unions and employers represented on the industrial councils to set wage rates for unrepresented African workers. Amendments to the Wages Act also cut off the avenue by which some unions had endeavoured to represent unorganised non-white workers by requiring the signature of every affected worker on an application for a wage determination. In addition the Minister of Labour instructed the Wage Board not to make determi-nations for the unskilled.

But the determination to prevent use of the laws to advance the case of African workers ran up against other considerations. The Department of Labour wanted to divert African members of unions not recognised under the industrial law away from political and towards industrial matters. The Wages Board chairman, Lucas, observed that there was much African discontent about the structure of industrial relations laws which prevented them from benefiting from the Industrial Conciliation Act, and which, under the Native Labour Regulation Act, and the masters and servants law, prohibited them from striking (UG 22 1932: 304–5). The Department of Labour was, therefore, not adamantly averse to the representation of African workers by regulated trade unions, whether they were black unions or segregated branches of white unions (Wickins 1978: 138). In 1928 the Secretary of Labour wrote:

> I believe that the Native has been told and come to believe that the White man regards him as a menace and fears him . . . The counter for an attitude of this kind – in regard to industrial matters *with which alone my remarks are concerned* – is by administrative methods to accept the Native – who *de facto* takes so large a share in our industries – as being there *de jure* and entitled to participate according to his standing and abilities in the protection and opportunities afforded by law to other workers. (Duncan 1995: 207–8)

The department's aim was to 'draw the teeth' of the ICU, and prevent 'communist infiltration' of black unions, by bringing African workers under the aegis of white-led unions (Duncan 1995: 186–7). The white union movement, however, was divided. Defeat in the 1922 strike had been a crushing blow, and had resulted in substantial falls in membership. (For a general account see Lewis 1984.) From 1930 a 'fragile unity' was established in the union movement under the aegis of the South African Trades and Labour Council which adopted 'an explicitly non-racial stance,' and called for 'full legal rights for African trade unionists' (Lewis 1984: 1). Nonetheless, as the 1935 commission pointed out, the 'problem of colour' posed a 'serious obstacle' to effective union organisation in South Africa with non-whites not being accepted as union members outside the Cape and Natal (90). While not addressing segregation directly, it proposed that those excluded should be given some sort of administrative representation in the industrial council system through a member of the Department of Native Affairs, and one from the Department of Labour to represent those who did not fall within the definition of 'employee' (95).[6]

But there was no ultimate common interest between white and black workers. Writing in 1936 Reedman reproduced the market-based arguments of Clay, Mills and Martin and argued that the industrial legislation 'intended to preserve an earlier order which . . . refuses to remain'. There was a range of skills and lack of skills across all races, he wrote, but 'a legal fiction' preserved the notion that all white labour was skilled, and this increased the poor-white problem. While the wages legislation was in theory on a par with the British Trade Board structure and could be said to aim at the prevention of exploitation, Reedman wrote, the industrial conciliation legislation was 'quite different' in that it was based on the restrictive action of certain groups and promoted the interest of white trade unions. The 'fundamental issue' was that a small section of workers thereby maintained 'monopoly earnings' at the expense of a large section. While unskilled wages were between 50 and 75 per cent of skilled earnings in Australia, France, Canada and the UK, they were only between 10 and 30 per cent of skilled earnings in South Africa. This 'extraordinary disparity' underlay all the unresolved issues of industrial legislation (222–5).

---

[6] See Duncan (1995: 160ff.) for an account of the disagreements between the Departments of Labour and Native Affairs on the inclusion of Africans within the operation of the industrial and wage laws. He writes that the Native Affairs Department opposed raising African wages through the Wage Board because it would attract more Africans to the towns. The department also saw itself, and not trade unions, as the appropriate representative of African workers.

18

A rule of law

In 1924 Arthur Keith wrote that 'Throughout the Empire the system of government is distinguished by the predominance of the rule of law' (Keith 1924: 136). Starting here provides a framework for understanding: South Africa was a part of the British Empire which was both an international political and constitutional system, as well as both a worldwide legal system and a dominant and coherent legal culture. In using the phrase 'the rule of law' Keith was invoking Dicey's formulation which exercised a complete dominance over the discourse of public law in this area. It meant, according to Dicey, the 'absolute supremacy' of 'regular law', as opposed to 'arbitrary power' and even excluded 'wide discretionary authority' on the part of government. It meant the 'equal subjection of all classes to the ordinary law of the land administered by the ordinary courts'. And it meant that the principles of the common law, not a constitution, were the source of individual rights (Dicey [1885] 1959: 183–202). South African constitutional and administrative law developed within these contexts, and was powerfully influenced and constrained by them. Innes, as South Africa's Chief Justice, proclaimed that 'one of the features of the English Constitution, a feature re-produced in the self-governing Dominions, is the absolute supremacy of the law' (*Krohn v Minister of Defence 1915 AD 191* at 196).

Throughout the empire war, class struggle, racial rule, and ethnic division meant that the verbal formulae of the rule of law were highly qualified by statutory and emergency powers. In qualification of his general formula Keith also noted that in all the British Dominions the rule of law had been 'severely curtailed' in wartime (1924: 271). Of the courts in the empire as a whole he observed that during the war

> The Courts . . . took the most favourable view throughout of the wide extent of the authority conferred by Acts of Parliament dealing with War

Measures or War Precautions, enactments to this effect being held in all the Dominions to authorise the passing of regulations of the greatest variety and scope. Doubtless in their decisions the Courts were activated, as in the United Kingdom, by reluctance to seek to fetter the discretion of the executive in times of stress. (Keith 1921: 271)

In Britain the Defence of the Realm Act of 1914 placed extremely wide curbs on civil liberties. The courts were co-operative. In 1916 Lord Parker declared that 'those who are responsible for national security must be the sole judge of what national security requires' (*The Zamora. 1916 AC 1917* at 42). In *R v Halliday ex parte Zelig 1917 AC 260* the House of Lords supported the suspension of *habeas corpus* by delegated legislation. Peacetime did not end the British state's compulsions to add to the common law of sedition and conspiracy. The Emergency Powers Act of 1920 allowed for the proclamation of a state of emergency. In relation to industrial disputes, after the general strike of 1926, the Trade Disputes and Trade Unions Act of 1927 made strikes that had the objective of coercing the Government by inflicting hardship on the community illegal (see Cornish and Clark 1989: 349–50). In Australia the High Court had declared during the 1914–18 War that the limits of the Commonwealth's defence powers were 'bounded only by the requirements of self-preservation' and that the state could legally preserve 'at all hazards and by all available means' its 'inviolability' (*Farey v Burvett 1916 CLR 21*; quoted in Cowan 1967: 168). In 1926 the Australian Crimes Act made it possible for the government to proclaim a state of serious industrial disturbance in which strikes would be a criminal offence. These and other imperial statutes were examples for South African lawmakers, as were the decisions of the Privy Council on matters such as martial law (Cowan 1965: 10–11). In *Bhagat Singh v King Emperor 58 Indian Appeal PC 1931* the imperial approach was made plain. The Governor-General of India had absolute powers during emergencies, the Privy Council said, without any necessity to give reasons for his actions.

Looking back in 1938 Keith observed that, true to the British tradition, the Dominion constitutions 'ignore entirely the question of defining the rights to be enjoyed by subjects' (1938: 567). And he noted that

in the Dominions in general it has been necessary by law to make inroads on the rights which can be enjoyed by subjects, and to strengthen the common law provision against treason, sedition and like offences. The same causes which evoked the British legislation of 1920 to confer emergency powers on the executive have resulted in the enactment being copied overseas. (561)

He noted the use of special courts in Ireland and South Africa to 'prevent the defeating of the ends of justice by jury trial in cases of contravention of the law regarding riotous gatherings, the dissemination of seditious propaganda, and the use of violence in industrial disputes' (ibid.). In general, he found that 'growing unrest throughout the Dominions is increasing the difficulty of recognising as widely as formerly the liberty of the subject' (568).

The supreme courts of South Africa during this period struggled with the questions that affected courts throughout the Dominions: the relationship between their role as guardians of a rule of law; their function as agencies through which government policies were ultimately enforced; and the overriding need to assist in the protection of the security of new states plagued by insecurity and severe political divisions. I have already discussed the ways in which South African law developed in relation to political conflict and opposition (see part II). This chapter will be devoted to other aspects of the rule of law in South Africa. We shall see that it developed primarily along the racial frontiers: in relation to a racially driven immigration law; to the enormous enterprise of controlling African movement into and rights of residence within urban areas; and to the politically bitter struggle over Asian residence and trade.

Administrative law

In addition the South African courts were living through a period in which a new state was being constructed, growing in size, and increasing the reach of its regulatory activities and ambitions. The large number of major new statutes through which the new state was being made were by and large based on British or other Dominion statutes, and, even when they were not so in content, reproduced their form. This form incorporated ever-growing use of delegated legislation, and the granting by parliaments of wide discretions of a quasi-judicial kind to ministers and subordinate officials. These legal developments which resulted from the growth of the state were not singular to South Africa, and they produced huge challenges for lawyers educated within the Diceyan constitutional world view with its distinctive understanding of the division of powers, and its tendency to deny many of the realities of the new administrative state. Nonetheless there clearly were special characteristics of the growth of the state in South Africa which were distinctive. While a largely British constitutional and legal imagination governed many of the responses, the new state to which South African lawyers were responding had a significantly different focus: race. Consequently a substantial proportion of the legislation under which and cases through which the 'administrative law' was developed concerned the racially discriminatory policies of the new state. While the legal doctrines that developed were familiar and orthodox, they developed in a complex counterpoint to the contexts in which they were enunciated. The judges (and the legal writers) have paid attention to the judicial dicta, and to judicial ruminations, in order to show the development of principles. But it is also important in this area to focus on the particular problems out of which the approach taken by the South African courts developed. It is in these areas that there were the most occasions for clashes between government and courts; between the demands of elected legislatures, both central and local, and the judges' development of principles.

Like the courts in England the South African courts had to attempt to define the limits of their powers to interfere with decisions made by officials. Like the English courts they hesitated as to how far they would go, for example, in finding behaviour so unreasonable that it went beyond lawful authority. They tended to apply tests similar to those in England to a wide range of cases involving planning applications, licences and business dealings between government and private citizens, in which there were no racial considerations. It is useful to look briefly at the ways in which contemporary dilemmas were handled in England in an era riven by class war because the courts in England, like those in South Africa, were driven to search for a form of insulation from politics and to emphasise the internal self-sufficiency, objectivity and logic of law. As early as 1883 the Lord Chancellor, Selborne, proclaimed that judges were 'bound by the law, and . . . not at liberty to place strained constructions upon it even from feelings of *indulgence* which you may entertain towards those whose liberty is in danger' (Stephen 1979: 115 note 51; my emphasis). The English judges' experience of vehement political attack, and the willingness of the English parliament to legislate to reverse the effect of judicial decisions, inclined them towards taking refuge in a formalist disengagement from substantive political content in decision making, and to avoid confrontation with the legislature (see in general Dangerfield 1970; and Stephen 1979: 118ff.). It was from the English judges (who themselves drew it from their hostility to the increase in collectivist social legislation) that the South African judiciary derived the doctrine that existing property rights could not be taken away by parliament unless the language of an Act would admit no other meaning. The *quid pro quo* was to be more accommodating towards other collectivist legislation. In the words of Lord Loreburn, the Liberal Chancellor, in 1910, the House of Lords 'sitting judicially does not sit for the purpose of hearing appeals against Acts of Parliament' (*Vickers Sons and Maxim Ltd v Evans 1910 AC 444* at 445; quoted in Stephen 1979: 168). This approach involved determined use of the literal mode of interpretation to give credence to the appearance of political neutrality. Stephen discusses Lord Haldane's response to the politically sensitive legislation on trade union immunity. In *Vacher and Sons v London Society of Compositers 1913 AC 107* he would not speculate about the intention or 'motive' of parliament. The topic, he said, was not one judges could properly or profitably entertain. They could only construe language. If they tried to go further and entered 'the other province which belongs to those who, in making the laws, have endeavoured to interpret the desire of the country, they are in danger of going astray in a labyrinth to the character of which they have no sufficient guide'. Haldane, says Stephen, was 'the first in a line of liberal intellectual Law Lords who sought to lead the House, and hence the legal system, away from any semblance of competition with the political system' (1979: 220, 222). We may compare Haldane's dictum with that of Innes in *R v Mchlery 1912 AD 199* at 220: 'the discretion to judge what measures are conducive to peace, order and good government lies with the lawgiver and not with the Courts . . . Such a task would be in the highest degree invidious and difficult, and it is fortunate that the spirit of our constitution does not impose it upon the Judges.' As he said explicitly in 1914, 'The functions of a court are to decide the limits of authority, not the manner of its exercise' (*Gertzen v Middelburg Municipality 1914 AD 544* at 556).

The House of Lords in this period also stepped explicitly away from exercising substantive control over administrative decision making. The superior courts, as Cornish and Clark point out, were nowhere equal to the task of non-market allocation. The judges did not like their role in workmen's compensation cases to which they 'brought an elaborate procedure and a heightening of tensions . . . They were accordingly given no equivalent role in the new institutions of social security. Old age pensions, sickness insurance, unemployment insurance, would all breed special tribunals for determining the challenges by claimants to unfavourable decisions by administrators' (1989: 280). In an era of increasing government intervention and regulation the issue of how decisions could be reviewed was complex. Judges, Cornish and Clark write, had to accept bureaucratic decision making and tribunals, and in return claimed to be 'ultimate arbiters upon the scope of legal powers' granted by statutes, and also insisted that quasi-judicial decisions had to adhere to the rules of natural justice (95). In *Board of Education v Rice 1911 AC 179* the House of Lords disclaimed a role in exercising substantive control over discretion, admitting only to the possibility of procedural due process. Even over this they were compliant. As Lord Loreburn put it, administrators had to act in good faith and listen to both sides, but need not 'treat such a question as though it was a trial'. This approach was followed by the South African courts (see Baxter 1984: 542 note 5). In *Local Government Board vs Arlidge 1915 AC 120* Lord Shaw observed: 'That the judiciary should presume to impose its methods on administrative or executive officers is a usurpation. And the assumption that the methods of natural justice are *ex neccesitate* those of courts of justice is wholly unfounded' (138). He was quoted with approval by Solomon in *Fernandez v South African Railways 1926 AD 60* at 69. Of *Arlidge*'s case Stephen remarks that it 'removed any serious threat that the Courts might exercise even procedural due process over Departments of Central Government' (1979: 192).

The period was also characterised by concern over the huge volume of delegated legislation that marked the constitutional development of British states in the early twentieth century. Legislators, judges and commentators worried about the constitutional rectitude of devolving the legislative power to the executive. Early on Innes had even expressed doubts as to whether this could be done: 'Assuming that it can be validly done,' he said, 'it must surely be stated in the clearest and most unambiguous language' (*Crow v Aronson 1902 TS 247* at 256). South Africa's legislators discussed the issues in relation to the kinds of statutes that typically required extensive delegated legislating. In the debate on the Public Health Bill in 1919 members expressed themselves to be 'shy of the continual tendency of the Government to regulate the various activities of the country by means of regulations'; and opposed to the 'very bad system of creating small criminal offences by regulation.' In the following year parliament had before it the Profiteering Bill, which was modelled on the British Profiteering Act. It established a board of control which was given the power to establish reasonable prices and unreasonable profits, to pass regulations and to prosecute for their breach. It was vigorously opposed by Hertzog: 'He would never agree to a Bill which left it up to a tribunal to define a crime as it thought fit'. This could only be done by parliament (Hansard 22/4/20). But as in others areas of South African law these concerns were affected by race. The disquiet about delegated legislation did not apply to legislation concerning Africans. The Native Labour Regulation Act, which parliament had passed in 1911, created, by delegated regulation, an entire empire of control of mine workers, including a separate system of crime and punishment. In 1917 Botha introduced into parliament the first version of the Native Administration Bill (which was eventually to find its way onto the statute book in 1927). It was proposed, he announced, to legislate for African areas entirely by proclamation. Only Merriman had a principled objection to the strategy that 'most of the legislation in regard to segregation was to be done by regulation' (Hansard: 13/3/17; 3/4/17). In 1923 the Urban Areas Act delegated the power to legislate over all areas of African urban life to municipalities. (Most in practice used model regulations drawn up by the Native Affairs Department.) When Hertzog steered the 1927 Native Administration Bill through parliament he made a positive virtue of the fact that all legislation under the Act could henceforth be proclaimed by the Governor-General. He was supported by Smuts. Constitutional defence of the right of the legislature to legislate was weak. It was left to Drummond Chaplin to record that he objected strongly to the House giving to government departments power to make rules according to their discretion. But 'In dealing with legislation relating to natives . . . I cannot think that objection applies so much' (Hansard 29/4/27).

In the courts' judgments during this period it was emphasised that courts were not arbiters of the reasonableness of administrative decisions unless the unreasonableness was so gross and striking that *mala fides* or that the official had not properly applied his mind to the matter could be inferred (see Baxter 1984: 477ff.). This relatively 'hands off' view, deriving from, mainly, the English courts' growing reluctance to interfere with the organs of elected representative governments, was not necessarily satisfactory in responding to the growing tide of racially discriminatory decisions

made under legislation which did not specifically mandate such discrimi-
nations. Much of the development of South African administrative law
arises out of attempts to deal with this problem. South African courts,
already hampered by self-limiting doctrines, were forced to retreat from
attempts to categorise discrimination as unreasonable by the growing tide
of racial legislation, by the increasing frequency of administrative action
which simply assumed that discrimination was justified and by the
determination of legislatures to insist on discrimination in areas in which
there were serious clashes with the judiciary. This story illustrates well the
socially structured nature of reasonableness (see Baxter 1984: 483) and
how what is reasonable can change according to political and social
context. Discrimination against Africans was accepted as reasonable far
more easily than discrimination against coloureds and Asians, but over
the period covered here an extended acceptance of discrimination took
hold. There were, nonetheless, many cases in which discrimination when
not explicitly authorised was rejected by the courts (see Baxter 1984:
505–6 note 136). South African courts were also tied into a particular
style of statutory interpretation by the British constitutional framework
within which they worked. In the first decades of the twentieth century, as
we have seen, the contested nature of the State, and the drive for segregation, produced large numbers of politically contested and contentious
statutes. How these were to be read by the courts was clearly politically
crucial. Establishing and maintaining a 'rule of law' for a largely English
overseas audience and in terms of legal traditions, both English and
Roman-Dutch, which were taken seriously by the legal elites, was not easy
to reconcile with the increasingly shrill demands made by the white
electorate and politicians, nor with the urgent administrative agenda of
state building.

The tactic of reading statutes with close attention to literal meaning
only at first provided a way of limiting the statutory erosion of civil
liberties and of the extension of racial discrimination. But literalism was a
two-edged sword, the most useful edge of which was soon blunted as
parliament became more and more specific and overt in the wording of
statutes. Furthermore the habit of ignoring legislative intention and
purpose was also easily adaptable to a judicial attitude which detached
itself from responsibility for its rulings. In the first decades we can see a
dual and connected process in which the judiciary began cautiously and
became more creative and bold in relation to the development of private

law, but in relation to public law, after beginning bravely, became more timorous. While it continued to maintain an attachment not just to legalism but to an accompanying set of values, in relation to the criminal law, an inhibited formalism came to dominate its approach to statutory interpretation and administrative law.

The English case of *Kruse v Johnson 1898 2 QB 91* provided a framework for the South African judiciary in confronting their dilemma of how to react to delegated legislation. But it was one full of dangers, offering both the opportunity for activism and the justification for restraint. In a passage frequently referred to, Lord Russell admitted that there might be cases in which courts might have to find by-laws invalid on the grounds of unreasonableness.

> But unreasonable in what sense? If, for instance, they were found to be partial or unequal in their operation as between different classes; if they were manifestly unjust; if they disclosed bad faith; if they involved oppressive or gratuitous interference with the rights of those subject to them as could find no justification in the minds of reasonable men, the Court might well say 'Parliament never intended to give authority to make such rules; they are unreasonable and *ultra vires*'. But it is in this sense, and in this sense only . . . that the question of unreasonableness can properly be regarded. A by-law is not unreasonable merely because a particular judge may think it goes further than is prudent, or necessary or convenient. (99–100)[1]

Russell's formulation was intended to limit the cases in which intervention of the courts would be legitimate by describing a series of uncommon characteristics. But in the South African context partial and unequal operation between different classes, far from being uncommon, was often intended, and oppressive and gratuitous interference with rights, and racial discrimination, often appeared to administrators and judges to be simply common sense. This made the application of the formula somewhat unpredictable. It could be argued that Russell had formulated a necessary accommodation by the courts to the process of the democratisation of British government during the latter part of the nineteenth century. In considering the by-laws of 'public representative bodies', he said, 'they ought to be supported where possible . . . "benevolently" interpreted' (91). 'Surely it is not too much to say', he went on,

---

[1] For comprehensive references to the application of this formulation by the South African courts see Baxter 1984: 479 note 13.

'that in matters which directly and mainly concern the people of the country, who have the right to choose those best fitted to represent them in their local government bodies, such representatives may be trusted to understand their own requirements better than the judges' (99). This was a new path. As the dissenting judge pointed out there were no precedents for this view (111). But transported to South Africa, Russell's precept meant that the judges had to accept white legislatures and councils as legitimately representative of the population as a whole. In their frequent invocations, it was the verbal formula, not the philosophy, that they applied.

The Kruse test, as Baxter points out (479 note 13), was applied to all sorts of delegated legislation. But it was not applied to the exercise of discretion by a minister. Stratford formulated it in this way in 1928: 'The unreasonableness of a Minister . . . affords no grounds for a Court's interference with the exercise of his discretion.' The unreasonableness had to be 'so gross that something else can be inferred from it, either that it is "inexplicable except on the assumption of *mala fide* or ulterior motive" . . . or that it amounts to proof that the person on whom the discretion is conferred has not applied his mind to the matter' (*Union Government v Union Steel Corporation (South Africa) Ltd 1928 AD 220* at 236–7; see also *Sachs v Minister of Justice 1934 AD 11* above).

In *JCI Investments Co. v Johannesburg Town Council 1903 TS 111* Innes set out, in a judgment which was to be much quoted in the future, the attitude of the Supreme Court towards the review of decisions made by administrative bodies. The broader context of the case needs to be considered. One of the major grievances of the opposition in the mining and commercial worlds to the administration of Kruger's Republic was the laxity and corruption of administration. (see Marais 1961). One of the major promises of Milner's new regime was administrative efficiency and integrity, and the new Transvaal Supreme Court was to be seen as a guarantor of the new order. The case concerned an application to have valuations made by a valuation court reviewed on the grounds that they were excessive. In a sweeping statement, for which he gave no authority, Innes asserted that the right to review, set aside and correct decisions was 'a right inherent in the Court' (115). However he decided that in the absence of irregularity the court could not correct a decision not made by a court of record. Solomon dissented at the narrowness of the position taken. The court, he said, had no right to limit the full meaning of the word 'review' (126). But apart from its immediate context, the case marks an effective beginning of a long history of the attitude of South African courts to administrative jurisdiction. In Innes's case, as in the attitude he subsequently developed towards the discretions of officials, it was a story marked by wide dicta asserting the scope and power of review, combined with a narrower reluctance actually to exercise the powers claimed.[2]

Another issue of huge importance in the growing administrative state, with its separate racial empires, was how far the courts would claim control over the administrative decisions of officials. The Transvaal court had to consider this in the context of the racially charged question of the presence of Chinese labourers. The relevant laws gave powers to the Superintendent of Labour to order the return to the country of origin of 'any labourer who he has reasonable grounds to believe is a danger to the exercise of proper control of labourers in any mine'. If the man refused to go he could be arrested without warrant and brought before a magistrate for confirmation of the order. Li Kui Yu was arrested and deported, after he was denied access to friends or lawyers and to a court. Mason observed that the ordinances conferred 'enormous powers' on officials, and that it was their duty 'to keep strictly within these powers'. It was the 'absolute duty' of the court 'to see that laws of this kind are not stretched beyond the powers which they really give and are intended to give'. None of the officials had the power under the law to use force. 'One can quite understand why such a power should not be put even into the hands of officials, as distinguished from a judicial authority.' He ordered the reversal of what he called a 'tyrannical exercise of power'. Li Kui Yu was returned from Natal so that he might go through the deportation process required by the ordinances (*Li Kui Yu v Superintendent of Labourers 1906 TS 181*, at 185–7). A similar attitude was taken in *Ho Si v Vernon 1909 TS 1074*. While legislation required Asians to produce their certificate on

---

[2] The supreme courts were also not eager to interfere with other judicial sub-systems. The Prisons and Reformatories Act, for example, gave to the Superintendent of Prisons powers to try offences by his officers. A right of appeal lay to the Minister. What was contemplated, said the court, was not a judicial proceeding, but an 'administrative discipline', which could not be overruled by the courts (*R v Digue 1922 TPD 312*). This question of the nature of administratively created boards of enquiry was confronted by the Appellate Division in *Dabner v South African Railways and Harbours 1920 AD 583*. Innes ruled that a 'Statutory Board' created by the Railways and Harbours Act, no. 28 of 1912, was 'not a judicial tribunal' but a 'domestic tribunal' and that there was no authority establishing a right of legal representation before tribunals other than courts. (I have not found any sign that the law societies or the Bar commented on this restriction.)

demand by a police officer, the court found illegal the practice of forcibly entering a house to demand it. Such entry was not provided for in the legislation, said Innes. 'These are disabling Acts, and, as the Court has pointed out over and over again, must be strictly construed' (1077, 1080).

Nonetheless the tradition of judicial interpretation which bent towards the liberty of the subject was adhered to with differing degrees of enthusiasm. Wessels contended in *Sodha v Rex 1911 TPD 52* that the rule that statutes should be interpreted

> in favour of the liberty of the subject [is] a well known rule of interpretation; but it is one which we must deal with very carefully . . . If it is used to show the sympathy of the Court with certain individuals, or for the purpose of conforming to ideas which may be prevalent for the moment, then it is certainly a very dangerous method of interpretation. If, however, that rule of interpretation is restricted in this way – that the Court will not presume that the Legislature intended to curtail the rights of citizens – then it is a sound rule.

Otherwise, he went on, the court 'might allow itself to be savaged by popular clamour or by sympathy for individuals it considered to have been badly treated by the Legislature; and these are not the functions of a Court of law' (55–6).

The issues of bringing officials' power within the law (and of Wessels' attitudes) came up shortly after Union in the *cause célèbre* of *Whittaker v Roos and Bateman 1912 AD 92*. The plaintiffs had been arrested during unrest on the Reef, accused of placing dynamite on the tram tracks. They were segregated in solitary confinement in punishment cells, without access to legal advisers or visitors for a period of six weeks prior to their trial. They were later acquitted, and brought an action for damages against the Prisons Department. Wessels in the Transvaal court was unsympathetic. He thought they were 'not persons with whom we ought to sympathise'. In the Appellate Division, however, the three senior judges, de Villiers, Solomon and Innes, strongly rebuked both Wessels and the government. The principle, to Innes, was unlawful abuse of authority. Punishment and deprivation of rights could only begin after the guilt of a person had been established by a court of law. In private correspondence Wessels castigated his appellate colleagues as showing 'Pickwickian innocence and simplicity' and 'credulity' (see Katz 1976: 313). Most importantly, however, Whittaker and his co-plaintiff, Morant, were white. The case arose out of white political conflict. It was the occasion for a very strongly worded attempt to establish a rule of law in a new state by reigning in the abuse of powers by state officials. Its dicta would live on, sometimes invoked, sometimes not.

Like judges elsewhere the South African Bench expressed its growing dismay over the design of modern statutes. The question of immigration was one of the areas of contention between judiciary and executive. Decisions about the rights of individuals to enter the country always involved the exercise of a discretion, and these decisions were taken in a highly racially charged atmosphere, under the authority of statutes which had racial motivations, but avoided racial wording. Clearly the judges themselves could not make the decisions in the first instance. But what sort of control or review could they exercise? But prior to that was another question. For the executive tried, so far as it could, to exclude the judiciary from a role in immigration decisions. Section 3 of the Immigration Act provided that 'except on a question of law reserved by a Board' no court should have jurisdiction in relation to any order, restriction, removal or detention; and could not review, reverse or interdict any order of a board. In *Ismail v Union Government and Registrar of Asiatics 1912 AD 605* Innes expressed his concern:

> I fully share the view which the Judges, both here and in England, have of late years frequently had occasion to express as to the dangerous latitude to which the practice of passing skeleton statutes, leaving all the operative machinery to be supported by regulations, and giving the widest discretion to administrative officials, has of late years extended . . . the tendency, and apparently in some cases the design, is to supplant the function of both the Legislature and the Judiciary by the action of the Executive. (617–18)

He returned to the question in *Shidiack v Union Government (Minister of Interior) 1912 AD 642*. Here, though it did not affect the ultimate result of the case, which was the exclusion of the appellant's children from the country, the court found that where the statute required that the Minister be satisfied in relation to evaluation of an education test, regulations providing for the satisfaction of a subordinate official were *ultra vires*. There was, said Innes, 'a growing tendency in modern legislation to clothe with finality the decisions of public officials in matters which seriously affect the rights of the public, a tendency probably due to the increasing power and influence of Departmental officials. The effect is in such matters to oust the jurisdiction of the Courts.' Attention had recently been drawn to this question, he went on, by high judicial authority in England. It could lead to a 'serious menace' to the liberty of the subject. Nonetheless, as he was obliged to acknowledge, the court could not assert a jurisdiction which had been taken away (653).

The huge increase in the powers of administrators over the lives of ordinary people contained in the Urban Affairs Act of 1923 also created a potential for an active interventionist review by the courts of the ways in which these powers were exercised. In accordance with their earlier willingness to review 'judicial' proceedings they could well have classified the process before which a person could be banished from an urban area to a work colony as 'judicial'. But as we have seen above in *Hashe*'s case they declined to do so. The Urban Areas Act generated an enormous amount of subordinate legislation, regulations and by-laws, and consequently much litigation and many rulings on questions of validity, interpretation, the powers of officials and administrative law matters generally. The controls and limitations put on the urban residence of Africans thus contributed hugely to the making of South African law in a general sense. When one considers the overall framework and purpose of the legalism of the Urban Affairs apparatus one is struck by its use as an instrument of imposing uniformity of regulation on the many local authorities in the country. Regulations, centrally drafted, covered virtually every matter. While legal adjudication of the breach of many could not but give rise to the defence of some rights by decisions by the courts which limited official powers in specific instances, the overall effect was to put in place a mechanism of detailed control the elements and details of which were substantially the same for all urban areas. This extended the control of central government and ensured that all urban authorities operated the same system of controls. The role of the law, as I have observed already, was to create, regularise and authorise power, rather than to restrict it. In the years immediately following the passing of the Urban Areas Act the courts ruled that areas for African residence could not be proclaimed, nor people forced to live in them where no adequate residential accommodation yet existed. The Act gave great powers to local authorities to make regulations to control the condition and terms of residence, the management and control of locations, erection of buildings, the nature of services provided, the control of movement into and out of locations, the control of meetings, and the provision of penalties. In many areas breaches of even minor regulations could result in ejection and loss of the right of residence. It was part of the structure of the Act, in other words, that it produced a large number of detailed by-laws, relatively inaccessible, and often very broadly drawn, conferring great powers on local officials, and giving them wide discretions. (Though Section 23 of the Act provided that local authorities 'shall cause' the regulations to be translated into the African languages used in the area and copies posted in conspicuous places, this was held by the Appellate Division to be directory and not imperative, and non-compliance did not render the regulations invalid (Davis et al. 1959: 70).)

In 1930 (Act 25, sec. 19) parliament specifically gave powers to impose a general curfew. The Governor-General, at the request of a local authority, could declare that no African could be in any public place during any night hours specified without a permit signed by an employer. Tindall was to remark in 1930, reflecting on the loose and wide drafting current in regulations that 'the present practice of legislating by means of regulations might well be accompanied with the same care in drafting that is bestowed on the statute under which the regulations are made' (*Tshelza v Brakpan Municipality 1930 TPD 734*). It was a pious hope. In the nature of things, few were ever challenged. Regulations in law had to be consistent with the Act, and to determine whether they were the Appellate Division had ruled that the whole of the enabling statute must be looked at to determine what the intention of the legislature was (*Louvis v Municipality of Roodepoort-Maraisburg 1916 AD*). While the courts troubled themselves about whether the power had to be expressly given, or whether 'necessary implication' was sufficient, or whether powers which were 'reasonably ancillary' would be implied (66), they were not quick to rule that local authorities had exceeded their powers under the Act. The spirit of the approach may be summed up in van der Heever's test that courts, before 'interfering . . . must find that the subordinate legislature acted in a manner which the delegating authority could not have contemplated' (*R v Humphreys 1939 OPD 163*). In relation to the Urban Affairs Act, in which the contemplation in terms of policy of the Act was very wide, this was not much of a constraint, certainly a far lesser one than 'necessary implication'. It was generally the case that the superintendent of a location, or similar official, was given power by regulation to authorise who should enter or remain and to eject those he considered undesirable. These very far-reaching powers were not restricted in their administration by the superior courts. In the leading case of *Smith v Germiston Munici-*

pality the court showed how far a reasonably implied power could be taken (see below). In *Tutu and others v Municipality of Kimberley 1918–23 GWLD 64* the court considered a regulation empowering the superintendent not only to remove people from an area, but to order their huts destroyed if they were not moved within twenty-four hours. The regulation, the court said, was neither *ultra vires* nor unreasonable. Municipal by-laws ought to be supported where possible, it said, and credit should be given that those who had to administer them would do so reasonably. The conferring of arbitrary and despotic powers was not sufficient to make a by-law unreasonable, unless it was shown that the laws were arbitrarily and unreasonably exercised. A regulation making persons using alcohol liable to expulsion was held to be within the power 'to make regulations for the effectual supervision of such locations' (*Sdumbu v Benoni Municipality 1923 TPD 289*). Regulations could also confer wide discretionary powers on officials. Courts allowed these where a skilled official had to bring judgement to bear on a complicated situation; and where actual circumstances could be said to require immediate decisions (*Farah v Johannesburg Municipality 1928 TPD 169*). (In general see Davis et al. 1959.)

In 1927 Lourie published a overview of 'Administrative Law in South Africa', the first such treatment the subject had ever been given (Lourie 1927). He noted how the growth in the modern state had collapsed the Diceyan paradigm, and that Dicey's concept of the rule of law had been diminished in all English-speaking countries by the giving of quasi-judicial authority to officials. All these states had given officials duties of management of new and wide-ranging kinds, and had passed statutes in a form that frequently excluded the jurisdiction of the Courts over the discretions exercised. He noted that the development of South African law had been along English patterns so far as principles went, but that there were differences in the nature of the areas which attracted state supervision. Mines, in South Africa, were 'a favourite subject of administrative supervision', as were immigration, irrigation, phthisis compensation, police, civil service and licensing. Within the general framework of English administrative law, the specifics of the South African legal culture in this area developed around the elemental connections between race and issues of public policy. It was in immigration regulation that 'executive freedom from judicial control reaches its greatest extent', and many of the principles of South African administrative law had been established in conflicts on this terrain. Section 3 of the Immigration Act of 1913, he noted, excluded the jurisdiction of the courts in more emphatic terms than any other statute. In a series of cases in this area the courts had had to acknowledge that jurisdiction had been lost. This was, to Lourie, 'natural' because 'matters of public policy . . . outside the domain of the Courts are here a primary consideration' (12). The issue of policy was, of course, the racial make-up of the Union's population. He also commented on the growing number of cases 'peculiar to South Africa' where the official or quasi-judicial body had allowed itself, without statutory authorisation, to be guided by racial considerations (16). The courts, as Lourie said, would not necessarily assume that the power to discriminate racially had been given by the statute. Yet in *Padsha*'s case (see below) the Appellate Division had accepted that the terms 'economic grounds or on account of standard or habits of life' allowed explicit racial discrimination against all Asians. Thus while on the one hand the South African courts developed an administrative law along English lines, this was increasingly one that, like that in England, took the courts out of the way of administrative authority. And in the circumstances peculiar to South Africa, in an ever-intensifying racialisation of public policy, it was implicit that an administrative law would develop which virtually excluded blacks from judicial supervision of the power exercised over them. While therefore it was true to say that the South African courts had 'not been slow to express their dislike of the vast extension of the powers and functions of the executive' which had been 'accompanied often enough by a derogation from their own function' (23), they accepted the extension of power and the derogation from function far more readily when it related to the exercise of state control over all but whites.

Lourie's analysis was a sign of growing professional concern about administrative law. 'The mass of regulations is in itself of startling proportions,' said the *South African Law Times* in May 1933, 'professional opinion on the subject can hardly be said to have formed. We are still groping in the dark. Meanwhile the flood of administrative law and regulation threatens to engulf us.' The editorial expressed no fear of 'undue exercise of power', but stressed the need for 'certainty and uniformity'. Like Lourie, the writer thought that the Diceyan view that administrative law was a matter for the ordinary courts had become outmoded, and he concluded that 'the time had come, and the need was there, for the setting up of a special tribunal'. This was not done. Indeed such a suggestion was seen by many as a threat to the entire structure of the legal system. A leading barrister linked the recent appointments of civil servants to the Bench and the 'removal of important legal questions from the Bench to departmental tribunals' as 'being importations from the Continental system' which differed completely from that prevailing in Britain and South Africa. As Kennedy and Schlosberg remarked two years later, the system of administrative law was 'almost in its infancy in South Africa' and was 'divorced from the general rule of law' (1935: 420).

Asian traders: joining the discourses

If we are to appreciate the making of the South African rule of law we must hear voices other than those of the judges, and listen to, as I have said, politicians, the administrators and the public. This process can be illustrated by focusing on one of the major areas in which the principles of administrative law came into conflict with the racial imperatives of South African politics and society – the growing attempts to limit the rights of Asian traders. The problems in maintaining a court-inspired 'rule of law' in the face of a political determination to discriminate racially were dramatically illustrated. For here the issues were to some extent different from those affecting legal discrimination against Africans. Asians could not be relegated to a different, backward state of civilisation; they did not have chiefs and customary laws and reserves through which a veneer of justification for the application of different legal principles could be justified by the white legal system. In the Transvaal, where much of this legal struggle was fought out, they were part of the urban community, actively integrated into its commercial life. In 1904 the Transvaal Supreme Court ruled that instructions given by the government to revenue officers to refuse licences to Asian traders were illegal, and that no discretion existed to refuse anyone who tendered payment of the licence money. The attempt to exclude Asians revealed much about the spirit of the new British administration of the Transvaal. In spite of Law no. 3 of 1885 providing for segregation of Asians 'for sanitary purposes', Motan had traded before 1899 outside the area designated for Indian residence. The new government turned down his licence application, citing the 1885 law (*Motan Habib v Transvaal Government 1904 TS*). Innes said that statutes imposing serious disabilities had to be strictly interpreted. The old Transvaal view had been that because of the provision in the *grondwet* (constitution) that there was to be no racial equality, the law should be interpreted against Asians rather than in their favour (410). This view could no longer be argued. He concluded: 'It does strike me as remarkable that, without fresh legislation, the officials of the Crown in the Transvaal should put forward a claim which the Government of the Crown in England has always contended was illegal under the statute' (412). The government of the Transvaal duly responded legislatively. The Transvaal Local Government Ordinance (section 90e) gave to municipal councils powers to refuse licences to trade 'if in the opinion of the Council the applicant is not a desirable person'. The jurisdiction of the Supreme Court was excluded: appeal lay only to a magistrate. Consistent refusal of licence applications followed.

This was one part of the story. The other was the continuation in force of the Republican Gold Law which prohibited non-white occupation of proclaimed areas on the Reef. Given the situation on the Reef both before and after the war an absolute prohibition had been impossible to enforce. This was recognised under the revised version of the Act in 1908 which allowed the mining commissioner to permit occupation where vested rights had been established. The intense struggle that followed over rights of residence, rights to license to trade, immigration, the status of Indian marriages, and the intervention of the imperial government cannot be related fully in this book (see Joshi 1942; Pachai 1971). I shall take up the story with the settlement arrived at in which the Union government, while retaining the framework of discriminatory laws against Asian trade and residence in Natal and the Transvaal, undertook to respect the 'vested rights' existing, though it was not made clear what this meant. After that, within the framework of the licensing laws and the *Motan* decision, many new Indian businesses were opened. White-controlled municipalities resisted, and the struggle was fought on two legal grounds, the right to occupy land and the right to trading licences. Magistrates, to the chagrin of local councils, were capable of taking a formalist view of council reversal of licences, and appeals to them sometimes succeeded (SC 11 1919). Municipalities then had resort to the Gold Law to try to deny Indian merchants access to premises.

At the same time ways were being found to frustrate the racial bans on occupation of land. One practice was to register the title in the name of a white person, while the Indian 'owner' held a mortgage bearing no interest for the full value of the property. This was succeeded as a practice by the neater procedure of forming a limited company with Indian shareholders, and acquiring the title to the land in the name of the company. It was a legal device, according to evidence given to parliament, learned from practice in Japan, where law forbade Europeans owning land, and from British-ruled Singapore, which had similar prohibitions on Chinese land ownership (SC 11 1919: 23–4; evidence of Julius Wertheim). Three hundred and seventy such companies were formed in the Transvaal between 1913 and 1919. White reaction was quick and powerful. A federation of ratepayers' associations was formed to maintain the status quo. Hitherto, they pointed out, the law had been strong enough to prevent Indians acquiring land for trading purposes and it had been supported by the practice of the large township companies which had included in their title deeds provisions making it illegal to transfer or sublet leasehold stands to Indians, or allowing them to trade or live on them. In 1916 the Transvaal Supreme Court had declined to intervene, following the view taken by the English courts about German-dominated companies, that a company was an entity which had no nationality, and that there could be no enquiry into the nationality of shareholders (*Reynolds v Oosthuizen 1916 WLD 103*). The ratepayers' associations responded hysterically. If the device of using companies was legitimate, they claimed, touching on a wider and more hallowed question, 'there is every reason to believe they will be equally successful against the white farmer. There is nothing to stop the Indians there . . . there will be an end to the white farmer' (30–1). There was agitation not only for an amendment to the Companies Act, but for the application to the Indian companies of legislation on the model of the trading with the enemy laws which had applied to German companies, so that the Indian landholding companies could be compulsorily wound up. Forms of confiscation and forfeiture were often suggested, but on the whole respect for property rights was to prevail.

There were approximately 150,000 Indians in the Union, of whom, according to the 1921 census, only 13,405 were resident in the Transvaal. Further immigration, and inter-provincial immigration, were prohibited. Nonetheless the issue was presented by white agitation in terms of a battle on the frontiers for racial existence. Wertheim told the select committee:

> We are concerned with the economic side of the whole question and I do not think that it is quite right to say that we object to their colour. It all

opens up a very big question – the question of white versus coloured, the question of how the white man is to exist properly as against another person . . . who is able to under sell and under live him. (SC 11 1919: 33)

Another witness likewise cast the issue of trading licences in terms of whether South Africa was to be a white man's country. 'We are holding the borders of the white man's area' (34).

At heart what was at stake appeared to be commercial competition. One local Member of Parliament observed that farmers and other consumers generally dealt largely with Asian traders because they were cheaper (38). South African common law was premised on contractual freedom and market principles. But the premise did not seem relevant to economic competition between races. 'The Indian', Wertheim asserted, 'should not be allowed to enter into competition with the white man' (33). Krause, who represented the Indian traders before the parliamentary enquiry, pointed to the contradictions. 'Until such time as our economic ideas regarding competition have entirely altered', he argued, 'competition [is] the soul of any community'. Without it you had monopoly and there was 'a pretty general feeling that monopolies are responsible for high prices, and are in conflict with public interest'. His clients, he said, 'do not understand what you mean by unfair competition' (46ff.). Undercutting the rhetoric about holding the white man's borders, Krause posed the issue as being one in which traders on the town councils (in this case Krugersdorp) were 'really taking action against rival traders' (73). But theorising about economics did not seem to interest the Members of Parliament. One asked whether Indians ate meat; another how many were enlisted for military service (73). One should also perhaps not overestimate the simple question of economic competition. As in so many discussions on law and policy attention strayed, as we have seen, to race conflict as a whole, and to matters of sexual relations between white and non-white. On behalf of the Johannesburg ratepayers Wertheim said that there were public objections to dealings between Indian hawkers and white housewives involving the extension of credit. 'It leads to closer intercourse between the white housewife and the Indian and to greater familiarity than seems wise in the absence of her husband' (28). The extension of credit itself was seen as having the potential to undermine proper race relations. 'Where an Asiatic gives credit to the young people it has a bad effect, because immediately they owe him money he treats them as social equals' (SC 7 1930: 19). There was objection to the extension of credit by Asians to the group whose status was most at risk, the poor whites (40). In 1930 T. H. Leslie, objecting to Asian traders on behalf of the Vereeniging town council, told the select committee that Asian traders employed white girls who worked 'cheek by jowl with coloured men. Such girls must, eventually, lose their sense of superiority over the Asiatics' (SC 7 1930: 9–10). The danger spread beyond Indians, weakening the whole white position. 'Do they [the government of India] realise', asked Major Rood, 'there is a danger in allowing the Indians to mix too freely with the Europeans here and that that feeling of superiority which we have over the native may gradually disappear and endanger our social position' (233). Furthermore, the upsetting threats to status operated also at the other end of the social spectrum. Indian traders, it was said, had an unfair advantage because they were too nice to Africans. 'The native likes to go into their shops because he is allowed to sit on the counter and talk and take his time . . . and he enjoys himself' (40). It is in this atmosphere of wide-spread racism, and fierce competition for shares of the urban consumer trade, that much of South African administrative law was born. As with the immigration cases, the flourishing of non-racial judicial dicta and the development of principles from the surrounding penumbra of English administrative law operated within the context of widespread anti-Asian sentiment and the willingness of parliament to legislate to support it.

It is worth pursuing further the question of Asian trade and land-holding in the Transvaal for through it a number of important themes can be illustrated. We may come back to the point made earlier about the efforts that had to be made at official levels to impose racial separation. Once again we can see a drive to segregate on a number of official and political levels and official deployment or support for racist rhetoric, in the face of a persistent tendency of many of all races to ignore the official pressures. In the case of the Transvaal this extended also to local admin-istration. There were difficulties in administrative enforcement of politi-cally inspired legislation to separate the races. Huge administrative tasks were imposed by the scope of detailed intervention required, for which the existing administrative and policing machinery were not always adequate. There was no congruence between statute law and enforcement; or between court decisions and legal policy; or between statute law and court decisions and the facts on the ground. The languages of adminis-trative law, of policy and of politics were all different. In 1930 a parliamentary select committee took upon itself the task of reviewing how far the intentions of parliament 'indicated' in Act 37 of 1919 had been given effect to (SC 7 1930: vi). They found that there was a 'serious' position in that between 60 and 75 per cent of trading licences had been issued to people in illegal occupation of premises. While Act 37 of 1919 had protected vested interests, 'ever since . . . there has been no effective enforcement of the existing laws to restrict Asiatic occupation and trade . . . laxity on the part of the authorities cannot constitute a valid exercise for breaking the law' (vii). They complained that 'there can be no doubt that failure to enforce the law has been largely due to defects in the machinery of administration. No department of State hitherto considered itself to be entrusted with the duty to guard the public interest against contraventions, members of the public, individually and collectively, were averse to risking costly litigation' (viii). More specifically there were objections to the use of the legal system by Asians, which was characterised as illegitimate. Leslie for the Transvaal Municipal Association remonstrated that 'very large sums of money have been spent by Europeans and Asiatics in fighting cases in the Law Courts, and it is thought that Government should put a stop to such fighting in the same way as it would put a stop to any other fighting between sections of the community' (10). While litigation as a form of political unrest was bad enough, it had had other yet worse consequences. 'The effect of the cases fought in the Courts has been mainly to entrench the Asians more firmly than ever amongst the Europeans by defining rights on their behalf which were hitherto never clearly defined' (ibid.).

The president of the Transvaal Municipal Association, H. J. Crocker, referred with approval to the continuity and legitimacy of policy in the Transvaal, dating from republican legislation, which was to refuse to allow non-whites to own land in towns. He complained that the situation in which race alone could no longer be the grounds for a refusal of a licence to trade defeated the 'real intention' of the laws, which should now be made 'clear and unmistakable'. Leslie also endorsed 'the Republican standards' in relations between Europeans and Asians. The regrettable fact that they had not been maintained was the fault of the courts, which had decided that segregation applied to residence, and not trading, and had allowed the exploitation of other 'loopholes' (11). Europeans, Leslie said, were determined to oust the Asian, and like Crocker he wanted racial criteria made explicit in legislation. Court decisions, he said, 'are always in favour of the Asiatic . . . We have been so far misled in trying to make laws in which we were not honest. We have given the municipalities certain powers, but the Asiatic was never specifically mentioned. If we had done what we intended in the open we would never have had this trouble' (10).

Legislative attempts had been made to reverse the effects of the courts' decisions in reviewing the refusal of licences by the authorities. In 1926 the General Dealers Control Ordinance went further than the Local Government Ordinance. An application for a new licence could now be refused without reasons being given. 'Now nothing could be stronger than that,' said M. G. Nicolson, the secretary of the Transvaal Municipal Associations (15). But expectations were disappointed. Councils began to refuse licences, and decisions were contested. Some litigation by Asians was withdrawn because of lack of funds, but finally the Transvaal court had ruled that discretion was not properly exercised where it was clear that it had been exercised on racial grounds alone. 'We immediately recognised', Nicolson went on, 'that the provision was not worth the paper it was written on.' Frustrating applicants by simply not acting administratively was one course open. The Johannesburg city council simply deferred acting on licence applications made under the General Dealers Ordinance.

The victories gained by Asian traders in the courts had exposed some of the limitations of the white public's attachment to the rule of law. They suggest that even in cases that did not arise from extremes of political conflict, such as the Rand rebellion, the legitimacy of the courts' decisions was not easily accepted. The use of the power of parliament to command the courts to reach the desired results appeared the natural course. 'These people are continually creeping beyond the intention of the law,' M. D. Harrison told the 1930 committee. 'We appeal for the protection which the ordinary interpretation of the law seems to entitle us.' Rood, far from impressed by court decisions that Indians were within their rights under the law, claimed that they had found 'unusual and ingenious ways' of avoiding the principles of the law of 1885. 'They have evaded the law in respect of this question of purchase of land by means of what one can only call subterfuge. I do not think that anyone can question that: they may have acted within the four corners of the law, but anyone will admit that what they did was done by means of subterfuge' (339).

In Act no. 37 of 1919 parliament had sought to address the outcry by whites about the growth of the numbers of Asian-controlled companies acquiring land and escaping from the provisions of the Gold Law, by laying down that the controlling interest in a landholding company must be European. But it had not affected European nominees holding for Asian principals, nor addressed the situation in which Asians controlled by virtue of retaining and exercising management. Also, as Harrison said, 'one of the weaknesses of the [Act] lies in the fact that it is left to any member of the public to initiate action. The public in general is averse to entering into what may prove to be most costly litigation' (43). Several senior state officials who gave evidence to the 1930 select committee made it quite clear that they sympathised with what they, and the white public, thought was the purpose of the law, and were quite out of sympathy with the courts, but complained that the law gave them no adequate means of enforcement. The Registrar of Deeds pointed out that he had no access to information about the make-up of companies which applied to register land holdings, though the Registrar of Companies passed on to him information which 'may be at his disposal' when Indians had an interest. 'He is not compelled to furnish me with such information; it is merely an understanding between us' (94). He had no sympathies with the legalities. The law was a 'farce'. Worse still, said the Registrar of Deeds, many attorneys sympathised with Indians. 'Why should I worry about a man's race', one said, 'if that was a requirement it would be stated in the Act?' A personal friend of his had acted as a conveyancer for Indian clients. When reproached for assisting evasion, 'he admitted that although morally they were wrong, legally they were right'. Companies, the Registrar urged, should have to make six monthly returns of shareholders and it should be made a criminal offence for a European to transfer his shares to an Asiatic (95–6). The Registrar of Companies spoke to the committee of the great difficulties in controlling the racial character of companies, the problem of share transfers and the problem of the character of foreign companies. It all seemed too hard. 'I suppose Indians desire to acquire property in order they may carry on business . . . I would say that my own view of a satisfactory solution is expulsion from the country. If you cannot expel them you cannot prevent them from earning a living.' For him it was a dilemma. If the law was amended to criminalise the holding by Europeans of shares on the behalf of Indians 'it would create a few more criminals'. The penalty of confiscation of property of Europeans holding on behalf of Indians would be 'a very grave risk . . . but . . . can we do that?' (276–7).

The Commissioner for Immigration and Asiatic Affairs was no more sympathetic towards Asians. What he had to say pointed up the grievances of whites. To them it was clear, and right, that public policy was discriminatory, and that the law ought to support it. Inasmuch as Indians resisted by invoking what remained of their legal rights, they were, he complained, acting outside of the 'spirit' of the law, and were therefore at fault. A 'certain section' of the Indian community resented 'any differentiation' between themselves and Europeans and were 'determined to press every advantage . . . to evade any laws . . . Undoubtedly they want to make it as difficult as possible to carry out those laws restricting them. It is almost second nature with a certain class of Indian to try to beat the law' (269). He became a little carried away. 'There are Indians who at times will do an illegal act to obtain something which he could obtain quite legally without any trouble at all' (ibid.). Giving evidence on behalf of the Indian community P. K. Desai asked:

> Is it a matter for surprise that a class whose natural and healthy energies are suppressed by artificial restrictions should seek by ingenious devices to find loopholes and vents through which to overcome them? Legislation may properly be directed to the eradication of pests; towards the suppression and correction of crime and immorality. Are we a pest? Are we criminal? (163)

From across the spectrum of the official community the answer was a resounding 'yes'.[3]

The complaints against the law and the courts came, then, not just from potential trading competitors, or the white public and their political representatives, but from the highest levels of the Civil Service who felt frustrated in their efforts to carry out what they saw as 'policy'. In such a climate there was little scope for a defence. The Acting Agent of the Government of India in South Africa, J. D. Tyson, pointed out that there were only 4,324 Indians engaged in trade in the Transvaal, a small figure in relation to the hysteria about infiltration (283). No Transvaal government had ever, as a 'matter of fact', seriously enforced the segregation laws

---

[3] Official fantasies about a 'solution to the Indian problem' burgeoned. An enquiry was set up to determine where the Union's Indian population (80 per cent of which was South African born) should be re-settled. Overseas Indians, it observed, 'have for the most part remained outside the circle of citizenship in their new homes' (UG 23 1934: 5). Recommending North Borneo, New Guinea and Guyana as places to which South Africa's Indians could go, the committee concluded that the place for Indians in South Africa's economy was 'gradually closing'.

against Indians: not after the law of 1885; nor after the Gold Law of 1908; nor again after the law of 1919. It was because the authorities had never enforced the law that vested interests had grown, even since 1919. If they were not protected, he said, there would be a 'certainty of dissipating the atmosphere of inter-dominion understanding' (310–11). Whenever there were laws restrictive of elementary rights purely on the grounds of race, he said, 'a certain resistance' had to be expected. There could be no complaint, he thought, if the resistance was legal. 'It would be a pity to grudge the Indian his right of appeal to the Courts . . . certain witnesses seem to grudge the Indian recourse . . . because the Indian gets fair play and sometimes wins his case' (296). The General Dealers Ordinance, he noted, 'places enormous power in the hands of the class from whom the Indians' trade rivals are drawn' (297).

In 1932 parliament responded by amending the 1919 Act. Vested rights acquired before May 1930 were recognised. Ways of getting around the provisions of the 1919 Act were attacked: the expression 'fixed property' was extended to mortgage bonds to the value of more than half of the value of the property at the time of the registration of the bond, and leases in excess of ten years, and holding property on behalf of Asians or Asian companies were proscribed. Property registered in the name of Asians or Asian companies in contravention of the law was in the future to be declared forfeit to the state unless it was transferred to a European.

Under the amended Transvaal Ordinance, no. 11 of 1925 an applicant for a licence had to obtain a certificate of suitability from the local authority or licensing board. Local authorities had no hesitation in refusing certificates on racial grounds. Could they be overturned? In terms of Innes's often-quoted judgment in *Shidiack*'s case (above), they could not. There the court had said that the reasonableness of a decision was not a matter which the court could review. Unless bad faith could be shown, it could not be set aside. This decision had been reluctantly made in an immigration case in which the jurisdiction of the courts had been aggressively excluded. But the dictum was endorsed sixteen years later by the Appellate Division in another context when Stratford said that the 'law does not protect the subject against the merely foolish exercise of a discretion by an official, however much the subject suffers thereby' (*Union Government (Minister of Mines and Industries) v Union Steel Corporation (SA) Ltd 1928 AD 220* at 236–7). It had turned into settled doctrine: in short, as Krause J said, 'a decision could not be set aside simply because no reasonable man would have reached it' (*City Council of Johannesburg v Turf Store (Pty) Ltd 1930 TPD 513*; see Dean 1983: 213–18). Rationality was only one issue. If the courts would not review on those grounds, could they review on the grounds that irrelevant criteria had been taken into account when the decision was made? Was race an irrelevant criterion? In the case of trading licences in the Transvaal the issue was opened by the legislation under which reasons for refusal were given. Some racial reasoning was found to be in order, some was not (Dean 1983: 214–17). Dean writes that courts found it proper for officials to consider evidence of racial matters when taking decisions, though on occasion they rejected gross discrimination on purely racial grounds for the reason that it was not the only relevant criterion that the Act required be taken into account. Even where there was no overt mention of racial discrimination, but where it had clearly played a part in decisions, judges were ready to set the determinations aside. But the courts had to give way before new legislation. In 1932 the new ordinance laid down that no grounds for the decision to grant or refuse a certificate need be given, which the Transvaal Supreme Court found also meant that there need be no disclosure of the evidence taken into account. In *Jooma v Lydenburg Rural Licensing Board 1933 TPD 477* it found that the ordinance conferred absolute discretion on the board. The court, it said, could not be concerned with the wisdom of the legislation, but must give effect to its 'necessary implications'.

Reading the law: statutory interpretation

As I have suggested the field of administrative law is better thought of not as a matter of courts versus executive or as an opposition between legal and political decision making. All of these are in one continuum: judicial and political reasoning, and executive and judicial powers are interlocking discursive areas. Thinking about discretions and delegation falls into this area, as do the processes of reading statutes. While it is hard to disentangle the pieces, I shall try in this section to consider how the culture of statutory interpretation developed.

The Westminster framework of parliamentary supremacy within which the judges worked meant that statutes could not be tested for validity by the courts against any constitutional instrument. Thus the way in which they read was a major constitutional mechanism, the only avenue for a 'defence' of rights. For while the will of parliament had to be put into practice, implementing the words in which that will had been expressed was far from automatic. Complexly constructed and worded legislative instruments are difficult to read. In this system they must be read both in relation to other statutes, and in relation to a broad set of principles of common law, and there is room for considerable acceptable variation in the way in which meaning may be imputed to a particular law and the sovereign will of parliament understood and implemented.

The prevailing feature of the interpretative practices of the English courts in this period was towards a so-called 'strict interpretation'. Built on the principle that common law was 'real' law, and statutes a form of intrusion, they were narrowly read as changing the law only insofar as was necessitated by their explicit words. A broad purpose, intention, or spirit of the legislation, however obvious to the policy makers who had conceived it and the legislators who had passed it, was not read into the law. This approach was an essential part of a formalism which was supposed to separate the judiciary from the policy of the law and was a part of the accommodation to parliamentary supremacy: judges would be bound by the words of the law, but would not implement anything but those words. Within this culture of reading not all statutes came to be read in the same way. Statutes that created criminal penalties, and, even more so, statutes that interfered with private property rights, and taxation legislation were read literally and narrowly. Others, even those dealing with individual liberties, were read more generously towards the executive. But the judges insisted that their reading was necessarily apolitical, that they did not speculate on parliamentary motives, and only construed language. Their approach fed directly into South Africa's judicial practice. Chief Justice de Villiers had established in 1875 that 'in considering statutes made in the Cape Colony after the cession to the British Crown, the Courts should be guided by the decisions of the English Courts and not by the Roman-Dutch authorities' (*de Villiers v Cape Divisional Council 1875 Buch* at 64). There was little challenge to this over the following fifty years.

In commenting on the developing South African practice I shall look at which kinds of statutes were narrowly read, and which were not, because otherwise it is possible to fall into the error of citing dicta proclaimed in one context as if they had validity in others. And I shall also consider what contexts the judges chose to place words in, in order to give them meaning. This was especially important where race was concerned (all the major cases), where judges often strayed into what Lord Haldane had called 'the other province' and where 'interpreting the desire of the country' was a part of statutory interpretation in South Africa (see above). Many of the major appellate decisions in which interpretation was an issue concerned legislative restriction of the rights of Asians. In the dual state courts were able to argue comfortably in the case of Africans that different criteria applied. Both otherness and dangerousness were obvious to them. The existence of tribal institutions and a separate system of law and administration, as well as firm agreement on segregation politically and subordination economically, meant that it was relatively easy to read implications validating these into legislation which had failed to mention them. But in the case of Asians things were less clear cut. Gradually both otherness and dangerousness were established by decisions relating to marriage (see *Seedat* above) and immigration (see *Padsha* below). This process was contributed to by the lively public discourse on the economic threats posed by Asian traders; and the health threat posed by Asian ways of life. But Asians were not economically segregated in the same way as Africans, particularly on the Reef. They were not either farm labourers, domestic servants or enclosed in mine compounds; many were abroad in the market as retail and wholesale traders. This meant that the legal assumptions were that their business activities came under the same private law as those of whites, and it was therefore harder to read legislation against a background of presumed intent to discriminate on the grounds of race, or allow officials to do so.

I have traced above some of the story related to Asian property rights in the Transvaal. The cautious approach when property interests were at stake is less evident in other areas. Decisions relating to Asian immigration into the Transvaal leaned more towards the executive. These were intensely political cases, decided in the atmosphere of Asian passive resistance to the anti-Asian laws and policies of the Transvaal. The assertion of the right of entry and residence in the Transvaal was fiercely opposed by whites and by the Milner regime. In *Babhu v Rex 1906 TS 600* a man who had been entitled to live in the South African Republic under its laws was imprisoned for entering the Transvaal Colony without a permit. Transvaal Ordinance no. 5 of 1903 required that Asians have a permit to enter 'this colony'. The case turned on the meaning of 'this colony'. Did it include the late Republic? As Babhu's counsel pointed out, the policy of the court had been essentially to support continuity, and to treat Republican statutes as of continuing validity unless discontinuity was clearly stated in new law. In this case, however, Innes found for discontinuity. This colony, he said, 'means to enter this colony after it became a colony – not to enter the late Republic'. It was a hard case on the facts, he said. *Prima facie* a person entitled to live in the Republic was entitled to a permit to live in the colony. But, he said, that was a matter for the administration. 'We can only construe the law, which in my opinion is perfectly clear' (603).

Even where an economic interest was involved, it might give way to a larger security interest real or imagined, or one concerning racial inter-mingling. I have described in the account of land law *Tsewu*'s case which said that Africans had ordinary common-law rights unless they were explicitly taken away. However, in *Mamabalo v Registrar of Deeds 1907 TS 76* the same court ruled that Africans could not own the 'occupation farms' established in African areas by the republican law of 1886. In this case the court explicitly resorted to a historical method of interpretation to deny the common-law rights in question. Solomon admitted that 'in that law there is no express prohibition' on African ownership. This, in the light of earlier dicta might have been enough. But he went beyond the wording to the history of the legislation, and the intention of the legislature that could be derived from it. The policy of the law had been to establish a 'buffer' of white-owned farms against 'large hordes of barbarian natives'. Africans could not therefore be owners (78–82). Wessels agreed (83). Mason in dissent insisted that meaning had to be derived from the language of the statute alone (ibid.) but this was not the way in which statutory interpretation along the racial border was to develop.

The nature of the choices that the new Transvaal court would make is well illustrated in *Smith v Germiston Municipality 1908 TS 240*. The legislation in question authorised municipalities to lay out locations for occupation by Africans. It authorised the making of regulations for the supervision of locations. In terms of these powers regulations were made forbidding trading by Europeans in locations. The court found them to be *intra vires*. Krause, counsel for the appellant, pointed out in argument that there was no mention of trading in the statute and therefore no explicit power to render an ordinary and legal activity illegal on racial grounds. Feetham, appearing for the municipality, urged that the overall intention was to provide for segregation, and that the regulations had to be considered in the light of that intention. The court agreed. It bent easily before the winds of policy, as in the occupation farms case, a policy of separating African and European lives. Solomon ruled that the power to prevent trading was included in the phrase 'effective supervision' in the statute. What about the racial barrier? He referred to *Kruse v Johnson 1898 2 QB 91*, the classic case in which the English court proclaimed its reluctance to interfere with regulations passed by local authorities. But there the court suggested occasions on which such interference might be necessary. These were that the regulations were unequal in operation between the classes; in bad faith; manifestly unjust; or oppressive interference with rights. To Solomon segregatory rules about trade did not fall into these categories. 'It would be extremely difficult to supervise the conduct of natives in locations if white persons were freely allowed to trade there' (251). The imperatives of 'effectual supervision' (ibid.) had overridden all.

The case of *Dadoo Ltd v Krugersdorp Municipality 1920 AD 530* was the occasion for one of the last great clashes in this period between the restrictive attitudes towards statutes, which limited meaning to the exact wording, and a far more generous judicial attitude towards giving effect to legislative intention. Asians, as we have seen, were forbidden to buy land in the Transvaal, and to occupy certain areas. Dadoo formed a company, of which he owned 149 out of 150 shares, which acquired and registered title to land. There was no doubt that this had been done so that he could get around the prohibition. But was it illegal? What the courts had to say was in the final analysis not of lasting importance, as even before the Appellate Division had given its judgment parliament had already amended the law to the effect that land could not be owned by companies in which Asians had a controlling interest (Act 37 of 1919), and this may well explain the willingness of some of the Appellate Division judges to pronounce as they did. But the clash in attitudes towards racial legislation is nonetheless instructive. In the Transvaal Provincial Division Wessels had no hesitation in declaring Dadoo's attempt to be an illegal attempt to evade the operation of the law. He agreed that there was no express prohibition of what had been done but argued that nonetheless it fell within the mischief aimed at in the Act.

> To ascertain the exact scope of a prohibition we must not confine ourselves to the particular words of a particular section, but we must take into consideration the whole Act so as to arrive at what exactly the Legislature intended to prohibit. In order to determine the wish of the legislator we must see what acts he did not wish to be done even though he did not

prohibit them in special terms. For this purpose it is often necessary to examine carefully the past history of the law. (Quoted at 533–4)

For Wessels the underlying intention of the Act was clear, and it was to be derived from the basic constitutional principle of the South African Republic, whose law it originally was. Wessels specifically invoked the racist basis of article 9 of the *grondwet* which he quoted in Dutch as if to give it special scriptural force. '*Het volk wil geene gelijkstelling van gekleurden met blanke ingeztenen toestaan noch in kerk noch in staat*' (The people will accept no equalising between coloured and white neither in church nor in state). Asians to him did not fall within the group of subjects that Mason's approach would have protected. Rather the category of the subject was divided between *gekleurden* (coloured) and *blanke* (white). That the legislation as a whole was meant to prohibit Asians getting control of land followed from this and prevailed over any technicalities of interpretation of specific wording.

When the case was appealed, Innes rejected this approach. Every statute, he said, embodies some policy. But, he said, a judge could not place a meaning on language 'of which it is not reasonably capable, in order to give effect to what he may think to be the policy or object of the particular measure'. The intent of a law could not operate beyond the limits of its language. Innes accepted that Dadoo had acted to escape the provisions of the law. But a company was a separate juristic entity. Nothing had been done which was forbidden. Solomon likewise admitted that it was legitimate for a judge to examine the whole statute and its history to arrive at a meaning but warned that policy could not be extended beyond the limits laid down. How far the policy laid down in the *grondwet* was meant to operate depended on exact wording of particular laws. De Villiers, on the other hand, developed an approach far closer to Wessels, presaging a Roman-Dutch justification for giving effect to legislative intent which was at odds with the English approach that had until then been dominant in the Appellate courts. He quoted *Peckius ad Regulam*, 84, 1 (570–1).

Since in the regulation of all things, private as well as public, it is just that the written word should yield to the intention, and since the *ratio legis* is law, and the words of the law-giver should not be snatched at, but due regard should be had to his intention, it has therefore been decreed with great wisdom that when anyone is forbidden to do a thing in one way, he should not be allowed by taking advantage of the wording to act against the intention of the law.

It was said, he continued, that to adopt this approach was to go beyond the rules of interpretation which had often been applied by the Appellate Division. But while these rules were 'useful', he said, they could not be allowed to override principles and the 'principle of our law' was that '*voluntas legis* governs'.[4]

The issue of Asian immigration provided another fruitful field for pronouncements about interpretation. How far would the courts allow considerations of 'policy' to enter into their construal of statutes? In a case heard shortly after Union de Villiers CJ pronounced that

> It is not part of the duty of the courts . . . to criticise the policy pursued by the Legislature in its enactments, nor do I wish now to offer any criticism of the policy of the Act relating to Indian immigration . . . however . . . however desirable it may be to restrict Indian immigration, this Court must apply the same rule of construction which it would apply to Acts with less desirable objects. The maintenance of the liberty of the subject is of more importance than even the prevention of undesirable immigration, and, if the Legislature desires to place restrictions upon the liberty of any class of subjects, whether they be Europeans, or Asiatic or natives, it should do so in language which admits of no doubt as to its intention. (*Chotabhai v Union Government and Registrar of Asiatics 1911 AD 13* at 25)

It is worth reproducing this statement at length, because the inclusion of all within the embrace of the phrase 'liberty of the subject' in the early years of the state, when the courts were trying to establish the boundaries of accepted constitutional practice, did not survive the bruising decade that followed.[5]

The most significant case in this area of law is *R v Padsha 1923 AD 281* and it illustrates not only a qualification of the idea that unequivocal language was needed to restrict liberties but also of the claim that external and policy considerations had no place in the interpretation of statutes.

---

[4] It was this dissent of de Villiers that was pronounced to be the exemplary method of statutory interpretation by L. C. Steyn in his landmark book on interpretation (Steyn 1946). Under Steyn as Chief Justice during the apex of the apartheid period, the Appellate Division enshrined de Villiers' approach (see Cameron 1982).

[5] For a fuller account see Corder (1984: chapter 7). As Corder shows the decision in *Chotabhai* was the exception in a series of cases in which the Appellate Division made different choices about the 'liberty of the subject', but quotable dicta tend to live on as emblematic.

Section 4 of the Immigration Regulation Act of 1913 provided that 'any person or class of persons deemed by the Minister on economic grounds or on account of standard or habits of life to be unsuited to the requirements of the Union' would be a prohibited immigrant. In accordance with accepted practice throughout the white states of the British empire the purpose of the Act, which was to exclude immigrants on racial grounds, was to be achieved by an apparently non-racial categorisation.[6] The formula was a departure from the more common imperial model in which literacy in a European language was required, and which had been the criterion in the immigration laws of the Cape and Natal. Acting under the new law the minister (Smuts) declared that 'every Asiatic person' fell within the new category. Could the minister, under this section, deem a whole class of people, in this case all Asians, to be unsuited on economic grounds? Solomon, de Villiers and Juta JJA said yes; Innes and Kotze said no, as had the Cape Provincial Division. On this basis at least the language used was not that which 'admits of no doubt'.

The history of the Act was a complex story involving prolonged internal disorder and an imperial intervention. In interpreting it judges connected their reasoning to the world beyond the court in different ways. Gardiner in the Cape Provincial Division had said that by prohibiting all Asians the minister had clearly used racial grounds and not the economic grounds specified in the Act. But Solomon thought that the word 'economic' could be used in a wide or a narrow sense. In spite of the earlier dicta about interpreting discriminatory legislation narrowly, he was of the opinion 'that in this case it is used in a very wide sense'. The word derived etymologically, he said, from the meaning of managing a household, and therefore, in the broader sense related to the well-being of the state. To Solomon it was simply obvious that the introduction of 'other coloured persons' into the Union was not conducive to the well-being of the state. It was not because they might be poor; or even, to take up the main point in political discourse, that they would compete with other labour or

[6] See Huttenback (1976) for a comprehensive account of the development of the legal defences of the white-ruled colonies and Dominions against non-white immigration. Immigration law is a good lens through which to view both the British empire as a legal system and the pretensions of a non-racial rule of law. The solution that was acceptable to, and fostered by, the imperial government was the so-called Natal formula, which was a *de facto* racial barrier based on a linguistic test in which the choice of language and judgement of ability was in the discretion of the immigration officer. For an account of South African immigration law and policy in this period see Joshi 1942.

traders. Even Asians who became successful professional men were in the broad sense economically undesirable. At this point Solomon abandoned the strict construction of the language of the Act for a belated judicial reprisal against the passive resistance movement. Lansdown, in presenting the government's case, had specifically raised the question of the influence of Asian agitators on race relations. This was taken up by Solomon. A 'person of that [professional] class,' Solomon reasoned, 'exercising influence over his fellow Asiatic, may become a disturbing factor in the industrial processes of the country, as actually happened in the now historic case of Gandhi' (288–9). Juta agreed, contending that highly educated and civilised Asians had already proved to be a threat to industrial relations. He based his reasoning in terms of a mapping of the Union's population. There were large numbers of Africans, 'far outnumbering' the small number of Europeans. Then there were the added complexities caused by the coloureds, and the 'disproportionately large class' of poor whites. The introduction of coloured Asians, he thought, 'must inevitably complicate these problems'. De Villiers found that the minister had the power to define 'economic' in any way he liked.[7] But he was less sympathetic to the view taken of the racial dilemmas, taking an acid view of the tactful compromise that had produced a piece of racial legislation cast in non-racial terms which were satisfactory to the imperial government and the government of India, regretting that parliament had been 'induced to forsake the traditional habit of calling things by their names' (294). But in the court's willingness to say what it was that parliament had not called by its name, the 'traditional habit' of interpretation had also been forsaken. Innes's dissent shows that a different conclusion would have been reached if the hitherto accepted canons of interpretation had been adhered to. 'Grounds which in truth are not economic', he said, 'do not become so by virtue of an administrative pronouncement. Economic . . . signifies belonging to the development and regulation of the material resources of a community.' There was nothing in the Act to show that the ordinary meaning was not intended.

---

[7] In the early 1920s, Patrick Duncan, then the Minister of the Interior, began to apply the 'economic grounds' test to exclude Jewish immigrants. Jews, like Asians, were also viewed as subverters of proper race relations. In 1930 a Quota Act was passed to limit Jewish immigration. Again, like Asians, they were seen as a threat to national homogeneity: – in the words of D. F. Malan an 'undigested and unabsorbed and unabsorbable minority' (Shain 1994: 109; 126; 136).

The categorisation that the minister had made was therefore racial (466).[8]

Yet the story of the development of the culture of interpretation is not simple. While the Appellate Bench might have adopted a broad reading of a statute at the expense of the liberty of the subject in *Padsha*'s case they took a rather different tack in *R v Detody 1926 AD 198*. This was also a case of great political and practical importance in which the court found that Transvaal ordinance no. 43 of 1902 – which required 'natives', defined as those who belonged to aboriginal races south of the equator, to carry passes – was not applicable to women. The Transvaal Provincial Division had read the ordinance in a simple way, based on plain language, and concluded that women were included. But there were ironies when the case reached the Appellate level. Here Innes, Solomon and de Villiers invoked *Law Society v Wookey 1912 AD* in which the court had decided that women could not be admitted to the Bar because existing practice showed that, contrary to the ordinary rule, 'persons' did not include women when it came to the right to practice law. They applied the same reasoning to *Detody*'s case. The history of the application of the law showed that it had not been applied to women, and had therefore been understood to have a restricted meaning. It is clear that the decision could have gone either way in this case. More judges overall, when the Provincial Division decisions are taken into account, thought that the ordinance covered women. Argument was largely dominated by conflicting technical versions, one favouring the precedent in *Wookey*'s case, the other the technical rules of interpretation. There was some reference to what the ordinance might have meant in 1902 in the light of the history of pass laws in the Republic, and the problems faced by the new administration. But this was the extent of consideration of 'reality'. No weight was given to the effects of deciding either way, and this distinguishes it from *Padsha*'s case with its very broad speculations about the hypothetical effects of Asian immigration. But perhaps what was not said was as important as what was. In *Padsha*'s case the Appellate Division could talk about political matters because the issue was not one contested in white politics in the Union. All detested Asian immigration, and the class of persons affected

---

[8] Yet Innes himself was not consistent in strict construction of statutes in immigration cases. In *Ah Yet and others v Union Government 1921 AD 97*, in denying an appeal against a deportation order, he 'extracted the maximum sense from a statute which drastically affected human liberty, by an extensive interpretation' (Corder 1984: 140).

were outside the country. But it could not reason aloud politically about passes without transgressing upon 'native policy'. There was a history of opposition to passes for women; the pass laws had been justified in so many ways that their underlying purpose was not clear; and 'native policy' generally was very much at the heart of politics, especially in the mid-1920s when Hertzog's 'solutions' were absorbing parliament and public.[9] Thus technicalities were resorted to when political issues before the court were live and disputed, while substance could be acknowledged when they were not. From the point of view of the court it was a rational, perhaps necessary, discursive strategy.

To understand legalism in South Africa, as the above account shows, we need to consider the complex relationship between the different ways of conceiving the law. In considering overall the response of the South African courts to the growth of legislation, and the general problem of the relationship of the courts to the will of the legislature – to the question of the relationship between law and politics – it is also worthwhile considering a comparative context. South African judges have been judged (see Corder 1984) for their ultimate failure to stand in the way of the racialised content of South African legislation. But they inhabited, as I have noted, a larger legal universe which, in the public law area, was dominated by British courts. Not all context is immediate and local. British legal debate, ideas and the decisions of British courts of appeal on public-law matters were a part of the context in which South African decisions were framed. Compared to the general drift of the English courts the South African decisions appear in a different light. It could be argued that in the first decades of the twentieth century South African judges were, even in the circumstances of a strongly contested political order, and the highly politicised nature of many of the appellate cases, bolder in their defence of some of the 'liberties of the subject' than their English counterparts. The acceptance of legal formalism by both judges and politicians was eventually also a feature of the South African legal system. It gave to the judges, after three turbulent decades of controversy, both a limited degree of independence and an enhanced prestige. By the 1930s the fundamental

---

[9] The decision in *Detody*'s case was made against the background of strong anti-pass agitation of which the judges must have been aware. The appeal was financed by the African National Congress (see Eales 1991: 107). As Eales notes, passes for women were resisted in the name of African patriarchy. 'The Native man is himself the arbiter of his woman's conduct', said *Umteteli wa Bantu*. 'Should not my wife be armed with a written sanction from me?' asked an African clergyman (108–9).

divisions in white politics, which had been a feature of the years of state building, had softened. Those outside a central white consensus, which accepted the British connection, segregation of landholding and the workforce, were marginalised. The Supreme Court Bench became increasingly professionalised, its members dedicated more to the elaboration of a distinctive South African private law than to playing a part in the making of the South African polity. On the political sidelines, and increasingly immune from the vituperative criticism they had earlier attracted, the judges in their formalist cloaks lent a non-political prestige to the enforcement of the now routinely discriminatory statute law, while continuing to use the language of justice and equity in the private law. For the politicians the appearance of correctness which the growing formalism gave to the careful but unquestioned judicial enforcement of the statute law was a small price to pay for the acknowledgement of judicial independence in carrying out this role.

PART VI

Consideration

19

Reconstructing the state: legal formalism, democracy and a post-colonial rule of law

Henry Maine observed that 'sometimes the Past is the Present; much more often it is removed from it by varying distances, which, however, cannot be estimated or expressed chronologically' (quoted in Cocks 1988: 204). In the period of the reconstruction of the South African state the time of its first making is, in spite of the decisive break with the past, in many ways closer than the chronologically more recent years of its disintegration. While recent analyses of the dilemmas facing South African law have, understandably, focused on the recent past and the present, I offer in this book a different perspective, one based on a consideration of South African law as a part of the construction of the state. The premises on which the state is now being reconstructed are dramatically different, yet the problems are hauntingly similar. Establishing 'law and order' was a primary issue then as it is now; the relationship between white and African common laws remains to be resolved; differential land-tenure regimes have not faded away; and now a new global context, as empire did then, profoundly shapes the constitutional framework and also restricts local solutions to the relationships of law and market. Perhaps above all the wide gulf between the ambitions of the state and its capacities is still present. The differences are profound. With the end of racist rule and the expansion of political democracy the state is no longer in a potential state of war with most of its inhabitants. In considering law in the context of the construction of the state, I have tried to generate an idea of legal culture and to consider the relationship, in the period of the making of the white state, between the formalism of the superior courts and of professional legal ideologies, and the other legal discourses and practices which existed both inside the state and beyond it. Legal formalism purports to separate the 'legal' from the 'political' both institutionally and in terms of justification for decision making. Legal decisions, in this paradigm, made according to legal rules and doctrines and determining rights and entitlements according to these rules, are considered to be different from substantive decisions in which political and other considerations govern. Lawyers in South Africa, as elsewhere, write Zimmerman and Visser, 'tend to create law primarily with reference to the intellectual concerns raised in statutory documents, authoritative court decisions, and learned treatises' (1996: 6). To understand South African legal culture one must start with its own formalist self-image, and acknowledge also that without the centrality of formalism a state cannot be based on a 'rule of law'. But in the period of reconstruction a methodological emphasis on the relationship between legal formalism and the wider range of discourses about law can contribute to the change from an authoritarian to a democratic legal culture. By emphasising that 'law' is not confined to the law talk of limited professional sites, that there is no easily made separation between law and talk about law, or between popular and professional concepts, and by widening and emphasising the essential unity of the broader field thus constituted, the concept of legal culture could have an inherently democratising effect. The new South African constitution, Etienne Mureinik has said, provides a bridge 'from a culture of authority . . . to a culture of justification . . . a community based on persuasion not coercion' (quoted in Currie 1999: 138 note 2). Dennis Davis has written of a 'culture of reasoned argument' (1999: 398). But who is to participate in this reasoned argument, whose voices are to be heard and what premises will found the 'culture of justification'? In the period of transition these remain open dimensions. How can South Africa develop a democratic legal culture which is open to dialogue yet retains the distinctive characteristics of a 'rule of law'?[1]

There is the further consideration that the concept of legal culture may

---

[1] It is too soon to consider the impact on South African legal culture of the work, and theatre, of the Truth and Reconciliation Commission, which introduced a new set of voices, and new forms of dialogue, into South African legal culture, and which, through political necessity, abandoned many of the usual features of 'law'. This has been a profound intervention and the counterpoint between its model of accounting and that of law and courts will continue. There is some irony in the fact that while the politic elites chose to deal with the aftermath of some political conflicts by means of 'reconciliation', there were strong voices among the victims of apartheid violence for the more formalist and more punitive methods of the ordinary criminal law (see *Azapo People's Organisation vs President of RSA (1996 (8) BCLR 1015 CC)*).

It is also as yet too early to deal usefully with the question of language, which is central to any legal culture. Languages other than English and Afrikaans will find their way into court through lawyers and judges and new and different meanings will become possible. In this respect the analyses of *ubuntu* in *S v Makwanyane 1995 (3) SA 491 CC* are instructive.

be peculiarly appropriate to the analysis of radical transition when in the glaring light more of the legal landscape becomes plainly visible. As long as the hold of the political centre is longstanding and unchallenged, the claims of formalism, restricting 'law' to rule formation, application and the professional discourses connected to these, are very powerful. The common responses to the dominance of formalism – materialist, realist and post-modernist analyses – have been forms of 'unmasking', of trying to pierce the formalist veil to reveal the parts of 'law' that it conceals. But at a time when the centre's grip has weakened and all features of the legal system are in contention, the claims of formalism have been diminished and the unmasking has already been done. The complexity and interrelationships of the component parts are more easily seen. The dominant sound of the formalist voice has been momentarily diminished, and this should allow the other voices to be heard.

It was a peculiarity of much of transition rhetoric in South Africa, at least among the political classes, that it proclaimed that the political processes would be subject to and regulated by a new legality. The idea of the 'rule of law', however bizarrely actualised, was an important component of the colonial state and white rule, and it has remained central to the making of a new state in the era of global constitutionalism. The protracted constitution-making processes were accompanied by a counterpoint of violence which, paradoxically, led to exaggeration of the security that would be provided by a new legality. As it had been nearly a century earlier, South Africa was colonised in the 1990s by a new kind of internationally sanctioned state: this time not the 'Westminster system' but the 'Constitutional State'. A form of political liberalism, which had notably failed over the whole history of the South African state to attract significant support from any segment of the population, found its philosophy entrenched at the heart of a new constitution. The constitution inflated the role of law, and the political power of judges, in an attempt to remedy the faults of the previous state's version of the 'rule of law'. Parliamentary sovereignty was subjected to a Bill of Rights which served, reflecting the end of both the cold war and apartheid, as both a post-Calvinist catechism, and a post-Marxist manifesto (Chanock 1999b). Yet the new legal order for South Africa is still likely to struggle to develop within a context of political turbulence. If we are to think about the legal future we must imagine that this instability will not go away after a brief 'teething' period, and will not be unquestioningly mediated by the

constitution's bill of rights. The South African state has never been stable.
Its political legitimacy has been under challenge since the first process of
formation, and South African legal culture has had much experience of
the accommodations between legalism and violence.

Thinking about the basic characteristics of South Africa's legal discourse and practices may also help us to think more clearly about what
'newness' in a legal system could mean. Legal discourses, as we have seen,
do not exist insulated from other social discourses. The legal construction
of race, for example, could hardly be understood apart from the wider
discourses, scientific, political and popular, about race. Similarly the legal
construction of rights is attached to a broader cultural and political
discourse. And, most importantly, a legal culture cannot be understood by
reference only to judges, or even more broadly to lawyers. It is carried on
in other fora. Politics is the most obvious, but perhaps the most important
that has been discussed in this book is bureaucratic. In any highly bureaucratised state the main generators and users of law are the bureaucracy,
and they are a major influence on the growth of a legal culture.

Legal culture: political conflict and the development of formalism

In the state built after 1902 law and order were secured by the creation of
a paramilitary police force which was to combine the roles of policing and
internal occupation. The new magistracy combined the political roles of
district administration and surveillance with adjudication. Over these
institutions, both of which blurred the boundaries between administration
and law, was placed a judiciary with an overstated and self-styled separation from the world of the political. Thus, while most of the legal business
of the state was carried out by institutions and personnel which were part
of the coercive bureaucratic apparatus, the top of the system embodied a
symbolic separation between 'law' and other aspects of state power. After
1902 the new regime faced several fundamental challenges to 'law and
order'. Two basic features of the state's response can be noted. One was
the determination of the government to crush its opponents without
compromise or concession, and the consequent enactment of what it
hoped were the necessary statutes. The second was the supreme courts'
response, in terms of their formalist mission, which was to limit the
actions of officials closely to the powers granted by the new laws, by a

literalist style of interpretation. These were responses that did not, as we have seen, sit easily together. But more than simple judicial literalism was at work. We must remember other contexts: the faith put in formalism in relation to the external reputation of the country and its mining industry; the sensitivity of the judges to political criticism (the targets of the anti-labour action were white voters); and, in relation both to Indians and trade unions, the fact that the country was not yet fully independent and that there were persistent voices on their behalf at Westminster. There was also allegiance to the idea of the 'rule of law' which the unresolved balance between white political groups made for them a necessary shield. The idea did have roots in the white self-narrative of civiliser of the barbarian; and it could still be flourished, with weakening effect, at the articulate elites of the subject races. Appeal to the Privy Council remained as a form of guarantee of commercial and property rights. The weakness of the state and the fundamental political and racial divisions gave to law a crucial role in controlling debate and outcomes. The result of this for law was to produce a model of judges divorced from 'politics', yet attached to 'law'. This could only mean an entrenchment of the literal style of formalism.

Yet the Bench was highly political, and it had to operate in an intensely politically charged environment. Most of the senior judges had had political careers of note (Corder 1984: chapter 1). They were plunged immediately into a series of crises. These events, involving as they did numerous politically related prosecutions in the courts, had important ramifications for legality in the new state, establishing early the role of the courts as a political arena. On the one hand they began what was to become a familiar dialogue between government and the courts. The courts were not generous to the executive in their interpretations either of the common law relating to sedition and treason or of the statute law. They forced the government into either detailed legislative changes de-signed to tighten up controls over political activities or towards 'legalised' ways of bypassing the ordinary courts altogether. The new riotous assembly laws were one way; the proclamation of martial law followed by Acts of indemnity, or simply illegal executive action so excused, another. The pattern continued. Special courts were created to hear the charges arising out of the rebellions in 1914/15 and 1922. New legislation to control strikes and speech was passed in the 1920s. When the latter was strictly interpreted by the courts, recourse to the courts in these matters was put beyond the reach of much of the population via the mechanisms of the Native Administration Act. By the time the National Party government came into power in 1948, the rules of the game seemed well established. Over the next forty years the government dealt with setbacks in the courts by constantly producing more detailed restrictive rules, and by multiplying measures to exclude courts' jurisdiction by the extension of the creation of emergency powers and by quarantining ministerial discretions (Forsyth 1985; Dugard 1978; Davis 1987).

In retrospect there are questions to be asked about this process. What did the courts achieve, and why did they act as they did? It was the functioning of a deeply divided white democracy which kept the courts politically open. And to me more interesting, what effect did this (serious) play have on the nature of legality? In one sense both sides won: the judiciary reaffirmed a major tenet of their view of law, while the government eventually achieved its aims within the law and could be confident of doing so once it had arrived at the right verbal formula. Individual litigants often won also, which is an important consideration. The government lost little prestige and not much effectiveness. But the effect was to keep the possibility open for individual litigants to use the courts against the government's attempts to use law to control their political opposition. This had a number of consequences in that it simultaneously strengthened the notions over the long term that a 'rule of law' prevailed; that the essence of the defence of the 'rule of law' was a judicial style; and that the law courts were usable arenas of political struggle, but within the confines of form, not by challenging substance. One outcome of the decades of bitter struggles for rights in the courts was, therefore, the embedding of a formalist approach to rights and interpretation within the legal culture.

Two other themes from the early political confrontations were to be of continuing importance. One arose from executive efforts simply to exclude the jurisdiction of the courts from politically sensitive areas. The early battle, won by the executive, was sharply fought over the Immigration Act. The second concerned the role of the courts when state security was threatened. In this instance it was the cases arising out of the Afrikaner rebellion that drew from the courts the affirmation of the doctrine *salus reipublicae suprema lex est*. In both cases the course taken by the South African courts was hugely influenced by developments in similar contests between courts and executive in Britain, and similar statutory models in Britain and elsewhere in the empire. The British judges, caught in the intense struggle over the beginnings of the welfare state, tried to define themselves out of the line of fire. Under the impact of two world wars they subordinated themselves entirely to the demands of the executive in security areas. South Africa's judges did the same. Part of the point here is that the choices were constrained and that neither sets of judges had much option in the substantive directions taken, but they could affect detail and degree. But a larger point is that, while the choices were forced upon South African judges by specific local conflicts, the directions of their solutions, and how they thought about and verbalised them, drew extensively on external discourses and examples. For South African legal history we must acknowledge the powerful effects of the Diceyan paradigm. The formalist reasoning the judges adopted existed in a relationship with other legal discourses. Judges could be formalist and 'above' politics because they knew that others were not. They knew that in the Diceyan world they did not settle substantive political issues, and that the judges' role was only to keep the executive within the powers defined by the legislature.

Judges

Both the ideology of legal formalism and the prevailing South African legal narratives emphasise a role for the judiciary that is 'above' politics. Yet the judges were the targets of public criticism throughout the life of the white state, particularly in the decades during which not all whites accepted the full legitimacy of the state. Indeed one of the features of South African legal culture in the first decades was the intensity of public criticism of the courts. In spite of the continuing public disapprobation, however, the judiciary was virtually beyond criticism inside the profession and in its journals, where a deferential and congratulatory sense reigned virtually without interruption. Judicial prestige was also protected during the apartheid years (partly by the judges' use of the contempt power) largely because they offered to opponents of the regime a slender hope of justice, while to the government's supporters judges were an embodiment of its propriety. And it was not until then that the judiciary became so much a focus of discussions of law. The judges throughout, with some exceptions, adhered to a weak version of civil liberties. If we wonder why such a stance should have developed, the answer lies chiefly in the divisions among the ruling white elite. In the period covered by this book nearly all the beneficiaries were white opponents of the government. Indeed it is to the existence of white trade unions, and the white Labour Party, and to the continuing activity of Afrikaner republicans, all strong forms of white opposition that had to be accepted as legitimate, that South Africa owes its 'rule of law' tradition. African opposition did not receive the same respect from law.

But it was in the period after 1948 that the issue of the proper judicial role in constitutional and public life became perennially controversial. The constitutional confrontation of the 'old' appellate judges and the new National Party government over the removal of coloured voters from the common voters' roll had an enduring impact on South African legal life. Of the judges who ruled against the government it can be said that their political intentions were honourable, their ambition to thwart the government impossible, and their contrived legal reasoning in part responsible for the accelerated politicisation of the court. Liberals and the 'Left' have praised the decisions, writing a story of defeat with honour (though the defeated judges did not resign over this or other issues related to apartheid). It is not my view that the decisions were 'wrong' because I do not think there are right or wrong decisions in this sense in law. But the judges certainly tested the limits of expected behaviour and reasoning, which exist in any legal system (for a summary of the cases see Forsyth 1985: chapter 2). Their defeat also gave rise to a powerful belief that if only the South African judges had had a bill of rights to wield against the government's statutes, they would have prevailed. After their defeat what role was possible, in relation to public law, for a judiciary which was broadly supportive of government, yet which operated self-consciously within the confines of legal formalism? With the broader moral/legal avenues closed, all that opposition could wring from the law depended on the interpretation of statutes. A literalist approach by a judiciary is usually a way of delaying and perhaps frustrating an executive bent upon change, while a strategy of interpretation more sensitive to giving effect to the purpose and policy of legislation is one that facilitates executive ambitions. During the twentieth century, the British courts, protective of the status quo against legislative changes arising out of the labour and welfare agenda, had developed, and passed on to South Africa's judges, the tactics of obstructive literalism. The voice of legal progressives in the United Kingdom had long urged an approach to interpretation based on the intention of the legislature. In the 1950s the South African judges began to free themselves from the grip of literalism, with progressive generosity towards the intentions of the legislation of apartheid (see in particular *Minister of Interior v Lockhart 1961 (2) SA 785 A* and *Roussow v Sachs 1964 (2) SA 551 A*). The vast scope of apartheid's agenda, which involved detailed interference in every aspect of the country's life and economy, spawned a legislative style heavily dependent on delegated legislation and regulations, and on ministerial and official discretions. Sometimes the administrative ambitions were so far reaching (or impossible of perform-ance) that, even with generosity, they could not, within the formalist paradigm, possibly be held to come within the compass of legislation. Sometimes too the exercise of official discretions was baulked at, but for two decades after the crisis of the mid-1950s the courts on the whole lived comfortably with the government.

As opposition to apartheid intensified, this accommodation was to begin to cause discomfort. The strength of black political opposition meant that increasing numbers of cases involving the use of ever more widely drawn repressive political statutes were funnelled into the courts. No longer were they able to bask beneath a mantle of legal impartiality, which had been bestowed in part by the acquittal of those charged with treason in 1956. More and more they became instruments of punishment, their reputation among whites for legal correctness being exploited by the government, and consequently dwindling swiftly in the eyes of the ma-jority of the population. Parts of the legal profession were filled with an anxiety which became an important ingredient in legal discourses. One strand of this was expressed in concern for the legitimacy of 'Law' as an abstract entity in the eyes of black South Africa. In its worst form the nightmare (or the threat) was that 'They' would just cease to believe in it altogether and that a terrible harvest would consequently be reaped (Davis 1987). Another strand was the debate that developed over the moral position of judges. Cogent calls were made for them to resign on the grounds that the 'true' function of a judiciary could no longer be carried out (see Wacks 1984), but went unheeded. However, among those lawyers who did not support the regime, another powerful, and strategically attractive, line of argument was mounted (Dugard 1978). This claimed that the judges could do different things *without departing from the formalist paradigm* because there were different paths inherent within South African common law itself.

Legal culture 2

One of the effects of these struggles within the law was, then, the almost exclusive focus on the judiciary as vectors of law. (Both of the important and substantial historical reviews of South Africa's legal system produced in this period, Corder (1984) and Forsyth (1985), focused on the judges of the Appellate Division (see also van Blerk (1988).) But it is important to set the judges not just within the framework of the political system of the country, as has usually been done, but within the larger legal culture of which they were a part. As I have emphasised the most important of the other legal discourses in South African legal culture existed within the bureaucracy, or within the dialogue between bureaucrats and politicians, both of which are distinct from the discourse among lawyers, or that between lawyers and the public or politicians and public on legal matters. South African law in this century has essentially been the atmosphere in which the bureaucracy breathed. The state was a (large and sophisticated) colonial state in the sense that it was throughout self-consciously involved in the project of using its power to recreate a society and remake an economy. We can usefully think of two periods of such construction, one following 1902 in which the basic endowments of a twentieth-century Anglo-colonial state were put in place, and a second great endeavour from the 1950s to create apartheid. The creation and working of vast statist enterprises of this kind used law for effective centralised management of officials, and achievement of policy goals. I repeat these obvious things only to be able to point out that from the perspectives of those governing these processes, judges, common law and the like were peripheral in the making and administration of law. In these 'internal' discourses when judges appear it is but occasionally and as irritating obstacles. In the culture that created and used the larger part of the legal universe, law was policy-oriented command.

From this standpoint the controversies about the role of judges must be re-ranked in importance. For a more complete picture of legal culture we must ask ourselves about administration. Writers about law do of course frequently consider administration, but they tend to adopt the perspective of administrative law, a perspective which assumes that the rules that limit the ways in which officials exercise power are the main game, and that the judiciary is responsible for making these rules. But if we adopt the bureaucratic perspective of policy goals, efficient management and effective achievement of ends, the place of the judges and their rules looks different. To comprehend South Africa's legal culture we must be sensitive to this perspective as the state is poised to embark on an even larger venture of (re)construction. The impatience of the administrative state with legal formalism is not just a South African theme but an important strand in the history of twentieth-century law (see e.g. Horwitz 1992: chapter 8). Each legal culture develops its own ways of accommodating the ideal worlds of lawyer and administrator, and the differing concepts of legal process and rights involved. What of South Africa's accommodation? Here again one must recall the Diceyan framework with its limitation of the remedies for redress against official actions to rights in common law and the 'natural justice' tests, and the absence of the wider contemporary repertoire of rights and remedies. In any case Africans were not citizens in this respect but were the objects of state action and received scant protection from administrative law. Legislation largely affecting Africans gave greater and wider discretion to officials, and at lower levels, than that affecting others. In particular, from the 1920s onwards the Urban Areas Act and the Native Administration Act gave to officials far-reaching powers over personal liberty, bypassing the formalities of criminal and administrative law, and these methods were endorsed by the courts. The limited protection of the courts (which was used, for example, by Asians faced with economic discrimination by officials), was not extended to major predicaments of African life. And here it must be emphasised that an understanding of a legal culture extends not simply to what officials may, or must, legally do, but how they do it. In the submission of Justice Pius Langa, currently South Africa's senior African judge, to the Truth and Reconciliation Commission (TRC) he stressed that the repressive laws on the statute books were 'exacerbated' by 'crude, cruel' officials. 'There was a culture of hostility and intimidation . . . [The] face presented by authority . . . was of a war against people who were unenfranchised' (quoted in Dyzenhaus 1998: 61).

It is also important to recall that the areas in which legal regulation grew in tropical profusion were those in which the state failed to achieve its aims. The major legal/administrative ventures were not successful. Severe attempts to limit political expression failed to suppress opposition. Black consumption of alcohol surged despite the fervid attempts at prohibition; African urbanisation increased rapidly in tandem with the incrementally complicated prohibitions and controls on movement and urban residence.

Hindson claims that 'the implementation of the Urban Areas Act had little, if any, impact on the pace of African urbanisation' (1987: 42; see too Greenberg 1987: 34). Even in the most politically sensitive area, land, van Onselen reminds us that sharecropping contracts 'were widespread for nearly half a century after they were officially abolished by the Natives Land Act' (1996: 7). We cannot gauge the effects of these laws because we do not know what the outcomes would have been had it not been passed, but we can see that intensive legal regulation did not easily achieve its most central ends, and that it was these failures that had a marked effect on the temper of the legal culture. The increasingly hyperbolic elaboration of restrictive legislation and regulations, and the growth of resort to wide administrative discretions, were attempts to cope with the intractability of the society to immense regulatory ambitions. The decline of legal liberalism was due not to original sin but to its inapplicability to the regulatory tasks of the colonial state. Similar failures await the new state. However resort to legislative hyperbole and sweeping discretions may be ruled out by the bill of rights and democratic political processes.

In South Africa the broader public discourse about the role of law was dominated for much of the existence of the white state by an affirmation of a liberal idea of a neutral law on one level, with a pragmatic acceptance of, indeed insistence on, the use of law to secure racial advantage. One response of African elites was to try to hold 'law' to its empty promises. But in the closing period of white rule the response that alarmed white lawyers was the envisioning, and the beginnings of the practising, of a completely different kind of law. In the last decade, in particular as the white state began to lose control of African areas, informal courts under the control of local militants began (sporadically) to operate (e.g. Burman and Scharf 1990). Various forms of popular justice have not been successful in Western countries where, whatever the obvious failings of state institutions, the state's courts and police have maintained a central relevance to people's conceptions of law and justice. In those situations the development of alternatives in the area of dispute resolution have more to do with perceptions of cost and convenience than rejection of the state's law. But in South Africa where the state's legal processes have been at best irrelevant to the needs of most of the population for mechanisms for disputing, alternative courts might hold an appeal even once the fuel of revolutionary rhetoric has run out. Another part of the breaking of the unity of the old set of practices has been the development of new forms of legal practice. The growth of, for example, the Legal Resources Centre, involving not an impatient discarding of legal forms, but an effort to realise the promises of law on an entirely new scale, might create a far broader consciousness of the possibilities of 'legal rights'. This may not always be compatible with 'popular justice' (Legal Resources Centre *Annual Reports*; White 1988). In this context one might also think of the growth of, and successes of, labour law during the 1980s. While the jurisprudence evolved in this area departed in many respects from the traditional forms and sources of South African law, nonetheless labour struggle and trade union activity was funnelled into and mediated by legal institutions. While this may suggest a strengthening of 'law' in what was an unlikely area for success, the willingness of labour to use this arena may have arisen because it was the only effective and available means of pursuing goals available then, and was open on good terms. Now that the labour leadership is a part of the ruling elite, and the labour movement a vital part of the governing constituency, it could well pursue its goals in the political rather than the legal arena. Conflicts between labour and government, as the latter embraces the employers' agenda of increased productivity, are unlikely to be resolved in the courts.

In the South African revolution neither Bastille nor Winter Palace were stormed, and no Nuremberg trials held, and the image projected in the absence of such dramatic symbolic events has been one of a managed and consensual transition. This has had effects on the ways in which the legal future has been imagined. The emphasis on continuity has not been uncontroversial. The then Minister of Justice, Dullah Omar, while sensitive to the issue of 'representativity' for the new judiciary, told the TRC of the 'dismay of our colleagues and friends, comrades in struggle' at the slowness of change, and of the new government's commitment to the building of a 'tradition and culture' in which politicians would not 'dictate' judicial appointments (legal hearings, October 1997: truthorg.za./HRVtrans/legal/legal htm).[2] But of course the real meaning

---

[2] During the 1998 election there were hints from the governing party that it would change the process to speed up transformation of the judiciary if it received the necessary two-thirds majority to change the constitution. Between 1994 and 1998 there were ninety-one new judicial appointments. Of these twenty-four were African (three of these women) and thirteen Asian (one a woman). Six white women have also been appointed (Malleson 1999). There has been much commentary around the issue of the experience required before appointment but none of the new appointees remotely approaches the lack of experience on appointment of the 'boy judges', de Villiers and Kotze, Chief Justices of the Cape and the South African Republic.

of the political transition has yet to unfold and may well prove to be more far reaching than envisaged. Limitations on our ability to imagine the future may falsify all prevision. I raise these questions in order to pursue the question of a legal culture in another way. How far can the existing practices and meanings stretch? Even if we do not think of these as constraints, but as resources to be drawn upon (as is implied, for instance, in the strategy of grounding rights thinking in the existing common law), how far can they continue to be usable as a part of a fundamental rejection of the order of which they were a part? Asking this question implies that there is or will be something else to use, something new. A good deal of the reformist (not a critical word) thinking, activity and scholarship about the legal future has been occupied with scouring the legal resources of the world for models with which to proceed. Much of South Africa's legal revolution may be made, like the legal system of the original Union, by bringing in answers from outside. There may well be an eagerness among lawyers to take this road, rather than to look to the development of local discourses, if only because these ideas have already been validated as 'law' elsewhere, by courts, or in conventions. Two connected questions emerge here. One is how large the legal repertoire available and suitable to a late twentieth-century industrial state really is. Is it not a purpose of the reconstruction to make South Africa's legal system look like those of other 'normal' countries? The second concerns the nature of the new state's relationship with the emerging globalisation of law. What place is there, as a widening range of uniformities are developing in the world's law, for specific local transformations? Increasingly caught in a tightening web of international agreements, conventions and expectations, which have become the textual universe of a new positivism, how relevant can the specific cultural features of local meanings and practices, narratives and purposes, be for any legal system (Klare 1998)?

The states created in Asia and Africa by the European empires, of which South Africa is one, all developed systemic legal pluralism. At the end of empire the anticipation was that, as foreign and racial rule receded, the plural legal systems would be both modernised and indigenised into single, culturally appropriate, national legal systems. But it is not easy to fit post-war developments anywhere in the former empires into this narrative. Indeed in both Asia and Africa the gap continues to persist between an externally oriented sector of law with global content and working within a formalist paradigm, and local law for the local population and local transactions, less formal and more culturally specific. There may be nothing 'wrong' with this at all; it is just that it was not expected by lawyers who have always had centralising ambitions and illusions. It does give us some insight into the possible development of South African legal culture. Current debates about the remaking of South African law have envisaged that a new accommodation may have to be made with African law; and that courts will have, to some extent, to reflect a greater degree of public accessibility and participation; but that these developments will take place within a single 'system', governed by the constitution's bill of rights. But perhaps the paradigm will fragment, leaving formalism confined to the elite and economic sectors using a global legal culture, while the keeping of order and the settlement of local disputes is abandoned to the realms of ministerial discretion and executive action (with the attendant dangers of political corruption), or to varying forms of popular court and customary law. There are important 'frontiers' between global and local legal cultures to be considered. One is property in land, which is essentially local, yet hard to separate from the 'rights' in property protected by the externally oriented sector. Another is 'family law', highly sensitive to local cultures, yet subject to the new scrutiny of international rights standards. Changes to land law are of particular importance in the current transition because they tell so much about the limits on sweeping change in this environment. A symbolic restitution of land seized by the white state (going back to 1913) will not in itself resolve the tensions between land as symbol of community and security, and land as economic asset. What kind of 'title' anyone, white or black, will have poses a real challenge for legal thinking and will be a complex matter to link with a global economic order. The lack of quick success (in spite of politically responsive and legally sophisticated efforts) in redefining communal tenure, in coping with the role of chiefs, in securing the tenure of farm workers, or altering the effects of urban segregation raise the spectre of a ship, reclaimed from a pirate crew, yet adrift on the same rocks (Chanock 1996). Similarly the urgent demands of 'law and order' may soon create limitations on the emergence of a 'rights culture'.

If South Africa is to avoid the pitfalls involved in a 'cult' of courts and judges (the word is Brigham's: 1987) it must take seriously that part of a legal culture which has been given least consideration in formal legal literature so far – the discourses about law in the culture at large, about institutions, practices and values. Here we might recall Robert Cover's remark, of particular value to those who instinctively look towards the judges as the source of creativity in the legal system: 'Judges characteristically do not create law, but kill it. Theirs is the jurispathic office. Confronting the luxurious growth of a hundred legal traditions, they assert that *this one* is the law and destroy or try to destroy the rest' (Cover 1983: 53). Reasoning with law, talking about law, working with law, and imagining law is not confined to the courts. The judges alone cannot be the source of the new legal culture. A formalist approach to writing about law has been most likely to separate the wider areas of legal discourse from consideration of law itself as being largely irrelevant to the professionalised internal methods of the legal world. Indeed there is much sense in separating internal professional legal discourses from discourses about law as their categories and ways of reasoning can be, and have often been in the South African case, not only very different but also more just. But one needs to do this without forgetting, and when necessary exhuming, the relationship between the discourses internal to law, and those about law. An exaggerated formalism is in many circumstances developed as a response to demands from the public for 'substance', while public and political demands made of the law's processes have often been a response to the perceived failures of an unrealistic formalism. The formalist style of South African law owes much to its complex relationship with these 'external' or popular discourses about law. Inasmuch as formalism represents a claim not just to authority over decision making in a particular area, but to the values according to which the decisions will be made, and to the intellectual materials that can be invoked in making them, it involves both a denial of and a response to alternative claims and pressures. These have been constantly present in the history of a polity where the drive to establish and maintain the advantages of racial rule drove public discourses about the law. An overall summing up of how this dialogue developed in South Africa would be too crude. Colonial law, depending on towards whom it was facing, could be either arbitrary or legalist, discriminatory or fair: its forms contained both stances. Its essence can perhaps be best captured by appropriating Bhabha's phrase 'a spirit of calm violence' (Bhabha 1995). Some features can be noted. One is the unsurprising observation that the state conducted the dialogue very largely with whites, not blacks. Black criticisms of the discriminatory enforcement of law (especially criminal law, the labour and pass laws, and land law) were constant and vocal, and were, until the last years of the

1980s, rarely even denied, but simply ignored. The result was that there were many areas of substantial overlap between discourses internal to law and those about law, but the dialogues that helped to shape the formal law excluded most of the population, even in the area of customary law.

Race

Considered historically rather than mythologically, South Africa's Roman-Dutch law was invented during the opening decades of this century. In the context of the overwhelming influence of English legal forms, of English as the language of the courts and the profession, of English public law, and of the paucity of Roman-Dutch legal sources available to judges (and scholars and barristers), the success of the venture was not assured, nor was it unquestioningly accepted by the profession. While in another contemporary new state Australia's judges in these decades were to align its common law closely to England's to reap the advantages of uniformity and experience, an alternative white nationalism in South Africa made this course unattractive. Roman-Dutch law was created in opposition to English law (and African law) as part of the writing of a national self-narrative. Voices calling for a codified civil-law system for South Africa were weak and ignored, and neither a European-style code nor even American-style re-statements were embarked on. Instead the local common law was developed by the judges, case by case, in rambling judgments. Excluded increasingly from the political realm by frequent bruising public criticism and executive determination, the judiciary's prestige and independence were developed in the core areas of common law, in which they were granted a wide degree of latitude. This was an integral part of the development of white cultural nationalism, taken up with renewed vigour when nationalist-minded judges finally took command of the appellate courts in the 1950s and 1960s.

This process also contributed to the entrenchment and projection of an autonomous formalism in the legal culture. Yet the national self-narrative in the Roman-Dutch law was exclusive. As we have seen, another common law was created by native administrators and magistrates, and it was one that drew on a differently imagined past and which did not share the institutional contexts that contributed to the formalism in the Roman-Dutch law. It is with this way of formulating the historical formation of the culture of South Africa's systems of common law that we can begin to approach the issues around transition. We must grasp the legal creativity of the period of the making of white statehood. The evolution of the different system of common laws embodied national, cultural and political narratives specific to time and circumstances, but this has not ever been its self-image. Even at the time in which the legitimacy of the heritage of the Roman-Dutch law was being called into question it was defended as the embodiment of 'scientific, abstract and generalising methods' (van der Walt 1995: 172). The current period of transition is an opportunity to revive creativity and some of the subordinated narratives, as the sources of common law are no longer tied by a nationalist and racist search for non-English, non-African roots. The voices, like Z. K. Matthews, that called for the parity of treatment and incorporation of African law into the common law can now be heard as a racialised dual system is called into question. Most significant for the future of the common law will be the constitutional provisions (secs. 8 and 39) aimed at achieving a congruence between the bill of rights and the values of the constitution and the common law. This will pose significant challenges to the place of 'scientific' reasoning based on the principles of civil law (see van der Merwe 1998). There will also be new external sources which will impact on the ways in which common law develops. Indeed experience elsewhere suggests that a culture of rights needs to be closely connected to the rights in the common law and not confined to a political/public law sphere. But this may not happen quickly for it involves changing a perception that the common law was an innocent component of the legal system.[3]

The issue of the place of race in the common law is best illustrated through the overlapping discourses in South African legal culture. If we confine our consideration to discourses internal to law it is not difficult to catalogue the frequent occasions on which non-racial principles were declared by judges, who placed the 'responsibility' for racism on statutory commands made to the courts. But if we consider the dialogue between the white discourses the legal culture has been permeated with a sense of struggle against the country's non-white population. Before we convict

---

[3] See the intriguing evidence given to the Judicial Commission by van Heerden JA in 1996 in which he was concerned to establish that he heard only one case in which a 'so-called apartheid law figured' while a judge in the Orange Free State (1996: 122). What Dyzenhaus (1998) has called the '95 per cent defence' – that nearly all judicial work had nothing to do with apartheid and was therefore innocent in relation to it – was also invoked by others in the hearings of the Truth and Reconciliation Commission.

the judiciary of the white state of excessive formalism we should underline how much they entered into extrinsic dialogue. The key appellate decisions in *Moller* and *Padsha* illustrate the close engagement between popular and judicial racism. The most basic self-conception of the legal enterprise was that it was inherent to white government and white civilisation and from this most other things flowed. The criminal law was informed by a criminology underpinned by racism, evolutionism and eugenicism, which focused increasingly on the inherent differences and dangerousness of Africans. We have seen that one of the largest legal/racist enterprises, the attempt to impose prohibition of alcohol on Africans, was founded on these fears. Even if we were to leave aside the huge enterprise of coercion which used the apparatus (institutions, personnel and language) of the criminal law to enforce economic and political discipline on Africans through a range of racially discriminatory statutes, the administration of the common law relating to crime was inseparable from racial rule. The basic axiom of white political discourses was that whites and Africans had different capacities, and this provided the justification for their exclusion from political rights. It is hardly surprising that these themes overlapped with the legal discourses that were founded on such differences. In the separate legal regimes which whites defined as belonging to Africans, they were seen to be not simply different, but deficient. Africans, in the white view, conceived of holding land in common because they had not yet reached the stage of understanding that it ought to be held individually. Africans were polygamous because of moral backwardness, not economic or cultural difference. Similar reasoning was applied to Africans' perceived inability to understand contract. The elaboration of, and continued working with, plural systems of common law were a part of a regime of subordination, not equality. Roman-Dutch law which developed as part of the bifurcation was anything but racially innocent, its identity being celebrated in its European origins (Chanock 1994).

Those elements of racial discrimination that were added by statute produced some complex problems. But most of the formal doctrinal difficulties for the courts were caused when discrimination was enacted against Asians, in immigration, in rights to property, in residence and licensing. It is on this frontier that the courts were boldest in their requiring specifically discriminatory instructions from statutes. This underlines the point made about the inherence of the narratives of difference in the common law. Asian legal rights in relation to property could not so easily be isolated into a separated legal realm as those of Africans. They could be in relation to marriage, where the possibility of polygamy in Hindu and Muslim religious law provided a sufficiently different cultural narrative in which to situate a common-law discrimination against Asian marriages.

No account of the place of race within South Africa's legal culture can ignore the questions of racial classification by law, and the issues of interracial sex and marital relations. It was not simple, given the complex racial make-up of the country, and the multifarious purposes of discrimination on the basis of race, to arrive at, or administer, racial definitions. The definitions of excluded groups tended to vary from law to law, depending on its purposes, but their most common feature is that they were originally based on a social definition of racial identity, not a genealogical or a biological one. South African legal definitions, not for want of knowledge of the examples, steered away as we have seen from the inheritance-based definitions which prevailed in American state legislation (particularly, though not exclusively, in the South). Clearly also there was no development of the German example of 'scientific' determination. South African tests and processes were cruel, but pragmatic. Courts and administrators applied tests of appearance, circumstances and habits of life, and social acceptance, as determinants of racial status. Despite the flourishing discourses of biological racism in the broader culture (Dubow 1995), they were strangely rare in the discourses internal to law.

Racism in South African legal culture was always objected to from the standpoint of legal liberalism which opposes discrimination between those who ought to be equal rights bearers. In emphasising a history of pervasive and dominant racism it is by no means my aim to exclude from the story the constant projection of the alternative path of non-discrimination maintained by some at all levels. Liberal legalism was a powerful rhetorical weapon in the struggle to de-legitimise apartheid, because it was perhaps the only non-racially based doctrine with significant purchase among nearly all parts of the white elite. Even so, a display of the limited repertoire of liberal legal dicta from cases past should not be allowed to distort the picture of the racial foundations and purposes of South Africa's law. This lesser tradition of non-racism in law appeared to be about to have its historic moment as the apartheid state collapsed. Legal aspects of racial discrimination were dismantled, those relevant to racial identity itself in personal law being among the first to go. What could seem more obvious than to conclude that liberalism had been triumphant in law, and that the legal culture could, and henceforth would, be constructed along lines in which racial identity was irrelevant? Where law had seen little but race, race would now become legally invisible. But a society of acutely self-conscious racial identities remains. Can one imagine a legal culture reconstructing itself which could or should not see them (see e.g. Robinson 1997)?

Two things were at once obvious. One was that a law based upon a complete and formal ignoring of race as a factor in constituting rights would contribute to entrenching the economic status quo unless and until the 'market' put it right. A second, and also politically charged, problem was that of the accommodation of cultural difference within a framework of legal uniformity. Apartheid was born at the beginning of the end of the era of European colonialism. After 1948 South African legal culture had swung more determinedly towards a racially based law in the period when legal systems elsewhere in the world were moving towards a formal non-racism. Similar ironies are presented now. As multi-national states begin to fragment elsewhere, South Africa seeks to create one. This does not, of course, necessarily invalidate the enterprise. It serves only as background to the point that the apparent historical moment of a non-racial legalism is fraught with difficulties. A liberal rights discourse which emphasises rights as the basis of entitlement to equal treatment, and which had long been part of the conceptual basis of the aspirations and objectives of liberals in South African law, now competes with other concepts of rights which are gaining strength in those external discourses on which the debate about re-construction in South Africa relies so heavily.

A liberal rights order is challenged by other powerful versions of rights. While the informing historical trajectory of the Marxism that was an important part of the liberation struggle has lost credibility, and the vocabulary of Marxist jurisprudence has forfeited its persuasive capacities, the obvious power of an emphasis on substantive economic right as a necessary part of a rights order remains. The nature of the transition from white rule, and its conceivable outcomes, are markedly different from those envisaged by many who fought for liberation. But historical trajectories formerly envisaged are unlikely suddenly to be erased from consciousness. The way they interact with unfolding circumstances will provide the context for the influence of substantive concepts of economic rights.

The second, increasingly influential, challenge is the post-liberal dis-course of rights which insists that recognition of difference rather than a fictional sameness be the basis for the assertion and recognition of rights (see Andrews 1999). These conceptualisations, developed primarily in the evolution of a new rights culture in the USA which demands the acknow-ledgement and effective recognition of the gender and race of rights bearers, have instant purchase in South African debates. The search for ways in which the need for affirmative action in relation to jobs and property rights can be fitted into an equal-rights paradigm draws its essential intellectual support from these new rights. And in South Africa now there are other more complex cross-currents. The assertions of gender equality, and of a greater sensitivity towards cultural rights, and a growing confidence in an African-defined customary law, may not fit easily together. The purity of the liberal legal paradigm has already been shattered by laws on affirmative action and a unified family law which recognises polygamy.

There are diverse strategies with which to meet the challenges of an inheritance of hierarchical legal pluralism. One could be to seek unity, the other to recognise diversity based on equality. The new constitution points invitingly in both directions: it is prescriptive as to rights to which all law – statutory, common law, and customary law – must conform, yet specific in its recognition of the right to observe, and have applied, law appropriate to cultural identity and religion (see secs. 15, 30, 39 and 211; and Himonga 1998; Bennett 1995). In 1997 the Cape Supreme Court flatly rejected the cardinal discriminatory decision in the history of South African common law, *Seedat*'s case (see above) which had been endorsed by the Appellate Division as late as 1983 (Himonga 1998: 12). The court invoked the values of 'equality' and 'diversity' in the constitution, yet contestation can be expected between the diversity in society and the monologic leanings of (even) rights jurisprudence and of state law making. In contrast to the rejection of the concept of a unified marriage law after the formation of Union, the new Law Commission in 1996 began by positing that the post-apartheid state, based on equality, 'should in principle have one marriage law' (quoted by Himonga 1998: 20) but it has so far stumbled over diversity, and the relationship between customary laws and internationally inspired rights jurisprudence may take long to settle.

Finally in relation to race one can return to the question of the future of formalism, for issues relating to race are one of the most testing frontiers of the contest between form and substance. They involve, as do issues relating to gender, the basic question of how the legal subject is perceived. In the first decades of the Union South Africa's legal culture grappled with, and essentially rejected, the constitution of Africans as rights bearers in law. The rejection of the 'Cape' policy is often discussed in terms of political rights only. But it also involved the rejection of the assumption that the legal regimes for whites and Africans would eventually be assimilated into one (the European). There turned out to be an essential connection (which some judges had tried to avoid) between political and common-law rights. Once Africans were not members of the community constituting the state, and as it became plain that they would never be so considered, so legal assimilation was abandoned and Africans relegated to a separate legal regime. The reconstitution of Africans as full legal actors and bearers of rights in a new state will strengthen liberal legalism, providing for the first time a political base for the recognition of equal rights in law.

Legal culture 3

I have dwelt at some length on the violence that preceded and followed the creation of the Union in 1910, for it was in this period that South Africa's formalist legal culture was created. The end of the white state has produced for South Africa's legal culture a powerful challenge to the brand of legal formalism discredited by its association with apartheid. But in a turbulent political environment the problems of balancing form and substance will not go away. The current constitution has ushered in a realm of what might be called the 'new formalism', in which a bill of rights, and its associated global jurisprudence, will be used to provide exhaustively the primary and secondary texts of the new 'rule of law'.[4] However people with all their eggs in the new rights-based formalist basket will be disappointed. Neither law nor rights will trump politics, particularly as both may depend on an administrative capacity that the

---

[4] It is noteworthy that there is a search for new interpretative methodologies which the new court and its wide range of possible authorities seem to call for. These involve reconsideration of the old 'scientific' style of reasoning, and 'literal' statutory interpretation. There has been a philosophical resort to the (conflicting) indeterminacies of hermeneutics and deconstruction. (See the essays in *Acta Juridica* 1998.)

state may not have. And conversely those who might celebrate the discarding of form in the dash for change will soon discover the exposure and vulnerability that such a strategy involves for its protagonists. It seems to me that at least an awareness of this issue in all its complexity should be a part of the process of the growth of the new legal culture.

Can there be a formalism without the claim of legal professionals to control validity in reasoning about law? Is it possible to maintain the integrity of the processes and judgments of the courts, while at the same time denying the claim of judges and courts to constitute and control the discourses of the legal culture? While all legal systems need to consider this question, it is especially important in a system in so profound a transition. There will be obvious fears for a 'rule of law' if the narrow claim to control the definition of law is abandoned, and the danger of the possible rejection of law if it is maintained. Pragmatists who treat 'reconstruction' as exercises in 'what is to be done' may be irritated by such questions. The tensions that exist, and must be accommodated in any legal system, between painstaking care in relation to rules and process and the sweeping rhetoric of justice, are much stronger in these circumstances. A new rhetoric of rights, as it will not be accompanied by commensurate economic changes, could increase cynicism about and rejection of law unless it learns to become both less exclusive and less absolutist.

One of the most important features, in some eyes the saving grace, of legalism in South Africa in the closing decades of the white state was the way in which the courts became the arena in which vital political positions were manifested and battles were fought (see in particular Abel 1995). Statements made from the dock became a component of the political heritage and legal culture that cannot be overlooked. Even though there will now be other places in which these causes can be heard, it is likely that, given the new rights jurisprudence and the need to give it meaning in practice, the courts, in particular the new Constitutional Court, will continue to be a focus for 'political' cases. The experience in other 'new' states after the end of colonialism has been that the legal repertoire of actions and choices is limited. The role of the highest court is constrained by its need to ensure that the new order 'works'. Politically this limits its freedom in proclaiming rights. Given that this is so, it is important that such a court does not become the only focus for new legal discourses or practices. The sensitivity of judges to broader fields of discourse has been clearly apparent in South Africa in the past decade. While the final period of apartheid opened with a judiciary alive to the government's belief in 'total onslaught', it had partially metamorphosed in apartheid's closing years along with government policy, reversing previous doctrines and practices. The already demonstrated sensitivity to political prevailing winds now has a new institutional setting in the Constitutional Court. Politicians and lawyers have positively welcomed the involvement of a new court, which is in an exposed position. Obviously not all sides want the same things from such a court. For the whites who relinquished political power it represented a possible shield, and a symbolic guarantee of a state governed by law. For the new rulers it will be the means by which policies receive the ultimate stamp of legitimacy. Like any court of last resort, but in an especially acute way, it will be caught between the paradigms of form and substance. An uncompromising formalism has never been appropriate either to the settlement of constitutional disputes or in the interpretation of a rights instrument, which is one of the major avenues by which the broader legal culture will find its way into the decisions of courts.

In the white state many South African lawyers struggled to maintain a legal liberalism implied by the forms they had inherited. It is important to acknowledge both parts of the story: that some tried and that the effort usually failed. In the new state where there are urgent political necessities, unresolved historical antagonisms, many wants and much anger, can an attempt to maintain formal 'liberal' law of the type envisaged in the new constitutional arrangements be successful? There are many obvious things to be thought about if a version of formal liberal law is this time to be more successful. Some are already in process: a lower-court system not entirely dominated by public officials; a return to forms of lay participation in judgment; a less remote Bar; a less exalted judiciary more widely chosen; a more comprehensible and accessible common law; different forms of legal practice. G. Simpson argued at TRC legal hearings that what was needed was 'to break the tradition of distanced judging in our society'. All of these are a part of situating the existing narrow notion of law in a wider legal universe of practices, and part of a rescuing of the law from both politicians and judges. The gulf between the limited professional legal discourses and other ways understanding law was exemplified in the statement of Z. Hussein to the legal hearings. The judges (and lawyers) he said had in a 'technical legal polemic' portrayed themselves as 'victims' of parliamentary sovereignty. But, as he said, 'We are not asked to explain ourselves within a narrow context which we set for ourselves . . . legal positivism is not an answer to the community' (truthorg.za/HRVtrans/legal/legal.htm).

There are other basic issues with which this book began. From the point of view of the experience of most South Africans 'law' has meant, primarily, 'police'. In recreating a legal culture, a new policing may mean more on the ground than does a new constitutional discourse. But the political transition has been accompanied by a perceived experience among all communities of a collapse of effective policing and a rising tide of politicised gang rule, crime and violence. The old state, eroded from within by rampant corruption, had lost control over substantial areas of South African life before it was replaced, and this has not been recaptured by the new one (see Ellis 1999). There was a long tradition of non-state policing and courts in the black urban areas, and in the 1980s this developed from a rejection of the state's police and courts into the widespread establishment of people's courts and local self-policing (see Brogden and Shearing 1993: chapter 6). There has been ambitious think-ing about building on this in reconstruction through a sharing of 'sover-eignty' between community and state in policing (Sachs in Brogden and Shearing 1993: x). This theoretical reaction to the colonial model of policing on which the old state was founded has necessarily been radical, but has not effectively informed practice. The perception of anarchy poses the greatest threat to the emergence of a more responsive legal order, and it is more far reaching than a question of a response to crime, chaos and disorder. Law depends on administrative efficiency, rights upon a strong state, not a weak one. A declining effectiveness of the state's administrative machinery and a growth of corruption at a time in which new rights are being proclaimed would weaken any new legal order. An effective, yet accountable, administration and a confident democracy could be better guarantees for a new legality than a bill of rights. For lawyers a simple neo-realism which paid greater attention to the processes of law making and administration, rather than to philosophies of interpretation, could provide a better understanding.

There is an inspiring contrast between 1910 when the Department of Justice report laconically remarked that 'the year of Union has been a hanging year' (UG 35 1911: 10) and the abolition of the death penalty by the Constitutional Court in its first case (*S v Makwanyane 1995 (30) SA*

391 CC).[5] There can be glorious moments for an appellate judiciary in which judges are able in unique historical junctures to reach out beyond unjust principles, legally established, to re-found a legal order. But these instances are rare: the inspiring statements of principle with which the new order is necessarily declared do not easily translate into solutions for social conflicts, and engender long-drawn-out litigation to haunt those judges who have the daily task of deciding difficult cases for litigants according to known rules of law. There are also the well-canvassed problems of justifying judicial power of this sort in a democracy: it is unlikely that any of these decisions would have been made had a majoritarian voice been decisive. Yet in spite of the increase in judicial power around the world as new constitutional states spread and the discovery of 'rule of law' and 'governance' issues become a part of the language of globalisation, the judicial voice, even when it rises to inspiring heights, cannot alone bear the burden of envisioning the new legal order.

We may return now to where we began, with a new state, the Union of South Africa, being constructed after prolonged violence and a spectacular reconciliation between (white) elites. A new constitutional order built on an external model of parliamentary supremacy, and based on a 'rule of law' was the foundation. A new binary private law was evolved, which struggled with the problems of uniformity and diversity. A huge task of legislative re-making of the country was embarked upon to provide it with the institutions of a twentieth-century state. This idealised legal order rapidly degenerated in the face of political realities. And the attachment of state law to the 'market' and its 'law' was drastically modified to protect and advance partial economic interests. The parallels, as the new South African state embarks upon its task of legislative reconstruction, transforming a terrible legacy into a democratic post-colonial order, are both close and distant. Parliamentary supremacy has been rejected in the name of a new, externally inspired, culture of constitutionalism. Colonial racial supremacy has gone. In sharp contrast to the absence of women in the processes of law and state that I noted at the outset, not only was the rhetoric of gender equality a part of transformation, but half of those who took part in the negotiating process of 1993 were women, as were a quarter of the first post-apartheid parliament (see Murray 1994). Yet the

---

[5] Similarly we can contrast the widespread use of the reverse onus of proof that underlay much of the criminal law discussed in this book with the Constitutional Court's finding that such reversal was contrary to the bill of rights.

development of legal culture in a conflictual political culture in a state that has never been united or stable will be focused around the old matrices – of international acceptability and internal economic struggle; centralisation, disunity and diversity – and new ones – popular justice and democracy and constitutionalism. Legal liberalism faltered as an instrument with which to construct the old state which had political premises and institutions that were hostile to it. The construction of a legality compatible not only with the conquest of both violence and immense economic inequality but also with the tensions between individual rights and collective identities remains the challenge for all those who talk about law. As I have emphasised throughout, the state made at the beginning of the century was integrated into a global empire: and the state now being constructed is a part of a new globalised legal order. Lawyers simultaneously face internally and externally, dealing with the inherited legal culture within the context of a global liberal democratic order which has both weakened the state and reduced its ability to control the market; and enhanced the role of 'law' as a guarantor of stability. 'Law' is seen as the means through which solutions to conflicts, which the political processes may have failed to compromise, are to be found. Yet a vigorous rights discourse is evidence of the prevalence of wrongs. And the idealising language of law conceals not only the ambitions of the state, but also its incapacities, which are the major threat to a rule of law.

BIBLIOGRAPHY

Abel, R. (1995) *Politics by Other Means: Law in the Struggle against Apartheid, 1980–1994*. New York, Routledge

Anderson, D. M. and D. Killingray eds. (1991) *Policing the Empire. Government, Authority and Controls 1830–1930*. Manchester, Manchester University Press

Andrews, P. ed. (1999) *Gender, Race and Comparative Advantage*. Special issue of *Law in Context* 15(2) 1999

Arnold, T. (1935) *The Symbols of Government*. New Haven, Yale University Press

Ashforth, A. (1990) *The Politics of Official Discourse in Twentieth Century South Africa*. London, Oxford University Press

Atiyah, P. S. (1970) *Accidents, Compensation and Law*. London, Weidenfeld & Nicolson

Bain, G. C. (1938) *Crime, the American Negro and the Urban Native in South Africa*. Pretoria, Carnegie Corporation

Basner, M. (1993) *Am I an African?* Johannesburg, Witwatersrand University Press

Baxter, L. (1984) *Administrative Law*. Cape Town, Juta

Beinart, W. (1986) 'Settler Accumulation in East Griqualand from the Demise of the Griqua to the Natives Land Act'. In Beinart, Delius and Trapido eds.

Beinart W., P. Delius and S. Trapido eds. (1986) *Putting a Plough to the Ground: Accumulation and Dispossession in Rural South Africa 1850–1930*. Johannesburg, Ravan

Beinart, W. and P. Delius (1986) 'Introduction'. In Beinart, Delius and Trapido eds.

Bennett, R. (1934) *Up for Murder*. London, Hutchinson

Bennett, T. W. (1991) *A Source Book of African Customary Law for Southern Africa*. Cape Town, Juta

(1995) *Human Rights and African Customary Law*. Cape Town, Juta

Berger, I. (1992) *Threads of Solidarity: Women in South African Industry 1900–1980*. Bloomington, Indiana University Press

Bhabha, H. K. (1995) 'In a Spirit of Calm Violence'. In G. Prakash ed. *After Colonialism*. Princeton, Princeton University Press

Blackburn, D. and W. W. Caddell (1911) *Secret Service in South Africa*. London, Cassell

Blackwell, L. (1962) *Are Judges Human?* London, Bailey Brothers & Swinfen

Blaine, C. H. (1931) *Native Courts Practice*. Cape Town, Juta

Boon, J. (1982) *Other Tribes, Other Scribes: Symbolic Anthropology in the Comparative Study of Cultures, Histories, Religions and Texts*. Cambridge, Cambridge University Press

Bourhill, C. J. (1912) 'The Smoking of Dagga among the Native Races of South Africa and the Resultant Evils'. Ph.D. thesis, Edinburgh University

Bradford, H. (1988) *A Taste of Freedom: The ICU in Rural South Africa, 1924–30*. Johannesburg, Ravan

Brigham, J. (1987) *The Cult of the Court*. Philadelphia, Temple University Press

Brogden, M. and C. Shearing (1993) *Policing for a New South Africa*. New York, Routledge

Brookes, E. H. (1924) *The History of Native Policy in South Africa*. Pretoria, Nasionale Pers

Brookes, E. H. and R. F. Currey (1930) 'The Administration of Justice'. In Brookes and Currey eds.

   (1933) *The Colour Problems of South Africa*. London, Kegan Paul

Brookes, E. H. and R. F. Currey eds. (1930) *Coming of Age. Studies in South African Citizenship and Politics*. Cape Town, Maskew Miller

Bryant, A. T. (1929) *Olden Times in Zululand and Natal*. London, Longmans

Burman, S. (1981) *Chiefdom, Politics and Alien Law*. Oxford, St Martin's

Burman, S. and W. Scharf (1990) 'Creating People's Justice: Street Committees and People's Courts in a South African City'. 24 (3) *Law and Society Review* 693–774

Cameron, E. (1982) 'Legal Chauvinism, Executive-mindedness and Justice: L. C. Steyn's Impact on South African Law'. 99 *South African Law Journal* 38–75

Carnegie Commission (1932) *The Poor White Problem in South Africa*. Stellenbosch, Pro-Ecclesia

Cd 714 (1901) *Papers relating to Certain Legislation of the Late South African Republic Affecting Natives*

Cd 2027 (1904) *Despatches from the Governor of the Transvaal Enclosing a Return with Regard to Magistrates of the Colony*

Cd 2399 (1903–5) *Report of the South African Native Affairs Commission 1903–05*. Appendices: Evidence, vols. 1, 2 and 3

Cd 2852 (1906) *Report of the Departmental Committee on Vagrancy*, vol. 1

Cd 5684 (1907) *Comparative Analyses of the Company Laws of the United Kingdom,*

India, Canada, Australia and New Zealand; with Memoranda Prepared for the Imperial Conference (1907) by the Direction of the Board of Trade

Chanock, M. (1977) *Unconsummated Union*. Manchester, Manchester University Press

(1985) *Law, Custom and Social Order: The Colonial Experience in Malawi and Zambia*. Cambridge, Cambridge University Press

(1989) 'Writing South African Legal History: A Prospectus'. 30 *Journal of African History* 265–88

(1991) 'Paradigms, Policies and Property: A Review of the Customary Law of Land Tenure'. In K. Mann and R. Roberts eds. *Law in Colonial Africa*. Portsmouth NH, Heinemann

(1994) 'The South African Native Administration Act of 1927: Reflections on a Pathological Case of Legal Pluralism'. In O. Mendelsohn and U. Baxi eds. *The Rights of Subordinated Peoples*. Delhi, Oxford University Press

(1995) 'Race and Nation in South African Common Law'. In P. Fitzpatrick ed. *Racism and Nationalism in Law*. Aldershot, Dartmouth

(1996) 'Making and Unmaking a Segregated Land Regime: Tenure, Market and Individual'. In S. Arnfred and H. Petersen eds. *Legal Change in North/ South Perspective*. Roskilde, International Development Studies

(1999) 'The Lawyer's Self: Sketches on Establishing a Professional Identity in South Africa, 1900–1925'. *Law in Context* (1)

(1999b) 'A Post-Calvinist Catechism or a Post-Communist Manifesto? Intersecting Narratives in the South African Bill of Rights Debate'. In P. Alston ed. *Promoting Human Rights through Bills of Rights: Comparative Perspectives*. Oxford, Oxford University Press.

Chisholm, L. (1989) 'Reformatories and Industrial Schools in South Africa: A Study in Class and Gender, 1882–1939'. Ph.D. thesis, University of the Witwatersrand

C.J.I. (1909) 'The Cry of the Abolitionist'. 26 *South African Law Journal* 43–53

Clifford, J. (1988) *The Predicament of Culture*. Cambridge MA, Harvard University Press

Clifford, J. and G. Marcus eds. (1986) *Writing Culture: The Poetics and Politics of Ethnography*. Berkeley and Los Angleles, University of California Press

Cobbey, A. S. (1990) *Class and Conciousness. The Black Petit-bourgeois in South Africa, 1924–1950*. Westport CT, Greenwood Press

Cockrell, A. (1996) 'Breach of Contract'. In Zimmerman and Visser eds.

Cocks, R. (1988) *Sir Henry Maine: A Study in Victorian Jurisprudence*. Cambridge, Cambridge University Press

Cohn, B. (1996) *Colonialism and its Forms of Knowledge: The British in India*. Princeton, Princeton University Press

Colonial Office. Confidential Prints Miscellaneous 138, London

Corder, H. (1984) *Judges at Work*. Johannesburg, Juta

Corder, H. ed. (1988) *Essays in Law and Social Practice*. Johannesburg, Juta

Corder, H. L. (1946) *The Truth and Nothing But*. Cape Town, Juta

Cornish, W. R. and G. Clark (1989) *Law and Society in England, 1750–1950*. London, Sweet & Maxwell

Cover, R. (1983) 'Violence and the Word'. 95 *Yale Law Journal* 1601–30

Cowan, D. V. (1959) 'The History of the Law Faculty of the University of Cape Town. *Acta Juridica* 1–20

(1961) *The Foundations of Freedom*. Cape Town, Oxford University Press

Cowan, Z. (1965) *Sir John Latham*. Melbourne, Oxford University Press

(1967) *Isaac Isaacs*. Melbourne, Oxford University Press

Creighton, W., W. Ford and R. Mitchell (1983) *Labour Law: Materials and Commentary*. Sydney, Law Book Company

Crush, J. and C. Ambler eds. (1992) *Liquor and Labour in Southern Africa*. Athens, Ohio University Press

Culler, J. (1988) *Framing the Sign*. Oxford, Basil Blackwell

Currey, R. F. (1930) 'Defence and Police'. In Brookes and Currey eds.

Currey, R. N. (1968) *Letters of a Natal Sheriff*. Cape Town, Oxford University Press

Currie, I. (1999) 'Judicious Avoidance'. 15 *South African Journal of Human Rights* 2, 138–65

Dangerfield, G. (1970) *The Strange Death of Liberal England*. London, Paladin

Davenport, T. H. (1971) *The Beginnings of Urban Segregation in South Africa*. Grahamstown, Rhodes University

Davenport, T. H. and K. S. Hunt eds. (1974) *The Right to Land*. Cape Town, David Philip

Davies, R. H. (1979) *Capital, State and White Labour in South Africa 1900–1960*. Brighton, Harvester Press

Davis, D. (1987) 'Post Apartheid South Africa. What Future for a Legal System?' *Acta Juridica* 220–36

(1999) 'Equality: The Majesty of Legoland Jurisprudence'. 116 *South African Law Journal* 2, 398–414

Davis, D. and M. Slabbert eds. (1985) *Crime and Power in South Africa*. Cape Town, David Philip

Davis, G., L. Melunsky and F. du Rand (1959) *Urban Native Law*. Port Elizabeth, Grotius Publications

Dean, W. H. (1983) 'Reason and Prejudice: The Courts and Licensing Bodies in the Transvaal'. In Kahn ed.

Denoon, D. (1973) *A Grand Illusion*. London, Longmans

Department of Justice (1914) 'Magistrates in the Transvaal'. Union Archives 3/317/111

de van Hart, N. (1915) 'Crime and Criminal Law under Socialism'. 32 *South African Law Journal* 226–40

de Villiers, M. (1918a) 'Legal Education in South Africa'. 35 *South African Law Journal* 155–60

    (1918b) 'Women and the Legal Profession'. 35 *South African Law Journal* 289–91

Devitt, N. (1934) *Memoirs of a Magistrate*. London, H. F. and G. Witherby

Dicey, A. V. ([1885] 1959) *An Introduction to the Study of the Law of the Constitution*. London, Macmillan

Doxey, G. (1961) *The Industrial Colour Bar in South Africa*. Cape Town, Oxford University Press

Dubow, S. (1989) *Racial Segregation and the Origins of Apartheid in South Africa 1919–1930*. Oxford, Macmillan

    (1995) *Scientific Racism in Modern South Africa*. Cambridge, Cambridge University Press

Dugard, J. (1974) 'The Political Trial: Some Special Considerations'. In Kahn ed.

    (1978) *Human Rights and the South African Legal Order*. Princeton, Princeton University Press

Duncan, D. (1995) *The Mills of God*. Johannesburg, Witwatersrand University Press

Dyzenhaus, D. (1998) *Judging the Judges, Judging Ourselves: Truth, Reconciliation and the Apartheid Legal Order*. Oxford, Hart Publishing

Eales, K. A. (1991) 'Gender Politics and the Administration of African Women in Johannesburg 1903–39'. MA thesis, University of the Witwatersrand

Ellis, M. (1999) 'The New Frontiers of Crime in South Africa'. In J. F. Bayart, S. Ellis and B. Hibou eds. *The Criminalisation of the State in Africa*. Oxford, James Currey

Evans, I. (1997) *Bureaucracy and Race: Native Administration in South Africa*. Los Angeles, University of California Press

Fagan, E. (1996) 'Roman-Dutch Law in its South African Historical Context'. In Zimmerman and Visser eds.

Finn, P. (1987) *Law and Government in Colonial Australia*. Melbourne, Oxford University Press

Forsyth, C. (1985) *In Danger for their Talents*. Johannesburg, Juta

G 4 (1883) *Report of the Commission on Native Laws and Customs*. Cape Town, Cape Government

Gandhi, M. (1928) *Satyagraha in South Africa*. Ahmedabad, Navijan Publishing House

Gardiner, G. G. and C. W. Lansdown (1924) *South African Criminal Law and Procedure*. Cape Town, Juta

Garland, D. (1985) *Punishment and Welfare: A History of Penal Strategies*. London, Heinemann

Garthorne, E. R. (1924) *The Application of Native Law in the Transvaal*. Johannesburg, University of Witwatersrand Press

Geffen, I. A. (1928) *The Laws of South Africa Affecting Women and Children*. Johannesburg, Esson

Gilman, S. (1985) *Differences and Pathology: Stereotypes of Sexuality, Race and Madness*. Ithaca, Cornell University Press

Goodrich, P. (1990) *Languages of Law: From Logics of Memory to Nomadic Masks*. London, Weidenfeld & Nicolson

Greenberg, S. (1987) *Legitimating the Illegitimate: State, Markets and Resistance in South Africa*. Los Angeles, University of California Press

Grundlingh, A. (1991) 'Protectors and Friends of the People: The South African Constabulary in the Transvaal and the Orange River Colony 1900–1908'. In Anderson and Killingray eds.

Hahlo, H. and E. Kahn eds. (1960) *The Union of South Africa: The Development of its Laws and Constitution*. Cape Town, Juta

(1968) *The South African Legal System*. Cape Town, Juta

Hailey, Lord (1938) *African Survey*. London, Oxford University Press

Hamilton, C. (1998) *Terrific Majesty: The Power of Shaka Zulu and the Limits of Historical Invention*. Cape Town, David Philip

Hancock, W. K. and J. van der Poel eds. (1962 and 1968) *Selections from the Smuts Papers*. Cambridge, Cambridge University Press

Hepple, B. A. (1960) 'Economic and Racial Legislation'. In Hahlo and Kahn eds.

Hewart, Lord (1929) *The New Despotism*. London, E. Benn

Higgins, H. B. (1915/16) 'A New Province for Law and Order'. 29 *Harvard Law Review* 13–39

Himonga, C. (1998) 'A Legal System in Transition: Cultural Diversity and National Identity in Post Apartheid South Africa'. *Recht in Afrika* 1–23

Hindson, D. (1987) *Pass Controls and the Urban African Proletariat*. Johannesburg, Ravan

Hiscock, W. J. (1924) 'The Bar and the BA Degree'. 41 *South African Law Journal* 262–8

Hoag, E. B. and E. H. Williams (1923) *Crime, Abnormal Minds and the Law*. Indianapolis, Bobbs-Merrill

Holdsworth, W. (1932–66) *A History of English Law*, vols. I-XVII. London, Methuen

Honore, A. M. (1974) 'Legal Reasoning in Rome and Today'. In Kahn ed.

Horwitz, M. J. (1977) *The Transformation of American Law 1780–1860.* Cambridge MA, Harvard University Press

(1992) *The Transformation of American Law.* New York, Oxford University Press

Hosten, W. J. (1983) *Introduction to South African Law and Legal Theory.* Durban, Butterworths

Hutchison, D. (1996) 'Aquilian Liaibility 11 (Twentieth Century)'. In Zimmerman and Visser eds.

Hutt, W. H. (1933) 'Economic Aspects of the Report of the Poor-white Commission'. 1 *South African Journal of Economics* 281–90

(1935) 'Logical Issues in the Study of Industrial Legislation in the Union'. 3 *South African Journal of Economics* 26–42

Huttenback, R. A. (1971) *Gandhi in South Africa: British Imperialism and the Indian Question 1860–1914.* Ithaca, Cornell University Press

(1976) *Racism and Empire: White Settlers and Colored Immigrants in the British Self-governing Colonies 1830–1910.* Ithaca, Cornell University Press

Innes Papers. Correspondence of Sir James Rose-Innes. South African Archives, Cape Town

Jeeves, A. H. (1985) *Migrant Labour in South Africa's Mining Economy 1890–1920.* Kingston and Montreal, McGill-Queens University Press

Jeppe, C. (1910) 'Undue Preference'. 27 *South African Law Journal* 564–73

Johnstone, F. A. (1976) *Class, Race and Gold: A Study of Class Relations and Racial Discrimination in South Africa.* London, Routledge & Kegan Paul

Joshi, P. S. (1942) *The Tyranny of Colour.* Port Washington NY, Kennikat Press

Junod, H. (1912) *The Life of a South African Tribe,* vol. II. London, D. Nutt

Kahn, E. ed. (1974) *Select South African Legal Problems.* Cape Town, Juta

(1983) *Fiat Justitia: Essays in Memory of O. D. Schreiner.* Cape Town, Juta

Kantor, B. (1972) 'The Evolution of Monetary Policy in South Africa'. In M. Kooy ed. *Studies in Economics and Economic History.* London, Macmillan

Kaplan, D. E. (1976) 'The Politics of Industrial Protection in South Africa 1910–1939' 3 *Journal of South African Studies* 70–91

Kaplan, L. V. (1984) 'The Development of Various Aspects of the Gold Mining Laws in South Africa from 1871 to 1967'. Ph.D. thesis, University of the Witwatersrand

Katz, E. (1974) 'White Workers' Grievances and the Industrial Colour Bar 1902–13'. 42 *South African Journal of Economics* 127–56

(1976) *A Trade Union Aristocracy.* Johannesburg, African Studies Institute, University of the Witwatersrand

(1994) *The White Death: Silicosis on the Witwatersrand Gold Mines 1886–1910.* Johannesburg, Witwatersrand University Press

Keegan, T. (1986) *Rural Transformation in Industrialising South Africa*. Johannesburg, Ravan

Keith, A. B. (1916) *Imperial Unity and the Dominions*. Oxford, Clarendon Press

(1924) *The Constitution, Administration and Laws of the Empire*. London, W. Collins

(1929) *The Sovereignty of the British Dominions*. London, Macmillan

(1938) *The Dominions as Sovereign States*. London, Macmillan

Kennedy, W. P. and H. J. Schlosberg (1935) *The Law and Customs of the South African Constitution*. London, Oxford University Press

Kircher, B. (1995) *An Unruly Child. A History of Law in Australia*. Melbourne, Allen & Unwin

Kitchin, S. B. (1927) 'The Lawyer's Place in the Commonwealth'. 44 *South African Law Journal* 142–6

Klare, K. (1998) 'Legal Culture and Transformative Constitutionalism'. 14 *South African Journal for Human Rights* 146–88

Klug, H. (1995) 'Defining the Property Rights of Others: Political Power, Indigenous Tenure and the Construction of Customary Land Law'. 35 *Journal of Legal Pluralism* 119–48

Knafla, L. and S. Binnie eds. (1995) *Law, Society and State: Essays in Modern Legal History*. Toronto, University of Toronto Press

Krause, F. E. (1939) 'Crime and its Punishment'. 36 *South African Journal of Science*

Krikler, J. (1993) *Revolution from Above, Rebellion from Below: The Agrarian Transvaal at the Turn of the Century*. Oxford, Clarendon Press

Lacey, M. (1981) *Working for Baroko: The Origins of a Coercive Labour System in South Africa*. Johannesburg, Ravan

La Hausse, P. (1990) 'The Cows of Nongoloza: Youth, Crime and *Amalaita* Gangs in Durban, 1900–1936'. 16 *Journal of Southern African Studies* 79–111

Laubscher, B. J. (1937) *Sex, Custom and Psychopathology: A Study of South African Pagan Natives*. London, Routledge & Kegan Paul

Le May, G. (1965) *British Supremacy in South Africa*. Oxford, Oxford University Press

Lee, R. W. (1915) *An Introduction to Roman-Dutch Law*. Oxford, Clarendon Press

(1923) 'Law and Legislation in the Union of South Africa'. *Yale Law Journal* 224–32; repr. in 40 *South African Law Journal* 442–50

(1924) 'Roman-Dutch Law in South Africa'. 40 *Law Quarterly Review* 61–75; repr. in 41 *South African Law Journal* 297–311

Legal Resources Centre, *Annual Reports*. Johannesburg

Lestrade, G. P. (1934) 'Some Aspects of the Economic Life of the South African Bantu'. 2 *South African Journal of Economics* 420–42

Lever, J. (1978) 'Capital and Labour in South Africa: The Passage of the Industrial Conciliation Act'. In E. Webster ed. *Essays in South African Labour History.* Johannesburg, Ravan

Lewin, J. (1947) *Studies in African Law.* Philadelphia, University of Pennsylvania Press

Lewis, J. (1984) *Industrialisation and Trade Union Organisation in South Africa.* Cambridge, Cambridge University Press

Lewsen, P. ed. (1969) *Selections from the Correspondence of John X. Merriman.* Cape Town, van Riebeeck Society

'Lex' (1908) 'The Position of Attorneys'. 25 *South African Law Journal* 152–6

Lifton, G. (1986) *Nazi Doctors: Medical Killing and the Psychology of Genocide.* London, Macmillan

Loram, C. T. (1921–2) 'The Claims of the Native Question upon Scientists'. 18 *South African Journal of Science*

Lourie, A. (1927) 'Administrative Law in South Africa'. 44 *South African Law Journal* 10–23

Lucas, F. (1933) 'The Determination of Wages in South Africa'. 1 *South African Journal of Economics* 49–57

Maclean, J. ([1858] 1968) *A Compendium of Kafir Law and Custom.* London, Frank Cass

Macmillan, W. M. (1930) *Complex South Africa.* London, Faber & Faber

Maitland, F. W. (1908) *The Constitutional History of England.* Cambridge, Cambridge University Press

Malan, F. S. (1951) *Die Konvensie Dagboek van F. S. Malan,* ed. F. Preller. Cape Town, van Riebeeck Society

Malleson, K. (1999) 'Assessing the Performance of the Judicial Service Commission'. 116 *South African Law Journal* 1, 30–49

Mamdani, M. (1996) *Citizen and Subject: Contemporary Africa and the Legacy of Late Colonialism.* Princeton, Princeton University Press

Mandela, N. (1994) *The Long Walk to Freedom.* London, Little Brown

Mandelbrote, H. J. (1936) 'Constitutional Development 1834–1858'. In *Cambridge History of the British Empire,* vol. VIII. Cambridge, Cambridge University Press

Marais, J. S. (1961) *The Fall of Kruger's Republic.* Oxford, Clarendon Press

Mardall, G. (1913) 'Our Prisons and Reformatories'. 30 *South African Law Journal* 427–32

Marks, S. (1970) *Reluctant Rebellion.* London, Oxford University Press

Marks, S. and R. Rathbone eds. (1982) *Industrialisation and Social Change in South Africa.* London, Longman

Matsetela, T. (1982) 'The Life Story of Nkgono Mma-Pooe: Aspects of Share

Cropping and Proletarianisation in the Northern Orange Free State, 1890–1930'. In Marks and Rathbone eds.

Matthews, E. L. (1921) 'South African Legislation relating to Marriage or Sexual Intercourse between Europeans and Natives or Coloured Persons'. 38 *South African Law Journal* 313–20

Matthews, Z. K. (1934) 'Bantu Law and Western Civilisation in South Africa'. MA thesis, Yale University

(1981) *Freedom for my People*. London, Rex Collings

Maud, J. P. (1938) *City Government: The Johannesburg Experiment*. Oxford, Clarendon Press

McGlendon, T. (1995) 'Tradition and Domestic Struggle in the Courtroom: Customary Law and the Control of Women in Segregation-era Natal'. 28 *International Journal of African Historical Studies* 527–62

(1997) '"A Dangerous Doctrine": Twins, Ethnography and the Natal Code'. 39 *Journal of Legal Pluralism* 121–40

McQueen, R. and W. Pue eds. (1999) *Misplaced Traditions*. Sydney, Federation Press

Menachemson, L. (1985) 'Resistance through the Courts: African Urban Communities and Litigation under the Urban Areas Act'. BA Hons. thesis, University of the Witwatersrand

Merry, S. (1990) *Getting Justice and Getting Even: Legal Consciousness among Working Class Americans*. Chicago, University of Chicago Press

Mertz, E. (1992) 'Language, Law and Social Meaning: Linguistic/Anthropological Contributions to the Study of Law'. 26 *Law and Society Review* 413–45

Milner, J. R. L. (1996) 'Ownership'. In Zimmerman and Visser eds.

Morice, G. T. (1911) 'Recent Mental Science and its Bearing on Law'. 28 *South African Law Journal* 20–8

(1920) 'The Administration of Criminal Law in South Africa'. 37 *South African Law Journal* 131–8

(1924) 'The Burden of Proof in Criminal Cases'. 41 *South African Law Journal* 132–8

Morrell, R. (1986) 'Competition and Co-operation in Middelburg'. In Beinart, Delius and Trapido eds.

Morris, H. (1948) *The First Forty Years*. Cape Town, Juta

Muirhead, J. M. P. (1911) 'The Treatment of Juvenile Offenders. *South African Journal of Science*

Muller-Hill, B. (1988) *Murderous Science. Elimination by Scientific Selection of Jews, Gipsies and Others, Germany 1933–45*. Oxford, Oxford University Press

Murray, C. (1992) *Black Mountain, Land Class and Power in the Eastern Orange Free State 1880's to 1980's*. Johannesburg, Witwatersrand University Press

Murray, C. ed. (1994) *Gender and the New South African Legal Order*. Cape Town, Juta

Nathan, M. (1919) *The South African Commonwealth*. Johannesburg, Speciality Press of South Africa

(1944) *Not Heaven Itself*. Durban, Know Publishing

Neumann, F. ([1942] 1963) *Behemoth. The Structure and Practice of National Socialism*. New York, Octagon Books

Olivier, Lord (1927) *The Anatomy of African Misery*. London, L. and V. Woolf

Pachai, B. (1971) *International Aspects of the South African Indian Question 1860–1971*. Cape Town, Struik

Packard, R. (1994) *White Plague, Black Labor: Tuberculosis and the Political Economy of Health and Disease in South Africa*. Berkeley, University of California Press

Paton, G. W. (1952) *The Commonwealth of Australia. The Development of its Laws and Constitution*. London, Stevens

Peires, J. (1987) 'The Legend of Fenner Solomon'. In B. Bozzoli ed. *Class and Conflict in South Africa*. Johannesburg, Ravan

Philips, R. E. (1938) *The Bantu in the City*. Lovedale, Lovedale Press

Plaatje, S. (1916) *Native Life in South Africa*. London, P. S. King

Pollak, H. (1933) 'Women Workers in Witwatersrand Industries'. 1 *South African Journal of Economics* 58–68

Posel, D. (1991) *The Making of Apartheid 1948–1961: Conflict and Compromise*. Oxford, Clarendon Press

Pratt, A. (1913) *The Real South Africa*. London, Holden & Hardingham

Radzinowicz, L. (1966) *Ideology and Crime*. New York, Columbia University Press

Reedman, N. (1936) 'The Industrial Legislation Commission'. 4 *South African Journal of Economics* 221–9

Reitz, H. (1946) *The Conversion of a South African Nationalist*. Cape Town, Unie Volksbeperk

Robertson, H. M. (1934) '150 Years of Economic Contact between Black and White'. 1 *South African Journal of Economics* 2, 403–25

Rogers, H. (1933) *Native Administration in South Africa*. Johannesburg, Witwatersrand University Press

Rose-Innes, J. (1949) *Autobiography*, ed. B. Tindall. Cape Town, Oxford University Press

Roux, E. (1948) *Time Longer than Rope*. London, Victor Gollancz

Sachs, A. (1973) *Justice in South Africa*. London, Chatto

Sachs, E. S. (1952) *The Choice before South Africa*. London, Turnstile Press

Sachs, W. (1933) 'The Insane Native: An Introduction to a Psychological Study'. 30 *South African Journal of Science*

Sampson, V. (1926) *My Reminiscences.* London, Longmans Green

SC 6 1910–11 *Report from the Select Committee on Closer Land Settlement.* Pretoria, Union Government

SC 3 1911 *Report of the Select Committee on the Native Labour Regulation Bill*

SC 6 1912 *Report of the Select Committee on the Incorporated Law Societies Consolidation Bill*

SC 10 1912 *Report of the Select Committee on the Miners' Phthisis Bill*

SC 6 1913 *Report from the Select Committee on Native Custom and Marriage Laws*

SC 9 1913 *Report of the Select Committee on European Employment and Labour Conditions*

SC 10 1913 *Report of the Select Committee on Garnisheeing Wages*

SC 1 1914 *First Report of the Select Committee on the Agricultural Land Bank*

SC 4 1914 *Report of the Select Committee on the Workings of the Miners' Phthisis Act*

SC 6 1914 *Report of the Select Committee on the Removal of Restrictions under Wills Bill*

SC 8A 1914 *Third Report of the Select Committee on Native Affairs*

SC 1 1916 *Report of the Select Committee on the Law Society (Cape of Good Hope) Private Bill*

SC 5 1918 *Report of the Select Committee on the Police Strike and Recruiting*

SC 11 1919 *Report of the Select Committee on the Disabilities of British Indians in the Transvaal*

SC 9 1921 *Report of the Select Committee on the Apprenticeship and Regulation of Wages Bills*

SC 3A 1923 *Report from the Select Committee on Native Affairs (re Urban Areas Bill)*

SC 4 1923 *First and Second Reports from the Select Committee on Suppression of Stock Thefts*

SC 14 1925 *Report of the Select Committee on the Wage Bill*

SC 4 1926 *Report of the Select Committee on the Usury Bill*

SC 12 1926 *Report of the Select Committee on the Enfranchisement of Women*

SC 10 1927 *Report of the Select Committee on the Subject of the Native Bills*

SC 7 1930 *Report of the Select Committee on Asiatics in the Transvaal*

SC 9 1930 *Report of the Select Committee on the Industrial Conciliation Amendment Bill*

SC 7 1931 *Report of the Select Committee on the Native Service Contract Bill*

Schapera, I. (1934) *Western Civilisation and the Natives of South Africa: Studies in Culture Contact.* London, Routledge & Kegan Paul

(1943) *Tribal Legislation amongst the Tswana of the Bechuanaland Protectorate.* London, London School of Economics

Scharf, W. (1985) 'Liquor, the State and Urban Blacks'. In Davis and Slabbert eds.

Seymour, W. S. ([1913] 1960) *Native Law and Custom*. Cape Town, Juta

Shain, M. (1994) *The Roots of Anti-Semitism in South Africa*. Johannesburg, Witwatersrand University Press

Shropshire, D. W. (1941) *The Bantu Woman under the Natal Code of Native Law*. Lovedale, Lovedale Press

Simons, H. J. (1936) 'The Criminal Law and its Administration in South Africa, Southern Rhodesia and Kenya'. Ph.D. thesis, London University

(1968) *African Women: Their Legal Status in South Africa*. London, Penguin

(1987) 'African Marriage under Apartheid'. Paper given at the Conference on Family Law Reform in Africa, Harare

Simons, H. J. and R. Simons (1969) *Class and Colour in South Africa 1850–1950*. London, Penguin

Simpson, G. N. (1986) 'Peasants and Politics in the Western Transvaal'. MA thesis, University of the Witwatersrand

Smith, K. J. (1988) *James Fitzjames Stephen*. Cambridge, Cambridge University Press

Stafford, W. G. (1935) *Native Law as Practised in Natal*. Johannesburg, Witwatersrand University Press

Statement of Policy under the Native Trust and Land Act (1937). Pretoria, Union Government

Stephen, R. B. (1979) *The House of Lords as a Judicial Body*. London, Weidenfeld & Nicolson

Steyn, L. C. (1946) *Die Uitleg van Wette*. Cape Town, Juta

Stubbs, W. (1929) 'Opening Address'. *Native Appeal Court Reports*, vol. 1

Sugarman, D. and D. R. Rubin (1983) 'Towards a New History of Law and Society in England 1750–1914'. In Sugarman and Rubin eds.

Sugarman, D. and D. R. Rubin eds. (1983) *Law, Economy and Society 1750–1914: Essays in the History of English Law*. Abingdon, Professional Books Ltd

Swainger, J. (1995) 'Wagging Tongues and Empty Heads: Seditious Utterances and Patriotism in Wartime Central Alberta'. In Knafla and Binnie eds.

Swan, M. (1985) *Gandhi. The South African Experience*. Johannesburg, Ravan

Swanson, M. (1977) 'The Sanitation Syndrome. Bubonic Plague and Urban Native Policy in the Cape Colony'. 18 *Journal of African History* 387–410

Tatz, C. M. (1962) *Shadow and Substance in South Africa*. Pietermaritzburg, University of Natal Press

TG 11 (1908) *Report of the Indigency Commission*. Pretoria, Transvaal Government

Thompson, L. M. (1960) *The Unification of South Africa 1902–10*. Oxford, Clarendon Press

Torpey, J. (2000) *The Invention of the Passport*. Cambridge, Cambridge University Press

Transvaal Strike Legal Defence Committee (1924) *The Story of a Crime*. Johannesburg, n.p.

Trew, H. F. (1938) *African Man Hunts*. London, Blackie & Son

Truro, C. (1910) 'Native Law and Custom'. 1 *Union Law Review* 338–53

UG 35 1911 *Department of Justice, Annual Report for 1910*

UG 10 1912 *Report of the Commission on Industries and Trade*

UG 62 1912 *Commissioner of Police, Annual Report*

UG 39 1913 *Report of the Commission Appointed to Enquire into Assaults on Women*

UG 44 1913 *Department of Justice, Annual Report*

UG 12 1914 *Report of the Economic Commission*

UG 37 1914 *Report of the Native Grievances Enquiry 1913–14*

UG 28 1915 *Annual Report, Department of Justice*

UG 19 1916 *Report of the Native Lands Commission*

UG 22 1916 *Native Lands Commission: Minutes of Evidence*

UG 25 1916 *Native Lands Commission. Minute to the Minister of Native Affairs by Sir W. H. Beaumont*

UG 19 1917 *Report of the State Mining Commission*

UG 36 1918 *Department of Justice, Annual Report for 1916*

UG 39 1918 *Department of Justice, Annual Report for 1917*

UG 46 1919 *Third Report of the Public Service Commission of Enquiry*

UG 35 1920 *Department of Justice, Annual Report*

UG 35 1922 *Report of the Martial Law Enquiry Commission*

UG 41 1922 *Report of the Interdepartmental Committee on the Native Pass Laws, 1920*

UG 42 1923 *Report of the Native Location Survey*

UG 14 1926 *Report of the Economic and Wages Commission*

UG 17 1927 *Report of the Native Affairs Commission*

UG 22 1932 *Report of the Native Economic Commission 1930–2*

UG 26 1932 *Report of the Native Affairs Commission 1927–31*

UG 3 1934 *Report of the Department of Native Affairs 1932–3*

UG 14 1934 *Report of the Tuberculosis Commission*

UG 23 1934 *Report of the Indian Colonisation Committee*

UG 37 1935 *Report of the Industrial Legislation Commission*

UG 45 1936 *Report of the Company Law Commission 1935–6*

UG 35 1937 *Report of the Commission of Enquiry Regarding the Cape Coloured People of the Union*

UG 38 1937 *Report of the Interdepartmental Committee on Destitute, Neglected, Maladjusted and Delinquent Children and Young Persons, 1934–7*

UG 52 1937 *Department of Health, Annual Report*

UG 30 1939 *Report of the Commission on Mixed Marriages in South Africa*

UG 47 1947 *Report of the Prison and Penal Reform Commission*

UG 31 1952 *Report of the Interdepartmental Committee on the Abuse of Dagga*

van Blerk, A. (1984) 'The Genesis of the "Modernist"–"Purist" Debate: A Historical Birdseye View'. 47 *Tydskrif vir Hedendaagse Romeinse Hollandse Reg* 255–79

(1988) *Judge and Be Judged*. Cape Town, Juta

van der Horst, S. (1971) *Native Labour in South Africa*. London, Frank Cass

van der Merwe, D. (1998) 'Roman-Dutch Law: From Virtual Reality to Constitutional Resource'. *Acta Juridica* 117–37

van der Walt, A. J. (1995) 'Tradition on Trial: A Critical Analysis of the Civil-law Tradition in South African Property Law'. 11 *South African Journal on Human Rights* 169–206

van der Walt, A. J. and D. G. Kleyn (1989) 'Duplex Dominium: The History and Significance of the Concept of Divided Ownership'. In Visser ed.

van Heerden, Justice (1996) Judicial Commission: transcript of interview (unpublished)

van Onselen, C. (1982) *Studies in the Social and Economic History of the Witwatersrand*. London, Longmans

(1985) 'Crime and Total Institutions in the Making of Modern South Africa: The Life of 'Nongoloza' Mathebula 1867–1948'. 19 *History Workshop* 62–81

(1996) *The Seed is Mine*. Cape Town, David Phillips.

van Rensburg, H. (1956) *Their Paths Crossed Mine*. Cape Town, Central News Agency

van Zyl Smit, D. (1989) 'Adopting and Adapting Criminological Ideas: Criminology and Afrikaner Nationalism in South Africa'. 13 *Contemporary Crises* 227–52

Venable, H. (n.d.) ' "Natives Land" Laws, Segregated Markets and the Economic Decline of African Landowning Communities in the Western Transvaal, 1900–1940'. Unpublished paper, New York University, Law and Society Colloquium

Vindex (1901) 'The Suggested Repeal of Roman-Dutch Law in South Africa'. 18 *South African Law Journal* 153–62

Visser, D. (1985) 'The "Absoluteness" of Ownership: The South African Common Law in Perspective'. *Acta Juridica* 39–52

Visser, D. (1989) 'The Legal Historian as Subversive'. In Visser ed.

Visser, D. ed. (1989) *Essays on the History of Law*. Cape Town, Juta

Wacks, R. (1984) 'Judges and Injustice'. 101 *South African Law Journal* 2, 266–85

Walker, E. A. (1925) *Lord de Villiers and his Times*. London, Constable

(1937) *W. F. Schreiner*. London, Oxford University Press

(1962) *A History of Southern Africa*. London, Longman

Watermayer, E. F. (1936) 'The Roman Dutch Law of South Africa'. In *Cambridge History of the British Empire*, vol. VIII. Cambridge, Cambridge University Press

Wells, J. (1982) 'Passes and Bypasses: Freedom of Movement for African Women under the Urban Areas Act of South Africa'. In M. Hay and M. Wright eds. *African Women and the Law: Historical Perspectives*. Boston, Boston University Press

Welsh, D. (1971) *The Roots of Segregation: Native Policy in Colonial Natal 1845–1910*. Cape Town, Oxford University Press

Wessels, J. (1928) 'Codification'. 45 *South African Law Journal* 5–20

Whitfield, G. M. (1930) *South African Native Law*. Cape Town, Juta

White, L. E. (1988) 'To Learn and to Teach: Lessons from Driefontein on Lawyering and Power'. 4 *Wisconsin Law Review* 699–769

Wickins, P. (1978) *The Industrial and Commercial Workers' Union of Africa*. Cape Town, Oxford University Press

(1981) 'The Native Land Act of 1913: A Cautionary Essay on Simple Explanations of Complex Change'. 49 *South African Journal of Economics* 105–29

Wiener, M. (1990) *Re-constructing the Criminal: Culture, Law and Policy in England*. Cambridge, Cambridge University Press

Wilson, F. (1971) 'Farming 1866–1966'. In M. Wilson and L. Thompson eds. *Oxford History of South Africa*, vol. XI. New York, Oxford University Press

Worger, W. (1987) *South Africa's City of Diamonds: Mine Workers and Monopoly Capitalism in Kimberley, 1867–1895*. New Haven, Yale University Press

Worsfold, W. B. (1912) *The Union of South Africa*. London, n.p.

(1913) *Reconstruction of the New Colonies under Lord Milner*. London, Kegan Paul

Wright, H. M. ed. (1972) *Sir James Rose-Innes: Selected Correspondence*. Cape Town, van Riebeeck Society

Yudelman, D. (1984) *The Emergence of Modern South Africa*. Cape Town, David Philip

Zimmerman, R. and D. Visser eds. (1996) *Southern Cross: Civil Law and Common Law in South Africa*. Oxford, Clarendon Press

No author (1910) 'Editorial'. *Union Law Review*

INDEX

Act of Union 39 n7
Addison, Richard 280
administrative law 29, 472–87; and Asian
traders 487–97; concern over growth of
486–7; court review of administrative
decisions 479–81; of new state 472–3;
immigration 482–3; review of 485–6; race
473, 476–7; test 477, 478–9; role of courts
476–7; statutory interpretation 477–8,
497–508; Urban Areas Act 483–5; see also
delegated legislation
Admission of Attorneys Bill (1926) 231
adultery, and African law 310
African law 28; and administration of 247, 274,
279–80, 281, 291–3, 296–8; adultery, 310;
African Christians 247–8; appeals from
260–1; as area of white expertise 243–4,
252–3; assimilation 253–4, 256, 258, 276;
assimilation into 'South African' law 356–7;
bride wealth 262–3, 264–5, 271, 277–8,
308–9; changing family structure 301–2;
codification 246–7, 248–9, 250–1, 254,
258–9, 273–4, 355; *Compendium* of 250–1,
282, 286, 292, 325; contract 307–10; criminal
law 254, 319–21; debt 303, 316–17, 317–18;
delict 306–7, 339; development of 292–3, in
Cape Colony 250–7, Natal 245–50, Transvaal
257; divorce 310, 311, 313–14, 315; economic
participation 336–40; enfranchisement 256;
evolutionary advancement 251; exemptions
from 342–5 individualism 298; influences on
292–3, 353; interpretation of 252–3, 354–6;
land ownership 383–4; land tenure 258,
304–5, 381–2; legal capacity 337; legal status
338–9; marriage 261–72, 310–16, 330–36,
348–51; Z. K. Matthews and 356–7; Native
Administration Act (1927) 273; Native Affairs
Commission (1903–5) 257–61; Native
Disputes Bill 275; polygamy 265–7, 270–2;
property relations 301–4; property rights
298–300; restriction of use of legal
practitioners 296–8; segregation of 278–82;
shift in control over 249–50; Stubbs on nature

of 351–2; succession 304–6, 340–1;
testamentary rights 305–6; variations in 248,
353–4; variable application of 328–30;
witchcraft 321–7; women 276, 277–8, 302–3,
309–10; women's property rights 299–301,
304–5, 308–9; see also chieftaincy, *and* Natal
Code of Native Law
African National Congress 60; protest against
jury system 120; and pass laws 417–18
African Survey 329
African Women 291
Afrikaner rebellion (1914) 48; government
response to 139
agriculture, and legal profession 232–3
alcohol, as cause of black crime 84–6; police
and control of 56, 58; see also prohibition
Alexander, Morris 109–10, 182
Anderson, Commissioner 457
Andrews, W. H. 443, 450, 463, 467
anthropology, relation to criminology 64
Appellate Division, and Roman-Dutch law
161, 163–4
arbitration, industrial 443–4
Arthur of Connaught, Prince, and Samuel
Long case 8–10
Asian traders, and administrative law 487–97;
company law 488–9, 494; courts 493, 494,
495; as economic threat 490; enforcement of
regulations against 491–2; Gold Law 488,
494, 496; land ownership 488–9, 492, 494,
496; refusal of licenses 487–8, 493, 496;
threat to white settlement 490–1; use of
legal system 492; white reaction to legal
victories of 493–4
Asians, and position in South African law 19;
and statutory interpretation 499
Assaults Commission, *see* Commission into
Assaults on Women
assimilation, 342; and African law 253–4, 256,
258, 276, 310, 333, 355–6; Cape Colony
250; criminal law 319; exemptions from
African law 343–5; land ownership 382–3;
native custom 318–19

555

INDEX OF LEGAL CASES CITED